Hangingout™ in Ireland

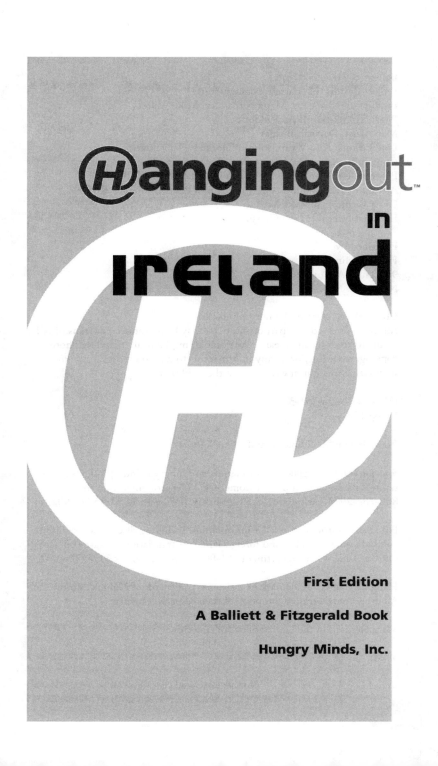

Hangingout™ in Ireland

First Edition

A Balliett & Fitzgerald Book

Hungry Minds, Inc.

Balliett & Fitzgerald, Inc.
Project Editors: Liz Barrett, Kristen Couse
Production Managers: Maria Fernandez, Mike Walters
Production Editor: Paul Paddock
Map Artist: Darshan Bhagat
Line Editors: Kim Wyatt, John O'Donnell, Will Tizard
Copy Editors: Kevin McLain, Will Tizard, Karen Dunn
Proofreaders: Donna Stonecipher, Vinnie Ferraro, Jodi Brandon
Associate Editors: Simon Sullivan, Lauren Podis, Nathaniel Knaebel, Chris Varmus, Alix McNamara
Editorial Intern: Joanna Cupano

Published by
Hungry Minds, Inc.
909 Third Avenue
New York, NY 10022

ISBN: 0-7645-6351-3
ISSN: 1531-7498

Book design: Sue Canavan and Mike Walters

Special Sales: For general information on Hungry Minds' products and services please contact our Customer Care Department within the U.S. at 800-762-2974, outside the U.S. at 317-572-3993 or fax 317-572-4002.

For sales inquiries and reseller information, including discounts, premium and bulk quantity sales, and foreign-language translations, please contact our Customer Care Department at 1-800-434-3422 or fax 317-572-4002.

Manufactured in the United States of America

5 4 3 2 1

CONTENTS

IRELAND

backmatter

maps

IRELAND xviii

The Northwest

Northern Ireland

a disclaimer

Please note that prices fluctuate in the course of time, and travel information changes under the impact of the many factors that influence the travel industry. We therefore suggest that you write or call ahead for confirmation when making your travel plans. Every effort has been made to ensure the accuracy of information throughout this book and the contents of this publication are believed correct at the time of printing. Nevertheless, the publishers cannot accept responsibility for errors or omissions or for changes in details given in this guide or for the consequences of any reliance on the information provided by the same. Assessments of attractions and so forth are based upon the author's own experience and therefore, descriptions given in this guide necessarily contain an element of subjective opinion, which may not reflect the publisher's opinion or dictate a reader's own experience on another occasion. Readers are invited to write the publisher with ideas, comments, and suggestions for future editions.

Your safety is important to us, however, so we encourage you to stay alert and be aware of your surroundings. Keep a close eye on cameras, purse, and wallets, all favorite targets of thieves and pickpockets.

an invitation to the reader

In researching this book, we discovered many wonderful places—hotels, restaurants, shops, and more. We're sure you'll find others. Please tell us about them, so we can share the information with your fellow travelers in upcoming editions. If you were disappointed with a recommendation, we'd love to know that, too.

Please write to:
Hanging Out in Ireland
Hungry Minds, Inc.
909 Third Avenue
New York, NY 10022

foreword

Most of us have had the experience of going to a new school or moving to a new neighborhood and not knowing a soul there, not knowing the laws of the land, feeling lost and uncool. But if you're lucky, someone comes along who invites you in and shows you where the action is. The same can be said for travel—unless you're committed to seeing Europe through the moving tinted window of a tour bus, pretty soon you're going to want to get past the initial strangeness and get with it. And to really be able to do that, you need someone or something to help you along, so that what could have been just another cute postcard turns into a new chapter in your life.

Going to Europe is infinitely more complicated-and ultimately more rewarding-than just going on a road trip. Without some help, you may repeatedly find yourself surrounded by a numbed-out tour group, scratching your head and wondering what all the fuss is about. We sent out our teams of writers with just that in mind. Go to where the action is, we instructed them, and tell us how to find it.

Of course we tell you how to see all the cultural and historical goodies you've read about in art history class and heard about from your folks, but we also tell you where to find the party, shake your butt, and make friends with the locals. We've tried to find the hottest scenes in Europe—where traditions are being reinvented daily—and make these guides into the equivalent of a hip friend to show you the ropes.

So, welcome to the new Europe, on the verge of mighty unification. The European Union (EU)—and the euro's arrival as a common currency—is already making many happy, others nervous, and setting the entire continent abuzz with a different kind of energy. As the grand tour of Europe meets the Info Age, the old ways are having to adjust to a faster tempo.

But even as the globe is shrinking to the size of a dot com, Europe remains a vast vast place with enough history and art and monuments to fill endless guides—so we had to make a choice. We wanted the *Hanging Out Guides* to live up to their title, so we decided to specialize and not only show you the best spots to eat, shop, sightsee, party, and crash, but also give you a real feeling for each place, and unique but do-able ways to get to know it better. So we don't cover *every single* town, village, and mountaintop—instead, we picked what we felt were the best and serve them up with plenty of detail. We felt it was crucial to have the room to go deeper, and to tip you off as to how to do the same, so that after you see the sights, you'll almost certainly end up in a place where you'll get to know the secret to the best travel—the locals.

Aside from the basics-neighborhoods, eats, crashing, stuff (shopping), culture zoo (sightseeing stuff), and need to know (the essentials)—we cover the bar scene, the live music scene, the club scene, the gay scene, the visual arts scene, and the performing arts scene, always giving you the scoop on where to chill out and where to get wild. We take you on some beautiful walks and show you great places to hang (sometimes for no money). Things to Talk to a Local About actually gives you some fun conversation openers. Fashion tells you what people are wearing. Wired lists websites for each city—some general, some cool, some out-of-the-way-so you can start checking things out immediately. It also takes you to the best cybercafes in each place. Rules of the Game lays out local liquor and substance laws and also gives you the vibe on the street. Five-0 does a quick sketch of cops in each city. Boy meets Girl dares to speculate on that most mysterious of travel adventures. And Festivals & Events lists just that. We also take you out to all the best outdoor spots, where you can hike, bike, swim, jump, ski, snorkel or surf till you've had enough.

Our adventurous team of writers (average age, 24) and editors let you in on the ongoing party. We want to make sure that your time abroad is punctuated by moments when you've sunk deep enough into the mix (or danced long enough to it), so that you suddenly get it, you have that flash of knowing what it's like to actually *be* somewhere else, to live there—to hang out in Europe.

Introduction

At first glance, Ireland may seem almost as familiar as Canada to American visitors. Everybody speaks English, young Dublin hipsters wear the same styles you see on the street in New York, and Big Macs and Dunkin' Donuts are more common than corned beef and cabbage. But don't let the global Burger King invasion fool you into thinking that Ireland is just America with an accent. Far from it. For one thing, Ireland is way older—and way younger—than the United States.

Ireland's age is obvious to anyone who ventures out of the main cities. Drive a few hours from downtown Dublin and you'll see Neolithic tombs, Bronze Age forts, early Christian monastic sites, Viking walls, Norman castles, Georgian estates—enough antiquity to make your head spin, all in plain sight, and as commonplace as Wal-Marts in the United States.

What's less obvious is how young Ireland is. The Republic itself, with its own constitution and currency, is barely 50 years old. And the people are even younger. Roughly half of the population is under 25, and nearly a quarter are under 15. So even though the culture may seem a bit traditional in terms of surface courtesies—men still open doors and give up their seats for women—make no mistake about it: Ireland is rapidly being redefined by its youth, whose sheer numbers and unconventional ways make the country one of the coolest destinations in all of Europe. More than six million people visit Ireland each year, a number that is almost double its population of 3.7 million.

Ireland

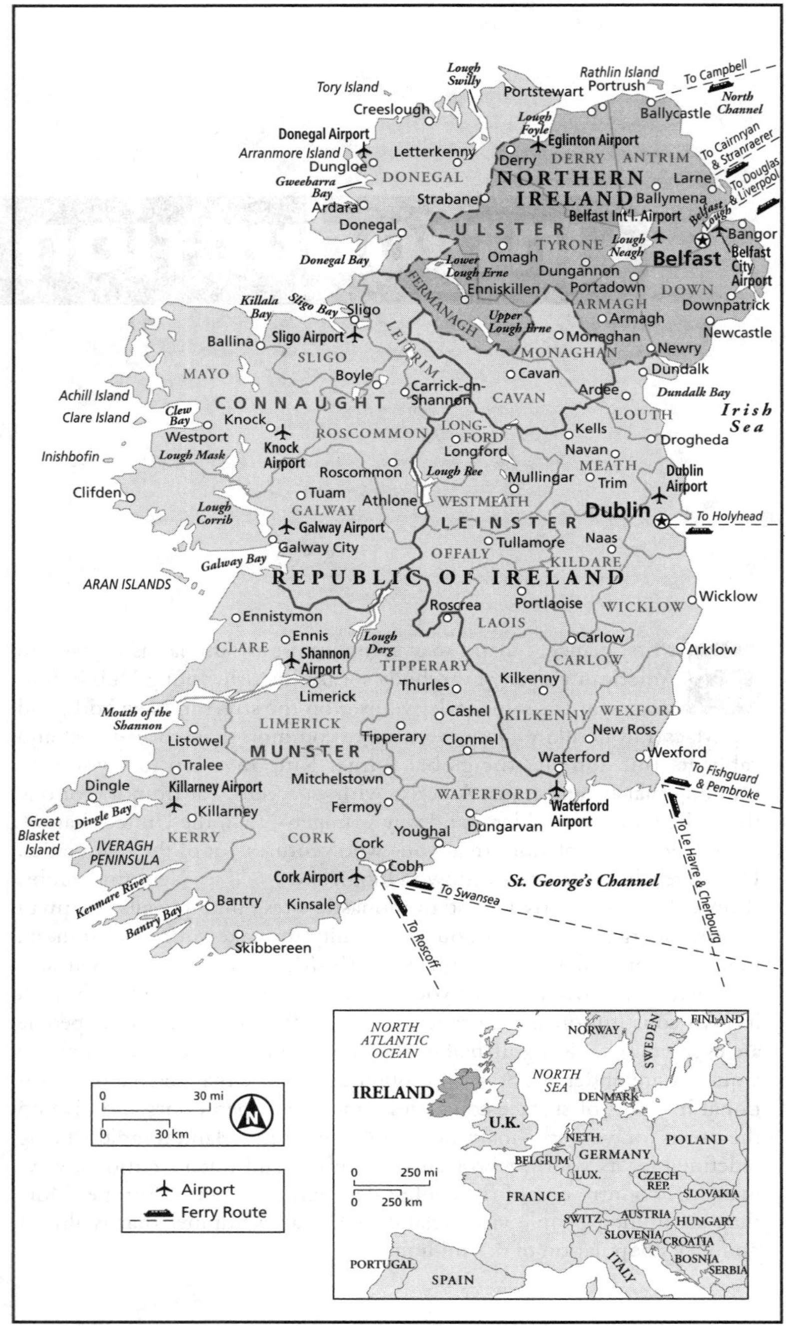

Tory Island
Lough Swilly
Rathlin Island
Portstewart
Portrush
To Campbell
North Channel
Creeslough
Ballycastle
Lough Foyle
Donegal Airport
Eglinton Airport
Arranmore Island
Letterkenny
Dungloe
Derry
DERRY
ANTRIM
To Cairnryan & Stranraer
Gweebarra Bay
DONEGAL
NORTHERN IRELAND
Larne
To Douglas & Liverpool
Ardara
Strabane
Ballymena
Belfast Int'l. Airport
Belfast Lough
Donegal
ULSTER
Bangor
TYRONE
Lough Neagh
Belfast
Belfast City Airport
Donegal Bay
Lower Lough Erne
Omagh
Dungannon
Enniskillen
Portadown
DOWN
FERMANAGH
ARMAGH
Downpatrick
Killala Bay
Sligo Bay
Sligo
Armagh
Upper Lough Erne
Ballina
Sligo Airport
LEITRIM
Monaghan
Newcastle
SLIGO
MONAGHAN
Newry
MAYO
Boyle
Cavan
Dundalk
Achill Island
Carrick-on-Shannon
Ardee
Dundalk Bay
CONNAUGHT
CAVAN
Clare Island
Clew Bay
Knock
LOUTH
Irish Sea
Westport
ROSCOMMON
LONGFORD
Kells
Inishbofin
Lough Mask
Knock Airport
Longford
Drogheda
Navan
MEATH
Roscommon
Lough Ree
Dublin Airport
Clifden
Mullingar
Trim
Tuam
Athlone
WESTMEATH
Lough Corrib
GALWAY
LEINSTER
Dublin
To Holyhead
Galway Airport
Tullamore
Naas
Galway City
OFFALY
KILDARE
Galway Bay
ARAN ISLANDS
REPUBLIC OF IRELAND
Roscrea
Portlaoise
WICKLOW
Wicklow
Ennistymon
LAOIS
Ennis
Lough Derg
Carlow
CLARE
Arklow
Shannon Airport
TIPPERARY
CARLOW
Kilkenny
Thurles
Limerick
Mouth of the Shannon
Cashel
KILKENNY
WEXFORD
LIMERICK
New Ross
Tipperary
Listowel
Clonmel
MUNSTER
Waterford
Wexford
Tralee
To Fishguard & Pembroke
Mitchelstown
Dingle
Killarney Airport
WATERFORD
Waterford Airport
Fermoy
Great Blasket Island
Dingle Bay
Killarney
Dungarvan
Youghal
To Le Havre & Cherbourg
KERRY
CORK
IVERAGH PENINSULA
Cork
Cobh
Cork Airport
St. George's Channel
Kenmare River
To Swansea
Bantry
Kinsale
Bantry Bay
To Roscoff
Skibbereen
0 30 mi
0 30 km
N
Airport
Ferry Route
NORTH ATLANTIC OCEAN
NORWAY
SWEDEN
FINLAND
NORTH SEA
IRELAND
DENMARK
U.K.
NETH.
POLAND
BELGIUM
GERMANY
0 250 mi
0 250 km
LUX.
CZECH REP.
SLOVAKIA
FRANCE
SWITZ.
AUSTRIA
HUNGARY
SLOVENIA
CROATIA
BOSNIA
SERBIA
ITALY
PORTUGAL
SPAIN

What makes Ireland such a great place to visit? That's an easy one: The best pubs in the world, great places to stay for cheap, extremely hospitable people who are actually fond of foreign visitors (really!), and a breathtaking landscape that has not been polluted or turned into commercial tourist traps. And despite the media scares about violence in Northern Ireland, Belfast is actually one of the safest cities in all of Europe in terms of street crime—and it's a blast in terms of partying.

One thing you'll learn right away is that to the Irish, there is really only one Ireland, *all* of it. The borders are now free of soldier-manned checkpoint searches and are significant only in finding your way through the country's history, along its roads, and amid its people. The basic division is between "the South" (the Republic of Ireland, Éire, or the "Free State") and "the North" (Northern Ireland, often referred to as "Ulster"). The South is a sovereign, independent nation made up of 26 counties, while the North, with six counties, is part of Great Britain. The line partitioning the land and people of Ireland into two political entities was drawn in the Anglo-Irish Treaty of 1921 and remains a matter of dispute. In practical terms for travelers, the line between north and south represents a national border, which basically means only that you have to exchange your Irish "punts" for British pounds in order to pay for a pint.

North or south, day or night, the mainstay of Irish social life is unquestionably the pub. There are more than 10,000 pubs throughout the tiny country, in every city, town, and hamlet, on every street and at every turn. The origin of pubs reaches back several centuries to a time when, for lack of trendy coffee bars or health clubs, neighbors would gather in a kitchen to talk and maybe sample some home brew. As a certain spot grew popular, word spread and people came from all directions, always assured of a warm welcome. Such places gradually became known as public houses, or "pubs" for short. The name of the person who tended a public house was often mounted over the doorway, and many pubs still bear a family or proprietor's name, such as Davy Byrnes, Doheny and Nesbitt, or W. Ryan. Many, in fact, have been in the same family for generations. Although they might have added televisions, pool tables, dartboards, or eve those horrible little touch-screen gaming machines, their primary purpose is still to be a stage for conversation and a warm spot to down a pint or pack in an inexpensive lunch of pub grub. Pub grub, by the way, is often a lot better than its name suggests; in recent years, many pubs have converted or expanded into restaurants, serving excellent unpretentious meals at prices you can lift a pint to.

Operating hours for pubs and other drinking establishments are regulated throughout Ireland. In the Republic, pubs are open 10:30am to 11:30pm Monday through Saturday from May through September. From October through April, hours are 10:30am to 11pm. Bars are open from 12:30 to 2pm and from 4 to 11pm on Sunday, year-round; nightclubs and discos close at 2am. In the North, pubs are open year-round from 11:30am to 11pm Monday through Saturday, 12:30 to 2pm and 7 to 10pm on Sunday. If a pub doesn't appear to be closing when the appointed hour arrives, it's because the official closing times are often not the *actual* closing times. Some laws, it seems, are made to be broken.

One thing you're bound to notice in the pubs—and throughout Ireland—is that smoking is still huge there. In public places, smokers often light up without hesitation directly under "no smoking" signs. In some pubs, gas masks might be a cool survival accessory if they didn't make it so tough to put back a pint. The rule is simple: Nonsmokers, fend for yourselves.

But you won't have to worry much about smoking, one way or another, when you get out into Ireland's great outdoors. The island is the perfect size for exploring: big enough to enjoy wide open spaces yet small enough to get around in a relatively short period of time. With a land mass of approximately 32,600 square miles, Ireland is roughly the same size as the state of Maine, though shaped somewhat differently. It's not more than 300 miles north to south, and 170 miles east to west. No point in Ireland is farther than 70 miles from the waters that surround it—the Atlantic Ocean, the Irish Sea, and the St. George and North channels.

And though it has a reputation for being rainy or at least misty (what the Irish called "soft days"), Ireland is by no means a country where people spend all day inside, huddling around peat fires. And the days are long gone when the most aerobic thing travelers did in Ireland was tracing their roots. Practically every corner of the country is packed with opportunities for outdoor pursuits, from daredevil hang gliding, whitewater kayaking, and surfing, to cruising the links a la Tiger Woods.

Ireland is also heaven for camping, hiking, and backpacking because of its many gorgeous parks and increasingly "green" policies that protect the island's natural beauty. Four major national parks are already open to the public—**Connemara National Park** in County Galway, **Glenveagh National Park** in County Donegal, **Killarney National Park** in County Kerry, and **Wicklow Mountains National Park** in County Wicklow—and others are planned, including **Burren National Park** in County Clare, which is currently under development.

To make the rounds of Ireland—North and South—you'll need at least two weeks, or better yet, three. But even if you have only one week, you can see enough to convince yourself and others you've been there. If it's your first time in Ireland, Dublin and Galway make great hubs. Both have major party and college scenes, and you can easily take short day-trips to small villages with picturesque thatched-roof stone cottages like the ones you see on postcards or make your way to a nearby park for an overnighter. Whether you decide to tour around or to stay put in the cities might depend on whether you're more interested in sights or stories. You'll see more sights if you cruise around, but you'll likely hear more stories—and hopefully create a few of your own—if you stick around awhile in any given spot.

Whatever you do, when in Ireland, do as the Irish do: Kick back a bit and enjoy yourself. As the locals like to say, "When God made time, he made plenty of it."

Sláinte!

the best of ireland

party spots

The Old Oak [Cork City]: Just about the hippest pub you'll ever find. It's packed to the rafters with Cork's most eligible young people on weekend nights, and the party's only just beginning when the rest of the pubs are ready for closing.

Guinness International Jazz Festival [Cork City]: THE place to be in late October if you just can't get enough of that wailing sax. It's one of the biggest, most popular festivals in Ireland.

Belfast: Surprisingly, this previously war-torn city has emerged as arguably the preeminent party center on the whole island. The Golden Mile and University area have more great traditional pubs, world-famous DJ's and slick clubs than you can shake a stick at.

McLynn's Pub [Sligo Town]: Simply cannot be beat for atmosphere and level of *craic.* Sing alongs are a nightly event. The kind of place where everybody knows everyone else by the time the bar closes.

Temple Bar [Dublin]: The winner and still champion! Sure it's a hedonistic display of alchoholic debauchery, but for the serious party animal there is arguably no other place in the world that can match it.

best of the outdoors

Kayaking [Union Hall]: Some of the best paddling you'll ever find. You can paddle at night, explore hidden coves, and do a bit of island-hopping.

Bicycling: Ireland offers some spectacular pedaling opportunities, the best of which are in **Killarney National Park,** around gorgeous lakes and through quiet hilly forests, or across **Inis Mór,** the largest Aran Island, among high cliffs, green pastures, ancient ruins, lonely beaches, and stormy sea and sky .

Killary Adventure Company and Delphi Adventure Centre [Killary Harbour]: Between them, these two mountain man meccas offer equipment for pretty nearly every adventure sport imaginable. It's all here—convenient, eh? Not to mention the scenery! The situation is perfectly ideal and ideally perfect.

Slieve League Cliffs and Horn Head [County Donnegal]: Two of the most breathtaking views in the country are located on opposite sides of its biggest county. It's a tossup as to which place will have you gasping for breath at the sheer grandure and awe of it all. Try to hit at least one of these places.

Croagh Patrick [County Mayo]: In a land where the mountains are barely hills, Croagh Patrick is one of the few serious hikes in the country. Join thousands of other pilgrims who come here to climb the steep, rocky face. Some come for the views, others come to bolster their Christian faith. Don't be surprised to see barefoot, elderly people climbing alongside youngsters in hiking boots.

culture

Cork City: The Irish are especially fond of the performing arts, viewing the theater with a sort of divine reverence, and nowhere is this better witnessed than in Cork City—and there are tons to choose from. While you're there, don't miss a play at the **Everyman Palace Theatre,** the **Cork Arts Theatre,** or the **Triskel Arts Centre.**

Glendalough [Wicklow Country]: If you only visit one monastic site while you're in Ireland, let it be Glendalough, set amidst the wild and totally spectacular beauty of the Wicklow National Park.

Maggie's [Kilkenny City]: This little pub has some of the best live trad sessions in the country. The ultratalented musicians here sing the old ballads with as much passion (or more!) as went into writing them in the first place, and ne'er a better bodhrán was ever played.

Black Taxi Tour of the Sectarian Murals [Belfast]: This tour will shake you but it's an absolute must-see if you're in Belfast. There is simply no better way to glimpse into the ongoing struggle for peace and the history of violence in Northern Ireland.

weird and bizarre

Galway Cathedral [Galway]: This place wins the peanuts for tackiest church in the whole country. Heck, it's even got a small mosaic of John F. Kennedy in a side enclave, complete with clasped hands and halo!

Buddhist retreat [Castletownbere]: *Om* your way to breathtaking views and maybe even a little piece of nirvana in West Cork. And how convenient: there's a hostel right next door!

Cong: Obsessed with John Wayne? Sure, we all are. Head for Cong, a village of less than 500, yet slavishly and singularly devoted to the memory of the film The Quiet Man, shot here in the 50's by Irish emigré John Ford. Visit The Quiet Man Cottage, eat at The Quiet Man Café, stay at The Quiet Man Hostel… You get the idea.

The races at the Curragh [County Kildare]: One of the coolest, and most idiosynchratic things you can do in Ireland. Here, you can place £1 bets on the finest horseflesh in the world, drink pints with a jovial crowd, and immerse yourself into an important part of Irish culture. And only an hour away from Dublin.

dublin and nearby

If your visit to Ireland were limited to just a week—which would be a major bummer—you could spend the whole time in the greater Dublin region and still get a feel for what makes Ireland tick: a wonderful combo of cool urban party life and awesome natural beauty less than an hour away. And we're not talking tree-lined suburban streets here, we're talking genuine wilderness, as in mountains and hiking trails and campgrounds.

This combination of city center and open country has been a very good—and a very bad—thing for the Irish. The good part is obvious (hike by day, party by night, get away for the weekend, etc.). The bad part is a little more complicated, especially when viewed from a broad historical perspective. The stretch of coast from **County Louth** (above County Dublin, bordering Northern Ireland) to **County Wicklow** (below County Dublin) has practically begged foreign invaders to come on in, and the rivers Liffey and Boyne made the opportunity even more inviting. Whoever controlled this area, known as "the eastern triangle," controlled the command center for the whole of Ireland. Within the area was **Tara,** the hill of kings; **Dublin,** the greatest of the Viking city-states; and the Pale, the English colonial fist that held the rest of Ireland in its grip (now you know where they got the expression "beyond the Pale"). Nearby were **Newgrange** and **Knowth,** among the most profound prehistoric sites in the world; **Kells,** where Ireland's greatest literary treasure was fished from a bog; and the valley of Boyne, where the Irish finally lost their country to the English.

Rimmed by the Irish Sea, the eastern triangle—every point of which is a short distance from Dublin—has less rain, less bog, and more history than any other region in the country. To the south, **County Wicklow** presents a panorama of gardens, lakes, mountains, and seascapes. To the east sit the flat plains of **County Kildare,** Ireland's prime pony country. In the north are **Counties Meath and Louth,** packed with historic sites.

But what about the party scene? Well, that would be in Dublin. And to appreciate the scene, you have to understand a bit about the city itself. Attracting a million visitors a year, Dublin is ground zero not just for partying but for all of the changes that are transforming Ireland into a prosperous and totally happening country. Pubs, restaurants, and hotels going up faster than you can say "shillelagh." Dublin is now among the most cosmopolitan cities in Europe—you'll find Asian fusion eats on the same street as traditional pubs. But what makes it such a great place to visit is that it is not just another I-could-be-anywhere big city splintered into the many characters of a diverse population. Dublin is unmistakably Irish.

You can still see parts of the Vikings' thousand-year-old cobblestone enclave in the Old City, but the Irish culture in Dublin is unflinching; a couple thousand years of having your butt kicked by foreign invaders will do that to you. The River Liffey divides the town as it once divided Viking from Celt and Norman from Norse. Most of the "new" Dublin lies south of the Liffey. An hour's walk from the top of Grafton Street down O'Connell and into north Dublin is a walk through time.

In Dublin, the Irish soul is reflected in its rich tradition of storytelling—be it the written word or song, the Irish are the masters. What else would you do when your history consists of being plundered on all sides? Storytelling has been the Irish peoples sanctuary, beginning with *the* book, the Book of Kells. And Dublin has provided some of the world's greatest writers: James Joyce, Oscar Wilde, George Bernard Shaw, and Samuel Beckett. They were the rock stars of their time.

Today's rock stars are, well, rock stars. The Irish music scene is undoubtedly one of Europe's best, partly because it forges the edgiest new music but is driven by the enduring Irish soul. Put Dubliners U2, Sinead O'Connor, or the Corrs from County Louth in your Walkman and stroll the city streets. Explore, get lost, and ask for directions—you may uncover a time capsule from the Dublin of a century ago.

If literature is the soul of Dublin, pubs are its heart. (Here comes the part about the party scene, at last.) Finding your favorite pub in Dublin is almost a rite of passage. The pubs are like Dublin's tribal fire, where people come to socialize and find out what's happening. The energetic new Dublin is contagious, and it ain't just the brew talking. A pint of Guinness in a cheery pub on a damp night, surrounded by friendly Dubliners, is good for what ails you. Step out to the Palace Bar, Kehoe's, or the Stag's Head and you'll see what we mean.

Although the temptation might be to party down in Dublin and then split, you can make the most of your bad self by taking a trip to the surrounding countryside. Within an hour in any direction you'll find some of the most important prehistoric sites in Europe, beaches and mountains. What more could you ask for? (Free advice: If the sun is shining, get outside. *Quick.* It probably won't last long.)

Dublin's wild expansion has continued beyond city limits; some call it sprawl, others call it progress. Just outside of Dublin are the seaside towns of **Howth** and **Dún Laoghaire.** You go here for the beaches, to stroll on a promenade, to swim off of sandy strands. Shake off the stink before you head back to Dublin for more nightlife, or on to the next chapter of your journey.

North of Dublin you'll find a land of legends, **Counties Louth and Meath.** If you have taste for ancient sites you'll be in hog heaven. And if you haven't yet acquired a taste, this place might just do it for you. Go to the **Hill of Tara,** 1,500 years ago the most happening spot in Ireland. Pre-

Travel Times

* By train
** Water-crossing required (by ferry usually)
*** By cable car

	Dublin	Howth	Dun Laoghaire	Bray	Drogheda	Monasterboice
Dublin	-	:25*	:20*	:40*	:50*	1
Howth	:25*	-	:50*	1:10*	:50	1:05
Dun Laoghaire	:20*	:50*	-	:20*	1	1:10
Bray	:40*	1:10*	:20*	-	1:05	1:15
Drogheda	:50*	:55	1	1:05	-	:10
Monasterboice	:55	1:05	1:10	1:15	:10	-
Mellifont Abbey	:55	1:05	1:10	1:20	:10	:10
Newgrange and Knowth	:45	:55	1	1:05	:20	:20
Kells	1	1:15	1:15	1:25	:45	:45
Trim	:55	1:10	1:10	1:20	:50	:40
Hill of Tara	:45	1	1	1:10	:30	:25
Kildare	:40	1	:55	1	1:20	1:25
Wicklow	:50	1	:40	:25	1:35	1:50
Glendalough	1	1:20	:50	:40	1:45	2

Mellifont Abbey	Newgrange and Knowth	Kells	Trim	Hill of Tara	Kildare	Wicklow	Glendalough
:55	:45	1	:55	:45	:40	:50	1
1:05	:55	1:15	1:10	1	1	1:10	1:10
1:10	1	1:15	1:10	1	:55	:40	:50
1:20	1:05	1:25	1:20	1:10	1	:25	:40
:10	:20	:45	:50	:30	1:20	1:35	1:45
:10	:35	:45	:40	:25	1:25	1:50	2
-	:10	:40	:45	:30	1:20	1:45	1:55
:10	-	:35	:35	:15	1:10	1:35	1:45
:40	:35	-	:35	:15	1:25	1:50	1:55
:45	:35	:35	-	:20	1:45	1:45	1:50
:30	:15	:15	:20	-	1:10	1:35	1:40
1:20	1:10	1:25	1:15	1:10	-	1:30	1:10
1:45	1:35	1:50	1:45	1:35	1:30	-	:30
1:55	1:45	1:55	1:50	1:40	1:10	:30	-

historic **Newgrange** will satisfy those seeking really, really old Ireland. One of the most incredible archaeological wonders of Europe, this burial mound built over 5,000 years ago sports 200,000 tons of stone carved with cool spiral, diamond, and concentric circles. The burial passage is 60 feet long, and is the place to be for a mystical winter solstice (unfortunately there is a waiting list for the next couple of years.)

Counties Kildare and Wicklow are where the wild things are. We're talking trees, trails, and lots of pretty ponies. The border of County Wicklow starts just a dozen or so miles south of downtown Dublin, and within this county you'll find some of Ireland's best rural scenery. If religious history or sacred sites is your thing, you'll want to make a pilgrimage

town of a thousand writers

You'll probably spend a fair amount of your time in Dublin soaking up the atmosphere in some of the city's famed pubs—as well you should. Indulging in some Guinness and a classic trad session is a great way to experience Irish culture. But don't make the mistake of thinking that Dublin's only contribution to the art world has been rowdy sing-a-longs fueled by all of those perfectly pulled pints. The city possesses a literary history of an astonishing richness and depth. While most places would be ecstatic just to claim Oscar Wilde and James Joyce as homeboys, overachieving Dublin has been the breeding ground for such prodigious (and disparate) talents as Roddy Doyle, Seamus Heaney, Sean O'Casey, Samuel Beckett, and Emer Martin.

Sean O'Casey (1880–1964)
Born into poverty as John Casey in Dublin, the Abbey Theatre playwright based three of his greatest works on his early life in Dublin tenements: *The Shadow of a Gunman* (1923), *Juno and the Paycock* (1924), and *The Plough and the Stars* (1926).

Brendan Behan (1923–64)
Playwright, travel writer, journalist, IRA activist, and raconteur, Behan is remembered for his flamboyant and boisterous ways as well as for his writings. His best works include his autobiography, *Borstal Boy* (1958), and the plays *The Quare Fellow* (1954) and *The Hostage* (1958), first written in Irish. The streets of his darling Dublin are the setting for many of his works. One of his most memorable and, indeed, myth-enhancing statements was his declaration of being "a drinker with a writing problem."

Samuel Beckett (1906–89)
Playwright and novelist, Beckett is probably known more for his work

to **Glendalough,** set in the wild beauty of the **Wicklow Mountains National Park,** where Saint Kevin lived, prayed, did a few things he definitely wouldn't write home about, and prayed some more. County Kildare and horse racing go hand in hand, or should we say neck and neck. If you fancy horses or the track, place your bets here.

getting around the region

For the most part, this region benefits from decent transportation. It's easy to get from Dublin by bus or train to most places you might want to mosey. If transfers are necessary, they are usually convenient. DART (Dublin Area Rapid Transit) links Dublin to Howth at its northern ter-

in developing the idea of absurdist theater than as an Irish writer, however, as a native of Dublin, he taught French at famed Trinity College. In 1938, he moved to France, where he served as a secretary to James Joyce (perhaps Dublin's most celebrated literary son), became involved with the Resistance, worked with the Irish Red Cross, and wrote. His most renowned drama, *Waiting for Godot* (1952), remains one of the definitive plays of the 20th century.

Roddy Doyle (Born 1953)
Dublin is not only author Roddy Doyle's birthplace and his home, it is at the heart of nearly all of his short stories, novels, and screenplays. As the foremost interpreter of contemporary working class life in Dublin, Doyle has had massive success with his short stories, "The Commitments", "The Van," and "The Snapper"(collected together as *The Barrytown Trilogy*). Doyle was awarded the Booker Prize in 1993 for his novel *Paddy Clarke Ha Ha Ha.*

Emer Martin (Born 1968)
One of the most talented envelope-pushers of the past few years is Gen-X powerhouse Emer Martin, whose debut, *Breakfast in Babylon,* was named Ireland's Best Book of 1996. Her work is steeped in her country's complex history and meditates on the price one pays for attempting to outrun the past—both personal and political. Her most recent novel, *More Bread Or I'll Appear,* has garnered similar acclaim.

minal, and goes south all the way to Bray, where you can catch a bus to Wicklow. Bus Eireann covers most of the region, the places you'll want to go anyway.

You definitely do not need a car while in Dublin. It's an easy town to walk, and there is always the city bus or a taxi if your feet get tired. To get a feel for the city, a two-day minimum is a must. There is so much to do here it would be a cryin' shame for you to spend any less time. Although you could easily spend your entire trip here and never get bored, it's best to venture out and get a taste of what the outlying towns and attractions have to offer.

Let's say you have about two weeks in Ireland. Unless you're burning to get to the Ring of Kerry or the Galway coast, you'll want to spend three or four days in Dublin. By night, seek out your signature pub, take in live tunes, and soak up the literary vibe. By day, roam the city streets and take day trips. Whether you want nature, history, or more pub crawlin', it's all within Dublin's reach, and you might want to take advantage of the relatively easy transportation. You could venture north or south on DART for a little r & r along one of the beaches. Or you could take the train to Drogheda in County Louth and from there take a bus to Tara or Newgrange. You can take a bus to one of Kildare's fine tracks and lay your money down. Tree-huggers may want to spend as much time on the Wicklow Way as they do in Dublin. If you're not inclined to hike, you can at least spend day cycling and picnicking near lovely Glendalough before heading back to Dublin.

If you only have a limited amount of time, say a week, you could make the most of it by spending two days each in Dublin and Belfast, and the rest of the time at the places that strike your fancy. If you're jonesin' to get on the road, you can visit Counties Louth and Meath on your way north, or hit Wicklow on your way to Counties Wexford, Waterford, and Kilkenny.

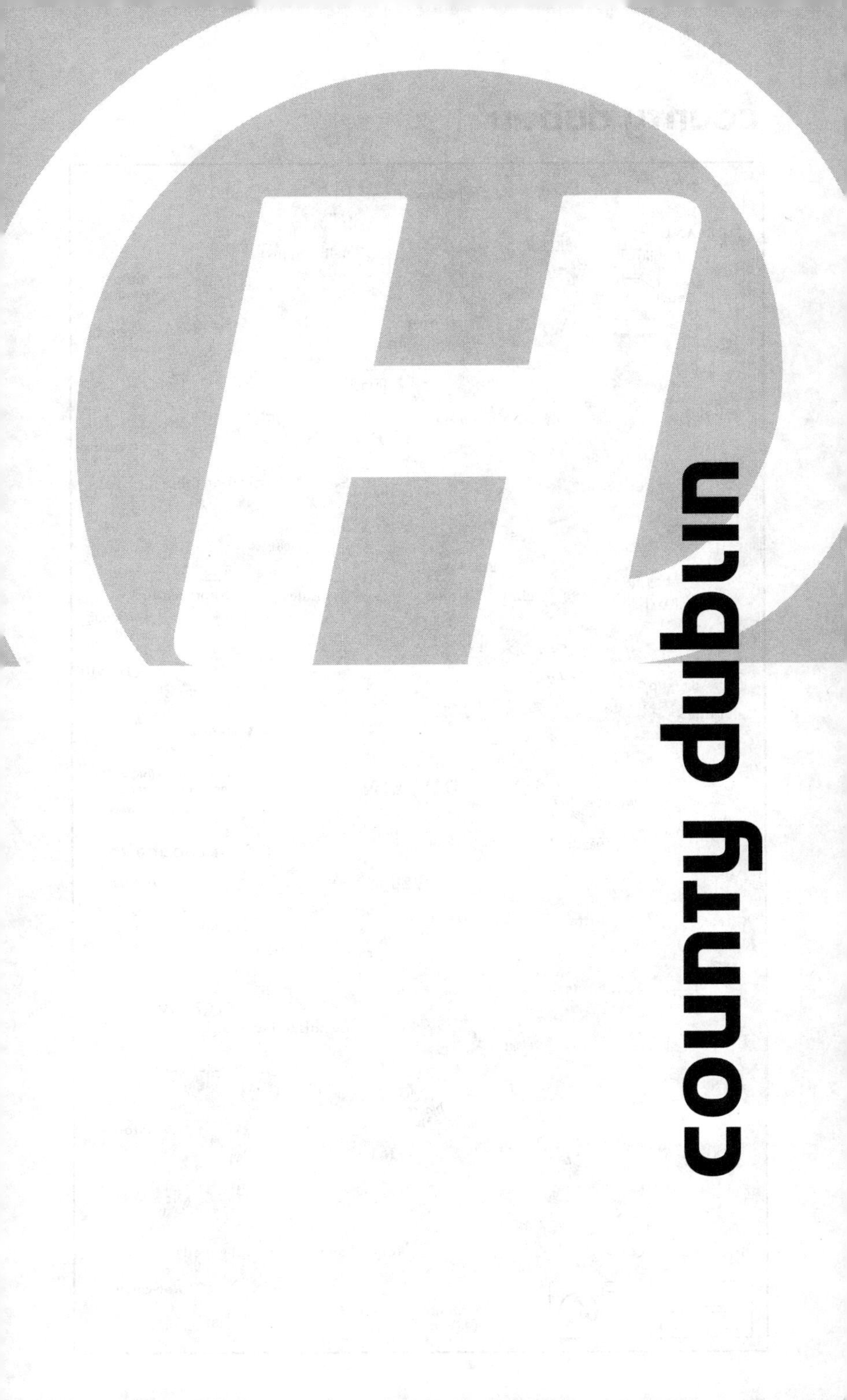
county dublin

county dublin

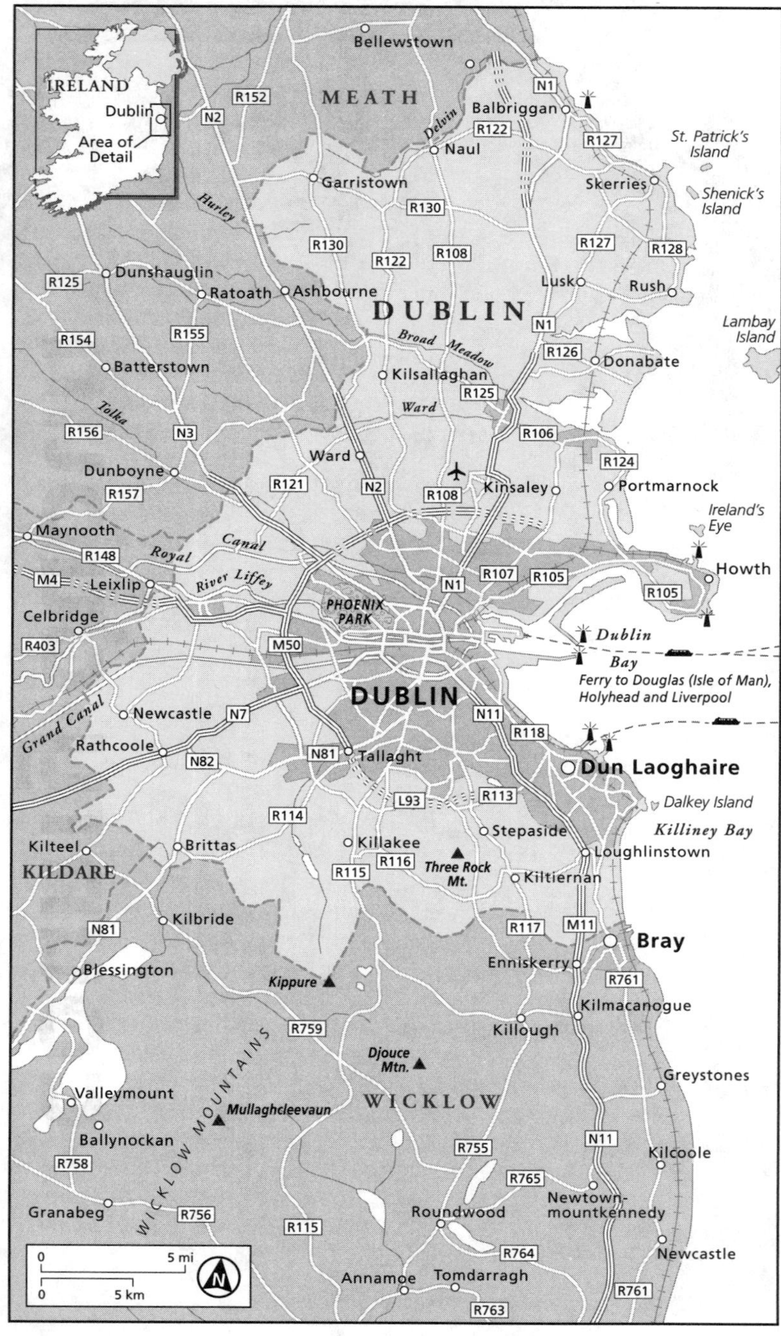

dublin

If you're young and out for a good time, the new Dublin beckons. This place is completely awash in money, and over half its population is under the age of 25. It'd be hard to find this kind of youthful, optimistic, hedonistic energy anywhere else on earth. Five years ago, an unprecedented economic boom started to sweep through Ireland, and things are moving along as strong as ever, with the capital city at the heart of it. Justifiably famous for its friendly, laid-back people, beautiful pubs, and small-city charm, the now cosmopolitan Dublin is even more inviting with packed clubs, vibrant theater and music scenes, great bars, and quiet cafes where you can kick back and watch Europe's wild west unfold.

You'll hear a lot of noise about Dublin's pubs, and though the hype can get a little overdone, the truth is that these establishments are, and always have been, the living heart of the town. Check out the special kind of friendly living-room vibe in a few comfy little beauties, and you'll see what all the fuss is about. The number of great places is astounding—the ones listed here only scratch the surface—and finding your own special pub is a Dublin rite. A lot of new places (often either slick "theme" bars or sort of Euro-loungey places) are also opening all over town, some say at the rate of dozen a day. Many Dubliners haven't quite decided what to make of these, but the international hipster contingent in town flocks to the best of them. The newer bars also usually offer more of a pickup/mingling vibe than the older pubs.

Dublin's generally a safe city, but the standard problems everywhere else are standard here, too: Just don't be careless. Pickpockets and purse-snatchers have been known to work busy shopping districts and crowded pubs, and it's not a good idea to embark on solo explorations down those temptingly dark, deserted side streets after hours. Lately, the local authorities have set up a pretty impressive network of 24-hour street surveillance cameras around town, so you might want to think twice about your own behavior under Big Brother's watchful eye.

Sources for arts and entertainment happenings in Dublin are legion: The glamour-glossy ***In Dublin,*** published bi-weekly and sold everywhere for £1.95, contains listings and articles on bars, music, clubs, flicks, theater, the gay scene, galleries, museums, and restaurants (plus the added bonus of always displaying a gratuitously bare, contorted babe and the word "SEX" splashed on the cover, not to mention the dominatrix ads in the back). The ***Event Guide,*** a free listings paper you'll find lying around most cafes and bars, does as good a job as In Dublin, minus the price, gloss, gay scene, and naked chick. The ***Hot Press,*** another £1.95 investment, also contains listings but is more of an organ for music-industry propaganda. The hefty ***GCN*** (Gay Community News), published monthly, can be found in gay-friendly places about town.

neighborhoods

Whatever you're up to, the city center will usually be the place for doin' it. The slow, walled-in **River Liffey** flows east-west through Dublin's core, and most main streets either flow from bridges at right angles to the Liffey, or branch out from these main thoroughfares and run parallel to its bending path. **O'Connell Bridge** lies at the heart of the center. **O'Connell Street,** the old commercial guts of the town, stretches north from the bridge and past the monumental **General Post Office** to **Parnell Square.** This is one of the most soulful parts of Dublin, with a lot of grand old architecture gone a little seedy and not a lot going on (although new development is brightening things up rapidly). To the south, there's **Temple Bar,** a web of cobblestone streets once a funky haven for artists, now a Disneyfied hotbed of touristy bars, clubs, shops, and restaurants. To the east, in the network of winding streets within the borders formed by **Grafton Street, Trinity College, Dublin Castle,** and Temple Bar, is one of the city's heaviest clusters of great bars, pubs, cafes, and live music: The Dublin where Dubliners party. To the southeast, down Grafton

five-o

Dublin police, called Gardai (that's "Gardee" or usually just "the Gard"), are a pretty straightforward, helpful bunch. Feel confident going to them if you need assistance, but also keep in mind that they can search anyone on reasonable suspicion of drug possession and hold them in jail for seven days without charge.

five things to talk to a local about

Dubliners need about as much prodding to talk as hemophiliacs do to bleed. A hearty "hello" should get you an earful with most any representative of this most friendly, loquacious race. Still, if you're worried, give the following openers a try:

1. The Irish seem generally obsessed with any and all of their **famous fellow-citizens,** especially the musicians: U2, the Cranberries, the Coors, Sinead O'Connor, etc. Drop a name and see where it takes you.
2. Anything touching on **drink:** Irish beers, Irish whiskey, and, of course, the great old pubs of Dublin.
3. Ask somebody about **Gaelic football** and/or hurling [see *gaelic games,* below].
4. These days, **the Celtic Tiger** is on everyone's lips. What is it, where did it come from, and how will it thrive in the future?
5. **Ireland** itself seems an inexhaustible subject for the locals. Ask someone to tell you what you should know about this fair island, but only if you've got a comfortable seat.

Street, there's **St. Stephen's Green** [see *hanging out,* below]. Here you get a lot of the fancier hotels and expensive shopping, plus the national gallery, museum, and the library complex. Further to the east of the Green, there are long, elegant rows of brick-faced townhouses arranged around well-manicured squares. Not a hot spot, sure, but something to see.

Public transportation in Dublin is in a bit of a transitional period at the moment. The current bus-centered system just can't keep up with the huge load brought in by Dublin's boomtown economy, nor do those big and beautiful double deckers exactly fly through the city's near-constant gridlock. To make matters worse, Dublin's regular transit routes shut down by 11:30pm, just when the party's getting started for most people. The DART system, which connects the suburbs to the north and south of Dublin, runs til midnight. A new system is currently in the government pipeline, but don't hold your breath. Fortunately, the bulk of stuff to see and do in town lies within a 20 minutes' walk of O'Connell Bridge. So save yourself a lot of wasted time and aggravation, book your digs as near as possible to the city center and take to the streets by foot. Bicycle rental is also an option [see *need to know,* below], but in Dublin's kind of urban mayhem, it's only for those who like to walk that fine line between bravery and stupidity.

First thing you gotta know when you come to Ireland is about *craic.* You may be shocked to hear people talking about how much good crack they have. You'll hear things like, "ooh, boy, did I have great *crack* last night!" You may wonder, since when did Dublin get hooked on the pipe? Well, don't fret, they're actually talking about *craic,* not *crack. Craic* (pronounced "crack") is not a *thing,* it's more of a feeling. When you go out with friends, sit around, have a couple pints, talk, gossip, laugh, maybe listen to music, well, that's *craic.* When you smoke a purified form of cocaine out of a little glass pipe, well that's just stupid. *Craic* is what makes Ireland the place it is. It's the resilient attitude that keeps the Irish Irish, the invisible glue that binds people together. How do you get local *craic?* It's really second nature, it's just a bit different in Ireland. Go out with friends old or new, spark up a conversation with a local, talk, laugh, drink and you'll be having *craic* in no time.

For info about where to find good *craic,* go to ***www.wheresthe craic.com.*** This entertainment guide features up-to-date listings of music gigs in Dublin, Cork, Kilkenny, Limerick and other places.

hanging out

Dublin's streetlife is kind of manic-depressive, with full bipolar swings depending on the weather's whims. Of course, the wet days can turn the outdoor hangout spots bleak and lifeless, but that's the perfect time to join everybody else in a cozy corner of the nearest pub. Meanwhile, even just an hour of warm sunshine guarantees crowds in the parks, cafes, and plazas. Spring fever comes on something fierce for the ray-starved Irish. You've got to get yourself to a park on these rare days: The vibe is electric.

The very best place in town for collective, ecstatic sun worship has got to be the **Trinity College Park** *(back of Trinity College, near corner of Leinster St. S. and Lincoln Place).* On sunny weekday mid-afternoons, the young and over-privileged gather to drink beer, watch cricket, and mingle. This is the best to pretend you're local or meet someone who is. The good times come complete with a patio of (sometimes) sun-kissed picnic tables at Trinity's **Pavilion Bar,** gorgeously manicured grass, and leafy colonnades of trees. If you get tired of gazing on white linens and melanin-deprived flesh, there's always the glowering imperial architecture for eye candy.

For that universal "My God, small world!" run-in with your old college roommate or to mix with other travelers from around the world, go sit on the steps of **Temple Bar Square,** right in the heart of Temple Bar. On a sunny afternoon, there'll always be someone here you'll want to talk to, even if you can't speak the same language. To add to the circus feel, summertime brings street theater to the square every weekday from noonish to 3pm.

For the local skate rats, it's gotta be the **Central Bank Plaza,** just down from Trinity College on Dame Street.

At the south end of Grafton Street, **St. Stephen's Green** is the most popular park in Dublin. Once a great spot for grisly public executions, now it's a tranquil haven for groping lovers. A mixed, anonymous, all-city crowd frolics here, amidst the landscaped flower beds, duck ponds, bridges, gazebos, and shady groves. Usually full of folks, but big enough so there's always a spot free.

Since this is Dublin, the key thing about **The Bailey** *(Duke St., D2; Tel 01/670-49-39; Bus 32X, 39X, 41X, 66X, 67X; Noon-11:30pm Mon-Sat, 4-11pm Sun; AE, V, MC, DC)* is those big heat lamps set up above the outdoor tables. In a pedestrianized enclave just off shoporama-central Grafton Street, these are the best (and most popular) sidewalk views in town. Regulars cultivate that "just slightly overdressed" look, both day and night. Lunch in leopardskin? They've done it—without raising an eyebrow. Slightly gay, pickings are good for all persuasions in the evenings, especially if you like trophy-wife-in-training types.

rules of the game

Public drinking gets you unfavorable attention, as does walking down the street with a joint. They don't mess around here when it come to drugs [see *five-o,* above]. Even so, the streets of Temple Bar crawl with sweat-suited teenage touts selling hash and E of questionable quality. Hard drugs, particularly cocaine and heroin, are getting bigger all the time around here. Heroin is more a part of Dublin slum life, while coke is big in the clubs, most epecially (it has been reported) in **P.O.D.** [see *club scene,* below], which has been called a "den of drugs" in the local papers. P.O.D. is a real dealers' hangout: One regular was recently picked up after bragging on the dance floor about his part in a grisly machine-gunner-on-motorcycle hit on a public prosecutor. These people are most definiteley not the "quaint Irish." They're not to be messed with.

dublin

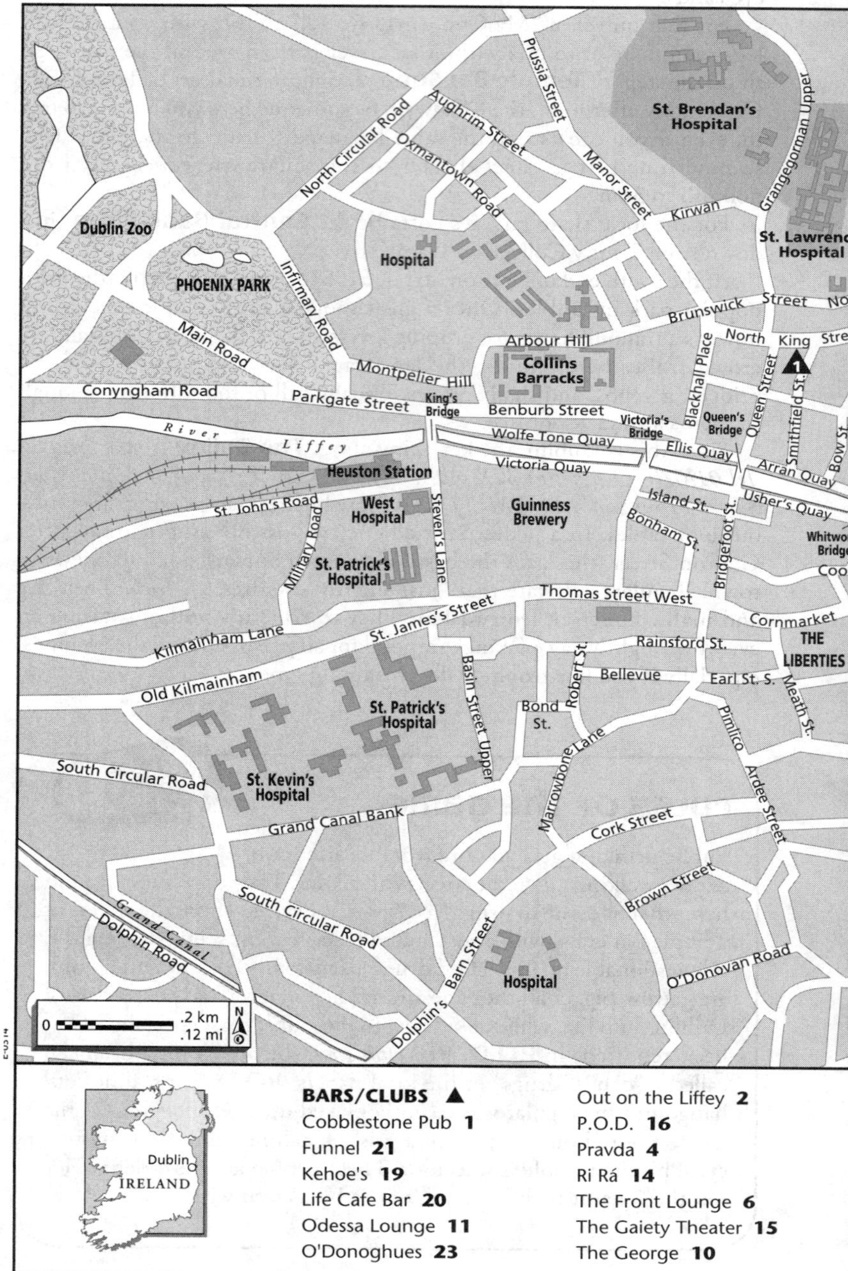
Prussia Street
St. Brendan's Hospital
Grangegorman Upper
Aughrim Street
North Circular Road
Oxmantown Road
Manor Street
Kirwan
St. Lawrence Hospital
Dublin Zoo
PHOENIX PARK
Infirmary Road
Hospital
Brunswick Street
North King Street
Main Road
Arbour Hill
Collins Barracks
Montpelier Hill
Blackhall Place
Queen Street
Smithfield St.
Conyngham Road
Parkgate Street
King's Bridge
Benburb Street
Victoria's Bridge
Queen's Bridge
River Liffey
Wolfe Tone Quay
Ellis Quay
Arran Quay
Bow St.
Heuston Station
Victoria Quay
Island St.
Usher's Quay
St. John's Road
West Hospital
Steven's Lane
Guinness Brewery
Bonham St.
Bridgefoot St.
Military Road
St. Patrick's Hospital
Thomas Street West
Kilmainham Lane
St. James's Street
Cornmarket
Rainsford St.
THE LIBERTIES
Bellevue
Earl St. S.
Old Kilmainham
Basin Street Upper
Robert St.
Meath St.
Bond St.
St. Patrick's Hospital
Marrowbone Lane
Pimlico
South Circular Road
St. Kevin's Hospital
Ardee Street
Grand Canal Bank
Cork Street
Brown Street
South Circular Road
Grand Canal
Dolphin Road
Barn Street
Hospital
O'Donovan Road
Dolphin's
0 .2 km .12 mi
N
Dublin
IRELAND
BARS/CLUBS ▲
Cobblestone Pub 1
Funnel 21
Kehoe's 19
Life Cafe Bar 20
Odessa Lounge 11
O'Donoghues 23
Out on the Liffey 2
P.O.D. 16
Pravda 4
Ri Rá 14
The Front Lounge 6
The Gaiety Theater 15
The George 10

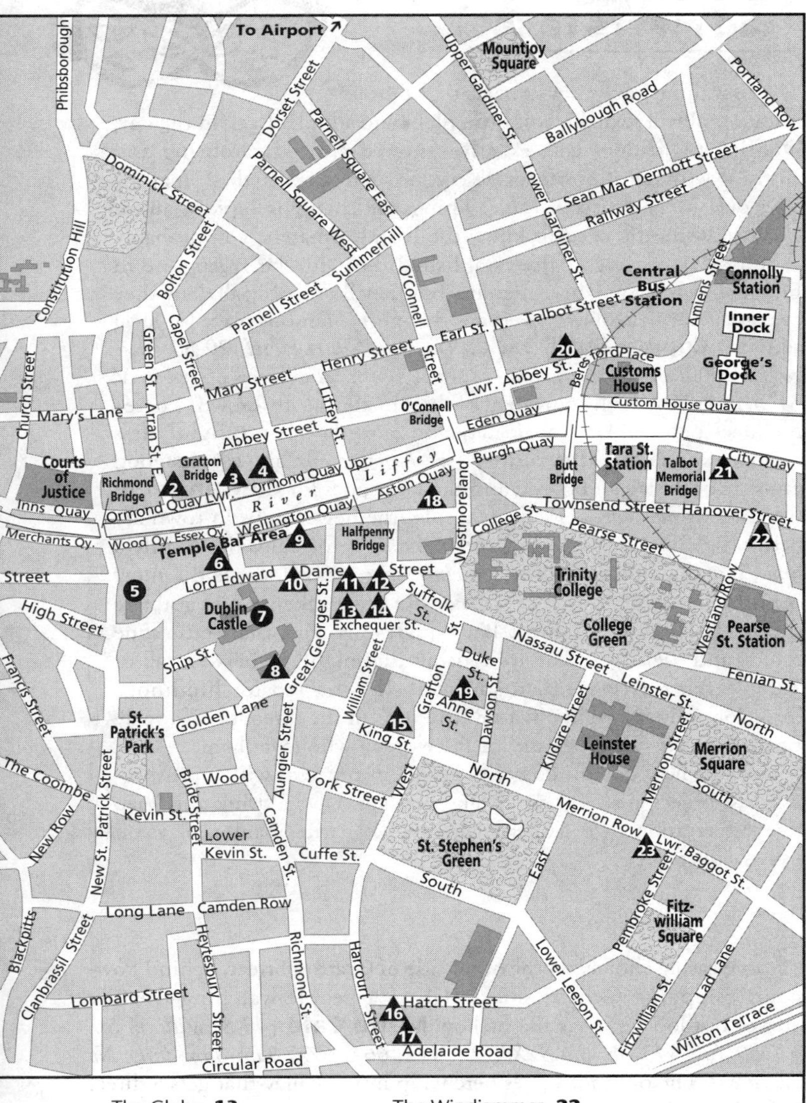

To Airport
Phibsborough
Dorset Street
Parnell Square East
Parnell Square West
Mountjoy Square
Upper Gardiner St.
Lower Gardiner St.
Ballybough Road
Portland Row
Sean Mac Dermott Street
Railway Street
Dominick Street
Constitution Hill
Bolton Street
Summerhill
Parnell Street
O'Connell Street
Central Bus Station
Connolly Station
Amiens Street
Talbot Street
Earl St. N.
Inner Dock
George's Dock
Beresford Place
Customs House
Custom House Quay
Lwr. Abbey St.
Henry Street
Mary Street
Capel Street
Green St.
Arran St. E
Church Street
Mary's Lane
Liffey St.
Abbey Street
O'Connell Bridge
Eden Quay
Burgh Quay
Butt Bridge
Tara St. Station
Talbot Memorial Bridge
City Quay
Courts of Justice
Richmond Bridge
Gratton Bridge
Ormond Quay Upr.
Ormond Quay Lwr.
River Liffey
Aston Quay
Wellington Quay
Inns Quay
Merchants Qy.
Wood Qy.
Essex Qy.
Temple Bar Area
Halfpenny Bridge
Westmoreland St.
College St.
Townsend Street
Hanover Street
Pearse Street
Trinity College
College Green
Westland Row
Pearse St. Station
Street
Lord Edward
Dame Street
Suffolk St.
High Street
Dublin Castle
Exchequer St.
Great Georges St.
Nassau Street
Fenian St.
Ship St.
Duke St.
William Street
Grafton St.
Anne St.
Dawson St.
Kildare Street
Leinster St.
Leinster House
Merrion Street
Merrion Square North
Merrion Square South
Francis Street
St. Patrick's Park
Golden Lane
Aungier Street
King St.
York Street
West
North
The Coombe
New Row
Patrick Street
Bride Street
Wood
Kevin St.
Lower Kevin St.
Camden St.
Cuffe St.
St. Stephen's Green
South
East
Merrion Row
Lwr. Baggot St.
Pembroke Street
Fitz-william Square
New St.
Long Lane
Camden Row
Blackpitts
Clanbrassil Street
Heytesbury Street
Richmond St.
Harcourt Street
Lower Leeson St.
Fitzwilliam St.
Lad Lane
Lombard Street
Hatch Street
Adelaide Road
Wilton Terrace
Circular Road
2
3
4
5
6
7
8
9
10
11
12
13
14
15
16
17
18
19
20
21
22
23

The Globe **13**
The Kitchen **9**
The Long Hall **8**
The Odeon **17**
The Palace Bar **18**
The Stag's Head **12**
The Windjammer **22**
Zanzibar **3**

CULTURE ZOO ●
Christchurch Cathedral **5**
Dublin Castle **7**

lad meets lass

The first thing you gotta know is that Dublin is undergoing a sexual revolution, plain and simple. Back in the day, Dublin's nightlife wasn't exactly centered around carousing and arousing with the opposite sex. Everyone went out with their "mates"- boys over here, girls over there. Things are changing rapidly, and if you really feel the need to know the Irish intimately, you probably should get yourself to the established meat markets. Anyone in Dublin can tell you where they are, but they'll probably all deny they ever go. They lie. Anyway, perhaps the most infamous place for local action is **Copper-Faced Jack's** *(Jackson Court Hotel, 29-30 Harcourt; 10pm-2:30am Fri, Sat, 11pm-2:30am Sun-Thur; £5 cover; V, MC),* full of the Irish equivalent of the Biff and Muffy crowd. There's no cover before 11pm on Friday and Saturday. For a slightly less intense experience, **The Bailey** [see *hanging out,* above] sees good cruising both day and night, and the same goes for **Café en Seine** [see *live music scene,* below]. As a rule, the newer pubs in town are better for mingling [see *bar scene,* above]. As for clubs, it's mostly a bust, but the vibe at **Rí-Rá** [see *club scene,* below] seems the most comfortable for meeting people. For the backpacker set, it's gotta be sunny afternoons at Temple Bar Square-flirt with that statuesque Swede and then set a date for a drink that night. Otherwise, all of Temple Bar's mass-tourism superpubs have a rep for libidinous behavior, most satisfying if your taste runs in the direction of rowdy English-soccer-fan-types and/or the women who love them.

So, just how do you do get yourself "in process" with a prospective lust object around here? Make sure you have a drink and keep the conversation *light.* Superficial is the key: witty banter, plays on words, jokes.

A more casual choice, on the other side of Grafton Street, behind Powerscourt Shopping Centre, smack-dab in a people-watching-friendly cluster of outdoor cafes, is the mellow **Metro Café** *(43 S. William St., D2; Tel 01/679-45-15; Bus 32X, 39X, 41X, 66X, 67X; 8am-8pm daily; No credit cards).* The outdoor tables here wrap into an alley that gets a direct solar hit in the afternoon.

Turning into an all-night party on weekends after the clubs close, **@ Home Cafe** [see *eats,* below] draws an international, gay-straight mixed crowd of hipsters in for grooves, tapas, and wine. This place can be hard to find and sometimes hard to get into (but definitely worth the effort), so make sure you know the where's and how's before you get wasted. Drop in during the day and get the lowdown from the ultra-friendly staff.

Lots of Latin jazz and some techno fills the night at **Kaffe Moka** *(39-40 S. William St., D2; Tel 01/679-84-75; Bus 32X, 39X, 41X, 66X, 67X; 8am-4am daily; No credit cards).* Check out the big couches and coffee tables in the third-floor "library." The crowd here is mostly young, stylish, and international—like the easy-on-the-eyes staff. Kind of a clearinghouse for Dublin's newest arrivals, this place gives a lot of folks their first job in town.

If you're feeling more philosophical on a Saturday at 3am, try **Sufi's Café** *(48-50 Lower Stephen St., D2; Tel 01/679-85-77; Bus 16, 16A, 19, 19A, 22, 22A, 155; 8am-11pm Mon-Thur, till 4am Fri, Sat, 10am-11pm Sun; No credit cards)* just up the street from Kaffe Moka, but with a much mellower, quiet-conversation vibe, with Persian poetry decorating the walls.

Another sweet, very social late-night spot is the ultra-modern **Juice** *(73-83 S. Great George's St., D2; Tel 01/475-78-56; Bus 16, 16A, 19, 19A, 22, 22A; 9am-11pm Mon-Wed, till 4am Thur, Fri, 11am-4am Sat, noon-11pm Sun),* serving a hip, post-club crowd till the late hours. Just across from **The Globe** [see *bar scene,* below].

bar scene

Dublin's bars generally serve beer and liquor, but most don't do much in the way of cocktails beyond a vodka tonic or two. Ask for a martini, and you're probably gonna get a blank stare. Beer is generally sold and drunk by the pint. For lightweights, there's a measurement called "a glass," which is something like a half-pint but not exactly. Prices are pretty

the tart with the cart

Dubliners love cheeky nicknames, especially when they mock public figures. They call the famous monument to fishmonger Molly Malone at the end of Grafton Street (around the corner from where she was baptized) "the tart with the cart" and the women at the Ha'penny Bridge "the hags with the bags." The O'Connell Street statue of Anna Livia, James Joyce's sensual symbol of the River Liffey in *Finnegan's Wake,* is better known as "the floozy in the Jacuzzi." And Joyce himself, who stands immortalized with his cane, frozen in cement across from the General Post Office on O'Connell Street, is lovingly referred to as "the prick with the stick" or "the dick with the stick." Take your pick.

dublin

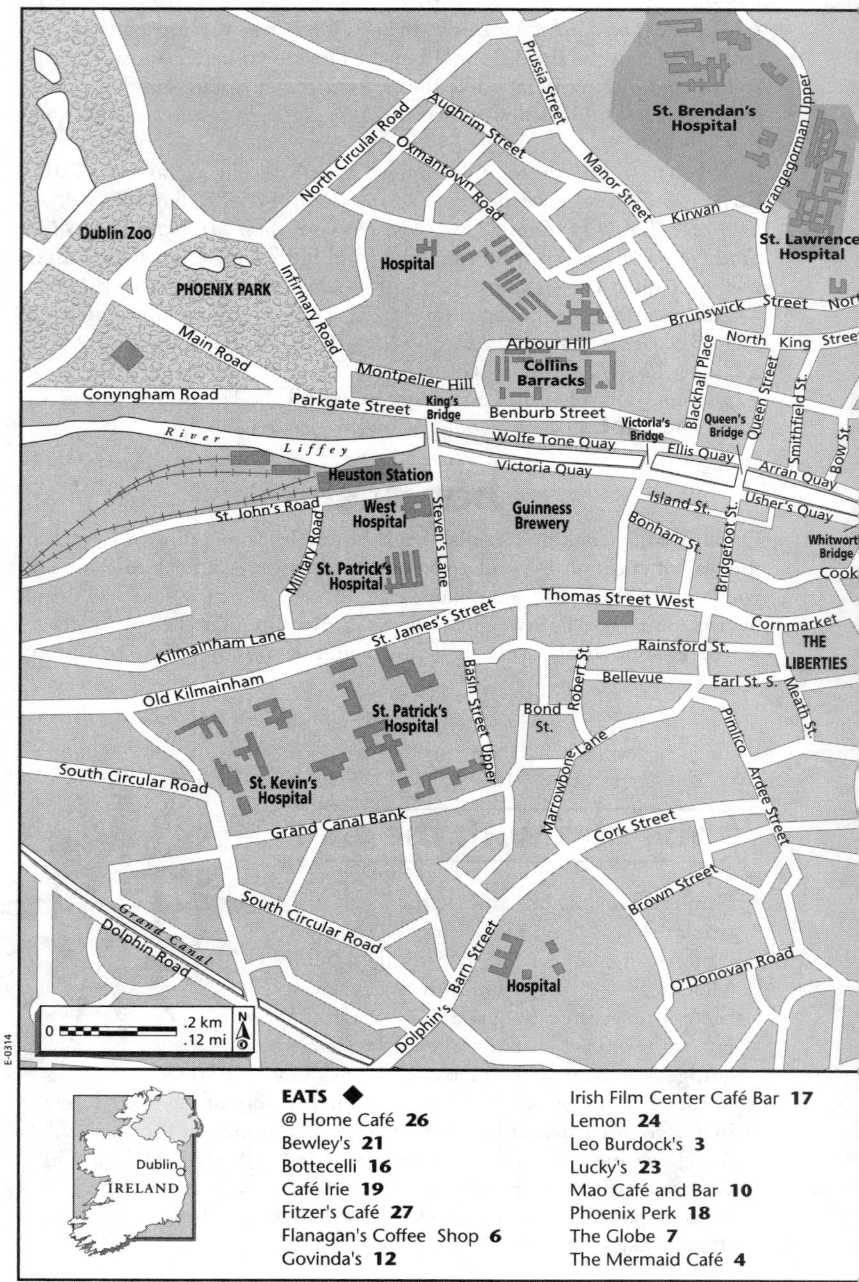
Prussia Street
St. Brendan's Hospital
Grangegorman Upper
Aughrim Street
North Circular Road
Oxmantown Road
Manor Street
Kirwan
St. Lawrence Hospital
Dublin Zoo
Hospital
PHOENIX PARK
Infirmary Road
Brunswick Street
North King Street
Main Road
Arbour Hill
Collins Barracks
Blackhall Place
Queen Street
Smithfield St.
Montpelier Hill
Conyngham Road
Parkgate Street
King's Bridge
Benburb Street
Victoria's Bridge
Queen's Bridge
River Liffey
Wolfe Tone Quay
Ellis Quay
Bow St.
Arran Quay
Victoria Quay
Heuston Station
Island St.
Usher's Quay
St. John's Road
West Hospital
Military Road
Steven's Lane
Guinness Brewery
Bonham St.
Bridgefoot St.
Whitworth Bridge
St. Patrick's Hospital
Cook
Thomas Street West
St. James's Street
Cornmarket
Kilmainham Lane
Rainsford St.
THE LIBERTIES
Old Kilmainham
Basin Street Upper
Robert St.
Bellevue
Earl St. S.
Meath St.
Bond St.
St. Patrick's Hospital
Pimlico
Marrowbone Lane
South Circular Road
St. Kevin's Hospital
Ardee Street
Grand Canal Bank
Cork Street
Brown Street
South Circular Road
Grand Canal
Dolphin Road
Barn Street
Hospital
O'Donovan Road
Dolphin's
0 .2 km .12 mi
N
E-0314
Dublin
IRELAND
EATS
@ Home Café 26
Bewley's 21
Bottecelli 16
Café Irie 19
Fitzer's Café 27
Flanagan's Coffee Shop 6
Govinda's 12
Irish Film Center Café Bar 17
Lemon 24
Leo Burdock's 3
Lucky's 23
Mao Café and Bar 10
Phoenix Perk 18
The Globe 7
The Mermaid Café 4

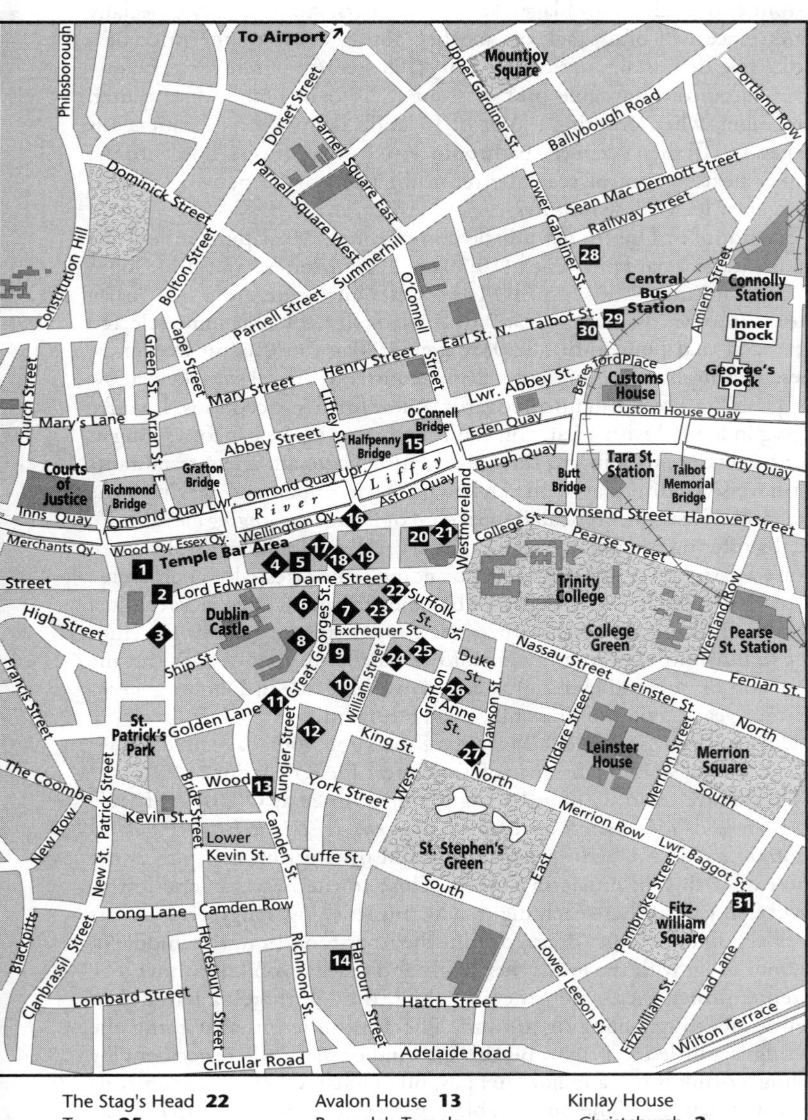

The Stag's Head **22**
Tosca **25**
Yamamori Noodles **8**
Wagamama **11**

CRASHING ■
Abbey Hostel **15**
Abraham House **28**
Avalon House **13**
Barnacle's Temple Bar House **5**
Fitzwilliam **31**
Glenn Court **29**
Harding Hotel **1**
Kelley's Hostel **9**
Kinlay House Christchurch **2**
Oliver St. John Gogarty's Temple Bar House Apartments **20**
Russell Court Hotel **14**
The Townhouse **30**

uniform in the city center: A shot of whiskey runs around £2.10, a pint of stout about £2.30, and lager £2.50. Late bars, clubs, or any especially swank place will often tack on another 30p or more to the price of a drink. The downstairs bar at **J.J. Smyth's** [see *live music scene,* below] serves the most affordable pint of stout (£2.15) in Dublin city center. Remember, when ordering a pint of Ireland's famous stout, patience is the key. Go freshen up in the bathroom, strike up a conversation with the drinker next to you, or scan the room for talent—the pouring process will take at least a few minutes.

Bar hours in Dublin get a little complicated. Most pubs follow the nationwide standard pub hours (10:30am-11pm Mon-Sat or till 11:30pm in summer and 12:30-2pm/4-11pm Sun), but there are a few "early houses" in town that start up at 7 or 7:30am all week and some selected "late bars" that pour until 12:30 or even 1:30am, mostly on weekends. These closing hours mean last call; the courteous Irish lawmakers allow you a half hour to finish up afterwards. A few further exceptions: If you're staying in a hotel with a bar, you can usually stay in the bar for as long as your bartender is willing to stay awake. Also, there are a few restaurants that have started to play with the law by staying open and serving wine (and food, at least theoretically) until 4am or later [see *hanging out,* above], thereby offering the added thrill of the very real possibility of a police raid. (Don't worry, you're not the one who's going to be arrested.) Then there's the old late-night standby: A row of basement dives on Leeson Street, just up from St. Stephen's Green, where the truly desperate go after the clubs close to buy bottles of rotgut wine for the ridiculous price of £20. But the expansion of pub and club hours has been a big issue in Dublin government for years now, so all this may change any minute....

Unless otherwise noted, all bars have the same hours, as stated above, and are within walking distance of Tara Street DART Station.

Don't leave town without having a pint or three at **O'Donoghue's** *(15 Merrion Row, just off St. Stephen's Green; Tel 01/661-43-03; 2pm-11:30pm daily; No credit cards).* A Dublin institution, this pub is the center of Irish folk music in Dublin, close to the hearts of the festive crowd that gathers here each night. The music is sing-songy, and visitors have been known to get dragged from their barstools onto the middle of the floor to jig with the locals. Just smile and act like you know how. The aforementioned locals are generally older, though there's a handful of twentysomethings hanging around. The atmosphere is rustic and the lighting is a little too bright, but it's the kind of place where accidentally spilling a drink is not a major faux pas, but a likely way to have someone buy you a new one. The only problem with O'Donoghue's is that it's so dense with harsh cigarette smoke that the clouds have almost condensed into liquid or solid masses. But it's almost worth getting laryngitis just to experience the fun of this place. Who says north of the Liffey ain't all that?

For those brave enough to walk the deserted streets after dark, or for those who can spare a couple quidros for a cab, the **Cobblestone Pub**

(North King St. on main square in Smithfield; Tel 01/872-17-99; open daily 'til 11:30pm; No credit cards) is an absolute must. Lacking the glammy grunge of Temple Bar's pubs, Cobblestone is a place for locals and those who love them. Enlightened and casual-cool students chat loudly amidst old-timers who look like they've been glued to the bar since the 1950s. There is superb traditional music here almost every night in one, two, or all three of its rooms. The main room is always busy, and musicians usually set up by the end of the bar and play acoustic only. The side bar on the first floor gets busy, but is darker and more atmospheric. If you come before 10pm, you may be lucky enough to catch a trad session with only a handful of people sitting around, wallowing in the beauty of a sad old melody. Upstairs the mood varies and is only open a few nights a week. If you want to see the Dublin that residents of Dublin see, come here.

Set in a stone courtyard off Dame Street that becomes an open street party in the summer months, the **Stag's Head** *(1 Dame Court, D2; Tel 01/679-37-01; Bus 16, 16A, 19, 19A, 22, 22A, 155; Open till 12:30am Thur, Fri; No credit cards)* is one of those great Dublin pubs that welcomes just about anybody, from students to construction workers. You couldn't find better atmosphere for lunch or a contemplative pint than the eerie, stained-glass-lit back room, accompanied by the resident stuffed fox-in-a-box. Weekends always get packed here, but so does everywhere else Dublin.

Some say the **Palace Bar** *(21 Fleet St., D2; Tel 01/677-92-90; Bus 46, 46A, 46B, 63, 150; No credit cards),* on the edge of Temple Bar, pours the best pint of stout in town. Behind those huge, swinging, frosted glass and wood doors, preside some of the finest old-school barmen in Dublin, always there to greet your order with a smile and a nod of the head. God bless 'em—they know how to make a body feel right at home. No wonder your drink tastes better.

The Long Hall *(51 S. Great George's St., D2; Tel 01/475-15-90; Bus 16, 16A, 19, 19A, 22, 22A, 155; No credit cards)* is the pub for nostalgic purists. There ain't much here that hasn't been in place since Queen Victoria ruled: from the ornate, hand-carved wood, to the dozens of filigreed mirrors, and to the crowd of friendly geezers. Take in a few pints at the extra-long bar and see if you can get anybody talking.

The upstairs at **Kehoe's** *(9 S. Anne St., D2; Tel 01/677-83-12; Bus 32X, 39X, 41X, 66X, 69X; V, MC, AE)* looks just like what it is: an old family home converted into a pub. Even the threadbare red wall-to-wall is still in place. First floor wins for coziest digs in town. The regular crowd shuffling up to the unvarnished bar is mostly made up of scruffy-looking arty types, perhaps because the **Kerlin** [see *arts scene,* below], Dublin's big-name gallery, is just up the street.

For those who need to know such things, and you know who you are, things are usually downright lively at **The Windjammer** *(111 Townsend St., D2; Tel 01/677-25-76; DART to Pearse Station; Open at 7:30am daily; No credit cards)* at the otherwise ungodly drinking hour of 8am. Behind the portholes and under the pictures of sailing ships,

Dubliners regularly partake in an alcoholic salutation to the dawn. Many here haven't had a job in years, but that just means they've had time to perfect their conversation skills.

Frequented by music industry folks, **The Globe** *(11 S. Great George's St., D2; Tel 01/671-12-20; Bus 16, 16A, 19, 19A, 22, 22A, 155; No credit cards)* is also Grand Central Station for Dublin's student/hipster community, somehow managing to be cool while still being unpretentious and friendly. Ever wanted to meet an A&R man? Now's your chance. A laid-back vibe, with big ol' wooden tables and a broad-beamed barn floor, plus a few Roman busts for no particular reason. Good coffee, great lunches, and a mellow Sunday afternoon jazz session. The Globe becomes part of **Rí Rá** [see *club scene,* below] after closing time.

The Front Lounge *(33 Parliament St., D2; Tel 01/670-41-12; Bus 46, 46A, 46B, 63, 150; V, MC)* is as Gotham as it gets in Dublin. The modern, art-museum interior fills with a fab-dressed, bite-me-I'm-beautiful crowd, given more flavor than your average Dublin watering hole by the presence of **The Back Lounge** [see *gay scene,* below], a second bar mostly for men who like men.

Housed in the old Harcourt train station, **The Odeon** *(57 Harcourt St., D2; Tel 01/478-20-88; Bus 14, 14A, 15A, 15B, 48A; 12:30pm-midnight Mon-Wed, till 1:30am Thur-Sat, 1pm-midnight Sun; V, MC, AE)* has to be one of the biggest bars in town, and it's packed with young, professional, late-twenties suburbanites every weekend, when the DJs bring in everything from jazz to disco. And they don't just come for the minimalist decor and cool Sunday afternoon cult movies in the winter—they come because this is the most likely spot to meet your Hibernian lover-to-be.

So, you like vodka and big, beautiful Soviet art? Make your way to the north side of the Ha'Penny Bridge, comrade. Cavernous, but still full of little nooks, **Pravda** *(3-5 Lower Liffey St., D1; Tel 01/874-00-90; Bus 25, 25A, 26, 37, 39, 39A, 66, 66A, 66B, 67, 67A, 60, 70X, 134; Noon-11:30pm Mon-Wed, Sat, till 1:30am Thur, Fri, 4-11:30pm Sun; V, MC, AE)* features about 20 different vodkas and DJs spinning mostly hip-hop and funk on weekends starting at 8:30pm. Food, too.

Just around the back of The Globe is the **Odessa Lounge** *(13-14 Dame Court, D2; Tel 01/670-76-34; Bus 16, 16A, 19, 19A, 22, 22A, 155; 5:30-11:30pm Mon-Sun; noon-4:30pm Sun; V, MC, AE)*. Head down into the basement dimness for "young, modern urbanites" sinking into leather couches and doin' the chill cocktail lounge thang. Very comfy but a little more expensive than most. Did we mention they do cocktails? Come for the hangover-curing Sunday brunch of stuffed sausages, Bloody Marys, and people-watching. Reservations recommended.

Remember how mellow watching your little aquarium used to make you feel? The people at the "late bar" **Life Cafe Bar** *(Irish Life Mall, off Lower Abbey St., D1; Tel 01/878-10-32; DART to Connolly Station or Bus 27B, 42, 43, 53, 53A; Noon-11:30pm Sun-Wed, till 1:30am Thur-Sat, till*

12:30am; V, MC) know all about that. The mid-twenties crowd lazing on the continuous blue wall couch under the big tropical fish mural are here for relaxing, conversing, and late-night drinking, but not for straining themselves while DJs spin loungey, laid-back grooves. One downside: Pints are pricey to begin with, at £2.50 to £2.75, and they do a 20p hike during the late hours.

live music scene

What Dublin's music scene lacks in variety it makes up for in atmosphere. More than a few Dublin pubs have grown from neighborhood locals to major city venues hosting international acts without losing their classic pub character. These intimate places naturally spark those indispensible connections between bands and crowds, and their general management style seems to follow a love of music, not specializing in any one musical style, so you'll often see weekly lists ranging from jazz to grunge to trad (traditional Irish music), and nobody seems to mind. Free jazz performances on Sundays are pretty standard in Dublin, so be on the lookout. Unless otherwise noted, these places follow the standard pub hours [see *bar scene,* above].

Whelans *(25 Wexford St., D2; Tel 01/478-24-20; Bus 16, 16A, 19, 19A, 22, 22A, 155; Bands play 8:30pm daily; whelanswex@tinet.ie; No credit cards),* down near St. Stephen's Green, is the scruffy little place in town every band wants to play and then play again, just to bathe in that certain special vibe that lives around the wooden stage in the back room. Unvarnished and unpretentious, seven nights a week here can be a musical education in itself: Gypsy fiddle players, salsa, pop, and rock, it's all here, and the talent (and crowd) is consistently the best in town.

The International Bar *(23 Wicklow St., D2; Tel 01/677-72-90; Bus 32X, 39x, 41X, 66X, 67X; No credit cards),* off the west side of the Trinity College Green, is just a real vintage Dublin pub and a superb one for so many reasons. Simon's been behind the bar here for 30 years, pulling pints under seven beautifully carved heads representing the rivers of Ireland. The nightly acts upstairs could be blues, R&B, acoustic folk, or even comedy and theater. David Murphy's Tuesday open-mike acoustic is an institution: More than a few who started here have been signed to the majors, and Friday's blues regulars back B.B. King when he's in town. Definitely a musician's hangout.

Trad has experienced a new blossoming in Dublin's music scene over the last decade. Listening to a really good trad jam is like listening to great jazz: It's wild, primal, and intoxicating. But forget the cheesy tourist trad sessions drowned out by drunken crowds in Temple Bar. The place to go if you want the real deal is the **Harcourt Hotel** *(60-61 Harcourt St., D2; Tel 01/478-36-77, 24-hour Gigline info 1850/66-44-55; Bus 10, 10A, 11B, 13, 20B; V, MC),* a classy old Georgian job just down the street from **P.O.D.** [see *club scene,* below]. They serve up the best in town for free (well, almost always) seven nights a week in one of their two wood-lined hotel bars. It's another musician's favorite, especially since they can drink after hours at the "residents only" bar. They're planning an expansion of their gigging space, so the intimate feel here may change some.

Black and beautiful, **J.J. Smyth's** *(12 Aungier St., D2; Tel 01/475-25-65; Bus 16, 16A, 19, 19A, 22, 22A, 155; No credit cards)* is another classic, family-owned local doing jazz and blues upstairs in a low-lit, smoky old bar with a no-nonsense, casual feel—no snooty twits here. All their nights are good, but the jazz on Thursdays is the real standout. Tuesday's an open jam session, so sign up in the afternoon for a spot. The benevolent J.J. may serve the cheapest pint of stout in the city center: £2.15 downstairs, 5p more upstairs.

Right between Trinity and St. Stephen's Greens, **Café en Seine** *(40 Dawson St., D2; Tel 01/677-43-69; Bus 32X, 39X, 41X, 66X, 67X; V, MC, AE)* does a deliciously mellow brunch/detox session at 1:30pm. Local legend Herbie fronts the Red Hot Jazz Trio, crooning out hypnotic renditions of Ella's and Billie's favorites under the twirling metallic vegetation of the Parisian Art Nouveau decor. Try **The Globe** [see *bar scene,* above] after 5pm for another particularly good Sunday jazz fix.

For info on the small jazz scene in Dublin, contact the **Improvised Music Company** *(Tel 01/670-38-85; imcadmin@tinet.ie),* a government-funded organization charged with developing jazz in Ireland. Cool job, eh? They arrange gigs around city and bring in a lot of international acts, as well as host the Pendulum jazz night at J.J. Smyth's every Sunday.

For people who prefer high-decibel electronic enthusiasm (i.e. feedback), **Eamonn Doran's** *(3A Crown Alley; Tel 01/679-91-14; Bus 46, 46A, 46B, 63, 150; V, MC)* is just off Temple Bar Square. This is more of a loud, grungy, young guitar-band venue than you'll find in the rest of the city; clashing chords are belted out downstairs in a vaguely honky-tonk looking bar done up in copper-chrome and red velvet. The place to go if you think no Irishman wears his hair long.

cLub scene

Dublin's club scene is small, but the town's clubbers more than make up for it with gung-ho drive—no blasé crowds here. Keep on the lookout for the frequent "one-offs": One-time special events often supplying the month's best party. For the real news, ask the folks at **Big Brother** or **TAG** [see *stuff,* below]. Something you may notice if you get around is that the postage-stamp-size dance floors at Dublin's "big clubs" suffer from long-bar-envy; drinking space is the priority here. If you dance, you gotta love the crush of bodies, and the open, promiscuous exchange of bodily fluids (mostly sweat but also the standard Irish public display of deep-tongue skills) is rampant. As The Man currently dictates, clubs are open 11pm-2am. Crowds move in around 12:30am.

P.O.D. *(35 Harcourt St., D2; Tel 01/478-01-66; Bus 14, 14A, 15A, 15B, 48A; 11pm-2am daily; Cover £5-8; V, MC, AE)* stands for Place Of Dance, in case there was a question about what people do here. A house-dominated joint in a former train tunnel, this one's a killer to get into. On

12 hours in dublin

1. Do what everybody else does. Take the bus tour to ease your guilt over squandering yet another opportunity to broaden yourself through enlightening intercultural exchange, then get to pub crawling with a vengeance. The open-topped double-deckers of **Dublin Bus Tour** *(59 Upper O'Connell St., D1; Tel 01/873-42-22; Departs every 15 minutes 9:30am-4:45pm daily; £6; V, MC)* tour the town and stop at most of the major cultural sites [see *culture zoo,* below]. One ticket lets you get on and off as much as you like during the day.

2. Check out the spectacular *Book of Kells* [see *culture zoo,* below].

3. Have a pint or two in the magisterial tranquillity of the **Palace Bar** [see *bar scene,* above].

4. Take in some great live music at **Whelans,** the **International Bar,** or the **Harcourt Hotel** [see *live music scene,* above].

5. Expose yourself to some good theater at **Project @ The Mint** [see *arts scene,* above].

6. Ease that hangover with some Billie Holiday, eggs Benedict, and a Bloody Mary at **Café en Seine** [see *live music scene,* above].

7. Dance 'round the tulips in **St. Stephen's Green.** [see *hanging out,* above]

8. Learn the words to *Molly Malone* by heart. (Check out her well-endowed statue at the north end of Grafton Street.)

weekends, it's regulars and their suppliers only, mate. Always dress to impress, but save yourself the poser-posturing aggravation and try the easier techno-driven Thursdays or free-entrance Sundays (if you arrive before 10pm in the adjoining, wrought-iron and blue-neon Chocolate Bar). Fridays claim a "totally queer" door policy, but some hets manage to slip in. Worth it for bragging rights more than anything else, and to test your mettle in the terrifying installation-art bathrooms.

As every Dubliner will tell you in tones of hushed sacredness: *"It's part-owned by U2."* Bono and the gang tried hard on the basement makeover of **The Kitchen** *(Clarence Hotel basement, E. Essex St., Temple Bar, D2; Tel 01/677-66-35; Bus 46, 46A, 46B, 63, 150; Cover £3-8; No credit cards),* coming up with a kind of Jabba's palace look; there's not a straight wall in the place, and this is probably the only dance floor in the world with a moat. Already damn tiny anyway but it's made smaller by a cordoned-off part to keep the quality away from the peasantry. The no-nonsense techno-babies' favorite, the place cooks on Tuesdays, fires fueled by £2 vodka and Redbull hits.

festivals and events

St. Patrick's Festival *(Mar 13-17; Tel 01/676-32-05):* Parades and festivities in celebration of Ireland's favorite snake-charmer.

Dublin Film Festival *(Mar; in the IFC, Savoy, and Screen cinemas; Tel 01/679-29-37):* Film screenings, lectures, seminars, and industry schmoozarama.

Bloomsday *(June 16; Tel 01/878-85-47; www.jamesjoyce.ie):* An annual, 24-hour-long party for James Joyce worshipers and anyone else who cares to join in.

Temple Bar Blues Festival *(late July; Tel 01/677-22-55):* International blues acts pack the pubs and streets of Temple Bar. Films and workshops, too.

International Puppet Festival *(mid Sept; Tel 01/280-09-74):* Puppeteers from around the world descend on Monkstown, County Dublin. Madness ensues.

Dublin Fringe Festival *(late Sept-mid-Oct; Tel 01/872-90-16; www.fringefest.com):* The best of international off- and off-off-Broadway theater hits town.

Dublin Theatre Festival *(early Oct; Tel 01/677-84-93; www.iftn.ie/dublinfestival):* Irish and international theater at its best.

If you just want a fun, hip place that won't turn you away, head for **Rí Rá** *(Dame Court; Tel 01/677-48-35; Bus 16, 16A, 19, 19A, 22, 22A, 155; No credit cards).* It's the enlightened middle road in relaxed cool, playing everything from hip-hop to disco. Dance floor thing in the basement; cult movies, projections, and mellower grooves in the upstairs **Globe Bar** [see *bar scene,* above]. Another good thing about this place: Unlike the other two "big rep" clubs in town, romantic encounters actually happen regularly here.

Humming with that unbeatable underground buzz, the two floors of **Funnel** *(24 City Quay; Tel 01/677-03-40; DART to Pearse Station or Bus 5, 7, 7A, 7X, 8; Bar 9am-6pm Mon-Fri, club 8:30pm-2am Wed-Sat; Cover £6-8; V, MC)* tuck into redeveloped riverside warehouses opposite the Custom House. Warm up in the curvy, uncannily vulva-like downstairs bar, then ascend to the heights of pleasure in the blacked-out upstairs dance floor and stage. There's a superb performer-audience vibe here, as the best in up-and-coming local DJs give their all, and the crowd gets down. The door staff is actually friendly.

An old Victorian theater full of salsa, reggae, and world music on three levels—how can you go wrong? **Salsa Palace @ the Gaiety Theatre** [see below] *(11:30pm-2am Fri; Cover £7)* is just a big funhouse; five Bogart-and-Bacall-classy antique bars, a couple dance floors, live bands, and cult movies in the vast theater, which incidentally is kept quite dark and is a "great place to snog." (That's Irish for kiss.) This place is a maze, so watch out: Get too hazy and you probably won't surface 'til morning.

Yes, they're beautiful and dress damn fine in **Zanzibar** *(34-35 Lower Ormond Quay, Tel 01/878-72-12; DART to Tara St. Station or Bus 25, 25A, 26, 37, 39, 39A, 66, 66A, 66B, 67, 67A, 70, 70X, 134; 10:30am-1:30am Mon-Fri, 11am-1am Sat, Sun; No cover; V, MC),* a 1,500-capacity, over-the-top, African-themed late bar replete with palms, mosaics, giant urns, and Arabian Nights-evocative paintings. A little cheesy, but hey, sometimes we all want that, especially since you don't have to pay to party. Also, it's a good place for meeting members of the opposite sex. Popular with foreign university students, who carouse and arouse to anything from techno to ABBA on one of the larger dance floors in Dublin. Get there before 10pm, it fills up fast.

arts scene

Dublin's art, fashion, and design world is just now starting to gain momentum. You've got to realize that it's only been in the last four or five years that there was any significant population in Ireland with money to spend, period. Some say this is the reason Ireland has had more than its share of great writers: Paper and ink are cheap; canvas, silver, or silks are not. Well, as a wise man said, money is the grease for creativity's wheels, and the wheels are spinning in Dublin. You're sure to get an earful on the subject, and perhaps an introduction to a few of Ireland's future groundbreakers at **The Clock** *(110 Thomas St., D8; Tel 01/677-55-63; No credit cards),* the local pub for Dublin's College of Art and Design, a few minutes walk west of the Temple Bar. Another spot drawing in a picture-peddling crowd is the venerable **Kehoe's** [see *bar scene,* above], just around the corner from Dublin's top gallery, the Kerlin.

▸▸VISUAL ARTS

Irish contemporary art is a little subdued compared with works from other parts of Europe. You'll see lots of subtle grays and blacks, muted colors, and straightforward, museum-like presentations. There's not much showboating going on. That wouldn't be the Irish way.

If art drama is what you're looking for, the most experimental of the big-name contemporary galleries in town is the warehouse-sized **Green On Red Gallery** *(26-28 Lombard St. East, D2; Tel 01/671-34-14; 11am-6pm Mon-Fri, till 3pm Sat; greenred@iol.ie; No credit cards),* a few blocks south of **Dublin Castle** [see *culture zoo,* below]. Here you're likely to see more installation art, from found materials to video, with a mixture of Irish and international artists.

Being the big cheese of the Dublin art scene, the **Kerlin Gallery** *(Anne's Lane, off S. Anne St., D2; Tel 01/670-90-93; 10am-5:45pm Mon-Fri, 11am-4:30pm Sat; gallery@kerlin.ie, www.kerlin.ie; No credit cards)* has the most impressive stable of established Irish artists working in photography, painting, sculpture, and prints. They also have the most impressive prices on works ranging from charcoal sketches of magnified clustered sperm to photographs of bleak urban wastelands. Don't be afraid to drop in for a look: The staff here are down-to-earth and friendly. Conveniently located between Trinity College and St. Stephen's Green.

For an edgier feel, try **Temple Bar Gallery and Studios** *(5-9 Temple Bar, D2; Tel 01/671-00-73; 10am-6pm Tues-Sat, till 7pm Thurs, 2-6pm Sun; www.paddynet.ie/tbgs, tbgs@indigo.ie; No sales)* a big concrete and industrial steel complex founded by a group of artists back in '94 in the hope of giving first-timers a chance. Mostly a publicly funded workspace for 30 artists, this is where they get up to those sometimes groundbreaking, sometimes "Screw your petty bourgeois conventions of taste! This filthy rag thrown in the corner is art!" kind of shenanigans.

Where the local DJs who do projection effects hang out, **Arthouse Multimedia Center for the Arts** *(Curved St.; D2; Tel 01/605-68-00; 9:30am-6:30pm Mon-Fri, 10am-5pm Sat; www.arthouse.ie, info@arthouse.ie; Free admission),* in Temple Bar, is about as hip as it gets in Dublin. Inside a big Bauhaus steel-and-glass fish tank, their official line is to "further the use of digital technologies in Irish artistic practice." According to them, they are the keepers of the "Artifact," a sinister object with unspeakable powers with which they will enslave the Earth. Actually, it's a CD-ROM of the work of over 800 local artists working in multimedia. They also do exhibitions, performance art, training, publishing, the whole digital kit-and-caboodle. Definitely worth a look-see, then kick back in their upstairs cafe [see *wired,* below].

▶▶PERFORMING ARTS

Irish theater seems to be a little obsessed with rural nostalgia these days. That means a lot of what you'll see on the main stages will be set in the same little thatched-farm kitchen with lines like: "Cup of tea?"; "Cow's gotten out again"; "It's the priest, the priest!"; and "Johnny's gone off to America, oh, how will we manage?!" repeated ad nauseam. Hopefully, it's just a phase. Thankfully, there's plenty of edge-cutting going down, too.

If you really want the whole footlights shebang in a nutshell, drop £10 on the ***Irish Theatre Handbook,*** a comprehensive guide to Irish drama and dance with descriptions of all known venues and companies. For the latest skinny on what's hot and what's not in local theater, check out ***Irish Theatre Magazine,*** a £4 quarterly. Both are available in **Waterstone's** [see *stuff,* below].

For the post-curtain crowd, the formula is to look for the comfiest pub nearest the theater. Practically connected to the back door of the Gaiety, **Neary's** *(1 Chatham St., D2; Tel 01/677-85-96; Bus 10, 11A, 11B, 13, 16A; No credit cards)* gets most all their thespian trade. **Brogan's Bar** *(75 Dame St., D2; Tel 01/679-95-70; Bus 50, 50A, 54, 56A, 77, 77A, 77B; No credit cards)* is convenient to the Olympia. And for a pow-wow of the big heads from the Gate and the Abbey, try the **Flowing Tide** *(9 Lower Abbey St., D1; Tel 01/874-41-06; DART to Connolly Station; No credit cards).*

The never-boring 3-person **Barabbas** group *(7 South Great George St.; Tel 01/671-20-13)* specializes in outrageous "what will they do next?" physical theater. Wunderkind Mikel Murfi was last seen talking out of his ass, artfully done up as a face and thrust through a stage floor. (It's a lot better than it sounds, really.) **The Corn Exchange** *(43-44 Temple Bar; Tel 01/679-64-44),* a theater, dance, and performance group, does a lot with stylish, experimental stagings. They're regular favorites at fringe festivals worldwide. **Rough Magic** *(Tel 01/671-92-78)* is the big deal in town for new Irish plays.

Otherwise, for consistently good stuff there's always the **Project Arts Center** *(39 E. Essex St., Temple Bar, D2; Tel 01/679-66-22; DART to Connolly Station; Shows 8pm; Tickets £5-8; www.project.ie, info@project.ie; V, MC).* Founded in '66 by artists wanting an alternative venue, the Project does theater, music, dance, and performance art. They've helped foster the likes of U2, Gabriel Byrne, Liam Neeson, and Neil Jordan, to name a few. In June 2000, they moved into a big, newfangled, Euro-money building, complete with 250-seat auditorium, gallery, bar, garden, and bookshop.

For theater on the cheap, there's the **Players Theatre** *(Upstairs in the Samuel Beckett Centre, Trinity College; Tel 01/608-22-42; DART to Tara St. Station or Bus 5, 7A, 8, 15A-C, 46, 55, 62, 63, 83, 84; Shows 1pm, 8pm Mon-Sat Oct-May; £3.50, £2.50 members, matinee £2.50/1.50; No credit cards)* showing works produced, directed, and performed by Trinity students.

The **Abbey and Peacock Theatres** *(26 Lower Abbey St.; Tel 01/878-72-22; DART to Connolly Station; Performances 8pm; Tickets £8-16; www.abbey-theatre.ie, abbey@indigo.ie; V, MC),* Ireland's national theater, were founded by Celtic revivalists back in 1904, and some might say things haven't progressed since then. Ground zero for Irish nostalgic self-absorption and the tourists who flock to see it. The Peacock is the Abbey's little studio, intended for more adventurous programming. Overall, this is not an exciting place, but the acting and production standards are truly world-class. They're getting a new (as yet undetermined) artistic director soon, so who knows what the future holds?

The Gate *(Cavendish Row, D1; Tel 01/874-43-68; DART to Connolly Station; Box office 10am-7pm Mon-Sat, shows 8pm Mon-Sat; tickets £12-14; V, MC, AE, DC)* is where a young Orson Welles cut his teeth. Same story as the Abbey: These days it's for suburban upper-middle-class consumption. Uh, I mean, this is where you can see definitive productions of the Irish classics.

John Scott's **Irish Modern Dance Theater** *(SFX City Theater, Upper Sherrard Street; Tel 01/874-96-16, Fax 01/878-77-84; imdt@iol.ie, www.adnet.ie/imdt)* is a contemporary theater specializing in offbeat and innovative productions and stagings of original works. Using Irish talent from around the world, the company strives to take dance in new directions, and is now incorporating multimedia into their work. In this year's *Off the Wall,* massive still images of dancers in motion were projected on top of trippy, ambient lighting effects on the wall of a Temple Bar lot. It's all a bit pretentious and who knows if it means anything at all, but it's cool as hell to see giant, half-naked girls and boys arabesqueing on a wall. They put on about two shows a year, generally in late fall and winter, but check their web site or give them a ring when you're in town. They perform all over Ireland and Europe as well. It's a good place to let the Guinness haze inside your head interact with the world.

You'll never know what's up at the **Gaiety** *(S. King St.; Tel 01/677-17-17; Box office 11am-7pm Mon-Sat, shows 8pm Mon-Sat, matinee 3pm Sat; Tickets £7-46; V, MC),* Dublin's oldest theater, set in a gorgeous old Victorian. Could be opera, ballet, concerts, or theater. Some good, some bad. It's worth the price of a ticket just to sit in the Dangerous Liaisons-like gilt-and-velvet splendor of the 1,000-seat hall. Same holds for Dublin's other, slightly smaller old Vic, the **Olympia Theatre** *(72 Dame St. D2; Tel 01/677-77-44; Bus 50, 50A, 54, 56A, 77, 77A, 77B; Tickets £15-30; V, MC, AE).*

Despite what the international phenom of Riverdance might lead you to assume, dance ain't so big in Dublin. For news, check in with the **Dance Theatre of Ireland** *(Tel 01/280-24-55)* or **Irish Modern Dance Theatre** *(Tel 01/874-96-16).*

The place for film geeks has got to be the **Irish Film Center** *(6 Eustace St., D2; Tel 01/679-34-77; Bus 21A, 78A, 78B; Screenings 2-11pm daily; Membership £10 per year, £1 weekly; Tickets £4.50 adults, £3 students; fii@ifc.ie, www.iftn.ie/ifc; V, MC).* It's the only place in town for art-house cinema and a pretty cool one at that, with a tasty restaurant and bar added in [see *eats,* below]. There's just one catch: You have to be a member. Fortunately, weekly memberships only cost £1 and can be purchased up to 10 minutes before any screening. Don't miss Flashback, their survey of Irish filmmaking, shown for free Wednesday through Sunday at noon.

For the latest Hollywood schlockfest, get your rocks off at the **Savoy** *(Upper O'Connell St., D1; Tel 01/874-88-22; DART to Connolly Station; Tickets £4.75, £3 before 6pm; V, MC)* a five-screener on the city's main drag, with the biggest screen in Ireland.

▸▸LITERARY SCENE

The history of Dublin's literary life is legendary. We all know that more than a few of the greatest European writers of this century came out of this little town. Well, times have changed, and the local talent these days seems less likely to be found sitting next to you at the pub and more likely to be heading for cities outside of Ireland, where them big publishers roam. A lot of what goes on these days amounts to ancestor worship with the venerable James Joyce getting the most flattering offerings made to his dead white maleness. If you want to sample some local authors still among the living, pick up The ***Stinging Fly,*** Dublin's literary journal, available at local bookstores. For other news, the free, bi-weekly *Event Guide* has a literary events section called "Literary Live" with all upcoming events listed. The *Irish Times* runs a definitive lit listings section every Saturday. To talk to another human being about it, contact the Irish Writers' Centre *(Tel 01/872-13-02; iwc@iol.ie, www.iol.ie/~iwc/)*. The staff here are so lethargically boho cool, they come off like those pesticide junkies in the movie *Naked Lunch*.

The place where things word-wise go down, the **Winding Stair Bookshop & Café** *(40 Lower Ormond Quay, D1; Tel 01/873-32-92; Bus 70, 80; 10am-6pm Mon-Sat, 1-6pm Sun; Cover £1.50-5; V, MC)* is the most frequent host for readings of contemporary poetry and prose in Dublin, usually in the evenings. The place has a great vibe, a chill cafe overlooking the Liffey, and...a very windy old staircase. Who knows? Maybe you'll meet tomorrow's Seamus Heaney scribbling away over a cup of joe.

Looking like the basement conversion Grandpa did for the benefit of his poker buddies, **Grogan's Castle Lounge** *(15 S. William St.; Tel 01/677-93-20; Bus 32X, 39X, 41X, 66X, 67X; No credit cards)* is an old man's pub where Dublin's bookish types come a-slumming. Actually, it's quite cool; darn attractive local artwork hangs on the walls above the green 1950s-vintage upholstery. The dominant color being green, calm meditativeness sets in pretty quickly here, especially after a pint or two. So come and lay the groundwork for your next novel or something.

gay scene

Compared with other European capitals, the gay scene in Dublin is none too big. Actually, with only two officially "gay" bars, it's pretty small. Even so, an enlightened Irish government gave the legal go-ahead to homosexuality a few years ago, and gay culture is thriving. For listings and other info, pick up the *GCN* (Gay Community News) at **Waterstone's** [see *stuff,* below]. In Dublin magazine also has a gay happenings section. There are a few places around town that regularly draw a good gay crowd: **Juice** [see *hanging out,* above] just up the street from the George; **@Home Café** [see *eats,* below], which hosts a gay night on Sundays; and **The Front Lounge** [see *bar scene,* above]. Some good numbers to know: Dublin Lesbian Line, Tel 01/872-99-11; Gay Switchboard Dublin, Tel 01/872-10-55; LOT (Lesbians Organizing Together), Tel 01/872-04-60; LEA (Lesbian Education and Awareness), Tel 01/872-04-60; and Out House, Tel 01/670-63-77.

The George *(89 S. Great George's St.; Tel 01/478-29-83; Bus 22A; 12:30-11pm Mon-Tue, till 2:30am Wed-Sun; V, MC)* holds the honor of being the first gay bar established in Dublin. Actually a bar and nightclub, the crowd here is mostly gay men, with some lesbians and an increasing number of straights walking on the wild side. The Sunday evening bingo here with dancing drag queen Penny Bridge has become a fine old Dublin institution.

Just downriver from the Four Courts, **Out on the Liffey** *(27 Upper Ormond Quay; Tel 01/872-24-80; DART to Tara St. Station or Buses 34, 70, 80)* is more of a lesbian hangout, in an old-style stained wood and bric-a-brac pub.

Gay nights in Dublin hot spots are not well-established. *HAM (Homo Action Movies)* at **P.O.D.** [see *club scene,* above] (£8) is probably the best night in town these days, drawing a ridiculously well-manicured, fab-dressed, mixed crowd. For the most up-to-date listings, check out *GCN.*

culture zoo

Trinity College and the Book of Kells *(College Green, D2; Tel 01/608-16-88; Bus 5, 7A, 8, 15A-C, 46, 55, 62, 63, 83, 84; 9:30am-5pm Mon-Sat, noon-4:30pm Sun Oct-May, 9:30am-4:30pm Sun Jun-Sept; Admission £3.50 adults, £3 students):* One of the funkiest illuminated picture books ever made, housed in a city-center, green haven of a campus.

National Gallery *(Merrion Square West, D2; Tel 01/661-51-33; DART to Pearse Station or Bus 5, 6, 7, 7A, 8, 10, 44, 47, 47B, 48A, 62; 10am-5:30pm Mon-Sat, till 8:30pm Thur, 2pm-5pm Sun; Free tours 3pm Sat, Sun; www.nationalgallery.ie, artgall@tinet.ie; Free admission):* Easy to get to and chock-full of old Irish art. Nice on a rainy day.

National Museum *(Kildare St. near St. Stephen's Green; Tel 01/677-74-44; 10am-5pm Tue-Sat, 2pm-5pm Sun; Free admission):* The National Museum is a must-see for those seeking knowledge about the history of this island. Particularly enticing to the curious visitor is the extensive collection of pre-Christian artifacts. These bronze- and stone-aged relics bring to life the religious customs and burial practices of the ancient Irish, and even shows how they ate. Check out the iron-age grave with a remarkably intact body that was found in a bog. Metalwork that dates from the introduction of Christianity in the 5th century onward is also incredible. The metal has distinct Celtic swirls and ornamentation; check out the biggest draw, the truly beautiful Tara Brooch. The good thing about the museum is that it's filled with booty from other parts of the country, so you can get an excellent picture of the cultural and archaeological history of the whole of Ireland without leaving Dublin.

Irish Museum of Modern Art *(Military Rd., Kilmainham; Tel 01/671-86-66; Bus 78A, 79, 90; 10am-5:30pm Tue-Sat, noon-5:30pm Sun; Free admission):* Beautiful building, nice garden, so-so art.

Chester Beatty Library and Gallery of Oriental Art *(20 Shrewsbury Rd., Ballsbridge, D4; Tel 01/269-23-86; DART to Sandymount Station or Bus 5, 6, 6A, 7A, 8, 10, 46, 46A, 46B, 64; 10am-5pm Tue-Fri, 2-5pm Sat; Free admission, free guided tours 2:30pm Wed, Sat; mryan@cbl.ie):* One of the finest collections of Asian art in Europe.

Dublin Castle *(Dame St. at Castle St.; Tel 01/677-71-29; 10am-5pm Mon-Fri, 2pm-5pm Sat-Sun; Admission £3 Adults, £2 Students):* Let's put it this way: do you enjoy torture? If your answer to this question is yes, plunk down the pound and take the guided tour of Dublin Castle. Even if your answer is no, the castle does have one thing going for it: the couches look very comfortable, so if you're about to fall asleep, maybe you can ask nicely and the tour guide will let you curl up on one. Better yet, just stick to the outside and read our brief history: Built in 1204 by Norman King

John, it was the seat of British power in Ireland until the early 20th century. The Easter Uprising led to 50 defeated insurgents being executed within the castle's walls. In 1938, the first President of Ireland was sworn in here. Nowadays, it's used as a government office and is the formal reception area for powerful political visitors to Ireland. The architecture is a questionable hodgepodge of 800 years of additions.

Christ Church Cathedral *(Christ Church Place; Tel 01/677-80-99; 10am-5:30pm daily; £2 suggested donation):* Dean John Patterson and his wacky band of clerics have cooked up a riotous helping of Cathedral zaniness sure to satisfy your appetite for the Big Man. But seriously, folks, the Christ Church Cathedral has a fascinating history and exudes an intimacy and sense of peace that you will find in few churches anywhere. It's much cooler than its neighbor down the street, the more grandiose St. Patrick's Cathedral. Perhaps it's because they don't have braggin' rights to St. Patrick having baptized people on their grounds, or maybe it's because of the church's history that they all seem more down-to-earth about the whole eternal salvation racket. In 1038, a group of Vikings, who had apparently taken a break from pillaging Ireland, saw fit to construct a little wooden church here. In 1171, the original structure was buffed out in stone. The present cathedral structure dates from the 1870s, when a massive restoration took place.

Bank of Ireland/Parliament House *(2 College Green, D2; Tel 01/661-59-33 x2265; All city centre buses; 10am-4pm Mon-Fri, 2-5pm Sat, 10am-1pm Sun; Free admission):* Come see the opulent former chambers of the only parliament that ever voted itself out of existence. The stylish

fashion

For a European capital, Dublin's a pretty casual town. The basic youth uniform looks like a Gap ad, minus the khakis (a piece of clothing curiously absent from Ireland, perhaps as a result of the long, cruel occupation by khaki-wearing British). Two things stand out in Dublin street fashion; the omnipresence of "combats" (known to folks in the U.S.A. as "cargo pants") and the absence of "runners" (aka sneakers). Everybody wears some kind of leather shoe. Sporting sneakers will probably get you barred from more than a few of the places mentioned in this guide. Seems many pubs have bouncers just to enforce the "no-runners" rule. Otherwise, you look great. Don't worry.

place to change money. With guided tours of the House of Lords Chamber *(10:30am, 11:30am, 1:45pm Tue, Thur).*

The General Post Office (GPO) *(O'Connell St., D1; Tel 01/872-88-88; DART to Connolly Station or Bus 25, 26, 34, 37, 38A, 39A, 39B, 66A, 67A; 8am-8pm Mon-Sat, 10:30am-6:30pm Sun; Free admission):* A symbol of Irish freedom. Story has it you can still see bullet holes from the 1916 Easter Rising in the pillars out front.

The Custom House *(Custom House Quay, D1; Tel 01/878-77-60; Bus 27A, 27B, 53A; 10am-5pm Mon-Fri, 2-5pm Sat, Sun; Admission £2):* One of Ireland's most dramatic architectual sites, more than slightly screwed up by a misplaced, hulking DART bridge: Beauty and the Beast. Check out the octagonal room on the first floor.

St. Patrick's Cathedral *(Patrick's Close, Patrick St., D8; Tel 01/475-48-17; Bus 50, 50A, 54, 54A, 56A; 9am-6pm Mon-Sat, 9am-4:30pm Sun; Admission £2 adults, £1.75 students):* The former haunt of Saint Patrick and Jonathan Swift—you find the connection.

Kilmainham Gaol Historical Museum *(Inchicore Rd., Kilmainham, D8; Tel 01/453-59-84; Bus 21, 78, 78A-B, 79, 123; 9:30am-4:45pm daily Apr-Sept, 9:30am-4pm Mon-Fri, closed Sat, 10am-4:45pm Sun Oct-Mar; Admission £2 adults, £1 students):* A fascinating and sometimes gruesome presentation of Irish prison history.

Guinness Hopstore *(St. James' Gate, D8; Tel 01/408-48-00; Bus 51B, 78A, 123; 9:30am-5pm Mon-Sat, 10:30am-4:30pm Sun Apr-Sept, 9:30am-4pm Mon-Sat, noon-4pm Sun Oct-Mar; www.guinness.ie; Admission £5 adults, £4 students or certified alcoholics (har, har)):* A tour of this site is obligatory for anyone who partakes of the dark stuff. Free pint (or two!) with admission.

The Old Jameson Distillery *(Bow St., D7; Tel 01/807-23-55; Bus 67, 67A, 68, 69, 79, 90; 9:30am-6pm daily, last tour at 5pm; Admission £3.50 adults, £3 students):* Get to know your whiskey history at this former distillery.

The Joyce Tower Museum *(Sandycove, County Dublin; Tel 01/280-92-65; DART to Sandycove Station or Bus 8; 10am-1pm/2-5pm Mon-Sat, 2-6pm Sun Apr-Oct; Admission £2.50 adults, £2 students):* James Joyce slept here.

great outdoors

If you want to work the physique in Dublin city center, your best bet is a gym. Otherwise, to avoid the constant congestion on the downtown sidewalks and streets, you could run with the deer in the vastness of Phoenix Park at the edge of the city or maybe do laps around St. Stephen's Green. There are two gyms in town that offer short-term memberships.

Right in the heart of Temple Bar, **Pulse Fitness Center** *(1-2 Temple Bar, D2; Tel 01/679-96-20; DART to Tara St. Station or Bus 46, 46A, 46B, 63, 150; 7:30am-10pm daily; Membership £7 per day, £15 per week, £55*

gaelic games

If you want to experience something truly, authentically Irish, without any mass-tourism b.s., you'll have to check out a **Gaelic football** or **hurling** match.

Dubliners, as well as the rest of Ireland, are madly passionate about these two sports. Both are considered home-grown, are played on an amateur basis only in Ireland, and evoke happy feelings of national identity. There's some history here: The **GAA** (Gaelic Athletic Association) was founded in 1884, as part of the Irish independence movement. But whatever the history, both sports also embody the kind of fast-paced, high-skill, and high-scoring events that any sports fan will immediately respond to. Gaelic football could be called a cross between soccer and rugby, while hurling looks something like lacrosse spliced with field hockey: The players carry big wooden sticks, which they can use like bats, but they can also handle the ball, called a *sliothar* (that's "shlither"). You're sure to see these sports on any pub TV screen in the summer.

For live blood, sweat, and tears, check out the elite inter-county games taking place in Dublin from mid-March to mid-September at **Croke Park** *(Jones Rd., D9; 01/836-32-22; Bus 3, 11, 16; Times and teams listed in Evening Herald; £2-6).* This is the finest Gaelic sport to be seen in the land, and the intense inter-county rivalry makes for an electric atmosphere. The season culminates in the All-Ireland Hurling and Football Finals, Ireland's Superbowl.

per month; Classes £3 at lunchtime, £3.50 evenings; V, MC) offers a smallish weight room with the basic machines and classes, plus a unisex sauna.

Why run when you can trot? **Ashtown Riding Stables** *(Navan Rd., Castleknock, D15; Tel 01/838-38-07; Bus 37, 38, 39, 70; 9am-5pm daily in summer; £15/hr riding or lesson; No credit cards)* will rent you a horse and let you wander as you please through the hills, forests, and fields of Phoenix Park, just at the edge of Dublin. (Don't worry, the park is quite safe and innocuous, except for Ireland's rampant public indecent exposure problem.) Don't know how to ride? Don't worry, they offer lessons, too. (Just kidding about the indecent exposure.)

Ah, a romantic row in a brightly painted, handmade boat, out to an uninhabited island, followed by a picnic by one of the old ruins.... Sure, 'tis a recipe for lovin'. Find **Aidan Fennel** (aka **The Ferryman**) *(Coliemore Rd., Dalkey, Co. Dublin; Tel 01/283-42-98; Ferry £3, rowboat rental £5/hour Jun-Aug, weather permitting; DART to Dalkey Station)* on the stone wharf next to the Dalkey Island Hotel.

If you're in town sometime during May and June, you owe it to yourself to check out the **Howth Castle Rhododendron Gardens** *(Howth, Co. Dublin; Tel 01/832-22-12; DART to Howth Station or Bus 31; 8am-sunset daily Apr-Jun; Free admission),* where 2,000 varieties of rhododendron will be blooming like heaven fallen to Earth in this 30-acre garden. Just checking out pretty little Howth Harbor and the view from the headlands above the town is worth the 20 minute DART ride.

Only a block south of St. Stephen's Green, but worlds away in atmosphere, is the serene, walled-in **Iveagh Gardens** *(Clonmel St., off Harcourt St.).* So few people come to its broad lawns, shady walkways, and fountains, it's almost spooky. You can feel like it's your own private garden in the middle of a sunny afternoon. Great for a picnic with a special friend; it closes at 6pm.

stuff

The places for a mainstream shopping fix in Dublin are around the pedestrianized Grafton and Henry streets. Grafton Street, on the south side of the Liffey at the edge of Temple Bar, is definitely more expensive and upmarket; it's Dublin's equivalent of Fifth Avenue. It's also much more touristy than Henry Street, where Dublin's north-siders go bargain shopping. But if you're trawling for goodies with some real character, you'll have to wander off the main track.

▶▶DUDS

If you want to blend with the in crowd at the clubs, get your socially acceptable uniform at **Hobo** *(4 Exchequer St.; Tel 01/670-48-69; 9:30am-6pm Mon-Wed, Fri, till 8pm Thur, till 7pm Sat, noon-6pm Sun; £1-150; V, MC),* which sells streetwear ("combats"—basically cargo pants—and tight T-shirts) to every hipster and skate rat in town.

Ten doors down, **Sabotage** *(14 Exchequer St.; Tel 01/670-48-69; 10am-6pm Mon-Sat, 2-6pm Sun; V, MC, AE)* does the phattest hip-hop wear.

One great thing about being a female is **No-Name** *(11 Suffolk St.; Tel 01/677-37-99; 9:30am-6pm Mon-Sat, till 8pm Thur, 2-6pm Sun; 99p-£24.99; V, MC)* a women's-only shop for labels like Calvin Klein and Kookai at discount prices. Snatch up two little numbers for £5 in the bargain basement.

You'll find the who's-who at the **Design Centre** *(Powerscourt Townhouse Centre, top floor, D2; Tel 01/679-57-18; 9:30am-6pm Mon-Sat, till 9pm Thur; www.designer-place.ie; £100-250; V, MC, AE),* a ready-to-wear "group showcase" for up-and-coming women's designers.

Oakes *(8 Dawson St., D2; Tel 01/670-41-78; 10am-6pm Mon-Fri, till 5pm Sat; oakes@tinet.ie; £70-350; V, MC)* specializes in collection-based, custom-fit high fashion at ready-to-wear prices. Calling their concept "customized-to-order," young design partners Donald Brennan and Niall Tyrell have attracted a worldwide following. Check it out.

For a slightly younger take on classic Hibernian beauty, try Marc O'Brien, upstairs at **Awear** *(26 Grafton St., D2; Tel 01/671-72-00; 9:30am-6:30pm Mon-Sat, till 8:30pm Thur, noon-6pm Sun; £85-130; V, MC).*

Definitely doing the iconoclastic side of local fashion, **Sé Sí** *(13 Temple Bar; Tel 01/679-05-23; 10am-6pm daily, till 8pm in summer; £15-90; V, MC)* features the kind of stuff that will stand out in any crowd. Pronounced "shay-shee," the name means "him and her" in Gaelic. Vibrant and innovative are the words for their clothing and accessories. The place to go for that purple velvet backpack with the fuzzy technicolor horns sticking out all over.

▸▸BOUND

Easons *(40 Lower O'Connell St., D1; Tel 01/ 873-38-11; DART to Connolly Station or Bus 25, 34, 37, 38A, 39A, 39B, 66A, 67A; 8:30am-7pm Mon-Wed, till 8:45pm Thurs and 7:45pm Fri, 1-6pm Sun; V, MC)* is Ireland's big chain bookstore, with branches all over the country. This particular one, off the Henry Street shopping area, has all the atmosphere you would expect of a big chain, but the selection, including imported newspapers and magazines, just goes on and on.

Hodges Figgis *(56-58 Dawson St., D2; Tel 01/677-47-54; Bus 10, 11A, 11B, 13, 20B; 9am-7pm Mon-Fri, till 8pm Thur, 9am-6pm Sat, noon-6pm Sun; V, MC)*—say that one five times fast. Just a hop south of Trinity College, this is the grand old man of Dublin's bookshops, now going all trendy with a comfy cafe inside. The stained wood interior is a great place for a free read on a rainy day.

Across the street from Hodges Figgis is **Waterstone's** *(7 Dawson St., D2; Tel 01/679-141-5; Bus 10, 11A, 11B, 13, 20B; 9am-8pm Mon-Fri, till 8:30pm Thur, till 7pm Sat, 11am-6pm Sun; V, MC).* This one has dark wood too, plus a slightly more piquant stock than its neighbor, doing gay stuff, New Age, and Women's Studies. These folks also host frequent, free readings by authors.

Dandelion Books *(74 Aungier St., D2; Tel 01/ 478-47-59; Bus 16, 16A, 19, 19A, 22, 22A, 155; 10:30am-6:30pm Mon-Sat; No credit cards)* is just a horde of cheap, used paperback thrillers. Pulp-lover's heaven.

Part of the host of book peddlers next to Trinity, **Hannas** *(27-29 Nassau St., D2; Tel 01/677-12-55; Bus 5, 7A, 8, 62; 9am-6pm Mon-Sat, till 8pm Thur; V, MC)* feels like a real bookshop, with high-shelved, oodles-o-books chaos and slightly naughty erotic art on the wall. Does new stuff too, but it's the secondhand we're interested in.

Don't let the creepy entrance tunnel scare you—**The Secret Book and Record Store** *(15A Wicklow St., D2; Tel 01/679-72-72; Bus 32X, 39X, 41X, 66X, 67X; 11am-6:30pm daily; V, MC)* is quite friendly, stocking secondhand and antique books in a small, comfortable space. You'll never know what you'll find here. They even have some old vinyl (hence the name).

▸▸THRIFT

The big mama of Dublin flea markets has gotta be **Mother Red Caps Market** *(Back Lane, off High St., D8; Tel 01/453-83-06; Bus 21A, 78A,*

78B; 10am-5pm Fri-Sun). "Da Mutha" lies sprawled in a big roofed-in space just a little trot past Christchurch Cathedral. You know the drill: Stalls selling anything from framed portraits of John Wayne to floral-print couches, henna tattoos, or your fortune. Good luck, and don't forget to haggle.

Dublin also has a slew of charity secondhand shops. There are a couple just around the corner from **Trinity College** [see *culture zoo,* above], including **Oxfam** *(S. Great George's St., D2; 10am-5pm Mon-Sat; 99p-£7; AE, V, MC).* Down the street is **Cerebral Palsy** *(Unit 8, S. Great George's St., D2; 9:30am-5pm Mon-Sat; £2.50-10; No credit cards).* On the north side, there's **C.A.S.A.** *(26 Capel St., D1; Tel 01/872-85-38; 9:30am-5pm Mon-Sat; Most items under £5; No credit cards),* which benefits the Caring and Sharing Association. Sounds nice, doesn't it?

Two parts of town have sprung up as secondhand zones, conveniently close to one another. **George's Street Arcade** *(S. Great George's St. near the corner of Exchequer St., D2; Bus 16, 16A, 19, 19A, 22, 22A, 155; 10am-6pm Mon-Sat)* hosts no fewer than three shops: **Jenny Vander** *(Tel 01/677-04-06; £10-250; V, MC)* has serious, Great Gatsby-esque vintage clothes and jewelry for women at some serious prices. Just up Jenny's stairs, **Rufus the Cat** does more men's clip-on ruffles, jumbo afro wigs, glittery gold platforms with 6-inch heels, and full '60s- and '70s-style suits. Both shops regularly equip the discerning partygoer with stylish rental outfits. Across the arcade, the **Big Whiskey** *(Tel 01/677-92-99; V, MC)* does your more standard secondhand stuff very well, and very cheaply, mostly for £5 or under.

There are even a couple of cheap secondhand shops in the well-touristed environs of Temple Bar *(Bus 46, 46A, 46B, 63, 150).* **The Eager Beaver** *(17 Crown Alley; Tel 01/677-33-42; 9:30am-5:30pm Mon-Fri, 9:30am-6pm Sat, till 7pm Thur in summer; £3.95-17.95; V, MC)* has two floors of unisex secondhand. **Damascus** *(2 Crown Alley; Tel 01/679-70-87; 10am-6pm Mon-Sat; Clothes £1-20; V, MC)* has men's and women's secondhand, plus some creepy totems from Indonesia and a fleet of wind chimes that's threatening to collapse the ceiling.

▸▸FOOT FETISH

Need some new treads? Try **DV8 Shoes** *(4 Crown Alley; Tel 01/679-84-72; Mon-Sat 10am-6pm, till 8pm Thur; £19.99-110; V, MC, AE).* They're all here: Shelly's of London, Bunker, Yellow Cab, Diesel, Vagabond, those yummy f—k-me boots, platform sneakers, and blue suede shoes. Stomp in style, baby.

▸▸TUNES

Remember, most of the records in Ireland are like the wine: brought in by ship. Still, there's a pretty good selection outside of those multinational-owned, pop-dominated megastores (which we won't talk about). The two floors of **Chapters Music Store** *(54 Middle Abbey St.; Tel 01/873-04-84; 9:30am-6:30pm Mon-Sat, till 8pm Thur, 1:30-6:30pm Sun; V, MC)* offer a wide selection of new and secondhand CDs and videos, plus vinyl and DVD.

Vinyl junkies and beat freaks, **Big Brother Records** *(Basement of 16B Fade St.; Tel 01/672-93-55; 11am-6pm Mon-Sat, till 6:30pm Thur; www.bigbrotherrecords.ie, bigbrother@connect.ie; V, MC)* is your home for everything in hip-hop, jazz, and electronica. In a cozy basement just a stone's throw from George's Street Arcade [see above], owner Killian "Heart-O-Gold" Murphy is ever-present, amicable, and knowledgeable, like a regular Bodhisattva of Beats.

Upstairs at the same address, **Road Records** *(16B Fade St.; Tel 01/671-73-40; 10am-6pm Mon-Sat; www.groov.ie/road, road@groove.ie; V, MC)* has what's new in indie vinyl, Chicago "post-rock," reggae, and ska in your basic hole-in-the-wall record shop.

For the drum 'n' bass, techno, and trance you heard the DJs spinning last night, head down the banks of the Liffey to small but slick **TAG Records** *(5 The Cobbles, Wellington Quay; Tel 01/677-97-05; 11am-7pm Mon-Sat; V, MC)*. The staff here are so obliging, it's almost eerie.

Just north of the Ha'Penny Bridge, **Abbey Discs** *(3 Meller Court, Lower Liffey St.; Tel 01/873-37-33; 9:30am-6:30pm Mon-Sat, till 8pm Thur; V, MC)* carries a very respectable selection of dance music, new vinyl, and budget CDs.

down and out

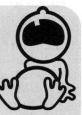

Got no money? Take the poor man's tour of Dublin on the **DART.** It works this way: You can ride the train from one end of Dublin Bay to the other, while only paying for travel to one stop (80p), if you tell the ticket seller when you get on that you're only going to the next station. Just make sure you do get off at that next stop when your "tour" is over. This is most convenient between Pearse and Tara Street stations in city center. The DART's comfy, green-upholstered, big-windowed wonders travel north to the Howth peninsula and south along the shoreline to Bray, passing over historic cityscapes, along sandy beaches, and through leafy village centers. Or, if you know you'll want to get off a few times, you can always get an all-day pass for £3.50.

Or take in a free flick. During July and August, there's a free screening every Saturday night in Temple Bar's Meeting House Square. Tickets (free but required) are available at **Temple Bar Information Centre** *(18 Eustace St., D2; Tel 01/671-57-17)*.

Otherwise, most of the major cultural sites in Dublin are free entry [see *culture zoo,* above]. You got no money for anything else, you might as well feed your head.

Pick up your black roses and Marilyn Manson key rings at **Rhythm Records** *(1 Aston Quay; Tel 01/671-95-94; 11am-6pm Mon-Sat; V, MC).* On Temple Bar's river side, this chaotic tourist bazaar features hard rock, punk, and goth secondhand, collectible CDs and vinyl.

eats

All the money flowing around Ireland, combined with a surge of immigration into the country from abroad, has brought some real cosmopolitan variety and quality to the Dublin restaurant scene. You can get anything from Mongolian to Mexican, but unfortunately you're likely to wait long stretches for just about everything. There's no such thing as snappy service in Ireland. Glacially slow is more like it. Your best strategy is to do like the Irish and keep a sense of humor. One tip: The wait staff will usually ignore you completely after they've dropped off your meal. If you want your check before the third millennium, it's probably better to go up to the "cash" and ask to pay there. Otherwise, resign yourself to gathering dust. If you do get a good waiter, tip as you would at home. They'll appreciate it. Unless noted, all spots below are within walking distance of Tara Street DART Station.

▸▸CHEAP

For a real Dublin pubgrub lunch done right, take a pilgrimage to the **Stag's Head.** Try the daily special for £4.50. **The Globe** serves up tasty and trendy lunchtime fare for under £5 between noon and 3pm [see *bar scene,* above, for both].

Eat lunch with the last of the independents in the cafe/bar at the **Irish Film Center** [see *arts scene,* above] a chill, almost homey bar connected to the IFC art-house cinema complex. The soup of the day (with a hearty slice o' bread) makes a good light lunch for under £2. Don't wait for the waiters to come to your table—place your orders at the bar, and you'll get the food faster.

Staffed by an international collection of friendly freaks, the **@ Home Café** *(Creation Arcade, off Duke St., D2; Tel 01/672-90-10; Bus 32X, 39X, 41X, 66X, 67X; 9am-11pm Mon-Thur, till 3am Fri-Sun; £1.20-7.95 all items; V, MC)* is a real gem. It's a laid-back, informal cafe with a kind of hip East Village feel, tucked away in a little mall between Grafton and Dawson streets, that serves absolutely delicious Mediterranean-style food, doing morning breakfast, lunchtime soups, killer salads, sandwiches, and exotic tapas in the evening. The Sunday brunch is great, too. Check it out anytime but especially late-night, after the clubs close.

A little upstairs hole-in-the-wall with a constant rock-steady and reggae soundtrack, **Cafe Irie** *(11 Upper Fownes St., Temple Bar, D2; No phone; Bus 46, 46A, 46B, 63, 150; 10am-6pm Mon-Wed, Fri, Sat, till 8pm Thur, noon-6pm Sun; 80p-£3.75 breakfast and lunch items; No credit cards)* might actually persuade you that the tourist-laden Temple Bar is still funky. Serving it up fresh and creative, they also have prices that can't be beat: A meal of soup, sandwich, and tea here can cost you well under £5. Go before the lunch rush at 1pm.

Doin' the cheapest Irish breakfast in town, **Flanagan's Coffee Shop** *(10 Castle House, S. Great George's St., D2; Tel 01/475-02-25; Bus 16, 16A, 19, 19A, 22, 22A, 155; 7:30am-4:30pm daily; All breakfasts under £3; No credit cards)* comes through with an egg, a sausage, and a rasher (Irish bacon), plus toast and tea, all for £1.50. Beat that. Tiny and purple, it's just across from **The Globe** [see *bar scene,* above].

For the best (and probably cheapest) slice of deep-dish 'za in town, made by Italians, naturally, hit Temple Bar's **Botticelli** *(3 Temple Bar, D2; Tel 01/672-72-89; Bus 46, 46A, 46B, 63, 150; V, MC).* For £1.50 to £1.80, they've got anything from sausage to smoked salmon on those slabs, and slices are available from noon to 3pm.

Eat your way to cosmic consciousness without dropping too much of your material world in the process at **Govinda's** *(4 Aungier St., D2; Tel 01/475-03-09; Bus 16, 16A, 19, 19A, 22, 22A, 155; 11am-9pm Mon-Sat; £1.25-4.50; MC, V),* just south of Temple Bar. One of a constellation of cheap, cafeteria-style, tofu-and-salad eateries connected to a meditation center/Krishna commune/what-have-you. Physical manifestations tastefully decorated in auras of red, green, and yellow.

The best thing at **Yamamori Noodles** *(71-72 S. Great George's St.; Tel 01/475-50-01; Bus 16, 16A, 19, 19A, 22, 22A, 155; 12:30-11pm Sun-Wed, till 11:30 Thur-Sat; £6.50-9.50 per entree; V, MC, AE)* is the 12:30 to 5:30pm lunch special: £5 for any dish of noodles (14 choices of ramen, soba, or udon) with a choice of tea, coffee, or fresh carrot juice. Their huge bowl of ramen, chock-full of veggies, meat, and seafood, never disappoints. It's "cool food, cool jazz, and sushi," and they get packed later for their more expensive, but still reasonable, dinners. Around the block from **Dublin Castle** [see *culture zoo,* above].

If you're in Dublin and you don't go to **Bewley's** *(78 Grafton St; Tel 01/676-761; 7:30am-11pm daily. 11/12 Westmoreland St.; Tel 01/676-761; 7:30am-7:30pm daily. 40 Mary St.; Tel 01/677-671; 7am-9pm Mon-Wed, 7am-2pm Thu-Sat, 10am-10pm Sun),* then you must be too high to know what's good for you. Bewley's is another Dublin institution—think of it as the yin to Starbuck's evil yang. The place is elegant while still being ultra-chill and inexplicably cheap (the all-day Irish breakfast of eggs, tea, toast, bacon, sausage, more sausage, and beans is only £3.95). The crowd is diverse, surprisingly so for a place that looks like only confirmed teetotalers would dare step inside. Angsty teens defiantly cloud the smoking section with their incessant puffing while little old ladies read the papers and sip tea. There are three locations in downtown Dublin, so wherever you are, you can find relaxation only minutes away.

Noodles are status symbols at **Wagamama** *(South King St.; Tel 01/478-21-52; noon-11pm Mon-Sat, 12:30-10pm Sun; £6-8).* This elbow-to-elbow style eatery is slick and attracts people who definitely want to be seen slurping their soba, but damn if the food isn't tasty. It's not even that expensive; a huge bowl of noodle soup could fill at least 1.5 people.

wired

***www.ireland.travel.ie* :** Irish Tourist Board
***www.eventguide.ie* :** *The Event Guide* Site
***www.iol.ie/~smytho/dublin/* :** Hedonist's guide to Dublin
***www.geocities.com/sunsetstrip/club/3008/* :** Dublin clubbing

Most hostels have at least one computer available, and Internet cafes seem to be taking over every basement in town. Try going well before noon or late evening unless you're OK with waiting.

Central Cybercafe *(6 Grafton St., D2; Tel 01/677-82-98; 8am-11pm Mon-Fri, 9am-11pm Sat, 10am-10pm Sun; www.centralcafe.ie; £5/hr, £4 students; No credit cards)* is a bright, second-story cafe with lots of big art and stained-glass windows, just packed with the latest equipment: 15 flat-monitored Pentium III's, plus a printer, scanner, and fax service. Plenty of food and designer coffee too, all on the menu for under £4. Basement-housed **Planet Cyber Café** *(23 S. Great George's St., D2; Tel 01/679-0583; 10am-10pm Sun-Wed, 10am-midnight Thur-Sat; £1.50/15 mins, £5/hr; £0.80-2.35 all food items; No credit cards)* offers 17 fast PCs, a scanner, and color printing; as well as coffee, sandwiches, pizza, and sweet stuff to munch on. Head north of O'Connell's statue to find **Global Internet Café** *(8 Lower O'Connell St., D1; Tel 01/878-02-95; 8am-11pm Mon-Fri, 9am-11pm Sat, 10am-10pm Sun; £5/hr; www.globalcafe.ie; No credit cards).* It's the bright and happy California vegetable still-life theme in yet another basement, this time with a mixture of swift PCs and iMacs, plus color printing, scanning, and faxing. **Bétacafé** *(Curved St.; Dublin 2; Tel 01/605-68-00; 10am-6pm Mon-Sat, noon-6pm Sun; £5/hr, £4 students; www.betacafe.com; No credit cards),* in the second-floor atrium of Temple Bar's Arthouse [see *arts scene,* above], is the cybercafe with the best ambiance but the worst hardware. The videoheads from Arthouse come here to sip cappuccinos but not necessarily to surf, so the crowd is more arty and sociable. The old black Macs here are only for the desperate. Otherwise, there's a printer and seven slightly aged PCs, built by Hyundai. When the others are full, try the north side's **Interpoint** *(67 O'Connell St., upstairs at Funland, D1; Tel 01/878-34-55; 9am-10pm daily; £5/hr, £4.50 students; V, MC).* No caffeine here but there's always a few speedy PCs open, and you can make cheap international calls from the phone booths, then play some pinball downstairs. A fax and laser printer are available as well.

Lucky's *(39 Dame St.; 8am-5pm Mon-Sat; £3.95 for a large breakfast)* is a great spot for whiling away the morning hours over greasy slabs of rashers (like bacon only thicker) and white pudding (hockey-puck-like sausage filled with god-knows-what). The "Big Breakfast" (fatty meats, anyone?) features tea, eggs, sausage, rashers, white pudding, and toast for a paltry £3.95—enough fatty acids to keep you trekking for hours. On a lighter note, you can get coffee and cappuccinos as well as a hearty assortment of pastries and croissants. The crowd is diverse in age, level of hep, and working status, but lands on the proper side of things. The comfy but smoky backroom has attractive ceiling windows to let in the sun, diffused by Dublin's ubiquitous clouds.

You've tried the rest, now stop messing around at those pretentious Temple Bar cafes and come to **Leo Burdock's** *(2 Werburgh St; Tel 01/454-03-06; noon-midnight Mon-Sat, 4pm-midnight Sun; £3-4.50; No credit cards),* hands down the best chip shop in the known universe. You'll recognize it by the queues running around the corner most days. Spitting distance from the Christ Church Cathedral, it's a toss-up as to which place will do more for your soul. An enormous filet of battered and fried cod is £3; chips are £1.20. Easily enough food for two adults, but with stuff this good, get your own, dammit. Get 'em with salt and vinegar or splurge for ketchup or tarter sauce (£0.15 for a little packet that you could probably get for free from Burger King). About the only thing Burdock's doesn't have is hot girls behind the counter. Too much of a good thing could kill you, after all.

Lemon *(66 S. William St.; Tel 01/672-90-55; 8am-late; £1.80-3.50 for crepes; No credit cards)* is a welcome addition to the new, gastronomically enlightened Dublin. Enjoy crepes sweet and savory in this slick, ultra-modern café. Imagine a lovely crepe with butter and sugar. Or tuna and cheddar. Or smoked salmon . Or Canadian maple syrup and bananas. Eat in the small back dining area or bask in the infrequent Dublin sun at outdoor café tables. The staff is friendlier than you'd expect for a trendy place in a trendy neighborhood.

Ah yes, the **Phoenix Perk** *(50 Dame Street; Tel 01/679-96-68; 10:45am-8:00pm Mon-Fri, 10:15am-8pm Sat-Sun; sandwiches £3-4; No credit cards).* Is there *anywhere* American pop culture has not laid a reminder of its ubiquitousness in the lonesome backpacker's path? Hard to say for sure. Phoenix Perk's logo is based on the logo for the coffee shop on TV's *Friends, Central* Perk, get it? Inside, it's pretty much the same as the show, except you won't see Chandler, Monica, Rachel, Joey, Phoebe, or Ross, and all the furniture is different, and the lay-out of the building is nothing like the set they show on TV. Nonetheless, the people that work here make you want to stay and hang out with your...friends! Kick it over tea and coffee, pretty good baguette and Panini sandwiches filled with a wide assortment of meats, cheese, and veggies, £3-4.

▶▶DO-ABLE

Taking Ireland's communist chic craze to its extreme, **Cafe Mao** *(2-3 Chatham Row; Tel 01/670-48-99; noon-late daily; entrées under £10; V,*

MC) attracts everyone from 40-year-old-mom-types on a Saturday out to fresh-faced coolios who like wearing sunglasses indoors. The noisy, busy, trendy spot has a well-lit interior thanks to large garage-style windows. Décor is a bit like an Ikea showroom, with brilliant bands of reds, blues, and yellows wrapping around mostly unadorned white walls. Warhollian silk screens in neon colors embellish the back walls and entrance (The staff is darn attractive, too). Try the Malaysian chicken with saffron rice and a side order of delicious, hot Lemongrass Nan bread. Finding good food that's not meat-based in Dublin is like trying to get high on Sleepy Time Tea, so this place should be a find for all of you hippie-dippy veggie-types. If you don't salivate over the flesh of caged animals, go for the red pumpkin curry with butternut squash and lemongrass, with vegetable spring roles as an appetizer.

The old standby for young Dubliners going out on the town, the popular local chain **Fitzers Café** *(51 Dawson St., D2; Tel 01/677-11-55; Bus 10, 11A, 11B, 13, 20B; 9am-11:30pm daily; £6.95-13.95 per entree; V, MC, AE)* serves everything from tandoori to chili in attractive, modern surroundings. This one is just south of Trinity College; another branch is at Temple Bar Square.

▸▸SPLURGE

The atmosphere at **Tosca** *(21 Suffolk St., D2; Tel 01/679-67-44; 10:30am-11pm Mon-Fri, 11am-11:30pm Fri, Sat, 1-4pm Sun; £8.95-15.95 per entree; V, MC, AE)* puts it in a category of its own. Everybody who thinks they're anybody comes here to rub shoulders with supermodels, rock stars, and any other young gods and goddesses of our media-obsessed world. Still, it's a comfortable place for mere mortals, conveniently right off Grafton St., and the Italian-style food is darn good. Best for dinner or the *Elvis Loves Eggs* Sunday brunch with live DJs.

The Mermaid Cafe *(69-70 Dame St., D2; Tel 01/670-82-36; Bus 15, 15A 15B, 83, 155; 12:30-2:30pm/6-11pm Mon-Sat, 12:30-3:30pm/6-9pm Sun; £8.75-13.75 per entree; V, MC)* is one of the places in town food critics flock to for the pleasure of it. On a sunny Temple Bar corner, and with lots of windows, chef/owner Ben Gorman puts up a different menu of creative seafood dishes every week. Try the giant seafood casserole with Thai aromatics or tuna tartare with white horseradish slaw and wasabi mayonnaise: It's craft cooking at its best.

crashing

Dublin city-center lodgings have been springing up like toadstools after a rain these last few years, responding to the massive influx of partying weekenders. Unfortunately, although many places are mediocre, even the dirty, overcrowded, and poorly run places are guaranteed full houses in summer because of the heavy demand. To avoid getting stuck in a dive, book well in advance, especially for weekends. Irish hotels are known to have a quirk about beds; budget or big-bucks makes no difference. They all seem to have a stock of mattresses strangely reminiscent of the island's geography:

pointy at the corners, bog-soft in the middle, and generally ancient. If you want a firm mattress, make sure you insist on one. And one more thing: There's lots of street noise in the presently construction-frenzied Dublin, so ask for a bed away from the road if that bothers you.

▶▶CHEAP

The hostels listed here all have comfy TV lounges, well-equipped kitchens, and serve a small breakfast (generally toast and tea) included in the crashing price.

Painted yellow and white, every window full of blooming flowers, the **Abbey Hostel** *(29 Bachelor's Walk, D2; Tel 01/878-07-00; DART to Tara St. Station or Bus 51, 51B, 68, 68A, 69, 69X, 78A, 79, 90, 210; info@abbey-hostel.ie, www.indigo.ie/~abbeyhos; £40-60 double, £13-17 4-bed, £11-16 6-bed, £8-14 10-bed; V, MC)* takes the prize as prettiest hostel in city center. Overlooking the Liffey at O'Connell Bridge, this hostel is about as central as it gets. With bathrooms in every room, the real power showers feel pretty damn good in comparison to the usual whimpy 30-seconds-a-push jobs. Friendly, clean, and relatively small, you can even practice your piano playing in the TV room. BBQ-o-rama on the back patio in the summer, charcoal provided.

Avalon House *(55 Angier Street; Tel 01/475-00-01, Fax 01/475-03-03; info@avalonhouse.ie; www.avalon-house.ie/index.shtml; £9-15 dorm)* is the Grand Central Station of hostels. This 300-bed backpacker Mecca welcomes the budget traveler with clean sheets, and free "breakfast in a bag" (a muffin, yogurt, and fruit). Avalon House sees over 100,000 guests a year and does so with remarkable efficiency. The place is giant, and so by its nature is a bit impersonal; some people complain about the service. But it has a full kitchen, 24-hour access, secure locker storage (£1), no curfew, pay Internet kiosks and helpful staff. Online reservations can be made at their web site and you can book ahead for other hostels here too. Doubles and singles are available, though they fill up fast; book well in advance.

Located in the heart of the hedonist's paradise, **Barnacles Temple Bar House** *(19 Temple bar, corner of Cecelia Street; Tel 01/671-62-77, Fax 01/671-659; templeba@barnacles.iol.ie; £18-25 per person twin room, £13-17 4-bed dorm, £11.50-£14 6-bed dorm, £10.50-13 10-bed dorm, £9-11 12-bed dorm)* is super-friendly and clean; it seems to be popular with gay and lesbian backpackers. This new hostel features en suite bathrooms, gratis continental breakfast, and moins cher laundry facilities. There is also a self-catering kitchen to boil your spaghetti.

Located just around the corner from the central bus station, **Abraham House** *(82 Lower Gardiner St., D1; Tel 01/855-06-00; DART to Connolly Station; Bus 27B, 42, 43, 53, 53A; £7.50-10.50 dorm, £13.50 quad, £18.50-19.50 double; V, MC, AE)* is everything it should be: clean, secure, and cheap. Most rooms have attached bathrooms, and everybody gets a towel.

The Dublin branch of the USIT NOW empire, **Kinlay House Christchurch** *(2/12 Lord Edward St., D2; Tel 01/679-66-44; DART to*

Tara St. Station or Bus 21A, 50, 50A, 78, 78A, 78B; kindub@usit.ie; £9-14 dorm, £14 quad, £14-17 double; V, MC) has a great location in Temple Bar, attractive interior, and clean communal bathrooms—so don't let the name scare you off. The big, cheap, sky-lit dorm rooms on the top floor are by far the nicest in Dublin.

The best of the super-cheap B&B's on Gardiner Street, **Glen Court** *(67 Lower Gardiner St.; Tel 01/836-40-22; DART to Connolly Station or Bus 27B, 42, 43, 53, 53A; £16 single, £30 double, £42 triple, £52 quad; No credit cards)* takes up a high-ceilinged old Georgian all done in dainty, light pink paint. It's hard to believe the hostel-comparable prices for private rooms include a full Irish breakfast plus soap and a towel, but it's true. The sparse rooms need a paint job and the furniture's secondhand, but it's all clean. Yep, you get a sink and phone booth-like shower all to yourself, too. The shared toilets are in the hall. There's also a nice little breakfast room and a chill satellite-fed TV lounge (pink, of course).

▸▸DO-ABLE

Right on Great George's nightlife strip and just over from Grafton Street, **Kelly's Hotel** *(36-37 S. Great George's St., D1; Tel 01/677-92-77; DART to Tara St. Station or Bus 16, 16A, 19, 19A, 22, 22A; kellyshtl@iol.ie; £30-45 single, £68-76 double; V, MC, AE)* has budget prices but gives you Old-World class and atmosphere. With its banistered staircases, mellow blue-and-white floral wallpaper, dark wood, and frosted glass, the place has a real "tranquil haven" feel. A small "student" single, with shared bathroom, goes for £30, breakfast included.

Harding Hotel *(Copper Alley, Christchurch, D2; Tel 01/679-65-00; Bus 21A, 50, 50A, 78, 78A, 78B; www.iol.ie/usitaccm, harding@usit.ie; £45 single; £50-£60 double or triple; V, MC)* has bright, spotless, and spankin'-new rooms complete with bathrooms, TV, and coffee/tea makers—smack dab in the middle of tourist central. No breakfast, but there is Darkey Kelly's, the hotel's restaurant/bar named after a famous old Dublin whore who had a heart of gold (but was unfortunately burned to death for murder). Connected by an inner courtyard to Kinlay House Hostel [see above], so sly use of their kitchen may be an option.

The Townhouse *(46-48 Lower Gardiner St., D1; Tel 01/878-88-08; DART to Connolly Station or Bus 27B, 42, 43, 53, 53A; gtrotter@indigo._ie; £40-52.50 single, £56-86 double, £72-96 triple, £12-17 hostel dorms, all including full breakfast; V, MC)* gives a lot of bang for the buck. Their rooms are truly stylin' (each one individually decorated by the owner), if small, and the huge breakfast is the best coronary-inducing Irish grub around. The tranquil little back garden has a Japanese look to it (Lafcadio Hearn, the "Supreme Interpreter of Japan to the West, and Vice Versa" lived here in the 19th century) and the staff is great. Private bathrooms with every room.

Other do-able options include **Kilronan House** *(70 Adelaide Rd.; Tel 01/475-52-66, Fax 01/478-28-41; info@dublinn.com, www.dublinn.com; Single £55, double/twin £96, breakfast included, private baths; V, MC, AE)* in the city center; **Charleville Lodge** *(268/272 North Circular Road; Tel*

01/838-66-33, Fax 01/838-58-54; Bus 10 to N. Circular Rd. and Rathdown Rd.; charleville@indigo.ie, www.charlevillelodge.ie; Nov-Apr: Single £35, Twin/Double: £27.50/person, Triple/family £25/person; May-Oct: Single £60, Twin/Double £45/person, Triple/family £35/person; Full Irish breakfast included, private baths; V, MC, AE) 10-15 minutes from the city center; and **Aston Hotel** *(7-9 Aston Quay; Tel 01/677-93-00, Fax 01/677-90-07; stay@aston-hotel.com, www.aston-hotel.com; Nov-Feb: Sun-Thur £34/person, Fri-Sat £40/person; Mar-Oct Sun-Thur £40/person, Fri-Sat £48/person; V, MC, AE)* in the Temple Bar area.

▸▸SPLURGE

Not the Ritz, but damn charming in its own way is the **Fitzwilliam Hotel** *(83 St. Stephen's Green South; Tel 01/478-21-33; Fax 01/478-22-63; £55-85 per person; AE, V, DIN)*. With only a handful of rooms (all with private bath), staying here makes you feel you're at someone's house. High Georgian ceilings give the small rooms a spacious feeling. The location can't be beat, a beautiful quiet street two seconds from St. Stephen's Green and nearby one of the best traditional pubs in Dublin, **O'Donnoghue's** [see *bar scene,* above]. Breakfast is served up hot and delicious downstairs in the dining room.

Russell Court Hotel *(Harcourt St., D2; Tel 01/478-49-94; DART to Tara St. Station or Bus Bus 14, 14A, 15A, 15B, 48A; £65 single, £100 double, £115 triple; V, MC, AE, DC)* is a big, classy, old-world hotel on a pretty Georgian street just off St. Stephen's Green, and it just happens to look like some beautiful fantasy bordello in a Hollywood movie. And you might even be able to afford it. In addition to the regular rates, there's a weekend special: two nights, one dinner, and two full breakfasts, all for £89 per person sharing. A lot of their rooms are actually (get this) suites, chock-full of old, faux-Chinese antique furniture, couches, canopy beds, and gas fireplaces. Rooms 111, 112, and 300 are especially sweet. There's a great beer garden in back, a superb residents' bar inside, and free entrance to the Vatican nightclub in the basement every night.

What could be better to start your party weekend than watching the sunset from a downtown Pimp Daddy rooftop penthouse? At the **Oliver St. John Gogarty's Temple Bar Penthouse Apartments** *(18-21 Angelsea St., Temple Bar, D2; Tel 01/671-18-22; DART to Tara St. Station or Bus 46, 46A, 46B, 63; £70-80 1-bedroom, £120-130 2-bedroom, £130-140 3-bedroom; V, MC, AE),* the dream becomes reality. These modern, lots-o-glass-and-hardwood apartments do the full kitchen, dining room, living room (with TV, video, and leather couches, no less), and bedrooms deal, plus there's a rooftop deck and balconies with sweeping views of the city. For this price (each bedroom is a double), it's a steal.

need to know

Currency Exchange The local currency is the **Irish pound (£),** aka the ***punt.*** A Bureau de Change within any bank will have the best rates.

Tourist Information Best bet is the centrally-located **Dublin Tourism Centre** *(St. Andrew's Church, Suffolk St.; Tel 01/605-77-00; 8:30am-*

7:30pm Mon-Sat, 11am-5:30pm Sun June-Sept, 9am-5:30pm Mon-Sat Sept-June; information@dublintourism.ie, www.visit.ie/dublin). Other offices include: **Irish Tourist Board** *(Baggot St. Bridge; Tel 01/602-40-00; 9:15am-5:15pm Mon-Fri; www.ireland.travel.ie)* and branches at the airport and ferry terminal. **USIT NOW** *(Aston Quay; Tel 01/677-81-17; 9am-5:30pm Mon-Fri, 10am-1pm Sat)* will help you find a hostel.

Public Transportation The primary public transit is **Dublin Bus** *(55p-£1.25),* operating between 6am and 11:30pm, with special NiteLink (£2.50) service from the center to outer areas on Thur, Fri, and Sat at midnight, 1am, 2am, and 3am. Free maps, schedules, etc., are available at **Dublin Bus Head Office** *(59 Upper O'Connell St., D1; Tel 01/873-42-22; 9am-5:45pm Mon-Fri; till 1pm Sat).* **DART** trains run through town and out to Dublin's suburbs. Tickets can be bought at the DART stations and at the **Rail Travel Centre** *(35 Abbey St. Lower, across O'Connell Bridge on the north side; single trip £3-12, weekly £12.50).* If you buy a single-trip ticket, you must specify your exact destination. Taxis are expensive and in short supply around town. It's especially bad late-night, when you can easily wait for an hour or more to get a ride. The standard taxi practice, with tourists and locals alike, is to take the most out-of-the-way route possible to jack up the fare, then play politely dumb if called on it—Dublin's maze-like setup makes this an easy scam. When getting in a cab, try to have an idea of how best to get where you're going or at least have a map handy to check that you're not being given the runaround. If you want vengance, take the taxi's roof sign number and call the **Garda Carriage Office** *(Tel 01/475-58-88).*

Bike Rental Rent a two-wheeler at **Cycle Ways** *(185-186 Parnell St., three blocks north of the Liffey; Tel 01/873-47-48).*

American Express *(116 Grafton St.; Tel 01/677-28-74).*

Emergency **Emergency** *999.* **The Mater Hospital** *(Eccles St.; Tel 01/453-79-41),* **St. Vincent's Hospital** *(Elm Park; Tel 01/209-43-58),* and **St. James' Hospital** *(James St.; Tel 01/830-11-22),* will all stitch you up.

Pharmacies **O'Connell's Late Night Pharmacy** *(21 Grafton St.; Tel 01/679-04-67; 8:30am-8:30pm Mon-Sat, 11am-6pm Sun)* and **Hamilton Long Late Night Pharmacy** *(5 Lower O'Connell St., Tel 01/874-84-56; Mon-Fri 8am-8pm, Sat 8:30am-6pm)* aren't that late-night, but they're open later than most.

Telephone Area code: *01;* information: *1190;* international operator: *114.* If you're going to be making many local calls, save yourself some money and aggravation and pick up a phone card. Both local and international calling cards can be purchased in almost any shop.

Airports **Dublin International Airport** *(Tel 01/704-42-22).* ***Dublin Bus Airlink,*** with a stop outside the arrivals terminal, will run you directly into the city center, Connolly Station or Heuston Station, departing about every 10 minutes *(7am-11pm daily; £3 adults, £1.50* *students).* **Dublin Bus CitySwift 41** also goes from the airport to Eden Quay in the city center with many local stops in between. It's cheaper, at £1.10, but much slower. Taxis to the center cost around £12.

Trains **Heuston Station** *(Kingsbridge, off St. John's Rd.),* out on the west side of town, serves south, west, and southwest. Take Stationlink Bus 90 into town. **Connolly Station** *(Amiens St.)* serves north and northwest, take a left out of the station, walk down Amiens Street, and you'll be smack in the middle of Temple Bar. **Pearse Station** *(Westland Row, Tara St.),* just east of **Trinity** College Green, serves southeast. **Irish Rail** *(Tel 01/836-62-22)* provides the trains.

Bus Lines Out of the City **Bus Eirann** *(Busárus, Store St.; Tel 01/836-61-11)* is right in the city center.

everywhere else

howth

On a clear day, you can look across the Irish Sea from Howth Head—nine miles northeast of Dublin—and see the mountains of Wales. H.G. Wells called the view "one of the most beautiful in the world." But the view is not the main reason most travelers go to the now-suburban town of Howth (rhymes with "both"). They go to see the famous 15th-century castle celebrated in the opening lines of *Finnegan's Wake*: "riverrun, past Eve and Adam's, from swerve of shore to bend of bay, brings us by a commodius vicus of recirculation back to Howth Castle and Environs." Don't worry, there are much simpler directions [see *culture zoo,* below].

The town of Howth, situated on the tip of the peninsula that forms the northern coast of Dublin Bay, is a small fishing village with a fascinating past and a laid-back present. It has been described as the Irish equivalent of a Greek fishing village, with white, craggy cliffs and whitewashed houses. At the end of the DART line, this town of 16,000 people is becoming Ireland's version of a yuppie sailing town—suburban but off the beaten track—where the houses have manicured lawns and the yacht harbor is next to the ruins of an ancient abbey. And of course, there still are the local boys whose sun-burnt red noses match their red down vests, even in the heart of summer.

Everything you'll want to see in Howth is within walking distance of the **DART station** on **Harbour Road.** The castle is across the street, and the harbor is just a short walk down the hill. During the week there's really nothing to do for excitement, but if you come on a Friday or Saturday afternoon you can hang out at the castle until sunset, then take a few steps over to the **Bloody Stream** [see *bar scene,* below], which is packed on weekends with a very young, very single crowd who are definitely ready to party. Fortunately, the last DART train doesn't leave until a few minutes after the pub closes, so there is no need to spend the night.

bar scene

Walk out the front door of the DART station, step down a few stairs, and you'll be face-to-face with the bouncer at the **Bloody Stream** *(14 West Pier, under Howth DART Station; Tel 01/839-507; Open daily; lunch under £10, dinner £10-20; MC, VISA)*. During the week, the small, brick-walled pub is quiet and the crowd is mostly working-class men over 30 out to enjoy a pint by the peat fire. But on weekends, a much younger crowd takes over—so young that the bouncer gets very serious about checking IDs at the door. The place gets totally packed and so loud that some people call it "the Bloody Scream." You won't find super-hip Dublin club rats here, but there is definitely lad-meets-lass potential.

Wondering about the name? Beneath the pub there's a stream where a knight of King Arthur's Round Table supposedly fought a battle with the ruling Danes. The pub owners say they also fought a constant battle there—against the stream flooding the bar while it was under construction. Hence the name: the Bloody Stream.

culture zoo

All of Howth's cultural attractions are within the **castle grounds,** just steps away from the DART station. Inside the gates are a castle, a monolithic tomb, an amazing rhododendron garden, and a transport museum.

Howth Castle *(off Howth Rd.; Tel 01/832-22-46; Howth DART station, 31 bus; 8am-sunset daily Apr-Jun,; free):* Pop legend holds that Grace O'Malley, a beautiful 16th-century pirate queen from Mayo, was on her way back from visiting Queen Elizabeth I when she stopped for a bite to eat at Howth Castle. The servants turned her away because the family was having supper, and Grace was so ticked off that she kidnapped Lord Howth's son and took him back to her castle in Clew Bay. The ransom she demanded was a promise from the Howth family that the gates of their castle would never again be locked and that an extra place would be set at the table each night for the head of the O'Malley clan, just in case. The gates remain unlocked to this day and there's always an empty plate at the table. Far be it from the Irish to tempt fate.

The castle is now partially in ruins. You can't go inside the castle itself, but you can go inside the gates and roam around the grounds, stroll through the 30-acre **Rhododendron Gardens** next to the you-can't-afford-it Deer Park Hotel (peak bloom time is May-June), visit **Aideen's Grave,** a monolithic tomb within the gardens. **National Transport Museum** *(Tel 01/847-56-23; 10am-5pm Mon-Fri, 2-5pm Sat-Sun; 50p students):* Howth had the world's last fleet of open-topped double-decked tram cars, which are now on display in this small museum.

great outdoors

For great views of the sea, of nearby Lambey Island, and the village itself, try the **Cliff Walk.** The whole trail is about seven kilometers long. It has a few steep spots, but it is a paved trail, so it's actually do-able. It starts at the end of the long harbor wall and heads up a steep hill to the edge of the cliff, then back down into the village and out again along the cliffs and the harbor to Baily's Lighthouse. It's just one trail, so you don't have to worry about where to turn or getting lost. One cautionary note, though: fences are being put up in spots where people have fallen—and died. Some locals claim the deaths weren't accidents and protest that the fences ruin the pristine view. Just watch your step and don't do it alone.

eats

Howth is famous for its fresh seafood, but it's a bit of a splurge in most of the fancier restaurants. A great way to sample the seafood without breaking the bank is to have a bowl of pub owner Michael Wright's home-made seafood chowder (£2.95) at the **Bloody Stream** [see *bar scene,* above]. Another good option is next door at **Pad Thai** *(12 West Pier, on the Harbour wall; Tel 01/832-22-55; 6-11pm Mon-Sat, noon-10pm Sun; lunch under £10, dinner £10-20; MC, VISA),* a small, casual spot where the only obvious clue that you're in a Thai restaurant is a bronze Buddha sitting on a shelf. There's more fish than Thai food, but it's all good and lunch is cheap compared to what you get at most of the other restaurants in town.

crashing

If you end up stuck here for the night, the town has a few do-able options, including **Gleann-na-Smol** *(Nashville Rd.; Tel. 01/832-29-36; Fax 01/832-05-16; rickards@indigo.ie; All rooms £21/person; Private baths; No credit cards),* a seven-minute walk from the train station and 10-15 minute walk from the town center. **Hazelwood** *(Thormanby Rd.; Tel/Fax 01/839-13-91; 101706.3526@compuserv.com, www.hazelwood.net; Shared rooms £22/person, single occupancy £30; Private baths; Breakfast included; No credit cards),* a short walk from the station, 15 minutes from the town center and 5 minutes from the cliff walk; and **Highfield** *(Thormanby Rd.; Tel. 01/832-39-36; Mar-Oct £25, Nov-Feb £22; private baths, some in-room and some out of room; Breakfast included; No credit cards),* about 10 minutes from the village center, high on a hill. As a last resort, try **St. Lawrence Hotel** *(Harbour Rd.; Tel. 01/832-26-43).*

need to know

Tourist Information The tourist office in **Dublin** [see above] can give you all the info you'll need on excursion to Howth.

Emergency The **Garda (police) Station** *(27 St. Lawrence Rd.; Tel 01/666-49-00)* is in the village.

Trains The **DART station** *(Harbour Rd.; Tel 01/850-36-62)*is across from the castle and above the Bloody Stream [see *bar scene,* above]. The DART ride to Dublin takes about 20 minutes; trains leave for Dublin every five to ten minutes during peak commute hours and every 15-20 minutes the rest of the time. The last train leaves for Dublin shortly after the Bloody Stream closes at night; don't miss it.

Bus Lines Out of Town The **Bus Éireann** *(Call Busáras in Dublin at Tel 01/836-61-11)* line 31 or 31b to Dublin stops on Lower Abbey Street in the village.

Postal The **Howth Post Office** *(27 Abbey St.; Tel 01/831-82-10; 9am-5:30pm Mon-Fri; 9am-noon Sat)* is the place to post letters, naturally.

dun laoghaire

Most travelers visit Ireland's oldest town, Dún Laoghaire (*Laoghaire* rhymes with "dreary"), not by choice, but because that's where the ferry drops them off after they've crossed the Irish Sea from Holyhead, Wales. Yet a lot of Dubliners go to the 1,500-year-old harbor town on purpose, just to get out of the city for a while and stroll along the town's West pier, where there's a panoramic view of Dublin across the bay. And, as in most of Dublin County, there is a "James Joyce slept here" site to visit as well.

Though Dún Laoghaire isn't likely to win any awards for being the most scenic spot in Ireland, the 15-minute DART ride from Dublin does offer some minor eye candy. First you'll past **Booterstown Marsh,** a wildlife/bird sanctuary, then you'll see long, sandy beaches and a clear vista of the Irish sea just outside the train window.

Finding your way around on foot is a snap. There are signs posted all around to direct you to the major sights, just as there are in Dublin. Once you get to town on DART, walk straight up the hill and you'll hit **Great Georges Street,** the main commercial drag. Though generally bustling, the street doesn't offer much of interest to young hipsters. Most of what you'll want to see and do is down by the water. Each of the two piers—the **East Pier** and the **West Pier**—is more than a half-mile long and ends at a lighthouse. On Sundays the West Pier gets fairly crowded and you might rub shoulders with some of Dublin's rich and semi-famous out for their daily exercise.

bar scene

There are several pubs scattered up and down Georges Street, mostly catering to weekend escapees from Dublin and locals who've been drinking there since they were big enough to climb up on the barstool. There's no real reason to go inside unless you're dying for a pint. But if you do decide to stop for a wee sip, try **Smyths Pub** *(180 Lower Georges St.; Tel 01/280-11-39; Open daily)*. The atmosphere is either old world or depressing, depending on how many pints you've had, but it's worth seeing because it's the only pub in town that still has a "snug"—a narrow little room next to the main bar which was once a major rendezvous spot for illicit love affairs because it was the only place where women were allowed to toss back a few pints.

A mile south of town, you can catch free trad music—and expensive but really yummy seafood—at the **Purty Kitchen** *(Old Dunleary Rd.;*

Tel 01/284-35-76; No cover for traditional music; Cover £5-6 for blues and rock in the Loft nightclub upstairs). The pub is housed in one of the few buildings left in what was the center of town before the harbor was built in the mid-1800s and Dún Laoghaire developed in a different direction. Inside, the atmosphere is friendly and homey—open brick fireplace, cozy alcoves, pub posters on the wall—but the crowd is unpredictable. It varies from 35-year-old Dublin nurses on a night out to a summertime mixed bag that sometimes includes young international travelers out to catch free trad (the schedule varies, so call ahead) and live blues and rock upstairs (Wednesday through Saturday, 9pm).

culture zoo

The main cultural attraction in the Dún Laoghaire area is one of Dublin County's many **James Joyce** shrines. You can find it by heading south along the water for about a half-mile to **Sandycove,** a pleasant little strip with a decent beach.

James Joyce Museum *(Take DART to Sandycove, then walk down to the coast, then take a right until you hit Martello Tower; Tel 01/872-20-77; 10am-1pm/2-5pm Mon-Fri; 2-6pm Sun, Apr-Oct; Admission £2.40):* A small collection of letters and personal effects—guitar, cane, glasses—that once belonged to the beloved writer is housed in Martello Tower, a 40-foot granite monument built in 1804 to withstand an invasion threatened by Napoleon. When Joyce spent a week there 100 years later, he was the guest of Oliver Gogarty, who had rented the tower from the army for £8 a year. You may recognize this place from your lit class as the setting of the first chapter of *Ulysses.*

eats

The big deal here is seafood, but anything more than fish 'n' chips could easily cost more than a shared room at a hostel. There are plenty of less expensive options in town, from a gooey slice at **Bits 'n' Pizzas** *(15 Patricks St.; Tel 01/284-24-11)* to Chinese at **Yung's** *(66 Upper Georges St.; Tel 01/284-21-56)*.. And if you're staying at the **Old School House** [see *crashing,* below], there's no better deal than the hearty Irish breakfast for £2 (dinner is £6).

crashing

If for some strange reason you do decide to stay overnight in Dún Laoghaire—some people do because it can be cheaper than Dublin—there are a few places that are adequate if unexciting, and conveniently close to transportation when you're ready to move on. The most popular place for young travelers is a friendly, convenient 180-bed hostel, **The Old School House** *(Eblana Ave. near DART station; Tel 01/280-87-77; £9 dorm, £26 twin, £28 double, £30 double with private bath, peak rates July-Sept).* It offers a community television room, free hot showers, currency exchange, lockers, laundry, and a restaurant. Rooms with two, four, six, and eight beds are available. The staff is friendly and maintains a photo scrapbook on the web at ***www.hostel.ie,*** where you can see a bunch of semi-clothed lads and lasses jumping into the nearby waters or get an idea of who you might run into in the hallway on your way to the shower.

Another option is the **Port View Hotel** *(Royal Marine Rd.; Tel. 01/280-16-63; Fax 01/280-04-47; portview@clubi@ie; Single £60; double £50/person; Private baths; Breakfast included; V, MC, AE),* in the town center, a two-minute walk from the train station. For traditional B&B accomodations, try **Rosmeen House** *(Rosmeen Gardens, No. 13; Tel. 01/280-76-13),* or any of several B&B's on Rosmeen Gardens.

need to know

Currency Exchange Since Dun Laoghaire is swarming with tourists just off the boat, there are banks all over town just waiting to grab a small fee for exchanging currency. Banks right on the main drag include **First Active** *(1 Upper Georges St.; Tel 01/284-12-74)* and **TSB** *(11 Upper Georges St., Tel 01/280-85-57).*

Tourist Information The **tourist office** *(10am-9pm daily)* is at the ferry terminal.

Health and Emergency Emergency (police, fire, ambulance): *999;* Marine emergency: *112.* The local police are based at the **Garda Station** *(Corrig Ave., Tel 01/666-50-00 or 01/280-12-85).* **St. Michael's Hospital** *(Lower Georges St.; Tel 01/280-69-01)* is one of several hospitals and clinics in town.

Pharmacies There are numerous pharmacies in town. On the main drag are **Burnett's Pharmacy** *(41 Lower Georges St.; Tel 01/280-11-24)* and **O'Mahony & Ennis** *(4 Upper Georges St.; Tel 01/280-11-63).*

Trains The **DART station** *(Tel 01/85-03-66-22)* is across the street from the Dún Laoghaire-Rathdown County Hall. The ride to Dublin takes just 15 minutes (£2.20 return); trains leave every five minutes during peak commute hours and every 15-20 minutes the rest of the time.

Bus Lines Out of Town **Bus Éireann** *(Call Busáras in Dublin at Tel 01/836-61-11 for information)* lines 7, 7a, and 8 connect Dún Laoghaire with Dublin; 45a goes to Bray. There are no direct bus lines to towns north of Dublin; you have to go back to the city by DART or bus to make a connection.

Postal The **post office** *(Century Court, Upper Georges St.; Tel 01/230-01-40; 9am-6pm Mon-Fri, 9am-5:30pm Sat)* is on the main drag.

bray

Popular with Dublin's working-class, **Bray** is a seedy, run-down resort town 45 minutes south of Dublin. Choked with tacky amusement arcades and shabby convenience stores, this place should win an award for being the cheesiest town in all of Ireland. So why go there at all? Answer: You have to, if you want to get to some of the beautiful spots in County

wired

If you're stuck in Bray and you desperately need a very strong cup of coffee—and you're starting to realize why they put the sick in homesick—stop off at **Braynet** *(Star Leisure Centre, Bray Seafront, Tel 01/286-1520; 10am-11pm daily)* an internet cafe where the coffee's good and you can log on to the internet to check your e-mail from home. Try not to totally escape into the web, though; it'll cost you £5 per hour.

Wicklow, as there is no direct bus service from Dublin. So think of Bray as a transfer town, a (hopefully) short stop on the way to where you really want to go. Have an hour to wait before your bus comes? Pity. Stuck for the night? *Ouch.*

Bray's not a terribly big town. There's a main drag (named, appropriately enough, "Main Street") brimming with rundown hotels, little coffee shops, and the like. To get there from the **DART** station (see *need to know,* below), walk toward town on Florence or Quinsborough Road; both cross the railroad tracks.

At the seafront (also appropriately named "Strand Road"), you'll find more of the same. The big attraction is the **National Sealife Centre** *(Strand Rd.; Tel 01/286-6939; open daily at noon; £4.95),* a big aquarium with the standard fare from sharks to shrimp. While you're wandering around the seafront area, look up the house that James Joyce lived in for a couple of years as a child—when his family was rather down and out—at **One Martello Terrace.** It later became the setting for a scene in *A Portrait of the Artist as a Young Man.*

eats

Surprisingly enough, there's a decent vegetarian restaurant in town, where you can also get a tarot card reading if the spirit moves you (suggested question: What am I doing here?). The outside wall of **Escape** *(1 Albert Ave., opposite Sealife Centre; Tel 01/286-6755; Mon-Sat noon-10:30pm, Sun noon-9; tarot readings Mon-Thur 7-11pm, Sat-Sun 2-6pm; dinner £8-12)* is decorated with pop art graffiti, which makes it obvious that this is not a granola and tofu joint but also tends to warn you that there's more than food inside. Escape is a combo café/gift shop/cutesy art gallery/candy store/fortune-telling salon, but the food's surprisingly inventive, with dishes like Sicilian crepes filled with Mediterranean vegetables in sundried tomato and cream sauce. The tarot and astrology readings are given by several different people, including an astrolger who writes daily horoscopes for tabloids like the *Star* and the *Examiner* (Ali, available Monday and Tuesday evenings).

bar scene

If you happen to be in Bray on a Wednesday night, there are free trad sessions at the **Harbour Bar** *(Bray Harbour, Seapoint Rd.; Tel 01/286-2274; trad sessions Weds., live music Sat., open daily).* The bar may not be all that exciting, but getting there is an adventure. From the DART station, turn right and walk to the end of the road. When you get there, you'll see a small parking lot and the high walls of Carlisle Grounds across the road. Between them is a small lane. Follow that lane and walk down the stairs at the end, then walk through the tunnel on the right. When you emerge from the tunnel, the Harbour Bar is the first building on the left—but you're not home free yet. You have to go around the corner to find an open gate, then pick a door. The left door will lead you to the bar, but take the middle one (which leads to the snug) if you want to bypass the tourist crowd.

crashing

If it's too late to go anyplace at all, you could try any of the bed and breakfasts on the Strand, which are more expensive, or those on Sidmonton Avenue or Meath Street, which are cheaper. For the most part lodging in this town's kinda dingy, and there are no hostels, so where you stay is pretty much a toss-up. Chances are, with all the forms of transport available (outside of any beasts of burden, that is), you won't stick around. With the DART train running into Dublin every five minutes at peak times and every twenty minutes at all other times, there is no reason to sleep over in Bray.

If you are really and truly stuck here, try **Ulysses** *(Central Esplanade; Tel/Fax 01/286-38-60; cojo@indigo.ie; April-Sep: Single with in-room bath £30, shared twin or double (all have in-room baths) £27.50/person, Single with shared bath: £25; Oct-Mar: Doubles/twins £25/person; Breakfast included; V, MC),* 7-10 minute walk from the DART station, right on the seafront, about 10 minutes from the town's main street; **Crofton Bray Head Inn** *(Strand Road; Tel/Fax 01/286-71-82; Open Jun- Sep only; £25 for all rooms; Breakfast included; V, MC),* a 10-15 minute walk from the train station on the seaside, not far from town center; or **The Westbourne** *(Quinsboro Road; Tel 01/286-23-62; Fax 01/286-85-30; www.dirl.com/wicklow/westbourne; £30 for all rooms; Private baths; V, MC, AE),* a short walk from the train station, in the center of town, near the seaside.

need to know

Currency Exchange There are a handful of banks on Main Street, including **Bank of Ireland** *(45 Main St.; Tel 01/282-8001).*

Tourist Info If for some incomprehensible reason you want to learn more about Bray, go to the **Bray Tourist Office** *(Main St., in the Heritage Centre, next to the Royal Hotel; Tel 01/286-71-28; 9am-5pm Mon-Sat June-Sep, 9:30am-4:30pm Mon-Sat Oct-May).*

Trains To get back to Dublin, take **DART** *(station is half a kilometer off Main St. by the strand; call the Bray train station at Tel 01/236-33-33 for information)* to Connolly Station. Or opt for **Irish Rail** *(same location as the DART train; Tel 01/236-3333)* which makes stops in Bray on the Dublin-Rosslare Harbour line.

Bus lines out of the city **St. Kevin's Bus Service** *(Tel 01/281-8119)* passes through Bray twice daily on the way to Glendalough—once at midday and once around half past six in the evening. There's also service to Dublin at 8am and 5pm. Call for exact times and pickup locations. You could also catch **Bus Éireann** *(call Busáras in Dublin at Tel 01/836-6111 for information)* and head up to Dublin (routes 45 and 84) or down through Wicklow Town and other towns on the coast to Rosslare Harbour (route 5), both several times daily.

Internet See *wired,* above

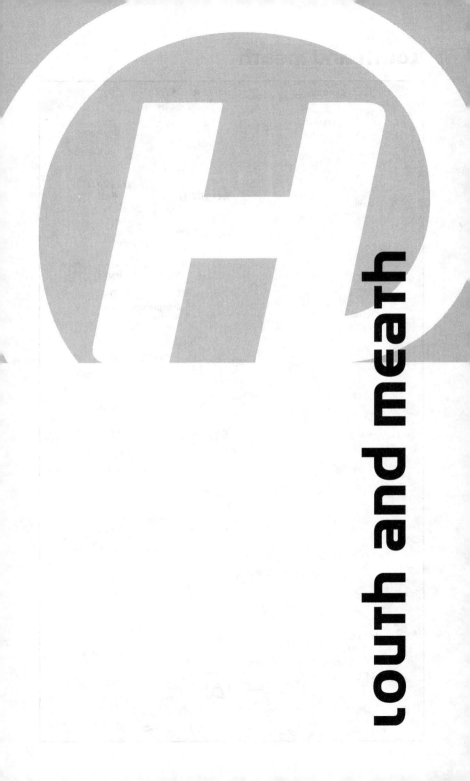
louth and meath

Louth and Meath

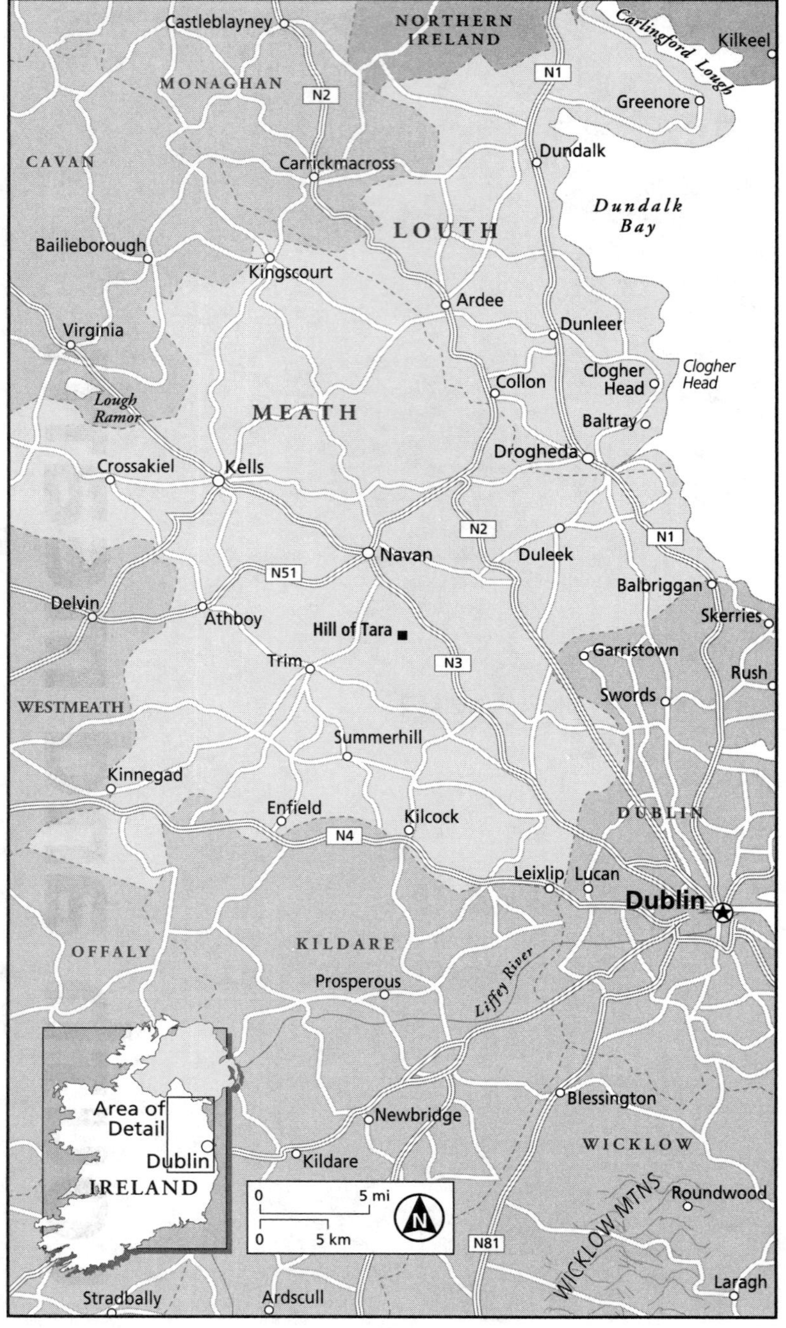

drogheda

With about 24,000 people, Drogheda is the largest and most happening town in the area. But remember, we're out in the country, where "happening" is a relative term. The town has an adequate nightlife and several decent restaurants, but is otherwise dead. There isn't much that is beautiful or enthralling about this town, but it's close to many of the ancient spots in the Boyne Valley and Louth areas, and will keep you busy, if not exhilarated, till the wee hours. The most compelling reasons to come here are the nearby sites, **Newgrange** and **Monastaireboice** [see *everywhere else,* below, for both]

bar scene

Drogheda offers a couple of popular pub-cum-disco places that are actually a lot of fun—especially once you accept the fact that they are your only options. Except for Number 4, which stays open till 2am, the pubs close their doors at 11:30pm, though you can usually hang out for up to an hour longer and swill one more pint.

Peter Mathew's/McPhails *(9 Lawrence St.; Tel 041/983-73-71)* is a popular pub with the local young folk and plays more "alternative" music than anywhere else in town. **Fusion** *(12 George St.; No phone; No credit cards)* spins mostly Top-40 remixes and funky classic-rock-type grooves for the uninhibited local youths. A clubby pub where you can dance and drink, **The Earth** *(Westcourt Hotel on West St.; Tel 041/983-09-69)* features a cool stone-age motif. **Number 4** *(Stockwell Lane; Tel 041/984-50-44; £1-5 cover on weekends; Open late),* goes for a slicker look, and is your best bet for late-night fun. Plus they have DJs and live music on weekends.

eats

You can pick up groceries at **Tesco** *(West St.; Tel 041/983-72-09; 9am-6:30pm Mon, Tue, and Sat, 9am-9pm Wed).* **Monks** *(Shop St. near river; Tel 041/984-56-30; Sandwiches £3-5)* is a cool cafe good for lunch or coffee drinks. **La Pizzeria** *(St. Peter's St.; Tel 041/983-42-08; Open Mon-Sat till 11pm; Dinner £5-7)* is popular with locals and is a good bet for dinner with tasty pizza and pasta dishes. Many pubs in town have lunch as well.

crashing

The **Harpur House Hostel** *(William St.; Tel 041/983-27-36; £8 per bed, £12 single; No credit cards)* is a small independent hostel situated comfortably in an old house with old marble fireplaces. From the town center, take Shop Street to Peter Street and take a right onto William Street. The hostel is the last house on the right. Your other option in Drogheda is the **Green Door Hostel** *(47 John St., a block from the bus station; Tel 041/983-44-22; £10 per bed; £13 single; No credit cards).* The

drogheda

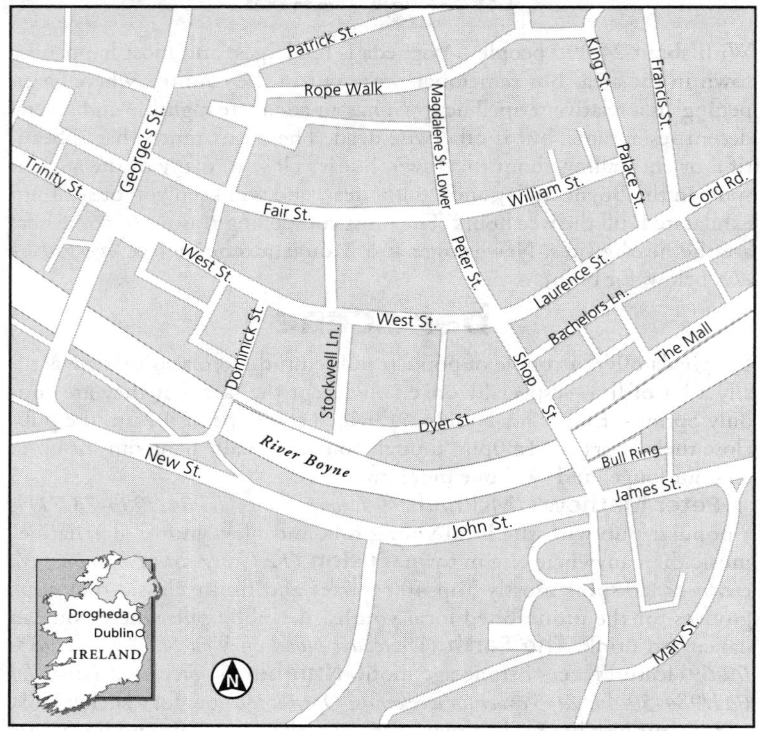

place is friendly and pretty comfortable, though you may feel like a sardine in the crowded rooms.

Other do-able options include **Harbour Villa** *(Mornington Rd.; Tel.041/983-74-41; Bus 101 or 103 in the direction of Layton will drop you off right at the house; Single £22, double without bath £20; Breakfast included; No credit cards),* three kilometers from Drogheda, right by the River Boyne; and **Boyne Valley Hotel** *(Dublin Rd.; Tel 041/983-77-37; Fax 041/983-91-88; reservations@boyne-valley-hotel.ie, www.boyne-valley-hotel.ie; Double £105, single £58, Private baths, Breakfast included; V, MC, D),* 5 minutes from the train and bus station, and a two-minute bus ride or 20 minute walk to the town center.

need to know

Currency Exchange TSB *(West St; Tel 041/983-87-03; 9:30-5pm Mon-Wed, Fri, 9:30am-7pm Thur)*

Tourist Information There is a tourist office in the **Bus Station** *(Danore Rd.; Tel 041/983-70-70; 9:30am-6pm Mon-Sat, 11:45am-5pm Sun).*

Health and Emergency Our Lady of Lourdes Hospital *(Windmill Rd.; Tel 041/37601).*

Trains and Buses You can catch a bus or train to Drogheda several times a day from Dublin or Belfast; check with Bus Eireann or the tourist office for a schedule. You'll be dropped off at the Drogheda bus station (see *tourist information,* above).

Laundry FM Launderette *(13 North Quay; Tel 041/983-68-37; 9am-6pm Mon-Sat; £4 wash/dry).*

Bike Rental Quay Cycles *(11 North Quay; Tel 041/983-45-26; 9am-6pm Mon-Sat; £8/day, £30/wk, £5/day with ISIC card).*

Postal The **Post office** *(West St.; Tel 041/983-81-57; 9am-5:30pm Mon-Sat)* is easy to find, in the middle of West Street.

monasterboice

If you see only one ruined religious site while in Ireland, make sure it's Monasterboice. Not only does it have a great round tower and a ruined church, it has two of the best Celtic crosses in existence: **Muiredach's Cross** (Muriedach was abbot of Monastaerboice until 922 A.D.) and the taller yet more beat-up **West Cross.** Probably used for teaching the gospel, the crosses are covered with carvings depicting well-known biblical events. Brush up on your biblical symbolism before you come here or you may miss the following on the faces of Muiredach's cross: *Eastern Face* (from bottom up): the Fall of Adam and Eve, Cain killing Abel, David (with sling) and Goliath, Moses bringing water from the stone, and the Wise Men. *Western Face* (from bottom up): Christ being arrested, Doubting Thomas, Christ passes the keys to St. Peter, the crucifixion, Moses with Hur and Aaron. And how do we know it's *Muiredach's* Cross? The inscription at the base translates "A prayer for Muiredach, for whom this cross is made."

You may notice that on two separate places on the cross, Christ's wound is in different places. This apparent screw up may be attributed to a simple mistake on the part of the sculptor, or could be the work of two different artists with poor communication skills, or it could be something else entirely. Vanity was considered a major sin to the 10th-century monks who lived and worked here, and it's very likely that the mistake was made intentionally to avoid making the cross perfect, lest others think they were being too lofty.

The **round tower** at Monasterboice is impressive as well. There's nothing in the tower anymore, though it was once used as a storehouse and possibly a refuge from invading bands of thugs. Built to have an entrance 14 feet off the ground, you may notice that the doorway is now much closer to the earth. What made the entrance lower? Well, for hundreds of years, people were buried around the tower, and as time went on, they began burying people on top of each other, gradually raising the ground level. Kind of gruesome.

need to know

Hours/Days Open The site is open dawn to dusk; come early or late to avoid the tourist hordes.

Cost Entrance is free.

Directions Monasterboice is located off N1, about 6 miles northwest of Drogheda. If you're going by car or bike, take the N1 road going north from Drogheda until you get to Dunleer exit (about 8 km/5 mi). Turn off the N1 at the Dunleer exit and follow the signs. You can reach Mellifont Abbey [see below] from Monasterboice via a narrow dirt lane.

mellifont abbey

St. Malachy, one of the first Cisterclans to reach Ireland from France, founded this abbey in 1142. It became the main Roman Christian outpost in the area and its center of religious activity until the 16th century. Originally run by imported French monks as a means of eliminating the corruption of previous Irish orders, the French quickly retreated back from whence they came after finding that they did not get along with the locals. Specifically, the abbey flourished until Henry VIII suppressed it in 1539. The monks, some 150 in all, fled in all directions, as the Tudor monarch ordered that the abbey be handed to his favorite, Edward Moore, ancestor of the earls of Drogheda. He had it turned into a private but fortified mansion. Over the years the mansion fell into shameful decline, and was attacked by Cromwell's forces. In Queen Victoria's day it was used as a pigsty.

The significance of the French influence is that the abbey was the first to reproduce a layout and architecture that was being used in mainland Europe. The abbey's ruins are not as impressive as Monastairboice [see above], though at the time of its construction, which spread across 15 years, its pillars were gargantuan, dazzling the local peasant population. Its blossoming of arches and vaulted ceilings was called "riotous" at the time. Today the broad stumps in the ground are the only visible clue to its former glory. There is a map at the site that lets you trace the outline of the original abbey. The gatehouse remains as the only part of a fortified wall that once ringed the monastery. The lavabo, the octagonal house monks used for washing, is indicative of the former splendor of the place.

need to know

Contact Information Tel *041/26459*.

Hours/Days Open The abbey is open daily 10am-5pm May-mid June and mid Sept-Oct; 9:30am-6:30pm mid June-mid Sept.

Directions The abbey is located off N1, about 6 miles northwest of Drogheda. If you're going by car or bike, take the N1 road going north from Drogheda until you get to Dunleer exit (about 8 km/5 mi). Turn off the N1 at the Dunleer exit and follow the signs. You can reach Monasterboice [see above] from Mellifont Abbey via a narrow dirt lane.

Cost Admission is £1.50 for adults, 90p for students.

newgrange and knowth

The two ancient sites most worth checking out while in Drogheda are Newgrange and Knowth. (Technically, they are in County Meath, but it's super-easy to get to them from Drogheda.)

Newgrange, a Neolithic passage tomb, is one of the coolest monuments in Ireland. Older than the pyramids, it dates from around 3200 B.C.E. It consists of a giant mound of earth and stone over 80 meters in diameter and 12 meters high. Inside, a narrow, not-for-claustrophobics tunnel leads back to the chamber, where several shallow stone discs sit, once used, some think, to lay out the recently departed. Very little is known of the people who created Newgrange or the swirling designs carved into the stone on the inside and outside of the structure, although there is definitely a sun-worshipping motif. Newgrange is a testament to the advanced understanding of its builders of the elements and the seasons. The roof hasn't leaked in more than 5,000 years. During winter solstice, a beam of light shines through a narrow opening, the roof box, above the entrance for about 20 minutes and casts an intense light all the way back through the tunnel. When you're back in the chamber, wait for the crowd of tourists to clear out, then get down on your hands and knees and you can see the roof box way down at the end of the tunnel. It should give you a little appreciation of how smart these people were. And to think most of them didn't live past 30.

Some people say Knowth is more impressive than Newgrange. It's rumored to have been a burial site for Ireland's high kings. It has two passage graves you can see, both discovered in the late 1960s, and some of the best megalithic art in the world inside the graves and on curbstones all around the base of the mound.

need to know

Hours/Days Open The sites are open daily 9:30am-5:30pm Nov-Feb, 9:30am-5:30pm Mar-Apr, Oct, 9am-6:30pm May and late Sept, 9am-7pm June to mid-Sept. Knowth is open May-Oct only.

Directions and Transportation Newgrange lies just north of the River Boyne, about 13 km south of Drogheda and 5 km southeast of Slane. Knowth is about 1 km northwest of Newgrange or almost 4 km by road. There are no direct buses to either of the sites. During most of the week, the closest you'll get is Slane, which is served by up to six buses daily Monday-Saturday from Drogheda. On Saturday, the bus from Drogheda stops at Donore, closer to the Center [see below], on its way to Slane.

Cost You can pick up tickets for Newgrange and Knowth at the **Center** *(Off N51, Slane, Tel 041/988-03-00).* Admission is £4 for adults, £2 for students.

KELLS

Kells is a quiet little village, but its central location makes it a great base to explore the region. Kells' claim to fame is the *Book of Kells* [see *culture zoo,* below]. Although it didn't originate here, it passed through and now sits in Trinity College, Dublin. The main attraction these days is probably the Round Tower, located smack in the middle of town. The tower dates to around 1076, when the high king of Tara was murdered inside. Also worth checking out are the high crosses in the churchyard [see *culture zoo,* below].

pub scene

O'Shaughnessy's *(Market St.; Tel 01266/41110)* is a decent pub in the traditional vein, as is **Monaghan's,** [see *eats,* below] which is in the same building as the **Kell's Hostel** [see *crashing,* below].

culture zoo

Kells was originally the site of a 6th-century monastic settlement, founded by St. Columcille (aka Columba), so the sights here (like much of rural Ireland) are mostly churches and crosses. Monks driven from the Scottish island Iona landed here in 807, with the Vikings hot on their heels. Reportedly, they carried a rough draft of the *Book of Kells,* which was stolen in 1007. But the thief in question only wanted its gold case, and the book was later found deep in a bog. The monks moved to Derry a few hundred years later, but you can still see ruins and lots of old crosses.

Cross of Patrick and Columba *(next to the Round Tower):* The best preserved cross from the period—the Cross of Patrick and Columba—is inscribed with scenes of Daniel in the lion's den, the fall of Adam and Eve...you get the picture.

Church of St. Columba *(inside the Churchyard, on the grouns of the ruins; 10am-5pm Mon-Fri, 10am-1pm Sat):* Within this Protestant church you'll find crosses from the 9th century bearing scenes of everything from the baptism of Jesus to Noah hitting the high sea.

eats

Your chow choices are limited. Pick up do-it-yourself eats at the **Tesco Supermarket** *(across the street from the Kells Hostel).* **Pebbles** *(Newmarket St.; 9am-5:30pm Mon-Sat)* is a decent diner that is popular with the locals. **O'Shaughnessy's** [see *pub scene,* above] also does pub grub lunches.

crashing

The **Kells Hostel** *(Carrick St.; Tel 01266/49995; hostels@iol.ie; £7.50 per bed in 7-bed dorm, £10 double; No credit cards)* is friendly and fun. They also rent bikes and can give loads of info on local sights and scenic rides. And with a pub next door—what more could you ask for?

If the hostel is full, or you just feel like a little more comfort and privacy, another option is the **Headfort Arms Hotel** *(John St.; Tel 01266/40063).*

need to know

Currency Exchange There is a branch of the **Bank of Ireland** on John Street *(Tel 046/40-032)* where you can change money.

Tourist Information The **Kells Tourist Information Center** *(Headfort Place; Tel 01266/49336; 10am-1pm/2pm-5pm Mon-Sat, 1:30pm-6pm Sun; info@meathtourism.ie)* is near the town hall.

Trains and Buses **Buses** to Dublin (£6.70 single £9 round trip) depart from opposite the Catholic church on the Dublin road three times daily (2pm, 6pm, and 8pm, roughly). Buy your tickets in Dublin or on Bus Éireann's Website, **www.buseireann.com.**

Trim

Trim is the second-largest town in Meath and home to the impressive 12th-century **Trim Castle** [see *culture zoo,* below]. Hundreds of years ago, Trim was home to several monasteries. Now it's a tiny town of 1,700 people whose tourist industry survives on visitors to Trim Castle. The **River Boyne** runs through the middle of town, and the downtown consists of four streets arranged in a rough square formation: **Watergate Street, Market Street, Bridge Street,** and **Mill Street.** Market Street is where you'll find most of the food and drink. The town is cute and sleepy and postcard pretty, a quintessential small Irish town, definitely worth a day-trip from Dublin.

pub scene

Trim has a small nightlife, but **The Bounty** *(Bridge St.; Tel 046/32640; 10:30am-11:30pm Mon-Wed; 10:30am-12:30pm Thurs-Sat; 10:30am-11pm Sun)* is a decent place to get a pint and offers up traditional flavored *craic.* They have trad sessions here some nights. **The Abbey Lodge** *(Market St.; Tel 046/31285)* also is a good bet.

culture zoo

Taxi drivers in Dublin have often joked that Irish directions are always given according to pubs and churches—turn left at the pub, right at the church, and so on. But in Trim, you'll be better off finding your way around by using castles as landmarks.

Trim Castle *(Castle St.; Free):* As Ireland's largest castle, the enormity and imposing skyline alone warrant a visit to Trim Castle. For several hundred years, it served as a chief fortification for Meath and for whoever occupied it. Though given its history, one wonders how secure it actually was. The first occupant, Hugh DeLacy, was kicked out in 1173, only a year after it was built. The keep stands almost 100 feet tall and the walls average 11 feet thick. The castle re-opened in November 2000 after extensive renovation, but don't expect it to be brand spankin' new. Most of the work involved unearthing buildings on the grounds that had been buried for centuries. Oh yeah, Hollywood heartthrob Mel Gibson shot part of *Braveheart* here in 1995-6. There aren't any fences around the castle, so it's open anytime you want to go.

Talbot Castle and **St. Mary's Abbey** *(High St.; Free):* Across the River Boyne you'll spy Talbot Castle and St. Mary's Abbey. In 1368, the abbey burned to a crisp, but was rebuilt and partially converted to Talbot Castle. Sir John Talbot, the original resident, was a scary guy known for kicking French booty (although in 1429, Joan of Arc took him down temporarily). Jonathan Swift, of *Gulliver's Travels* fame, also called the castle home for a year or so.

eats

There is a **Supervalu** *(Haggard St.; Tel 046/31505; 8am-7:30pm Mon-Wed, Sat, 8am-9pm Thur-Fri, 8am-6pm Sun)* food market for DIY meals. The **Abbey Lodge** [see *pub scene,* above] serves big pub lunches for around £4-5 from 12:30-2:30pm.

crashing

The **Bridge House Hostel** *(Bridge St. next to the Tourist Office; Tel 046/31848; Open Apr-Sept only; £10 per bed in 4-bed dorms, £25 double; No credit cards)* is a bit pricier than other hostels in the area, but it's the cheapest option in town. It's a decent place with is a cool TV lounge that used to be a wine cellar.

There are also B&Bs in town, if you have a bit more generous budget: **Friarspark** *(Dublin Road; Tel 046/31745; £17-20 per person; No credit cards)*, and **Brogan's B&B** *(High St.; Tel 046/31237; £20-25 per person),* which doubles as a pub. Other do-able options include **Echo Lodge** *(Dublin Rd.; Tel. 046/37945; Shared rooms £19/person, singles up to £25, private baths, breakfast included; No credit cards),* 15-20 minutes on foot from the town center, along the Dublin bus route; and **Tigh Cathairn** *(Longwood Rd.; Tel. 046/31996; mariekeane@esatclear.ie; Shared rooms £20/person, singles £25.50, private baths, breakfast included; No credit cards),* 10 minutes from town center. Take the bus to Trim Castle and walk 10 minutes or taxi to this B&B.

need to know

Currency Exchange Bank of Ireland *(Market St.; Tel 046/31230; 10am-5pm Mon, 10am-4pm Tue-Fri).*

Tourist Info The **Tourist Office** *(Mill St.; Tel 046/37111; 9:30am-*

12:30pm/1:30-5pm daily) sells a self-guided walking tour map for £2 that will help maximize your time in Trim.

Directions and Transportation **Bus Eireann** stops at the Castle, and returns to Dublin eight times a day Monday-Saturday, and Sunday three per day. The trip takes one to two hours.

Postal At the **Post Office** *(Market St.; Tel 046/31268; Fax 046/36099; Mon-Fri 9am-5.30pm, Sat 9am-12.30pm)* you can exchange currency and buy telephone calling cards in addition to all of the regular postal services.

hill of Tara

Unfortunately, the best view of the Hill of Tara is one you're unlikely to see, unless you A: can afford to hire a helicopter, or B: are Superman. If you really want an aerial view, you can always pick up a postcard at the **Tara Visitor's Center** [see *need to know,* below].

Fortunately, the most impressive thing about Tara isn't so much the big, concentric rings overgrown with green that rise up from the hill or the view, but its compelling history. The site is one of the most important in the history of Irish Christendom, and one of its mounds served as a passage tomb for Stone-Agers from about 2500 B.C. But the hill is best remembered as the royal seat of the high kings. By the 2nd century A.D., because of its strategic location and commanding views of the countryside, Tara was a seat of power for the most powerful pagan warrior kings in Ireland. The kings performed rituals, celebrated, and ruled their kingdoms from the hill. Every three years, a *feis* was held (basically a huge banquet), and more than 1,000 people—including princes, poets, athletes, priests, druids, musicians, and jesters—partied for a week. It wasn't all fun and games, though: This is also when laws were passed and tribal disputes settled. The last feis was held in 560 AD, and Tara fell into decline after Christianity took hold.

The Christian part all started back in the late 5th century. St. Patrick had been wandering the countryside for years, trying to convert the pagan Celts to Christianity (and having a tough time), when he came up with a pretty bright idea: Convert the king and it'll be a hell of a lot easier to convert everyone else.

Each autumn, a pagan festival commenced: The king would command his demesne to extinguish all their fires before sundown. At sundown he would light a giant fire at the Hill of Tara and only then could everyone else light their fires. It was a symbol of the power of the king and the allegiance of his followers.

Clever St. Patrick knew that there was one sure way to gain an audience with the king, and that was to piss him off. Right before the king was to light his fire, Patrick lit a big one on the nearby Hill of Slane. It worked. Dragged before the king, Patrick plucked a shamrock out of the ground, used it to explain the holy trinity and generally talked up the whole Christ thing. The king thought it all seemed like a good idea, and the rest is history.

need to know

Hours/Days Open Always open, always free.

Tourist Information **Tara Visitor's Center** *(Off the main Dublin road (N3); Tel 046-25903; 9:30am-6:30pm daily mid-June to mid-Sept, 10:00am-5:00pm daily May to mid-June, mid-Sept-Oct; Admission £1.50 including tour),* is located in the old church beside the entrance to the archaeological area.

Directions/Transportation To get to Tara, you can take the local bus from Dublin to Navan and ask the driver to let you off as close as possible to the site. From the drop off, it's about a 20-minute walk to the site. Also, many day-trip organized bus tours leave from hostels in Dublin such as the **Avalon House** [see **Dublin**] and go right to the site. If you're driving, from Trim take the R161 to Navan, then the N3 toward Dublin.

Eats and Crashing There are a number of hostels and eateries in nearby **Trim** [see above].

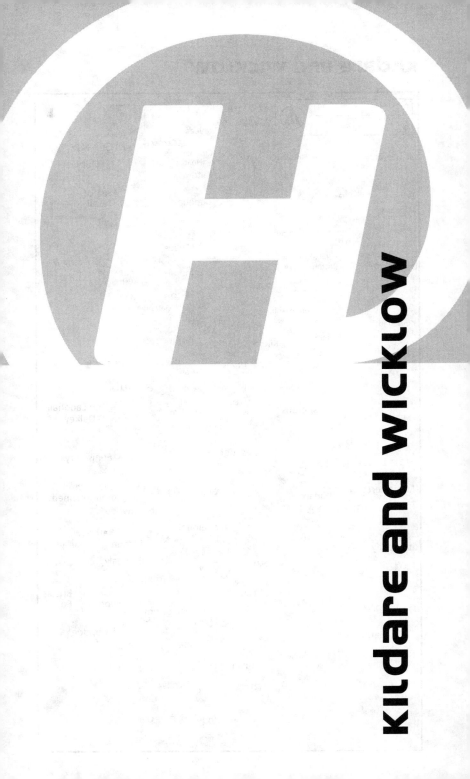
Kildare and Wicklow

Kildare and Wicklow

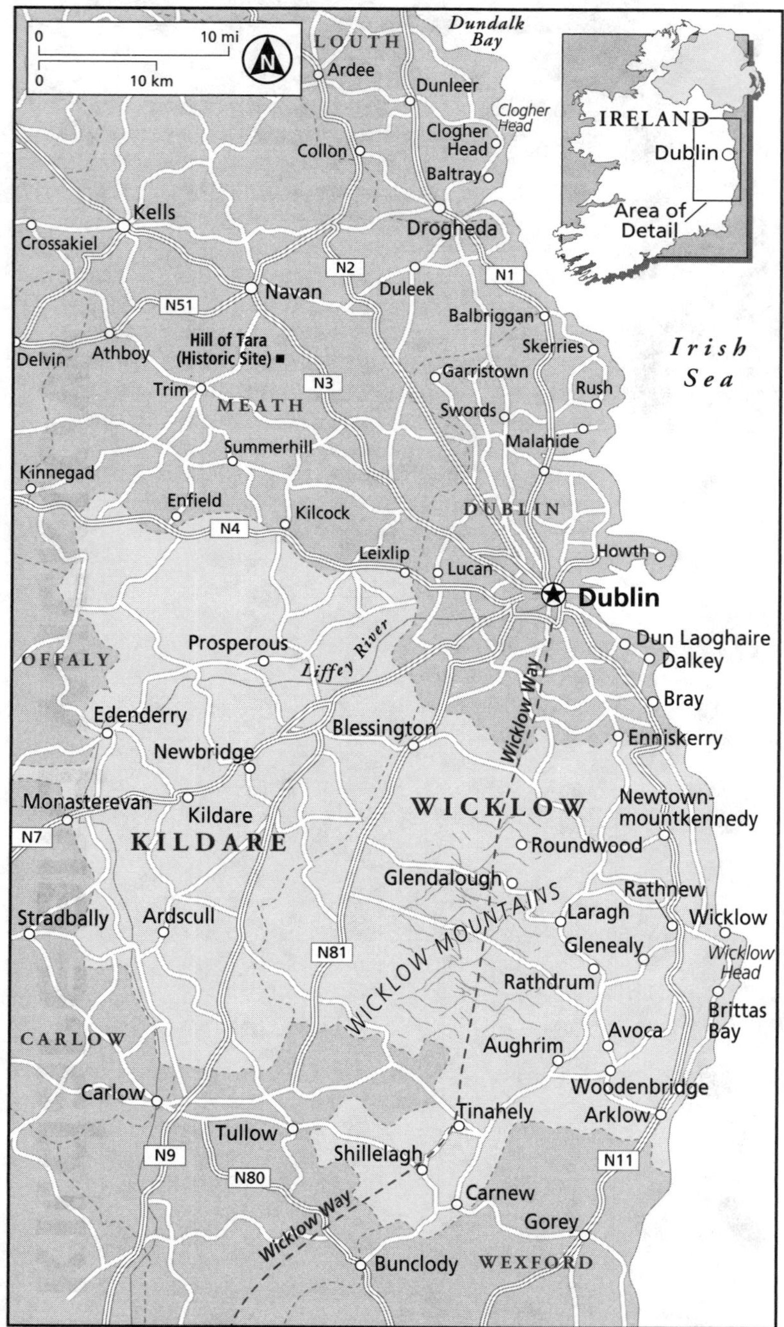

0
10 mi
0
10 km
N
Dundalk Bay
LOUTH
Ardee
Dunleer
Clogher Head
Clogher Head
Collon
Baltray
Kells
Crossakiel
Drogheda
N2
N1
Duleek
Navan
N51
Balbriggan
Skerries
Irish Sea
Delvin
Athboy
Hill of Tara (Historic Site)
Garristown
Trim
N3
MEATH
Rush
Swords
Malahide
Summerhill
Kinnegad
Enfield
Kilcock
N4
DUBLIN
Howth
Leixlip
Lucan
Dublin
Dun Laoghaire
Dalkey
Prosperous
Liffey River
OFFALY
Wicklow Way
Bray
Edenderry
Blessington
Enniskerry
Newbridge
Monasterevan
Kildare
WICKLOW
Newtown-mountkennedy
N7
KILDARE
Roundwood
Glendalough
Rathnew
WICKLOW MOUNTAINS
Stradbally
Ardscull
Laragh
Wicklow
Glenealy
Wicklow Head
N81
Rathdrum
Brittas Bay
CARLOW
Avoca
Aughrim
Woodenbridge
Carlow
Tinahely
Arklow
Tullow
Shillelagh
N11
N9
N80
Carnew
Wicklow Way
Gorey
Bunclody
WEXFORD
IRELAND
Dublin
Area of Detail

Kildare

If you've seen *Braveheart*, you've already caught a glimpse of the plains of Curragh near Kildare town. The seat of Irish horseracing and breeding, County Kildare was an ideal location for a Mel Gibson-on-horseback film shoot. On the other hand, the nearby Curragh Prison Camp—where many IRA soldiers have done time right next to your ordinary everyday murderers and rapists—served as a backdrop for the World War II POW drama, *The Brylcreem Boys*. So you might say Kildare has a little something for everybody, kind of an equal opportunity county.

Kildare is also famed as the birthplace of Brigid, Ireland's second patron saint [see *culture zoo,* below]. Brigid was a bit ahead of her time, founding a co-ed monastery in Kildare in the 5th or 6th century.

But let's stick with the horses. The only reason you'd stop in Kildare—an unremarkable town of less than 4,000 people, situated on the busy road between Dublin and Cork—would be to play the ponies, ride the ponies, or watch the ponies meet and fall in love (OK, maybe they aren't actually *in love,* but the stud farms do have a neutral zone where the fillies are allowed to calm down a mite before they breed).

culture zoo

St. Brigid's Cathedral *(Kildare town, Tel 045/441-654; 10am-5pm Sat, 2-5pm Sun, May-Sep; £2):* If the horse you bet on needs a little divine intervention, head on over to St. Brigid's. Aside from the ponies, this 13th-century Protestant cathedral is the main point of interest in Kildare. Built on the site of a Catholic monastery and convent founded by the town's patron saint, Brigid, in 490 A.D., the cathedral features a 10th-century round tower, the tallest climbable high tower in Ireland, offering a great view of the track.

And speaking of the tallest, highest, and mostest...the czar of world records, Arthur Guinness, was from Kildare. The famous brewer apparently was out to set a record of his own; he fathered 21 children, then opened the first Sunday school in Ireland (gotta get a day off somehow...).

city sports

The Irish National Stud thoroughbred breeding farm *(1.6 km (1 mi) northwest of Kildare town in Tully; Tel 045/522-963 or 045/521-617; 9am-6pm daily, Feb 12-Nov 12; £6 adults, Students £4.50)* was founded in 1900 by Scottish colonel William Hill-Walker, an astrology freak who had horoscopes charted for all of his horses and sold all the foals whose stars were ill-fated. He also had skylights built in all of the paddocks and stallion boxes so the horses could see the stars. The funny part is that the old geezer was remarkably successful, and the Irish Stud is still producing champions today. When you visit the Stud, take the 35-minute guided tour (offered hourly) to find out everything you ever wanted to know—and then some—about sex and horses. The best time to see newborn foals is January through June. And while you're there, don't miss the tiny Irish Horse Museum, where the skeleton of legendary steeplechaser Arkle, who won three straight British Cheltenham Gold Cups in the '60s, is on display.

Now, off to the races. It can be expensive, so if you can go to only one track, go to the home of the Irish Derby, the **Curragh Racecourse** *(North of Kildare town on the Dublin road (N7); Tel 045/441-205; 2pm-6pm Mar-Oct, call for race schedule; General admission £10, Irish Derby £15, combo race admission and return train fare from Dublin £12).* In addition to world-class horseracing, you'll see a crowd that looks like a cast of extras from *My Fair Lady,* all decked out for a day on the green. It's a far cry from the skanky off-track betting rooms back home. Busaras race buses from Dublin go directly to the track, as do Iarnrod Eireann trains from Heuston Station; the trip should take between an hour and an hour-and-a-half. From Kildare, take the No. 126 bus toward Dublin.

There are two other tracks nearby that are smaller and less expensive, but not really worth a trip from Dublin: the **Naas Racecourse** *(Tipper Rd., Naas, 6.5 km (4 mi) northeast of Kildare; Busaras race buses from Dublin go directly to the track; Tel 045/897-391; Call track for schedule; Adults £8-10, students £4-5)* and the **Punchestown Racecourse** *(Naas-Ballymoreustace Rd, off N7 Naas Rd., about 5 km (3 mi) north of Naas; Tel 045/897-704; Year-round; Call track for schedule and admission fees).*

eats

There's plenty of food at the racecourses, but if you want to chill in a little bistro instead of gulping it down while the horses pound the track, head back into Kildare town. There are lots of little pubs and cafés right in the center of town (all of which are within a radius of a few blocks).

Kristianna's Bistro *(Claregate St., Kildare; Tel 045/522-985; Lunch daily 12:30-2:30pm, dinner 6:30-10pm, Fri-Sat until 11pm; lunch under £10, dinner £10-20; MC, V)* specializes in seafood and has vegetarian fare as well. If you happen to be in town on a Friday, stop by the **Naas Country Market** *(Town Hall, Naas; Call chairperson Margaret Gillespie for info; Tel 045/862116; 10:30am-midafternoon Fri)* for homegrown fruit and veggies, homemade cakes, and other farm-fresh eats. They also sell hand-knitted sweaters made to order and are happy to give you free gardening advice even if you don't buy a thing.

crashing

In theory, you won't be spending the night here, but if horses turn you on, try Liz and Ned Fitzpatrick's **Castle View Farm** *(4 km (2.5 mi) from Kildare town, signs are posted all along the way from the center of town; Tel 045/521-816, Fax 045/521-816; Open Mar-Nov; 4 guestrooms with private bath, community TV lounge, £16.50-22.50; supper £7; V, MC).* They don't breed horses, but it's a short walk down an idyllic hedge-trimmed path from the main house to their working dairy farm. Hey, it's a farm. With animals. And delicious home-cooked meals. Plus it's a major photo op: The house looks just like the pictures of cozy Irish farmhouses you see on all the postcards.

Other do-able options include the **Lord Edward Guesthouse** *(The Square,Kildare; Tel 045/522-389, Fax 045/520-471; Singles £20, doubles £35, private baths; V, MC, AE, D),* about a ten-minute walk from the Kildare train station and a two-minute walk from the Kildare bus station, in the town center; **Curragh Lodge Hotel** *(Dublin Rd.; Tel 045/522-144, Fax 045/521-247; clhotel@iol.ie; All rooms £35/person, private baths; Breakfast included; V, MC, AE, Laser),* a 10-minute walk from Kildare train station and a short walk from the town center; and **St.Mary's** *(Maddenstown,Curragh ; Tel 045/521-243; All rooms £18/person, shared baths, breakfast included; No credit cards),* three miles from Kildare center, reachable by taxi from the train or bus station.

need to know

Currency Exchange There are several banks in Kildare town, including the **Bank of Ireland** *(The Square, Tel 045/521-276)* and the **Allied Irish Bank** *(The Square, Tel 045/522-001).* In Naas, try the **Bank of Ulster** *(44 N. Main St., Naas; Tel 045/897-355).*

Tourist Information The **Tourist Information Office** *(Tel 040/469-117; 9:30am-5:30pm Mon-Fri)* is on the main square in Kildare. **Kildare Fàilte** *(38 S. Main St., Naas; Tel 045/898-888; 9am-5pm Mon-Fri)* specializes in tourism for County Kildare.

Health and Emergency Emergency: *999*; Gardai *Tel 045/521-222 in Kildare, 045/884-300 in Naas.* There is one hospital nearby: **Naas General Hospital** *(off the Ballymore Road, Tel 045/897-221).*

Trains and Buses It takes about an hour-and-a-half to get from Dublin to Kildare town on **Iarnrod Eireann** *(Tel 045/521-224);* trains depart **Heuston Station** daily at 12:55pm. But there has been ongoing track work on the route for some time, which means you have to get off and take a bus part of the way. **DART trains** run to Newbridge, but you still have to take a bus from Newbridge to Kildare, so it's easier just to take the bus the whole way.

It takes an hour for the 12 bus to get from Dublin to Kildare on the **Dublin-Limerick-Ennis line;** buses depart Dublin hourly every day, 7:45am-7:45pm. Heading back to Dublin, the ride takes ten minutes longer because the 12 line adds a couple of stops, but it leaves Kildare hourly every day, 9:50am-9:50pm. The fare is £5.80 each way, students £4 *(Call Busáras in Dublin at Tel 01/836-6111 for information).*

Postal You shouldn't have any trouble finding the **Kildare Post Office** *(Dublin St., Kildare; Tel 045/521-346; 9am-5:30pm Mon-Fri, 10am-4pm Sat, closed for lunch Sat 1-2:30pm).* There's also one in Naas *(S. Main St., Naas; Tel 045/897-287; 9am-5:30pm Mon-Fri, noon-5pm Sat).*

WICKLOW TOWN

Despite the brightly painted buildings that line the streets, Wicklow Town is slightly drab and even a tad depressing. The beach might have something to do with it: it's strewn with shards of beer bottle glass and fast food wrappers. The construction sites by the seaside don't exactly provide for a picturesque view either. It's not necessary to overnight in Wicklow Town if you're heading to **Wicklow National Park** [see below], which can also be reached directly from Dublin, but if you've spent a few days hostelling and hiking there, Wicklow Town may come as a welcome breath of civilization, a place to dress up for dinner, catch a trad session in a pub, and tour a couple of historic sites, particularly those associated with Irish national hero Charles Stewart Parnell. The city also makes a good base for exploring the strands several kilometers to the south, such as **Brittas Bay** or the **Silver Strand** [see *great outdoors,* below], which seem gorgeous in contrast.

Wicklow Town's easy to master: it consists basically of one main street—which changes its name from **Abbey** to **Main** at **Fitzwilliam Square.** You just walk down the street from the bus stop or train station past the gas station—if you're walking downhill, you know you're going in the right direction—to reach the **Wicklow Bay Hostel** [see *crashing,* below]. At the Square, **Bridge Street** will lead you to the **Leitrim Lounge** [see *bar scene,* below], the hostel, and a lot of ugly construction sites. Perhaps by the time you read this, however, there will be plenty of spiffy new seaside condos, and you can walk along the quiet misty Wicklow shores wishing your own bedroom view could be so splendid.

As with most other smallish Irish towns, the social scene centers around the pubs, and there's not too much of a youth vibe to speak of (all

wicklow, how poetic

John Millington Synge wrote of Wicklow in a poem called "Prelude":

"Still south I went and west and south again,
Through Wicklow from the morning till the night,
And far from cities, and the sights of men,
Lived with the sunshine, and the moon's delight.
I knew the stars, the flowers, and the birds,
The grey and wintry sides of many glens,
And did but half remember human words,
In converse with the mountains, moors, and fens."

the college kids are off making merry in Dublin). By night, you'll find many of the town's 6,000 residents at **Philip Healy's** [see *bar scene,* below].

bar, club and live music scene

You'll find live trad very nearly nightly at **Philip Healy's** *(Fitzwilliam Sq.; Tel 0404/67380),* which serves up good pub grub and has the busiest social scene in town. This place packs itself to the rafters every night with young and old, native and tourist alike. The air's always buzzing with the strains of that unmistakable Irish brogue. **The Bridge Tavern** *(Bridge St.; Tel 0404/67718)* offers live music—country, trad, or pop—every night of the week at "The Crow's Nest." It has another doorway on the cross street, but it's the same pub. Other pubs in town include **O'Connell's** *(Abbey St. on Fitzwilliam Square)* and **Fitzpatrick's** *(Abbey St. on Fitzwilliam Square),* both on Abbey Street, and the **Leitrim Lounge** *(The Murrough, on the right side of the street near the Wicklow Bay Hostel),* which also serves good food. Don't come to Wicklow expecting an *exceptionally* fun time at night, and you won't be disappointed.

culture zoo

Wicklow's Historic Gaol *(Kilmantin Hill; Tel 0404/61599; 10am-5pm daily Apr-Sept, 10am-4pm daily Mar and Oct; wccgaol@eircom.net, www.wicklow.ie/gaol; Admission £4):* The best—if not only—reason to visit a jail on vacation is to see what it was like for *other* people. This former prison is filled with mannequins representing haggard and destitute prison inmates sporting melodramatic expressions and sickly gray painted faces. There are actors here, too, but they aren't quite so entertaining. The jail gives a rather interesting overview of Irish political history and daily life within horrific pre-reform prison conditions. Irish and British prison reformers, like Jeremiah Fitzpatrick, who called this particular jail "a very insecure, bad prison" in 1785, were inspired to call for prison reform after witnessing such atrocious sanitation and living conditions. The first laws were passed in the 1760s, although naturally it was quite some time before they were actually put into effect.

great outdoors

Luckily for all you mountain men and women, the **Wicklow Mountains National Park** [see below] is nearby, as is **Devil's Glen,** a fabulously secluded sylvan spot for a picnic. The glen is only a ten-minute bus ride from Wicklow Town; Take Bus Éireann [see *need to know,* below] to Ashford on the same route that goes on to Dublin, then walk two-and-a-half miles east to Devil's Glen, where you can take a hike through some rugged terrain to the **Devil's Punchbowl,** a gorgeous waterfall up in the northeast corner of the glen, about 3 miles from the entrance.

Back in Wicklow Town, you can walk on over and see the all-too-scant ruins (we're talking a couple of rocks here) of the 12th-century Norman **Black Castle,** on a hill to the right from the Wicklow Bay

charles stewart parnell

Charles Stewart Parnell, one of Ireland's most important nationalist leaders, was—ironically enough—the son of a Protestant landowner. An outspoken proponent of Home Rule, he was elected to the British Parliament in 1875, where he became a master at using filibusters to spread his message about the many problems facing the Irish people. His agitation spurred rebellions against the English landlords, and he was briefly imprisoned for having (indirectly, it's true) promoted the violence. Along with British prime minister William Gladstone, Parnell attempted to pass the first Home Rule Bill in 1886, and though that first shot failed, it certainly paved the way for inevitable Irish independence.

Parnell's political future seemed bright until he became involved with a married woman named Kitty O'Shea. Her highly publicized divorce case brought the love affair to center stage, and although it certainly wouldn't have fazed anyone in modern times, back then the scandal was enough to ruin Parnell's career. Kitty got her divorce and married Parnell, but his fall from grace broke him completely, and he died only four months after their marriage.

Hostel. The same path that leads from town out to the ruins—which begins at the Black Castle golf course—continues down to a lighthouse. The path ends there, but you can continue walking on the Silver Strand, a small beach.

If an invigorating walk is what you're after, head south out of town on the coast road, which will take you directly to the esteemed cliffs of **Wicklow Head,** teeming with sea lions. The walk out to the cliffs should take about 20 minutes.

For canoe rental, boat trips, and swimming lessons, go to **Aquasports** *(Wicklow Pier; No phone)*. Rent a bike from **Wicklow Hire** [see *need to know,* below] and ride down to the small-but-pretty **Silver Strand** about two miles south of Wicklow. Farther down, around 16 km (9.9 mi) south of Wicklow Town, you'll find fantastic **Brittas Bay,** which wins the Blue Flag Award every year from the European Parliament for the best beaches. (Dubliners flock here in good weather.) There aren't any shops or restaurants in the area, so definitely pack a picnic lunch. You can also take a cab to either beach for a few punts each way.

stuff

Desperate for something to read for your next train or bus ride? The selections at **Malone's Bookshop** *(Main St.)* and **Bridge Street Books** *(Bridge St.; 10am-6pm Mon-Sat)* could hardly be called comprehensive; they stock mostly Irish studies titles.

eats

All the pubs serve decent food; try **Philip Healy's** [see *bar scene*, above] till around nine. The food's more or less traditional Irish fare—you know, lamb, steak, lots of potatoes, the usual. Or you can take advantage of the hostel kitchen and buy groceries at the **Supervalu** *(Wentworth Place, off Church St; Tel 0404/61888)*.

powerscourt

The **Powerscourt Gardens, House Exhibition, and Waterfall** *(off the Dublin-Wicklow Rd., N11; Tel 01/204-6000; Gardens and house 9:30am-5:30pm Mar-Oct; 9:30am-dusk, Nov-Feb; waterfall 9:30am-7pm, Mar-Oct; 10:30am-dusk, Nov-Feb; house and gardens £5 Adults, £4.50 Students , waterfall £2 Adults, £1.50 Students)*, near Enniskerry in County Wicklow and about 8 kilometers (5 miles) from **Bray** [see **County Dublin**], has always been a popular tourist attraction. Parts of the grounds were used in several movies, including *Excalibur*. The gardens are immaculately landscaped, and the waterfall, a 6 km (3.7 mi) walk from the garden, checks in as the highest in Ireland at 400 feet. The house itself, built in the 1730s, lost much of its grandeur in a fire in 1974 and is still in the process of restoration. Powerscourt makes an easy afternoon trip from Dublin. To get there, take DART to the Bray station, then take Bus Éireann route 85 from Bray to Enniskerry, or take the route 45 bus directly from Dublin.

There's a good hostel a couple of miles from the garden, if you want to stick around: **Lacken House Hostel** *(Knockree, Enniskerry, Wicklow; Tel 01/286-4036; £7-£8 dorm; No credit cards)*, in a gorgeous restored 18th-century stone farmhouse with a little brook running right next to it. There is a lockout between 10:30am and 5:30pm unless the weather is bad. If you want, you can pick up the Wicklow Way nearby instead of starting at Glendalough.

For seafood, steaks, and all that stuff, you could try **Rugantino's River Café** *(South Quay; Tel 0404/61900; Wed-Sat 6-10pm; Sun brunch 1-5pm; Main courses £10-15; V, MC)*. It's romantically candlelit by night and always popular with Wicklow's upper crust, so make reservations before you go.

crashing

Opened in 1842 as a trade school, the **Wicklow Bay Hostel** *(The Murrough, Marine House; Tel 0404/69213; wicklowbayhostel@tinet.ie, www.angelfire.com/on/wicklowbayhostel; £8 dorm; No credits cards)* later served as a military barracks for both British and Nationalist soldiers, an orphanage, a school, a textile factory, and a Guinness bottling plant. Talk about history. Captain Robert Halpin, who laid the first transatlantic cable from the U.S. to Europe, held his celebration dinner here, and part of Pierce Brosnan's film *The Nephew* was filmed here—there's a picture above the reception desk of 007 himself holding the baby of the house. The hostel has ample kitchen facilities, an exceptionally friendly and helpful staff, and gorgeous sea views from the dorms. To reach the hostel, walk toward town from the bus or train stops, and at Fitzwilliam Square turn left onto the bridge, then another left. The large sunny yellow building with the "Marine House" sign straight ahead is where you want to go.

If you're going to splurge in Wicklow Town, there's no better place than at the **Old Rectory Country House and Restaurant** *(One mile off the N11 on the Dublin side of Wicklow town; Tel 0404/67048; Open Mar-Dec; mail@oldrectory.ie, indigo.ie/~rectory; £54 per person; V, MC, AE)*, a lovely old Victorian that's won awards for both its accommodations (including bathrooms en suite, a gym and sauna) and its excellent restaurant featuring fresh seafood and organic produce. The food's so good that it's been featured on several Irish television programs.

within 30 minutes

The birthplace of Charles Stewart Parnell [see *charles stewart parnell*, above], **Avondale House** *(Rathdrum, signposted off R752; Tel 0404/46111; 10am-6pm May-Sept, 11am-5pm Oct-Apr; Admission £3 adults, £2.50 students)* is now restored to the splendor known by its most famous owner. The house offers a good video introduction to Parnell's role in Irish history and a display of personal memorabilia, including copies of Parnell's love letters to his mistress, Kitty O'Shea. The town of Rathdrum is accessible from Wicklow Town via Bus Éireann or Irish Rail, about a 20-minute trip; the house itself is about a mile outside Rathdrum.

Reachable by Bus Éireann from Wicklow to Ashford about a 5-minute ride on, **Mount Usher Gardens** *(Ashford; Tel 0404/40116 or 0404/40205; 10:30am-6pm Mar 17-Oct 31; mount_usher.gardens@*

indigo.ie; Admission £4 adults, £3.50 students) has large tea rooms overlooking a lovely 20-acre garden that includes exotic trees, flowers, and streams meandering alongside shady paths. Rambling across wooden bridges and fields dotted with colorful wildflowers makes for a peaceful, scenic afternoon, and the views are certainly more postcard-worthy than any you'll find in Wicklow Town.

need to know

Currency Exchange Cash in those traveler's checks at the **Bank of Ireland** *(Main St.; 10am-5pm Mon 10am-4pm Tue-Fri)* or **AIB** *(Main St.;10am-5pm Mon 10am-4pm Tue-Fri),* which has an ATM.

Tourist Information Information abounds at the **Wicklow Tourist Office** *(Main St. on Fitzwilliam Sq.; Tel 0404/69117; 9am-1pm/2-6pm Mon-Fri, 9:30am-1pm/2-6:30pm Sat, Jun-Sept, 9:30am-1pm/2-5:30pm Mon-Fri, Oct-May).*

Public Transportation There are no city buses, but **Wicklow Tours** *(Tel 0404/67671)* runs minibuses to Glendalough twice a day June through August. If you're staying at the Wicklow Bay Hostel, it's especially easy to do a day trip on Wicklow Tours: The bus leaves the hostel at 10:30am every day in the summer and picks everybody up at Glendalough at 5pm for £6 round-trip. You can also try **Wicklow Cabs** *(Tel 0404/66888).*

Health and Emergency For medical treatment, head to the **Hospital** *(Colley St.; Tel 040/467108).* It's about a 10-minute walk north on Main Street on Kilmartin Hill.

Trains The **Wicklow Train Station** *(Church Rd.; Tel 040/467329 for information)* receives trains from Dublin-Connolly and Rosslare Harbour (three or four trains from each per day). The station's a bit of a walk (about 15-20 minutes) outside Wicklow Town. To get there, walk away from Fitzwilliam Square toward and past the Grand Hotel, then turn right at the gas station. If you need a cab, the station employers will call one for you (cabbies don't just linger outside the station)—for larger groups, call **Nick Dolan** *(Tel 040-467420).*

Bus Lines Out of the City **Bus Éireann** *(call Busáras in Dublin at Tel 01/836-6111 for information)* leaves from the Wicklow Gaol and the Grand Hotel and Main Street for Dublin or for Wexford, Rosslare Harbour, etc. Buses leave approximately nine times a day (six times on Sundays).

Bike Rental Rent a bike and feel the burn at **Wicklow Hiring** *(Abbey St.; Tel 0404/68149; 8:30am-1pm/2-5:30pm Mon-Sat; £6 per day, £30 per week).*

Laundry If it's time to fluff and fold, head to **Bridge Laundry** *(Bridge St.; Tel 0404/62535; Mon-Sat 9:30am-1pm/2-5:30pm).*

Postal Head to the **Wicklow Post Office** *(Main St.; Tel 0404/67474; 9am-5:30pm Mon-Fri, 9:30am-12:50pm/2:10-5:30pm Sat)* with your letters home.

glendalough and the wicklow mountains

A sizeable chunk of County Wicklow—some 50,000 acres of it—has been set aside as Wicklow Mountains National Park. If you've got a car, you've got it made here, spinning along the 82-mile-long **Wicklow Way**, which winds through the park's forested hillsides and valleys with dramatic mountain views. Otherwise, pull on your hiking boots and explore the mountains by foot—public transportation in the area is terribly scarce. The mountains here are a weird geographic oddity, a vast granite mass of hot rock that bulged up from the earth some 400 million year ago and started to chill out. Most of this rugged mountain terrain was "sculpted" during the Ice Ages. Dating from 1981, the trail through the park is the oldest marked trail in Ireland and

st. kevin

Saint Kevin, the guy who founded Glendalough in the early 6th century, is another of those Irish characters whose life is shrouded in interesting legends. Apparently he first lived here as a hermit for seven years, moved away to found another monastery, then returned to Glendalough to establish the monastery whose remains fascinate visitors today. What we're really interested in, though, is what happened while he was living here alone. Kevin was said to be, er, a very *attractive* man; a local woman (some say she was actually a queen) became smitten with him. So he did what any hotly pursued monk would do: he hid from her, retreating into a cave. Eventually she found him, one night while he was sleeping, and proceeded to...well...let's just say she let her hormones get the best of her. Of course Kevin woke up, and was so angry that he accidentally threw her off a rocky ledge, now aptly known as Lady's Leap. Of course she fell into one of the lakes and drowned, and poor Kevin spent the rest of his life repenting for what he had done. (And they still gave him a halo? *Yeesh.*) Other Kevin legends sound even wackier than that of a young man resisting female advances: it's said he employed an otter to catch salmon for him, and that once a blackbird laid an egg in his outstretched hand while he was praying. He supposedly stood motionless until the egg eventually hatched.

one of the most scenic, stretching all the way from Marlay Park (close to the border of Dublin) to Clonegal in County Carlow. Along the trail you pass heather-clad mountains and glacial valleys. To walk the whole trail generally takes about 10 days. We liked the little town of **Glenmalure,** one of the most scenic in the valley. Nearby you'll pass by **Lungaquilla,** highest point in the mountains. The scenery between **Sally Gap** and **Roundwood** (check it on your map) is some of the most spectacular in the park.

Those who aren't die-hard hikers usually just get a taste of the Wicklow Mountains' wild beauty by visiting the tiny town of Glendalough (glen-da-lock, meaning "glen of two lakes"), one of the most important monastic settlements in Ireland, founded by St. Kevin in the 6th century. The ruins of Glendalough includes a tall, well preserved round tower; a small cathedral; a few churches; and a graveyard that's still in use. The ruins are always open and always free. In summertime, gaggles of eager visitors walk along forested paths encircling the two gorgeous shimmering lakes—imaginatively named Upper Lake and Lower Lake—and lots of very cool monastic ruins, and then usually head off to the next destination on their itineraries. Glendalough's wonderfully serene vibe is ruined a bit, though, when there are too many tourists—so come early or late in the season if you can. Try to get away from the crowds: Look for the steep trail leading to a high waterfall with a big rock that makes an ideal spot for a little bit of quiet contemplation. Or, to attain the maximum creepy factor—and it's deliciously spooky, all right—visit the cemetery among the monastic ruins at dusk on a foggy night after a pint too many at the pub down the road from the An Óige hostel [see *crashing,* below]. You'll come back in the morning to a completely different place.

Some visitors do stick around and really start walking. While the mountain trails are not easy on the feet, they are well tended and there are also several hostels along the way [see *crashing,* below] that cater to rugged rambler types. The Visitors Centre [see *need to know,* below] identifies suggested trails, but most of them aren't marked. It also sells the indispensible *Wicklow Way Map Guide,* which should help you from getting too lost. You can walk anywhere you like in the park, as long as you don't fish, swim, boat, or otherwise disturb the park's natural state.

A leisurely 7-mile walk east of Glendalough you'll find **Devil's Glen,** the most bucolic valley in the park. There's a bizarre "sculpture garden" at the entrance to the glen, formed when local sculptors decided to create Celtic figures out of several old trees that had been knocked down in big storms. Once here, you can't leave without seeing the **Devil's Punchbowl,** one of the most breathtaking waterfalls in Ireland. It's at the northeast end of the glen, beyond some rugged terrain.

eats

If you're staying in Glendalough, pretty much your only choice for eats and drinks are the **Glendasan Restaurant** and the **Glendalough Tavern** *(both Tel 0404/45135; Restaurant: 8am-10am/12pm-3pm year-round, dinner 7pm-9pm Sun-Thur Feb-May and Sept-Jan, 7pm-9:30pm*

did you know?

- The Irish love their poetry, their per capita consumption of poetry surpasses that of any other English-speaking country. Not surprisingly, they've also churned out some decent verse in their time themselves.
- For certain scenic areas in Ireland, mobile phone "masts," as they're known, have been designed in the shape of trees, to cut-down the eye-sore factor on the Irish landscape caused by cell-phone revolution.
- On Irish coins, "heads" refers to the side bearing the harp, the national emblem. "Tails" is the side once occupied by the British monarchs, now replaced by animals, such as the cow, horse, and rooster. How's that for stickin' it to the throne.
- Katherine Kelly, one of Ireland's authenticated little people, was 34 inches tall and weighed 28 pounds when she died in 1735.
- The newt (Triturus vulgaris) is Ireland's only home-grown reptile.
- Robert Emmet is said to have been able to rattle off the English alphabet backward without taking a breath. This was not how or why he died.
- Little John, Robin Hood's got-to big-man met his end not in Sherwood Forest, but in Arbour Hill in Dublin, where he was hanged.
- Under that wacky Oliver Cromwell, it became law that the same bounty was offered for the head of a wolf and the head of a priest.
- The longest, and, indeed, most inane, formal debate on record anywhere in the world was conducted at University College Galway in 1995. The motion debated for 28 days read as follows: "This house has all the time in the world."
- In January 1997, the Irish government granted its first-ever divorce. The recipient was a terminally ill man, long separated from his wife, who sought to marry his current partner before he died. They did marry, and he died shortly afterward.
- When the Censorship of Films Act was passed in 1923, the first appointed censor was James Montgomery, who confessed to knowing little to nothing about films. He was quite clear, however, about his job, which, in his own words, was "to prevent the Californication of Ireland."
- In 2000, Ireland was ranked seventh among the world's most competitive nations, edging ahead of Germany, Britain, and Japan, and so giving new meaning to "the fighting Irish."

daily Jun-Aug. Tavern: 12pm-3pm/5:30pm-8:30pm daily, till 9pm Jun-Aug; Bar open 10:30am-11:30 pm Sun-Fri, till 12:30pm Sat. V, MC, AE, Din), located in the same building just outside the gated entrance to the park. The Tavern, frequented by the hostelling set staying a few minutes up the road, is a good place for a pint and a game of pool. The Glendasan Restaurant offers a better-than-average three-course lunch for around 12 punts.

crashing

Camping in national parks is forbidden, so if you're going to be traipsing around you'll need a place to stay.

In Glendalough, the recently renovated An Óige **Glendaloch Lodge Hostel** *(Glendalough; Tel 0404/45342; £11 dorm, £12.50 quad; lockout noon-5pm; V, MC)* has a super location right near the Glendalough ruins and lakes. Everything's clean and comfortable, if a tad sterile, and there's no pesky curfew. Breakfast is available for £3-5 and dinner for £5; if you'd rather cook for yourself you'll have to walk to nearby Laragh for groceries, which is a mile away. The Irish Writers' Centre of Dublin hosts traditional music and poetry sessions here three times a week during the summer months *(Admission £5, less with a student discount).*

If you're planning on doing some walking, there are several good hostels along the Wicklow Way: just find 'em on the *Wicklow Way Map Guide* and plan your route. **Aghavannagh House Hostel** *(Aughrim; Tel 0402/36366; Mar-Nov; No credit cards),* a lovely three-story stone house that once served as a military barracks, is set in the woods just off the Wicklow Way. There's absolutely no practical means of public transportation: The nearest bus stops are nine miles away, so as you can imagine almost everybody staying here is doing the heavy-duty hiking thing.

Situated in the national park, An Óige **Tiglin Hostel** *(Devil's Glen, Ashford; Tel 0404/40259; £6-7 dorm; No credit cards)* boasts the National Outdoor Training Centre next door. The outdoor centre can hook you up with expedition doing just about anything you'd want to do in the mountains—hiking, canoeing, rock climbing, fishing. . . . The biggest plus of staying at this hostel is its proximity to Devil's Glen. You can hear the rush and gurgle of the Devil's Punchbowl nearby. There's no place to get food within an hour's walk, unfortunately, but the hostel does have a small store. The public transportation options here are slightly better: from Dublin, you can take Bus Éireann [see *need to know,* below] toward Wicklow to Ashford (or from Wicklow to Ashford, only a ten-minute ride), and then it's about a three-mile walk west to the hostel on a tiny, unmarked road. If you're hiking from Glendalough, the hostel is about a four-mile walk to the northeast.

There are two more good hostels on the western side of the mountains. **Ballinclea Hostel** *(Ballinclea, Donard; Tel 045/40465 or 045/54657; £7-9 dorm; March-Nov; No credit cards),* a day's hike from Glendalough, is reachable pretty much only by foot or by car. If you're sick of walking by now, other activities, like horseback riding and orienteering, are available near the hostel. There's also **Rathcoran House Hostel** *(Baltinglass, Wicklow; Tel 0508/81073; £8.50 dorm, £19 double; No credit cards),* tucked in the midwesterly corner of the county, which is popular with those finishing the Wicklow Way. Buses bound for Dublin, Waterford, or Rosslare Harbour (routes 5 or 132) come through here. The hostel itself is a nice one: Breakfast is included, and bikes are up for rent.

need to know

Tourist Information **The Wicklow Mountains National Park Visitors Centre** *(Glendalough; Tel 0404/45425; 10am-6pm, May-Aug; 10am-6pm Sat-Sun, Apr and Sept)* is located by the Upper Lake at Glendalough. The Centre is the best place for information on trails, lodging, and so on. Hikers and drivers can get detailed maps here, though those are also available from any tourist office in County Wicklow. (Pick up the excellent *Wicklow Way Map Guide* for £4.50.) If the Wicklow Park Visitor Centre is closed, try the **Glendalough Visitor Centre** *(Tel 0404/45324; 9am-6:30pm, Jun-Aug; 9:30am-6pm, Sept-mid Oct; 9:30am-5pm, mid-Oct-mid-Mar; 9:30am-6:30pm, mid Mar-May; Admission to video presentation £2 adults, £1 students),* where the St. Kevin's Bus stops. If both visitor centers are closed and you need info right away, you can always call the park ranger's office at 0404/45561 or 0404/45338.

In Wicklow town, you can get information at the **Wicklow Tourist Office** *(Main St., Fitzwilliam Sq.; Tel 0404/69117; 9am-1pm/2-6pm Mon-Fri, 9:30am-1pm/2-6:30pm Sat, Jun-Sept; 9:30am-1pm/2-5:30pm Mon-Fri, Oct-May).*

Directions/Transportation From Dublin, the easiest way to get to Glendalough is with **St. Kevin's Bus Service** *(Tel 01/281-8119; 11:30am and 6pm Mon-Sat, 11:30am and 7pm Sun; approximately £8 round-trip),* which leaves twice daily from outside the College of Surgeons on the west side of St. Stephen's Green all year round.

When it comes to the Wicklow National Park, you can't really depend on **Bus Éireann** to take you wherever you want to go; you'll have to go to Baltinglass, in the southwestern corner of the county (Route 5), or to Wicklow Town (Route 2, 5, or 133) and then continue by foot or bicycle into the park. To get to Glendalough you have to take St. Kevin's Bus Service.

Bike Rental You can rent a bike from the **Glendaloch Lodge Hostel** [see *crashing,* above] for £7 per day, or £35 per week, plus a £30 deposit.

the southeast

After Dublin, the big question is: What next? The scenic coast of western Cork? The tourist-crunched Ring of Kerry? How about the spectacular Cliffs of Moher?

Not so fast. Before you zoom over to the West of Ireland for those popular travel destinations, consider the southeastern region of the country. **Counties Wexford, Waterford, Tipperary, Carlow,** and **Kilkenny** have a lot to offer. They are often referred to as Ireland's "sunny Southeast," because they generally enjoy more sunshine than the rest of the country. If you skip a visit to Ireland's former stronghold, medieval **Kilkenny City,** bypass the enormous fortress on limestone Rock of Cashel, or forego a scuba dive in the caves off of Hook Head, your Irish photo album will remain hopelessly incomplete. So spend at least a few days in the relatively tranquil, and relatively sunny, Southeast before heading west, where wild coastlines are tempered by heavy tourism and ubiquitous, smog-spewing travel coaches.

History comes to life in city walls built a thousand years ago, monuments to Irish heroes, and colorful villages lined with cobblestone streets. The larger towns of southeastern Ireland have a distinctly medieval flavor, particularly Kilkenny, **Cashel, Wexford,** and, to a lesser extent, **Waterford.** You'll walk through narrow, winding streets and find yourself rubbing up against imposing old stone buildings with facades that only begin to hint at the centuries they've witnessed and marauders they've survived—the Normans, Vikings, and Oliver Cromwell for starters. Wexford and Waterford were heavily influenced by Viking invasions in the second half of the first millennium A.D., and you can still see signs of the Viking presence in city walls. The **Hook Peninsula** was famous for shipwrecks and boasts a lighthouse dating to the 13th century. County Carlow (which bears the dubious distinction of being the second smallest county in Ireland), is the site of the bloodiest battle of the 1798 Uprising.

Sure, you'll find places of architectural, historical, and cultural interest in other parts of Ireland, but the feeling you get walking down these twisted old streets—a mild sense of claustrophobia, a quiet awe, an involuntary attitude of humility—is unique to the older cities of the Southeast. Toss back a pint in a pub rich with history, like Kilkenny's Kyteler's Inn, which dates to 1324 and was once the home of alleged witch Dame Alice Kyteler. Walk around the monuments in Wexford Town on a cool summer evening, or stand in the shadow of 12th century St. Canice's Cathedral in

Kilkenny City (or Jerpoint Abbey or **Kells Priory**) during a spell of cold, relentless rain, and you'll see what we mean.

County Wexford is a prime place to take advantage of the "sunny Southeast," with some remarkably good beaches—Curracloe Beach and Rosslare Strand are both easy day-jaunts out of Wexford Town—and super diving around the Hook Head peninsula. Okay, the Riviera it's not, but it's as close as Ireland gets to sun 'n' fun. And if you're heading on to the Continent, it's a convenient area to enjoy your last little bit of Ireland before catching a ferry to France out of Rosslare Harbour.

getting around the region

Ireland's convoluted public transportation routes don't allow you to just hop on a bus or train and go wherever you please whenever you please, and that will definitely shape your itinerary to a large degree. As for heading out to the smaller towns in each county, from Waterford City to Tramore or Wexford to New Ross, buses are the only way to go. Bicycling is ideal for village-hopping along the Barrow and Nore rivers, to Thomastown, Inistoige, Graiguenamanagh, and Bennettsbridge. Of course, if you have a car you can go wherever you please, but the cost of rentals can put a serious hole in your travel budget—and if you think gas is expensive in the States, wait till you start forking over the big bucks for Irish petrol, sold not by the gallon but by the liter.

Try taking a private bus service [see *need to know,* **Wicklow Mountains National Park**] from Dublin to Glendalough, where you can gaze at shimmering lakes and walk amid forested ruins. Then, if you want to get to Wicklow Town to check out the beaches, you'll have to take St. Kevin's back up to Bray, and then Bus Éireann or Irish Rail down to Wicklow Town. In fact, if you want to get anywhere from Glendalough you'll pretty much have to head back north to Bray or Dublin first. Once you're in Wicklow, you can take the train or the bus to Wexford Town; Wicklow and Wexford are both Irish Rail stops. From Wexford, Rosslare Harbour's just a short train trip away, but you won't be heading there until you're ready to take on the rest of Europe.

From Wexford, you can take the train or the bus to Waterford; if you'd rather skip Waterford and head on to Kilkenny instead, you're *still* going to have to stop in Waterford, because there's no direct route from Wexford to Kilkenny. After you've spent time in Kilkenny, where to next? Options are back to Waterford (again) or Dublin, or to Carlow Town to see Browne's Hill Dolmen, which is on the Waterford-Dublin bus route.

Going from Wicklow to Kilkenny involves another complicated route—as we've said, you'll find a lot of those in this country—so you've got to study the train and bus schedules and maps carefully before deciding on an itinerary. And if you want to get to Cork from the Southeast, don't take the train; taking the bus is a lot easier.

Travel Times

* *By train*
** *Water-crossing required (by ferry usually)*
*** *By cable car*

	Dublin	Wexford Town	Enniscorthy	Blackstairs Mountain	Hook Head Peninsula	New Ross	Rosslare Strand	Rosslare Harbour	Waterford City
Wexford Town	3*	-	:20	:45	1	:35	:20	:20	1
Enniscorthy	1:50	:20	-	:20	1:20	:40	:35	:40	1
Blackstairs Mountain	1:45	:45	1	-	1:40	1	2:15	:45	1:20
Hook Head Peninsula	3:10	1	1:20	1:40	-	:45	1:15	1:15	:20
New Ross	2:25	:35	:40	1	:45	-	:50	:50	:20
Rosslare Strand	3:20	2	:35	1	1:15	:50	-	:10	1:10
Rosslare Harbour	3:10	:35	:40	:45	1:15	:50	:10	-	1:10
Waterford City	2:30	1	1	1:20	1:10	:20	1:10	1:10	-
Dungarven	3:10	1:45	1:50	2:05	1:55	1:10	2	2	:45
Ardmore	3:35	2:10	2:15	2:30	2:20	1:30	2:25	2:30	1:10
Tramore	2:40	1:20	1:20	1:40	1:20	:40	1:30	1:30	:20
Comeragh Mountains	3:25	2:05	1:25	2:05	2:10	1:25	1:35	2:15	1
Carlow Town	1:10	1:30	1	:40	1:50	1:15	1:40	1:40	1:15
Cashel	2:15	2:10	2:15	2:10	2:25	1:30	2:30	2:30	1:20
Cahir	2:30	2	2	2;15	2:10	1:20	2:10	2:10	1
Kilkenny	1:50	1:30	1:20	1:05	1:45	1	1:45	1:45	:45
Thomastown	2:30	2:20	1:40	2:20	2:30	:35	2:35	2:30	1:30
Inistoige	2	:55	:55	1	1:10	:20	1:10	1:10	:40
Graiguenamanagh	2	1	1:40	:45	1:10	:25	1:15	1:15	:45
Bennettsbridge	1:50	1:20	1:15	1:05	1:30	:45	1:35	1:30	:45
Kell's Priory	2	1:20	1:40	1:20	1:35	:50	1:45	1:40	:35

Dungarven	Ardmore	Tramore	Comeragh Mountains	Carlow Town	Cashel	Cahir	Kilkenny	Thomastown	Inistoige	Graiguenamanagh	Bennettsbridge	Kell's Priory
1:45	2:10	1:20	2:05	1:30	2:10	2	1:30	2:20	:55	1	1:20	1:20
1:50	2:15	1:20	1:25	1	2:15	2	1:20	1:40	:55	:50	1:15	1:400
2:05	2:30	1:40	2:05	:40	2:10	2:15	1:05	2:20	1	:45	1:05	1:20
1:55	2:20	1:20	2:10	1:50	2:25	2:10	1:45	2:30	1:10	1:10	1:30	1:35
1:10	1:30	:40	1:25	1:15	1:30	1:20	1	:35	:20	:25	:45	:50
2	2:25	1:20	2:20	1:40	2:30	2:10	1:45	2:35	1;10	1:15	1:35	1:45
2	2:30	1:30	1:35	1:40	2:30	2:10	1:45	1:30	1:10	1:15	1:30	1:40
:45	1:10	:20	1	1:15	1:20	1	:45	1:30	:40	:45	:45	:35
-	:25	1	:15	1:20	1:30	1:10	1:30	1:30	1:30	1:35	1:30	1:25
:25	-	1:15	:40	2:30	1:50	1:30	2	2	1:50	1:15	1:55	1:50
1	1:15	-	1:15	1:30	1;40	1:20	1:05	1:45	1	1:10	1	:55
:15	:40	1:15	-	2:05	1:25	1:10	1:40	1:40	1:30	1:40	1:40	1:30
1:20	2:30	1:30	2:05	-	1:40	1:50	:35	1:50	1	:50	:40	:50
1:30	1:50	1:40	1:25	1:40	-	:20	1:10	:10	1:40	1:50	1:20	1:15
1:10	1:30	1:20	1:10	1:50	:20	-	1:15	:25	1:30	1:40	1:20	1:10
1:30	2	1:05	1:40	:35	1:10	1:15	-	1:20	:35	:45	:45	:20
1:30	2	1:45	1:40	1:50	:20	:25	1:20	-	1:55	2:05	1:30	1:25
1:30	1:50	1	1:30	1	1:40	1:30	:35	1:55	-	:15	:25	:30
1:35	1:45	1:10	1:40	:50	1:50	1:40	:45	2:05	:15	-	:30	:40
1:30	1:55	1	1:40	:40	1:20	1:20	:45	1:30	:25	:30	-	:15
1:25	1:50	:55	1:30	:50	1:15	1:10	:20	1:25	:30	:40	:15	-

anyone up for a little hurling?

Only in Ireland indeed! Hurling is a sport that predates just about all of them. Imagine an amalgamation of lacrosse, field hockey and perhaps a bit of cricket for good measure. Fifteen players carrying hurlies (the sticks) vie for control of a cork and leather sliotar (the ball). Points are amassed when a player puts the sliotar between the H-shaped posts of the goal: 1 point for going above the crossbar and through the post, 3 points for going under the crossbar, between the posts, and past the goalie.

Of course, in the process of attempting to score, a player can pass the ball with his hands, kick it with his feet, or toss the ball in the air and give it a good whack with the hurlie. If this isn't complicated enough, you can also charge your opponent from the side and put his or her ass on the ground if the situation calls for it (although there are no pads, players do at least wear helmets).

As far back as the 8th century, hurling was actually woven in to the basic law of the land; the game was used as a forum for settling inter-village disputes. Some matches became so heated that more than a few casualties resulted.

It was with the development of the GAA (Gaelic Athletes Association) in the late 19th century, however, a group believed to be as powerful as any political group of the time, that hurling became an influential part of Irish society and culture. It remains so, although perhaps in scarcer form, to this day.

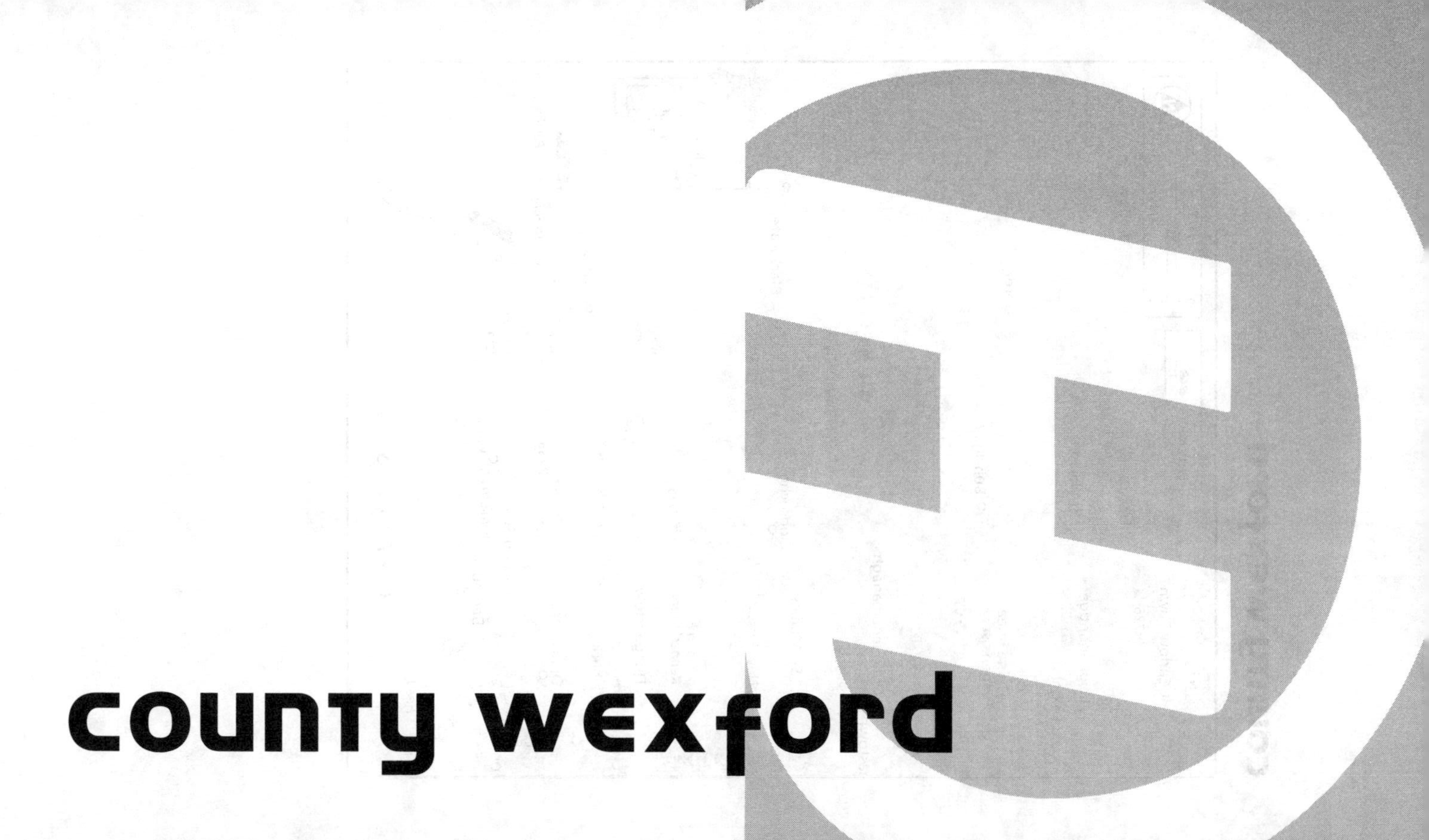
county wexford

county wexford

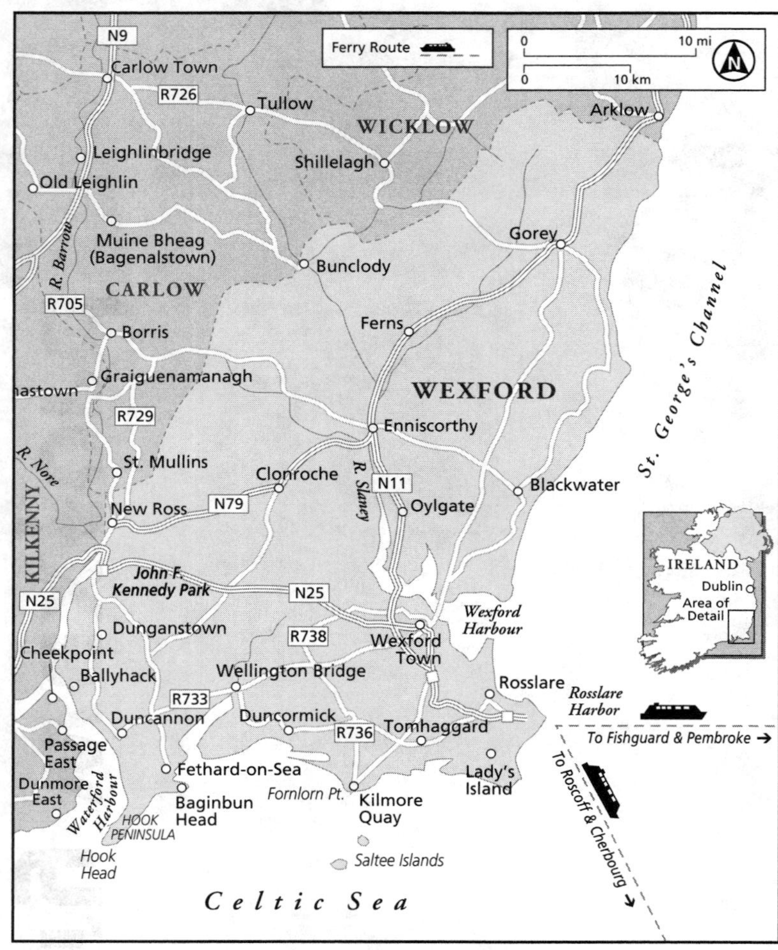

Ferry Route
0
10 mi
0
10 km
N
N9
Carlow Town
R726
Tullow
WICKLOW
Arklow
Leighlinbridge
Shillelagh
Old Leighlin
Muine Bheag
(Bagenalstown)
Gorey
R. Barrow
Bunclody
CARLOW
R705
Ferns
Borris
Graiguenamanagh
WEXFORD
R729
Enniscorthy
R. Nore
St. Mullins
Clonroche
R. Slaney
N11
Blackwater
St. George's Channel
KILKENNY
New Ross
N79
Oylgate
IRELAND
Dublin
Area of
Detail
John F.
Kennedy Park
N25
N25
Wexford
Harbour
Dunganstown
R738
Wexford
Town
Cheekpoint
Ballyhack
Wellington Bridge
Rosslare
Rosslare
Harbor
R733
Duncannon
Duncormick
R736
Tomhaggard
To Fishguard & Pembroke →
Passage
East
Fethard-on-Sea
Lady's
Island
To Roscoff & Cherbourg
Dunmore
East
Waterford
Harbour
Baginbun
Head
Fornlorn Pt.
Kilmore
Quay
HOOK
PENINSULA
Hook
Head
Saltee Islands
Celtic Sea

wexford

All too often dismissed by tourists hurriedly passing through on their way to or from the ferry port at Rosslare Harbour, Wexford Town radiates its own laid-back charm, with extra-friendly locals, extraordinarily narrow streets, and excellent pubs and restaurants. At first glance it doesn't seem like there's an awful lot to do here, but you could easily spend two or three days lounging on the nearby beaches and listening to some great trad sessions at night, especially at the **Centenary Stores** or the **Sky and the Ground** [see *bar scene,* below].

This town of 10,000 is well known in some circles: Wexford's fame originates from its annual Opera Festival [see *festivals and events,* below] in October, which attracts thousands of fans from all over the world, as well as its typically bloody Irish past. Over the centuries, Vikings, Gaels, and Normans all struggled for control of the little harbor of the mudflats (which is what *Waesfjord* means), and Oliver Cromwell, needless to say, left his mark in County Wexford. The historians in Enniscorthy have some interesting stories to tell [see **Enniscorthy,** below]. Although the waterways that once made this town a busy port are now filled with silt thanks to the River Slaney, the waterfront and miles of coastline still define Wexford.

neighborhoods

Wexford Town is small, compact, and easy to walk. Its wickedly narrow streets somehow still manage to accommodate both motor and pedestrian traffic. At the northern end of town, by the bus and train station, you'll find **Redmond Square,** which includes a monument and a small patch of

wired

You can get plugged in at the **Megabytes Internet Centre** *(Francis St.; Tel 053/23262; 9am-5:30pm Mon-Fri, 7-9:30pm Mon-Thur, 11am-4pm Sat; £4 per hour).*

neat green lawn where younger residents are known to sit around looking bored. By the sea, **Commercial Quay** stretches into **Custom House Quay,** where the road dips inland before coming back out into **Paul Quay.** This is known as **The Crescent,** and here you'll see a statue of native son and U.S. naval commander Commodore John Barry [see *culture zoo,* below].

Wexford's streets can get a little confusing; the Normans, Vikings, and Irish weren't exactly doing any city-planning together. Kinda-but-not-really parallel to the Quays, **Selskar Street** becomes **North Main Street,** which turns into **South Main Street.** The old **Cornmarket** is just off the intersection where Selskar becomes North Main, and inland of that you'll find **Abbey Street.** Several side streets branching off the main street lead into the residential areas, where you might find children playing with hurly sticks in the streets on warm dusky evenings.

bar, club, and live music scene

As is customary in any Irish pub, doors close at 11:30pm and patrons still drowning in their umpteenth pint are encouraged to make haste. Nightclubs are open until at least 1:30am, usually 2am.

Dim, youthful, and lively, **The Centenary Stores** *(Charlotte St. near Commercial Quay; Tel 053/24424)* meets with the approval of even the hippest Dubliners. Chill to the strains of some kick-ass trad on Monday and Wednesday nights and on Sunday afternoons. Folk music's the thing on Tuesday evenings. The hip will note that The Centenary Stores also has a nightclub spinning the usual techno and pop on Thursday through Sunday nights *(11pm-2am; Cover £5).* Not surprisingly, this pub's most popular with the "I've-been-living-out-of-my-backpack-for-the-past-three-months" crowd.

An older, quieter, more local crowd predominates at **The Sky and the Ground** *(112 S. Main St: near King St.; Tel 053/21273),* where you can hear live trad Sunday through Thursday nights, and sometimes Friday nights in the summertime. The music, the locals, and the quintessential Irish pub ambience make it a must.

Best known for its awesome award-winning pub food [see *eats,* below], **Tim's Tavern** *(51 S. Main St.; Tel 053/23861)* offers only occasional live trad sessions. Come for the delicious munchies and the colorful local crowd.

The rafters and floorboards at **Ó'Faolain's** *(11 Monck St.; Tel 053/23877)* are constantly vibrating with live music. You'll find trad on Sundays at noon, and on Friday, Saturday, and Sunday nights there's a nightclub with the typical trad music, decor, and characters swinging until 1:30am. Cover's £5, but you pay only £3 if you've been in the pub first.

Aside from The Centenary Stores, the best nightspot has got to be **Mooney's Lounge** *(Commercial Quay; Tel 053/24483)*. A popular pub with cheap lunches, Mooney's has live bands and frenzied dancing Thursday through Sunday nights. Most of the time there's no cover charge. Oh, and don't worry about that sign stating that only over-21s are allowed—as you'll find in many pubs and clubs in Ireland, it's just a lot of blarney.

arts scene

Housed in an unassuming Georgian building dating to 1775, the **Wexford Arts Centre** *(Cornmarket; Tel 053/23764; 10am-6pm Mon-Sat; open later if something's going on; wexfordartscentre@eircom.net; Free admission to art exhibitions, play tickets £3-5; No credit cards)* offers dance lessons, plays, concerts, art exhibitions, creative writing classes, and workshops on all sorts of creative endeavors, as well as a cafe with plenty of scrumptious eats. The Arts Centre is pretty much Wexford's only venue for the visual arts, but unfortunately the art exhibitions can leave much to be desired; don't come here expecting Jack B. Yeats. That said, it's the common man's theater—in other words, you should come here for an evening performance if you're not into opera, which is virtually all the Theatre Royal [see below] shows. There *are* trad sessions here Wednesday nights in summertime, but why pay a two-punt cover when you can get the same thing for free at most of the pubs in town?

Host to the infamous **Wexford Opera Festival** [see *festivals and events,* below] every October, the **Theatre Royal** *(27 High St.; Tel 053/22400 info, 051/22144 box office; £5-50)* sticks to opera much of the rest of year as well. Music and plays too, but Arts Centre performances are less expensive and more frequent.

culture zoo

Vikings, Normans, Cromwell—who hasn't been to Wexford? Like most other Irish cities, Wexford is rich in history and has the ruins and interesting old buildings to prove it.

Bull Ring *(off N. Main St. at Common Quay; Free):* A lot went down at the Bull Ring. First, Cromwell's men massacred almost two-thirds of the town's people here in the mid-1600s because they refused to surrender. The first declaration of an Irish Republic was made here in 1798—okay, so it didn't hold too much weight; it's the thought that counts. A statue here, The Lone Pikeman, was placed in remembrance of the Irish who fought during the 1798 Rebellion (the Bull Ring was an open-air

festivals and events

Chances are you weren't planning on making a trip to Wexford Town in late October, but just in case you were, be advised to book way in advance—we're talking several months ahead. The **Wexford Opera Festival** *(Call the Theatre Royal for details; www.wexfordopera.com; £50 tickets, available beginning in June)* attracts opera lovers from all over the world to the **Theatre Royal** [see *arts scene,* above].

weapons factory at the time). Later, Irish heroes like Daniel O'Connell and Eamon de Valera took to the podium here and riled up the crowds. So what about the name? In the 17th century, the town square was *the* spot for bull baiting, a sport introduced by the butcher's guild. Tradition has it that after a match the hide of the unlucky bull was presented to the mayor and the meat went to the poor. These days, a much tamer sport takes place here—shopping. A weekly market sets up here Friday and Saturday 10am-4:30pm. The best homemade cakes and fruit breads are sold by women bakers trying to earn a little extra money. You'll also find a wide array of flea market items such as new and used clothing, jewelry, antiques, and various souvenirs and crafts.

Commodore John Barry Statue *(The Crescent; Free):* A gift to Wexford from President Eisenhower on behalf of the United States in the mid-1950s, the Commodore John Barry Statue commemorates the Wexford native, American revolutionary, and first commander-in-chief of the U.S. Navy. If you're spending any time around the Crescent, you can't miss it. (Did you know that September 13 is Commodore John Barry Day in the U.S.?)

St. Iberius Church *(N. Main St.; Tel 053/43013; 10am-5pm May-Sept, 10am-3pm Tue-Sat Oct-Apr; Free):* Though it was built only in the mid-17th century, St. Iberius stands on the site of many houses of worship dating from Norse times, and it's rumored that a church founded by St. Patrick once stood here.

Church of the Assumption and **Church of the Immaculate Conception** *(Bride and Rowe Sts.; Tel 053/22055; 8am-6pm; Free):* Known as the twin churches, the faux-Gothic Church of the Assumption and Church of the Immaculate Conception with their super-tall spires dominate the Wexford skyline when seen from a distance. Okay, they don't make the greatest landmarks while you're *in* town, since the narrow streets make it hard to spot them from many angles. Still, they're worth visiting for their 19th-century Gothic Revival architectural detail, complete with mosaics and stained-glass windows depicting biblical scenes.

Selskar Abbey *(Off Temperance Row at Westgate St.; Free):* The ruins of 12th-century Selskar Abbey are worth noting because the very first treaty ever between the English and the Irish was signed here in 1169. The gate might be locked, but there'll be a sign telling you where to find the key, if you'd like to look around. Supposedly, during the time of Henry III, Alexander Roach founded and erected this Abbey after his star-crossed lover fled his arms and joined a convent. There's not much left to see here other than some arches—now in ruins—adjacent to the Westgate Heritage Tower. Why is the place in such bad shape today? Cromwell's wanton troops paid a visit to the abbey in 1649.

great outdoors

Ever see *Saving Private Ryan*? Remember that pretty beach where the D-Day troops landed in the extremely bloody first scene? No, it's not actually in Normandy. It's **Curracloe Beach,** at 12 miles long the longest beach in Ireland. Walking out to Curracloe from town takes about 4 hours, but it's assuredly lovely; you can also bike out, or take a taxi one or both ways. For directions, check with the Wexford Tourist Office [see *need to know,* below] or ask at Kirwan House, the local hostel [see *crashing,* below]. Kirwan House also offers guided walks from town to the **Wildfowl Reserve, Raven Point** (another nature reserve) and Curracloe Beach.

A good way to see all Wexford has to offer is to join the **Wexford Hill-walkers Club** *(£1 membership fee; Call Kirwan House for information: Tel 053/21208)* for a day; it meets Sundays at 9:30am and Wednesday nights at 6pm during the summer months. Check with Kirwan House to verify days and times. The club meets at the Old Library Car Park near the Wexford Arts Centre [see *arts scene,* above] at the Cornmarket. It's a good way to meet people—rugged, athletic people, mostly in their late twenties or early thirties—since walks are limited to between 15 and 30 people.

stuff

Wexford is by no means a shopper's heaven; you'd do better to save your traveler's checks till you get out west. Still, you can find good music and

TO market

If fine dining is getting to be a bit much, **Dunnes Stores** *(Redmond Sq.)* is the place to stock up on munchies.

wexford town

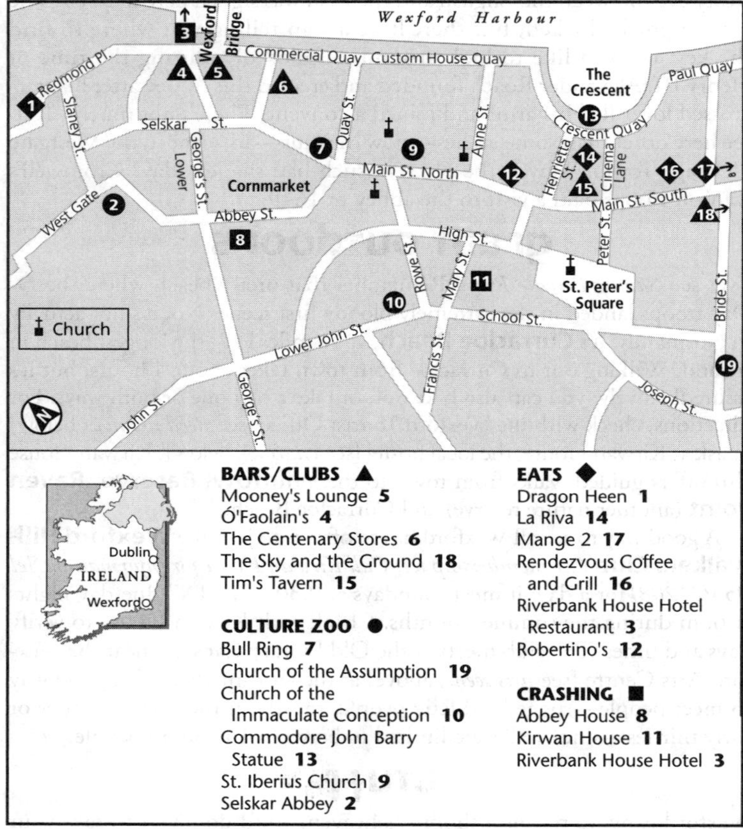

lovingly beat-up old paperbacks to while away the hours spent on long Bus Éireann rides.

▶▶TUNES

It's not very big, but you can still satisfy your craving for the Corrs at **Square Discs** *(Redmond Sq.; V, MC)*.

▶▶BOUND

Reader's Paradise *(3 Selskar St.; 9:30am-6pm Mon-Sat, also Sun July-Sept)* epitomizes the hole-in-the-wall used bookstore. Or are you a book snob? Gotta have 'em new? Try **The Book Centre** *(5 S. Main St.; Tel 053/23543; V, MC)* or **The Wexford Bookshop** *(31 N. Main St.; Tel 053/22223)*.

▶▶DUDS

The Closet *(111 North Main St.; Tel 053/21969; 2-6pm Sun, 9am-6pm Mon-Thur/Sat, 9am-7pm Fri; V, MC, AE)* stocks cool clothes for gals in cheerful sherbety colors. And you can find deliciously tacky, skintight "Mickey's Topless Bar" T-shirts in assorted bright colors at the unisex **Union** *(44 S. Main St.; Tel 053/23808; V, MC).*

eats

Wexford has a great reputation for fine dining, but there aren't a ton of cheap places to eat if you're on a tight budget. Check out the excellent (and inexpensive!) pub grub at Tim's Tavern or at most of the other pubs in town (although Tim's *is* undisputedly the best).

▶▶CHEAP

Tucked away in a dinky little mall called Lowney's, **Rendezvous Coffee and Grill** *(S. Main St., in Lowney's Mall; Tel 053/22220; Under £5)* offers the best cheap breakfast in town. You'll find the name hilariously inappropriate—this place, a vague reminder of an American diner in appearance, is crawling with families with young children—but the food's an excellent value. Plunk down £3.50 for a generous plate of bacon and cabbage along with potatoes and veggies. You'll find inexpensive sandwiches and other breakfast choices, too. It's cheap, authentically Irish, and highly recommended by the local bacon-and-cabbage set.

As for good pub grub, **Mooney's** [see *bar scene,* above] offers a traditional lunch for around three to five punts—not a bad deal, eh? The food at **Tim's Tavern** [see *bar, club, and live music scene,* above] is constantly winning all sorts of awards. Generous helpings of delicious traditional Irish fare are up for grabs at a mere five punts. As always, lunch presents a better value than dinner; lunches are served between noon and 6pm daily. You could also try the pub food at **The Sky and the Ground** [see *bar, club, and live music scene,* above], which likewise serves till the Angelus rings.

▶▶DO-ABLE

Want to eschew the traditional for a taste of Chinese? Lusting for egg rolls and vegetable-fried rice? A three-course lunch at **Dragon Heen** *(Redmond Sq.; Tel 053/21332; 12:30-2:30pm/5-11:30pm daily; AE, MC, V)* will run you about £7. Main courses go for £9-13, so it's a pretty good deal.

Is it Italian you're after? **Robertino's** *(19 S. Main St.; Tel 053/23334; MC, V)* offers the requisite pasta and pizza for around six punts. Good, but not exactly a taste of *Roma.* What did you expect? This is Ireland, not Italy.

The **Riverbank House Hotel Restaurant** *(Wexford Bridge; Tel 053/23611; Open daily noon or 1-9pm; river@indigo.ie, www.riverbankhouse.ie; Main courses £5-12; V, MC, AE, DC)* defines the word "delicious." If you're searching for classy meals at prices that won't make you cringe—not to mention totally impeccable service—the Riverbank is the place to go. The menu's got steak, seafood, pasta, and a sprinkling of vegetarian options. Try the baked aubergine (£6.95), and for dessert, the lemon tart with strawberries marinated in lime and ginger sauce (£2.95). You'd swear you were in absolute heaven if you didn't know any better. (Do they play Nancy Sinatra in heaven? I think not.)

▸▸SPLURGE

Upscale Italian's the menu at **La Riva** *(Crescent Quay; Tel 053/24330; Main courses £10-17; V, MC),* and if you can afford it this is *the* place to splurge. (Well, one of *the* places. There are tons of great restaurants in this town.) Oddly enough, for an Italian restaurant, you won't find any pasta on the menu, just seafood, poultry, and steak. La Riva makes one sweet little place for a romantic dinner: dark red walls festooned with abstract art, a lovely view of the harbor, and an intimate (that is, it's just one small room) candlelit setting. As for recommendations, try the lime-baked salmon with pink peppercorn sauce (£12.95). Similarly luscious desserts go for £3.25. The chocolate marquis drizzled in white chocolate sauce bears a remarkable resemblance to a pile of dung on a porcelain plate, but I can assure you it tastes nothing like it.

It's got a French name and an awesome Mediterranean-flavored menu: At **Mange 2** *(100 S. Main St.; Tel 053/44033; 6-10:30pm daily, closed Mon in winter; balyt@gofree.indigo.ie; Main courses £10-15; V, MC),* try the grilled beef filet with *pommes anna* (those are just fancy potatoes) and leek compote with wild mushroom and sun-dried-tomato sauce.

crashing

▸▸CHEAP

It's the only hostel in town, but luckily it's far better than fine. You couldn't find a friendlier staff in all of Ireland than at **Kirwan House** *(3 Mary St.; Tel 053/21208; www.hostelaccommodation.com; £8 dorm; No credit cards).* The common room is every bit as comfortable as your family room at home, and after chatting with everybody here you'll feel as though you've been here for weeks instead of mere minutes. Owner Richard Barlow makes it a personal mission to keep all of his guests at ease and totally well informed about everything there is to do and see in Wexford Town. The social vibe here just can't be beat; you'll never want for a drinking buddy (or two, or three, or more) as long as you're staying at the Kirwan House. If you're lucky, you'll catch an informal Irish language lesson going on as well. Rooms have beds for 2 to 8 people; you have the option of staying in either co-ed or single-sex rooms. There are two rooms with private baths; everything else is communal. There is no curfew.

▸▸DO-ABLE

There are plenty of bed-and-breakfasts in Wexford Town, but **Abbey House** *(34 Abbey St.; Tel 053/24408; £32 en suite double, £20 single; V, MC, AE),* just across the way from Selskar Abbey [see *culture zoo,* above], is one of the better ones, since it's right in the middle of town. You might think the rooms here won't be as quiet as those in the B&Bs on the northern end of town, but roads there are heavily trafficked, while the streets in the center of Wexford are too narrow to accommodate much more than pedestrians. Anyway, it's got all the goods: bedrooms with comfortable beds, televisions and bathrooms, and good breakfasts.

If the Abbey House is booked, try **McMenamin's Townhouse** *(3 Auburn Terrace, Tel 053/46442; Fax 035/346-442; mcmem@indigo.ie, www.wexford-bedandbreakfast.com; £35 single, £27 per person shared; pri-*

vate bath, breakfast included; V), in the town center; or **Mount Auburn** *(Auburn Terrace, Tel 053/24609, Fax 053/24609; £30 single, £22-25 per person shared; private bath, breakfast included; V, MC),* right across the street from the train station.

▸▸SPLURGE

With new management and remodeling job, the **Riverbank House Hotel** *(Wexford Bridge; Tel 053/23611; river@indigo.ie, www.riverbankhouse.ie; £40-50 double, £55 on bank holidays or during the Wexford Opera Festival; V, MC, AE, DC)* gives you countless totally excellent reasons to splurge (especially if you count every single item on the restaurant menu [see *eats,* above]). You might want to investigate the weekend special, which costs £70 (yikes! £135 in summertime) for two nights of bed and breakfast and one evening meal. The views of the river from the bedrooms and exceptional customer service give you even more reasons to stay the night, and the Wexford pub scene's just a short walk across the bridge.

need to know

Currency Exchange Line up for punts at **TSB Bank** *(73/75 N. Main St.; Tel 053/41922; Mon-Wed, Fri 9:30am-5pm, Thur 9:30am-7pm)* or **AIB** *(N. Main St.; Tel 053/22444; 10am-5pm Mon, 10am-4pm Tue-Fri),* both of which have ATMs. You can also change money at **Sam McCauley's Pharmacy** [see below], but you will get the best rates at the banks.

Tourist Information The **Wexford Tourist Office** *(Henrietta St. and the Crescent; Tel 053/23111; 9am-6pm Mon-Sat Apr-June and Sept-Oct; 9am-6pm Mon-Sat, 11am-5pm Sun July-Aug; 9:30am-5:30pm Mon-Fri Nov-Apr)* is located near the center of town.

Public Transportation Wexford's not big enough for inner-city public transportation. If you need a taxi, try **Walsh Cabs** *(Tel 053/41449)* or **Noel Ryan** *(Tel 053/24056).*

Health and Emergency **Garda Station** *(Roches Rd.; Tel 053/22333).* You can also call **Wexford General Hospital** *(New Town Rd.; Tel 053/42233)* for medical attention.

Pharmacies **Sam McCauley's Pharmacy** *(4/6 Redmond Sq.; Tel 053/22422; 9am-9pm Thur-Fri, 9am-7pm Sat-Wed)* has a Bureau de Change, hair studio, and beauty salon.

Buses and Trains **Bus Éireann** and **Irish Rail** depart from **O'Hanrahan Station** *(Tel 053/22522)* at Redmond Square on the Quay. Wexford's on the Dublin-Rosslare Harbour line; trains depart in either direction three times a day. There are seven or eight buses to Dublin a day (four on Sundays), at least nine a day to Rosslare Harbour, four a day to Limerick, and during the summer months there are direct routes to Galway and Waterford.

Bike Rental Both **Haye's Cycle Shop** *(108 S. Main St.; Tel 053/22462; 9am-6pm Mon-Sat, bikes also available Sun; £10 per day, £40 per week, deposit £50 or ID)* and **The Bike Shop** *(N. Main St.; Tel 053/22514; 9am-6pm Mon-Sat; gordon@iol.ie; £8 per day, £30 per week, £40 deposit, £12 extra for one-way option)* offer rentals.

Laundry Head to **Padraig's Laundrette Ltd.** *(4 Mary St., next to Kirwan House; 9:30am-6:30pm Mon-Fri; Sat 9am-9pm; wash and dry under £4)* for the old fluff and fold.

Postal Postcards from the edge get mailed at **Wexford Post Office** *(Anne St.; Tel 053/22123; 9am-5:30pm Mon and Wed-Sat, 9:30am-5:30pm Tue).*

Internet See *wired,* above.

everywhere else

enniscorthy

This cute little town, situated 15 miles north of Wexford, is notable mostly for its role in the 1798 Uprising. Here a priest named Father Murphy led Irish nationalists who managed to hold off the Brits up on **Vinegar Hill** for almost two weeks before surrendering. The **National 1798 Visitor Centre** does a brilliant re-enactment of the battle [see *need to know,* below]. Vinegar Hill's only a couple of miles outside of town and makes a pleasant scenic walk. At the top of the hill, a panoramic view of Enniscorthy and Wexford countryside evokes memories of the mount's many martyrs (We know you don't remember them, cause you didn't know who they were in the first place, but you can at least stand here and take in the gorgeous view).

Don't miss the excellent **Enniscorthy walking tour** led by Maura Flannery *(Castle Hill, Enniscorthy; Tel 054/36800 or 086/816-23-01; tours begin at 10am; call to reserve a spot; £3)*—she's full of gossip that's hundreds of years old and still hasn't lost its juice. Tours leave on the hour from the craft shop on Castle Hill.

For your fill of history, check out **Enniscorthy Castle,** which houses the **Wexford County Museum** *(Castle Hill, Enniscorthy; Tel 054/35926; 10am-6pm June-Sept, 2-5:30pm Oct-Nov and Feb-May, 2-5pm Sun Dec-Jan; £3 adults, £2 students).* In the center of town overlooking the Slaney River, this Norman castle dates from the 13th century and remains in excellent condition due partly to recent renovation. Tons of people have owned it over the centuries, most notably the poet Edmund Spenser. Elizabeth I supposedly gave it to him for writing *The Faerie Queene,* which was of course steeped in shameless flattery of the "virgin" queen. Previously it had served as a monastery after the original owners vacated. Damaged by Cromwell in 1649 and having served as a prison during the 1798 Uprising, the castle now houses interesting exhibits on both the 1798 and 1916 rebellions.

The **Antique Tavern** *(14 Slaney St.; Tel 054/33428; £1.80 sandwiches, £2.25 Guinness, £3-5 full lunch)* serves hearty fare to complement your post-castle pint. This 200-year-old pub, richly decorated with antiques and Enniscorthy artifacts, has twice been named Wexford County "pub of the year." Every day there is a different lunch menu, most often including lasagna, quiche, soup, or sandwiches.

need to know

Tourist Information The **National 1798 Visitor Centre** *(Mill Park Rd. off the N30 & N11; Tel 054/37596 or 054/37597; 9:30am-6pm daily, last admission 45 min. before closing; £4.50 adults, £3.50 students)* is definitely cooler than the average heritage center. The Battle of 1798 at Vinegar Hill really comes alive through such audio-visual presentations as a 3-D video and a human-scale chess board used to show the nuanced power structure of the time.

Buses It's easy to get to Enniscorthy from Wexford Town via **Bus Éireann** route 2. The ride lasts 25 minutes, and there are at least seven buses every day.

the blackstairs mountains

A long, rounded ridge of peaks, the Blackstairs form a border between the cities of Carlow and Wexford. As of yet, these mountain trails are completely unspoiled by tourism, and there are beautiful walks in several directions. Pick up a guide called "Walking the Blackstairs" at the Wexford tourist office [see *need to know,* below], which includes trail descriptions along with information about plant and wild life.

Blackstairs is a vast landscape flooded with peaceful farming communities. The best walks in the area are the "Blackstairs Walk" (10 km round trip) or the "Sculloge Gap" walk (26 km round trip). Half- or full-day walks can be planned. To join in guided walks, call Michael Kietlly of **Wexford Walking Club** *(Tel 053/22642).*

The Blackstairs reward you not only with virgin forest walks but also with panoramic views in most directions. About three miles upriver of Graiguenamanagh is the hamlet of **Borris,** a good center for exploring the mountains. There are rugged heathery slopes in all directions, and the most luxuriant forest cover on the eastern slopes.

The area is presided over by Mount Leinster at 2,610 feet. If you have a car, you can actually follow the roadway right up the summit of Mount Leinster, but the Wexford Walking Club strongly encourages people to hike up instead. Most trails are rated easy, but there are challenging routes if you are so inclined.

The Blackstairs have been left untouched by the tourist rush, leaving its plush landscapes and gray-blue skies exactly how nature intended. These mountains are not regulated by anyone but the humble surrounding villages. Camping is allowed as long as it's outside the property lines of any farms. An honor system prevails: If you clean up after yourself, you can camp overnight wherever you please.

need to know

Tourist Information Ask at the Wexford Tourist Office for more details on the mountains or in the base town of Bunclody.

Directions and Transportation If you've got a car, it's a 30- to 45-minute drive from Wexford: Take R370 out of Wexford to a sleepy little village called Kiltealy, and from there follow the signs for the Mount Leinster Scenic Drive. Reaching Mount Leinster by bus takes more doing: Catch a **Bus Éireann** bus to Enniscorthy (a 25-minute ride, with at least seven departures a day) and change buses at Enniscorthy for Bunclody (two buses a day, at 9am and 6pm). **Bus Éireann** goes to Bunclody, at the foot of the mountain, from Enniscorthy (route 5). If you're heading to Borris, you'll head about 9 miles southwest of Bunclody on foot or by bike.

hook peninsula

Jutting out into the sea like a long finger pointing at you (if you were standing out in the middle of the ocean, that is), County Wexford's Hook Peninsula gave rise to the expression "by Hook or by Crooke." When Cromwell said it, he was referring to two possible pieces of geography at which to land his troops—Hook Peninsula or the town of Crooke. The peninsula's landscape, characterized by rocky headlands and beaches at secluded coves, draws some of the most rugged sightseers in the British Isles, especially divers. The area's underwater scenery is varied and spectacular, including deep caves and gullies, although the water's not too deep—15 meters at most—and the sea is often rough around the very tip of the peninsula. The best spots for deep-sea sightseeing are right around the **Hook Head Lighthouse,** which is reputed to be the oldest lighthouse in Europe, if not the whole world; the flame was first lit by monks in the 5th century. (A word of warning: The cliffs near the lighthouse are pitted with blowholes, so watch your step.) You could also try exploring the underwater coast around **Churchtown,** which is located a kilometer back from the peninsula's tip. **Slade Harbour,** 2 kilometers up from the Hook Head, is also a popular diving spot. The **Hook Sub-Aqua Club** *(Slade, County Wexford; Tel 051/388-302)* provides a full range of diving facilities and equipment. Call for rates and directions.

In addition to divers, the peninsula attracts birders (who show up to observe the spring and fall migrations), bikers, and hikers. The terrain is especially good for biking (bring along a picnic) as the roads are flat and straight. "The Hook" also makes for some historic sightseeing, as you meander among its old forts and historic abbeys, with lighthouses to guide the way.

You rarely escape the wind here—the summer's bracing sea breeze gives way to fierce winter winds. "That's why we have so many pubs along the coastline," an old-timer told us. "The pubs are our safe havens in the storms." The people you meet here are among the warmest and friendliest in Ireland. At times many of them have great humor but they can get philosophical too. They always seem to have time for a chat or to tell tales about days gone by.

The southernmost point of Hook Peninsula is **Hook Head.** Northeast up the coastline lies another hamlet, **Baginbun Head,** close to **Bannow Bay** and the point where the Normans landed in 1169. Between the two sits the tiny fishing village of **Slade Harbour,** dominated by its ruined castle, or the village of **Duncanon,** a little summer resort with a sandy beach and a Norman fort. Four kilometers up the opposite coast of the peninsula, to the northwest of Hook Head, is the little town of **Ballyhack,** where a ten-minute ferry ride can take you and your car across the harbour to Passage East in County Waterford.

culture zoo

While you're in Ballyhack, check out 12th-century **Dunbrody Abbey** *(New Ross Rd., 3.2 km (2 mi) northeast of Ballyhack; Tel 051/388-603; visitors center open 10am-7pm, July-Aug; 10am-6pm, May-June and Sept; Admission £1.50).* One of the few abbeys that Cromwell must've overlooked, Dunbrody is amazingly well preserved, and you can pretty much explore its winding staircases and maze of rooms as you please. Speaking of mazes, the caretakers planted a maze of hedges in 1992, also open for your childlike amusement. The bushes are still pretty short, though, so if you want to get lost your best bet would be to crawl through on your hands and knees.

eats

There really isn't any place to eat in Arthurstown, where the only hostel is, so it's best to stock up on groceries back at Ballyhack, the town just north of Arthurstown. Stop first in Ballyhack at **Byrne's** *(At the Ballyhack ferry port; Tel 051/389-107; 9:30am-9:30pm Mon-Sat, noon-2pm/4-7pm Sun; No credit cards),* a small pub and grocery store. You can also get sandwiches in the pub for around £2.

crashing

You've got one choice in the way of budget accommodation on the Hook Peninsula, and that's the **Arthurstown Hostel** *(Arthurstown, 1 km (0.6 mi) south of Ballyhack; Tel 051/389-411; £7 dorm; No credit cards).* Located on the western coast of the peninsula, it's pretty average in the way of An Óige hostels: curfew at 10:30pm (hey, you didn't come here for the pub scene!), lockout between 10:30am and 5pm, and helpful staff. Call ahead to book.

There are plenty of places to stay on the eastern side at Fethard-on-Sea, including the ever-popular **Hotel Naomh Seosamh** *(Main St., Fethard; Tel 051/397-129; £20 per person for B&B; V, MC, AE),* whose nightly (in season; weekends only in off-season) entertainment is the best in the area. The hotel and its pub draw a young, fun-loving crowd who can enjoy a pub grub meal for £5 or a beer for £2, while listening to the traditional Irish music performed here. There is no other hotel along the coast that gives you such a glimpse of Gaelic life.

need to know

Tourist Information Surf your way to ***www.thehook-wexford.com*** or e-mail ***hookinfo@iol.ie*** for information about the peninsula and all possible activities, or try the **Wexford Tourist Office** *(Henrietta St. and the Crescent; Tel 053/23111; 9am-6pm Mon-Sat Apr-June and Sept-Oct; 9am-6pm Mon-Sat, 11am-5pm Sun July-Aug; 9:30am-5:30pm Mon-Fri Nov-Apr).*

Directions and Transportation **Bus Éireann** *(O'Hanrahan Station, Wexford Town; Tel 053/22522)* runs local route 370 only once daily, if that, from Wexford to Fethard-on-Sea, which is still at least 5 miles away from the diving facilities at the edge of the peninsula. Your only viable option is to drive from Wexford Town: Take R733 and R734 to Fethard-on-Sea and proceed south from there.

new ross

Best known as the birthplace of President John F. Kennedy's grandfather, Patrick Kennedy (all right, so he was actually born in Dunganstown just south of New Ross—it's close enough), the New Ross area has little in the way of scenery or cultural attractions to offer visitors besides the **John F. Kennedy Park and Arboretum** *(Tel 051/388-171; 10am-5pm daily, Oct-Mar; 10am-6:30pm, Apr and Sept; 10am-8pm, May-Aug; £2)* and the **Kennedy Homestead** *(Tel 051/388-264; May-Sept 10am-5:30pm daily; 6 km south of New Ross, off R733; £2.50),* which doesn't live up to the name in the least; the original Kennedy homestead no longer stands. However, this building does house exhibits on the history of the illustrious Kennedy family.

John F. Kennedy was proud of his Irish ancestry: He visited New Ross during his presidency and made glowing speeches about the people, his family, and the country. As the United States' only Irish Catholic president, he has been elevated to a near-godlike status in this country. (Next time you're in Galway check out that mosaic of his likeness in the Galway Cathedral, complete with clasped hands, halo, and angelic expression.)

Another reason to stick around New Ross: The **Shielbaggan Outdoor Education Centre** *(Ramsgrange; Tel 051/389-550 or 051/389-552; £50 deposit per person),* technically on the Hook Peninsula, offers canoeing, sailing, snorkeling, orienteering, rock climbing, hill walking, archery, and horseback riding in New Ross. There's no public transportation to the Centre, but they can help you arrange charter bus pick-ups for groups.

need to know

Directions and Transportation The homestead and park are difficult to reach without a car, since they're a few miles away from the bus stop in New Ross. Are you a sucker for that crazy Kennedy mystique and ready to walk it? Wexford to New Ross **Bus Éireann** routes 40 and 55 depart seven to nine times daily. The trip takes about 40 minutes.

rosslare strand

Don't confuse Rosslare Strand with Rosslare Harbour. The two places might be separated by mere kilometers, but the spot you'll actually *enjoy* spending time in is Rosslare Strand. A perfect day trip from Wexford, the beach is safe and sandy, and was awarded a Blue Flag by the E.U., which means local waters are not polluted. However, the water may be too cold for you at any time of year. The southeast coast of Ireland does get more sunshine than any other part of the country, but don't take the "sun trap of Ireland" tourist ballyhoo too seriously, though; it could very well rain the entire time you're here—after all, this is Ireland. The resort boasts 5 miles of sandy beaches considered safe for swimming and ideal for windsurfing. People don't spend all their time in the water, as there are ample opportunities for horseback riding, pony trekking, golf, water sports, angling, and canoeing. If it's not a good day for the beach, stroll north to **Rosslare Point** for a scenic view. If Irish families frolicking in the sea is not your idea of a good time, you'll want to press on to more sophisticated climes after a day here—if the caravanners don't run you down first.

Rent sailboards and wetsuits at the **Rosslare Watersports Centre** *(On the beach; Tel 053/32101);* shallow waters make Rosslare Strand perfect for windsurfing.

One of the best and most reasonably priced restaurants in the tiny resort town is **Lemon Tree** *(Tel. 053/32124; Main courses £10-15; daily 6:30-9:30pm; AE, DC, MC, V),* inside the Cedar's Hotel. Once you arrive in the center of town, the hotel is clearly visible, right on the water, although there is no sea view from the dining tables. Clients range from young windsurfers to Irish families. The food is good and fresh, and portions are generous. It's true home-style cuisine prepared by fresh-faced Irish lasses who, though hardly budding Julia Childs, know how to prepare straightforward fare, including fresh fish.

If you choose to spend the night the best place to lay your head would have to be **The Iona** *(turn left onto the main Rosslare Strand Road from the* *train station road, it's on the right; Tel 053/32116; £20-22 per person, £25 single, includes full breakfast; No credit cards).* Staying at this ample white Victorian is like sleeping over at your grandma's house—that is, providing your grandma had a nice house and was fun to stay with. Everything has that lovely old worn-in, well-loved feeling. The Iona offers full breakfast, and all rooms have bathrooms and televisions—but why bother with the remote when that lovely golden strand awaits?

need to know

Tourist Information The tourist office representing the area is **Rosslare Harbour Tourist Office** *(Ferry Terminal, Rosslare Harbour; Tel 053/33623; Mon-Sat 9am-5pm).*

Directions and Transportation Rosslare Strand is but a 10-minute train ride from Wexford Town. There are three trains per day. To get to the beach, turn left immediately as you exit the station, and walk for about 5 minutes.

Bike Rental Business is really too slow here for full-time bike rental outfitters to exist. However, most of the local hotels keep bikes for the use of guests only (not the general public).

rosslare harbour

Rosslare Harbour isn't exactly the nicest place to be; chances are, if you're here it's because you've either just arrived in Ireland (from Cherbourg, Le Havre, Fishguard, or Pembroke) or you're ready to leave. If you tell people you're here for the sightseeing, don't wonder why they look at you like you're out of your gourd—you probably are (out of your gourd, that is).

If your ferry isn't leaving too early, you might want to consider staying over in Wexford instead. It only takes a half-hour to get from Rosslare Harbour to Wexford by train, and the scenery around Wexford, as well as the accommodations, are much more pleasant.

eats

Your options for chow are slim. Many of the nearby hotels serve food, but your best (and most cost-effective) bet might be to pick up groceries or a sandwich at **Lambert's Quik Pick Foodstore** *(Rosslare Harbour village center; 8:30am-9pm daily)* or the **Supervalu** *(Kilrane Rd.; 9am-1pm/2-5:30pm Mon-Fri, 9am-1pm Sat).* If you do want to be served hot food, head to the restaurant at the **Hotel Rosslare** *(Rosslare Harbour village center, Tel 053/33110; 11am-11:30pm daily; Lunch £7.50 and up).* They also have a pub that runs on the same hours and serves slightly less expensive grub. The pub is actually a neat place to while away your time here—it doubles as a museum of town history, so the walls are covered with great old black and white photos.

crashing

If you're coming to or from France or the British Isles, you'll most likely get your first or last night's sleep in Ireland at the **Rosslare Harbour Hostel** *(Goulding St., Rosslare Harbour, Wexford; Tel 053/33399; £6-8 dorm; V, MC, AE)*, situated on a hill overlooking the ferry port. This hostel has a midnight curfew, but why would you be out later than that in this town, anyway? The facilities are purely utilitarian: sufficient, but by no means fantastic. The reception desk is open during the night to accommodate people getting off the ferries. The hostel is up the hill from the ferry port; walk up the steps from the terminal, make an immediate left after Hotel Rosslare. You can call the hostel if a pick-up is necessary.

There are two other slightly more expensive options around town, if the hostel is full (not bloody likely, but you never know...): **St. Anthony's** *(St. Martin's Rd.; Tel 053/33599; £23 single, £17.50 per person shared, all with private bath, breakfast included; V)*, in the town center, and **Carragh Lodge** *(Station Rd.; Tel 053/33492; £19 single w/private bath, £17 w/out private bath, breakfast included; No credit cards)*, which is cheaper but less central, a 10-minute walk from the town.

need to know

Currency Exchange Line up for your punts at the **Bank of Ireland** *(Kilrane Rd.; Tel 053/33304; 10am-12:30pm/1:30-4pm Mon-Fri)*, which has an ATM if you arrive in the off-hours. There's also a Bureau de Change in the post office, which is located (oddly enough) in the **Supervalu** [see *eats,* above] on that same street.

Tourist Information The **Rosslare Harbour Tourist Office** *(Tel 053/33622; Open to meet all sailings except the 6:30am, Apr-Sept)* is at the ferry terminal.

Trains and Boats **Rosslare Harbour Rail Station** *(at the ferry port; Tel 053/33114 or 053/33592)* is located a half-mile from the Rosslare Harbour Hostel [see *crashing,* above]. There are several trains daily to and from Waterford, Wexford, Dublin, and Limerick. If you're planning to arrive or leave by ferry, you're either going to or coming from Le Havre or Cherbourg, France (taking a full 24 hours) or Pembroke, Wales (4 1/2 hours). For those destinations, take **Irish Ferries** *(Tel 053/33158; www.irishferries.com)*; from Fishguard, Wales (3 hours), take the **Stena Line** *(Tel 053/33115 or 053/33330)*.

Bus Lines Out of the City **Bus Éireann** *(at the ferry port in the same office as Irish Rail; Tel 053/33592)* buses leave for Wexford, Waterford, Dublin, Cork, Limerick, Tralee, and Galway via Waterford. There are around 10 buses per day to Wexford (£2.50, 20 minutes) and Dublin (£9, 3 hours), and around two or three to all other locations.

county waterford

county waterford

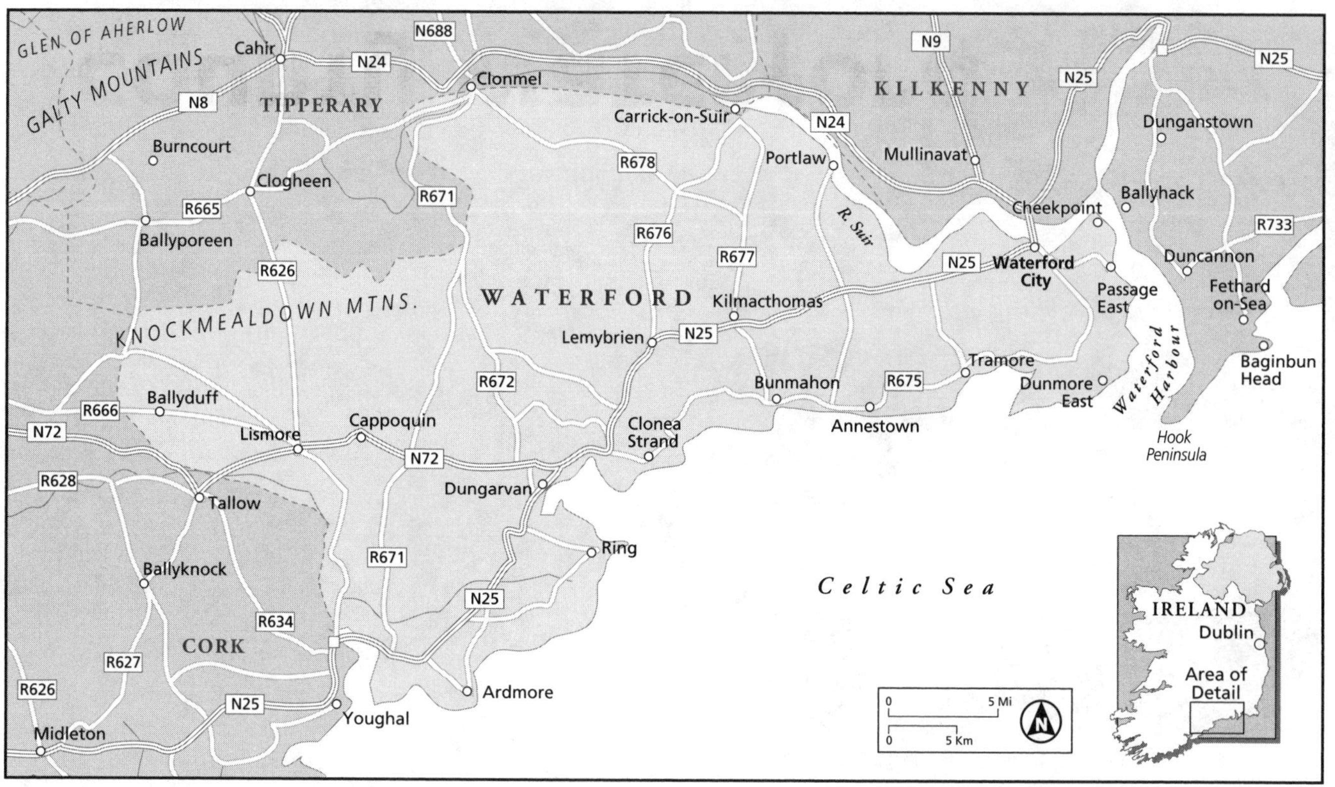

waterford city

If you're headed for Waterford City, chances are—well, it's as certain as the Irish love their Guinness, really—that you're here for the crystal. Most travelers, and natives for that matter, find this major working port city of the Southeast cloaked in a vague cloud of drabness, and nobody really opts to linger for too long. The industrial appearance of the waterfront does hide a charming old, narrow-laned town center with an identifiable youth scene, but Waterford is hardly the most exciting or colorful city in Ireland—not by a long shot. You probably won't spend more than a day here; you'll soon be off to prettier scenery and livelier goings-on, though very likely laden down with the crystal vase you promised to buy for your grandma (although it'd probably be better to get it shipped home—or to buy it at your last shopping stop before you leave the country, as you can find it everywhere, and at the same price). **The Crystal Factory** [see *stuff,* below] does have an incredible staff of craftspeople whom you can watch doing their glassblowing magic on factory tours. Founded in 1783, the place supplied all the decanters the British aristocracy could hoist until the Famine hit; the factory closed in 1851 and wasn't reopened until 1947.

There are also a few great pubs around here worth checking out, and the Waterford coastline makes a nice side trip. It might not have all the charm of Kilkenny, but Waterford City's air is also distinctly medieval. Chunks of the original city wall, built by the Vikings in the 700s, are still standing, and one of the coolest pubs in town, **T & H Doolan's** [see *bar scene,* below], actually incorporates the battlements into its building structure.

wired

www.munster-express.ie: Munster Express, Southeast Ireland's newspaper.

www.waterford-guide.com: A guide to the city and county.

www.waterford-today.ie: Waterford's weekly newspaper.

www.amireland.com/waterford_tourism: Pretty much self-explanatory.

The blatantly misnamed **Voyager Internet Café** *(Parnell Court, Parnell St., in a shopping center off John St.; Tel 051/843-843; www.voyager.ie; 8:30am-12:15am Mon-Wed, 8:30am-3:30am Thur-Sun; £6/hour; No credit cards)* offers no food at all. Nope, not even coffee. Voyager might be little more than a hole in the wall, but at least it's open late enough for you to catch some of your friends at home online, the music's good, and the computers are reasonably fast.

You can use the computers at the **Waterford Library** *(Ladylane, no street number; tel. 051/873-506; 11am–1pm 2:30-5:30pm Tue, Thur, Sat; 2-8pm Wed, Fri; closed Mon)* for free, but you've got to book at least an hour in advance. They aren't as speedy as those at the Voyager, but large windows letting in natural light and potted plants on the windowsill make a considerably nicer environment in which to immerse yourself in cyberspace.

neighborhoods

The streets in Waterford City's old center can be a tad confusing—evidently the Vikings had no concept of gridlines or tidy street numbering. As is typical of a rough-and-ready port city, **the Quay** is where most of the action is and all the main streets shoot off from there. As is also typical, it changes names several times: **O'Connell Street,** which runs east-west, parallel to **Merchants Quay,** becomes **Great George's Street,** which morphs into **High Street**, which eventually ends up at a tangle of little streets between **Henrietta,** and **Greyfriar's**, two side streets off the Quay. **Barronstrand Street** and **The Mall** head off the Quay inland to the south, then join up to create a large triangle meeting at **Parnell House** on **Parnell Street,** which is the same street as The Mall. Barronstrand turns into **Broad,** which turns into **Michael Street,** before it meets the end of the triangle. Most of the hip places to be are in or on this triangle of sorts. And it's all walkable, which makes things simple. A short cab ride can get you anywhere a little farther out.

hanging out

The intensity of Waterford's youth vibe, orbiting around the **Waterford Institute of Technology,** on Cork Road, just off the eastern end of the main highway, almost makes up for its minuscule size. So there *are* at least a few spots that are trendy enough for even the best of you. **Geoff's** [see *bar scene,* below] leads the list of "come to be seen" pubs in Waterford; actually, it's pretty much the *only* "come to be seen" pub in this city, so if you're young, hip, and just too cool for your Doc Martens, you'll inevitably wind up here.

The coziest cafe in town is **Café Luna** [see *eats,* below]. The **California Café** [see *eats,* below] has potential as a prime chilling spot as yet undiscovered by resident hipsters, but isn't exactly hopping at all hours of the night yet. Still, it's sparkling, the servers are friendly, and the eats are yummy and reasonably priced.

Waterford doesn't have any leafy, pseudo-sylvan dog-walking and people-watching spots. Most folks opt to lounge on the benches in the triangular space where Broad, Barronstrand, and George's streets meet, one block off the Quay. Everybody ends up here at some point or other, sipping a soda or a cup of coffee while gazing off dreamily in a seaward direction. Late afternoon is best for this, of course.

bar scene

Supposedly the oldest pub in the city, and with a chunk of the original Viking-built city wall to prove it, **T & H Doolan's** *(32 George's St.; Tel 051/841-504),* right in the town center northwest of the cathedral, is a venerable mainstay in Waterford City. It's fabulously traditional and a great spot for live music sessions: An as-yet-undiscovered Sinead O'Connor once played in this crypt-like space and the crowd is just as bold and on the lookout for new phenoms today.

A splendid spot for inexpensive pub grub, **Egan's** *(36-37 Barronstrand St.; Tel 051/875-619)* is similar to T & H Doolan's, but not as old. You probably won't find any trad here, but be forewarned: There *is* the occasional karaoke session.

All the beautiful twentysomethings in Waterford City make appearances at **Geoff's** *(9 John St.; Tel 051/874-787),* a 5-minute walk south of

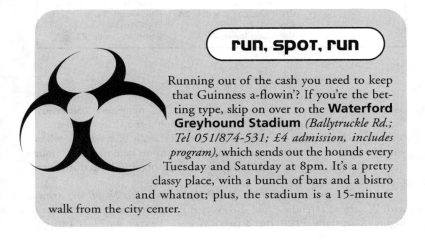

run, spot, run

Running out of the cash you need to keep that Guinness a-flowin'? If you're the betting type, skip on over to the **Waterford Greyhound Stadium** *(Ballytruckle Rd.; Tel 051/874-531; £4 admission, includes program),* which sends out the hounds every Tuesday and Saturday at 8pm. It's a pretty classy place, with a bunch of bars and a bistro and whatnot; plus, the stadium is a 15-minute walk from the city center.

waterford city

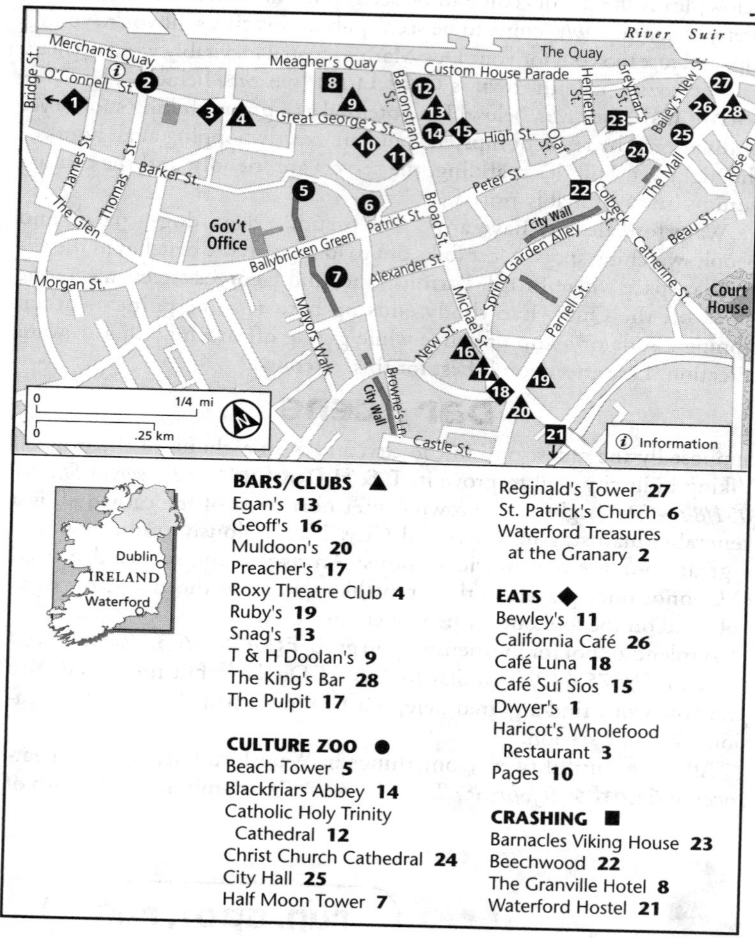

the town center, known as the "city's hippest bar" by general consensus. Waterford's hip young things sit around looking just a little bored and a bit too cool for the rest of the town. (But can you really blame them, when you can squeeze absolutely everything there is to do here into a 24-hour spree?) The surging vibe makes Geoff's the best place in Waterford for a little local cruising action, at least.

Right next door to Geoff's, **The Pulpit** *(John St.; No phone)* brims with Waterford's trendiest mid-20s every night of the week. It also hosts a nightclub upstairs, **Preacher's** [see *club scene*, below], which is a trippy ascent into a weird Gothic fantasy—though one with a mixed-ages crowd of easy-to-meet locals.

Muldoon's *(John St.; Tel 051/856-924 or Tel 051/844-180; Lunch noon-3pm, dinner 5:30pm-late; V)*, just a few steps from Geoff's, has a dark spacious sports-bar feel, so it's surprising that the food here is so fancy. The menu's got stuff like marinated chicken in a Thai green curry sauce or dark and white chocolate mousse with blueberry compote. (That's just fruit whip in a sugary sauce.) There are occasional folk and trad sessions, and it's open the latest of all the pubs—1:30am or later. You can get free basic bar snacks after 11:30pm.

live music scene

Feeling more refined than your rumpled well-worn jeans and big bulky backpack would suggest? **The Symphony Club of Waterford** *(Cork Rd.; Tel 051/302-809; Fax 051/302-293; £6-10)* often hosts classical concerts at the Waterford Institute of Technology.

The King's Bar *(8 Lombard St.; Tel 051/870-949)*, a 10-minute walk east of the pubs of John Street, offers a trad session every Friday night, and all musicians are welcome. Take Parnell Street, which becomes the Mall; turn right on Lombard Street. This historic landmark pub, which has an old wood-burning fireplace, is popular not only with music lovers but also among the kind of sportsmen who like to place bets on horse races and then watch them on wide-screen TV's. Also check out **T & H Doolan's** [see *bar scene,* above] for nightly folk or traditional music; it's got solid creds. There's also trad on Sunday nights at **The Woodman,** the bar at Ruby's [see *club scene,* below].

club scene

Probably the liveliest club in town and definitely the most bizarre, **Preacher's** *(Upstairs at the Pulpit, John St.; 11pm-2am Wed-Sun; Girls*

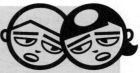

lad meets lassie

If you're here and ready for action, just be advised that a small-scale youth vibe in this city means the pickings can be slim. Save your serious prowling efforts for the larger, more vibrant cities on your itinerary. In the meantime, get yourself to **Geoff's** [see *bar scene,* above] for a leisurely pint first—there's one of your best chances to hook up with some of Waterford's finest specimens; afterwards, check out **Preacher's** [see *club scene,* below], arguably the best nightclub in Waterford. If nobody catches your eye—hey, you're probably on the first bus to Cork City in the morning anyhow.

free Thur before midnight, no cover Sun) has this Goth thing going on in the decorating scheme that some would think fabulous and others downright scary. Take your pick. At any rate, the club goers are, in contrast, upbeat and unpretentious.

Continuing with the pub-cum-club thing, **Snag's** *(upstairs at Egan's, 36-37 Barronstrand St.; Tel 051/875-619; Usual club hours Fri-Sun;* is more of a generic nightspot, but still good for laughs.

"Neat dress essential" at **Ruby's** *(Parnell House, Parnell St.; Tel 051/858-128; 11pm-2am seven nights; Cover £3-6)* means sport jackets for guys and skintight black leather for girls. It's a decent, if undistinctive, nightspot overall, though, with handy utilitarian food available at the adjoining bar, **The Woodman,** during daylight hours and still more trad by night. No teenyboppers need apply: Supposedly they're pretty strict about the over-23's-only rule.

arts scene

Just about the only all-purpose arts venue in town is the **Garter Lane Arts Centre** *(22a O'Connell St.; Tel 051/855-038; 10am-6pm Mon-Sat, later for evening events; admin@garterlane.ie; Tickets £6-12),* which offers pretty standard fare: plays, screenings of old movies like *High Society,* concerts, and exhibitions of painting, sculpture, and photography. There isn't an event scheduled every night, and plays usually run only a night or two; pretty disappointing, especially if you've just come from Cork City.

▸▸VISUAL ARTS

The **Waterford Municipal Art Gallery** is housed in **City Hall** *(The Mall; Tel 051/873-501, ext. 489 to make an appointment),* with a fairly dry collection of your typical Irish standbys by Yeats, Lamb, and Keating. Hours are sporadic and by appointment only.

▸▸PERFORMING ARTS

The other theater in town is the **Theatre Royal** *(The Mall; Tel 051/874-402),* which stages the city's **Light Opera Festival** in October [see *festivals and events,* below].

The Waterford Show *(City Hall; Tel 051/358-397 or 051/875-788, after 5pm 051/381-020 or 087/681-71-91, bookings at the Tourist Office* [see *need to know,* below] *or at the Waterford Crystal Visitor Centre* [see *stuff,* below]; *Tue, Thur, Sat, shows 9pm May-Sept; admission £8; AE, V, MC)* consists of Irish music, stories, and dancing in a big classy ballroom at Waterford City Hall, which is behind Reginald's Tower on The Mall. You get a glass of Bailey's before the show at 8:45pm and a "complimentary" (oh, *please*) glass of wine during the performance. But not so bad, considering you'd pay almost £8 for a glass of Bailey's and a glass of wine at a pub anyway. The dancing and music's quite passable, too, and the experience as a whole isn't as cheesy as it sounds.

gay scene

You might not find all the happy people of Waterford frantically waving their rainbow flags, but there is a small gay community here in the city,

festivals and events

The **Spraoi** *(e-mail spraoi@voyager.ie for info)*, pronounced "spree," is Ireland's biggest street festival, taking place on the bank holiday weekend in early August. There's a huge parade, among many other festivities. There's no real occasion for celebrating (and maybe that's the best reason of any to party).

Did the prospect of that internationally renowned Wexford Opera Festival send you looking for your tuxedo and funny little binoculars? The **Waterford International Festival of Light Opera** sends the fat ladies singing at the Theatre Royal on The Mall *(late September; Tel 051/874-402)*.

Calling all Yeats- and Wilde-wannabes: The **Seán Dunne Weekend,** "a festival of spoken and written word" *(early to mid-April; Tel 051/309-983)* offers street theater performances, even more live music than usual on the streets and in hotels and pubs, special art exhibitions and plays, debates, book readings, and writing awards.

thanks mostly to those frisky young'uns at the Waterford Institute of Technology, which has a support group called the **GLAM Society** (www.angelfire.com/wa/glamwit; glamwit@angelfire.com). GLAM sometimes sponsors events open to the general public; if you know you're going to be in the area, e-mail for more information. While you're at it, take a peek at the monthly *Gay Community News* (homepage.tinet.ie/~nlgf).

Call the **Gay and Lesbian Line South East** *(Tel 051/879-907; GLSE_@hotmail.com)* to find out about what's going on in Waterford, Wexford, Kilkenny, and Tipperary.

There is now a gay nightclub running the first Friday of the month at the **Forum Regal Room** *(The Glen, Waterford; fly.trap.tripod.com)*.

culture zoo

Ancient Waterford's got plenty in the way of medieval buildings and relics up for show, although most of it isn't as spectacular as you might find elsewhere; there aren't a lot of absolute must-sees on this list. While you're walking around town, be sure to check out the remnants of Waterford's city walls, originally built by the Vikings back at the start of the first millennium. The ruins are scattered around the city, most notably near the Theatre Royal and Reginald's Tower. Some of the walls' built-in towers are also still standing: **Half Moon Tower** *(Patrick St.)*, **Beach Tower** *(Jenkin's Lane)*, and **Watch Tower** *(near Railway Square)*.

Waterford Treasures at the Granary *(Merchant's Quay; Tel 051/304-500; 10am-5pm Sept-May, 9:30am-9pm June-Aug; mail@*

waterfordtreasures.com, www.waterfordtreasures.com; Admission £4/£3 students): Reopened as a museum in 1999, the whole place has a cool futuristic decor. It has some pretty neat artifacts from throughout the town's thousand-year history, and the audiovisuals on mythology, medieval happenings, and all that jazz are definitely worth a look. The same building houses the town's Tourist Office.

Reginald's Tower *(On the northern end of the Mall, on the Quay; Tel 051/873-501; 10am-5pm Mon-Fri, 2-6pm Sat-Sun, open Easter-Oct; Admission around £2):* The most recognizable medieval fixture in the city, Reginald's Tower is part of the original city fortification. Built in the 1100s by the Vikings, it's had a pretty colorful history as a prison, an arsenal, and a mint; several English kings stayed here, too. There are some highly atmospheric exhibits on ancient royal charters that testify to Waterford's importance to the British crown, but if 900-year-old government documents aren't your thing, you can get just as good an idea of the Tower's history by taking a leisurely stroll through it.

Christ Church Cathedral *(Cathedral Sq., follow Henrietta St. away from the Quay; Tel 051/396-270; Free admission)* and **Holy Trinity Cathedral** *(Barronstrand St.; No phone; Free admission)*: The star Baroque architect John Roberts designed both the Protestant (Christ Church) and Catholic (Holy Trinity) churches. Both are worth a visit: Christ Church is Europe's only Neoclassical Georgian cathedral, and Holy Trinity has an amazing carved pulpit and crystal (Waterford, of course) chandeliers. Roberts's popular flourishes also grace the late-18th-century **City Hall** *(The Mall; Tel 051/873-501; Free admission)* and the **Theatre Royal** [see *arts scene,* above]. Christ Church offers a presentation on the city's history, but it costs £3 and your punts would probably be better put to use in one of the pubs.

Blackfriars Abbey *(Arundel Sq.; No phone; Free admission):* Some of the oldest ecclesiastical ruins in the city can be found here. It centers around a 13th-century square tower that's truly a ghostly sight by night.

St. Patrick's Church *(Jenkins Lane; No phone; Free admission):* This elegant 18th-century church was a holdout in times of religious oppression and thankfully survived with grace to spare. It's worth a visit for a peek at its melancholy Spanish-influenced interiors.

city sports

For most things outdoorsy, you'll really need to venture outside the city [see **everywhere else**]. However, if you're hot to trot, gallop on over to the **Killotteran Equitation Centre** *(Old Kilmeaden Rd., Waterford; Tel 051/384-158; Open all year, closed Sun; Fees average £10 per hour),* which offers riding lessons and treks through pretty Waterford landscapes.

stuff

Buying a fancy piece of glass at any *other* place in Ireland just wasn't good enough? (They do sell Waterford crystal all over the country, you know.) Go for a tour and a shopping excursion at **Waterford Crystal Factory**

and Gallery *(Cork Rd.; Tel 051/373-311; Tours 8:30am-4pm Apr-Oct, 9am-3:15pm Mon-Fri Nov-Mar; Showrooms 8:30am-6pm Apr-Oct, 9am-5pm Mon-Fri Nov-Mar; Tour around £4/£2 students).* The whole deal consists of a 20-minute video and a half-hour tour of the factory. The factory is about a mile's hike outside of town so cabbing it might be best for this one.

If you want the goods but don't want to bother with the factory tour, just go to any "fine" department store in Waterford, or check out the **Waterford Design Centre and Gourmet Store** *(44 The Quay; Tel 051/856-666; wdc@tinet.ie)*, which is also great for designer threads, leather, and craftsy earthenware.

If you really *really* need new clubbing clothes, you could try the **City Square Shopping Centre** *(Arundel Sq.; Tel 051/853-528),* but only if you really *really* need something. This place is crowded with crossword-wielding retired people and stroller-pushing mommies with 10 kids hanging off of each leg. It's easy to get squished. It is, however, the best place in Waterford for trendoid shopping. Pick up that new CD at **Golden Discs** *(City Square Shopping Centre).* There are also plenty of stores, like Benetton and whatnot, around Barronstrand and George's streets.

If you'd rather spend your money on the latest Maeve Binchy novel for that next long Bus Éireann trip, hop on over to **The Book Centre** *(5 S. Main St.; Tel 051/873-823),* a generic but well-stocked local book-worm mecca.

Because you've been hunting all over for Irish beanie babies (so they don't make 'em here, so what?), you simply have to stop in at **Irish Treasures** *(121 The Quay; Tel 051/844-009; 9am-6pm Mon-Sat; 2-6pm Sun),* which sells pottery, crafts, CDs and tapes, T-shirts, and "souvenirs for every taste"—read: kitsch. Don't you love it? You had to buy one of those "Kiss me, I'm Irish" T-shirts for your brother anyway.

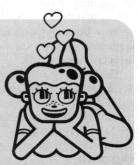

fashion

The young people in Waterford, though few, seem bolder and louder than those in other Irish cities, for some reason, and their bright trendy clothes reflect the attitude. Wear anything you've seen in a teeny-bopper fashion magazine at least a hundred times already—flared pants or jeans and tight-fitting T-shirts and sweaters for girls, and windpants, rugby shirts, and sneakers for guys—and you'll fit right in.

eats

There's not exactly an abundance of inexpensive places to eat in this city. Well, there are several places, but most lack *atmosphere*—unless you consider the Golden Arches to be atmosphere.... The eminently classy **Café Luna** and the **California Café** are your best choices if you don't want fries with that.

▸▸CHEAP

Generally known as Waterford's hippest spot for coffee, salad or a sandwich, and some laid-back conversation, **Café Luna** *(53 John St.; Tel 051/834-539; 11am-12:15am Mon-Wed, 11am-3:30am Thur-Sun; www.cafe-luna.ie)* attracts what few bohemians there are in this city—and a few wannabes, too. Don't come exclusively for the food, though; while it's decent, some dishes even perfectly good, by the end of the day the kitchen can be out of whatever it is you want to order—and this place is open till 3:30am most nights of the week. During busy times the management has been known to impose a £3.50 minimum charge, which means you'll have to add a salad or croissant to that coffee-and-journal-writing-at-noon plan. And you'll have to order something else, too, if you're going to stay long enough to hear that Eric Clapton CD on the stereo revert back to track one—they don't like loiterers here.

Chill to the strains of Tracy Chapman and a bright Pacific green decor at the new **California Café** *(8 The Mall; Tel 051/855-525; 10am-8pm, Mon-Sat; Items under £5; V, MC)*, which offers tasty food that's dirt cheap. Try a sandwich named "Hollywood," "Beverly Hills," or "Los Angeles," (the menu's as cheesy as Monterey Jack), or try the potato and leek soup for £2—the chef'll ask you if you liked it. This would be the perfect place to hang out, read a book, or chat with a friend, except that it closes way too early.

Try "sitting down" (that's what the name means in Irish) at **Café Suí Síos** *(54 High St.; Tel 051/841-063; All items under £6)*. The cafe offers an inexpensive yet thorough breakfast menu; lunch and dinner options consist mainly of sandwiches and pasta. Set on the town's main street, it's a sunny, bustling spot, ideal for a healthy breakfast of muesli, yogurt, and fresh fruit (£1.50); carnivores will want to order the typical full Irish breakfast (around £4).

Find cheap but yummy pub grub anywhere on Barronstrand Street: Try **Egan's, T & H Doolan's** or **Muldoon's** on John Street [see *bar scene,* above].

Generic but inexpensive spots for lunch include the two locations of the local chain **Pages** *(Upstairs at The Book Centre, Barronstrand St.; 5 S. Main St.; Tel 051/873-823; V, MC, AE)*.

▸▸DO-ABLE

There aren't too many middle-of-the-road spots for munchies, but **Haricot's Wholefood Restaurant** *(11 O'Connell St.; Tel 051/841-299; 10am-8pm Mon-Fri, 10am-5:45pm Sat; Main courses around £5-6;*

V) is one that both veggie-lovers and carnivores can appreciate, offering a surprisingly eclectic menu of vegetarian, vegan, seafood, and meat dishes. A relaxed, very earthy clientele can always be found here, wearing whatever they threw on today.

▶▶SPLURGE

Widely regarded as *the* best restaurant in town, **Dwyer's** *(8 Mary St.; Tel 051/877-478; 6-10pm Mon-Sat; AE, MC, V, DC)* has regular prices that'll make your head spin, but get there between 6 and 7:30pm and a full dinner will only set you back around £15. The menu's deliciously elegant (and deliciously delicious, of course): Just picture the waiter laying down a steaming wild salmon in filo pastry garnished with cucumbers and fennel. It's a homey old place run by a delightful local couple.

There's also the fixed-price dinner at **The Granville Hotel** [see *crashing,* below], which is yummy but bank-breaking: an eye-popping £22.50 for three courses and tea or coffee. How about mussels *marnières* on the half-shell, poached in white wine and cream with fresh herbs and onions for a starter? Follow that with honey-roasted Duck Mount Congreve with lardons of bacon and apple cream along with vegetables or salad. Then top that off with a dish of tiramisu with caramel sauce or chocolate roulade with strawberry coulis for dessert. And why not, if you've got the parental plastic?

crashing

Waterford is very much lacking in good affordable accommodations, perhaps because there's just not enough demand. You can choose between a few really fancy (and really expensive) hotels, a small handful of mostly mediocre B&Bs, or a couple of lukewarm hostels, but that's about it. You probably won't be spending more than a night here anyway, so it's not such a big deal.

▶▶CHEAP

There are only two Bórd Fáilte-approved hostels in Waterford City. *Do not stay at any other hostel in town*—unless you're okay with filthy bathrooms and bedrooms and God-knows-what-else. We're talking skanky at best.

Barnacle's Viking House Hostel *(Greyfriars/Coffee House Lane, The Quay; Tel 051/853-827; ireland.iol.ie/~lalco/page7.htm, viking@barnacles.iol.ie; £8-12 dorm, £24-31 double; V, MC, AE)* is the comfiest hostel in town. This place has a hundred beds, so it's unlikely that you'll be turned away. But if you are and there's no room at the **Waterford Hostel** [see below] either, don't look for another hostel. Splurge on a B&B. Seriously. Anyway, the Viking House is definitely your safest bet in Waterford, although an impersonal atmosphere and icky puke-colored walls make it far from the nicest hostel you'll come across. On the other hand, continental breakfast is included, along with 24-hour reception, a Bureau de Change, relatively spacious dorm rooms (many with en suite bathrooms), and a nice common room with a 16th-century fireplace the owners unearthed while setting up the place.

If the Viking House happens to be full in the summer, and you can't afford to splurge a little, head straight to the **Waterford Hostel** *(70 Manor St.; Tel 051/850-163; £7 dorm, no private rooms; Open June to mid-Sept; V, MC, AE)*, which has only 20 beds. The Waterford Hostel is open for only a few months in summer and isn't as big or as comfortable as the Viking House, but we're really serious about the skank hostels warning, so it's worth considering. There is no lockout or curfew, and the hostel is a 5-minute walk from the city center.

▸▸DO-ABLE

Among the best of the bed and breakfasts in Waterford City, **Beechwood** *(7 Cathedral Sq., follow Henrietta St. off the Quay; Tel 051/876-677; About £20 singles, around £32 doubles; No credit cards)* is a place you'll love for several reasons: The charming, traditional rooms are quiet, thanks to a good old-fashioned home-and-B&B combo, and the square, spread out in front of **Christ Church Cathedral** [see *culture zoo,* above], allows only pedestrian traffic.

A couple other relatively affordable options are **Corlea House** *(2 New St., Tel 051/875-764; £16 per person, single or "family" rooms; No credit cards),* in the city center, and **Derrynane House** *(19 The Mall, Tel 051/875-179; Open Easter-Nov.1; Rooms with private bath £18 per person; without private bath £17 per person; No credit cards),* about a 20-minute walk from the city center.

▸▸SPLURGE

Living off Mommy and Daddy's credit card? Lucky you—you can afford to stay at **The Granville Hotel** *(The Quay; Tel 051/305-555; double rooms only; £55 per person, £70 single occupancy, Oct-Apr; £65 per person, £80 single occupancy, May-Sept; weekend special £95 for two nights; full Irish breakfast included; V, MC, AE),* no doubt some of the classiest digs in town. This hotel's got all the typical upscale trappings, including a ritzy *prix fixe* dinner menu [see *eats,* above], classy modern rooms, and an inviting lobby that says, "You've arrived." If you can't afford to stay here but want to pretend that you can, the ultra-refined hotel bar makes a great place for a quiet pint.

need to know

Currency Exchange AIB *(The Quay; Tel 051/876-607; 10am-5pm Mon, 10am-4pm Tue-Fri)* and **Bank of Ireland** *(The Quay; Tel 051/872-074; same hours),* both with ATMs; the Tourist Office also has a Bureau de Change, but the banks usually have the better rates.

Tourist Information Waterford Tourist Office *(41 The Quay; Tel 051/875-788; 9am-6pm Mon-Sat Apr-June and Sept, 9am-6pm Mon-Sat and 11am-5pm Sun July-Aug, 9am-5pm Mon-Sat Oct, 9am-5pm Mon-Fri Nov-Mar).*

Public Transportation Bus Éireann operates daily bus service within Waterford and the surrounding area; flat fare is 70p. Taxi ranks are outside Plunkett Rail Station and along the Quay opposite the Granville Hotel. To call a taxi, try **City Cabs** *(Tel 051/852-222),* **Cab**

873 *(St. John's Park; Tel 051/873-873)*, **Metro Cabs** *(Tel 051/857-157)*, or **Parnell Cabs** *(Tel 051/853-791)*.

Health and Emergency Garda Headquarters *(Tel 051/874-888)*; **Holy Ghost Hospital** *(Cork Rd.; Tel 051/374-397)* or **Waterford Regional Hospital** *(Ardkeen, Dunmore Rd.; Tel 051/73321)*.

Pharmacies Gallagher's Pharmacy *(29 Barronstrand St.; Tel 051/878-103)*, or **Mulligan's Chemists** *(40-41 Barronstrand St.; Tel 051/875-211; and City Square Shopping Centre Unit 12A, Tel 051/853-247)*.

Airport Waterford Airport *(off R675, 6 miles outside of town; follow the Quay, make a right at Reginald's Tower, then follow the signs; Tel 051/875-589)*, has service to England. No public transportation is available to the airport, so take a taxi.

Trains and Buses Irish Rail at Plunkett Station *(Ignatius Rice Bridge; Tel 051/873-401)*; **Bus Éireann**, nationwide service from the Plunkett Station Depot *(Across the bridge from the rail station on The Quay; Tel 051/873-401)*.

Bike Rental Wright's Cycle Depot *(19-20 Henrietta St., off Parade Quay; Starting at £10 per day)*.

Postal General Post Office *(Parade Quay; Tel 051/874-444; 9am-5:30pm Mon-Fri, 9am-1pm Sat)*.

Laundry Duds 'n' Suds Laundromat and TV lounge *(Parnell House, Parnell St.; Tel 051/841-168 or Tel 051/858-790; 8:30am-8pm Mon-Sat)* or **Washed Ashore** *(The Quay; 8am-9pm Mon-Fri, 8:30am-6:30pm Sat)*.

Internet See *wired*, above.

everywhere else

dungarvan

There might not be a whole helluva lot to see here in the old port town of Dungarvan, situated 48 km (30 mil) west of Waterford City, but its tremendous ocean views, pretty (if rocky) beaches, and excellent pub scene assure you a pleasant afternoon and evening. The harbor itself is in need of a huge cleanup effort, but the picturesque forests, hills, and location where the River Colligan meets the sea are totally snapshot worthy. Most of the town's pubs are on the waterfront or mere steps from it.

bar scene

Back when Dungarvan's harbor was a thriving commercial port, merchants came to **The Moorings** *(The Quay; Tel 058/41461; V, MC, AE)* to discuss business. This pub's more than 150 years old, and its walls are covered with photographs attesting to its former status as a mariner's gathering place. These days it's a comfortable magnet for most of the adventuresome sorts who visit Dungarvan.

Minnie's *(Abbeyside; Tel 058/42161)* is definitely what you'd call posh—it's a pretty classy place. The pub grub here is good, but you can only get it at lunchtime (12:30 to 2:30pm); come for the trad music sessions on Wednesday nights. On Sunday nights there's a nightclub for over-21's, sometimes with live bands.

Widely regarded as the liveliest pub in town, **Davitt's** *(Davitt's Quay; Tel 058/449-000)* offers live trad and rock music almost every night of the week. Visitors have lauded Davitt's as a "rambling Gothic-style emporium" that still manages to feel warm and cozy, with large stone fireplaces and plenty of comfy seating. Much of the furniture and decorations were lifted (legally, of course) from churches across the European continent. Davitt's also has a restaurant serving pizza and Mexican food all day [see *eats,* below].

Another good spot for live trad is **The Anchor** *(The Quay)* which showcases local bands on the weekends. But look around—you'll usually find other equally good options all along the waterfront.

culture zoo

Not too much to see in Dungarvan Town, except for **King John's Castle** *(By the Quay; Free admission),* built in the late 12th century. It doesn't really rank star status among the area's many fine ancient stone fortifications, but it's right in town, it's free, and it is, after all, a castle.

city sports

How does a leisurely trot on horseback through rolling green hills strike you? Call **Colligan Equestrian Centre** *(Crough, Colligan; Tel 058/68261; Open all year Tue-Sat; Prices start at £9 per hour)* and you're all set. You might want to try booking ahead, since there are only a dozen horses and the place gets really busy during the summertime due to its fantastic location overlooking Dungarvan Bay.

And of course there's always the beach. Dungarvan's own is stony, but just 3.2 km (2 mi) east of town, the lovely and sandy **Clonea Strand** is a big draw in summer. Though you may find the waters too cold at any time of the year, even in July and August, the waters fronting the beach are often good for surfing. In summer, Clonea Strand is popular mainly with Irish families and college-age visitors. While on the beach, check out the "women of Dungarvan," famed in legend and lore for being among the most enticing in Ireland. It is said that in 1649 one Dungarvan woman so charmed Cromwell that he spared the Irish who lived in the area his usual wanton violence.

eats

All the pubs in town offer decent food at reasonable prices. Try **Davitt's** [see *bar scene,* above] if you're in the mood for pizza; the fajitas are edible but would never be mistaken for Tijuana chow. There are also a few inexpensive cafes in town: Try the creatively named **An Bialann**—it means "the restaurant" *(Grattan Sq.; Tel 058/42825)* for informal traditional Irish grub served at rustic wooden tables and benches.

festivals and events

If you're lucky, your time here will coincide with the **Féile na nDéise** *(http://dungarvan.com/feile/feilepag/schedule.htm),* a traditional-music festival sending local pubs into foot-tapping frenzies the first weekend in May.

crashing

When I tell you this hostel used to be a monastery, you'll likely conjure up visions of a small, restored medieval stone building in a forest clearing, or something equally romantic. No such luck, I'm afraid. **Dungarvan Holiday Hostel** *(Youghal Rd.; Tel 058/44340; homepages.iol.ie/~clonanav/, clonanav@iol.ie; £7 dorm, £15-17 double; No credit cards)* actually looks pretty modern (and pretty boring, considering what you might have been expecting). It's perfectly fine for a night, though. The hostel rents bikes, and it's located within mere spitting distance of the town's beaches and pubs. Guests do interact with each other, though it's not quite a love-in. There's no curfew or lockout, as guests all have keys. Bathrooms are, for the most part, shared, though there is one room with a private bath.

Other do-able options include **Abbey House** *(Friars Walk, Abbeyside; Tel 058/41669; £20 per person, private baths, breakfast included; No credit cards),* 10 minutes on foot from the town center, by the sea; **Seaview** *(Youghal Rd.; Tel 058/41583; Fax 058/41679; fahyn@gofree.indigo.ie, www.amireland.com; £25-30 singles, £20-25 per person shared; private baths; breakfast included; V, MC),* overlooking Dungarvan Bay, in the countryside, a 5-minute drive from the town center; and **Lawlor's Hotel** *(T.F. Meagher St.; Tel 058/41122; Fax 058/41000; info@lawlors-hotel.ie, www.lawlors-hotel.com).*

within 30 minutes

A good place to fall under the spell of Irish language and culture is **Ring (An Rinn)**, only a 5-minute drive—or a pleasant 20-minute walk—south of Dungarvan. This tiny village is part of the Gaeltacht, and traditional Irish music just doesn't get any more authentic than what you'll find here. Summer festivals are held often and without warning, with music ringing through the streets and pubs celebrating Irish culture. Even when there's no festival, there's live traditional music to be found at least one night every week. One particularly popular spot in Ring is **Mooney's** *(Tel 058/46204; 10:30am-12:30am daily; Entrees £2-4, beer £2.30-£2.50; No credit cards).* Live music is played here every night during the summer, creating a nostalgic aura. In addition to beer, they offer pub grub and steak and chicken dishes. This very old rustic pub is also frequented by the Clancy Brothers, praised throughout Ireland and the world as one of the top folk acts around. Head down to **The Marine Bar** *(Tel 058/46455; 11am-12:30am daily, closed Wed in summer, closed Mon and Sat in winter; Entrees £5-15; V, MC)* for another taste of traditional Irish nightlife of Ring. This friendly warm-hearted pub, with stone walls and a huge open fireplace, offers food ranging from grilled steaks to scrumptious seafood dishes. Every night you can hear the soft echo of a flute and banjo singing the melodies of the Emerald Isle. If you hang out here at night you'll have to take a taxi to get back to Dungarvan.

need to know

Currency Exchange **AIB** *(Meagher St.; 10am-5pm Mon, 10am-4pm Tue-Fri)* and **Bank of Ireland** *(The Square; Same hours)* both of which have ATMs.

Tourist Information **Dungarvan Tourist Office** *(The Square; Tel 058/41741; 9am-9pm Mon-Sat June-Aug, 9am-6pm Sun, 9am-6pm Mon-Sat Sept-May)* or try the helpful ***dungarvan.com*** website.

Bike Rental **Dungarvan Holiday Hostel** [see *crashing*, above] *(£6 per day),* **O'Mahoney's Cycles** *(Abbeyside; Tel 058/43346; Hours vary; Call ahead; £5 per day),* or **Murphy Cycles** *(Main St.; Tel 058/41376; £10 per day, £40 per week),* a Raleigh Rent-A-Bike dealer, which means you can return the bike to any other Raleigh bike shop in the country.

Bus Lines Out of the City **Bus Éireann** *(Tel 051/79000)* runs routes 4 and 40 to Waterford (a 50-minute ride, almost a dozen per day). Route 40 goes on to Cork City (five to seven buses a day), hitting Youghal and Midleton [see **Southwest region**] in between; it's about an hour and 20 minutes from Dungarvan to Cork. Buses leave from Davitt's Quay in Dungarvan.

Postal **Dungarvan Post Office** *(Bridge St., off The Square; Tel 058/41210; 9am-5:30pm Mon-Fri, 9am-3pm Sat).*

ardmore

Though Ardmore boasts beautiful sandy beaches, many people come here not for the beaches, but to visit the brooding ruins of **St. Declan's Monastery** on his feast day, July 24. According to legend, Declan was preaching the gospels in Ireland in the 5th century, before Patrick even arrived. Remains include a cathedral, round tower, and well, in addition to a mysterious rock overlooking the beach. They say the rock floated across the sea from Wales when Declan returned from his visit there. Grave markers in the cemetery bear ogham letters, which comprised the first written Celtic language.

This quiet, sleepy village consists of no more than cottage rowhouses, a pub or two, a few "caffs" (cafes), some souvenir shops, and beautiful sandy beaches with dramatic jagged cliffs towering above. Directly east of the village, a path will lead you to St. Declan's Well, which overlooks the sea. The freshwater spring, which pilgrims once used to wash themselves, still runs. Next to the well you can see the ruins of the ancient Dysert Church. A fun thing to do is take the 5-km walk from here past the well and along the jagged cliffs. If you've got the energy, you can walk all the way to Whiting Bay (about 2-1/2 miles), where you can drown your thirst in a pub. Ardmore is also the start of the 95-km St. Declan's Way, an old pilgrimage trail stretching all the way to the Rock of Cashel in Tipperary.

The trail—some parts of which are unchanged since the time of St. Declan, 1600 years ago—runs smoothly across the gently rolling countryside before climbing up into the mountains.

Paddy Mac's *(Main St.; Tel 024/94166; Main courses £8-£15; AE, DC, MC, V; June-Sept daily noon-1:30am; off-season daily noon-8pm),* is the "hot spot" of town, the place all party people head to for pub grub, ale, and good times. Just off the beach, this rustic, wood-paneled eatery serves food that's more filling than spectacular. Their specialty, believe it or not, is potatoes cooked in their skins—they call them "jacket potatoes." If you hit the joint early in the evening, there's a good chance you'll stay until closing—live music of varying styles is presented in the peak summer months.

If pleasant seaside views and quiet, relaxing atmosphere are your thing, check into the **Ardmore Beach Hostel** *(Main St.; 024/94501; £8 dorm, £30 double),* where you'll find more of the same. The lone private room is a splurge as private hostel rooms go, but it's unusually nice.

need to know

Tourist Information The tourist office *(Tel 024/94444; June-Aug 11am-1pm, 2-5pm daily)* sits in the parking lot by the beach. Its structure resembles a sandcastle some weird kid made.

Buses Ardmore is located 35 miles southeast of Waterford on the **Bus Éireann** route from Cork. Three buses run daily to and from Cork year-round Monday to Saturday (only one on Sunday). In the peak months, there are two daily buses to and from Waterford via Dungarvan. Off-season, buses serving Waterford run only on Friday and Saturday. All buses let you off on Main Street in the center of town.

tramore

If you're headed for Tramore, odds are you're all for boards, wetsuits, and big curls. **Oceanic Manoeuvres Surf School** *(3 Riverstown, Tramore; Tel 051/390-944; oceanic@tinet.ie; open all year; surfboards £5 per hour, wetsuits £5 per hour, board and suit £8 per hour, bodyboards £3 per hour, bodyboard and suit £6 per hour; 2-hour lessons £6-25, depending on group size)* will set you up, even if you're just starting out.

Tra Mhór, the town's traditional name, means "big strand," and this 5-km stretch of beach is aptly named. It's one of the most popular holiday resorts in Ireland—and, yes, a bit tacky—with lots of family-oriented tourist joints, including fast food fish 'n' chip eateries and amusement arcades. You can skip most of these and head for the beach. If the water is too cold (highly likely) you can take one of the most dramatic walks in the area, the **Doneraile Walk,** which begins at the tourist office and follows **Cliff Road Walk** for some of the finest panoramic coastal scenes in the area. You'll pass sheltered coves and inlets, including **Newtorn Cove** and **Guillamene.**

At the old train station depot on Railway Square is the **tourist office** *(Tel 051/381-572; June-Sept 9am-6pm daily).* Several buses run here daily from Waterford, letting you off right in the center of town near the beaches. The bus ride from Waterford takes only 15 minutes. The beaches are set against a backdrop of high dunes, some rising 30 meters, especially at the eastern end. Tramore faces the bay with Great Newton Head to the southwest and Browntown Head to the northeast, which both make for great views.

The town has a youth hostel, **The Monkey Puzzle** *(Upper Branch Rd.; Tel 051/386-754),* lying close to the tourist office. It's rather bare but clean, with dormitory beds for £8 a night. If you want more privacy, ask for one of two double rooms, which cost £20 a night. Otherwise, there is a string of B&Bs along nearby Cliff Road, the best of which is **Cliff House** *(Cliff Rd.; Tel 051/ 381-497; £24 singles, £36 doubles; Open Mar-Nov).*

The town's best pub is **The Sea Horse** *(Tel 051/386-091)* on Strand Street. It also has the best pub grub in town, costing about £5 a meal, and served daily from noon to 9pm. The pub has the resort's most convivial atmosphere with a lot of young Irish people here in July and August, mingling with vacationing locals from Waterford and Cork County.

Skip the tacky eateries near the beach and head for the traditional favorite, **Cunningham's Fish & Chips** *(Main St.; 5pm-midnight daily in summer; Meals from £5; No phone),* which serves the town's best seafood.

After a good "tuck in," as they say locally, head for **The Hiberninan** *(Tel 051/386-396),* at the junction of Strand Street and Gallwey's Hill. In summer there's live Irish music in the pub which gives way to dancing at **Hi B** *(Open Wed-Sun until 1am, in season; £5 cover),* the dance club next door.

Another popular hangout at night is **The Victoria House** *(Queens St.; Tel. 051/390-338),* a three-floor pub where the young, the rowdy, and the restless gather on the ground floor. As you ascend to the top, the crowd grows older and more sedate.

need to know

Directions and Transportation **Bus Éireann** runs buses between Waterford and Tramore around 15 times a day.

comeragh mountains

In the center of County Waterford, Comeragh attracts climbers and hill walkers to one of the finest ranges in Ireland. The mountains offer a rich variety of terrain—everything from the precipitous Knockanaffrin Ridge to the glacial amphitheater of Lough Coumshingaun. The highlight of this area is **Mahon Falls,** which lies off R676 between Dungarvan and

Carrick-on-Suir. They are signposted at the hamlet of Mahon Bridge, some 15 miles south of Carrick-on-Suir—you'll turn onto Comeragh Drive and follow it west to the falls; after 3 miles, you reach a parking lot along the banks of the Mahon River. The trail to the falls leaves from here; walking time is about 20 minutes each way.

You can around the entire lake at Coumshingaun, in the eastern part of the mountains which is surrounded by dramatic rock faces that are known as some of the best climbing routes in Ireland.

For a deeper exploration of the mountains—where the going gets rougher, steeper, and tougher—a guide is recommended. The **Dungarvan Walking Group** is willing to show you the Comeraghs. Organizer Michael Powers (who can be reached at: Powers Book Shop, Tel 058/41617, in Dungarvan) will brief you on all of the provisions you might need for a day in the great outdoors, and then lead you out into the wild. The group meets at the TSB Bank on Main Street in Dungarvan for its 10am Sunday walks. These walks, lasting about 5 hours and covering rugged terrain, are not for the faint of heart.

If this sounds like altogether too much walking, you can also explore the mountains on horseback. We've gone horseback riding in the Comeraghs, and you can too if you call Melody's in Ballymacarbry *(Tel 052/36147)*, where horses can be rented at the rate of £12 per hour. Ballymacarbry is northwest of the park, halfway between Clonmel and Dungarvan.

It's possible, and not illegal, to go camping in these mountains, although locals tell us this is almost never done. If you do decide to camp out on the land, you of course have to bring your own provisions and gear. And be sure to carry away any litter that might pile up around your tent.

Instead of camping, a more viable option might be to stay at the tiny **Coumshingaun Lodge at Kilclooney** *(Tel 051/646-238; £20-26; V, MC)*, lying at the base of the mountains. "Lodge" is a bit of an exaggeration: There are only three rooms, each containing one queen size and one single bed. The cost is £20 per person if you're traveling with a group or £26 per day if you need the room for yourself. It's bone-bare but clean and comfortable, and lies only 200 yards from the base of the Comeraghs, so there are views in all directions. The price includes an Irish breakfast made in the old-fashioned kitchen.

need to know

Directions and Transportation The Comeragh Mountains are a 7-mile drive north of Dungarvan on the N25. The road is flat for most of the way except for three hills. You can walk it but it's a bit of an effort, especially if you want to conserve energy for hiking the mountains themselves. Unfortunately, there are no buses.

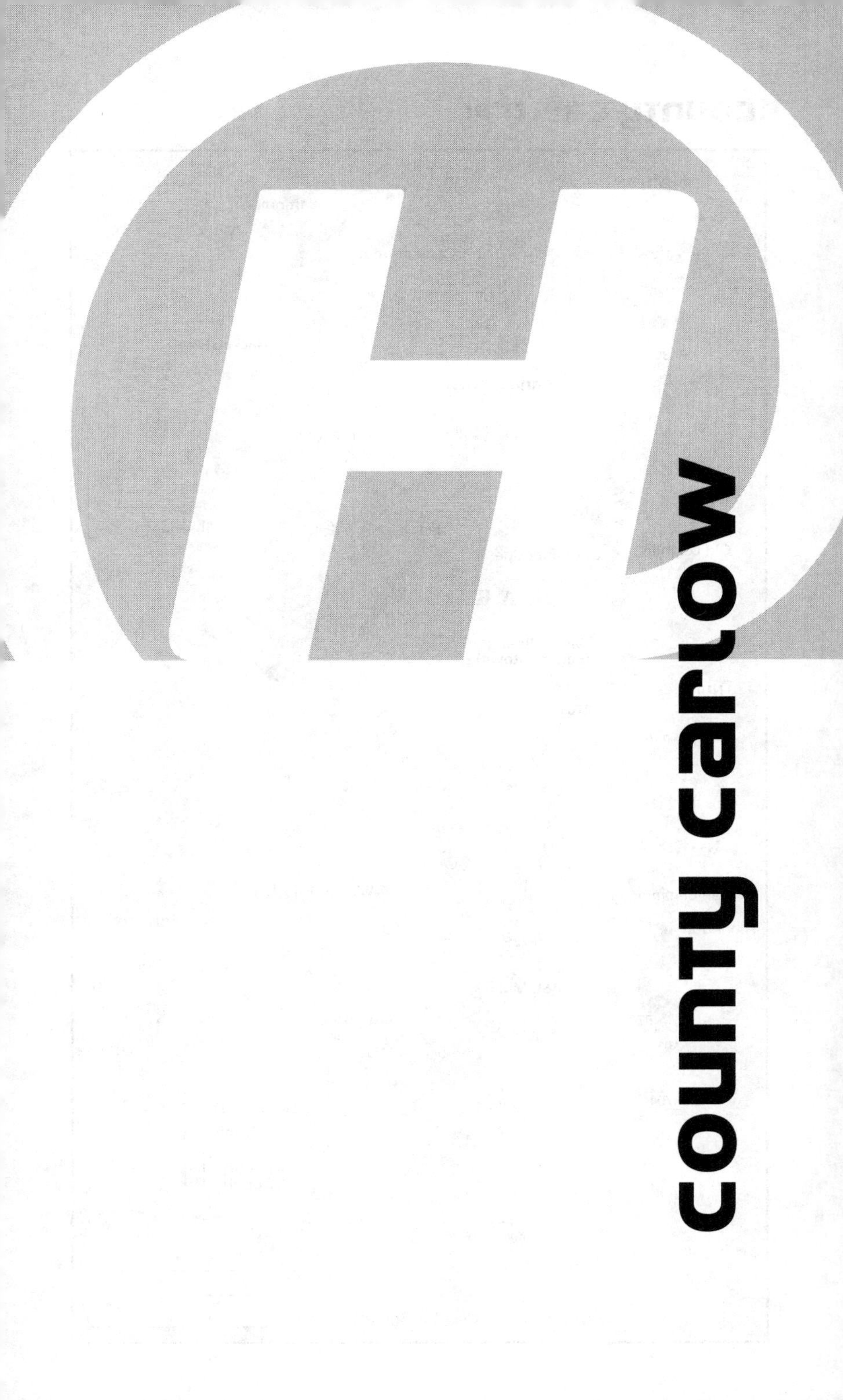
county carlow

County Carlow

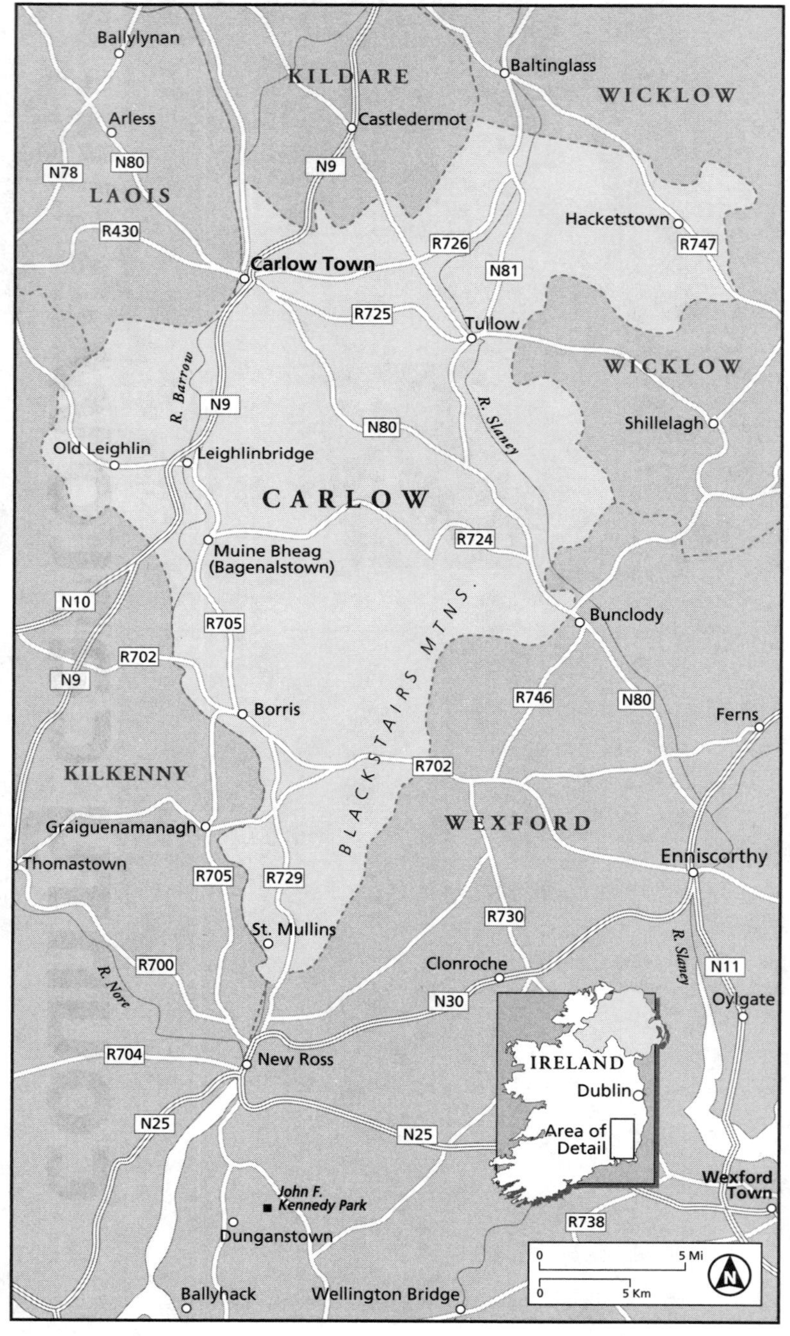

Ballylynan
KILDARE
Baltinglass
WICKLOW
Arless
Castledermot
N78
N80
N9
LAOIS
Hacketstown
R430
R726
R747
Carlow Town
N81
R725
Tullow
R. Barrow
WICKLOW
N9
R. Slaney
N80
Shillelagh
Old Leighlin
Leighlinbridge
CARLOW
R724
Muine Bheag
(Bagenalstown)
BLACKSTAIRS MTNS.
N10
Bunclody
R705
R702
N9
R746
N80
Borris
Ferns
R702
KILKENNY
WEXFORD
Graiguenamanagh
Thomastown
Enniscorthy
R705
R729
R730
St. Mullins
R. Slaney
R700
Clonroche
N11
R. Nore
N30
Oylgate
R704
New Ross
IRELAND
Dublin
N25
Area of
Detail
N25
Wexford
Town
John F.
Kennedy Park
R738
Dunganstown
0
5 Mi
0
5 Km
N
Ballyhack
Wellington Bridge

carlow

As you can pretty much figure out at first glance, Carlow Town isn't party or culture central. The main attraction here is **Browne's Hill Dolmen,** a huge and ancient stone structure within easy walking distance of the town [see *culture zoo,* below]. Another draw is Ireland's second longest river, **River Barrow,** where canoeists, rowers, and kayakers flock in good weather [see *great outdoors,* below].

With a population of about 12,000, Carlow is not a big town, and getting around is a piece of cake. Here's what you need to know: **Dublin Street** is the main thoroughfare, stretching north and south. **Tullow Street,** the main shopping—and drinking—drag, branches off at an angle. That's it.

bar, club, and live music scene

After a day of walking, paddling, or pedaling you can toss back a pint at one of Carlow's pubs. Many are packed in on Tullow Street, and there's something for everyone: food, dancing, tunes. And, of course, tasty brew.

Dinn Rí *(Dinn Rí Hotel, Tullow St.; Tel 0503/33111; Open until 2am; Cover £5-6; V, MC, AE)* is a pub of extremely impressive proportions—it stretches across the entire block between Tullow Street and Kennedy Avenue, morphing into a fantastic disco that admits a whopping 2,000 people on Saturday nights. The nightclub's open Friday through Sunday, but there is fun to be had on other nights, too. Everybody and their (hip) uncle in Carlow Town is here, man.

Other cool Carlow pubs include **Scragg's Alley** *(12 Tullow St.; Tel 0503/42233; No credit cards),* with good pub grub and even better live rock music on Wednesday nights (at the very least—you might get lucky

bottoms up

"Here's to a long life and a merry one.
A quick death and an easy one.
A pretty girl and an honest one.
A cold pint—and another one!"

on another night, too). The **Nexus** nightclub *(Cover £5-6)* upstairs from Scragg's is open Friday and Saturday nights, but after the scene at Dinn Rí, you're bound to be disappointed. At **Teach Dolmain** *(76 Tullow St.; Tel 0503/31235; No credit cards)* the grub's even won awards, and it's always lively at night (whoever isn't at Dinn Rí just might be here instead). At **Tully's** *(149 Tullow St.; Tel 0503/31862; No credit cards),* another perennial Carlow favorite, you can find live trad sessions—but, sadly, only sporadically. Whip out your own guitar to prod them along a bit.

culture zoo

You'll be surprised at how rich this town's history is (B.C., baby!). Check it out!

Carlow County Museum *(Town Hall, Centaur St., off the Haymarket; 11am-5pm Tue-Fri, 2-5pm Sat-Sun; £1):* This dinky two-room display houses locally found Celtic artifacts and town history displays.

Browne's Hill Dolmen *(3 km (1.8 mi) east of town on the Hacketstown road; Free):* Within easy walking distance from town, this megalithic tomb was reportedly used for religious rites over 4,000 years ago, and some say it's the burial site of a local king. It's very big, very old, and very, very heavy—the top stone weighs an inconceivable 100 tons. Take the path around the field, and ponder what our hairy ancestors made of this enormous rock.

Carlow Castle *(Castle St., eastern bank of River Barrow):* 12th-century Carlow Castle surprisingly survived Cromwell's extended temper tantrum, and it would be totally preserved today if some genius hadn't first converted it into an insane asylum and then blown it to smithereens in 1814 for some no doubt brilliant reason. Now all that's left is a stone wall and two tattered towers; you can't actually go inside.

Celtic High Cross: During early Christian times, Carlow's river valleys were home to monastic settlements, most of which were pummeled by the Vikings. Carlow's strategic position between Kilkenny City and the coast has contributed to the county's more recent violent history. During the 1798 Uprising (the last gasp before Ireland officially became England's booty), more than 600 rebellious Irishmen were massacred in

Carlow Town on what is now Tullow Road. The bodies of the slaughtered "Croppies" (they cropped their hair to show allegiance to the cause) are commemorated by a Celtic high cross across the river from Tullow Street, marking the spot where most of the victims are buried.

Cathedral of the Assumption *(College St.; Free):* The Cathedral is relatively new—1830s—but the stained-glass windows and statue of a certain Bishop Doyle, whose work in pursuit of the Catholic emancipation was obviously much appreciated, are worth a quick look.

great outdoors

Birds, butterflies, and fish beckon in the Carlow countryside; a bit of exercise, a nap on the shore, and a plunge into cool water might be good for what ails you (especially if you were out too late the night before). Rent a canoe from the **Otterholt Riverside Hostel** [see *crashing,* below] for around £14 for a half-day, or phone **Adventure Canoeing Days** *(Tel 0509/31307)* to arrange a tranquil paddle down the River Barrow. Individual canoe hire and guided group trips are available. If you rent a canoe from the hostel, you can put into the river from the backyard. You can also rent a bike from the hostel or **Coleman Cycles** [see *need to know,* below] for a spin through Carlow.

eats

There aren't too many options here; it might be a good idea to cook at the hostel instead of eating out. The **Superquinn** *(Carlow Shopping Centre, between Kennedy Ave. and Tullow St.; Tel 0503/30077; 8:30am-7pm Mon, Tue, and Sat, 8:30am-9pm Wed-Fri)* is your new best friend, as long as you're not looking to shop on a Sunday.

Bradbury's Coffee Shop *(144 Tullow St.; Tel 0503/43307; 8:30am-6pm Mon-Sat; No credit cards)* serves good cheap lunches; a meal of soup and bread is only £1.20. You can get a full Irish breakfast at **Sally's** *(Tullow St.; Tel 0503/43455; 8:30am-5:30pm; Under £5; No credit cards)* for £4. You can find excellent traditional Irish pub grub at **Scragg's Alley** or **Teach Dolmain** [see *bar scene,* above]. Even better, the prices go easy on your wallet.

crashing

The **Otterholt Riverside Hostel** *(Otterholt, Kilkenny Rd.; Tel 0503/30404; otter@iol.ie; £10 dorm, £13 double; No credit cards)* far surpasses any of Carlow's other accommodations, which is pretty decent considering it's a hostel. You want splendid views of the river? How about bike rental? And what about those gorgeous gardens out back? You can even rent a canoe here and launch it from the hostel's own back door. The Otterholt also boasts a campsite and a grill. The building itself is a charming Georgian house built in the early 19th century. This hostel makes a splendid place to spend the night.

If the hostel is full—or you're just tired of sleeping dorm-style—there are other options: The **Red Setter House** *(14 Dublin St., Tel 050/341-*

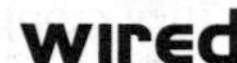

Communicate Now *(Carlow Shopping Centre, between Kennedy Ave. and Tullow St.; Tel 0503/43700; 10am-6pm Mon-Wed and Sat, 10am-9pm Thur-Fri; £6 per hour)* can get you connected.

848; £24 single with private bath, £20 single with shared bath, £22 per person double or triple with private bath; No credit cards), just a couple minutes' walk from the train station, or **Barrow Lodge** *(The Quay, Tel 050/341-173; georgepender@aircom.net; £21-23 per person, all rooms with private bath; No credit cards),* in the town center on the banks of the River Barrow.

need to know

Currency Exchange If you need some cash while in Carlow, try the **AIB** *(Tullow St.; Tel 0503/31758; normal bank hours).*

Tourist Information For info on all things Carlow, go to the **Carlow Tourist Office** *(Kennedy Ave.; Tel 0503/31554; 9:30am-1pm/2-5:30pm Mon-Sat).*

Trains and Buses You can reach Carlow on **Bus Éireann** *(Tel 01/836-61-11),* route 4 on the Dublin-Waterford line, with connections to Athlone and Kilkenny. The bus stops at Barrack Street eight times a day, four times on Sunday, on the way to Waterford. The **Carlow Train Station** *(Railway St., NE of Carlow; Tel 0503/31633)* is on the Dublin-Waterford route as well, making three to five stops daily. It's a bit of a walk (about 20 minutes) from the train station into the center of town: From the station, walk straight down Railway Road, make a left onto Dublin Road, and another left onto College Street.

Bike Rental Pedal your cares away at **Coleman Cycles** *(19 Dublin St.; Tel 0503/31273; 8:30am-7pm Mon-Sat; £5 per day, £25 per week, £40 deposit).*

Postal Drop your mom a line from the **Carlow Post Office** *(corner of Kennedy Ave. and Dublin St.; 9am-5:30pm Mon and Wed-Sat, 9:30am-5:30pm Tue).*

Internet See *wired,* above.

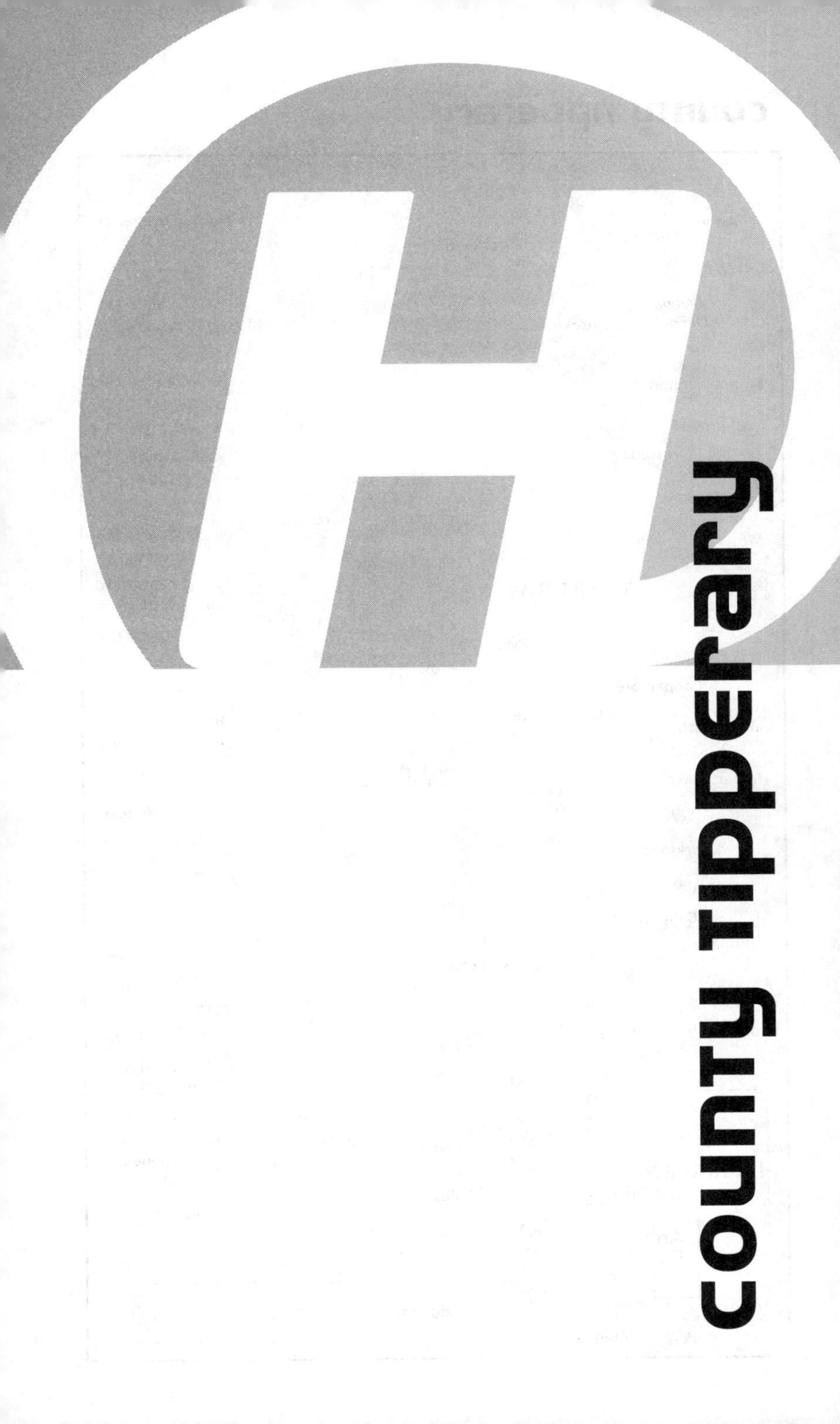
county tipperary

County Tipperary

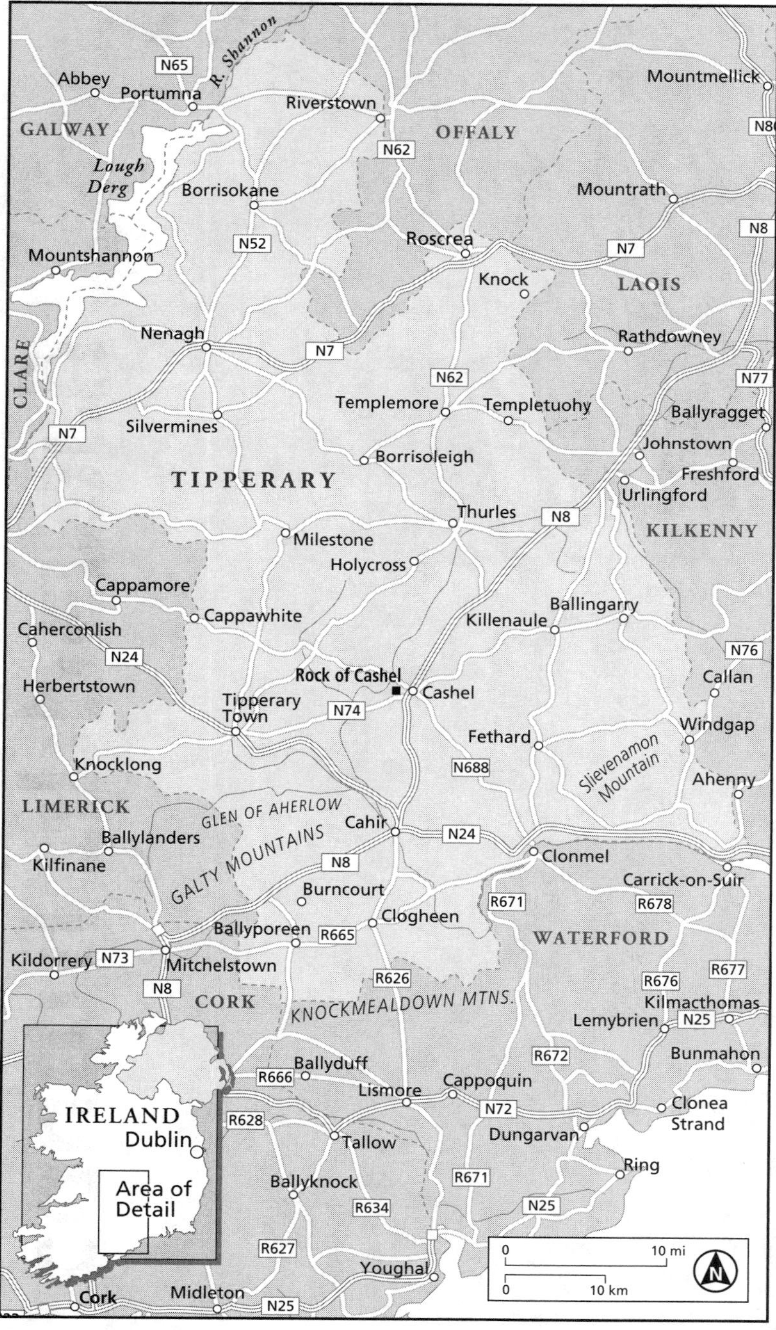

N65
Abbey
Portumna
R. Shannon
Riverstown
Mountmellick
GALWAY
OFFALY
N62
Lough Derg
Borrisokane
Mountrath
N8
N52
Roscrea
N7
Mountshannon
Knock
LAOIS
Nenagh
N7
Rathdowney
CLARE
N62
N77
Templemore
Templetuohy
Ballyragget
N7
Silvermines
Johnstown
Borrisoleigh
Freshford
TIPPERARY
Urlingford
Thurles
N8
KILKENNY
Milestone
Holycross
Cappamore
Ballingarry
Cappawhite
Killenaule
Caherconlish
N76
N24
Callan
Rock of Cashel
Herbertstown
Cashel
Tipperary Town
N74
Windgap
Fethard
Slievenamon Mountain
Knocklong
N688
Ahenny
LIMERICK
GLEN OF AHERLOW
Cahir
N24
Ballylanders
GALTY MOUNTAINS
Clonmel
Kilfinane
N8
Carrick-on-Suir
Burncourt
R671
R678
Clogheen
WATERFORD
Ballyporeen
R665
Kildorrery
N73
Mitchelstown
R677
R626
R676
N8
CORK
KNOCKMEALDOWN MTNS.
Kilmacthomas
Lemybrien
N25
R672
Bunmahon
Ballyduff
R666
Cappoquin
Lismore
Clonea Strand
IRELAND
R628
N72
Dublin
Dungarvan
Tallow
Area of Detail
Ring
Ballyknock
R671
R634
N25
R627
0
10 mi
0
10 km
N
Youghal
Cork
Midleton
N25

cashel

Unless you're visiting your old Uncle Paddy in County Tipperary, if you're in Cashel it's a pretty safe bet that you've come just to see **the Rock** [see *culture zoo,* below], which is actually an ancient fort atop a huge hill. Looking up from the bottom of the hill, you feel about the size of a fruit fly in comparison. The views inside the fortress's walls are awe-inspiring as well. There are guidebooklets available in English, Irish, French, German, Italian, and Spanish, and an audio-visual presentation, "Stonghold of the Faith," which lasts 17 minutes and is available in English, French, German, and Italian. There are several independent tour operators that bring large groups out to the Rock, and the staff at the Rock itself also offers a 45-minute tour, available on request, for groups of as many as 60 people. Note that all groups should be pre-booked. The tour guides are actually full of compelling stories about the Rock, supposedly dropped by the devil in a futile attempt to slow down plucky St. Patrick. Paddy, for his part, brushed the assault aside, picked up a shamrock and made it a symbol for the holy trinity—and all Ireland.

Cashel's identity really centers on the Rock—there isn't much more to the surrounding area except serviceable places to flop and chug. It can be reached from Dublin, Limerick, Cork, or Waterford via **Bus Éireann** [see *need to know,* below]. Once off the bus, just follow the signs for the Rock of Cashel. Aside from the Rock, there's not a whole lot to do in this town, although you could certainly fill the evening after your visit with a good old-fashioned pub crawl or a spruced-up trad and folk session at **BrúBorú** [see *bar and live music scene,* below].

bar and live music scene

Cashel's center for traditional Irish music, **BrúBorú** *(Rock Lane; Tel 062/61122; 9am-5:30pm Oct-Apr, 9am-11pm May-Sept; Free admission to center; £8 show),* looks like a fairly dull community center but offers ripping music performances from mid-June to mid-September on Tuesday through Saturday nights at 9pm. You can have a big ole traditional Irish mutton platter spread during the show for £25 (includes show); the admission price may seem hefty, but it's some of the best live music around, and it makes for a foot-stomping night. BrúBorú also has a heritage center with an evocative mini-museum, self-service cafe, and gift shop peddling fortress-y sorts of wares. Dress nice.

Although Cashel won't win any awards for its pub scene, there are still several places to drink the evening away if you'd rather not fork over £8 for the BrúBorú show. **Ryan's** *(76 Main St.; Tel 062/61431; No credit cards)* has a really cool beer garden and live trad or rock most nights. **Feehan's** *(Main St.; Tel 062/61929; No credit cards)* is a lively little pub with trad on Thursday nights only. Some folks say comfortable **Dowling's** *(Also on Main St.; Tel 062/62130; No credit cards)* serves the best pints in town. Heck, pick any old pub on Main Street and you'll be doing fine. These are all a good deal more relaxed and low-key than Brú Ború, so showing up in your jeans is fine.

culture zoo

If somebody were to compile a list of the "Seven Wonders of Ireland," the rock would probably be on it, judging from the way everyone gushes about its coolness, but don't forget to also check out the town's library.

Rock of Cashel *(Cashel; Tel 062/61437; 9am-7:30pm mid-June to mid-Sept, 9am-4:30pm mid-Sept to mid-Mar, 9am-5:30pm mid-Mar to mid-June; £3.50/£1.50 students):* Set atop a hill overlooking miles of Tipperary countryside, the fortress, known as the Rock, was in the beginning—since about the year 360—the seat of the Kings of Munster. Much later, in 1101, one of the kings granted it to the church. It's sometimes known as "St. Patrick's Rock" because St. Patrick is said to have baptized King Aengus here in 448. By night, when floodlit, the Rock looks even more like the stuff fairy tales are made of. Among the Rock's features are a medieval chapel, round tower, cathedral, graveyard, castle, and a completely restored choral hall, now used as the visitor's center. **Cormac's Chapel,** to the south of the Cathedral, gets our vote for the Rock's Most Remarkable Piece. The interior of the Chapel, begun in the early 12th century, is small, dark, and designed in the Romanesque style, which is extremely unusual in Ireland. Ethereal carved stone heads decorate the walls; it's said that the craftsmen often formed the likenesses of people who owed them money as a not-so-subtle reminder. Mere scraps of fresco remain on the walls today; in 1647, after the Roundheads' invasion devastated the compound, Cromwell had the walls painted over. Only recently, the layers of paint were carefully removed to salvage as much of this medieval work as possible—unfortunately, as it turned out, it wasn't very much.

The **round tower** dates from the 11th or 12th century; it's the oldest building on the Rock, standing 28 meters high. The doorway was built 3.5 meters above the ground to make invasion all the more difficult: While attackers attempted to scramble through the entry, the watchmen at the top of the tower could buy time by hurling rocks at them.

The 13th-century **cathedral** is a Gothic wonder that dominates all the other buildings on the Rock. The western end forms a 15th-century castle that was supposed to serve as the Archbishop's residence, but its cold, damp, dreary interior soon left it deserted. During a storm in the 19th century, a chunk of the building fell to the ground. It still lies there today to give visitors an idea of the extreme width of the walls. Hint: Don't ask if this chunk is the actual "rock"; it's not.

The **Hore Abbey,** built by Cistercian monks in the 13th century, sits across the street from the Rock. To reach it, you take a pleasant walk downhill from the Rock, over a fence, and through a stretch of farmland. The ruins are mildly interesting but by no means fantastic; take a look if you have the time.

GPA-Bolton Library *(John St.; Tel 062/61944; 9:30am-5:30pm Mon-Fri, 2:30-5:30pm Sun; Admission £1.50/£1 students):* Attention, all

the sexton of cashel

There's a story about a certain caretaker of the Rock of Cashel who didn't leave the place for the 60 years preceding his death. The tale begins in County Clare, where Paddy O'Sullivan, the handsomest boy in town, fell in love with a sweet girl named Nora O'Moore, who didn't ever say much. As the *seanachie* (traditional storyteller) who told me this story said, "There are rivers that are quiet on top because they're deep, and more that are quiet because they're not deep enough to make a ripple; when a woman is quiet, it's not easy to say if she's deep or shallow. But Nora was a deep one, and as good as ever drew a breath." Anyway, the feeling was mutual, and Paddy and Nora were planning to marry, when Nora's father decided to promise her to a family from Tipperary Town with a whole lot of sheep and an eligible son who wasn't terribly bright. Nora refused to marry anyone but Paddy, but her putz of a father insisted.

The two lovers planned to elope, but before they were able to, O'Moore tried to take his daughter to Tipperary to marry her off—while pretending that they were going to Ennis for a fair. Nora realized her father was lying to her and tried to escape, but he held onto her too tightly. Luckily, as it would seem, the father took a wrong turn and ended up in Cashel, right beneath the Rock. Nora found her chance to escape while her father was feeding his horse, but he caught up with her as she ran. After a long struggle they both fell down a steep riverbank to their deaths. Nora was buried in Cormac's Chapel and people came from miles around to extol her virtues. Her father was buried in the chapel's graveyard as far away as possible, right near the wall.

Heartbroken, Paddy didn't speak or move for weeks. Eventually Nora's ghost prompted him to leave for Cashel, where he tended to the graves in the graveyard—especially Nora's—for the remainder of his life, communing every night with the spirits of Nora and all the kings and bishops buried there.

The souls of Paddy and Nora may be resting peacefully now, but there must be plenty more who aren't so blissfully reunited with their loved ones. It's probably just as well the Rock isn't open at night for all the ghosts that no doubt linger around the ruins in the moonlight.

bibliophiles: While you're in Cashel, you've gotta check out the GPA-Bolton Library, which boasts the smallest book in the world and many extremely old first editions by Dante, Swift, Newton, and Machiavelli, among others.

eats

Don't come to Cashel expecting gourmet city. The second-floor **Coffee Shop** *(Main St.; Tel 062/61680; 8am-9pm Mon-Sat, 9am-9pm Sun; No credit cards)* may not have a very evocative name, but it offers good quiches, lasagna, sandwiches, and pie for under £5. It's a decent spot for a late lunch if you're waiting for the bus—which stops right outside.

You can also try **Pasta Milano** *(Ladyswell St.; Tel 062/62729; Noon-11pm Mon-Thur, noon-midnight Fri-Sun; £6-11 mains; V, MC)*. Its orange roof is so bright and garish you'll notice it immediately when you're up on the Rock looking down on the town. Fortunately, the pasta and pizza are much more tasteful than the exterior decor.

Come to think of it, your best bet might be to make good use of the hostel kitchen. If you're looking for groceries, the **SuperValu** *(Main St.; Tel 062/61555; 8am-6pm Sun-Wed, 8am-9pm Thur-Sat)* has the largest selection; the **Centra Supermarket** *(Friar St.; No phone; 7am-11pm)* is smaller.

crashing

Going to stay the night? Lucky you: Both Cashel hostels are well above average. **Cashel Holiday Hostel** *(6 John St.; Tel 062/62330; cashelho@iol.ie; £8.50-10 dorms, £24 doubles; No credit cards)* is close to both the Rock of Cashel and the bus stop. If you book far enough in advance, you can get a room with a private bathroom; otherwise, you'll have to share. The hostel has a kitchen for guests to use and a lounge/TV room. There is no curfew or lockout. Two thumbs up: Everything's clean, comfy, and convenient. What more can you ask for? A charming converted stone barn with an attached coach house, **O'Brien's Holiday Lodge** *(St. Patrick's Rock, Dundrum Rd; Tel 062/61003; £10 dorms, £30 doubles; No credit cards)* also is a safe pick. It's practically right under the Rock, just across the street from **Hore Abbey** [see *culture zoo,* above], and you can camp outside and rent bikes. (Although that really isn't necessary to see all there is to see here. In fact, you can just about see the extent of it from the window of your dorm room.) There's no curfew, and there is a kitchen and dining/lounge area. Call ahead; this lovely little spot has only 14 beds.

Other acceptable options include **Bailey's** *(Main St.; Tel 062/61937, Fax 062/62038; info@baileys-ireland.com, www.bailey-ireland.com; £45 single, £35 per person shared, all with private bath, breakfast included; V, MC, AE)*, **Maryville** *(17 Bankplace; Tel 062/61098, Fax 062/61098; www.maryvill.com; £20 per person, all rooms with private bath, breakfast included; V, MC, AE)*, **Ashmore House** *(John St.; Tel 062/61286; Fax 062/62789; ashmorehouse@aircom.net, www.ashmorehouse.com; £27 single,*

miler mcgrath, ace pluralist

The story of Miler McGrath never fails to elicit gasps of surprise and disbelief from visitors to the Rock of Cashel. McGrath served as an archbishop at the Rock between 1571 and 1621; he served simultaneously as a Catholic bishop near Belfast, as well. The man was filthy stinking rich by the end of his life, and after he died it was discovered that he enjoyed income from at least 72 different sources and had embezzled large sums of money from both the Protestant and Catholic churches. As if that weren't enough, this man of God had two wives—one Catholic, one Protestant, each blissfully unaware of the other's existence—and several children by each. Nobody had the faintest idea that anything fishy was going on until they read McGrath's epitaph was read, in which he boasted that he was able to exist in two places at once....

£22-23 per person shared, all with private bath, breakfast included; V, MC, AE), and **Abbey House** *(Dominic St.; Tel 062/61104, Fax 062/61104; geachnamainisteach@aircom.net; £25 single, £20 per person shared with private bath; £25 single, £18 per person shared without private bath, breakfast included; V, MC, AE)*, all in the town center.

need to know

Currency Exchange AIB *(Main St., Cashel; 10am-12:30pm/1:30-4pm Mon-Wed and Fri, 10am-12:30pm/1:30-5pm Thur)* has a Bureau de Change and an ATM.

Tourist Information Cashel Tourist Office *(Town Hall; Tel 062/61333; 9:30am-5pm May-June and Aug-Sept; 9:30am-6pm July)* and **Cahir Tourist Office** *(Castle St., next to Cahir Castle; Tel 052/41453; 10am-6pm daily July-Aug, 9:30am-6pm Mon-Sat mid-Apr through June and Sept)*.

Buses and Trains Bus Éireann *(Tel 062/62121)* runs four buses per day from Main Street, Cashel, to Dublin; three per day to Cork (two on Sundays); four per day to Cahir; and four per day to Limerick. Four or five buses also leave for Waterford every day from Cahir. The bus stop in Cahir is at Cahir Castle. The **Cahir Train Station** *(Off Cashel Rd.; call the Thurles station at 0504/21733 for information)* has one daily stop, Monday through Saturday, on the Waterford-Limerick Junction line. In addition, **Kavanagh's buses** *(Tel 062/51563)* travel

Monday through Saturday between Cashel and Dublin, making stops at Tipperary and Cahir.

Bike Rental McInerney's *(Main St., Cashel; Tel 062/61225; 9:30am-6pm Mon-Sat; £7 per day, £30 per week).*

Postal Cashel Post Office *(Main St.; Tel 062/61418; 9am-1pm/2-5:30pm Mon and Wed-Fri, 9:30am-1pm/2-5:30pm Tue, 9am-1pm Sat).*

cahir

Cahir (pronounced "care") probably isn't going to be an *optional* side trip if you're riding Bus Éireann to get to Cashel. If you're coming from Limerick, you have to switch buses at Cahir to get to Cashel, and because the public bus system here in Ireland is (as we often remind our dear readers) oh-so-efficient, you'll probably be waiting for at least a half-hour, and probably more.

The only place of real interest here is **Cahir Castle** *(Main Cahir St.; Tel 052/41011; 9:30am-5:30pm mid-Mar to mid-June and mid-Sept to mid-Oct, 9am-7:30pm mid-June to mid-Sept, and 9:30am-4:30pm mid-Oct to mid-Mar; Admission £2/£1 students)*, a 13th-century fortress that looks totally out of place next to the bus depot and the little modern shops all around. If you've got awhile, it's definitely worth a look; take a self-guided tours of the castle itself, built on a rock in the River Suir by the Irish chieftain Conor O'Brien. There's also a guided tour of the dramatic grounds, as well as a fascinating 20-minute video on its dark history. You can't miss the castle; the bus drops you off right in front of it.

need to know

Tourist Information The **tourist office** *(Town Hall; Tel 052/41453; Apr-Sept 9:30am-1pm/2-6pm Mon-Sat, July-Aug; also open 11am-5pm Sun)* is right in the center of town.

Directions and Transportation The ubiquitous **Bus Éireann** makes stops in Cahir on several different routes *(Tel 061/313-333 or 062/51-555 for schedules)*. You can also use bus Bernard Kavanagh *(Tel 056/31189 for more information)*, which runs a line from Dublin to Cahir Monday through Saturday. It's around a 2 1/2 hour ride, including all stops.

county kilkenny

County Kilkenny

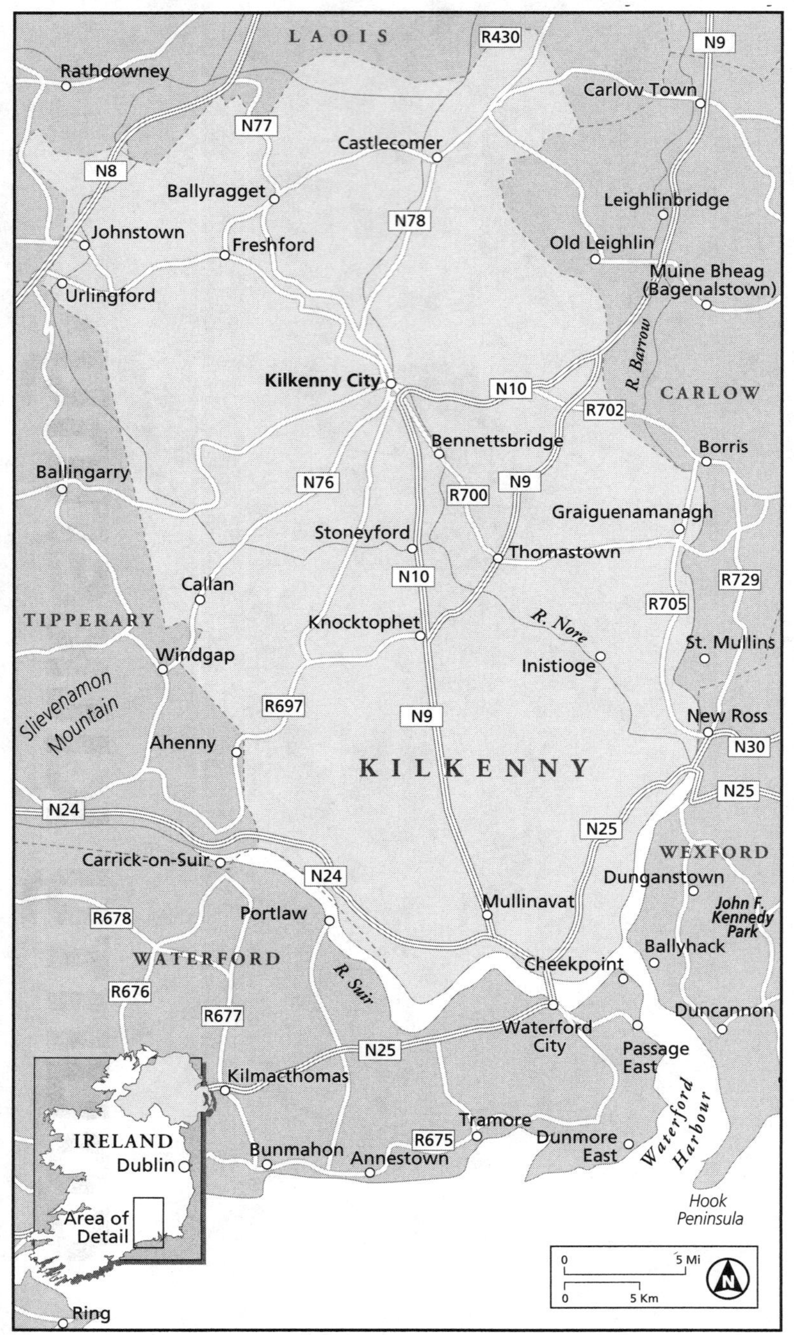
LAOIS
R430
N9
Rathdowney
Carlow Town
N77
Castlecomer
N8
Ballyragget
Leighlinbridge
N78
Johnstown
Freshford
Old Leighlin
Muine Bheag
(Bagenalstown)
Urlingford
R. Barrow
Kilkenny City
N10
CARLOW
R702
Bennettsbridge
Borris
Ballingarry
N76
N9
R700
Graiguenamanagh
Stoneyford
Thomastown
N10
R729
Callan
R705
TIPPERARY
R. Nore
Knocktophet
St. Mullins
Windgap
Inistioge
Slievenamon
Mountain
R697
New Ross
N9
Ahenny
N30
KILKENNY
N25
N24
N25
WEXFORD
Carrick-on-Suir
N24
Dunganstown
John F.
Kennedy
Park
Portlaw
Mullinavat
R678
Ballyhack
WATERFORD
Cheekpoint
R. Suir
R676
Duncannon
R677
Waterford
City
Passage
East
N25
Kilmacthomas
Waterford
Harbour
Tramore
IRELAND
Dunmore
East
Dublin
R675
Bunmahon
Annestown
Hook
Peninsula
Area of
Detail
0
5 Mi
0
5 Km
N
Ring

KILKENNY

Like an old black-and-white movie so charming you'd see it over and over again, Kilkenny, Ireland's foremost medieval city, gets better with age. True, it was more important then than it is now, but you just can't help falling in love (or at least in some serious like) with Kilkenny's quaint little streets, imposing old stone structures, and fantastic pub scene. If you're going to linger in the Southeast, make it a point to spend a good-sized chunk of your time here.

Much of Kilkenny's great architecture has been preserved, and the town hasn't really changed much over the centuries. The River Nore sweeps through the city north to south, with **Kilkenny Castle** [see *culture zoo,* below] dominating the bank. Bridges and waterways add to the city's considerable charm, and the lush countryside offers plenty of opportunities for outings.

neighborhoods

It's a walkable city of narrow streets and arched lanes, with a relatively simple layout: The main street changes names a few times, as is typically Irish, and a bunch of little lanes branch off to the west. Just don't confuse **The Parade,** which fronts Kilkenny Castle, with **Patrick Street.** The Parade and Patrick Street form a sort of lopsided quadrilateral on the map with **Rose Inn Street** at the top. Follow Patrick Street north and it becomes **High Street,** which eventually turns into **Parliament Street.** This street-in-an-identity-crisis is where most of the action is. It ends at **St. Canice's Cathedral** [see *culture zoo,* below], a 13th-century masterpiece of medieval architecture built on the site of the original Church of St. Canice. Face

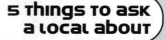

5 things to ask a local about

1. **"What's up with the cats?"** The sporting teams have cats as mascots and the Cat Laughs [see *bar scene,* below] is the most popular comedy venue in town. Any local worth his Kilkenny brew will begin to recite the age-old limerick that begins, "There once were two cats from Kilkenny...."

2. All the gossip might be a little old by now, but nobody's gotten tired of **Dame Alice** yet, especially since her house is still one of the most popular hangouts in town [see *the witch of kilkenny,* below].

3. Ask about the history behind any of the **buildings in town that date from the Middle Ages,** a particularly good topic of conversation should you happen to be at Kyteler's Inn [see *bar scene,* below].

4. As always, you can't miss when asking about the best ***ceol agus craic***—that is, music and fun, although the ubiquitous *craic* doesn't really have a perfect translation. There's a great buzz about the **Whiskers of Lichen,** Maggie's in-house band [see *live music scene,* below].

5. Ask for a **sex on the beach** at Langton's [see *bar scene,* below] and the owner will look at you as though you mean it literally. Good for a laugh.

south on Parliament Street and the street forks into **St. Kieran's Street,** on the left, and High straight ahead. St. Kieran's is home to a few of the coolest pubs in town: **Maggie's,** which hosts fantastic trad sessions several nights a week [see *live music scene,* below], and **Kyteler's Inn** [see *bar scene,* below], now-restored home of the infamous "Witch of Kilkenny" [see *the witch of kilkenny,* below]. For local news and info—and a giggle or two—check out the ***Kilkenny People***, the city's weekly newspaper, available in most places around town.

hanging out

Although 20,000 people call Kilkenny home, the town lacks a central hanging-out spot like the parks or popular little artsy cafes in other cities. The Kilkenny Castle gardens [see *great outdoors,* below] make a good spot for lounging around and taking in the fantabulous Irish scenery. The pubs have especially warm and spirited atmospheres; Kilkenny's younger crowd favors **Ryan's,** the **Pumphouse,** and **Widow McGrath's** [see *bar scene,* below] on weekends; all are great places for kicking back with a few pints and some more or less scintillating conversation.

bar scene

Kilkenny makes pub crawls just too easy. Some of the best are lined up in a row on Parliament Street across from the Watergate Theatre [see *arts scene,* below] and the Kilkenny Tourist Hostel [see *crashing,* below]. Could they have made it any more convenient for us immoderate world-traveling hooligans?

If you're in a medieval mood, check out **Kyteler's Inn** *(27 St. Kieran's St.; Tel 056/21064; V, MC, AE).* It's one of the oldest buildings in the city, dating to 1324, and was once the home of Dame Alice Kyteler, the "Witch of Kilkenny". You can cozy up to a large open fire on a chilly night, or take your pint out into the courtyard when it's sunny (which isn't too often). The pub grub's a bit iffy though; you'll have to take your chances on the Irish stew. The steak might be a safer option.

Bursting at the seams every night of the week, **Caisleán Uí Cuain** *(2 High St.; Tel 056/65406)*—let's call it "Puppy Castle"—is a bit tight size-wise, but it's a comfortable enough place to have your pint. Caisleán Uí Cuain is the pub-bastion of the Irish language in Kilkenny, so you can hear it spoken liberally here. When there's not a trad session going on, the Corrs serve as ear candy.

the witch of kilkenny

Far and away the most colorful character in Kilkenny's history, Dame Alice Kyteler had four husbands—not all at once, naturally—each of whom died under mysterious circumstances. Evidently no one bought that it was a mere coincidence, and since the Church already disapproved of her very lucrative money-lending business, it appeared that she was pretty much headed for the stake. She was formally charged of witchcraft in 1324, but friends in high places imprisoned the accusing bishop in Kilkenny Castle for 17 days. After his release the bishop set up court and, not surprisingly, Dame Alice and her servant girl, Petronella, were sentenced to be thoroughly cooked. The aforementioned friends in high places aided Dame Alice's escape the night before, however, and left poor Petronella to suffer the same fate as a sirloin steak. Dame Alice's son, William Outlawe, bought his way out of a hanging by re-roofing the choir stalls in St. Canice's Cathedral. Her house, supposedly the oldest in town, was restored in the '60s and is now one of the most popular pubs in town [see *bar scene,* above].

wired

Budding Kilkenny entrepreneurs have yet to cash in on the net cafe boom. There are options if you want to check your e-mail, but they aren't terribly comfy or convenient.

You can surf the net at the **Carnegie Library** *(John's Quay; Tel 053/22021; 10:30am-1pm/2-5pm/7-9pm Tue-Wed; 10:30am-1pm/2-5pm Thur-Fri; 10:30am-1:30pm Sat; katlips@iol.ie)*. It'll cost you £5 an hour if you're not a member—and you're not—but for £10 you can become one and get unlimited use. If you're going to be sticking around for awhile, it might make sense to fork over the tenner. You might get lucky, but it's wise to call ahead and make an appointment anyway.

A less comfortable option is **Compustore** *(Market Cross Shopping Centre, unit 12, second floor; Tel 056/71200; 10am-6pm Mon-Wed; 10am-9pm Thur-Fri; cstorekk@iol.ie; £5 per hour)*. There's a solitary clunky machine sitting on a store shelf, sans chair.

For general information about Kilkenny and its environs, check out these websites:

www.kilkenny.ie: Kilkenny information page

homepage.eircom.net/~ocarrold/kilkennycity/index.html: the Kilkenny directory

www.kilkennycraic.com: the "definitive" guide to Kilkenny

kilkenny.gaa.ie: Kilkenny's chapter of the Gaelic Athletic Association

www.kilkennypeople.ie: Kilkenny's weekly newspaper

Hear the *bodhrán* at its best at **Maggie's** *(60 High St.; Tel 056/61017),* which is, at least unofficially, the coolest pub in the city due to its old-style pub atmosphere and excellent live trad. Kilkenny lads and lasses showcase some of the best vocal chords on the island four nights a week, along with the *bodhrán,* lute, guitar, and tin flute. On Wednesdays and Thursdays from April to October the resident band, the Whiskers of Lichen, shakes the floorboards with some lively folk and traditional music. The musicians sing the old ballads so passionately you'd swear they were the ones who wrote them. It's no surprise that this place is hopping like a jackrabbit on steroids. Good luck finding a seat. FYI: Just to confuse you, there are two separate facades—one for Jim Holland's and one for Maggie's—but they both lead to the same pub.

Across St. John's Bridge on the east side of the Nore River, is **Edward Langton's** *(69 John St.; Tel 056/65133; V, MC, AE).* Decked out with a sleek horseshoe-shaped bar, posh booths, sofas, and an elegant, modern ambience, it's not your typical pub. It's best not to try the pub grub though; the prices are high, the service is poor, and the food itself is rather bland. It's a bit of a surprise that it's won so many awards, for "best pub in Ireland" and whatnot; it's nice, but not *that* nice.

Nobody's grieving at **Widow McGrath's** *(29 Parliament St.; Tel 056/52520),* a popular hangout for Kilkenny youth, especially on the weekends. The Widow's is much more spacious and modern than Caisleán Uí Cuain or Maggie's. The beer garden out back makes a nice place to enjoy an especially good lunch menu with a nice lukewarm pint on sunny days.

If you want to linger for awhile at any one pub on the Parliament strip, let it be **The Pumphouse** *(26 Parliament St.; Tel 056/63924; No credit cards).* The pool table, dartboard, cheap sandwiches, and lively vibe make it a popular spot with rowdy young Irishmen. The Pumphouse has one of the best pub grub menus, and the live rock, blues, and folk sessions on Sunday nights make a nice change from the ubiquitous trad. It's definitely one of the coolest places for meeting people and hanging out.

Set on a side street off the southern edge of High Street, **Andrew Ryan's** *(3 Friary St.; Tel 056/62281)* is your quintessential Irish pub, with live trad Thursday and Friday nights year-round, a young local crowd, and a beer garden out back. The music isn't quite as typical as the atmosphere, though: Sessions have been known to include Australian aboriginal sounds. If you're up for it, bring your own guitar or violin—all musicians are welcome.

On the northwest periphery of the old town, the **Cat Laughs** *(Dean St.; Tel 056/64398),* as you might guess, is run by the organizers of Kilkenny's annual Cat Laughs Comedy Festival [see *festivals and events,* below]. The bar's got a cool cosmopolitan feel, although the place is best known for its theater, the Mouse Trap, with comedy acts several nights a week [see *arts scene,* below]. You can usually find a live band playing here on a Saturday night as well.

Want less drink and more laid-back conversation? **Tynan's Bridge Bar** *(2 Horseleap Slip, at St. John's Bridge; Tel 056/21921),* a well-preserved Victorian pub, is the perfect place. Red oil lamps and watercolors adorn the walls, and Sinatra songs play softly on the stereo. You could spend all night drinking Bailey's at the classy horseshoe-shaped bar while discussing the meaning of life with your travel buddy, if that's your thing. Tynan's won't be jamming, maybe because it's a bit off the beaten path, but that's why it's so darn likeable. Upcoming renovations will provide more space that'll be used for live music sessions; it's a little too small to accommodate musicians as is.

live music scene

You won't be hard-pressed to find music in Kilkenny—most nights of the week trad spills from the pubs. Music usually begins between 9 and 9:30pm in the pubs, although some musicians take their sweet time setting up, especially at Caisleán Uí Cuain—you might have to wait awhile before hearing any music other than what's coming out of the CD player. The best places in town for trad are **Maggie's** *(Mon-Thur)* and **Ryan's**

(Thur-Fri) [see *bar scene,* above, for both]. **John Cleere's** [see *arts scene,* below], in addition to an entertaining open mic night on Wednesdays, has the longest-running trad session in Kilkenny on Monday nights.

You can also find live trad at the **Widow McGrath's** on Wednesdays, **Langton's** on Mondays, Fridays, and Saturdays, and at **Caisleán Uí Cuain** on Mondays and Tuesdays [see *bar scene,* above, for all]. **Kyteler's** [see *bar scene,* above] also has trad on Thursday and Sunday nights. Sometimes the music schedules vary, but there's definitely live music at least a few places every night of the week, so you won't be disappointed.

There's also a super-popular live rock, blues, and folk happenin' at **The Pumphouse** [see *bar scene,* above] on Sundays beginning at 9:30pm.

club scene

There are only a few nightclubs here in Kilkenny, but with such a fabulous pub scene, nobody notices. Times are 11pm-2am across the board. Expect to pay more here for drinks than you would in the pubs.

Taking its name from the best-loved emperor in Roman history, **Nero's** *(St. Kieran's St.; Tel 056/21064; 11pm-2am Thur-Sat; Cover £5-7)* is part of Kyteler's Inn (that Alice was one shrewd businesswoman). The setup is pretty traditional for a disco: top 40 and cheesy '70s hits on two floors, full bar, and a relatively strict dress code—no "runners" or "trainers" allowed (that's sneakers and wind-pants to you). Nero's gets packed, especially on weekends, so be sure to wear your Arrid Extra Dry.

Locals consider **Langton's** *(69 John St.; Tel 056/65133; Tue, Thur-Sun; Cover £5-8)* to be the nicest club in town, probably because it's situated in the posh reception hall in Langton's Hotel. The music's pretty much the same as at Nero's, with the same dress code. The bar and seating area is separate from the dance floor, which is nice if you'd actually like to hear what your partner is saying to you.

The Flagstone Winebar *(Parliament St.; 11:30pm-2am Thur-Sun, Wed-Sun in summer; Cover £5, no cover Sun)* is the coziest club in town.

lad meets lassie

Perhaps the best place to meet people in Kilkenny is...what's this?!...the library? Since everybody goes to the **Carnegie Library** *(John's Quay; Tel 053/22021; 10:30am-1pm/2-5pm/7-9pm Tue-Wed; 10:30am-1pm/2-5pm Thur-Fri; 10:30am-1:30pm Sat)* to check e-mail, it's almost guaranteed you won't have to hang out too long before running into somebody else who's looking to put the "hot" back in "hotmail."

festivals and events

Kilkenny Arts Week *(mid-Aug; Tel 056/63663; http://www.kilkennyarts.ie; tickets free-£12 per event, some student discounts):* This is Ireland's longest-established and best arts festival, drawing all ages to its program of street theater, classical and contemporary music, jazz, and film events. There are innumerable art exhibitions. Young people from all over Ireland and Britain, including many international travelers, show up here as well, not just for the main festival itself, but for "The Fringe Festival" that has grown up in recent years around the main festival. The Fringe Festival is more cutting edge and youth oriented. Amateur musicians show up; there is spontaneous open-air theater, poetry readings, displays of provocative art, a general sense of fun and outrageousness. The town is booked to the gills during the festival and advance reservations are important. Festival time is the most fun and happening time for a young budget traveler to show up.

Murphy's Cat Laughs Comedy Festival *(early June; Tel 056/63416 for info, 056/63837 for booking; laughs@iol.ie, www.murphyscatlaughs.com; £8-14):* Kilkenny's best-loved comedy venue brings you Kilkenny's best-loved comedy festival early every summer. It brings together some of Ireland's funniest comedians as well as several from abroad. You might have seen Jeremy Hotz, Harland Williams, or Ed Byrne on Conan O'Brien's show, and that's just the beginning of a very long list. Comedians perform at the Mouse Trap as well as at the Watergate [see *arts scene,* below], in addition to several pubs in town. Don't wait to get your tickets, and book your room way in advance even if you aren't into stand-up—plenty of other people are, and they'll all be here.

You can dress down here, but there's no beer, so skip it if you've just gotta have that Kilkenny brew. The bar serves wine, cider, and alcoholic soft drinks. There's none of that hokey disco stuff here; the music of choice is techno, and live bands play on Thursday nights.

arts scene

▸▸VISUAL ARTS

There are two galleries inside Kilkenny Castle [see *culture zoo,* below]: The **Long Gallery** *(Tours conducted hourly as part of the guided tour of the castle; £3.50 adults, £1.50 students)* houses a large collection of Butler family portraits—they lived here from 1391 to 1935—in a wing of the castle with cool tapestries and ceilings painted with Celtic motifs. The

Butler Gallery *(Kilkenny Castle, Tel 056/61106; 10:30am-5pm Apr-May; 10am-7pm June-Sept; 10:30am-12:45pm/2-5pm Mon-Sat, 11am-12:45pm/2-5pm Sun Oct-May; butlergal@indigo.ie; Free)* shows some of the best Irish and international contemporary art outside of Dublin, with about 11 exhibitions a year. The **Watergate Theatre** [see *performing arts,* below] also houses visiting exhibitions of contemporary Irish art.

▸▸PERFORMING ARTS

John Cleere's *(28 Parliament St.; Tel 056/62573)* has a darkened back room and stage to encourage local gigs. The open mic night on Wednesdays is always well attended but has a £2 cover charge. Most shows start around 8:15pm or 9:30pm. You can catch poetry readings, plays, and comedy sessions here in addition to rock, blues, and trad music.

The Mouse Trap *(Dean St.; Tel 056/64339)* at the Cat Laughs pub [see *bar scene,* above] offers popular comedy acts on Wednesday nights, as well as musical events on Tuesdays, mostly trad and blues.

The Watergate Theatre *(Parliament St. near St. Canice's Place; Tel 056/61674; watergatetheatre.homepage.com; £4-10)* is one of Ireland's newest, was opened in 1993 by then-prez Mary Robinson. Both local and visiting professional theater companies grace its stage in a comfy little 328-seat theater. Performances range from drama to musicals, ballet, opera, and popular music concerts. Hey, they even do Rodgers and Hammerstein! There's a performance pretty much every night, and it's a good choice if you're all pubbed out.

culture zoo

Because Kilkenny is Ireland's major medieval city, the city and surrounding area are filled with impressive old structures bearing histories richer than chocolate mousse.

Pat Tynan *(Tel 056/65929; 9:15am, 10:30am, 12:15pm, 1:30pm, 3pm, 4:30pm Mon-Sat, 11am, 12:15pm, 2pm, 3pm Sun, Mar-Oct; 10:30am, 12:15pm, 3pm Tue-Sat, Nov-Feb; tynantours@eircom.ie; Admission £3 adults, £2.50 students):* You can take an hour-long walking tour of the city with local historian Pat Tynan. Pat's walking tours are loaded with

run, spot, run

If greyhound racing's your thing, check out **St. James' Park** *(Freshford Rd.; Tel 056/21214; Races begin at 8:15pm Wed and Fri; £3 Wed, £4 Fri).* The price of admission includes a race card and the park is open all year. Betting windows are available, but the place is relatively sleaze-free.

local anecdotes and lore, and rich with the twinkling-eyed humor of a genuine Irish wit. Tours depart from the tourist office on Rose Inn Street [see *need to know,* below] pretty much every hour daily from March to October; check with the Tourist Office.

The Black Abbey *(Abbey St. off Parliament St.; Tel 056/21279; 7:30am-7pm Mon-Sat, 9am-7pm Sun Mar-Sept; 7:30am-5:30pm Mon-Sat Oct-Mar, no visits during worship; Free):* The Black Abbey might sound like a good name for a Goth nightclub, but it's actually a 13th-century Dominican church. Oliver Cromwell did quite a number on the abbey in the mid-1600s; after he was done using it as a courthouse there wasn't much left. Fortunately, it was fully restored in 1979. Nobody's entirely sure why it's called the Black Abbey—perhaps it's either because of the Dominicans' black habits or because the Black Plague in the mid-14th century significantly decreased their number. A bit of a stretch. At any rate, it's worth a look.

St. Canice Cathedral *(Coach Rd. near north end of Parliament St.; Tel 056/64971; 9am-1pm Mon-Sat and 2-6pm daily Easter-Oct, 10am-1pm Mon-Sat and 2-4pm daily Oct-Easter; stcanicescathedral@eircom.net; £1 donation requested):* The second-largest medieval cathedral in Ireland, St. Canice Cathedral was built in the 13th century on the site of the 6th-century Church of St. Canice. It's just packed with cool stuff: 3,000 books from the 16th and 17th centuries, stone carvings, stained-glass windows, and a round tower (possibly belonging to the original church) with excellent views that you can climb for £1. The tower's 100 feet high and 14.6 feet in diameter—not for acrophobes. Or claustrophobes. The acrophobes who also happen to fear tight spaces should *definitely* stay at ground level.

Kilkenny Castle *(The Parade; Tel 056/21450; 10:30am-5pm Apr-May; 10am-7pm June-Sept; 10:30am-12:45pm/2-5pm Mon-Sat and 11am-12:45pm/2-5pm Sun; Admission £3.50 adults, £1.50 students):* Kilkenny Castle is the most historically important structure in the city, a splendid mishmash of Gothic, Tudor, and Classical architectural styles. Built in the early 13th century and home to many long-dead men with fancy titles, the now-restored castle houses both the Long Gallery and the Butler Gallery [see *arts scene,* above], gardens, a bookshop, and a tearoom during the summer months. The Long Gallery showcases the family portrait collection of the Butler family, the industrial barons who transformed the castle from a drafty fortress into a glamorous showcase of 19th-century gilded-age wealth. The gallery's wooden hammerbeam roof is profusely decorated in the Pre-Raphaelite style, the creation of John Hungerford Pollen in 1861. It's a gay romp of exotic beasts, birds, and cannibalistic-looking plant life. The Long Gallery can be visited only as part of an hourly guided tour of the castle itself. The Butler Gallery, in the castle's former kitchens, houses changing exhibitions of contemporary art. Entrance is free with admission to the castle.

Shee Alms House *(Rose Inn St.; Free):* The Kilkenny tourist office has taken over the Shee Alms House, which once served as a poorhouse beginning in the late 16th century. The only freebies you can get here now are maps of the city.

Kilkenny

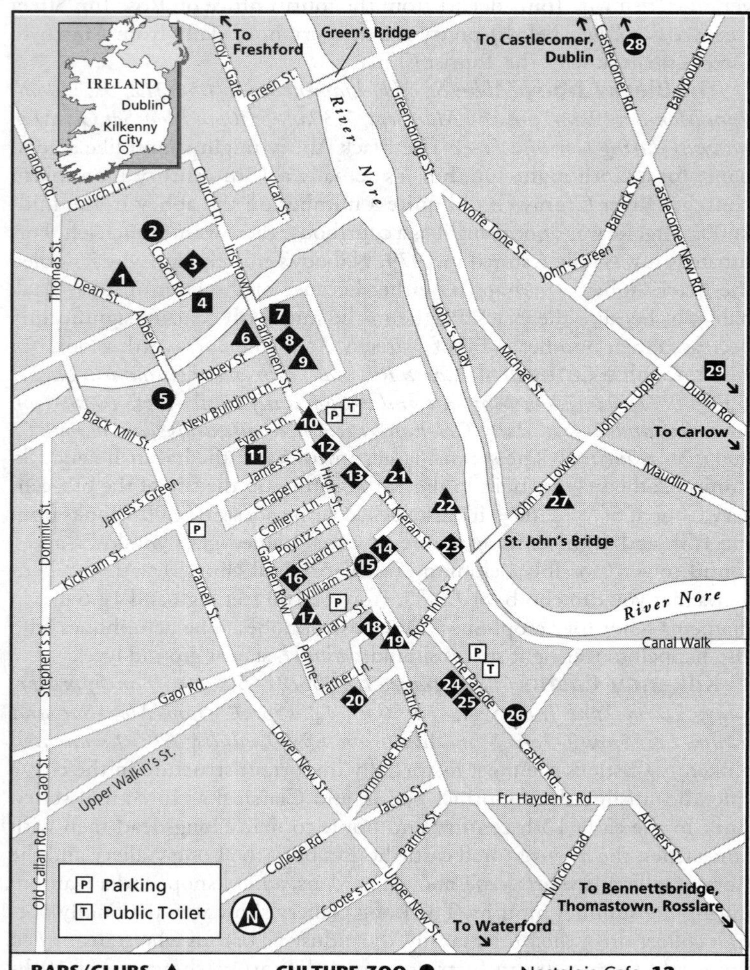

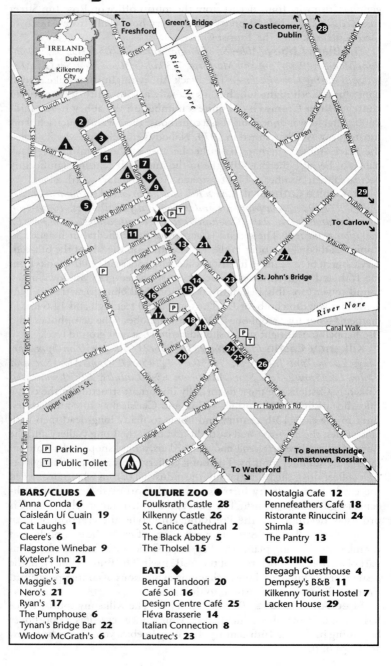

BARS/CLUBS ▲
Anna Conda **6**
Caisleán Uí Cuain **19**
Cat Laughs **1**
Cleere's **6**
Flagstone Winebar **9**
Kyteler's Inn **21**
Langton's **27**
Maggie's **10**
Nero's **21**
Ryan's **17**
The Pumphouse **6**
Tynan's Bridge Bar **22**
Widow McGrath's **6**

CULTURE ZOO ●
Foulksrath Castle **28**
Kilkenny Castle **26**
St. Canice Cathedral **2**
The Black Abbey **5**
The Tholsel **15**

EATS ◆
Bengal Tandoori **20**
Café Sol **16**
Design Centre Café **25**
Fléva Brasserie **14**
Italian Connection **8**
Lautrec's **23**
Nostalgia Cafe **12**
Pennefeathers Café **18**
Ristorante Rinuccini **24**
Shimla **3**
The Pantry **13**

CRASHING ■
Bregagh Guesthouse **4**
Dempsey's B&B **11**
Kilkenny Tourist Hostel **7**
Lacken House **29**

The Butter Slip You'll probably pass through the Butter Slip, which connects High and St. Kieran's streets. For centuries, this was where you went to buy butter on market days. The short, narrow alleyway bears some of the aura of its medieval construction, but with a series of side-by-side small shops that today include a stationery store and a hairdresser.

The Tholsel *(High St. near tourist office; Free):* The Tholsel, built in 1761 out of black Kilkenny marble, is a rather odd-looking building with a clock tower and front arcade—great for rainy days when you need to check the map. It originally served as a tollhouse and often hosted social gatherings, but the kegs and party hats have given way to the city's municipal archives. Dame Alice Kyteler's maid, Petronella, was burned at the stake here in 1324 for alleged witchcraft [see *the witch of Kilkenny,* above].

St. John's Priory *(John St. across St. John's Bridge; Free):* Built in the early 13th century, St. John's was once known for its exquisite windows. Though the outlying sections now lie in ruins, thanks to that pesky Cromwell character, the central part remains intact. Religious services are still held here, and it's a vital part of the religious fabric of Kilkenny. It's one of the most evocative sights of Ireland's finest medieval city—fun to prowl about the manicured lawns and imagine what life used to be like here.

Kilkenny College *(John St. near St. John's Bridge):* Around the corner from St. John's Priory is Kilkenny College, the alma mater of Jonathan Swift. Built in the mid-17th century, it is now Kilkenny's county hall.

Rothe House *(Parliament St.; Tel 056/22893; 10:30am-5pm Mon-Sat, 3-5pm Sun Apr-Oct; 1-5pm Mon-Sat, 3-5pm Sun Nov-Mar; heritage@heritage.iol.ie; Admission £2 adults, £1.50 students):* Rothe House was once a merchant's home in the late 16th century. Now it showcases a collection of period costumes and artifacts belonging to the Kilkenny Archaeological Society as well as visiting exhibitions. No playing dress-up here, but it's still worth a brief detour.

St. Mary's Cathedral *(James St. near Blackmill St.; Free)* was built between 1842 and 1856, during the darkest period of the Potato Famine. Consequently, there's not much transcendent joy in the rather pedestrian architecture of this somber-looking church. Even so, it's one of the most beloved and best-attended Roman Catholic churches in town.

St. Mary's Parish Church *(behind the Tholsel; No phone; Free):* This early-13th-century church is yet another example of medieval Kilkenny. (Are you sick of this stuff yet?)

Smithwick Brewery *(Parliament St. near the Kilkenny Tourist Hostel; Tel 056/21014; Tours at 3pm, Mon-Fri May-Sept; Free):* Ah, this is more like it. The Smithwick Brewery, dating from 1710, occupies the site of what was once a Franciscan monastery. Behind it, the 13th-century **St. Francis' Abbey,** ruined by—you guessed it—Cromwell, is open to the public as well. Rumor has it the monks were pretty good brewsky-makers. As for the brewery itself, pick up a free ticket from the tourist office and you can sit in for a "show." Read: free beer tastings. How can you pass that one up?

modification

There are no tattoo parlors here, but for ear and nose piercing, try the **Jewel Box** *(54 High St.; Tel 056/21055; 9:30am-6pm Mon-Sat; jewelbox54@hotmail.com; V, MC, AE),* which provides a discount for those staying at the Kilkenny Tourist Hostel—just mention the sign on the notice board. There's no better way to take the plunge into pierced-hood than at the hand of a friendly old Irishman. (Don't worry; he's sober.)

great outdoors

If you're looking to give your upper arms a workout, call Charlie and Clem Horan, who operate **Go with the Flow River Adventures** *(Tel 0509/31307; £25 per day, special rates available; www.gowiththeflow.ie),* a tour company specializing in excursions on rivers throughout Ireland. In this region, most tours will be on either the Barrow or the Nore rivers, but there are other alternatives. Tours are individually arranged and must be set up several weeks or (in low season) a week in advance. Their headquarters lie in the hamlet of Rosecrea, northwest of Kilkenny, but you don't ever have to show up there—once advance arrangements have been made, you're informed of the starting point of the tour.

The **Countryside Leisure Activity Centre** *(Bonnettsrath; Tel 056/61791),* 2 miles northeast of the center, offers archery, quad motor bikes, indoor rifle target shooting, and—what's this?—clay-pigeon shooting. Don't worry; it's perfectly humane. Unfortunately no public transportation runs to the Activity Centre, so you'll have to hoof it.

After you've checked out the races at **Gowran Park** [see *gowran park,* below], you can do your own riding at **Top Flight Equestrian Centre**

gowran park

Gowran Park *(Mill Road, Gowran; Tel 056/26120),* a bit of a hike (about 8 miles) from Kilkenny City, is a small but choice racetrack that attracts some of the biggest names in horseracing. It is popular with gamblers and equestrian types alike, and cultivates some very stylish, elite socializing around the subject of horsebreeding.

You can catch a bus to the track for a few punts; **Foley's bus service** *(Tel 0503/24410; Mon-Sat)* connects Kilkenny to Gowran Park. Races are only once or twice a month; call the race course or ask in the Kilkenny tourist office for dates and times.

(Warrington, off Bennettsbridge Rd.; Tel 053/22682; Open year-round; £10 per hour), just south of Kilkenny.

All right, so it's not technically outdoors, but if by chance you're feeling Piscean it's your only feasible option. **James Stephens' Swimming Pool** *(John's Quay, off Michael St.; Tel 053/21380; 7am-10pm Tue-Sat, 10am-9pm Sun)* is public and just down the street from the library. Opening times can vary though, so call extension 222 to verify hours.

Surrounded by acres of lawn, flowers, and fountains, the **Kilkenny Castle gardens** *(Kilkenny Castle, The Parade; 10am-8:30pm daily in summer; Free)* are free to enjoy and open until dusk. It's the perfect place for a picnic. For picnic food, check out one of the gourmet food stores in town [see *eats,* below]. The walk along the canal is picturesque and quiet (because nobody else is as well-informed as you are).

Rent a bike from **Kilkenny Cycles** or **J.J. Walls Bike Hire** [see *need to know,* below] and pedal on through that pretty Kilkenny countryside—it's fairly level riding with a few tiny hills here and there. Kells Priory, Jerpoint Abbey, and Duiske Abbey are within a few miles and the riverside villages—Thomastown, Inistoige, Bennettsbridge, and Graiguenamanagh—are all lovely places to spend an afternoon.

STUFF

This city's a great place to find Irish crafts from all over the country. The **Kilkenny Design Centre** *(Castle Yard, The Parade; Tel 056/22118; 9am-6pm, closed Sun Jan-Mar; V, MC, AE),* located in what were once the stables and coach house across from Kilkenny Castle, stocks really nice wool sweaters with Celtic designs, pottery, crystal, and jewelry. Yeah, it's all here, and it might be expensive but it's really, really nice. There's also a cafe upstairs [see *eats,* below].

For odds and ends, try the 40 or so shops at the **Market Cross Shopping Centre** *(Off High St.; Tel 056/52666; 9am-6pm Mon-Sat, 9am-9pm Thur-Fri).*

P. T. Murphy Jewelers *(85 High St.; Tel 056/21127; www.gemnet.co.uk/ptmurphy)* is a good place to find Irish *claddagh* jewelry. In addition to nose rings, the **Jewel Box** [see *modification,* above] sells Irish handmade jewelry. The silver, gold, and platinum designs of **Rudolf Heltzel** *(10 Patrick St.; Tel 056/21497; 9:30am-1pm/2-5:30pm Mon-Sat; V, MC)* are funky and unusual.

Kilkenny Irish Crystal *(Canal Sq.; Tel 056/61377; V, MC)* is said to be cut at a deeper angle than Waterford, so locals claim it's of a finer quality. You be the judge.

Browsing in **Yesterdays** *(30 Lower Patrick St.; 9:30am-6pm Mon-Sat, open Sun July-Aug; V, MC, AE, DC)* is like entering a Victorian time warp. Period-inspired jewelry, perfume bottles, blankets, porcelain dolls, dollhouse furniture, teddy bears, framed prints—it's fun even if you're too old to play with dolls.

At **Seamus Malone Pottery** *(Castle Yard; Tel 056/63335; seamusmalone@tinet.ie; V, MC),* there's something you don't see every day in the typical Irish craft shop: hand-carved one-of-a-kind mirrors. Oh yeah, and pottery too.

▸▸TUNES

Pick up the latest pop single at **Top 20** *(St. Kieran's St.),* which also serves as a Ticketmaster outlet. **Irish Heartbeat** *(High St.; Tel 056/52949; 9:30am-6pm Sat-Wed, 9am-9pm Thur-Fri)* sells only Irish and country music.

▸▸BOUND

You can pick up a used book at **Ossory Bookshop** *(67 High St.).* If you prefer a cup of joe with your literary pursuits, **The Book Centre** *(10 High St.; Tel 056/62117; V, MC)* has a well-stocked Irish studies section, a selection of international newspapers, and a cafe upstairs [see *eats,* below].

▸▸FOOT FETISH

How about a pair of china blue and lavender high-heeled leather mary janes? **Graham Shoes Ltd.** *(13 High St.; Tel 056/21183; V, MC)* must be hip—they've got a store in Dublin as well.

eats

There's no shortage of great places to eat in Kilkenny City, and the presence of two gourmet food stores ensures you'll be eating well no matter what. For picnics, try **The Gourmet Store** *(56 High St.),* in the center of town, which makes delicious hot and cold sandwiches for under £2. The other option is the funkily named **Shortis Wong's** *(75 John St.; Tel 056/61305),* which serves a wide variety of well-stuffed sandwiches and baked goods. If you need a change of pace, they also sell spring rolls and samosas. Most items are under £3. For dinner, you could cop out and pick up a frozen pizza and a club orange at **Dunnes Stores** *(St. Kieran's St.; Open till 7pm Mon-Tue and Sat, till 9pm Wed-Fri, till 6pm Sun)* or **Superquinn** *(Second floor, Market Cross Shopping Centre, off High St.; Open till 7pm Mon-Tue, till 9pm Wed-Fri, till 6pm Sat).*

All the pubs serve decent food, too. Expect to pay £4-7 for lunch and £5-10 for dinner. Try **The Pumphouse** or **Caisleán Uí Cuain** [see *bar scene,* above]; both serve food till around 8pm.

▸▸CHEAP

The Pantry *(St. Kieran's St.; Tel 056/62250; Dinner main courses £4.50-6.50, most items under £4)* has food that's fast but not fast food. It's cheap and convenient, but the food is by no means spectacular. Laugh at the servers in their funny white hats while munching on a burger and chips for £3 or a full Irish breakfast for £4.

Pennefeathers Café *(10 High St., second floor; Tel 056/64063; 9am-5pm; Under £5),* above the Book Centre, is a good choice for breakfast or lunch. The fare's pretty much standard, with all sorts of sandwiches for only a few punts and a full Irish breakfast for £3.95. Its functional, almost spartan decor reflects the thrift and no-nonsense simplicity of life in 1930s Ireland.

All that shopping wear you out? The upstairs **Design Centre Café** *(The Parade; Tel 056/65905; 9am-5pm Mon-Sat Jan-Apr; 9am-6pm Mon-Sat May-Dec; Under £7; V, MC, AE, DC)* sure is convenient for lunch. It's a cool, laid-back place to hang out, with white walls, circular windows, and a high-beamed ceiling. The menu's pretty standard—seafood and meat dishes, salads, soups, and pastries—but it's all fresh.

Café Sol *(William St. off High St.; Tel 056/64987; 10am-6pm Mon-Sat, noon-4pm Sun, 7-10pm Wed-Sat; Lunch £4-6; V, MC),* known far and wide as one of Ireland's best restaurants, is the place to go to enjoy a quiet meal. The food's got a definite Mediterranean bent to match the sunny decor, and it's totally delicious. Full Irish breakfast goes for £4.50, or try the vegetable curry and yogurt for less than £5 along with a nice cold glass of homemade lemonade. Don't miss out on dessert. Heck, order anything on the menu and you'll be happy.

Other inexpensive options include **Fléva Brasserie** *(84 High St.; Tel 056/70021; Noon-4pm Tue-Wed, noon-4pm/6-8pm Thur-Sun; Lunch £3-5, dinner from £7; AE, MC, V),* where the menu ranges from the traditional (Kilkenny meatloaf with potatoes, £5) to the "modern Irish" (a toasted baguette filled with hot chicken in lemon dill sauce for under £5), and the **Nostalgia Café** *(High St.; Tel 056/63374; 8am-6pm self service, 6-11pm table service; £4-10 per entree),* hands-down the kitschiest joint in the city.

▸▸DO-ABLE

In the mood for pasta but trying to skimp? **Italian Connection** *(38 Parliament St.; Tel 056/64225; Noon-11pm daily; £5-15; V, MC)* is perfectly adequate, although it's not quite as good as the pricier Ristorante Rinuccini [see below]. Between noon and 3pm, you can grab a lunch special here for five or six punts. The decor's artful yet warm minimalism might have been inspired by a decorator in Milan: wine casks, dark woods, crisp linens. Italian Connection is popular as a pre- or post-theater option, since it's so close to the Watergate Theatre [see *arts scene,* above].

Does a six-punt three-course lunch sound like heaven to you? Skip merrily to **Lautrec's Bistro** *(9 St. Kieran's St.; Tel 056/62720; Noon-10:30pm; Dinner £6-15; V, MC, AE),* where the menu consists of expertly concocted Italian and Mexican dishes, as well as fresh seafood. As always, lunch is a much better value, so come in the early afternoon and bring your appetite. Decorated in a simplified modern version of Art Nouveau, the place has the warm, appealing ambience of an Irish wine bar and bistro.

Looking for something a bit more exotic? Kilkenny's got two classy Indian restaurants: **Bengal Tandoori** *(Pudding Lane; Tel 056/64722 or 056/64707; Noon-2:30pm Mon-Sat, 6-11pm Mon-Thur, 6pm-midnight Fri-Sat, 5-11pm Sun; V, MC),* which offers an all-you-can-eat lunch for £8 between 1pm and 5pm on Sunday, and **Shimla** *(6 Dean St.; 056/23788; Under £10).*

▸▸SPLURGE

Located across the street from the castle, **Ristorante Rinuccini** *(1 The Parade, Kilkenny Circle; Tel 056/61575; Lunch £4-8, dinner £8-15; V, MC, AE, DC)* is highly recommended by everybody who's ever eaten there. No wonder: The Italian and Irish owners try hard to please and the atmosphere is intimate, elegant, and romantic. That's not even mentioning the food—fresh seafood and meats and homemade pasta. Lunch is a better value than dinner, unless you get there early for the specials between 6 and 7pm; try the tomato and basil soup along with vegetable pasta and Italian meatballs for lunch.

crashing

While there's no shortage of B&B's, there aren't a lot of hostels to choose from in Kilkenny, although the ones that are here are better than average. Hotels get extremely pricey here; a lot of the guesthouses are less expensive and just as luxurious. During the summer and comedy and arts festival weeks, they can fill up; try to book in advance.

▸▸CHEAP

When in Kilkenny, your absolute first choice ought to be the **Kilkenny Tourist Hostel** *(35 Parliament St.; Tel 056/63541; kilkennyhostel@tinet.ie; £10 dorm, £11.50-£13 per person doubles or quad; No credit cards),* in an 18th-century Georgian townhouse within spitting distance of half-a-dozen of the best pubs in the city. Bright comfortable decor, friendly staff, clean spacious dorms, and a spirited social vibe make the Kilkenny Tourist Hostel the best place to stay in the city. An excellent and informative events board in the front room, updated daily, will tell you where to find trad sessions, plays, and whatever else is going on that night. There's even more information in an alphabetized box of index cards on the sitting-room table. Most hostellers prefer to cook in the

kilkenny history

Kilkenny, or *Cill Chainnigh,* means "St. Canice's Church." It was founded in the 6th century by none other than the illustrious St. Canice herself. The city, like most others in Ireland, was dominated by the Normans beginning in the 12th century. The Statutes of Kilkenny are one of the first recorded forms of apartheid, starting in 1366 between the Normans and the Irish. Because of the city's central location on the banks of the River Nore, Kilkenny flourished as a walled city, and many parliaments attended by stuffy old men were held within its walls. Kilkenny was the center of the resistance against Cromwell in 1642, but from the looks of some of the buildings it's obvious it wasn't terribly successful. It's a matter of sheer luck that so much of the city's brilliant medieval architecture has actually survived—with a little touching-up here and there, of course.

bright airy kitchen and eat in the dining room that's always abuzz with activity, even impromptu music sessions. You just can't say enough about this place: It's graced with candles, mellow music on the CD player, incense burning, and one of the most comfortable sitting rooms in any hostel in Ireland. There's always a fire burning in the fireplace on a cold rainy night (which is basically every night). Did we mention how great this place is?

Foulksrath Castle *(Jenkinstown, 13 km (8 mi) north of Kilkenny; Tel 056/67144 or 056/67674; Mar-Oct; £5.50-7.50 dorm, continental breakfast £2.50; No credit cards)* is Ireland's oldest hostel in two ways: This Norman-style tower house dates from the 15th century, and it was opened as a hostel in 1938. This place is absolutely beautiful, but the tower, huge dining hall, fireplaces, and spiral staircase come with a price: The dorm rooms can be cold and echoey. You'll deal with it for the sake of the authentic atmosphere. ("Hey Ma, I stayed in a *castle* for ten bucks!") **Buggy's Coaches** *(Castlecomer, Tel 056/41264, buggy@indigo.ie, indigo.ie/~buggy; £1 one-way)* runs a shuttle service to the castle every day but Sunday. Buses depart Foulksrath for Kilkenny at 8:20am and 3:05pm, and leave from The Parade in Kilkenny for Foulksrath at 11:30am and 5:30pm. Don't stay here if you want to do a pub crawl; there's a 10:30pm curfew and the shuttle doesn't run late anyway.

▸▸DO-ABLE

You won't find frills at **Dempsey's B&B** *(26 James St.; Tel 056/21954; £15 single, £34 double with bathroom; No credit cards),* but clean, nicely decorated rooms and friendly service make it a fine choice. Another bed-and-breakfast option is **Bregagh Guesthouse** *(Dean St.; Tel 056/22315; £20 single, £36 double; No credit cards),* right across the street from St. Canice's Cathedral. Each of the townhouse's 15 rooms is modern, clean, and comfortable with private bath.

▸▸SPLURGE

Lacken House *(Dublin-Carlow Rd.; Tel 056/61085; £60 double, rate includes full breakfast; V, MC)* is a restored Georgian home and one of Kilkenny's nicest guesthouses. All the rooms were renovated in 1998, and they aren't huge, but they're brightly furnished and quite comfortable with private baths and color TV. The lush little garden in the back is a nice plus. It's a 10-minute walk from the action on High and Parliament streets, and the train station's only a hop, skip and a jump away. Lacken House also serves a fixed-price dinner for the eye-popping price of £25 a head.

need to know

Currency Exchange Having a cash flow problem? Head to the **Bank of Ireland** *(Parliament St.; Tel 056/21155; 10am-5pm Mon, 10am-4pm Tue-Fri),* or any of the other banks at the Parade/High St. intersection.

Tourist Information Questions? There are answers to be had at the **Kilkenny Tourist Office** *(Shee Alms House, Rose Inn St.; Tel*

056/51500; 9am-5pm Mon-Sat Nov-Mar; 9am-6pm Mon-Sat Apr and Oct, 9am-6pm Mon-Sat, 11am-1pm/2pm-5pm Sun May-Sept; Open till 7pm July-Aug).

Public Transportation **Kavanagh's Rapid Express** *(Depart from The Parade; Tel 01/679-1549 in Dublin, 056/31106 in Kilkenny; £4 one-way)* coaches run between Kilkenny and Dublin. Call **Kilkenny Cabs** *(Tel 056/52000)* for a taxi.

Health and Emergency **Garda Stations:** *(Dominic St.; Tel 056/22222).* **St. Luke's Hospital:** *(Freshford Rd., take Parliament St. towards St. Canice's Cathedral, make left onto Vicar's St., then another left onto Freshford Rd; Tel 056/51133).*

Pharmacies **John Street Pharmacy** *(47 John St.; Tel 056/65971),* **John O'Connell** *(4 Rose Inn St.; Tel 056/21033),* or **White's Pharmacy** *(5 High St.; Tel 056/21328)* will serve your pharmaceutical needs. All pharmacies open 9am-6pm Monday-Saturday, with a rotation system on Sunday. White's is big on cameras, offering one-hour film processing along with a free roll.

Trains The **Kilkenny MacDonagh Station** *(Dublin Rd.; Tel 056/22024; information desk open 8am-9:30pm Mon-Sat; 9am-9pm Sun)* is about a quarter-mile east of the town center, across the River Nore. Kilkenny is a stop on the Dublin-Waterford line, which runs about 4–5 trains a day.

Bike Rental Pedal fanatics should head to **Kilkenny Cycles** *(Lower Michael St., off John St.; Tel 056/64374; 9am-6pm Mon-Sat; £7 per day, £35 per week)* or **J.J. Walls Bike Hire** *(Maudlin St.; Tel 056/21236; 9am-5:30pm Mon-Sat, arrange to pick up bike Sat for use Sun; £7 per day; ID deposit required).*

Laundry It's a bit off the beaten path, but if you need clean duds head to **Brett's Laundrette** *(Michael St. near John St.; Tel 056/63200).*

Postal The **Kilkenny District Post Office** *(73 High St.; Tel 056/21813; 9:30am-5:30pm Mon-Fri, 9:30am-1pm Sat)* is the place for cards and letters.

Internet See *wired,* above.

everywhere else

thomastown

Thomastown, about 18 kilometers (11 miles) southeast of Kilkenny City and located on the Dublin-Waterford bus and train routes, is a great choice for a day trip. From here you can rent a bike [see *need to know,* below] and explore a string of pleasant villages along the River Nore, especially Inistoige and Bennettsbridge (both below); it makes a lovely ride through green countryside. Biking fanatics may want to move on to Graiguenamanagh (also below), which is more of a trek; those of us who don't have calf muscles that look like grapefruits will have to stick with the bus or a car. Besides the considerable **Jerpoint Abbey,** it's worth a stop at **Grennan Mill College**. An interesting fact: George Berkeley, of UC Berkeley fame, was born here. A local castle bears the Berkeley family name. There aren't any hostels and not a lot of accommodation choices in the area. If you don't have a car, you can rent a bike for the day or take the train from Kilkenny and return for the night.

culture zoo

Jerpoint Abbey *(Thomastown; Tel 056/24623; 10am-5pm Mar-May and Sept 14-Nov 1; 9:30am-6:30pm June-Sept 13; 10am-4pm Nov 16-Nov 30; Admission £2 adults, £1 students):* This 12th-century abbey is totally impressive and definitely worth the trip from Kilkenny City. The abbey showcases unusual Irish Romanesque details, a cloister arcade, early medieval effigies, and one beautiful east rose window. Its dilapidated appearance—the roof is missing on its left side—creates an eerie effect, compounded by an old, weathered tree greeting you at the entrance. It's 2.5 km (1.5 mi) south of Thomastown. From Kilkenny you can drive the Waterford Road (N9) to the abbey, or you can ride the train or bus from Kilkenny to Thomastown and walk the mile and a half from the station.

great outdoors

If you can't get enough of the River Nore valley, check out **Noreside Adventure Centre** *(Woollengrange, Bennettsbridge and Thomastown area; Tel 056/27273)*. It offers canoeing, hiking, orienteering, and abseiling, with full- and half-day excursions available. Call for specifics.

stuff

The **Jerpoint Glass Studio** *(Near entrance to Mount Juliet golf course, Thomastown; Tel 056/24350; Studio open 9am-5pm Mon-Thur, 9am-2pm Fri; Shop open 9am-6pm Mon-Fri, 10am-6pm Sat)* creates and sells totally gorgeous hand-blown glass in bright colors and pretty designs. Americans, better get that vase for Aunt Hilda shipped—this and any other craft shop will deduct the VAT refund for non-E.U. visitors right on the spot.

You'll find gemstones, crystals, and fossils at the offbeat **All That Glistens** *(Ladywell Corner, Thomastown; Tel 056/24081)*, which also has a shop in Kilkenny City *(Ormonde St.; Tel 056/56111)*. Drool over the jewelry, unusual pottery, glassware, and all of that natural history stuff, most of which probably won't fit into your bags.

eats

The Water Garden *(Ladywell St., Thomastown; Tel 056/24690; 10am-5pm Tue-Sat, noon-6pm Sun and holidays; Garden admission £1; No credit cards)* is a charming garden and cafe run as a fundraiser by the Camphill community for disabled adults and children. Lunches are made with the organic food raised at the community farm. Good food and good views for a good cause.

crashing

The best thing to do, really, is to make Thomastown a day trip and head back to Kilkenny to sleep, but if you do want to stay—or get stuck here—try the **Abbey House** *(Waterford Rd.; Tel 056/24166, Fax 056/24192; £20-30 single, £36-50 double, all rooms with private bath, breakfast included; V, MC, AE)*, a lovely 10-minute walk from the train station.

need to know

Currency Exchange The **Bank of Ireland** *(Market St.; Tel 056/24213 9:30am-4pm Tue-Sun, 9:30am-5pm Mon)*, in the center of town, has an ATM.

Tourist Information You can pick up information about the villages on the River Nore at the Kilkenny tourist office *(Shee Alms House, Rose Inn St.; Tel 056/51500; 9am-5pm Mon-Sat Nov-Mar; 9am-6pm Mon-Sat Apr and Oct; 9am-6pm Mon-Sat and 11am-1pm/2pm-5pm Sun May-Sept; Open till 7pm July-Aug)*.

Trains **Irish Rail** *(McDonagh Bus and Train Station, Dublin Road,*

Kilkenny; Tel 056/22024) serves Thomastown from Kilkenny on the Dublin-Waterford Route. Trains leave four times a day; five times on Friday and twice on Sunday. The trip takes 15 minutes and costs £4.50 one way.

Buses Bus Éireann *(McDonagh Bus and Train Station, Dublin Road, Kilkenny; Tel 056/64933)* runs several buses a day from Kilkenny into Thomastown (trip time: 25 minutes). The buses begin running daily at 8:15am, with frequent returns from Thomastown. The last bus from Kilkenny to Thomastown departs Kilkenny at 6:30pm. The one-way bus fare is £2.

Bike Rental For the feel of the wind in your hair and two wheels under your feet, head to **Treacy's Hardware Shop** *(Main St., Thomastown; No phone; Mon-Sat only; £5 per day, £25 per week, £20 deposit).*

inistoige

Recognize those quiet tree-lined streets and quaint little shops? You must remember them from *Circle of Friends,* which was filmed in Inistoige ("inish-TEEG"), a pleasant village not far from Kilkenny.

You'll enjoy biking around the lovely little streets, but you can also check out the **Woodstock Estate Forest Park** *(Mount Alto, 1 km (0.6 mi) south of Inistoige; Always open; Free),* with its lush and extensive gardens in the shadow of the ruined Woodstock House. The house burned down during the Troubles in 1922, and Woodstock is now a state park, packed with acres of trees, river walks, and picnic areas.

eats

Inistoige has one really nice restaurant, **The Maltings** *(Bridge House, Inistioge; Tel 056/58484, Noon-3pm/7-9:30pm Tue-Sun, reservations required; Dinner main courses £11-15; V, MC),* which offers yummy food (if you're not a vegetarian, that is) in a romantic country house overlooking the River Nore. The dinner menu includes roast duck, filet steak, and grilled salmon. Don't worry if you're biking; dress is casual.

need to know

Tourist Information Kilkenny tourist office *(Shee Alms House, Rose Inn St.; Tel 056/51500; 9am-5pm Mon-Sat Nov-Mar; 9am-6pm Mon-Sat Apr and Oct; 9am-6pm Mon-Sat and 11am-1pm/2pm-5pm Sun May-Sept; open till 7pm July-Aug).*

Directions and Transportation Inistoige is about 24 km (15 mi) southeast of Kilkenny. Because buses run just once a week, the best way to get here is by car—or by bike if you're up to the 5 mile (8 km) ride from Thomastown, or the 15 mile ride from Kilkenny. There are bike rental shops in both Kilkenny and Thomastown.

graiguenamanagh

It might be spelled a few different ways, but it's all the same place: Graiguenamanagh ("greg-nah-MAH-nah"), which means "village of the monks." Apt, since Graignamanagh is home to **Duiske Abbey** [see *culture zoo,* below], a 13th-century religious establishment which, although not quite as cool as either Kells Priory [see below] or Jerpoint Abbey [see **Thomastown**], is definitely worth a visit. The town lies on the River Barrow at the foot of Brandon Hill. The setting is idyllic, especially in spring, summer, or fall, and both locals and visitors gravitate to the riverbanks to hang out, taking in the 18th-century arched bridge. There are pleasant walks in all directions, notably up Brandon Hill—you are rewarded with one of the most panoramic views of the Barrow Valley from its heather-clad summit. You don't have to be a skilled mountain climber to walk to the top at 1,703 foot summit, as the climb is not terribly steep except in a few places.

culture zoo

Duiske Abbey *(Graiguenamanagh; Tel 0503/24238; 10am-5pm Mon-Fri, 2-5pm Sat-Sun June-Aug; Free):* Pronounced like "douche" with a k at the end (those Irish place names never fail to amuse, do they?), Duiske Abbey, right in the center of town, was built in the early 13th century. Recently restored, it's known for a large effigy of a knight affectionately referred to as "the Crusader" by locals (and that's almost certainly what he was). You'll find a few Irish high crosses of note here, as well. The Abbey's visitor center provides space for art exhibitions and sells Christian-themed sculpture, tapestries, and paintings—no doubt inspired by the abbey itself.

stuff

Duiske Glass Factory Shop *(High St.; Tel 0503/24174; 9am-5pm Mon-Fri, 10am-12:30pm Sat; V, MC, AE)* offers—you guessed it—. Unfortunately, the factory itself isn't open to the public. Another spot for cool Irish crafts is the **Cushendale Mills** *(High St.; Tel 0503/24118; 8:30am-12:30pm/1:30-5:30pm),* an ultra-traditional spinning and knitting mill, churning out colorful sweaters and the like. The mill shop is on High Street in the village next to the mill; there are no tours—if you want to learn to spin, befriend a Graiguenamanagh grandma.

need to know

Tourist Information Kilkenny tourist office *(Shee Alms House, Rose Inn St.; Tel 056/51500; 9am-5pm Mon-Sat Nov-Mar; 9am-6pm Mon-Sat Apr and Oct; 9am-6pm Mon-Sat and 11am-1pm/2-5pm Sun May-Sept; open till 7pm July-Aug).*

Directions and Transportation Graiguenamanagh is around 27 km

(17 mi) southeast of Kilkenny, 11 km (7 mi) east of Thomastown. It's located at the foot of Brandon Hill, on the South Leinster Way walking trail, which winds through Counties Carlow and Kilkenny starting in Kildavin. It's hard to reach if you don't have a car or you're not a heavy cyclist, as buses don't run very regularly here. Ask at the Kilkenny tourist office for maps and bus schedules.

bennettsbridge

Just a leisurely 5-mile ride north of Thomastown (south of Kilkenny), the quiet little village of Bennettsbridge is a potter's paradise, known for its great craft workshops. If it's authenticity you're after, come and get it. No room left in your bags for cool souvenirs? Have it shipped!

stuff

Bennettsbridge is a major Irish center for handmade pottery. **The Bridge Pottery** *(Chapel St., Bennettsbridge; Tel 056/27077)* offers hand-painted pottery. The water-powered **Nicholas Mosse Pottery Factory** *(Thomastown/New Ross Rd., Bennettsbridge; Tel 056/27105 factory, 056/27505 shop; 9am-6pm Mon-Sat, closed for lunch, 1:30-5pm Sun; frances@nicholasmosse.com, www.NicholasMosse.com),* a business that's been in the Mosse family for 11 generations. Nicholas Mosse's colorful pottery (he's been a potter since age seven) is all hand-thrown and hand-decorated. The shop also sells locally made linens and glassware.

And just outside of Bennettsbridge, there's **Stoneware Jackson Pottery** *(On the R700, 2 km (1.3 mi) north of Bennettsbridge; Tel 056/27175; 10am-6pm Mon-Sat),* which sells all sorts of pottery, even lamps, in rich earthy colors.

There's some manufacturing done at **Dyed in the Wool Knitwear** *(The Old Creamery Yard, Bennettsbridge; Tel 056/27684; 9:30am-6pm Mon-Fri, 10am-6pm Sat, 2-6pm Sun),* but most of the products are made in the old cottage-industry style—by hand.

Chesneau Leather Goods *(The Old Creamery, Bennettsbridge; Tel 056/27456; 10am-6pm Mon-Sat, 1-5pm Sun)* is surprisingly cosmopolitan for its location in such a tiny village. The owner and designers are of French origin, and fashionable stores all over Europe and the U.S. stock Chesneau's designs. Cool, huh? What you can see in the Bennettsbridge shop today will be in stores the following season.

eats

If all that shopping has left you drained and hungry, try **Café Nore** *(Main St., Bennettsbridge; Tel 056/27833; 10am-6pm Tue-Sat, 2-6pm Sun, closed Jan),* a great little place for a sandwich and a cup of cappuccino.

need to know

Tourist Information Kilkenny tourist office *(Shee Alms House, Rose Inn St.; Tel 056/51500; 9am-5pm Mon-Sat Nov-Mar; 9am-6pm Mon-Sat Apr and Oct; 9am-6pm Mon-Sat and 11am-1pm/2-5pm Sun May-Sept; open till 7pm July-Aug).*

Directions and Transportation Bennettsbridge is 4-1/2 miles south of Kilkenny on the R700 road. Bus service is available from several providers, including **Bus Éireann** *(Tel 051/873401),* which makes a stop in Bennettsbridge on its Rosslare–Limerick line, once a day in each direction. It doesn't work for day trips from Kilkenny, however, since the bus leaves Bennettsbridge before the bus from Kilkenny arrives. If you want to make it a day trip, it's best to take a taxi one way. Try **O'Brien's** *(Tel 056/61333)* in Kilkenny.

kells priory

If you think you've seen one set of ruins, you've seen them all, you're wrong. More than just another pile of really old rocks, the ruins of the once-fortified Kells Priory are some of the most spectacular in all of Ireland—some call it the country's best-kept secret. This large Augustinian priory—not to be confused with its even more famous namesake in County Meath—founded in the late 12th century sits on the bank of the Kings River, spreading out over 3 acres. The compound was fortified by an extensive outer wall and seven towers; inside, you'll see a bunch of medieval ecclesiastical structures. There are no set hours, and no entrance fee—you'll be sharing the place only with sheep. It's decidedly worth the trek out of Kilkenny; you can pick up a self-guided tour for £3.50 at the Kilkenny tourist office if you like.

If you find yourself stuck here, one option is the **Headfort Arms Hotel** *(John St.; Tel 0126/640063; www.boyne-valley-hotel.ie, reservations@boyne-valley-hotel.ie; £58 single, £105 double, private bath; V, MC, DC),* about a 20-minute walk (or 2-minute bus ride) from Drogheda's town center and a 5-minute walk from the bus and train station.

need to know

Hours/Days Open Always open—the sheep appreciate the company.

Directions and Transportation 13 km (8 mi) south of Kilkenny; ruins are 800 m (0.5 mi) east of Kells on the Stonyford road. Take N76 south to R699. The best way to get there if you're not driving is to board **Bus Éireann** bound for Waterford and request a stop at either Ennissnag or Stonyford, then walk approximately 2 miles to the Priory. Follow Stonyford Road west until you reach the hamlet of Kells. From here, the ruins of the priory are but 800 meters away, and are clearly signposted.

the southwest

Counties Kerry and Cork are all about countryside, about charming coastal villages and unspoiled islands, about lakes nestled into mountain ranges, and miles of scenic roads for hiking and cycling. Yes, and about convivial pub evenings in small towns where the locals are friendly and the trad music unadulterated. Even the heavily touristed areas such as the **Ring of Kerry** and Killarney National Park, remain thrillingly beautiful (kinda like Yosemite, where you just have to get a little off the tourist-beaten paths), and less-discovered spots like the **Dingle Peninsula** become your own incredibly lovely secret. With the green hills behind you and the blue ocean stretching endlessly before you, you can't help but feel in tune with the universe. Ascend the dozens of super-steep steps on Skellig Michael and wonder how the hell those monks went up and down those stairs every day without going into cardiac arrest; sit on a rock in the middle of the Lower Lake in Killarney National Park and ponder the secrets of the universe.

If you crave urban excitement, of course, **Cork City** is a very good option; Cork has a European flavor because of its centuries-old port, and its excellent theaters rival Dublin's best. After a night of culture, check out Cork's growing club scene (thanks to the University College Cork student population). Be sure to sample the local brews—Beamish and Murphy's—perhaps at a cool bar like the Old Oak.

Major travel tip: When faced with the question "to kiss or not to kiss the Blarney Stone" (a mere 5 miles outside Cork City), just say no. It's a major tourist trap, and when you think about who and what has been there before you, it makes putting a handful of old subway tokens in your mouth seem almost sanitary.

West Cork holds some of Ireland's most remote and wild coastal regions, perfect for testing out the stormy surf or basking on the golden sand. It's even better than the Iveragh Peninsula's 110-mile Ring of Kerry, where the astoundingly beautiful scenery—crashing waves, towering mountains, intriguing little villages—is often marred by big, ugly, motor-coaches belching out stinky gasoline fumes and packed to the gills with tourists. Biking the Ring used to be a great option, but now that Ireland has become one of Europe's most popular travel destinations, cyclists here run the very great risk of being shoved of the road by the tour buses; you'd be better off exploring the area on public transportation. But don't let that scare you off altogether—a visit to the island monastery of **Skellig Michael** alone will make any amount of traffic you encounter worth it.

And then there's **Killarney.** Let's be frank: It's a beautiful national park plagued by a town that's ultimately just a money-grubbing tourist-magnet. Pass through town swiftly to resupply or gawk at the spectacle of it, and then get thee to **Killarney National Park.** Provided you can keep from setting eyes on any other human being for fifteen minutes straight (and that's not always an easy task), you might just swear you've found heaven. Cycling through the intense vistas of the Gap of Dunloe, or hiking through dense woodlands may make Killarney Town a distant memory.

You'll certainly want to linger on the Dingle Peninsula for a few days at bare minimum. It's wonderfully rich in early ruins to clamber around, and the views are just astounding. The charming little we-refuse-to-surrender-completely-to-tourism Dingle Town makes an ideal base for exploring an area so amazingly rich in cultural and natural beauty.

getting around the region

You'll want to plan on spending at least a few days in each county, but give yourself plenty of wiggle room in case you fall under the region's spell. So we begin with Cork: you won't want to miss out on all the great stuff going on out on the western coast, and Bus Éireann's the way to go. Hitchhiking is a common practice, but that doesn't necessarily make it a safe one (although hitchhiking in Ireland is a heck of a lot safer than it is in the States). Anyway, tons of buses leave every day from Parnell Station in Cork City, bound for Youghal, Kinsale, Baltimore, Skibbereen, Schull, Bantry, and plenty of other places. If you want to go from one little coastal

take a hike

There are some fantastic long-distance walks to be had in Counties Kerry and Cork—but don't let the "long distance" part frighten you; you can walk as little or as much of it as you wish. Try the **Kerry Way** or the **Dingle Way** in Kerry, or the **Sheep's Head Way,** the **Beara Way,** or the **Blackwater Valley Way,** the last of which is in north Cork. You'll find the **Ballyhoura Way** winding through part of northern Cork as well. Naturally you'll be needing maps, and plenty of 'em; stop by any tourist office in Cork or Kerry; the **Killarney Tourist Office** *(Beech St.; Tel 064/31633; 9am-8pm Mon-Sat, 9am-1pm/2:15-6pm Sun, Jul-Aug; 9am-6pm Mon-Sat, 10am-6pm Sun, Jun, Sep; 9:15am-5:30pm Mon-Sat, 9:15am-1pm Sun, Oct-May)* has lots of information. Make a beeline for the *Long Distance Walking Route Guide* for Cork and Kerry.

Travel Times

* By train
** Water-crossing required (by ferry usually)
*** By cable car

	Dublin	Cork City	Cobh	Castletownberehaven	Dursey Island	Midleton	Union Hall	Youghal	Schull	Skibbereen
Cork City	2:50**	-	:25*	2:35	3:05***	:20	1:40	:45	2:10	1:45
Cobh	4	:25*	-	3:05	3:35***	:20	2:10	:45	2:40	2:10
Castletownberehaven	6:25	2:35	3:05	-	:30***	1:45	2	3:20	1:45	1:50
Dursey Island	6:55***	3:05***	3:35***	:30***	-	2:15***	2:30***	3:50***	2:15***	2:20***
Midleton	3:50	:20	:20	1:45	2:15***	-	2	:25	2:35	2:05
Union Hall	5:30	1:40	2:10	2	2:30***	2	-	2:20	:45	:15
Youghal	3:40	:45	:45	3:20	3:50***	:25	2:20	-	2:55	2:30
Schull	6	2:10	2:40	1:45	2:15***	2:35	:45	2:55	-	:30
Skibbereen	5:35	1:45	2:10	1:50	2:20***	2:05	:15	2:30	:30	-
Baltimore	5:50	2	2:30	2:05	2:35***	2:20	:30	2:45	:45	:15
Cape Clear Island	6:35**	2:45**	3:15**	2:50**	3:20**	3:05**	1:15**	3:30**	1:30**	1**
Kinsale	4:20	:35	1	3:05	3:35***	:55	1:20	1:20	2	1:30
Clonakilty	4:55	1:05	1:30	2:30	3***	1:25	:35	1:50	1:10	:40
Sherkin Island	6:05**	2:15**	2:45**	2:30**	2:50**	2:35**	:45**	3**	1**	:30**
Killarney Town	3:20**	1:20	1:50	1:50	2:20***	1:45	2:05	2:05	2	2:05
Killorglen	4:50	1:50	2:20	2:20	2:50***	2:10	2:35	2:35	2:30	2:35
Cahirsiveen	5:40	2:40	3:05	2:45	3:15***	3	2:50	3:20	3:10	3:15
Valentia Island	6:05**	3:05**	3:30**	3**	3:30**	3:25**	3:45**	3:50**	3:25**	3:30**
The Skelligs	6:10**	3:35**	3:55**	4**	3:40**	4**	4:20**	4:15**	4:10**	4:10**
Waterville	6	3	3:25	2:30	2:30***	3:20	3:10	3:40	2:50	3
Cahirdaniel & Derryname	6:15	2:40	3:05	2:10	2:10***	3	2:50	3:20	2:30	2:40
Sneem	5:35	2:15	2:40	1:40	1:40**	2:30	2:20	3	2:05	2:10
Dingle	5:30	2:55	3:20	3:20	3:20***	3:15	3:40	3:40	3:30	3:35
Tralee	4*	1:50	2:20	2:20	2:20***	2:15	2:40	2:40	2:30	2:35
Dunquin & the Blasket Islands	5:50**	3:15**	3:40**	3:40**	3:40**	3:35**	4**	4**	3:50**	3:55**

Baltimore	Cape Clear Island	Kinsale	Clonakilty	Sherkin Island	Killarney Town	Killorglen	Cahirsiveen	Valentia Island	The Skelligs	Waterville	Cahirdaniel & Derryname	Sneem	Dingle	Tralee	Dunquin & the Blasket Islands
2	2:45**	:35	1:05	2:15**	1:20	1:50	2:40	3:05**	3:35**	3	2:40	2:15	2:55	1:50	3:15**
2:30	3:15**	1	1:30	2:45**	1:50	2:20	3:05	3:30**	3:55**	3:25	3:05	2:40	3:20	2:20	3:40**
2:05	2:50**	3:05	2:30	2:20**	1:50	2:20	2:45	3**	4**	2:30	2:10	1:40	3:20	2:20	3:40**
2:35***	3:20***	3:35***	3***	2:50***	2:20***	2:50***	3:15***	3:30***	4:30***	2:30***	2:10***	1:40***	3:20***	2:20***	3:40***
2:20	3:05**	:55	1:25	2:35**	1:45	2:10	3	3:25**	4**	3:20	3	2:30	3:15	2:15	3:35**
:30	1:15**	1:20	:35	:45**	2:05	2:45	3:30	3:45**	4:20**	3:10	2:50	2:20	3:40	2:40	4**
2:45	3:30**	1:20	1:50	3**	2:05	2:35	3:20	3:50**	4:15**	3:40	3:20	3	3:40	2:40	4**
:45	1:30**	2	1:10	1**	2	2:30	3:10	3:25	4:10**	2:50	2:30	2:05	3:30	2:30	3:50**
:15	1**	1:30	:40	:30**	2:05	2:35	3:15	3:30**	4:10**	3	2:40	2:10	3:35	2:35	3:55**
-	:45**	1:45	:55	:15**	2:20	2:50	3:35	3:40**	4:10**	3:15	2:55	2:30	3:50	2:50	4:10**
:45**	-	2:30**	1:40**	1**	3:05**	3:35**	4:20**	4:25**	4:35**	4**	3:40**	3:15**	4:35**	3:35**	4:55**
1:45	2:30**	-	:45	2**	1:50	2:20	3:10	3:35**	4**	3:25	3:05	2:40	3:20	2:20	3:40**
:55	1:45**	:45	-	1:10**	1:50	2:20	3:05	3:35**	4**	3:25	2:40	3:05	3:20	3:20	3:40**
:15**	1**	2**	1:10**	-	2:35**	3:05**	3:10**	3:55**	4:25**	3:30**	2:45**	3:10**	4:05**	3:05**	4:25**
2:20	3:35**	1:50	1:50	2:35**	-	:30	1:20	1:45**	2:10**	1:40	:35	1:40	1:30	:45*	1:50**
2:50	3:35**	2:20	2:20	3:05**	:30	-	:50	1:20**	1:50**	1:05	1:05	1:30	1:15	:30	1:35**
3:35	4:20**	3:10	3:05	3:10**	1:20	:50	-	:10**	2:40**	:20	1:05	:40	2	1:20	2:20**
3:40**	4:25**	3:35**	3:35**	3:55**	1:45**	1:20**	:10**	-	2:45**	:35**	:50**	1:20**	2:30**	1:45**	2:40**
4:10**	4:35**	4**	4**	4:25**	2:10**	1:50**	2:40**	2:45**	-	3**	2**	3:05**	:40**	1:40**	1:45**
3:15	4**	3:25	3:25	3:30**	1:40	1:05	:20	:35**	3**	-	:20	:45	2:20	1:40	2:45**
2:55	3:40**	3:05	3:05	3:10**	1:40	1:30	:40	:50**	2**	:20	-	:25	2:40	2	3**
2:30	3:15**	2:40	2:40	2:45**	:35	1:05	1:05	1:20**	3:05**	:45	:25	-	2:25	1:30	2:50**
3:50	4:35**	3:20	3:20	4:05**	1:50	1:15	2	2:30**	:40**	2:20	2:40	2:25	-	1:05	:20**
2:50	3:35**	2:20	2:20	3:05**	:45	:30	1:20	1:45**	1:40**	1:40	2	1:30	1:05	4*	1:25**
4:10**	4:55**	3:40**	3:40**	4:25**	1:50**	1:35**	2:20**	2:40**	1:45**	2:45**	3**	2:50**	2:50**	1:25**	-

town to another, though, you might have to go back to Cork first; plot out your route thoughtfully. Another option is to find a Raleigh Rent-A-Bike dealer, cycle from one place to the next, and pay an extra twelve punts or so for the privilege of dropping off the bike in a different spot. From Cork City, try heading southwest to Clonakilty first, then further out to Skibbereen, and upon your arrival there you can take another bus to Baltimore or to Schull. As for Castletownbere, famed for its Buddhist-retreat-next-door-to-hostel set-up, it might just be easier to get there from Killarney instead of Cork; the bus ride's shorter than if you were to take route 46 from Cork and through Bantry to Castletownbere. (On the other hand, the Killarney-to-Castletownbere route only operates in the summertime.)

Another option is to begin in Cork City and go West-Cork-coastal-village-hopping, taking the summer-only Bus Éireann route on to Kenmare, at the end of the Ring of Kerry, and then to Killarney. (Insert your Ring of Kerry trip before or after reaching Killarney—although most people start in Killarney and end in Kenmare, not the other way around.) Irish Rail links Cork with Killarney and with Dingle's entry city, Tralee. From Tralee, take Bus Éireann out to the Dingle Peninsula and back. Moving onto Limerick [see The West], it'd be easier to take a bus there from Tralee rather than a train—that'd be yet another convoluted route.

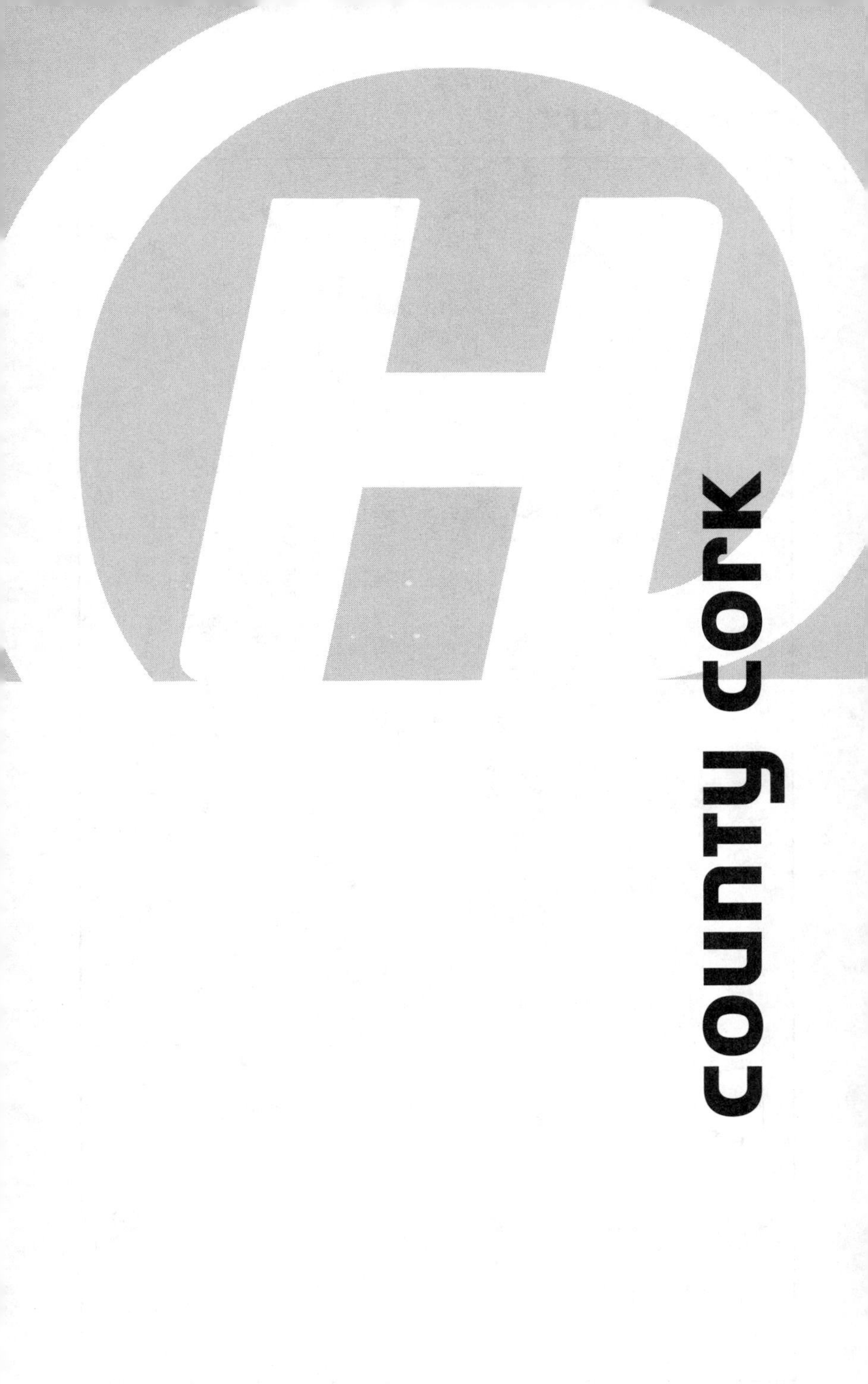
county cork

County Cork

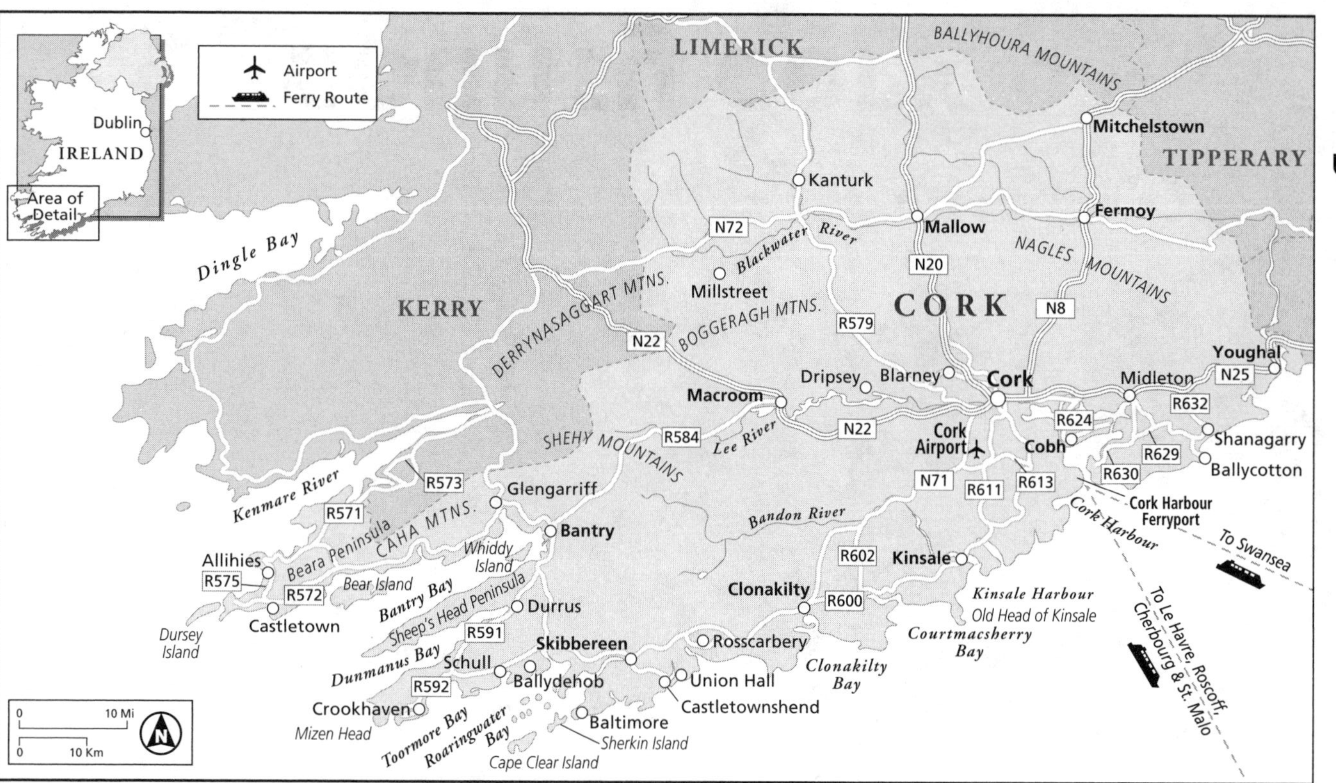

Airport
Ferry Route
Dublin
IRELAND
Area of Detail
LIMERICK
BALLYHOURA MOUNTAINS
Mitchelstown
TIPPERARY
Kanturk
Mallow
Fermoy
N72
Blackwater River
N20
NAGLES MOUNTAINS
Dingle Bay
Millstreet
CORK
N8
KERRY
DERRYNASAGGART MTNS.
BOGGERAGH MTNS.
R579
N22
Youghal
Dripsey
Blarney
Cork
Midleton
N25
Macroom
R632
R624
N22
Cork Airport
Cobh
Shanagarry
SHEHY MOUNTAINS
R584
Lee River
R629
Ballycotton
R630
R573
N71
R611
R613
Kenmare River
Glengarriff
Cork Harbour Ferryport
R571
CAHA MTNS.
Bandon River
Cork Harbour
Bantry
To Swansea
Whiddy Island
Beara Peninsula
R602
Kinsale
Allihies
R575
Bear Island
R572
Bantry Bay
Clonakilty
R600
Kinsale Harbour
Sheep's Head Peninsula
Durrus
Old Head of Kinsale
To Le Havre, Roscoff, Cherbourg & St. Malo
Castletown
Dursey Island
R591
Courtmacsherry Bay
Skibbereen
Rosscarbery
Dunmanus Bay
Schull
Ballydehob
Union Hall
Clonakilty Bay
R592
Castletownshend
Crookhaven
Baltimore
Mizen Head
Toormore Bay
Roaringwater Bay
Sherkin Island
Cape Clear Island
0
10 Mi
0
10 Km
N

CORK

Cork's the second largest city in the Republic, and while it may lack Dublin's sprawl or Galway's sparkle, the city certainly possesses its own sort of quiet charm. Don't believe anybody who says that Cork is boring. You could easily spend at least a week here hanging out in the cafes and in the park during the day, and seeing plays and going to clubs and pubs by night—and on the walk home you might even catch a flame-thrower or two.

Cork has been likened to Manhattan or Venice more than once, but aside from all three being port cities surrounded by waterways, there's really no comparison. Cork, with a population of just 127,000 mostly no-nonsense working souls, shows its roots as an old shipping town in many ways. But it's also modern enough to pride itself on culture and diversity, with a significant university scene and lots of outstanding theaters. You can't go wrong plunkin' down your pounds at such venues as the Everyman Palace Theatre, Cork Arts Theatre, Granary Theatre, or the Half Moon Theatre. You can snag a ticket, usually even at the last minute, for only £6-8, and watch a performance in a cozy old black box with an audience only two or three times the size of the cast. We're talking perfectly fine quality productions, just a more intimate (and therefore even more enjoyable) experience than you'd get in the big theater capitals.

Over the centuries all sorts of European cultural flavors washed into Cork's harbor along with goods for sale, and you'll find that reflected in Cork's diverse range of topnotch restaurants and cafes. Most of what you'll see is quintessentially Irish, though, from the bright enthusiasm of its residents to the lively trad sessions in the pubs at night to the

12 hours in cork city

1. Ring the **Shandon Church** bells [see *culture zoo,* above], and feel like the Master of the Universe, at least for as long as your song lasts. The entire city can hear what you play, so try not to mess up.

2. Buy a cup of hazelnut ice cream from **Gino's** [see *eats,* below].

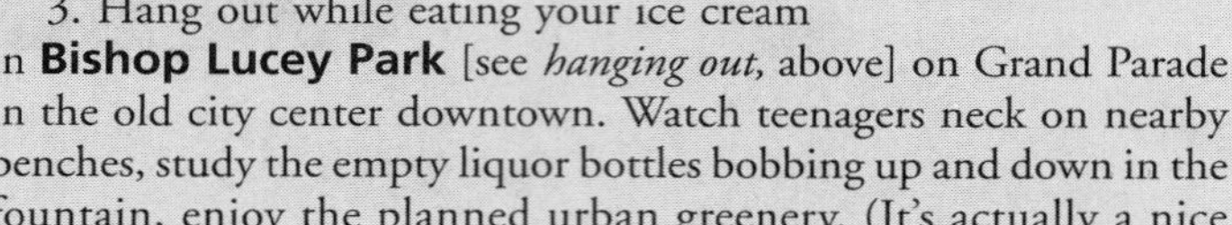

3. Hang out while eating your ice cream in **Bishop Lucey Park** [see *hanging out,* above] on Grand Parade in the old city center downtown. Watch teenagers neck on nearby benches, study the empty liquor bottles bobbing up and down in the fountain, enjoy the planned urban greenery. (It's actually a nice place, honest!)

4. See a play or concert at the **Everyman Palace Theatre,** the **Cork Arts Theatre,** the **Cork Opera House,** or **Triskel Arts Centre** [see *arts scene,* above]. Curtain time is usually 8pm.

5. For your obligatory pub crawl, don't miss **The Old Oak** [see *bar scene,* below] for a pint and an idle flirtation or two, and then catch the live music sessions at **The Lobby, Charlie's,** or **Gallagher's.**

6. Do s'more hanging around at some of the trendier bars, like **Bodega** or **The Roundy** [see *bar scene,* below].

7. As long as you can keep from slurring your words, call home with your Spirit card and tell them all about the fascinating cultural attractions you haven't actually seen. Inform them also that you haven't touched a drop: it might not be true, but at least they'll sleep easy tonight.

trusty old Beamish & Crawford beer factory still brewing on South Main Street.

neighborhoods

The River Lee divides Cork City into three sections. The **North Bank** encompassing Shandon [see *culture zoo,* below], features some of the steepest streets outside San Francisco. **Downtown,** between where the River Lee and its Southern Channel meet, is where almost all the action can be found, including pubs, clubs, theaters, and shops on **Patrick Street, Washington Street, Oliver Plunkett Street, Grand Parade, Main Street,** and **South Mall.** It's all very walkable, jumbled and enchanting. Finally, the **South Bank,** across the Southern Channel and on further south, includes the oldest streets in Cork, most of University College Cork's campus, City Hall, and St. Finnbarre's Church, on the site of the lone monastery that got this whole town started in the 7th century.

hanging out

Bishop Lucey Park, a narrow green strip wedged between Grand Parade and South Main Street, is the fave hangout spot of pretty much everybody, from cell phone-toting teeny-boppers to mothers with more kids than they can handle to business professionals and seasoned old people-watchers. The park's your place for an outdoor lunch, and everybody's here even on days that aren't perfectly warm and sunny (which, of course, is the great majority of them). High school and college students do their homework on the park benches, rowdy footballer-types push their friends around, and the terminally bored sit and stare at the rubbish floating in the fountain.

As for pubs, most of them are great for nursing a pint and contemplating the mysteries of the universe. Particularly good pubs to semi-productively pass the time are **Bodega, The Roundy,** and any pub branded an official collegiate hangout: **Rosie O'Grady's, Rearden's,** etc. [see *bar scene,* below]. Otherwise, the centrally located **Gloria Jean's**

five things to talk to a local about

1. **"Have you seen the new play at the Everyman yet?"** Corkonians are extra-specially proud of their performing arts resources and will eagerly discuss the finer points of dialogue, scenery, and all that theatrical stuff with you. This may, however, mean that you have to go to the theater yourself first to keep up your end of the conversation.

2. Ask about any of the events on Cork's jam-packed **festival calendar,** especially the jazz or film festivals. It's an especially hot topic at arty hangouts like Yumi Yuki, the Half Moon, or Bodega [see *bar scene* and *club scene,* below].

3. **"Who won the game this afternoon?"** Corkonians are even more passionate about their sporting teams than other Irishmen. Start a conversation out this way and it could go on for hours.

4. Mention the **Beamish Brewery** on South Main Street. Mention anything on the subject of drinking, really, and you're set for an earful.

5. If all else fails, resort to **Brit-bashing.** Every Irishmen's up for *that.*

wired

To get a general feel for things, check out ***www.cork-guide.ie*** and ***www.whazon.com,*** a monthly guide to events and eating out in Cork City.

The newly opened **Webworkhouse** *(Winthrop St.; Tel 021/4273-090; 10am-10pm daily; mail@webworkhouse.com, www.webworkhouse.com; £5 per hour, £4 per hour for students; No credit cards)* is really the only totally acceptable place in town for email access. Unfortunately, it's frequented by hardcore gamers who apparently don't realize that it'd be cheaper just to buy their own computers, so if there's a line, it moves *veeeery* slowly. And in the evenings, when net access costs only a punt or two, that line's almost unbearable. Bring something to read while you're waiting. Nevertheless, ultra-speedy PCs, cool, spacious, modern-minimalist surroundings, and Lauryn Hill on the CD player—not to mention those prices—make it by far the best place in town to surf once you do get online. Webworkhouse also offers net-to-phone service, which seems like a thrifty alternative for long distance phone calls.

If you do get sick of waiting, though, you could try **The Favourite** *(122 Patrick St.; Tel 021/4272-646; 9am-10:30pm; £6 per hour),* a newsagent offering coin-operated computers. Bring £1 coins. Another option is **The Q Room** *(Little Hanover St.; Noon-11pm; £6 per hour),* a bar and pool hall with a row of a half-dozen slightly aged computers. It's the best—well, the *only*—place if you want to enjoy a pint while reading all the emails from your buddies stuck back at home. You can also get lunch here between 12:30pm and 2:30pm.

(84 Patrick St.; Tel. 021/4270-555) provides sufficient seating, gourmet coffee, and freshly made breakfast munchies. Bring a newspaper or the novel you started on the plane ride over and chill through the morning hours sipping your banana mocha coffee on ice amid local studious types. This is also a great spot to pick up the local events weekly, ***The List***, and make your plan of attack for later.

bar scene

As per usual in Ireland, almost every pub in Cork stops letting people in around 11:30pm and starts nudging patrons out the door soon after. Things only really get going around 9pm, too, so for a couple of hours the pace is fairly furious. Make The Old Oak [see below] the last stop on your pub-crawling list, since it's open one hour later than the rest.

Frequented by both obnoxious rugby-types and fun-seeking travelers, **Gallagher's** *(MacCurtain St.; Tel 021/4551-526),* northeast of the historic core, a two-minute walk north from St. Patrick's Quay, immediately south of Wellington Road, offers three-pint pitchers of beer for the sweet price of £6 on "backpacker nights," every Monday and Tuesday. You can hear live modern folk music on those nights as well, and it's good enough to really pack 'em in; even on quieter nights finding a seat is like looking for nudists at the North Pole. Bright yellow, red, and green walls, pithy quotes painted on the shelf above the bar ("Dream as though you'll live forever; live as though you'll die today"), and the latest Backstreet Boys single over the loudspeaker create an atmosphere that's fun and lively—or a tad irritating, depending on your temperament.

Arguably the best pub in the city, **The Old Oak** *(113 Oliver Plunkett St; Tel 021/4276-165)* has a lively, youthful social vibe. Frequented by Cork's students and young professionals, this is *the* place to see and be seen. There's barely any room to breathe on weekend nights, but nobody really notices—it's all a big party under an incongruously elegant stained-glass dome, with Pearl Jam, U2, and Dave Matthews music blasting from every speaker. The Old Oak also closes an hour later than the rest of the pubs in the city, thus further promoting its exuberantly festive spirit. The only live music here is "live modern" on Sunday nights—no cover!—and on occasion cover bands like the Police II or Abbaesque play here. Did I mention that this place is perfect for mingling [see *lad meets lassie,* below]? Just be sure to bring your clingy tops and blackest jeans, and if at all possible don't blow the look by wearing sneaks.

Established in 1779, **An Spailpín Fánac** *(28-29 S. Main St.; Tel 021/4277-949)* is one of the oldest pubs in the city with traditional, if dreary, decor. You'll find every hand here curled around a pint of Beamish, since the brewery is located right across the street. *An Spailpín Fánac* could be roughly translated as "the wandering migrant worker" (kinda redundant, guys) and from the looks of the crowd, it must have been named for its patrons. No doubt you've heard a lot about this place, since some of the oldest and reportedly excellent trad sessions occur here Sunday-Friday. For those reasons (in addition to cheap pub grub) it might

rules of the game

Let's not be stupid. Public drinking isn't acceptable anywhere in Ireland (or at least that's what they tell us). Drinking on the street in Cork City gets you a minimum £25 fine on the spot, with a maximum fine of £500. Get caught littering and cough up another £50. So, toss an empty liquor bottle into the street with the gardaí nearby and you're back *at least* £75. Ouch.

JUST ONE TIP. DON'T.

Tipping the bartender or waiter isn't customary in Ireland; in fact, some might even consider it insulting or think you've left your money on the table by mistake. Cheaper for you, maybe, but on the other hand, some waitresses aren't quite so concerned about being friendly or providing good service as they would be in the States.

be worth a look, but the *craic* everybody's talking about just isn't found here. Could be it's too loud for talking or maybe folks are just a wee bit *too* into the music. It may also depend on the night you go, but there are definitely warmer, livelier pubs around town.

Definitely one of the coolest bars in town, **Bodega** *(46-49 Cornmarket St.; Tel 021/4272-878; V, MC),* in the exact center at Coal Quay Market just west of Paul Street Plaza, gets its young funky vibe from its converted warehouse status, two-story mirrors behind the bar, and brightly-painted car hoods and doors chained to the walls as much as it does from who comes here: the local college scene's hippest of the hip. Walk into Bodega and you'd swear you were in Greenwich Village if you didn't know better. Bodega's your best bet if you're a claustrophobe—plenty of space upstairs and down mean there's always room to breathe even at the busiest times. It's s magnet for the young and stylish, with a crowd that skillfully tread that fine line between not-scruffy and not-dressed-up. Think classy secondhand and body-hugging black threads. You can get bar snacks here as well, but nothing as substantial as the usual hearty "pub grub" offered in most of the other drinking joints in town. The soundtrack's more funky rock than trad, and the drinks—well, they do the job, though some seem a bit high-priced.

Small and sleekly modern, no doubt named for its shape, **The Roundy** *(Cornmarket, off Paul St.; No phone),* around the corner from Bodega, offers a jazzy laid-back vibe that Cork's young hipsters just can't get enough of. Some drinks here are noticeably more expensive than their equivalents at other bars in town; at Charlie's [see *live music scene,* below], for example, you can get a Bailey's coffee for £2, and here you'll have to fork over £3.20. Think of as a surcharge for the sleekly modern atmosphere. Mellow tracks on the sound system are loud enough to function as a cool soundtrack while still allowing folks to talk. Pick up a delish toasted sandwich before 8pm while you're checking out what everybody else is wearing.

Like Christmas only without the tree, **Sin É** ("*That's It*") *(Coburg St. opposite City Limits Comedy Club; Tel 021/4502-266; No credit cards),* just north of St. Patrick's Bridge, glows with cozy fires in winter, white icicle lights above the peninsular bar, and jovial pint-bearing locals. Avant-garde movie posters adorn scarlet walls and candles flicker in old wine bottles. It does get a bit tight in the evenings; the place isn't terribly big but it is terribly popular.

One of the most popular downtown student hangouts, dim and rustic **Rosie O'Grady's** *(S. Main St., off Washington St.; Tel 021/4278-253; www.rosieogrady.ie)* also offers live trad on Sunday, Monday, and Wednesday. When there's not live music, you'll hear the typical bubble-gum pop tunes at high volume. Watch the inebriated try to make phone calls in the big old-fashioned red telephone booth that's only for show. It's easy enough to get that way with the cheap drink prices in effect. Not much to eat, either.

Pseudo-medieval touches and what look like cave paintings make up the incongruous decor at **John Rearden and Son** *(26 Washington St.; Tel 021/4271-969 or 021/4278-054; info@reardens.com, www.reardens.com)*, a huge watering hole just around the corner from Rosie O'Grady's that serves up good cheap pub grub and an Irish version of Sheryl Crow on Wednesday nights. It's another popular spot with the university crowd, so snag a big comfy booth in the back or to the side, and you'll be all set for a night of mixing with the beautiful local boys and girls.

Across the street from Rearden's is another UCC nightspot, **The Washington Inn** *(30-31 Washington St.; Tel 021/4273-666; No credit cards)*. Smaller and definitely not as comfortable as Rearden's, it's pretty standard, really: pop music on the stereo, bare brick walls plastered with ads for clubs and plays (pick up concessions, those favorite promo coupons for discounted entry and specials, if you can find them), and the usual old-style beer ads. Reasonable for dropping in if you're on the block, but probably not worth a long trek.

Along with Rearden's, Rosie's, and The Washington Inn, other popular CIT and UCC hangouts include **The Goat Broke Loose** *(Grand Parade, across from the tourist office; No phone; No credit cards)*, and **Nancy**

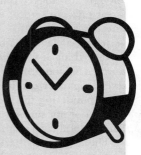

irish time

Always expect an Irishperson at least an hour later than the time you've agreed upon. It's "Irish time": nobody thinks anything of telling you they'll be there at 2pm and then showing up at 3:30pm (that's "half-three" in Irish/Anglospeak, by the way). It's just the way things are done. Oh, and don't bank on that bus arriving on time, either; many a tired and cranky traveler has waited for a half-hour or more after its scheduled stop, wondering if the bus would *ever* come.

Spain's *(48 Barrack St.; Tel 021/4314-452;),* south of the central part of the South Bank, both with occasional live trad sessions.

If you want to hang out at a typical Irish pub, don't go to **Deja Voodoo's** *(20 White St.; Tel 021/4313-080; www.iol.ie/~omalcork/DejaVoodoos).* on the South Bank near Loafer's. This pub would seem offbeat anywhere, but in Ireland the atmosphere comes across as especially eccentric. That said, it's totally fun and funky, with a bright cobalt blue facade, a bartop lined with freaky wooden dolls—which partly inspired the name, no doubt—and a huge traffic light hanging in the corner, always flashing a green for patrons to keep on drinking. But wait, there's more. White Christmas lights, primary-colored walls, a pool table in the back, African masks, and—*gasp*—this has got to be the only pub in Cork, if not in all of Ireland, playing hip hop music! (Maybe Cork's cooler than you suspected.) Surprisingly, the crowd's pretty run-of-the-mill for a place that looks like a counterculture den.

The sleekest wine bar in town is **ThExchange** *(George's Quay; No phone),* on the South Bank, a few blocks south of South Channel. The crowd here's a tad older and the atmosphere more, shall we say, *refined*—it's a *wine bar,* after all—so don't expect a party. Still, it makes a nice place to sample a glass of Tuscan wine and some laid-back conversation.

If you were too lazy to get yourself to the stadium, you can always watch the game on TV at the prototypical sports bar **The Hairy Lemon** *(Oliver Plunkett St.; Tel 021/4278-678).* We don't know how they got that name and we don't want to know.

live music scene

An Bodhrán *(42 Oliver Plunkett St.; Tel 021/4274-544; No credit cards),* in the center of downtown, hosts trad sessions Tuesday and Wednesday nights beginning at 9pm. A large stained-glass window with designs inspired by the Book of Kells brightens up this otherwise traditional pub.

The Gables *(32 Douglas St.; Tel 021/4313-076; V, MC, AE),* a few blocks south of ThExchange [see *bar scene,* above], has trad sessions good enough for local connoisseurs Wednesday and Thursday nights. Great pub grub, too [see *eats,* below], but you gotta order before the music starts.

Jerry Garcia wanna-be's with graying ponytails and tie-dyed T-shirts do their thing at **Charlie's** *(2 Union Quay; Tel 021/4965-272; No credit cards),* next door to City Hall where you'll hear blues, folk, or trad bands several nights a week. It's a cozy, if crowded, place to soak up a pint or two while pondering the meaning of the bizarre artwork on the walls and whether or not someone should break the news to The Medicated Blues Band (a local fave) that marijuana still isn't legal.

The downstairs bar's nothing to rejoice over, but upstairs at **The Lobby** *(1 Union Quay; Tel 021/4319-307; enquiries@lobby.ie, www.lobby.ie; Cover £5; No credit cards),* across the street from Charlie's, you'll find totally excellent live music every single night of the week. If it's at all a conceivable musical genre, they're hosting it: folk, trad, bluegrass,

lad meets lassie

In addition to Cork's many nightclubs, the best bar for cruising is decidedly the Old Oak [see *bar scene,* above], especially on the weekends. Think of it as a meet market rather than a meat market. If you're a girl looking for some local action, you've got it made. Irish guys are anything but shy, and you can usually get—at the very least—a few free drinks in exchange for a bit of conversation. The Cork girls aren't so easily won over, though; offer a girl a drink and she might actually refuse. Don't take it personally. Many a rosy-cheeked Kansas boy has been shunned for no apparent reason; just be persistent and you just may win out eventually.

blues, jazz, Gypsy, rock, classical, New Age—yup, all of it. Big names like Beth Orton frequent the gig list, and Cork native Sinead Lohan got her start playing upstairs at the Lobby as well. (Never heard of her? Shame on you! Pick up her latest, *No Mermaid,* at any record store.) Most consider the Lobby to be *the* best live music venue in Cork, so it might be worth that sizeable cover to check it out. Find out what's up for any given night in the ubiquitous Cork calendar magazine, *The List.*

The Shelbourne *(16-17 MacCurtain St.; Tel 021/4509-615; info@shelbourne-bar.com, www.shelbourne-bar.com; V, MC, AE),* a few blocks north or St. Patrick's Bridge, offers live music sessions every Monday between 9:30 and 11:30pm; sometimes it's trad, and other times you'll hear modern folk. Either way, the warm soft golden lighting, comfy seats, and a big old fireplace encourage listeners to stay for a while.

Hear live trad at **Sin É** [see *bar scene,* above] beginning at 9pm Tuesday nights and 6pm on Sundays. **An Spailpín Fánac** [see *bar scene,* above] has live trad sessions Sunday-Friday beginning at 9:30pm, and there's rarely a cover charge. The **Shandon Craft Centre** [see *stuff,* below], on the north bank of the River Lee, a six-minute walk from the historic center, directly south of St. Ann's church, hosts free concerts in June, July, and August, from 1–2pm. The music is folk, trad, jazz, or classical. **The Crawford Gallery** [see *arts scene,* below], in the exact center of the historic old city, immediately east of Paul Street Plaza, serves up classical concerts once a week in May and June beginning at 1:15pm. Admission is £5; pick up info at the gallery gift shop.

club scene

Cork's nightlife just keeps getting livelier and livelier, and you could easily stay a week and do a different nightclub every night. If you aren't much for sweaty crowds and deafening techno or pop, there are artsier choices as well. Pick up a copy of *The List,* the local listings magazine, almost any

what'd he say

A quick primer on the ins and outs of Irish slang:

Did he just ask for a *snog?* Kiss him if he's not too frog-like.

"How's the *craic?*" If there's lots of fun to be had, you tell 'em it's good.

If there's a live *trad* sesh here tonight, you'll be hearing some Irish folk music, complete with *bodhráns,* guitars, fiddles, and maybe even a set of *uilleann* pipes.

If it seems like a local is pulling your leg, he may very well be *slagging* you—that is, teasing you or giving you misleading information for a laugh at your expense.

Cheers is often used to mean "thanks," as well as "bottoms up!" and *no worries* is another way to say "you're welcome."

If somebody asks you to call, they don't mean on the phone—they're expecting you to visit. Use the phone if they ask you to ring. This little bit of slang vastly differs from American as well: To *knock somebody up* means to knock on their door, not to...well... you know.

place around town to see what's happening when and where. But beware: not all clubs are clean or completely safe—in fact, some of those not listed here can be downright foul. Whichever one you choose, stick to the main streets and away from dark alleys late at night, even if somebody who looks just like Mr. Rogers offers you a lollipop.

Rugby boys and preppy-types predominate at **The Red Room** *(17 Liberty St., off Washington St.; Tel 021/4251-855; Tue, Thu-Sun; Cover £3-5).* This club, on the western edge of the historic center near the junction of Washington Street and North Main Street, supposedly admits people over 23 only, which for some means the crowd's just too old to party properly. The scene gets better on a Tuesday night though, when you'll find more students getting hot and tipsy to loud, loud music. Get in for free before 11:30pm on Thursday and Sunday nights. It'll do, but it's by no means the greatest.

A perennial favorite, **Sir Henry's** *(S. Main St.; No phone; Wed-Sat; www.freakscene.com; Cover £2-11),* next to An Spailpin Fánac [see *bar scene,* above] is a winner of the "Best Dance Club in Munster" award. The drug scene brought the fuzz—err, the *gardaí*—in a few years ago, but the security's better nowadays and it's totally safe. Anyway, the mix here's as eclectic as the music: everything from indie dance to jazz, disco to eighties pop to techno, on four different venues with half-a-dozen DJ's. *Freakscene* on Wednesdays and *Planet of Sound* on Fridays are especially popular. First established as a rave club, Sir Henry's was a pioneer in the genre in Europe. Nirvana, among other legendary bands, played here, back when grunge was still cool. Even jaded veterans of big-city scenes should find this a suitably intense clubbing experience. Don't be a chump and pay full price; a little scouting and you should be able to find concessions, those coupons for free entry and specials, at the hostels, pubs, and at lots of other places around town.

The most popular club with Cork's students, **Gorby's** *(74 Oliver Plunkett St.; Cover £2-5)* reaches absolute maximum capacity every night of the week. Hot and sweaty local college peeps grind and saliva-swap to a mix of pop, alternative, and indie tunes. Get yourself there before 11pm and save a few punts; girls get in for free on Sunday nights.

The **City Limits Comedy Club** *(16 Coburg St.; Tel 021/4501-206; Comedy at 9pm, club 11pm-2am Fri-Sat; Cover £5-8),* in the North Bank, is a super-popular outing on Friday and Saturday nights after the comedy act's finished. Buy a ticket for both the show and the club before 8:30pm; if you'd rather just go to the club, come around 11pm. Most club-goers are at least in their early twenties, but the DJ has been known to spin a few moldy oldies in between the new pop singles.

Get dressed up for **Cubin's** *(Hanover St., off Washington St.; 11pm-2am, Tue, Thu-Sun; Cover £5),* but don't act as though you've tried. The wall murals follow a sort of *Gladiator*-chic ancient Rome theme, and the crowd here's nearly all working professional (over 23), aside from a few seasoned students. Locals say it's where the "cliquey posers" come to stand around and look pretty, in between Ricky Martin songs.

Nearby **Havana Brown's** *(Washington St.; Tel 021/4279-105; Cover £5),* part of Rearden's pub, [see *bar scene,* above] is much the same deal: a sweaty pop-infused meat market, for people over 23 only, which means you'll be rubbing elbows mostly with the "I-graduated-last-year-so-me-mum-made-me-move-out-and-get-a-job" set. Not that there's anything wrong with that....

Were you looking for a more refined nightspot frequented by artsy, intellectual types? Or how about just a place with a live band every so often? **The Half Moon Club** *(Half Moon St., behind the Cork Opera House; Tel 021/4270-022; Midnight-2am Thu-Sun; Cover £5),* in addition to showing some of Cork's coolest plays, also hosts a nightclub on weekends. There are at least three different rooms to choose from, and the DJs go beyond mainstream tunes. Often live bands deliver refreshingly offbeat sounds, like Afro-Celt music and other styles with a distinctly international flavor. No teeny-boppers here; the Half Moon's prized by Cork's cosmo-thirsty boho crowd, however small it may be.

By day, **The Yumi Yuki Club** *(Tobin St.; Tel 021/4227-577; 11pm-2am Tue-Sun; yumiyukiclub@oceanfree.net; Cover £3)* is a trendy new small but super-stylish Japanese restaurant, a self-described "Sushi Sake Café Bar," on the second floor of the Triskel Arts Centre. It's open before, during, and after the performances downstairs. By night, the tables are pushed aside and the classy art-hung walls vibrate with funk, jazz, and all that's *not* pop. Art students and members of Cork's general bohemia frequent the Yumi Yuki, making it a perfect alternative for those who don't like the ring of words like "mosh," "grind," or "Britney Spears."

arts scene

▸▸VISUAL ARTS

If only Cork's galleries could match the vibrancy of its fantastic old theaters—it'd be an artists' heaven. Oh, well. There's still stuff to see, most notably **The Fenton Gallery** *(Wandesford Quay; Tel 021/4315-294; nualafenton@eircom.net; www.artireland.net),* on Waterfront near Clark's Bridge, the latest addition to Cork's short list of commercial art galleries. It's fairly impressive, too: A huge gallery showcasing the most brilliant and unusual specimens in contemporary Irish art opens into a spacious courtyard. It's a hip, hip place, especially with a wine bar and cafe inside as well.

The **Triskel Arts Centre** [see *performing arts,* below] includes two small galleries for traveling art shows among its other happening arts events. Given the plugged-in nature of this complex, anything here is worth checking out.

The **Crawford Municipal Art Gallery** *(Emmet Place; Tel 021/4273-377; 10am-5pm Mon-Sat; www.synergy.ie/crawford; Free),* at Paul Street Plaza shows a small handful of works by Yeats and Keating as well as many by contemporary Irish artists. It also hosts frequent visiting exhibitions, both Irish and international. It's a bit disappointing, since there's not a whole lot to see, but it's worth a quick look and a leisurely lunch in the cafe.

The Cork Arts Society, aka the **Lavitts Quay Gallery** *(5 Father Matthew Quay, off South Mall; Tel 021/4277-749; 10am-6pm Mon-Sat; Free)* is a solid commercial gallery with exhibitions of contemporary work by well known Irish artists.

▸▸PERFORMING ARTS

For its size, the arts scene is amazingly vital in Cork, and theater is the star player. The place to start nosing around for plays, or anything else artsy, is fortunately no further than Main Street. Although there is no theater district per se, all theaters lie within an easy walk of each other. There is no central ticket office, so tickets must be purchased individually for each theater.

Triskel Arts Centre *(Tobin St., off S. Main St.; Tel 021/4272-022; 10am-5:30pm Mon-Sat, open 7:30pm for evening performances; triskel@iol.ie, www.iol.ie/triskel; V, MC)* is a fantastic venue for art and theater workshops, comedy acts, poetry and book readings, concerts, and plays. Two small galleries house visiting art exhibitions, and the Triskel Cinematek has frequent screenings of artsy international films. **Kino** *(Washington St. West)* is another venue for indie foreign films.

The **Everyman Palace Theatre** *(MacCurtain St.; Tel 021/4501-673; Most performances begin at 8pm; £6-10; V, MC)* hosts classic plays, like *Dr. Faustus* and an adaptation of *Gulliver's Travels,* as well as contemporary

festivals and events

Even if you aren't interested in this stuff, know that it will affect hotel availability: If you plan to be in town on these dates, book your rooms well in advance.

Intermedia *(May; Tel 021/4272-022)* is a month-long festival of experimental art forms by international artists, including "sound sculpture," improvisation, video, and performance art. Events take place in venues all over Cork City, in addition to Triskel Art Centre [see *arts scene,* above], which sponsors the festival.

An important gathering of jazz artists from around the world, the **Guinness International Jazz Festival** *(Mid-late Oct; call the tourist office at Tel 021/4272-595 for info www.corkjazzfestival.com)* attracts everybody who's anybody in the jazz world: Past participants have included Ella Fitzgerald, Wynton Marsalis, B. B. King, and Dizzy Gillespie. You'll find music at every conceivable venue in the city, even in the streets. Listen to top-notch performers for free in the pubs.

The high-profile and long-established **Murphy's Cork Film Festival** *(Early Oct; call the tourist office at Tel 021/4272-595 for info; www.corkfilmfest.org)* screens films—international, documentary, experimental—at Triskel and the Opera House [see *arts scene,* above], highlighting works by young directors and offering seminars and workshops for filmmakers.

Every pub and theatre in town is shaking to the old tunes during **The Cork Folk Festival** *(Sep; call the tourist office at Tel 021/4272-595 for info),* when local and international performers put their heads together to create art, theater, music and Irish heritage events.

The Cork International Choral Festival *(Late Apr; Tel 021/4308-308; www.corkchoral.ie; £10-12)* brings choral concerts and competitions to City Hall, **Jury's Hotel** *(Western Rd.; Tel 021/4274-477),* the Cathedral of St. Mary, and the Shandon Church [see *culture zoo,* above]. Tickets are available from the booking office at **Merchant's Quay Shopping Centre** *(Merchant's Quay; Tel 021/4270-169)* or at **Pro Musica** *(20 Oliver Plunkett St., Tel 021/4271-659).*

Irish productions in a cozy, intimate, well-worn theater. See whatever's playing and go out for a drink afterward; it makes for a nice evening, and your mother will be proud that you got a bit o' "culcha" in between drinking your wits away. Catch any play in previews and you'll pay only £5.

Like the Everyman, the nearby **Cork Arts Theatre** *(Knapp's Sq., off Camden Quay; Tel 021/4508-398; Most performances at 8pm; £8; V, MC)*

cork city

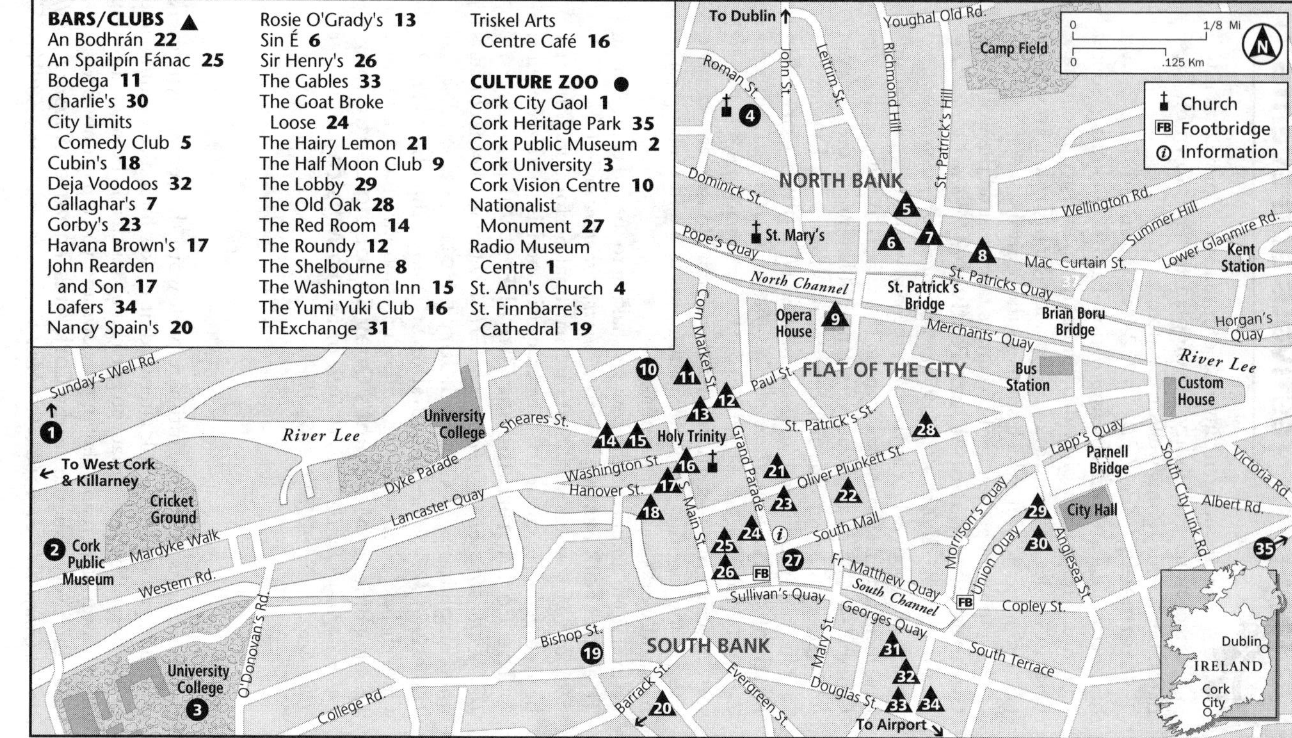
BARS/CLUBS
An Bodhrán 22
An Spailpín Fánac 25
Bodega 11
Charlie's 30
City Limits Comedy Club 5
Cubin's 18
Deja Voodoos 32
Gallaghar's 7
Gorby's 23
Havana Brown's 17
John Rearden and Son 17
Loafers 34
Nancy Spain's 20
Rosie O'Grady's 13
Sin É 6
Sir Henry's 26
The Gables 33
The Goat Broke Loose 24
The Hairy Lemon 21
The Half Moon Club 9
The Lobby 29
The Old Oak 28
The Red Room 14
The Roundy 12
The Shelbourne 8
The Washington Inn 15
The Yumi Yuki Club 16
ThExchange 31
Triskel Arts Centre Café 16
CULTURE ZOO
Cork City Gaol 1
Cork Heritage Park 35
Cork Public Museum 2
Cork University 3
Cork Vision Centre 10
Nationalist Monument 27
Radio Museum Centre 1
St. Ann's Church 4
St. Finnbarre's Cathedral 19
0
1/8 Mi
0
.125 Km
N
Church
FB Footbridge
i Information
To Dublin
Youghal Old Rd.
Camp Field
Roman St.
John St.
Leitrim St.
Richmond Hill
St. Patrick's Hill
Dominick St.
NORTH BANK
Wellington Rd.
Summer Hill
Lower Glanmire Rd.
Kent Station
St. Mary's
Pope's Quay
Mac Curtain St.
St. Patricks Quay
North Channel
St. Patrick's Bridge
Brian Boru Bridge
Horgan's Quay
Corn Market St.
Opera House
Merchants' Quay
River Lee
FLAT OF THE CITY
Paul St.
Bus Station
Custom House
Sunday's Well Rd.
University College
River Lee
Sheares St.
St. Patrick's St.
Holy Trinity
Grand Parade
Lapp's Quay
Parnell Bridge
South City Link Rd.
Victoria Rd.
To West Cork & Killarney
Dyke Parade
Washington St.
Oliver Plunkett St.
Hanover St.
S. Main St.
Cricket Ground
Lancaster Quay
Morrison's Quay
City Hall
Albert Rd.
South Mall
Union Quay
Anglesea St.
Cork Public Museum
Mardyke Walk
Western Rd.
FB
Fr. Matthew Quay
South Channel
Sullivan's Quay
Copley St.
Georges Quay
O'Donovan's Rd.
Bishop St.
SOUTH BANK
Mary St.
South Terrace
Dublin
IRELAND
University College
Cork City
Barrack St.
Evergreen St.
Douglas St.
College Rd.
To Airport

stages a wide range of productions on a small scale with both local and traveling theater companies.

Cheap tickets and offbeat performances make the **Granary Theatre** *(Mardyke Quay; Tel 021/4904-275; Most performances at 8pm; £3-7)* a definite contender. Plays here tend to probe and explore; recent productions have covered everything from cutthroat Hollywood to free love to Noah's wife's take on the whole flood deal. The Granary also stages fresh new scripts, even some by ambitious UCC students.

Don't rule it out just yet: the **Cork Opera House** *(Emmet Place; Tel 021/4276-357; Most performances at 8pm; V, MC)* has more to offer than overweight drama queens belting out songs in Italian. This place does drama, classical and popular concerts, and ballet, as well as opera. It's a pretty conservative venue—not the place for any edgy experimental work. Be prepared to dress up or be stared at. With an average ticket price of £12 and the cheapest going for a mere £6, you won't miss the student discounts and half-price coupons found in other cities. Standing room is available only at the last minute. Recent productions have included *Hamlet* and Oscar Wilde's *The Importance of Being Everest.* If you just can't handle that level of culture, duck around to the excellent **Half Moon Theatre** *(Cork Opera House; Tel 021/4270-022; Most performances at 8pm; £10; V, MC)*, which showcases concerts and both comedy and drama, featuring classic plays like Sophocles' *Antigone* that alternate with contemporary Irish-hatched productions. After weekend shows, the Half Moon caters to Cork's artsier club-goers [see *club scene,* above].

For laughs, try **City Limits Comedy Club** [see *club scene,* above], a really popular venue on Friday and Saturday nights. Ticket prices depend on how well known the comedian is; buy yours before 8:30pm. The price includes both the show and entrance to the nightclub afterwards.

Just north of the historic center on the same block of St. Ann's Church, The **Firkin Crane Centre** *(Shandon; Tel 021/4507-487)* is the best place for classical and contemporary dance productions performed by local and touring companies. Yup, that's pretty much it.

gay scene

Cork might not be at the very top of the list of openminded cosmopolitan cities, but you'll find it's as good, if not better, a place than Dublin to do your own thing. There are actually a few B&B's in County Cork catering *exclusively* to gays and/or lesbians, and there are lots of gay-friendly nightspots in town.

For information or support, call the **Cork Lesbian Line** *(Tel 021/4271-087; 8-10pm Thu)* or **Gay Information Cork** *(Tel 021/4271-087; 7-9pm Wed, 3-5pm Sat).* There's an **Irish Gay and Lesbian Film Festival** in mid-October; call the Gay Information Cork line for information about exact dates, times, and locations. Online resources include **Cork's Lesbian Community Online,** *www.explode.to/corklesbians,* and the **OASIS** page at University College Cork, *www.ucc.ie/ucc/socs/oasis/contact.htm.*

the rainbow connection

Did you know that homosexuality wasn't legalized in Ireland until 1993? Ouch! Don't cross Ireland off your itinerary just yet though—the country might not be quite as accepting or tolerant of alternative lifestyles as the United States, but there are still plenty of cool places to hang out and "be yourself" in the big cities: Galway, Cork, and Dublin.

The Other Side Café and Bookshop *(8 S. Main St.; Tel 021/4276-582; 10am-5:30pm Mon-Sat)* functions as a bookstore, cafe, and drop-in center; pick up a copy of *The Gay and Lesbian News, Munster Edition*, here. Around the corner, **The Other Place** *(7-8 Augustine St.; Tel 021/4278-470)*, a vegetarian cafe popular with local gays and lesbians, has a pub open Tuesday-Sunday after 7pm and a dance club on Fridays and Saturdays from 11:30pm to 2am; cover is £4. The first Friday of every month is girls-only. Definitely call for information before stopping by, since they've got this funny "membership" thing that's sometimes in force.

Along with The Other Place, **Loafers** *(26 Douglas St; Tel 021/4311-612)* about a five-minute walk south of the old town near the Red Abbey ruins, is Cork's official pub for gays and lesbians, although every so often the place goes "out of style" and the rainbow crowd decides to frequent another pub in town. The regulars at *that* pub then go someplace else until the unofficial Loafers boycott ends.

As for clubs, try the *MÓRdisco* on Tuesday nights or *Fetish* one Friday a month, both at **Zoë's** *(Caroline and Oliver Plunkett St., above the Black Bush; Tel 021/4270-870; Open nightly till 2am; Cover £5)*. They're always tremendously popular with gay men. **The Half Moon** and **The Yumi Yuki Club** [see *club scene,* above] are also good places to "just be yourself," and **Bodega** and **The Roundy** [see *bar scene,* above] make excellent pub hangouts.

All the Cork hostels are gay-friendly, but you might want to check out **Roman House** *(3 St. John's Terrace, Upper John St.; Tel 021/4503-606; rhbb@eircom.net, www.interglobal.ie/romanhouse; £25 single, £18 per person)*, a five-minute walk north of the old town, which provides accommodation exclusively to gay and lesbian travelers. Heteros will never know what excellent vegetarian breakfasts and super-comfy rooms they'll be missing.

The **Nadrid House** *(Inniscarra Lake, Coachford, County Cork; Tel. 021/4831-115; £17-22/person; Full Irish/veggie breakfast included; V)*, formerly the Amazonia B&B for Women, is moving in May 2001, to a grand

Georgian mansion set on a picturesque lake half an hour from Cork City, near the airport. In addition to the changes in name and setting, this gay B&B will also be opening its doors to men. Sporting equipment—bikes, kayaks, tennis rackets, etc.—is available for *free,* and so are pick-ups from the Cork Airport or ferryport. The owners also offer a vegetarian dinner, complete with *homemade wine.* Can this place possibly get any cooler? Another B&B that caters to gays and lesbians is Mont Bretia, in Skibbereen, on the coast [see **Skibbereen**].

The Sauna *(36 Lower John St.; Tel 021/4502-484; £10 admission)* caters to gay, bisexual, and "interesting" men. The price of admission allows for exit and re-entry, any time, all day.

culture zoo

Even if you skip the museums and churches—and Cork has a pride of them—make sure to stop by the **university**, where you can ooh and ahh over the incredible stained glass windows in the chapel then walk back out onto the campus and hook up with the city's lively student scene.

Nationalist Monument *(South Mall; Free):* This monument across the street from the tourist office, [see *need to know,* below], was erected in the memory of the Irishmen killed during the 1798 and 1867 rebellions against those awful English.

The Shandon Church aka **St. Ann's Church** *(Shandon; Tel 021/4505-906; 9:30am-5:30pm daily Jun-Sept; 10am-3:30pm daily Oct-*

down and out

Short on cash? You can still see a play at **The Granary Theatre** [see *arts scene,* above] for as little as £3. Check out the flyers around town or look in *The List* for what's playing.

Check your email for only £1 an hour at **Webworkhouse** [see *wired,* above] on Sunday evenings and for £2 an hour every other night of the week, but be prepared to wait.

Looking for action but suffering from an empty wallet? Girls get in free at **Gorby's** [see *club scene,* above] on Sunday nights, and most nights anybody can get in for only a punt or two before 11pm.

At **The Red Room** [see *club scene,* above] on Friday nights starting at 6pm you can hear the Courthouse String Quartet play—a little formal, sure, but there's free food! On Thursday and Sunday nights, get into the club for free before 11:30pm.

Rearden's [see *bar scene,* above] occasionally hosts wine-tasting sessions along with piles of great food, all for free. Casually and sweetly ask the bartender if there's one coming up anytime soon.

cork city

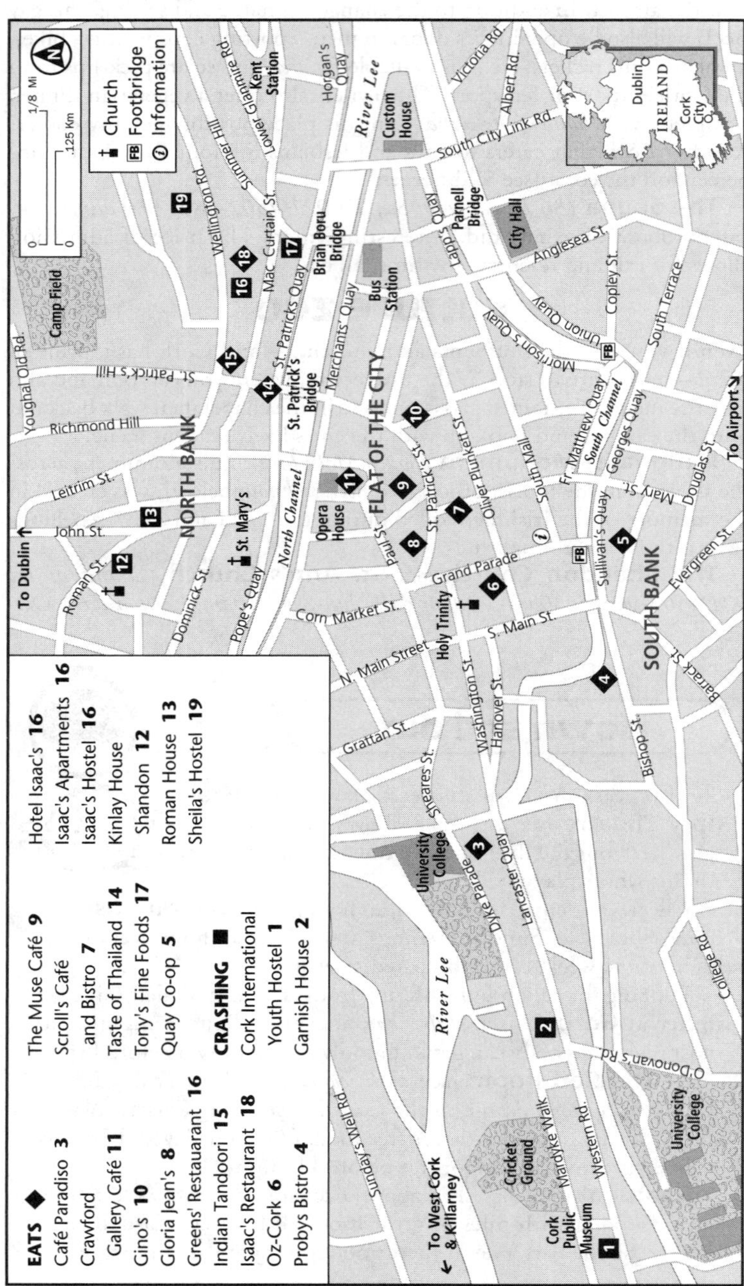
EATS ◆
Café Paradiso 3
Crawford Gallery Café 11
Gino's 10
Gloria Jean's 8
Greens' Restaurant 16
Indian Tandoori 15
Isaac's Restaurant 18
Oz-Cork 6
Probys Bistro 4
The Muse Café 9
Scroll's Café and Bistro 7
Taste of Thailand 14
Tony's Fine Foods 17
Quay Co-op 5
CRASHING ■
Cork International Youth Hostel 1
Garnish House 2
Hotel Isaac's 16
Isaac's Apartments 16
Isaac's Hostel 16
Kinlay House Shandon 12
Roman House 13
Sheila's Hostel 19
Church
FB Footbridge
Information
0
1/8 Mi
0
.125 Km
N
Dublin
IRELAND
Cork City
Camp Field
Youghal Old Rd.
Wellington Rd.
Summer Hill
Lower Glanmire Rd.
Kent Station
Horgan's Quay
River Lee
Custom House
Victoria Rd.
Albert Rd.
South City Link Rd.
Parnell Bridge
City Hall
Lapp's Quay
Anglesea St.
Mac Curtain St.
Brian Boru Bridge
Bus Station
Merchants' Quay
St. Patricks Quay
St. Patrick's Hill
St. Patrick's Bridge
Richmond Hill
Leitrim St.
John St.
To Dublin
Roman St.
Dominick St.
St. Mary's
Pope's Quay
North Channel
NORTH BANK
Opera House
FLAT OF THE CITY
Paul St.
St. Patrick's St.
Oliver Plunkett St.
Morrison's Quay
Union Quay
Copley St.
South Terrace
South Mall
Fr. Matthew Quay
South Channel
Georges Quay
To Airport
Douglas St.
Mary St.
Sullivan's Quay
SOUTH BANK
Evergreen St.
Grand Parade
Holy Trinity
Corn Market St.
S. Main St.
N. Main Street
Washington St.
Hanover St.
Barrack St.
Bishop St.
Grattan St.
Sheares St.
University College
Dyke Parade
Lancaster Quay
River Lee
College Rd.
O'Donovan's Rd.
Sunday's Well Rd.
To West Cork & Killarney
Cricket Ground
Mardyke Walk
Western Rd.
Cork Public Museum
University College

May; Admission £3 adults, £2 students, £3 to climb the tower): A visit to the 18th-century Shandon Church is, according to its curators, "an occasion of pure delight!" (How poetic.) The admission price might sound hefty, considering it's just an old church, but it's totally worth it: Upon climbing the tower you can see the whole city, and even better, you can do the Quasimodo thing and ring the bells yourself! Where else can you—yes, *you personally*—ring real actual church bells, and play songs that the entire city will hear? Sheet music—that is, the 1-6-8-8-7-9-1-kinda thing—is provided. Just make sure you're not up there when someone else is ringing them, unless you don't mind your ears buzzing for the rest of the day. The church also harbors a collection of very, very old books. Notice, also, how the four clocks on each side of the Shandon tower don't read the same time any longer, earning it the nickname of the "four-faced liar." Mass takes place Sunday mornings at 10am, in case you're interested in repenting for all that wild carousing you engaged in over the previous week.

St. Finnbarre's Cathedral *(Bishop St.; Tel 021/4963-387; 10am-1pm/3-5:30pm Mon-Fri; Free):* This late 19th-century cathedral occupies the site of Finnbarre's original church and school from the year 600, so it still qualifies as the founding stone of Cork—a city that even the Vikings couldn't succeed in finishing off. The building you see today dates mainly from 1880, when it was constructed in the pseudo-French-Gothic style popular at the time. Its trio of gigantic spires form one of the most prominent features of the Cork cityscape. Though there is no treasure trove of art to be found inside, the cathedral is richly ornamented, and best known for its mosaics.

Cork Public Museum *(Fitzgerald Park; Tel 021/4270-679; 11am-1pm/2:15-5pm Mon-Fri, 3-5pm Sun; Open till 6pm Jul-Aug; Free Mon-Fri, 75p Sun):* The museum houses some mildly interesting archaeological artifacts from early pagans, plus good scoop on local Republican heroes (remember, Republican here does not mean the G.O.P.); stop in for a quick look after your prowl of UCC across the street [see below].

University College Cork *(Western Rd.; Tel 021/4902-758 or 021/902-371 for tours; 9am-5pm Mon-Fri; Free):* UCC is the glorious epicenter of student life in Cork. Founded by Queen Victoria in 1845, the university is housed in a quadrangle of Gothic Revival style structures surrounded by beautiful, tree-lined gardens and lush lawns. The campus has walled college enclosures in the style of Trinity Dublin, a sort of Gothic look. characterized by sharp jagged angles and V-shaped door archways. While you can certainly prowl around on your own and see everything, the tour (£15 regardless of group size) will explain to you what you're looking at and provide historical lore about the college. You are free to enter the Central Student Center and meet local students while grabbing a bite to eat. For information about student-oriented goings-on, pick up the weekly "Eolas Diary," available free at many points all over the campus. While you're at UCC, check out the gorgeous **Honan Chapel** *(UCC grounds; Free)* and its terrific stained-glass windows.

Cork Heritage Park *(Bessboro Rd., Blackrock; Tel 021/4358-854; 10am-5pm Sat-Sun, Apr; 10:30am-5:30pm Sat-Sun, May-Sep; closed Oct-*

Mar; Admission £3.50 adults, £2.50 students): Set beside an inlet of Cork Harbour in a 19th-century courtyard, Cork Heritage Park offers several *mildly* interesting exhibits on Cork's maritime history, the history of the Pikes (a Quaker banking and shipping family who used to own the house), the environment, archaeology, and the history of Cork firefighting between 1450 and 1945. It's only two miles south of Cork's city center, but you can also take Bus Éireann Route 2. Academiaphobes should avoid it.

Cork City Gaol *(Sunday's Well Rd.; Tel 021/4305-022; 9:30am-6pm daily, Mar-Oct; 10am-5pm daily, Nov-Feb; Admission £3.50, adults, £3 students, joint ticket to Gaol and Radio Museum £7):* Fans of the gruesome bits of history should enjoy themselves very nicely at the Cork City Gaol, whose regal facade seems a total cover-up for the wretched conditions within-in the 19th century, at least. Exhibits strive to recreate the prison experience as accurately as possible, though the politically correct angle is added with presentations in several languages that intently explain how economic conditions of the period forced many Irish to resort to crime.

Radio Museum Experience *(Cork City Gaol, Sunday's Well Rd.; Tel 021/4305-022; 9:30am-6pm daily, Mar-Oct; 10am-5pm daily, Nov-Feb; Admission £3.50 adults, £3 students, joint ticket to Gaol and Radio Museum £7):* If you're already going to the Cork City Gaol [see above] you might as well buy a joint ticket anad take in the Radio Museum upstairs as well. This museum deals with the impact of the invention of radio on everyday life, and has cool exhibits on the early days of Irish radio. A bit more interesting than idle nose-picking.

Cork Vision Centre *(N. Main St.; Tel 021/4279-925; 10am-5pm Tue-Sat; visioncentre@eircom.net; Free admission):* No, it's not an optometrist's shop but a civic p.r. display that'll tell you everything you want to know about Cork City and a whole lot more. A scale model of the city is the focal point, and there are also frequent visiting exhibitions, films, photographs, interactive computers, and a café. Not a bad intro to the city.

modification

Although it looks kinda intimidating from the outside, the service at **Raven Tattoos** *(Paul St.; 11am-5pm Tues-Sat),* in the center of town north of St. Patrick's Street, is friendly and clean—always a plus wherever needles are involved—and the "art" is high quality. Go ahead and shock your family.

The Santal Hair Group *(Oliver Plunkett St.; Tel 021/4276-544; 9am-5pm Mon-Sat; V, MC)* offers half-price cut-and-color for students on Mondays, Tuesdays, and Wednesdays. If you were considering going blond, now's the time!

city sports

Hurling and Gaelic football matches are held on Sundays at 3pm in the summer at the **Pairc Uí Chaoimh Stadium** *(Marina Walk; Tel 021/4385-876 or 021/963-311).* Take Bus Éireann Route 2 and tell the driver you're going to the stadium. If you were wondering how to pronounce the name of the stadium, it's like "park ee queev," with a guttural spin on the "queev." However you pronounce it, you shouldn't miss this; no trip to Ireland is complete without seeing at least one hurling match or football game. The sweaty, roaring crowds, the cute hot-headed players, the liberal flow of Guinness—the *craic* just doesn't get any better than this. Call the stadium or check with the local newspapers for times and other info. Tickets to these games can be steep (£13-15), and it may be nearly impossible to find any for the most important matches, but there are also evening games on Sundays, Saturdays, and Wednesdays that cost £4 or less per ticket.

Don't ask why, but the Irish are crazy for dog racing. Brand-spanking new **Cork Greyhound Stadium** *(Curraheen Park, Curraheen Rd.; Tel 021/4543-095; cork@igb.ie, www.igb.ie;£3)* hosts greyhound racing at 8pm on Wednesday, Thursday, and Saturday. This surprisingly unsleazy place has a bunch of bars, restaurants (where waiters will give you advice on which dogs are the best bet, no doubt), and shops, and even live entertainment as well as a bureau de change.

great outdoors

Perhaps the best way to see the city is to walk it, but you can always rent a bike: try Rothar Rent-A-Bike, Cyclescene, or Irish Cycle Hire [see *need to know,* below for all]. A special "tourist trail" will lead you to most of the major cultural attractions in Cork City; it would make a nice afternoon walk. Get the info at the tourist office [see *need to know,* below].

For aquatics and scenic hikes and the like, you'll have to venture out of the city for a day at the very least. Try **Atlantic Sea Kayaking** in Union Hall, West Cork [see **Union Hall**]; scuba diving, windsurfing, or kayaking

a trip to the zoo

This is no ordinary zoo; you won't find any cages here. Featuring 90 different species of wildlife from five continents, **FOTA Wildlife Park** *(Carrigtwohill; Tel 021/4812-678; 10am-6pm Mon-Sat, 11am-6pm Sun, Mar 17-Sep 30; Open weekends Oct-Mar; £4.80 Adults, £2.50 students; V, MC)* may bring back memories of school field trips, but it's a good deal cooler, with picnic areas, gardens, video shows, a gift shop, and a cafe. Some of these animals are so exotic, it's impossible even to pronounce their names, and the arboretum boasts plants and trees every bit as exotic as the animals. It's easy to get to: take an Irish Rail train from the station in Cork City—there are 19 trains Monday-Saturday and nine on Sunday.

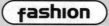

fashion

You won't find too many trendsetters—at least not when it comes to fashion—in Cork City. Posh and preppy is the style of choice for girls, and guys seem to be sticking with Adidas. Whatever you wear, though, the ensemble simply isn't complete without a cell phone. You get bonus points for a flashy color and an especially irritating ring ditty.

in Kinsale [see **Kinsale**]; or go deep-sea diving off the Baltimore coast (that's in County Cork, not Maryland), where you can explore a whole bunch of shipwrecks [see **Baltimore**]. That's just the beginning of a long list; being the biggest county in Ireland and quite peninsular, Cork's got quite a long stretch of beach to play on.

stuff

Stores full o' goodies abound on Patrick Street. You can probably find what you're looking for at one of the shopping centers in Cork City: Merchant's Quay, Paul Street, Savoy, or Grafton, all which offer a decent range of gift shops and boutiques for finding teeny-bopper or clubbing clothes or a hip pair of kicks.

▸▸CRAFTS

Housed in the old Butter Exchange dating from 1730, **Shandon Craft Centre** *(Cork Exchange, John Redmond St.; Tel 021/4508-881)* features craftspeople displaying their creations. Along with the usual pottery, glassware, jewelry, and clothing, some even sell handmade instruments like violins and cellos. During the summer months, free folk, trad, classical, and jazz concerts are held at 1pm.

Bound Waterstone's Booksellers *(Entrances on 69 Patrick St. and 12 Paul St.; Tel 021/4276-522; 9am-8pm Mon-Thu, 9am-9pm Fri, 9am-7pm Sat, noon-7pm Sun; V, MC),* in addition to everything else, stocks the usual selection of volumes on Ireland and the local scene. Another mondo-bookstore chain where you're sure to find almost anything, including local papers, is **Eason's** *(113/115 Patrick St.; Tel 021/4272-681; www.easons.ie; V, MC).* The Muse Café on the second floor serves inexpensive sandwiches and salads [see *eats,* below].

The bookshelves at **Mainly Murder** *(2A Paul St.; Tel 021/4272-413; 10am-5:30pm Mon-Sat)* are stuffed with...well...it's pretty self-explanatory.

Vibes and Scribes *(3 Bridge St.; Tel 021/4505-370)* sells new and used books and CDs. It's a great place to flip through stacks while consulting the encyclopedically informed staff.

▸▸BAZAAR

Coal Quay Market *(Cornmarket St.; 9am-5pm Mon-Sat)* has all the usual flea market stuff—clothing, furniture, jewelry, books, whatever—all of it secondhand and worth digging through for a few great finds.

Dating all the way back to the 17th century, **The Old English Market** *(Grand Parade, enter from Grand Parade, Princes, Plunkett, or Patrick Sts.; 9am-6pm Mon-Sat)* sells fresh, fresh, *fresh* (as in *still moving*) fish, meats, vegetables, and fruits, as well as some really gross stuff you can only get in authentic local markets, like tripe (animal stomach), drisheens (blood sausage), and crubeens (pig's feet). Come here for the bustling atmosphere even if you don't need groceries.

eats

Not surprisingly for a relatively large city with European influences, there's no shortage of great places to eat in Cork.

▸▸CHEAP

There's excellent pub grub to be had at **John Rearden and Son** [see *bar scene,* above]. Lunch is served between noon and 2pm during the week, noon to 6pm on Sundays, and dinner's from 3pm onward. Try the steak on hot garlic baguette with lettuce and mushroom sauce for £5.50, or penne pasta with garlic bread and tomato fondue for a mere £5.

The Shelbourne *(16-17 MacCurtain St.; Tel 021/4509-615; info@shelbourne-bar.com, www.shelbourne-bar.com; lunch noon-2:30pm, £5; V, MC)* also has a good lunch menu with the standard soups, sandwiches, and salads for under £5.

As traditional as a pub gets, **The Gables** [see *live music scene,* above] serves extraordinarily good pub grub, such as hearty ploughman's lunches, between noon and 3pm, then again between 5pm and 9pm.

A smart choice for breakfast or lunch, the **Crawford Gallery Café** *(The Crawford Gallery, Emmet Place; Tel 021/4274-415; 10am-5pm Mon-Sat; all items under £8; V, MC)* is stylish in a laid-back Victorian sort of way, attracting suited business-lunchers and bohemian art-lovers alike. Here you'll find fresh seafood dishes, baked goods, and open sandwiches. Good for meat-and-potatoes types, too, the café also serves more traditional Irish fare, like steak and kidney pie. The food's so good because the

bottoms up

"May you have the hindsight to know where you've been,
The foresight to know where you are going,
And the insight to know when you have gone too far."

place is run by some serious chefs, whose fancy hotel in the nearby small town of Midleton [see **Midleton**, below] even offers cooking classes.

Does browsing the bookshelves make you hungry? Pick up a cheap sandwich or salad at **The Muse Café** *(113-115 Patrick St.; Tel 021/4272-681; all items under £4; V, MC)*, a small cafe on the second floor of Eason's bookstore.

The perfect place for a late breakfast after a long pub crawl the night before, modest but comfortable **Tony's Fine Foods** *(8 MacCurtain St.; No phone)* offers a substantial full Irish or vegetarian breakfast for only £3.25. You can pick up pizzas, burgers, and the like here as well. It's just a hop, skip, and a jump from Sheila's or Isaac's hostels [see *crashing*, below].

Bright and serviceable, second-floor **Scroll's Café & Bistro** *(6 Princes St.; Tel 021/4270-251; Noon-6:30pm Mon, noon-10:30pm Tue-Sat, 9:30am-6:30pm Sat-Sun; under £6; V, MC, AE)* has just what you need: good, cheap food. Prices are even lower if you opt for take-out. Eat-in prices are all under £6 for standard cafe fare: lasagna or meat dishes, sandwiches, soups, and full Irish breakfasts on weekends.

Gino's *(7 Winthrop St., between Patrick and Oliver Plunkett; Tel 021/4274-485; Noon-11pm Mon-Sat, 1pm-11pm Sun; £5; V, MC)* makes the best pizzas in town, and the ice cream here is Cork's tastiest. Try hazelnut. (Just don't expect a cone.)

For something cheap, greasy, and exotic, try **Indian Tandoori** *(MacCurtain St.; No phone; under £5; No credit cards)*. Chill out with Indian music in this fluorescent yellow hole-in-the-wall, or call for take-out.

▸▸DO-ABLE

Ah, a taste of the Emerald City on the Emerald Isle! But Dorothy never ate as well as you will at chill pacific-hued **Oz-Cork Bistro** *(73 Grand Parade; Tel 021/4272-711; 8am-11pm Mon-Fri, 9am-11pm Sat-Sun; main courses £5-7; V, MC)*, although you'll have to tolerate the head waitress' wicked witch act. Aside from the service, the pizza, pastas, and salads are totally outstanding—an upscale bistro with upscale food at not-so-upscale prices. Reservations are absolutely essential, because the place is beyond super-popular. Cork's resident hipsters flock here at all hours of the day and night. The staff obliges by trying to get people in and out as quick as possible, which is too bad—otherwise it'd be a great place to hang out and people-watch over a pesto and sun-dried tomato pizza and a glass of red wine. Try the lasagna—ginger is the not-so-secret ingredient that makes the dish especially good. How come no one at home ever thought of that?

The **Quay Co-Op** *(24 Sullivan's Quay; Tel 021/4317-660; 9:30am-10:30pm daily, table service 6:30-10:30pm daily; lunch £4-6, dinner £5-8; V, MC)* dishes out the sort of vegetarian food that makes self-denial a non-issue. Besides standard dishes like lasagna or pizza, served with two salads or cooked vegetables, the menu offers more exotic and unusual treats like lentil and coconut soup or spinach and sun-dried tomato roulade. The Co-Op operates just like your grade-school cafeteria by day (except with much, much better food), but has regular table service by night. Feeling inspired after your meal? An organic-food grocery store is downstairs. The Quay Co-Op is enormously popular, and not just with countercultural types.

Near St. Finnbarre's Cathedral, **Probys Bistro** *(Probys Quay, Crosses Green; Tel. 021/4316-531; info@probysbistro.com, www.probysbistro.com; Lunch noon-2pm, dinner 6-10:30pm; £4.50-8 lunch, £9-15 dinner; V, MC)* might be a splurge for dinner, but lunch is a good value. Put together super-fresh local seafood, meats, and veggies with Mediterranean-style cooking and you've got a winner. Probys has a full bar as well, so enjoy a glass of red wine—or a Guinness—along with your penne puttanesca (tossed in tomatoes, onions, capers, black olives, roast peppers, and parmesan cheese, naturally), and don't miss the cream-topped strawberry and cinnamon tart for dessert.

For the best Thai in Cork (granted, it's the *only* Thai in Cork), go to **Taste of Thailand** *(8 Bridge St.; Tel 021/4505-404; 6-10:30pm daily; V, MC)* before 7:30pm for the £10 three-course early bird menu. You'll find lots of veggie options and especially good service.

▸▸SPLURGE

Café Paradiso *(16 Lancaster Quay; Tel 021/4277-939; 12:30-3pm/6:30-10:30pm Tue-Sat; Dinner £11-13; V, MC),* is often called *the* best vegetarian restaurant in the whole country (it even sells its own cookbook, for £20 yet), but this is one of those superlatives that actually might be deserved. You won't find a more inventive menu anywhere else; even hard-core carnivores feel satisfied here. Picture a salad with balsamic-roasted cherry tomatoes, goat's cheese, pine nuts, lentils, and grilled aubergine (that's the Euro term for eggplant) doused in basil, washed down with a glass of red wine, and a dish of strawberry baked Alaska for dessert. Dining in Cork just doesn't get any finer than this.

The hotel restaurant at Isaac's [see *crashing,* below], **Greene's** *(48 MacCurtain St.; Tel 021/4552-279; Breakfast 7:30-10am, bar food noon-6pm, dinner 6-10:30pm daily; greenes@isaacs.ie; dinner entrees £10-14; V, MC, AE)* might be a splurge, but the leftovers will feed you for at least another day. The early bird special, between 6pm and 7pm daily, makes an especially good deal: for around £13 or £14, you can get a three-course meal (a three-course Sunday brunch is also available for the same price). Try the superb potato and leek soup for a starter, followed by the (large) filet steak that comes with a Jenga-tower of perfectly crispy golden-brown french fries—er, *chips*—decorated in parsley, along with a hefty helping of fresh veggies. For dessert, the lemon tart and ice cream are good bets. The main courses are mostly seafood, but there are several vegetarian options, too, and the service is as excellent as the food. Providing the weather's cooperating, you can have dinner in the courtyard next to a waterfall that's romantically floodlit by night. If you're staying at the hostel next door, you'll save cab fare too (you know you can justify this if you try hard enough...).

crashing

▸▸CHEAP

The Cork International Youth Hostel *(1/2 Redclyffe, Western Rd.; Tel 021/4543-289; £8 dorm),* a recently renovated Victorian, is definitely nicer than the average An Óige hostel, but the location's far from ideal, unless you're going to be spending a lot of time at UCC, right across the street. The hostel has all en suite dorms, a bureau de change, full breakfast for £4, and an immaculate dining room, kitchen, and common room. It'd be perfect if only it were closer to downtown. Although you *could* walk here, you can also take city bus 8 from the Parnell Place Bus Station out to Western Road; you can also take that bus back into the city (it stops every 15 minutes outside the hostel).

The operators of centrally located **Sheila's Hostel** *(3 Belgrave Place, Wellington Rd.; Tel 021/4505-562; www.sheilashostel.ie, info@sheilashostel.ie; £7 6-bed dorm, £8.50 4-bed dorms, £21 double)* seem to have thought of everything: The friendly, helpful reception desk serves as a sort of general store, offering snacks, breakfast, and lunches; there's a bureau de change, video rental, barbecue facilities, Western Union, open fireplace, and Internet access (albeit a clunky kiosk). Heck, this place even has a sauna where you can purge away your impurities at £1.50 for 40 minutes. It's undoubtedly the best hostel in Cork City, although the rooms are a bit small and the

irish soda bread

What makes traditional Irish food so good is its earthy simplicity, the classic example of which is hot, wholesome, Irish soda bread. To make it yourself, preheat the oven to 450 degrees (Fahrenheit) and sift four cups of flour, one teaspoon of salt, and one teaspoon of baking soda into a bowl. Pour in one and two-thirds cups of buttermilk or sour milk (to sour fresh milk, add a few teaspoons of lemon juice—don't use fresh milk, or the bread won't rise) and mix the ingredients together by hand. Put the dough on a floured board and knead lightly for a minute until the dough is smooth, then shape it into a mound about an inch-and-a-half high. Cut a deep cross into the dough and place on a floured cookie sheet. Bake at 450 degrees for 15 minutes, then at 400 degrees for another half-hour. Let cool before enjoying with a generous dollop of creamy butter and a nice hot sweet cup of tea. *Voilé!*

shower facilities leave room for improvement. It's a five-minute walk from St. Patrick's and the main train station.

Like its counterparts in Galway and Dublin, **Kinlay House Shandon** *(Bob and Joan Walk; Tel 021/4508-966, kincork@usit.ie, www.iol.ie/usitaccm; £9-10 dorm, £12-13 4-bed dorm, £16 single, £12 per person double and triple; £30-36 double; V, MC)* in the old residential area of Shandon, close to St. Ann's Church, isn't a terrible option, but it just can't shake that orphanage feel. Reception could be a bit nicer, and the prices are on the high end. On the other hand, continental breakfast is included, there is a self-catering kitchen, a laundry, security lockers, a luggage storage area, a TV/video lounge, and you can get Internet access for £5 an hour on—gasp—a real computer! Not *bad,* but definitely not great.

Recently renovated, **Isaac's Hostel** *(48 MacCurtain St.; Tel 021/4508-388; corkhostel@isaacs.ie, www.isaacs.ie/isaacs_hostel_cork.htm; £8-10 dorm; V, MC),* part of the same complex as Isaac's Hotel [see below], now boasts all en suite rooms and a convenient central location. The biggest perk, though, has got to be the people: Isaac's is tremendously popular with backpackers, so you're sure to meet plenty of potential drinking buddies. Hostellers are also welcome to chill in the pretty lil' courtyard between the hostel and the hotel.

▸▸DO-ABLE

You'll find a big selection of B&B's on Western Road near the University College Cork campus, but don't just pick any old one. **Garnish House** *(Western Rd.; Tel 021/4275-111; garnish@iol.ie, www.garnish.ie; £25 and up single, £40 and up double)* is among the very best of the B&B's in Cork. Not only do the owners greet you with tea and scones upon your arrival, they'll do your laundry for free, and some of the double rooms even have Jacuzzis. (Those rooms cost around £50.) Rooms are festooned with fresh flowers and the beds are luxuriously comfortable. As if that isn't enough to convince you to stay here, a look at the mile-long breakfast menu will do the trick. If you want to cast off the backpacking mindset, Garnish House would make a perfect—not to mention romantic—choice.

Another idea, if you're traveling in a group of four or more, is to stay in one of the do-your-own-cooking **Isaac's Apartments** *(MacCurtain St.; Tel 021/4500-011; cork@isaacs.ie, www.isaacs.ie/~cork; £80-100 per night for 5-7-person apt.; V, MC),* which you can rent for as little as a single night. Not only are the apartments quiet and beautifully furnished, with a kitchen, living room (with TV, of course) and three bedrooms, it's significantly cheaper than the hotel for pretty much the same thing. A three-bedroom apartment sleeping five to seven people goes for £100 a night in the high season and £80 in the low. divide that five to seven ways and you've got a good deal. You can also get a two-bedroom apartment, sleeping four people, for £18-22 per person.

Other do-able options are **Antoine House** *(Western Rd.; Tel. 021/4273-494, Fax 021/4273-092; Shared rooms £25/person, singles £35,* *private baths, breakfast included; V, MC, AE),* right in the center city—buses stop outside the house, and the train station is only a few minutes away; and **Kent House** *(47 Glanmire Rd. Lower; Tel 021/4504-260).*

▸▸SPLURGE

You can't get any more central than **Hotel Isaac's** *(48 MacCurtain St.; Tel 021/4500-011; cork@isaacs.ie, www.isaacs.ie/~cork; £49 single, £70 double; V, MC),* a restored tobacco-drying plant with the original hardwood floors, friendly service, and immaculate and cozy rooms. Kick back and plan your evening in the comfy sitting area near the reception desk, complete with fireplace and plush sofas, or outside in the courtyard next to a picturesque, albeit fake, waterfall. The hotel restaurant, Greene's [see *eats,* above], serves fantastic three-course specials—meat and seafood mostly—between 6pm and 7pm for around £14. Could it be any more convenient? The **Everyman Palace Theatre** [see *arts scene,* above] is just across the street.

within 30 minutes

Blarney Castle *(R617, Blarney; Tel 021/4385-252; 9am-6:30pm Mon-Sat, 9:30am-5:30pm Sun, May and Sept; 9am-7pm Mon-Sat, 9:30am-5:30pm Sun Jun-Aug; 9am-sundown Mon-Sat, 9:30am-5:30pm Sun, Oct-Apr; Admission £3.50 adults, £2.50 students)* is at the top of the list of Irish tourist attractions for an absolutely ridiculous reason—need it be said?—the Blarney Stone. A priest-turned-poet in the 1830s was silly enough to write that this stone bestowed the gift of eloquence on whomever kissed it, and it's been swarming with tourists ever since. Maybe he got that idea from Lord Blarney's talent for talking his way out of dealings with Queen Elizabeth in the 16th century—who knows, but at any rate the superstition is now permanently cemented in everyone's tribal memories. The castle itself is worth a visit, but as for the stone, it's blackened by decades of smooching, and don't think the staff ever even sprays the damn thing with disinfectant, either—it's as dirty as that pair of underpants you've been wearing for three weeks straight. Use your common sense for once, and JUST SAY NO. If you insist, Blarney is reachable by Bus Éireann route 154 for £3 round-trip; buses leave rather frequently from the bus station to meet constant demand. This site also boasts the highest concentration of cheesy souvenirs per capita in all of Ireland (and that's saying something). As for the town of Blarney itself, there's really nothing else of interest, but if you want to stay overnight, you can try **Blarney Tourist Hostel** *(Killarney Rd., Blarney; Tel 021/4385-580 or 021/4381-430; £7 dorm; No credit cards),* in an old farmhouse.

Now that we've cleared that up and you're not going to Blarney Castle, you have time for some other delightful day trips to nearby towns like **Cobh**, the port from which your ancestors may have sailed for America; **Midleton**, a mecca for all lovers of Irish whiskey; and the scenic fishing village of **Kinsale**, all of which are covered later in this chapter.

need to know

Currency Exchange You can change money at the **Cork Tourist Office** [see below] or **Sheila's Hostel,** the **Cork City International Hostel** [see *crashing,* above], or at any bank. There are several banks along the main streets, including Patrick Street, North Main Street, and Bridge Street, all with typical bank hours.

Tourist Information The **Cork Tourist Office** *(Grand Parade; Tel 021/4273-251;)* is the main location for picking up maps and useful advice. There is a Budget Car Rental office here as well.

Public Transportation **Bus Éireann** operates a Cork City bus service; Route 8 hits most places in town, and it's useful if you're staying out on Western Road and don't want to lug your bags. Otherwise it makes more sense to walk everywhere.

Health and Emergency Police: **Garda Headquarters** *(Barrack St.; Tel 021/4316-020).* **Bon Secours Hospital** *(College Rd.; Tel 021/4542-*

the lord protectorate

Say what you will about Oliver Cromwell: intriguing, misguided, melancholy, heroic. Just make sure what ever you say about him while in Ireland includes the words ghastly, savage, and evil.

In 1649, Oliver Cromwell arrived in Dublin as commander-in-chief and lord lieutenant of Ireland, and set about destroying all opposition. One of the most brutal and effective butchers any empire has ever enlisted, Cromwell simply devastated Ireland, which still bears the scars of his savagery. To this day, some Irish spit when they say his name. Cromwell left no doubt about who was in charge. His campaign lasted only 7 months, but his brutal, bloodthirsty methods broke the back of all resistance. In his siege of the town of Drogheda alone, 3,552 Irish were killed, while Cromwell lost only 64 men. After subduing all but Galway and Waterford, Cromwell left Ireland and its administration in the care of his lieutenants and returned to England. His stamp lingered for centuries, and the memory of it still burns.

The Irish were offered a choice after the massacres: Anyone suspected of resisting the English forces could leave the country, give up their lands and resettle in Connaught or County Clare, or die.

Britain's hold on Ireland was thus solidified and would persist until the Easter Rebellion of 1916 and the War of Independence that would soon follow.

807), **Cork University Hospital** *(Wilton St.; Tel 021/4546-400)* and **City General Hospital** *(Infirmary Rd.; Tel 021/4311-656)* all provide medical attention.

Pharmacies For needs pharmaceutical, get thee to **Duffy's Dispensing Chemists** *(96 Patrick St.; Tel 021/4272-566;)*, **Phelan's Late Night Pharmacy** *(9 Patrick St. Tel 021/4272-511)*, or **Murphy's Pharmacy** *(48 N. Main St.; Tel 021/4274-121)*.

Airport **Bus Éireann** links the city center with **Cork International Airport** *(Cork City; Tel 021/4313-131; www.corkairport.com)* 12 times daily for £2.50 one-way. Buses leave from the bus station at Parnell Place. Two airlines service Britain and Europe for Cork: **Aer Lingus** *(Tel 021/4327-100)* and **Ryanair** *(Tel 01/609-7800)*. Flights from Cork Airport to the Americas and Asia are less frequent.

Trains and Bus Lines Out of Town **Irish Rail** *(Tel 021/4506-766)* and **Bus Éireann** provide nationwide service from **Parnell Place Bus Station** *(Tel 021/4508-188)*. Taxis are plentiful along Patrick Street and South Mall; to call for one, try **ABC Cabs** *(Tel 021/4961-961)*, **Shandon Cabs** *(Tel 021/4502-255)*, **Supercabs** *(Tel 021/4500-511)*, or **Tele-Cabs** *(Tel 021/4281-100)*.

Boats Ferry services from Cork depart from **Ringaskiddy Terminal,** 10 miles southeast of Cork, serviced by Bus Éireann for £3. Service is available to Swansea/Le Havre or Roscoff/Cherbourg via **Brittany Ferries** *(Tel 021/4277-705)*, **Irish Ferries** *(Tel 021/4504-333)*, or **Swansea Cork** *(Tel 021/4271-166)*.

Bike Rental There are several places to rent bikes in Cork: **Irish Cycle Hire** *(At the train station; Tel 021/4551-430)*; **Rothar Rent-A-Bike** *(2 Bandon Rd., Barrack St.; Tel 021/4313-133; rct@tinet.ie, rct.foundmark.com; £10 per day, £40 per week, £15 one-way service, £50 deposit; V, MC)*; or **Cyclescene** *(396 Blarney St.; Tel 021/4301-183; 8:30am-6pm Mon-Sat; £10 per day, £40 per week, £50 deposit)*. If you rent from the last two locations, the bike can be returned to any Raleigh Rent-A-Bike location nationwide.

Laundry If you're smelling funky, head to **Duds 'n Suds** *(Douglas St.; Tel 021/4314-799; 8am-9pm Mon-Fri, 8am-8pm Sat; wash and dry under £4)*. They also offer dry cleaning.

Postal Send those lovely postcards from the **General Post Office** *(Oliver Plunkett St.; Tel 021/4272-000; 9am-5:30pm Mon-Sat)*.

Internet [see *wired,* above]

everywhere else

cobh

Cobh—that's "cove" to you—is a good option for a day trip out of Cork City. There's not too much going on here these days, but until the 1960s it was Ireland's principal transatlantic port, the last bit of the old sod seen by countless Irish emigrants fleeing the Famine in the 1840s, and where the *Titanic* made its last stop in April 1912 before beginning its fateful America-bound voyage. When the *Lusitania*, a British ocean liner, was sunk by a World War I German submarine in May 1915, the survivors (as well as the bodies which could be recovered) were brought to Cobh, and a memorial still stands in Casement Square, near a mass grave.

There's not an awful lot of interesting stuff to do here, but there are a few good pubs and a couple of heritage museums that might (or might not) be worth a look, such as the Queenstown Story, with its haunting exhibits on the *Titanic* and *Lusitania* disasters. Otherwise, if you've got a drop of Irish blood in you, it can be very emotional just to see the last place in Ireland your ancestors saw before leaving; a brand-new museum provides plenty of information for a nominal fee.

The Queenstown Story *(Next to the Cobh railway station; Tel 021/4813-591; 10am-6pm daily, last admission at 5pm; Admission £3.50 adults, £2.50 students)* covers the *Titanic* and *Lusitania* wrecks, the topic of Irish emigration, and the overall role of Cobh (once known as "Queenstown") in maritime history. **St. Colman's Cathedral** *(On the waterfront; 7am-8pm daily)* is also worth a visit; its neo-Gothic spire dominates the Cobh skyline, but unfortunately you aren't allowed to climb the tower. Begun in 1868 by the famed neo-Gothic architect A.W.N. Pugin, the cathedral was finally completed in 1915 and revels in having the largest harmonized bell system, or carillon, in the country; there are 47 bells, and they weigh a total of 7,700 pounds. (Now you know why no one is allowed up into the spire.)

Cobh is best experienced as an afternoon excursion out of Cork City. It really doesn't make much sense to stay the night, since there are precious few accommodations here and **Irish Rail** *(Cork City station; Tel 021/4506-766)* runs back and forth 20 times a day (eight times on Sundays).

eats

There are several places to eat right in the village. If you want cheap eats, you can get reliable—but not thrilling—coffee shop fare at **O'Brien's Coffee Shop,** *(8 Pearse Square; Tel 021/4814-091).*

need to know

Tourist Information For Information, try the **Cobh Tourist Office** *(On the waterfront, up the hill from the train station; Tel 021/4813-301; 9:30am-5:30pm Mon-sat, 11am-5pm Sun).*

castletownbere

Castletownbere is worth visiting for a very un-Irish attraction—a secluded little Tibetan Buddhist retreat perched high on a cliff overlooking the sea. Wait...is this still *Ireland* we're talking about? Yep. Along with breathtakingly beautiful ocean views from the lovely Beara Peninsula, you can reach nirvana (meaning the spiritual state, not Kurt Cobain's band) at the temple known as the **Dzogchen Beara Retreat Centre** *(Garranes, Allihies; Tel 027/73032, Fax 027/73177; weekly stay £175-£350; Oct-Apr 2-3 nights £100-£160; very limited space in cottages for 2-6 people; advance reservations strongly recommended).* And right next door is the excellent **Garranes Farmhouse Hostel** *(Cahermore; Tel 027/73147; £5 dorm; 20 beds, no private rooms; No credit cards)*—clean, comfy, and oh-so-convenient for temple visiting. The Buddhists (who aren't officially connected with the hostel) welcome visitors who'd like to meditate in their wonderfully atmospheric, candle-lit space. Betcha get goose bumps just thinking of meditating in this dramatic setting, right? Unfortunately, tons of other people have the same idea, especially July-August. Book way ahead.

need to know

Directions/Transportation Another problem, aside from the fact that the retreat is far from secret: it's hard to get to if you don't have a car. **Bus Éireann** *(Tel 64/30011)* runs from Killarney (Route 282, summer only) or Cork (Routes 46 and 236) to Castletownbere, but the hostel and retreat are a five-mile walk or cycle from here. They really want to make sure you're serious about the need to *om.* When you call ahead to reserve your room, you can always try asking for a pick-up from the bus station.

dursey island

A mere 250 meters (820 feet) off the coast of the Beara Peninsula in West Cork, Dursey Island is the final destination of Cork's most memorable **cable car** *(Allihies; Tel 027/73017; Runs on demand 9-11am/2:30-5pm/7-8pm Mon-Sat, varies Sun; around £3 round-trip).* The 10-minute ride to the island is a little unsettling, but hey, it sure beats swimming! There are a few things you need to know: Bikes aren't permitted on the cable car—they're not necessary, anyway: the island is only a few miles long. Cows get precedence over people on the cable car—yes, it's big enough for bovines. And on Sundays, the cable car runs primarily to shuttle the islanders to church service on the mainland.

The island's biggest claim to fame is a totally tragic story: in 1602, 300 Irish people fled to Dursey to escape the English. But they were followed, and every single person was thrown over a cliff into the sea by the unbelievably cruel English troops. It's yet another example of why the Irish have a chip on their collective shoulder when it comes to the Brits.

Obviously you won't find any big parties going on here—you'll find only seven actual island residents and a helluva lot of sheep—but it's a perfect place for some quiet, romantic reflection, and Dursey's got *the* best views on the Beara Peninsula.

eats and crashing

There is nowhere—literally not a single place—to get anything to eat on the island, so it's definitely BYO lunch. You can freelance camp here wherever you find a spot no one's using, but unless you're prepared to rough it, it's probably better to make it a day trip and stay in Allihies, instead.

If you're waiting over for the cable car and need a light meal, drinks and sandwiches for your trip, or a place to crash, you can go to the **Windy Point House** *(Allihies; Tel 027/73017; Food served 11am-6pm; Double rooms £18.50/person; Breakfast included)* near the cable car station. Rooms in this modern house are simply but comfortably furnished, and you can relax in summer outside in the patio watching the cable car come and go. Food and drink can be ordered in the dining room overlooking the water. There's also a public lounge for telly-watching.

If you're trapped here, and the Windy Point House is full, you can always crash at the **Village Hostel** *(Allihies Village; Tel 027/73107; £8 for a bed, £18 for a private room),* a standard IHH hostel that will do you just fine for a night or two.

need to know

Directions and Transportation Allihies, the former site of a large copper mine, is the mainland town nearest to Dursey Island. If you don't have a car, it's difficult to reach this remote part of Ireland. A private bus company, **Berehaven** *(Tel 027/70007),* offers infrequent service, mainly in summer. You'll have to call to see how to hook up with this service. At any rate, you'll be delivered only to the village of Allihies, 5 miles from the actual cable-car station.

Bike Rental Instead of making the long walk, you can go to a place called **O'Sullivan's** *(Tel 027/73004; 9am-9pm daily),* along the main road at Allihies, where you can rent a bike (£6/day). You can also pick up the makings of a picnic here.

midleton

Midleton is all about one thing: Irish whiskey. Though the Jameson family's original distillery was established in Dublin, their finest whiskey is made at Midleton Distillery. If you aren't into whiskey, skip it. If you are, you'll love the little village and the local pub as well.

Every year since 1984, the distillery has produced a very limited bottling (100 cases) of Midleton Very Rare, but you won't be getting any free tastes of that at the **Jameson Heritage Centre** *(Midleton; Tel 021/613-594; 10am-6pm, Mar-Nov; Admission £4 adults, £3.50 students).* What you will get is a one-hour tour detailing the craft and history of whiskey production that ends with a free glassful of the good—but not best—stuff. After that, you may want to stop off at a local pub for more than a wee sip. It's definitely worth a day trip from Cork.

bar scene

For live trad music sessions to accompany your newfound taste for whiskey, try **The Meeting Place** *(Connolly St.; Tel 021/631-928; Cover £2)* or **The Town Hall Bar** *(74 Main St.; Tel 021/631-155).*

bottoms up

The Gaelic for whiskey is *uisce beatha,* ("ISH-keh BAH-ha") or "water of life"—and naturally the Irish claim that the French could never have come up with brandy without them. It's common knowledge, they will tell you, that the Irish were distilling the stuff first, and the French words for brandy—*eau de vie,* or "water of life," betray this. (The Irish do have a poetic way of putting *everything,* don't they? And like a lot of poets, they sometimes tend to mistake whiskey for water.)

eats

There's also great traditional Irish grub to be had at **Finin's** *(Main St.; Tel 021/631-878; 10am-10pm Mon-Sat, closed on bank holidays).*

crashing

If you do want to stay here, try **An Stór Hostel** *(Just off Connelly St., Midleton; Tel 021/633-106; £7 dorm, £10 per person double and twin; V, MC, AE).* The name means "the treasure" in Irish, and while it's not the best hostel in the world, you might consider it a small treasure anyway, with its blooming window boxes, friendly staff, and clean, airy, and comfortable atmosphere. And you gotta love that £2 laundry service.

need to know

Directions/Transportation Midleton is only a 25-minute **Bus Éireann** ride from Cork City (at least ten a day, eight on Sun).

union hall

This sleepy but delightful little town on the road to Skibbereen is a highly recommended stop, especially for nature-lovers, thanks to the beautiful West Cork coastline. A great way to explore it is with **Atlantic Sea Kayaking** *(Union Hall; Tel 028/33002; atlanticseakayaking@tinet.ie),* which offers arguably one of the best outdoor experiences in Ireland. The coastline is especially conducive to exploring: think small deserted islands, sea caves, secluded coves, and lots of varieties of colorful marine life. Atlantic Sea Kayaking offers overnight tours, too, as well as eerily cool night-paddling excursions. Accommodations and (good!) dinner and breakfasts are provided. Beginners are welcome, too. Don't wuss out—you'll be glad you didn't, especially if you come in the summer months and are lucky enough to catch mild weather (it does take some luck). The other great reason to stop in Union Hall is **Maria's Schoolhouse Hostel** [see *crashing,* below], a gorgeous old converted stone schoolhouse in idyllic surroundings.

eats

You want gourmet vegetarian *and* meat dishes? You got 'em at (where else) **Maria's Schoolhouse Hostel.** A three-course meal costs £15; breakfast is £3-5. Better still, Maria's has a wine license and there are people who say this place stacks up fine against some five-star hotels. So if you're in the area, this one's worth a diversion.

crashing

The place to stay is obviously **Maria's Schoolhouse Hostel** *(Cahergal, Union Hall; Tel 028/33002; Mar 15-Dec 31; mariasschoolhouse@tinet.ie; £8 dorm, £20-30 double; V, MC)*. Maria's consistently takes the top spot on many "Best Hostels in Ireland" lists, and it's easy to see why. It's immaculate and beautifully furnished, with high cathedral ceilings, sky-lit dorms, and a huge arched window in the airy and comfortable sitting room.

need to know

Tourist Information Tourist Office *(Town Hall; Oct-Mar 9:15am-5:30pm Mon-Fri; Apr-Jun 9am-6pm Mon-Sat; Jul-Sep 9am-7pm daily).*

Directions and Transportation Bummer that Bus Éireann doesn't stop in Union Hall—but no worries! Maria's will pick you up from the bus station in Skibbereen, where the bus *does* stop, eight kilometers away; just give a ring.

youghal

Texans will have no problem pronouncing Youghal—that's "y'all," y'all! The town's got a nice, if overcrowded, beach, and pretty coastal views that are spoiled somewhat by the unsightly sprawl of parked vacation caravans and RVs. The beach is blue-flagged, meaning the EU has dubbed them safe for swimming. It can be a decent place to spend the night if you're traveling between Cork City and Waterford and want to get some use out of that bathing suit. And the city's medieval charm (with Norman walls dating from 1275 surrounding the city) is as strong as its reputation as a beach holiday magnet. If Youghal can't quite compare to the amazingly beautiful—and surprisingly untouristed—towns of West Cork like Union Hall, at least one sorta cool thing going for it is that the movie adaptation of *Moby Dick*, with Gregory Peck, was filmed in Youghal in 1954. Another cool tidbit: It's said that Sir Walter Raleigh used to stroll these beaches (though probably not in a Speedo...).

culture zoo

A lone item of cultural interest, late-15th-century **Tynte's Castle** *(N. Main St.; Not open to the public)* is the only surviving example of a fortified residence in east Cork, and only one of two in the county. Originally it belonged to a wealthy Anglo-Norman merchant's family, but more recently served as a dry goods store before being purchased by a Youghal family.

youghal

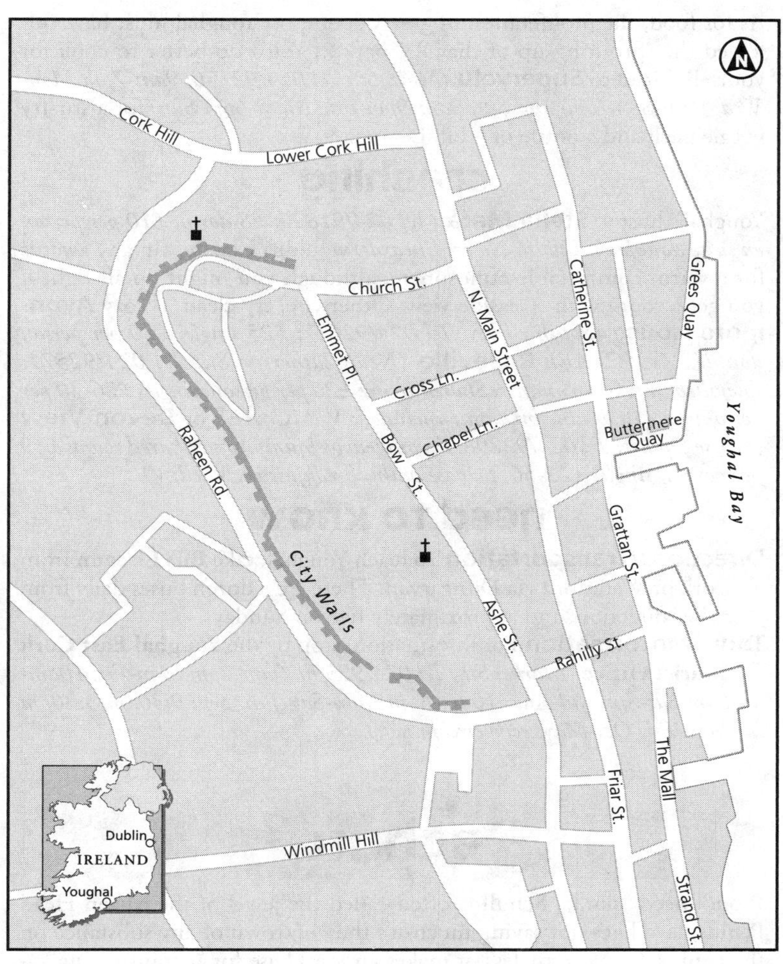
Cork Hill
Lower Cork Hill
Church St.
Emmet Pl.
N. Main Street
Catherine St.
Grees Quay
Cross Ln.
Chapel Ln.
Bow St.
Buttermere Quay
Youghal Bay
Raheen Rd.
Grattan St.
City Walls
Ashe St.
Rahilly St.
The Mall
Friar St.
Windmill Hill
Strand St.
Dublin
IRELAND
Youghal

eats

As for food, the proliferation of greasy spoons in Youghal must have followed the sprouting-up of that RV park.... You'd do better to cook for yourself. Head to **Supervalu** *(Main St.; Tel 024/92150; 9am-7pm Mon-Wed, 9am-8pm Thu and Sat, 9am-9pm Fri, 10am-6pm Sun)* for a stir-fry veggie pack and a bottle of Club Lemon.

crashing

Youghal's hostel, **Stella Mara** *(Tel 024/91820; £8 dorm; £10 per person en suite double and twin; No credit cards)* wouldn't exactly win any awards for a warm comfortable atmosphere, although you might do all right if you get a room with a seaside view. Otherwise, try clean 'n cozy **Avonmore House** *(South Abbey; Tel 024/92617; £25 single, £20 per person double; V, MC, AE)*; **Roseville** *(New Catherine St.; Tel 024/92571; rosevillebandb@aircom.net; Shared rooms £20 per person, singles £26-30 per person; private baths, breakfast included; V, MC, AE)*; or **Devon View** *(Pearse Square; Tel 024/92298; devonview.webjump.com; Shared rooms £19 per person, singles £22-50, private baths, breakfast included; V)*.

need to know

Directions/Transportation To reach Youghal, take **Bus Éireann** from Cork or Waterford via Dungarvan. There are a dozen buses daily from either direction, and approximately five on Sundays.

Tourist Information For information, stop by the **Youghal East Cork Tourist Office** *(Market Sq.; Tel 024/92390; 9am-7pm Mon-Fri, 10am-6pm Sat-Sun, Jul-Aug; 10am-6pm Mon-Sat, Jun, Sep; 9:30am-5:30pm Mon-Fri, Oct-May; ect@eircom.net;)*.

schull

Pronounced "skull," Schull is often called the jewel of the Mizen Head Peninsula. That's not saying much-it's the *only* town of any substance on the peninsula. Nevertheless, it makes an ideal base for "peninsulating"—that is, exploring the rest of what this finger of land has to offer, including an awesome lighthouse at Mizen Head and a beautiful beach near **Crookhaven** [see *great outdoors,* below]. While the Mizen Head peninsula is relatively quiet and untouristy, Schull itself gets a lot busier in July and August, so be prepared to share the pubs and beaches with those tour-busers who have no idea what it's like to live out of a backpack for weeks at a time. There are plenty of opportunities in Schull for biking, walking, and water sports; catch a ferry to Sherkin or Cape Clear Island if you're yearning for something more remote [see below for both]. Schull itself has only one busy street (named **Main Street,** appropriately enough), so you'll have the place down pat in no time at all.

bar, club, and live music scene

Unfortunately Schull isn't the best place to find live traditional Irish music; a couple of pubs do offer live folk music once or twice a week during the summer though.

Blessed with a blend of backpackers and locals, **An Tigín** *(Main St.; Tel 028/28830)* is one of the most popular pubs in town by virtue of its dartboard and live music sessions (twice a week during the summer, and once a week in the winter). As per usual, live music sessions in the pubs generally begin around 9:30pm and last for about two hours; ask around to find out which days they're happening this week.

A great place for pub grub and the occasional live folk session, **The Bunratty Inn** *(West End; Tel 028/28341; Meals served noon-8pm Mon-Sat; Main courses start at £3)* is your typical classy small-town pub. Check with the owners of the Schull Backpacker's Lodge [see *crashing,* below] to find out if the once-weekly music session is happening during your sojourn here.

culture zoo

Mizen Vision *(Mizen Head; Tel 028/35591 or 028/35115; 10:30am-5pm daily, mid-Apr-May and Oct; 10am-6pm daily, Jul-Sep; 11am-4pm Sat-Sun, Nov-mid-Mar; closed mid-Mar-mid-Apr and Jun; www.west-corkweb.ie; Admission £2.50 adults, £1.75 students):* This spectacular lighthouse looks out on a stunning combination of cliffs, ocean, and plenty of dolphins, whales, seals, porpoises, and birds. Tours, which cover the history of the Mizen Peninsula, are surprisingly colorful and informative. Even the drive out here is a joy. Take R592 southwest from Schull until it merges with the R591; when you reach Goleen, follow the signs for the lighthouse. Unfortunately, there really isn't any viable transportation alternative for those without cars. It's about 15km (9-10 miles) from Schull, and the highway makes for a pretty intimidating bike route.

Planetarium *(Colla Rd.; Tel 028/28552; 3-5pm Sun, Apr-May, 3-5pm Tue, Thu, Sat, Jun; 2-5pm Tue-Sat, 7-9pm Mon, Thu, Jul-Aug; Admission £3):* Rainy day? Never fear! Schull also offers what a lot of folks say is Ireland's best planetarium. It's part of the Schull Community College and it's right down the road from the Schull Backpacker's Lodge [see *crashing,* below]. The price of admission includes a 55-minute "star show" which begins at 4pm or 8pm.

great outdoors

You can rent a dinghy, windsurf, or dive from the **Schull Watersports Centre** *(By the pier; Tel 028/28554; 9:30am-8:30pm Mon-Sat; Dinghy rental £25 per half-day, windsurfing £10 per half-day).* The water's fine, and, as in Baltimore, there are plenty of old shipwrecks just waiting to be explored.

For those with wheels, you could take the R592 (which later becomes the R592) southwest to Crookhaven, a teeny little town located on a peninsula on the peninsula, and savor the gorgeous **Barleycove Beach,** which has been hailed as one of the finest in the region. The water might be just a tad chilly (okay, try totally freezing), but it makes a nice romantic spot for a picnic lunch.

You can also grab a ferry to Sherkin or Cape Clear Island; boats leave from the Schull pier at 5:30pm daily in June and at 10am, 2:30pm, and 4:30pm daily July-August. If you want to cover more of West Cork than just the Mizen Head, it'd be much quicker to take a ferry from Schull out to one of the islands and then take another ferry to Baltimore instead of returning to Schull.

eats

You can always make good use of the kitchen at the Schull Backpacker's Lodge [see *crashing,* below] by picking up groceries at the **Spar** *(Tel 028/28236; 7am-9pm Mon-Sat, 8am-8pm Sun)* or **Hegarty's Centra** *(Tel 028/28520; 7:30am-10:30pm daily),* both on Main Street.
That said, there are several excellent places to eat with prices that won't leave your wallet smoking. **The Bunratty Inn** [see *bar, club, and live music scene,* above], true to its claim, offers excellent pub grub. Garlic mussels set you back around £6, and happen to be some of the tastiest in West Cork.

There are also a couple of delectable bakery-cafes in Schull: **Adele's** *(Main St.; Tel 028/28459; Tea or lunch 9:30am-6pm Tue-Sun, dinner 6-10pm Thu-Sun; V, MC)* offers gourmet baked goods, sandwiches, soups, salads, and tea during the day, and pasta or seafood dishes during the evening. Who could resist an aromatic dish of tagliatelle with rosemary and parsley pesto? Owner Adele and her chef-extraordinaire son really are marvels, so be on the safe side and make reservations for dinner. Similarly gourmet is **The Courtyard** *(Main St.; Tel 028/28390; 10am-4pm Mon-Sat; dinner served 6:30-9:30pm; V, MC, AE),* offering up freshly baked bread, soups, sandwiches, and fancy cheeses, as well as meat, seafood, and pasta dishes in the evenings.

crashing

If you're looking to spend the night in Schull, there's really only one place you should ever consider: the **Schull Backpackers Lodge** *(Colla Rd.; Tel 028/28681; schullbackpackers@tinet.ie, homepage.tinet.ie/~schullbackpackers; £7.50-9 dorm, £20-25 double, £4-5 camping; Bike rental £7 per day, £35 per week; V, MC),* which never fails to make any travel critic's list of the best hostels in Ireland. Located in a pristine wooden lodge, the dorm rooms are clean, airy, comfortable, and—dare we say it?—cozy! Yes, the owners bend over backwards to make the place as homey as possible, and it shows in the high-quality bath and kitchen facilities too. Sure, you could stay at one of the B&B's in town but this place gives them a real run for the money. There are only 31 beds, though, so you should definitely book ahead, especially for July-August. To get here from the pier, walk right toward town, then make a left at the fork in the road, take another left when you come to the church; the lodge is well signposted. Another do-able option, just a five-minute walk from the bus stop in the town center, is **Schull Central** *(Main St.; Tel 028/28227; Singles with or without private bath £20-25, doubles with or without private bath £17 per person; Breakfast included; No credit cards).*

need to know

Currency Exchange Old reliable **AIB** *(Upper Main St.; Tel 028/28132; 10am-12:30pm/1:30-4pm)* has an ATM.

Bus Lines Out of the City Head back to Cork via **Bus Éireann** *(Cork City office Tel 021/508-188)* on one of the three buses Monday-Saturday or one on Sunday, June-September only. There's also one bus daily from Schull to Killarney.

Bike Rental **Freewheelin'** *(Cotter's Yard, off Main St.; Tel 028/28165; 10am-noon Mon-Sat; £8 per day, £45 per week)* will get you wheeling, but it isn't exactly free; unfortunately, that price is not a typo. You can always rent a bike at the **Schull Backpacker's Lodge** [see *crashing,* above], which is cheaper, with more convenient hours.

Laundry **Schull Backpacker's Lodge** [see *crashing,* above] also has this covered for £3.

Postal Stamp-lovers can go crazy at the **Schull Post Office** *(Main St.; Tel 028/28110; 9am-5:30pm Mon-Fri; 9am-1pm Sat; Closed on bank holidays).*

skibbereen

Skibbereen, the largest town in West Cork, with over 2,000 souls, offers plenty of sporting and lounging possibilities. If you're the outdoorsy type, don't miss the **Russagh Mill Hostel and Adventure Centre** [see *crashing,* below], making good use of the many sporting options on the nearby River Ilen. A couple of absolutely gorgeous gardens are just begging to be explored [see *great outdoors,* below] right outside Skibbereen, and there are plenty of pubs offering live music most nights of the week.

Being the largest town in West Cork does have its disadvantages; be prepared to brave the throngs of tourists who flock to Skibbereen during the summer months. Consider heading further south to Baltimore [see below] if you'd rather avoid the occasional traffic jam—whether it be on the street or in the nearest pub. Skibbereen is remembered by most Irish as one of the hardest-hit places during the terrible Famine in the late 1840s that you've heard so much about. The local publication *The Skibbereen Trail* (yours for a punt at any Skibbereen newsagent) offers plenty of information about local historical sites.

neighborhoods

It's quite a pretty little town, with brightly-colored buildings and a relatively simple layout: it's L-shaped, with **North Street** at the bottom and **Main Street** continuing upward to become **Bridge Street** after—you guessed it—the bridge.

bar, club and live music scene

One of the best pubs in town, **The Wine Vaults** *(73 Bridge St.; Tel 028/22110)* earned its popularity by serving up excellent pub grub on Friday nights, along with live folk music that's almost as good, all in a cozy rustic atmosphere. Twentysomething locals—as well as better informed pizza-loving visitors—pack themselves in like sardines on any night of the week. The Wine Vaults deserves solid praise for its scrumptious homemade sandwiches, soups, and pizzas—chow down before the music starts; the kitchen closes at 9pm during the summer and 8pm during the winter.

Another solid bet for live music is **Seán Óg's** *(Market St.; Tel 028/21573),* with trad sessions on Tuesday nights and often folk or blues sessions on the other days. It's particularly praiseworthy for its beer garden—but be reminded that Guinness doesn't grow on trees; you'll have to fork over a few punts for a pint. **The Cellar Bar** *(Main St.; Tel 028/21329; Disco 11:30pm to 2am; Cover £5)* is worth knowing about for a couple of reasons: one, it's got a pool table that locals make good use of, and two, it's got Skibbereen's only nightclub on Friday and Saturday nights. The pub-goers at **Baby Hannah's** *(Bridge St.; No phone)* aren't quite as young as the name would suggest; the place is plenty popular with twentysomething locals though, and if you're here over the weekend you'll probably be able to sit in for a live trad session.

great outdoors

Check it out! Even if you aren't going to stay at the **Russagh Mill Hostel and Adventure Centre** [see *crashing,* below], call to ask about joining in on the fun.

Gorgeous, splendid, *magnifique!* Don't miss the **Creagh Gardens** *(Creagh, on the R595 motorway 5.6 km (3.5 mi) south of town; Tel 028/22121; 10am-6pm daily, Mar-Oct; Admission £3),* which have been hailed as some of the most beautiful gardens in the whole country—and that's saying a lot. Mosey on over here after a leisurely breakfast in town, spend a few hours exploring the greenhouse and the meandering paths through explosions of brilliantly-colored wildflowers and trees, and then savor a "light lunch" of organic produce from the garden in the tearoom.

There's also another garden, **Liss Ard** *(1 km (0.6 mi) east of Skibbereen on the Castletownshend Rd.; Tel 028/22368; 9:30am-5pm Mon-Fri, May-Sep; Admission £3 adults, £2 students),* offering some surprises of its own. Along with plenty of wildflower meadows, woods, and small lakes, there's the "Irish Sky Garden," a fantastic and difficult-to-describe structure that's decidedly un-Irish but definitely not worth missing.

TO MARKET

On the cheap? Cook for yourself with groceries purchased at the **Supervalu** *(Main St.; Tel 028/21400; 9am-6:30pm Mon-Sat).*

arts scene

Stop in at **The West Cork Arts Centre** *(North St.; Tel 028/22090; 10am-6pm Mon-Sat; Free)* to visit any of the oft-changing contemporary Irish art exhibits or the permanent collection. While you're there, see if there are any poetry readings or concerts scheduled during your stay in Skibbereen.

eats

The peeps at **The Wine Vaults** [see *bar, club, and live music scene,* above] busy themselves daily with redefining the term "pub grub." They're known for their homemade pizzas, but the unusually tasty (for pub fare, that is) eats also include tomato and basil soup, sandwiches, and salads. You won't have to spend more than £5 or so. Food is served until 9pm in the summer and 8pm in wintertime.

Similarly delicious and inexpensive is breakfast or lunch at **The Stove's** *(Main St.; Tel 028/22500; 8am-6pm Mon-Sat),* where you certainly won't pay more than £4-5 for a hearty traditional Irish breakfast and enough freshly-baked scones to satisfy an army.

crashing

Situated in a restored 200-year-old corn mill, **Russagh Mill Hostel and Adventure Centre** *(Castletownshend Rd., about 2 km (1.3 mi) east of town; Tel 028/22451 or 028/21256; mid-Mar-Oct; £7-8 dorm, £20 double; No credit cards)* means total hostel heaven for outdoorsy types. Not only does the hostel double as an adventure center, but the staff is friendly, laid-back, and well-informed, and the dorm rooms are more spacious than average. Eight private rooms are also up for grabs. For around 10 punts, you can spend the day canoeing, biking, kayaking, hitting the archery range, or whatever else owner and expert mountaineer Mick Murphy has got planned for hostellers that day.

There's but one requirement for a reservation at **Mont Bretia** *(6 km (3.7 mi) east of town on Drinagh Rd.; Tel 028/33663; £18 per person, dinner around £10),* and unfortunately it's one that excludes most of us: you've gotta be a lesbian. It's such a nice place, though, that if you happen to be traveling with a female friend...well...nobody will really enquire too closely if you are or aren't "a couple." The owners provide extensive information on local sporting activities, free tea and coffee all day, vegetarian meals, and breakfast is served every day until noon. There's also a library with plenty of books and videos available for rainy days. To get here, drive east from Skibbereen on the N71 and make a left at the signpost for Drinagh Road.

Looking for something a little less rustic? The not-so-creatively-named **Bridge House** *(Bridge St.; Tel 028/21273; £18 per person; No credit cards)* is anything but boring on the inside: the whole place is decorated with splendid Victorian panache, and the breakfasts are similarly divine. It's easily the nicest B&B in town.

Other do-able options include the **Eldon Hotel** *(Bridge St.; Tel. 028/21300, Fax 028/21919; welcome@eldon-hotel.com, www.eldon-hotel.com; £28 per person and up, Oct-Apr; up to £45 per person, May-Sep; Private baths; Breakfast included; V, MC)* right across the street from the bus stop in the center of town; and **Ivanhoe** *(67 North St.; Tel 028/21749; Doubles/twins £15-20 per person, Singles £20-25; private baths, breakfast included; V, MC)*, a two-minute walk from the bus stop and the center of town.

need to know

Currency Exchange Try the usual suspects: **AIB** *(9 Bridge St.; Tel 028/21388; 10am-4pm Mon-Tue, Thu-Fri, 10am-5pm Wed)* and **Bank of Ireland** *(Market St.; Tel 028/21700; 10am-4pm Mon-Tue, Thu-Fri, 10am-5pm Wed)*.

Tourist Information The folks at the **Skibbereen Tourist Office** *(Town Hall, North St.; Tel 028/21766; 9:15am-5:30pm Mon-Sat, Jun-Aug)* will tell you anything you want to know. Promise.

Bus Lines Out of the City **Bus Éireann** *(Cork City; Tel 021/508-188)* to the rescue! The bus stops outside Calahane's Bar on Bridge Street. There are connections to Cork City on Route 46 twice a day Monday-Saturday, and once on Sundays. Route 46 hits Clonakilty three times a day Monday-Saturday, and twice a day Sunday. Route 44 serves Killarney once a day, June-September only. The bus to and from Baltimore follows Route 251 five times a day June-September, four times a day October-May.

Bike Rental **Roycroft Stores** *(Ilen St., off Bridge St.; Tel 028/21810; 10am-4pm Mon-Tue, Thu-Fri, 10am-5pm Wed; £8.50-10 per day, price includes helmet, £40 deposit)* will get you pedaling.

Laundry Spiff up your wardrobe at **Hourihane's Launderette** *(Ilen St., behind the Busy Bee fast-food joint; Tel 028/22697; 10am-10pm daily, £3.50 per load)*.

Postal Go to the **Skibbereen Post Office** *(The Square; 9am-5:30pm Mon-Sat)* with your cards and letters.

baltimore

How refreshing to find a coastal town where you can walk a whole mile without running into tourists! While the teeny population of 200 burgeons in summertime, almost everybody is coming to sail and dive, and we don't count those people as tourists—they're *travelers.* Baltimore's a splendid place to spend a day or two, especially if you're into water sports. It's also a jumping-off spot for the Sherkin or Cape Clear Islands [see below]. Divers just love Baltimore because of all the shipwrecks the little town has witnessed over the years. Ghostly underwater scenery, indeed.

bar, club, and live music scene

Baltimore's not the best place for lively pub goings-on and may not feature Ireland's finest traditional music, but there's still some *craic* to be had if you look in the right places.

Declan McCarthy's *(Above the pier; Tel 028/20159)* has the trad most nights of the week during summer. Unfortunately, there's sometimes a cover charge of around £5, which is definitely steep, especially when you consider that most Irish pubs offer live music for free. If you're here in Baltimore and you want some seriously foot-stomping old tunes to go with that pint, it's worth forking it over. It's no doubt the liveliest pub in town, attracting both hip hostellers and laid-back locals.

Also a hotel [see *crashing,* below], **Casey's of Baltimore** *(Baltimore; Tel 028/20197; caseys@tinet.ie, www.baltimore-ireland.com/caseys)* boasts a beer garden overlooking the bay.

festivals and events in west cork

Attention, poetry and classical music lovers: **The West Cork Chamber Music Festival** *(Bantry; late Jun; Tel 027/52788; westcorkmusic@eircom.net, www.westcorkmusic.ie; all events free)* consists of poetry readings, writing workshops, live classical music, and a crafts exhibition. Bantry lies 28 miles north of Baltimore. By car, head north from Baltimore along R595 for 8 miles to the junction of N71; follow the signs for Ballydehob, they will lead you also to Bantry.

Probably the best time to be in Baltimore is when the pubs offer fresh mussels and prawns and plenty o' live jazz during the annual **Seafood Festival** *(Baltimore; Third weekend of May; call Tel 028/21766 for info).*

culture zoo

Dún na Sead *(Overlooking the harbor; Free):* The ruins of the 16th-century "Fort of the Jewels" overwhelm the rest of the skyline at Baltimore Harbour. One of many built by the O'Driscoll clan, ubiquitous in these parts, the castle doesn't offer a terrible lot to see, perhaps because all of the jewels were long ago lost to the pounding of the sea.

great outdoors

A steady stream of treasure hunters hits the following dive centers, and while there's no guarantee you'll find any nuggets yourself, it never hurts to try, right?

The **Baltimore Diving and Watersports Centre** *(On the pier by the ferryport; Tel 028/20300)* offers diving instruction and equipment; the center plans diving expeditions around Baltimore as well as Sherkin and Cape Clear Island [see below]. Expect to pay around £45 for a three-hour dive (that includes equipment); beginner's courses run about £30.

Atlantic Boating Service *(At the end of the Baltimore pier; Tel 028/22734)* offers boat rental (ten to 15 punts an hour) and water-skiing (£20 or more for a half-hour session).

If you're not thrilled about getting wet, there are alternatives. Rent a bike [see *need to know,* below] and pedal eastward out of town to **Lough Ine** (the first part pronounced like "loch," meaning "lake," the second part just like "iodine" without the "iod"), the only saltwater lake in Ireland. Woods and hills surround the lake, and if you push yourself a little on those steeper trails you'll find some truly spectacular views on the hilltops.

You could also take a walk out to **The Beacon,** a lighthouse perched dramatically on a cliff overlooking the ocean with splendid views of Sherkin Island. Just follow the main road and you can't miss it.

eats

If you're headed out for Sherkin or Cape Clear Island, or if you're on a tight budget and want to eat in while you're in Baltimore, stop by **Cotter's** *(Main road by the harbor; Tel 028/20106; 9:30am-8pm Mon-Sat, 10:30am-8pm Sun),* a run-of-the-mill grocery store that actually opens on Sundays! Cue the choir music!

The best place in town for a delicious meal happens to be none other than **Café Art** *(Baltimore Hill; Tel 028/20289; 8:30am-9:30pm daily; main courses £9-12; V, MC),* run by the same people who bring you the delightful Rolf's Holiday Hostel [see *crashing,* below]. Heck, you might as well eat breakfast, lunch, *and* dinner here (if you can afford it, that is). Dinners include delicious and health-conscious treats like salmon, pasta, scones, and plenty of organic fruits and veggies. Even better, the place also serves as an art gallery with oft-changing exhibits of contemporary Irish painting and sculpture; Rolf's daughter Frederika is a sculptor herself.

On the other hand, if you happen by it, try **The Lifeboat Restaurant** *(On the harbor, in the post office building; Tel 028/20143; 10am-*

5:30pm daily), which offers pleasant views of the harbor and ultra-cheap soups, sandwiches, quiches, and the like.

Don't rule out the pubs in town. Not only a great pub, **Casey's of Baltimore** [see *bar, club, and live music scene,* above] is a great restaurant with some of the best seafood around—herring, wild Irish tuna, and the like, along with steaks and several vegetarian options. A plate of fish and chips'll set you back only £5 at **Declan McCarthy's** [see *bar scene,* above].

crashing

Lucky, lucky you. **Rolf's Holiday Hostel** *(Baltimore Hill, half-a-kilometer (a third of a mile) off R595, signposted just outside Baltimore center, 300 meters from the bus stop; Tel 028/20289; £7-8.50 dorm, £23 double, £3.50 camping; V, MC)* far transcends the word "cool." It's unusual, that's for sure: every dorm room is a separate 300-year-old stone cottage, and the same goes for private rooms. Reception couldn't get any friendlier, and the common room, kitchen, and dining room are clean and comfortable, offering marvelous views of the Baltimore Harbour and the surrounding countryside. Most likely you won't be making much use of that kitchen though, since the menu at Café Art [see *eats,* above] is totally delicious and reasonably priced. You can also rent bikes here.

Casey's of Baltimore *(Baltimore; Tel 028/20197; caseys@tinet.ie, www.baltimore-ireland.com/caseys; closed Feb 19-25, early to mid-Nov, and Dec 21-27; £58-65 single, low/high season, £39-47 per person double or twin, low/high season, lower weekly rates; V, MC, DC)* also offers bed-and-breakfast accommodation. Clean, cool, spacious, airy rooms look out onto the bay, and the breakfast itself is delicious: freshly-squeezed orange juice, fresh warm brown bread (which many guests rate as some of the best around), local farmhouse cheeses, cereal, and seafood—yes, for breakfast too! Of course, you can always ask for eggs and bacon or something else a little more to your liking.

need to know

Currency Exchange Oddly enough, pretty much the only place in town to exchange your cash for punts is at a *pub;* the idea is, of course, that you'll spend all of it just as soon as you get it—so beware. Luckily, **Declan McCarthy's** [see *bar, club, and live music scene,* above] is also the liveliest pub in town. There's also a bureau de change in the same building as the post office by the pier, but the hours are sporadic.

Tourist Information Check with the **Baltimore Tourist Office** *(By the pier; Tel 028/21766; Hours vary)* or the **Islands Craft Shop** *(By the pier; Tel 028/20347; Hours vary, usually 11am-5:30pm Mon-Sat, noon-5:30pm Sun Jul-Aug).* Both offer information about Baltimore, as well as the Sherkin and Cape Clear Islands.

Bus Lines Out of the City **Bus Éireann** *(Cork City office Tel 021/450-8188)* route 44 connects with Skibbereen and Cork City three or four times a day Monday-Saturday. Bus schedules are posted in the windows of the tourist office.

Bike Rental Bikes are available at **Rolf's Holiday Hostel** [see *crashing,* above] for around £7 a day.

Postal Mail stuff from the **Baltimore Post Office** *(Above the Islands Craft Shop; No phone; 9am-5:30pm Mon-Fri, 9am-1pm Sat).*

cape clear island

The southernmost inhabited island of Ireland, Cape Clear, only three miles long by one mile wide, has been called the country's last frontier. A 45-minute ferry ride from Baltimore takes you to this island, 8 miles off the coast of West Cork. Oh-so-scenic Cape Clear Island, population 150, is notable for its presence within the Gaeltacht, or Gaelic-speaking region, where lots of eager teen-aged students flock every year for summer language lessons. Serious cyclists will find the island a perfect setting for long rides through hills and farmlands. The island offers some of the most exhilarating coastal seascapes in Ireland, along with some of the country's best bird-watching possibilities. You'll have views to the sea of the often turbulent waters and of heather or gorse-clad hillsides inland. Cape Clear has about one-third of all the different plant species in Ireland, estimated to be about 1,000. So if you're serious about your flora, buy one of those plant identification books in Baltimore before taking the ferry over.

bar scene

Naturally you'll find much more in the way of outdoor excursions than you will nightlife, but the island's three pubs don't do such a bad job of livening things up after the sun sets. Get yourself to **The Night Jar's** *(Tel 028/39102),* **Club Chléire** *(Tel 028/39184)* or **Ciarán Danny Mike's** *(Tel 028/39172),* the last two of which offer live trad music most nights. Sessions at Club Chléire can and do last all night. You'll find that

festivals and events

The word "enchanting" describes **The Cape Clear Island International Storytelling Festival** *(Sept; Tel 028/39157)* perfectly. The festival offers four large concerts, workshops and seminars, cozy fireside storytelling sessions, and live music. Special boat trips, archaeological walks, and bird-watching excursions are also available.

nobody sticks to official hours here: the few shops and cafés on the island open and close pretty much as they please, and the pub owners aren't at all concerned about closing up at a "decent" hour like they would be at most other places in this country. Which is not to say these places are out-of-control rowdy, just thoroughly fun-loving.

eats

As for food, you don't have much choice other than **Cistin Chéire** *(Tel 028/39145; Noon-6pm/7:30-9pm),* the café below the Club Chléire pub, serving the usual sandwiches, soups, and pastries in the £3 range.

crashing

Your best bet for lodging is the **Cape Clear Island Hostel, aka Cléire Lasmuigh** *(South Harbour, Cape Clear Island, Skibbereen; Tel 028/39144; Easter-Oct; £6-7 dorm, no private rooms; No credit cards).* While the staff won't win awards for outstanding friendliness, the setting overlooking the fishing harbor is fantastic and you can't beat the sports center just next-door for workout convenience. Book early, because the hostel accommodates students learning Irish during the summer courses. The hostel is located one mile up from the pier. Keep left, and look for signs to the hostel.

If the thought of staying in one more hostel is too much for you, there is also the cozy **Cluain Mara House** *(Tel 028/39153; capeclearcottages@tinet.ie; £16-18 per person).*

the great outdoors

Ready to give those arms a workout? **Roaringwater Bay Centre** *(Tel 028/39198; 10am-4pm daily; Trips start at £25),* run out of the hostel, offers diving and sea-kayaking trips to local shoreline beauty spots. As you take in the craggy coastline with no trees to break the North Sea winds, be prepared: waters are likely to be rough even in summer. For your trouble, you're rewarded with an island of stark beauty, seen at its most colorful in May when thousands of wildflowers burst into bloom. Visits in October are even more dramatic because of the migrant bird colonies that land here, many flocking to North America for the winter. From July to September, you can view large colonies of seabirds during their nesting season. It is not uncommon to see dolphins or even a whale. On the island's western shore you'll sail by the ruins of O'Driscoll Castle dating from the 14th century. The scenic highlight is a series of windmills which until modern times were used to generate most of Cape Clear's electricity. The shoreline reveals patchwork farm fields divided by ancient, low stone walls. Everything from a two-hour trip around the island to a 5-day sea kayaking package is sold, the latter costing £175 and including meals, instruction, housing, and equipment. There are no rigid rules here; your individual boating needs can usually be accommodated. Bring along your own food and drink for short boat rides.

need to know

Tourist Information Before leaving Baltimore, ask at the tourist office for a useful map and brochure of Cape Clear Island. If you arrive on island in summer, you will sometimes find a small tourist information post at the pier where the ferry docks *(Tel 028/3919).* But don't count on anyone being there.

Directions and Transportation Cape Clear is reachable by ferry from Baltimore *(Tel 028/39135; two or three per day in the summer, one per day otherwise)* or from Schull during the summer months only *(5:30pm daily Jun; 10am, 2:30pm, 4:30pm daily Jul-Aug).* After disembarking from the ferry, turn left at the end of the pier and walk up the path to the town's cafes and pubs. The place is miniscule and in 20 minutes you'll quickly see where everything is.

Bike Rental Bikers should bring their wheels over from Baltimore on the ferry.

kinsale

Only 23 kilometers (18 miles) and a half-hour bus ride south of Cork City, Kinsale's an upscale fishing village turned national gourmet capital. Its population of about 1,800 residents quadruples during the summer months—if you're driving, the traffic jams throughout the narrow streets of the picturesque little town can definitely grate on your nerves. Better to skip the car and take the bus out of Cork City instead. It's so close that you could definitely base yourself in Cork City and just come out here for the day, but if sampling the restaurants is on your agenda, an overnight might be more in order. There's certainly enough else to do here to justify it. You can spend a dreamy afternoon walking out to the little-noticed James Fort across the harbor from the rest of the village (the coastline sort of curves around, dips down, and then comes back up, forming a peninsula of sorts that faces the Kinsale harbor) and chill for a while amid the ruins and grassy hills with a picnic lunch and a stack of postcards. There's also a tiny church nearby, also in ruins and, in the warmer months, submerged in a sea of wildflowers.

After the Battle of Kinsale in 1601—which the Irish and their Spanish allies lost, not surprisingly—the English dominated the area and banned Irish Catholics for the following 100 years; this battle is especially important in Irish history because most historians agree that it marks the start of the end of Gaelic Ireland. Not-to-be-missed sites include **Desmond Castle,** which the Spanish occupied at the time of that infamous battle in 1601; **Charles Fort,** dating to the late 1600s and built to protect the village from invasion [see *culture zoo,* below for both]; and the aforementioned James Fort.

kinsale

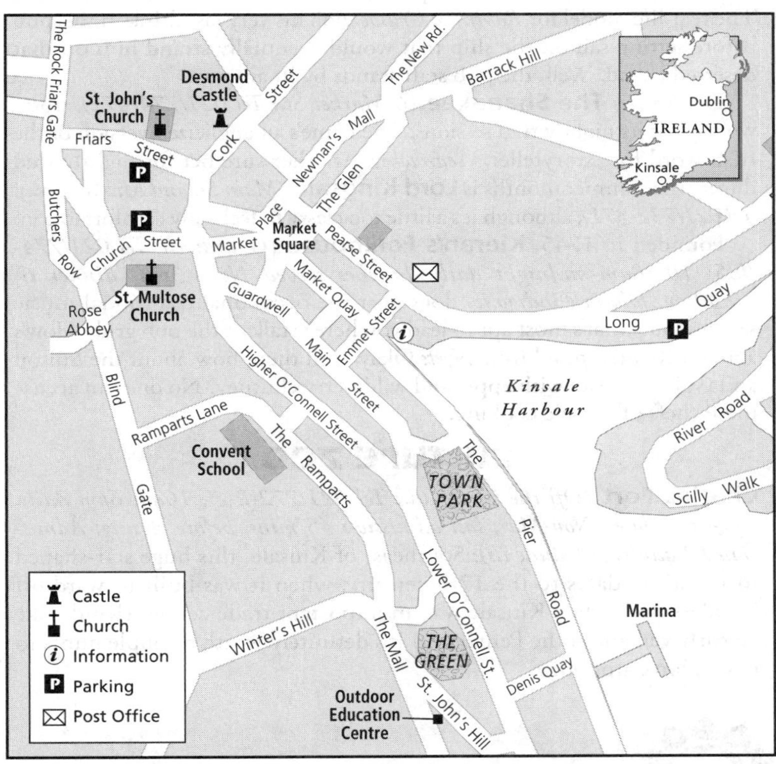

bar, club, and live music scene

Hands down one of the finest pubs in town, **The Spaniard** *(Scilly; Tel 021/4772-436; www.dragnet-systems.ie/dira/spaniard)* faces the harbor and is named after Don Juan del Aquilla, who led the Spanish troops during the Battle of Kinsale. There are three different bars to choose from—although they each serve the same stuff, of course—and it's one of the best pubs in town for catching a live music session. Don't come here if you're even a wee bit claustrophobic, though. In wintertime, the music sessions occur only on weekends; during the summer, there's a session every night. Mary Black, one of Ireland's most successful singers, has been known to play here on occasion. If you happen to be in town on a Sunday at any point in the year, don't miss the jazz session at 5pm. Naturally, The Spaniard serves good pub grub as well—from the traditional bacon and cabbage to roast farmhouse duckling with black cherry brandy sauce.

(Kinsale chefs clearly have a thing for farmhouse ducks [see *eats*, below].) Here's a little-known story that pub-goers here have been known to tell: The real-life model for *Robinson Crusoe* took his very last drink in this pub before setting sail on the ship that would eventually strand him on that deserted island. Well, the pub staff stands by it, anyway.

Don't miss **The Shanakee** *(6 Market St.; Tel 021/774-472)*, noteworthy for its nightly trad sessions. The name's an anglicized version of the Irish word for "storyteller," *seanachie*. Another sure bet for nightly trad during the summer months is **Lord Kingsale** *(Main St. and Market Quay, Tel 021/772-371)*, although it's a little too classy to feel truly comfortable in.

Founded in 1745, **Kieran's Folkhouse** *(Guardwell; Tel 021/774-085; 10:30am-midnight daily, lunches served Noon-3pm, dinner 6-10:30pm; folkhse@indigo.ie)* does host the occasional traditional music session, but what's most apt to lead you here is talk of the pub grub. How's about a Russian monkfish? *Nyet?* Okay, well then, how about the Stilton and Guinness paté with apple and wild berry chutney? No one can accuse these chefs of prosaic cooking.

culture zoo

Charles Fort *(Off the Scilly Rd.; Tel 021/772-263; 10am-6pm daily, Apr-Oct; closed Nov-Mar; last admission 45 mins. before closing; Admission £2 adults, £1 students):* Southeast of Kinsale, this huge star-shaped fortification dates to the 17th century, when it was built to ward off invaders back when Kinsale was an important trade center. (Kinda like an early version of the Pentagon.) It's definitely worth a couple punts to have a look around.

festivals and events

Held every September, the **Kinsale Arts Festival** *(Sept; Tel 021/4774-959 kinsalea@gofree.indigo.ie, http://gofree.indigo.ie/~kinsalea)* consists of concerts, plays, lectures, art exhibitions, and poetry and book readings at venues throughout Kinsale. Participants are well known throughout Ireland, although you might not have come across their names just yet (should I list some anyway? Hugh Tinney, Harold Wood, and Malcolm Proud). The Irish Chamber Orchestra has also performed here. Some events do require tickets, but the prices are "nominal." Check out the website for which events aren't free, and if you're interested try **Ticketmaster** *(Tel 01/4569-569; www.ticketmaster.ie)*. You could also try just showing up at the appropriate venue around a half-hour before the performance starts, but there's no guarantee that the event won't be sold out.

Desmond Castle *(Cork St.; Tel 021/774-855; 10am-6pm daily, mid-Jun-mid-Sep; 9am-5pm Mon-Sat mid-Sep-early Oct; 10am-6pm Tues-Sun, 10am-5pm Sun, mid-Apr-mid-Jun; closed mid-Oct-mid-Apr; Last admission 45 mins. before closing; Admission £1.50 adults, £1 students):* Dating from the early 16th century, the castle has played a lot of roles in Irish history, first as a Spanish stronghold in 1601, then as a prison for American sailors during the American Revolution, and later as a workhouse for Famine victims in the late 1840s. The castle has been renovated and now houses the **International Museum of Wine,** fitting not only because of Kinsale's gourmet status, but because the town was a designated "wine port" for several centuries. The museum underscores the "viniculturalcontributions of the Irish diaspora"; simply put, many an Irish expatriate went off to France and started his own winery, several of which are now internationally famous. Ask about a free wine tasting.

great outdoors

It's a 10-minute drive from Kinsale to **Ballinadee Trekking and Horse Riding Farm** *(Ballinadee; Tel 021/778-152),* which offers even you beginners a chance to reclaim your equestrian side. From Kinsale, drive across New Bridge and turn right. Go straight through Barrel's Cross, then take a right down the small lane to Ballinadee Village. The stables are about a half-mile from the village on Bandon Road. It's best to call ahead.

Biking along the water's edge is a super way to get some scenic exercise; rent a bike from Deco's on Main Street [see *need to know,* below]. There are plenty of well worn walking paths all over the village; pick up a free map at the tourist office [see *need to know,* below].

Sporting Tours Ireland *(71 Main St.; Tel 021/774-727; 9:30am-8pm daily, May-Sep; 10am-6pm Mon-Sat, Oct-Apr; £30 per scuba dive, £8 or more per hour for canoeing, etc.),* offers scuba diving, canoeing, and windsurfing.

stuff

Founded in 1991 by an ambitious Waterford craftsman, **Kinsale Crystal** *(Market St.; Tel 021/774-493; 9:30am-1:30pm Mon-Sat; V, MC)* allows shoppers to watch the crystal being made. Opt to have it sent home; most say the vase they bought for grandma didn't hold up too well in their bags.

The Dolan family runs **Kinsale Silver** *(Pearse St.; Tel 021/774-359; 9:30am-6pm daily; www.iol.ie/~dolan),* an excellent place to pick up a one-of-a-kind souvenir. You can watch Pat Dolan at work in the corner of the shop while you browse.

eats

Say what? You were looking for a *cheap* place to eat in Kinsale? Sorry, bub. This isn't the place for charming and inexpensive little cafes. This here is gourmet territory. If you're really trying to stick to a budget, there's always the **Supervalu** *(Pearse St.; Tel 021/772-843; 8:30am-9pm Mon-Sat, 10am-7pm Sun).*

For something a little less pretentious and a little less expensive than the typical Kinsale dining fare, stop by **The Greyhound** *(Market Sq.; Tel 021/772-889)*, an oh-so-picturesque little pub with pretty, colorful flower boxes in the windows and a cozy, inviting interior. The Greyhound offers the traditional Irish stew or shepherd's pie as well as a few anomalies, like seafood pancakes.

More affordable than many of its highbrow counterparts, **Max's Wine Bar Restaurant** *(Main St.; Tel 021/772-443; 12:30-3pm/6:30-10:30pm daily, closed Nov-Feb; Reservations recommended; 3-course dinner £12, main courses £6.50-£12.50; MC, V)* specializes in grilled mussels. It's one of your best bets if you're looking to sample all that gourmet Kinsale has to offer without using up the rest of your traveler's checks. Max's makes a good stop for veggie-lovers, too: goat cheese pasta is also on the menu.

Dinners at **The Cottage Loft** *(6 Main St.; Tel 021/772-803; 5:30-10:30pm daily, May-Oct; 6:30-10:30pm Tue-Sun, Nov-Apr; Main courses £6.50-18, fixed-price dinner £17.50; AE, MC, V)* have often been featured on British and Irish television, so reserve well ahead. Lucky for you that the seafood's as fresh as the house is old—and in a place built around 200 years ago, that's saying something. The menu also features a farmyard duck forever silenced in an apple brandy sauce, and here's something you won't find anywhere else: a dish called "Seafood Danielle," which consists of a salmon stuffed with crabs, prawns, and peppers with nettle sauce.

Jim Edwards' Steak and Seafood Restaurant *(Market Quay, off Emmet Place; Tel 021/772-541; 10:30am-11pm; Main courses £9-16; V, MC, AE)* is just as delish as the other places in town but with incredible decor. Along with stained-glass windows and plush red seating, there is a very cool clock over the door that shows the time with letters instead of numbers. The menu offers vegetarian dishes as well as several different kinds of steak and seafood. How about boneless duck with cassis and red currant sauce? Mmm, mmm, mmm.

Hint: **Chez Jean-Marc** *(Lower O'Connell St., near the Trident Hotel; Tel 021/774-625; 7-10:30pm Tue-Sun; 3-course dinner from £18, main courses £14-£16.95; AE, DC, MC, V)* doesn't serve Irish food and reservations are a very good idea. The menu is truly mouthwatering—how does salmon poached in court bouillon with crab toes and vermouth buttercream sauce sound? Or perhaps a duck in black currant liqueur? Jean-Marc supplies you with permission to die happy, as long as you don't do it in his restaurant.

If you're thinking it'd be best to make reservations before stopping in at **The Blue Haven** *(3 Pearse St.; Tel 021/772-209; Bar 12:15-3pm/5:30-9:30pm daily, restaurant 7-10pm daily; Bar, dinner main courses £5-£14; Restaurant, 3-course dinners from £23, main courses £10-£18; AE, MC, V)*, you're absolutely right. This is the restaurant by which all others in Kinsale are measured, and if you've got Mommy or Daddy's credit card you might as well use it here. How about a plate of farmyard duck with sage-and-onion stuffing, or salmon cooked over oak chips (a house specialty, naturally), or a bowl of especially delicious lamb stew? Picture yourself in culinary heaven, under a sign marked "The Blue Haven."

crashing

To get to the **Castlepark Marina Centre** *(Castlepark, Tel 021/774-959; mid-Mar-Oct; maritime@indigo.ie; £9 dorm, £22 double; V, MC),* you'll have to walk about 20 minutes from the center of town. But the location across Kinsale Harbour is excellent, just a few minutes' walk from the remains of James' Fort as well as a small beach—and it's right nextdoor to a pub. Bike rental, comfy beds, and lovely views make it a splendid place to spend the night. Naturally, there's also an excellent hostel restaurant (What did you expect? This is Kinsale). If you don't feel like walking, a ferry leaves every hour from the Trident Marina in Kinsale Harbour, but the walk really is manageable. The Castlepark Marina rivals the friendliness and cleanliness of any bed-and-breakfast, and it's a heck of a lot cheaper.

More moderate options include **O'Donovan's** *(Main St.; Tel 021/477-2428 £20 single, £22 per person suite June-Aug; £18 single £20 per person Sept-May; V),* **Shanakee** *(Market St.; Tel 021/477-4422 Avg. room £35),* and **Tierney's Guesthouse** *(Main St.; Tel 021/4772-205; Fax 021/477-4363; mtierney@indigo.ie, www.kinsale.ie/tierney.htm; Doubles £50 per person, singles £30 per person, private baths; Breakfast included; V, MC, AE).*

If you've still somehow got cash burning a hole in your pocket after dining out in Kinsale, check yourself into **The Old Presbytery** *(43 Cork St.; Tel 021/772-027; info@oldpres.com; £40 single, £60-£70 double; V, MC, AE),* a classy old Georgian right down the street from Desmond Castle and those great free wine tastings. The breakfast menu comes highly recommended.

need to know

Currency Exchange Head on over to the **Bank of Ireland** *(Pearse St.; Tel 021/772-521; 10am-5pm Mon, 10am-4pm Tue-Fri),* which has an ATM.

Tourist Information The **Kinsale Tourist Office** *(Emmet Place; Tel 021/774-234; 9am-6pm daily Mar-Nov)* has the answers you seek.

Public Transportation You'll be riding in style if you call **Kinsale Cabs** *(Market Sq.; Tel 021/772-642).* They've got a mini-bus and—can you believe it?—a Mercedes.

Health and Emergency Emergency: *999,* no coins required; Police, or Gardaí: *(Tel 021/772-302).* Call 021/772-1253 for the nearest doctor.

Bus Lines Out of the City **Bus Éireann** services Kinsale out of Cork City, with nine buses a day during the week and three on Sundays. The bus stops at the gas station opposite the tourist office on the pier.

Bike Rental **Deco's** *(Main St.; Tel 021/774-884; 9am-6pm Mon-Sat, 10am-6pm Sun, Jun-Aug; 9am-6pm Mon-Sat, Sep-May; around £7 per day, £2 per hour, £30 per week)* can hook you up with a set of wheels.

clonakilty

Clonakilty's principal claim to fame is as the birthplace of Irish rebel leader Michael Collins, whose story was told in the 1996 film of the same name film starring Liam Neeson. Automotive king Henry Ford was born here as well, but Clonakilty residents are much more proud of the Michael Collins connection. Clonakilty's got a nice beach, Inchydoney [see *great outdoors,* below], where locals and visitors alike hang out in the evenings before heading off to the pubs. And what splendid pubs they be! Clonakilty's well known for its vibrant taverns and excellent live trad sessions. Located just 45 km (28 mi) southwest of Cork City, Clonakilty makes a nice overnight stop on your way to or from Cork.

If you're lucky enough to be around in August for the annual music festival, the music sessions get even better. The exact dates are flexible; call the tourist office for info [see *need to know,* below]. You'll find yourself walking back to your temporary digs well after midnight with the strains of the fiddle and *bodhrán* (that quintessentially Irish goat-hide drum) still echoing in your head.

Interesting historical sidenote: The first Earl of Cork "re-founded" the town in the early 1600s with a hundred English families and attempted to force Irish Catholics off the land. Today, you'll note that his attempt was only temporarily successful: Clonakilty residents are Gaelic speakers and the Protestant church has been converted into a Post Office.

neighborhoods

Bus Éireann stops on **Pearse Street,** which continues west, becoming **Oliver Plunkett Street,** or east, becoming **Ashe Street, Wolfe Tone Street,** and **Strand Road,** in that order. Continue on the Strand Road and onto **Convent Road** to reach the **Lios na gCon** ring fort [see *culture zoo,* below]. Most of the nightlife action takes place on these main streets.

festivals and events

Check out **The Clonakilty August Festival** *(Aug; call Tel 023/33226 for info),* which offers street entertainment, live music sessions late into the night, and fireworks. **The Black and White Festival** *(Second week of July; call Tel 023/33226 for info)* offers a contest to see who can consume the most black and white pudding. No, that's not like chocolate and vanilla...it's blood sausage. If it makes you want to ralph last night's dinner just thinking about it, make sure you're not around to watch.

clonakilty

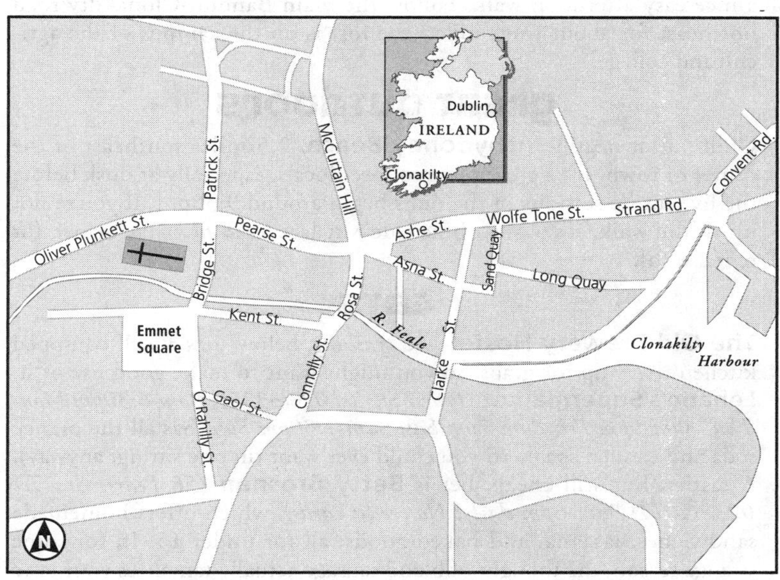

bar, club, and live music scene

One of the pubs most abuzz with great music and great conversation is **De Barra's** *(Pearse St.; Tel 023/33381).* Many super-famous musicians have visited here, including Paul McCartney, David Bowie, Bruce Springsteen, Sting, Ray Charles, and Ireland's most cherished silver-throated songstress, Mary Black—and there are plenty of old photographs hanging on the walls to prove it. There's a small stage and balcony, too, along with a harp, two centuries old, that's still being played during the trad sessions. If you come to Clonakilty, do *not* miss visiting this pub. It rates just about any glowing adjective you can think of, and there's never a night without music, winter or summer, hell or high water. Though if De Barra's is a bit too crowded for your liking, you could try **Shanley's** *(11 Connolly St.; Tel 023/33790)* or **An Súgán** *(Wolfe Tone St.; No phone),* also with live trad nightly. Or you could just close your eyes and follow your ears, really—there isn't a bad pub in town.

culture zoo

Naturally, you'll be wanting to find out more about the life—and sudden death—of Michael Collins, and tours of various relevant sites can be arranged through the Clonakilty Tourist Office [see *need to know,* below].

Lios na gCon: *(Clonakilty Agricultural College; 10am-4pm Mon-Fri; guided tours 11am-2pm; adults £2, children £1):* This ancient ring fort is located three miles east of Clonakilty. Recently "restored"—

although not many could vouch for its historical accuracy—it makes for a nice easy afternoon walk. Follow the main Bandon-Clonakilty road northeast for about three miles; the fort is on the campus of the agricultural college.

great outdoors

Chill out at nearby **Inchydoney Beach,** 2.5 miles southeast of the center of town. It's a great place to meet locals, especially at dusk before the live music sessions in the pubs begin around 9:30pm. If you're not up to the walk, it's a great bike ride out [see *need to know,* below, for rental info].

eats

The Old Brewery Hostel [see *crashing,* below] has a well equipped kitchen that's up for grabs, so you might want to make good use of it. **Lehane's Supermarket** *(Pearse St.; Tel 023/33359; 8am-6:30pm Mon-Thu, 8am-9pm Fri, 8am-7pm Sat, 9am-1:30pm Sun)* has all the orange soda and canned spaghetti you could ever want (in one sitting, anyway). A tastier, but still cheap, bet is **Betty Brosnan** *(58 Pearse St.; Tel 023/34011; 9am-6pm daily; No credit cards),* which offers homemade sandwiches, lasagna, and baked goods, all for under £5. If, for some strange reason, the thought of blood sausage actually tantalizes your taste buds, head for the local butcher's shop, **Edward Twomey's** *(16 Pearse St.; Tel 023/33365; 9am-6pm Mon-Sat).* He serves up some of the best black pudding in all of County Cork.

crashing

Definitely above-average when it comes to hostels, the **Clonakilty Old Brewery Hostel** *(Emmet Sq.; Tel 023/33525; wytchost@iol.ie; £8 dorm, £18 double; V, MC)* offers a well-stocked kitchen, bike rental, a warm social vibe, and spotless dorm rooms. It's located far enough away from the pubs that you don't have to hear the drunken mobs stumbling down the streets in search of their houses at two in the morning while you're trying to sleep. But it's close enough to be within only a few minutes' stumbling distance yourself. There are only 26 beds here, so definitely call well in advance during the summer, especially if the music festival's going on. From the bus stop at Pearse Street, make a left onto Bridge Street and a right onto Old Brewery Lane at Emmet Square.

Other do-able options include **Wytchwood** *(Emmet Sq.; Tel 023/33525; Fax 023/35673; wytchoust@iol.ie; Doubles £20-25 per person, singles £25-28, private baths, breakfast included; V, MC);* **O'Donovan's Hotel** *(Pearse St.; Tel 023/33250, Fax 023/33250; info@odonovanshotel.com, www.odonovanshotel.com; Doubles £35 per person, singles £40, private baths, breakfast included; V, MC, AE);* and **Emmet Hotel** *(Emmet Sq.; Tel 023/33394, Fax 023/35058; emmetshotel@aircom.net, www.emmetshotel.com;*

£45 per person Jun-Aug, £35 per person all other times, private baths, breakfast included; V, MC, AE).

need to know

Currency Exchange Try **AIB** *(Pearse St.; Tel 021/772-157)* or **Bank of Ireland** *(Pearse St.; Tel 021/772-521),* both of which are open during regular banking hours and have ATMs as well.

Tourist Information The **Clonakilty Tourist Office** *(Wolfe Tone St.; Tel 023/33226; 9am-6pm daily May-Dec)* has answers to all of your questions, especially about the summer music festival.

Bus Lines Out of Town **Bus Éireann** *(Tel 021/508-188)* connects Clonakilty to Skibbereen (two or three buses per day) and Cork City (around four per day). The bus stop is in front of the supermarket on Pearse Street.

Bike Rental Satisfy your urge to pedal at **MTM Cycles** *(Ashe St.; Tel 023/33584; £8 per day, £35 per week).*

Postal Parcels come and go at the **Clonakilty Post Office** *(Patrick St.; 9am-5:30pm Mon-Fri, 10am-4pm Sat).*

i'm the leprechaun!

Truth be told, Leprechauns really don't care much at all for pink hearts, yellow moons and such, their true passion is shoes. That's right—the wee little people of the Emerald Isle are cobblers at heart. Hammering away in seclusion, this offshoot of the elf family can make some classy footwear, not only for themselves, but for you, as well, if you stop pestering them for their bloody pot of gold!

The best place to track down one of these cantankerous little Irishman is the Glen of Cloongallon, an absolutely splendid part of Tipperary near the village of Thurles. According to the website *Ireland's Eye, www.irelandseye.com,* this area contains a 500ft (in diameter) "fairy ring," which is basically a hotbed for enchanted creatures of all types, including the Leprechaun. Nestled away in an oak tree in what is essentially a neutral zone between the ring and nearby Coogan's Farm, is a webcam that catches the everyday happenings of the little fellas. Sure, sure, I know what you're thinking, it's just a joke. Well, you know what they say, it's all fun and games until a Leprechaun kicks you in the shin. Check it out in person or try the direct link at *www.irelandseye.com/leprechaun/leprechaun.htm.*

sherkin island

There are all of about 70 residents on five-kilometer-long Sherkin Island, which sits peacefully off the coast of Baltimore [see above] in West Cork. You'll be happy to note that you will see more cows on the island than you will tourists—or people in general, for that matter. Visitors from all over Ireland come to Sherkin Island for its clean, quiet, sandy beaches, which you'll find on the side of the island opposite the pier.

bar scene

There are just two pubs on the island, the **Jolly Roger Tavern** *(From the pier, turn right just before the post office; Tel 028/20379)* and **Murphy's** *(Tel 028/20116)*, across the street from the Jolly Roger. The Jolly Roger offers trad sessions most every night in the summertime at around 9pm.

eats

The **Jolly Roger Tavern** and **Murphy's** [see *bar scene* above] are the only two places to eat out on the island; both serve good, cheap pub grub till late. You can buy groceries at **The Abbey** *(On the main road; Tel 028/20181; 9am-6pm Mon-Sat, noon-6pm Sun, Jun-Aug)*, but the pickings are slim—you may have to settle for bread and cheese.

crashing

There is no hostel here—the island's an easy enough day trip from Baltimore or Schull—but if you want to stay you could try the **Jolly Roger Tavern** *about £15 per person; No credit cards)*, which is also one of the island's two pubs.

need to know

Tourist Information The best source for tourist Information is the **Sherkin Island Post Office** *(on the road up from the pier; Tel 028/20181; 9am-1pm, 2pm-6pm Mon-Fri; No lunchtime closing Jun-Aug)*.

Transportation Getting to Sherkin is as easy as asking for a pint o' Guinness. Ferries leave from the **Baltimore Quay** *(Call the Island Craft shop in Baltimore for schedules; Tel 028/20347; £4 round-trip)* several times a day between 10:30am and 8:30pm, June-September. Two or three ferries a day leave from the **Schull Quay** *(Tel 028/28138 or 028/20125; £6-8 round-trip)*. It's actually faster to take the ferry from Baltimore to Sherkin and then catch a ferry to Schull from there than to make the trip by land.

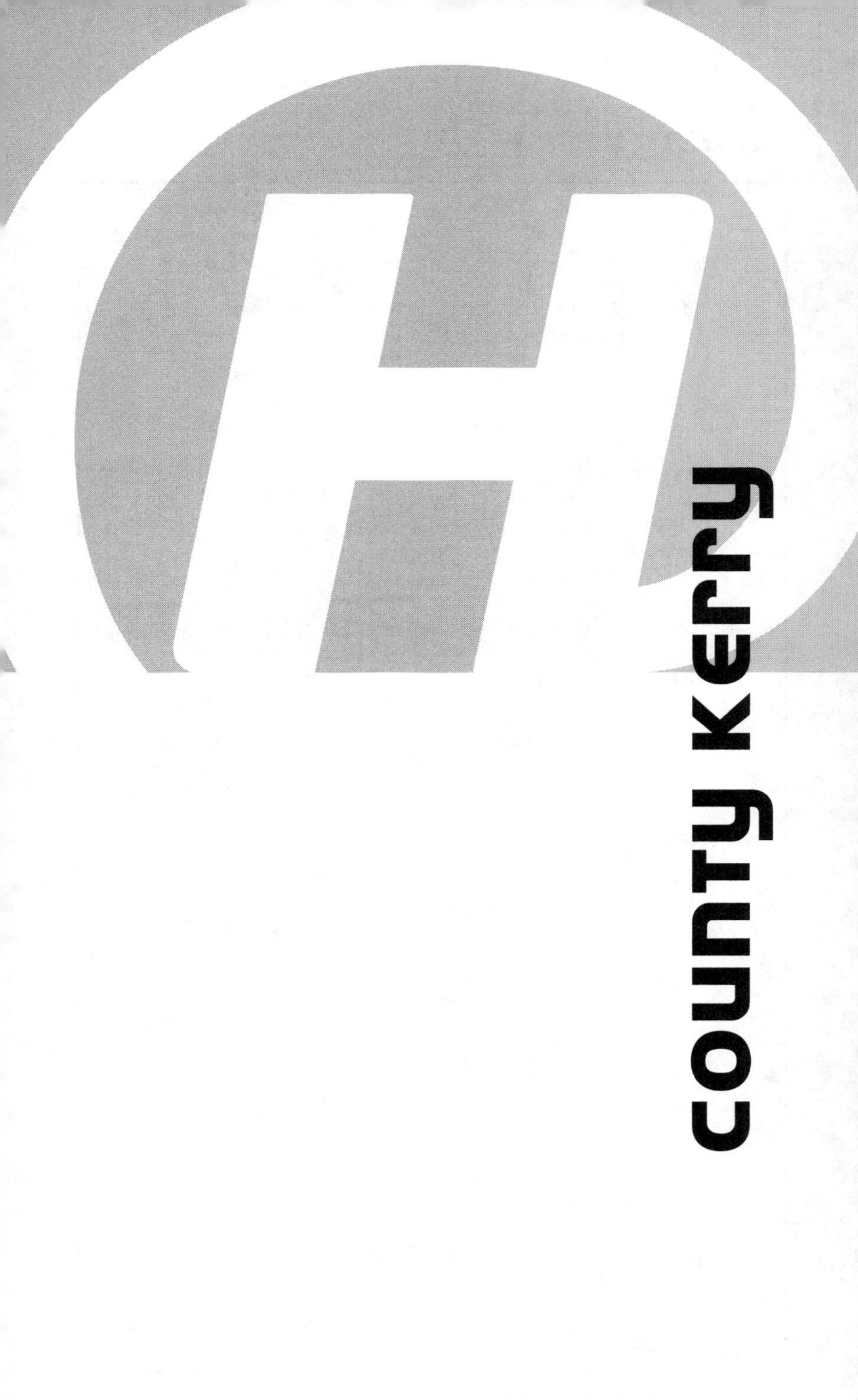
County Kerry

County Kerry

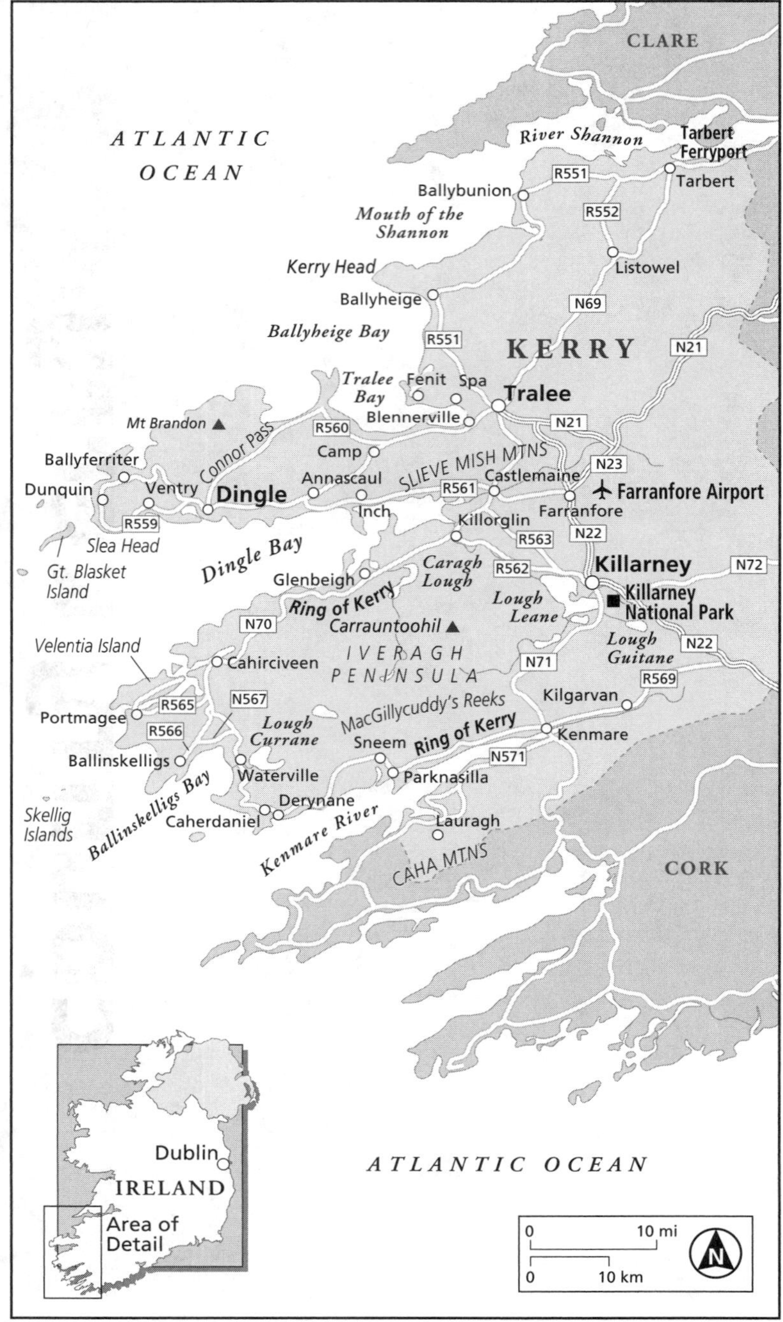

CLARE
ATLANTIC OCEAN
River Shannon
Tarbert Ferryport
Tarbert
R551
Ballybunion
R552
Mouth of the Shannon
Listowel
Kerry Head
Ballyheige
N69
Ballyheige Bay
R551
KERRY
N21
Tralee Bay
Fenit
Spa
Tralee
Mt Brandon
Blennerville
R560
N21
Connor Pass
Camp
SLIEVE MISH MTNS
Ballyferriter
N23
Dunquin
Ventry
Dingle
Annascaul
R561
Castlemaine
Farranfore Airport
Inch
Farranfore
R559
Killorglin
Slea Head
R563
N22
Dingle Bay
Gt. Blasket Island
Caragh Lough
R562
Killarney
N72
Glenbeigh
Killarney National Park
Lough Leane
Ring of Kerry
Carrauntoohil
N70
Lough Guitane
Velentia Island
N22
Cahirciveen
IVERAGH PENINSULA
N71
R569
R565
N567
MacGillycuddy's Reeks
Kilgarvan
Portmagee
Lough Currane
R566
Sneem
Ring of Kerry
Kenmare
N571
Ballinskelligs
Waterville
Parknasilla
Derynane
Skellig Islands
Ballinskelligs Bay
Caherdaniel
Kenmare River
Lauragh
CAHA MTNS
CORK
Dublin
IRELAND
Area of Detail
ATLANTIC OCEAN
0
10 mi
0
10 km
N

killarney

Ah, Killarney. On one hand, you have the Killarney National Park [see below], totally and awesomely resplendent in all the beauty of its lakes and mountains; on the other, you've got Killarney Town. The extraordinary popularity of the park has caused the adjacent town to balloon into a tourist mega-hub with tacky souvenir shops galore, pretentious restaurants, and more registered (and unregistered) accommodations than any other Irish town outside of Dublin.

As soon as you arrive, you pick up a distinct vibe that the place is motivated by the pursuit of the almighty punt. While this might not sound strange to an American, after a week in Ireland you'll probably have figured out that it's not the usual Irish way of doing things, and Killarney will feel jarringly different. As one disgruntled travel writer put it, Killarney is best seen through your rearview mirror. Though the national park is totally spectacular, the town inevitably leaves the traveler with a vague distaste.

Nevertheless, the town remains the most convenient base from which to explore the fantastic national park. Spend time in town when sleeping or drinking, and use all your daylight hours rambling in the wilderness. Try not to notice the motorboats and jaunting cars filled with camera-wielding tourists and you'll have a perfectly fine old time.

neighborhoods

Killarney is small and compact, with a population of about 7,200. The best way to get around is on foot. The town is built around one central thoroughfare, **Main Street,** which changes its name to **High Street** at midpoint. The principal offshoots of Main Street are **Plunkett Street,** which turns into **College Street,** and **New Street,** which, as its name implies, is still growing. The **Deenagh River** edges the western side of town, and **East Avenue Road** rims the eastern side, parallel to College Street. It's easy to walk in an hour or two.

The busiest section of town is the southern tip of Main Street, where it meets East Avenue Road. Here the road curves and heads to **Muckcross Road** and the entrance to **Killarney National Park.**

If you pull into town by train or bus, follow Park Road from the station to College Street (you'll pass the Fairview and the **Súgan** [see *crashing,* below] to your right on Lewis Road) till it turns into Plunkett Street. When it comes to a T at Main Street, hang a left and you'll see the tourist office, and the **Killarney Grand** [see *bar scene,* below]. If you go right on Main, make a left onto New Street to get to **Saint Mary's Cathedral** [see *culture zoo,* below], or for a roundabout way into the National Park.

hanging out

The **Súgan Hostel** front room [see *crashing,* below] can't be beat for a laid-back evening of roaring fires, guitars and gold fingers, steaming mugs of tea and quiet conversation. Otherwise, during the day, you've got the national park within a mere stone's throw. Make good use of it, why don't you?

bar and live music scene

Looking for a good old-fashioned rollickin' trad session? For the music, just follow your ears—it's all over, especially in the summertime. There's absolutely no such thing as a Killarney pub without live music. Most of the pubs here are pretty interchangeable, with nightly or near-nightly trad sessions, plenty of pub grub (many with adjacent restaurants), and all are full-to-brimming with tourists. Better picks include **Scruffy's** *(College St.; Tel 064/31038),* **Buckley's** *(College Street; Tel 064/31037),* **Murphy's** *(College Street; Tel 064/31294; Music Mon-Tue; V, MC, AE),* **O'Connor's** *(7 High St.; Tel 064/31115; castlelough@eircom.net),* **The Danny Mann Inn** *(New St.; Tel 064/31640),* and **Tatler Jack** *(Plunkett St.; Tel 064/32361).*

wired

The best place in town to check your e-mail is **Café Internet** *(New St.; Tel 064/36741; 9:30am-8pm Mon-Thu, 9:30am-7pm Sat; £5 per hour; V, MC),* a comfortable spot with speedy computers and lunch-'n-surf specials: get a Coke, toasted sandwich, and half-an-hour of net access for five punts. On the other hand, **Web-Talk** *(Main St.; 10am-10pm Mon-Sat, 2-8pm Sun; £5 per hour)* has more convenient hours, but the facilities are somewhat more austere. Don't come here if you're hungry, either.

The Killarney Grand, usually just known as **The Grand** *(Main St.; Tel 064/31159),* offers nightly folk and trad from 9:30pm until 1:30am, with no cover unless you arrive after 11pm. It's not the best live music you've ever heard, but most locals and backpackers who've been bumming around here awhile will tell you that it makes for a thoroughly enjoyable evening. It's a dimly lit pub with comfy seating, but if you want to sit down for the music you should get there early.

Next door to the **Súgan Hostel** [see *crashing,* below], **Kelly's Korner** *(Lewis Rd.; No phone)* conveniently will let you buy your pint and then take it back to the hostel so you can snuggle next to the fire and hear Pa play. (It sounds surprising, but even the most adventurous visitors would rather stay in at the Súgan than go out to any of the pubs!)

Several things distinguish **Yer Man's** *(Plunkett St.; Tel 064/32688)* from all the other pubs in town. The music is blues for the most part, not trad. It's the only pub in the country—hmm, make that the world—licensed to sell Guinness in jam jars—that's another great tidbit for your archive of useless information. It'll cost you a punt and a half, and you have to make a special request. The Strawberry Tree, once Killarney's finest restaurant, has been under the same ownership, but at the time of writing the owner's plans for reopening were still up in the air; all you need to know is that if you see the Strawberry Tree reopened (and you will), it's a delicious (if pricey) bet for dinner. Meanwhile, Yer Man's continues to serve up the Guinness with unusual style.

Can you say "tourist trap?" At **The Laurels** *(Main St.; Tel 064/31149; Cover),* that's precisely what you get. The nightly music sessions are lively, true, but they attract the aforementioned deep-pocketed tourists who think nothing of plunking down a hefty cover for admission. The music's more Lucky Charms than Guinness, sweat, and sawdust, although the ballad singers are kinda cool. Otherwise, it's a fine place for a pint.

club scene

If you're hot for the clubbing scene, then why are you here? Seriously, Killarney isn't the best place for your hoochie tube tops and smooth dance moves. Still all for it? There are a few options.

They'll tell you it's called **The Crypt** *(College St.; Tel 064/31038; 11pm-1:30am nightly; Cover £4-6)* because of its basement location and black decor, but it's actually because the club attracts people who were old enough to go clubbing when that ABBA single they're still playing first came out. (Heck, some of them were even over the hill *then.*) Over 23 only? Closed at half-past one? Dress code? *Please.* At least most of the music's decent, and some of 'em still know how to dance.

For those of us still wearing our Huggies disposables, there's always **Revelles** *(Kenmare Place, Tel 064/32522; Cover £5)* at the Killarney Avenue Hotel, pumping out the standard overplayed pop singles to Killarney's teeny-bopper crowd, who are trying a little too hard to look suave and sophisticated.

Killarney Town

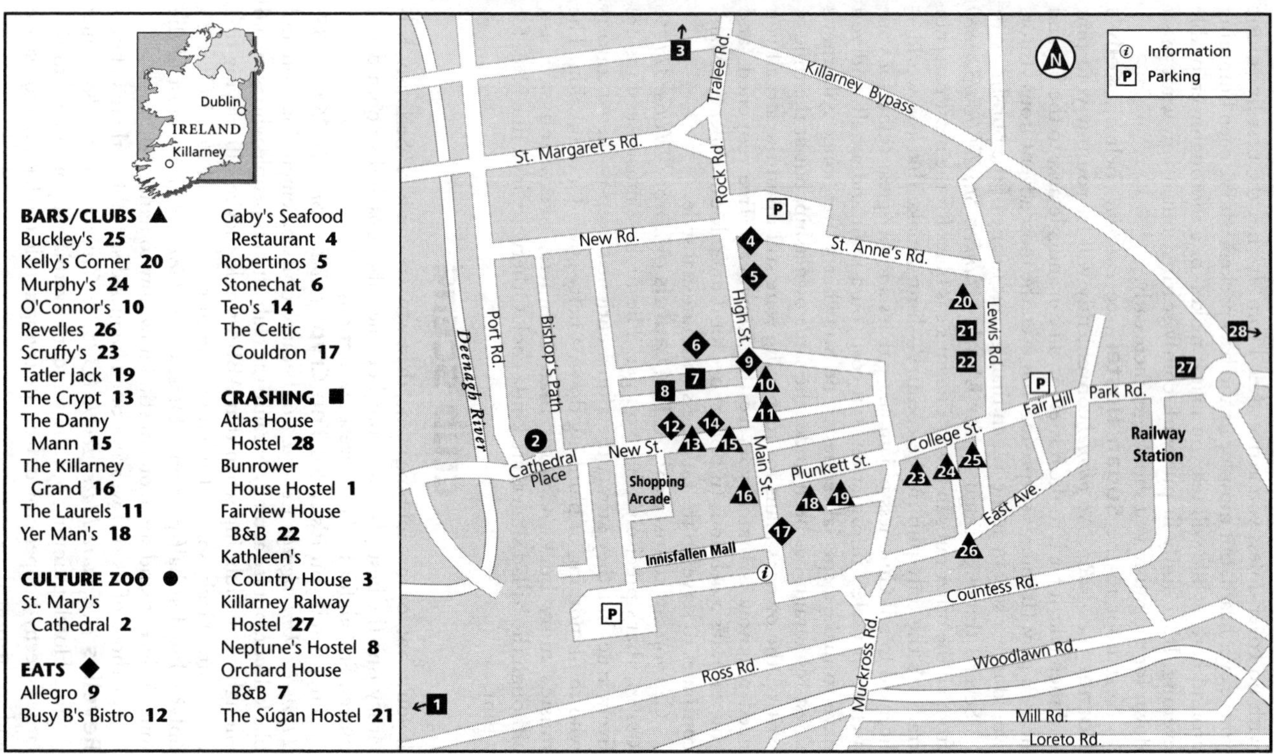

Information
Parking
Dublin
IRELAND
Killarney
Killarney Bypass
Tralee Rd.
Rock Rd.
St. Margaret's Rd.
New Rd.
St. Anne's Rd.
High St.
Main St.
Lewis Rd.
Port Rd.
Deenagh River
Bishop's Path
Cathedral Place
New St.
Shopping Arcade
Plunkett St.
College St.
Fair Hill
Park Rd.
Railway Station
East Ave.
Innisfallen Mall
Countess Rd.
Muckross Rd.
Ross Rd.
Woodlawn Rd.
Mill Rd.
Loreto Rd.
BARS/CLUBS
Buckley's 25
Kelly's Corner 20
Murphy's 24
O'Connor's 10
Revelles 26
Scruffy's 23
Tatler Jack 19
The Crypt 13
The Danny Mann 15
The Killarney Grand 16
The Laurels 11
Yer Man's 18
CULTURE ZOO
St. Mary's Cathedral 2
EATS
Allegro 9
Busy B's Bistro 12
Gaby's Seafood Restaurant 4
Robertinos 5
Stonechat 6
Teo's 14
The Celtic Couldron 17
CRASHING
Atlas House Hostel 28
Bunrower House Hostel 1
Fairview House B&B 22
Kathleen's Country House 3
Killarney Ralway Hostel 27
Neptune's Hostel 8
Orchard House B&B 7
The Súgan Hostel 21

culture zoo

Killarney's too busy bringing in the dough to worry about putting up pretty churches and other important buildings, but that's okay. You've got the park, and that's culture enough: Check out Ross Castle, Innisfallen Island, Muckross House, and all that good stuff [see **Killarney National Park**].

St. Mary's Cathedral *(at the end of New St.; Free admission):*19th-century St. Mary's Cathedral once harbored famine sufferers on its pristine emerald-hued lawn. Inside you'll find a cavernous neo-Gothic mega-church. This is definitely Killarney Town's most impressive building.

great outdoors

Killarney National Park. 'Nuff said. [see below]

eats

Aside from the greasy take-aways on the main streets of Killarney, there really aren't too many inexpensive options for eating out, and there are even fewer places for *good* cheap food. Almost every restaurant belongs in the splurge category. Be prepared to pay through your nose, especially at the restaurants on High Street, and don't expect generous plates; the prices sky-rocket as soon as a restaurant in these parts gets favorable reviews in a travel guide or magazine. If you want to keep a tight rein on your wallet, either go for lunch, which is always a better value, or cook for yourself [see *to market,* below]. All the pubs serve food, of course, and usually it's reasonably priced, though not always. Try **O'Connor's** [see *bar scene,* above] for some good, relatively cheap pub grub.

▸▸CHEAP

Decidedly the best place in town for a decently priced meal, **Stonechat** *(Flemings Lane, off High St.; Tel 064/34295, 10am-late)* makes a great laid-back spot for cheap yummy sandwiches, soups, and salads, for around £2. Enter through Dutch doors to find wooden tables in a cool, dimly lit room and a sweet little courtyard with a Plexiglas roof and a small garden.

markets

If you want to eat in or pick up supplies for the park, try **Richard Clifford** *(37 High St.; Tel 064/32151),* located downtown, or **Supervalu** *(Park Rd.; Tel 064/31400).*

Second-floor **Busy B's Bistro** *(New St.; Tel 064/31972; most items under £5; No credit cards)* has good prices but not all the chill atmosphere of Stonechat. It offers lasagna, Irish stew, cheeseburgers, and sandwiches. This ain't no gourmet palace, but it's decent food on the cheap.

▸▸DO-ABLE

Teo's *(88 New St.; Tel 064/36344; Noon-10:30pm; Main courses £6-13; V, MC, AE),* just fifty yards off Main Street, was once an inexpensive and delicious find. Since Teo's got all that good press, prices have inched their way up, so it's not such a great deal anymore. Nevertheless, if you want something a bit fancier than a tuna and tomato sandwich but don't want to fork over your student loan, check it out: vegetarian dishes go for around £7, pizzas for £8, and chicken or steak for £10-13. Teo's is also a good place for a large snack, like a stuffed spud for around four punts.

Not to be confused with that awful pizza grease-fest on Plunkett Street, **Allegro** *(9 High St.; Tel 064/32481; Noon-10pm daily; lunch under £5, all items £6-9; V, MC, AE)* offers burgers, pizza, and pasta in a typical Italian family-style atmosphere.

▸▸SPLURGE

Like seafood? *Love* seafood? You'll be in heaven at **Gaby's Seafood Restaurant** *(High St., Tel 064/32519; 6-10pm Mon-Sat, closed Christmas and late Feb-mid Mar; Main courses £13-30; V, MC, AE, DC).* If you can find it in the sea, you can find it at Gaby's, but at no small price: A fancy lobster cooked in fancy sauces—cognac, wine, cream, and spices—will cost you a bank-breaking thirty punts. The less expensive seafood dishes run around £14 to £20—shellfish, prawns, mussels, oysters, etc. There's also a single vegetarian option, usually pasta, for around £13 that's changed daily.

You have to ask for bread and butter at **The Celtic Cauldron** *(Plunkett St.; Tel 064/36821; 6-10pm Mar-Nov; Main courses £7-12; V, MC, AE),* but luckily they won't charge you extra. Here's the deal: this place has been written up dozens of times for its awesomely delicious and creatively prepared dishes from Ireland, Scotland, Wales, and Northern France, but the exact same dish that cost five punts one year will set you back eight the following. These people don't have any concept of the phrase "generous portions," either. That said, you'll find the food extraordinary: even an ordinary salad comes with stuff like walnuts, strawberries, and yummy mint dressing. Most main courses are meat, poultry, or seafood dishes, but a few options do exist for veggies. Don't buy a glass of mead wine here; a very, *very* small glassful will set you back three punts when you can get a whole bottle for around £8 at any off-license.

crashing

You'll find more rooms in Killarney than in any place outside of Dublin—plenty of hostels, tons of B&Bs (many of which are located over pubs), and plenty of pretentious super-hotels. The B&Bs included here are not over restaurants or pubs, meaning you'll get a much quieter night's sleep, and as for Kathleen's Country House, you couldn't find a nicer splurge anywhere in Killarney.

▸▸CHEAP

Seriously, you just can't say enough about **The Súgan Hostel** *(Lewis Rd.; Tel 064/33104; £9.50 dorm; No credit cards).* You want a hostel with atmosphere? You got it. Pa, the manager, is the closest you'll ever come to meeting a leprechaun, and the beds are among the most comfortable of any hostel in the country. Sure, the rooms are a tad pinched, but you won't notice or care; at a place with this much character (impromptu music and storytelling sessions a la Pa pretty much every night), you could forgive almost anything. Pa talks faster than a cheetah can run while he's giving you the standard tour of the hostel, so your head will be spinning giddily afterwards. He'll tell you about absolutely everything there is to do in this town, yet when nightfall arrives you won't want to leave the hostel. Most opt to buy a pint at Kelly's Korner [see *bar scene,* above] next door, bring it back to the Súgan, and relax at the oldest, coolest hostel in Killarney amid roaring hearth fires with Pa strumming his guitar and howling away. There is no curfew or lockout, and there is a large modern kitchen for guests. (By the way, *súgan* is the rope used to make traditional Irish chairs.)

Should the Súgan fill to capacity (that is, all of nine beds), you have several other decent options. You'll find **Neptune's Town Hostel** *(Bishop's Lane, off New St.; Tel 064/35255; neptune@tinet.ie, www.iol.ie/kerry-insight/neptunes/index.html; £8-9 dorm, £10 per person double; 10 percent discount with international student card; MC, V)* large and comfortable. You can do your laundry (five punts a load), check your email (although it's better to go to one of the net cafés in town), and have breakfast (for four punts or less).

Other choices include the clean-'n-comfy **Atlas House Hostel** *(The Park, off Cork Rd.; Tel 064/36144; call for pick-up from the train station; £15 dorm bed, £45 family suite; V, MC; no lockout; kitchen),* which offers continental breakfast (as it very well should, at these prices!), and **Bunrower House Hostel** *(Ross Road; Tel 064/33914; £8-9 dorm, £4 camping; no lockout; large kitchen),* a cozy spot with spacious dorm rooms and a common room with a fireplace on the road leading to Ross Castle. Want to camp? Do it here; it's the closest you can come to camping out in the national park.

By virtue of its location, the recently renovated **Railway Hostel** *(Park Rd., across from the train station; Tel 064/35299; £8-9 dorm, £12 per person double; No credit cards)* is certainly your most attractive option if you arrive at the train station totally exhausted in the pouring rain. Everything's clean, bright, and comfy. Most rooms have private baths—two rooms don't, and two rooms share a bath between them. You can rent bikes here for six punts a day, too. There's a 3am curfew, but it's highly unlikely you'd be tempted to break it anyway.

Otherwise, there are several good hostels in (or right outside) Killarney National Park if you'd rather spend the night outside of town [see below].

▸▸DO-ABLE

Most entrepreneurs in this town start with a pub, add a restaurant, and then figure, a B&B? Why not? We've got a second floor. What separates **Fairview House** *(College St.; Tel 064/34164; fairviewguesthouse@hotmail.com, www.geocities.com/fairview_guesthouse; £17-23 per person; V, MC)* from almost all the other bed and breakfasts in Killarney is that it's owner prides himself on a quiet establishment away from the noisy pubs and greasy take-aways—and it shows. The Fairview is immaculate, the beds and rooms are comfortable and homey, and the breakfasts are divine. If for some reason you want to take a coach tour of Killarney or the Ring of Kerry, the owners will take care of everything for you; if not, they're still good sources of local information. Most importantly, you get the feeling that they're genuinely concerned that their guests are comfortable and content.

Same deal with **Orchard House** *(Flemings Lane; Tel 064/31879; £16-18 per person; No credit cards).* It's clean, quiet, hospitable, and more focused on service than incoming cash flow. It's a cute little house tucked away on Fleming's Lane off High Street, across from Stonechat [see *eats*, above]. The keyword here is "little," so make sure to book ahead, even in low season. Orchard House is really close to all the pubs, yet you don't have to sacrifice a quiet night's sleep.

Other options include **Killarney View Guest House** *(Muckross Rd.; Tel 064/33122)* and **Carriglea Farmhouse** *(Muckross Rd.; Tel 064/31116, Fax 064/37693; carriglea@coeanfree.net; £21/person, private baths, breakfast included; V, MC),* overlooking the lakes a few miles out of town—take a taxi from the bus or train station.

▸▸SPLURGE

Forget about those huge impersonally pretentious mega-hotels in Killarney Town (that won't be hard for you to do, because chances are they're way out of your price range anyway). If you're up for a reasonable splurge, there's absolutely no better place than **Kathleen's Country House** *(Tralee Rd.; Tel 064/32810; info@kathleens.net, http://kathleens.net; £60-85 double; V, MC, AE),* a gorgeous, sprawling guesthouse set on the road out of Killarney Town. It's won so many awards it'd take forever to list them all here. Ads boast that it's "easy to get to and hard to leave," and nobody could possibly argue. Three acres of lush gardens surround the house, and the rooms are fabulously furnished with stylin' contemporary artwork—not those cheesy floral prints or bland dentist's-waiting-room kind of "art," either. Each room has a private bath and TV.

need to know

Currency Exchange Are you kidding? Do we have to tell you all the places that will jump at the chance to take your money, or can you just walk down the street and find someplace with your eyes closed? Plenty of places have bureaus de change, but banks give the best exchange rates. Your choices include **AIB** *(Main St.; Tel 064/31047; 10am-4pm Mon-Tue and Thu-Fri, 10am-5pm Wed),* **Bank of Ireland** *(New St.; Tel*

064/31050; 9am-4pm Mon-Tue and Thu-Fri, 9am-5pm Wed), or **TSB** *(New St.; Tel 064/33666; 9:30am-5pm Mon-Wed and Fri, 9:30am-7pm Thu),* all of which have ATMs for your shopping convenience.

Tourist Information The **Killarney Tourist Office** *(Beech St.; 9am-8pm Mon-Sat, 9am-1pm/2:15-6pm Sun, Jul-Aug; 9am-6pm Mon-Sat,*

the words of love, irish style

Whisper this in your little lad or lassy's ear, and from the pub you will flee, off to more amorous spots you will soon be!

"No sickness worse than secret love
It's long, alas, since I pondered that
No more delay; I now confess
my secret love, so slight and slim

I gave a love that I can't conceal
to her hooded hair, her shy intent
her narrow brows, her blue-green eyes
her even teeth and aspect soft

I gave as well—and so declare—
my soul's love to her soft throat
her lovely voice, delicious lips
snowy bosom, pointed breast

And may not overlook, alas,
my cloud-hid love for her body bright
her trim straight foot, her slender sole,
her languid laugh, her timid hand

Allow there was never known before
such a love as mine for her
there lives not, never did, nor will,
one who more gravely stole my love

Do not torment me, lady
Let our purposes agree
You are my spouse on this Fair Plain
so let us embrace"

—15th Century love poem, Anonymous

10am-6pm Sun, Jun and Sep; 9:15am-5:30pm Mon-Sat, 9:15am-1pm Sun, Oct-May) is just off Main Street, and provides info for the whole of County Kerry.

American Express *(East Avenue Rd.; Tel 064/35722; 8am-7:30pm Mon-Fri, 9am-6pm Sat, May-Sep; also open 9am-7pm Sun, Jul-Aug; 9am-5pm Mon-Fri, Feb-Apr).*

Health and Emergency **Garda Station** *(New Rd.; Tel 064/31222).* **District Hospital** *(St. Margaret's Rd., down High St. about a mile; Tel 064/31076)* provides medical care.

Pharmacies If you need to stock up your first aid kit before you head into the wild, try **Sewell's Pharmacy** *(New and Main Sts.; Tel 064/31027; 9:30am-6:30pm Mon-Sat, Sep-Jun; 9:30am-9:30pm Mon-Sat, Jul-Aug).*

Trains **Irish Rail** pulls into and out of **Killarney Station** *(off Park Rd. near East Avenue Rd.; Tel 064/31067 or 066/26555),* with four or five trains per day headed for Cork, Dublin, and Limerick.

Bus Lines Out of the City **The Bus Éireann depot** *(Tel 064/34777)* is behind the big outlet mall on Park Road, adjacent to the train station, but you can't get directly from one to the other. Buses leave for pretty much every place: Dingle, all stops on the Ring of Kerry (Cahirsiveen, Waterville, Sneem, etc.), Cork, Limerick, the Shannon Airport, Dublin, Galway, and Sligo. At least three buses a day leave for all destinations in summertime.

Bike Rental **O'Sullivan's** *(Bishop's Lane off New St.; Tel 064/31282; 8:30am-6:30pm; around £6 per day)* or **Killarney Rent-A-Bike** *(Outside the Súgan Hostel; around £6 per day)* will set you up with wheels.

Laundry **J. Gleeson's Launderette** *(College St.; Tel 064/33877; 9am-6pm Mon-Wed and Sat, 9am-8pm Thu-Fri; around £5 per load)* is probably the only laundromat on the island with an aggressive advertising campaign. Sheesh.

Postal For all your postal needs, head to the **Killarney Post Office** *(New St.; Tel 064/31288; 9am-5:30pm Mon and Wed-Fri, 9:30am-5:30pm Tue, 9am-1pm Sat).*

Internet See *wired,* above

killarney national park

The Irish landscape doesn't get much more breathtaking than this. Killarney National Park boasts over 25,000 acres of gardens, lakes, mountains, forests, as well as a rich variety of plant and animal life—some indigenous, some exotic. It's an absolute heaven-on-earth.

Unfortunately, tourists love it too. Disgruntled nature-lovers are pushed to the sides of the roads winding through Killarney National Park by smelly horse-drawn jaunting cars filled with gaping sightseers. Just about every day, no matter whether it's dry or rainy weather, loud motorboats or "water buses" break the sweet serene silence that lingers around the lakes. Ah, well. Try not to let it spoil your afternoon.

The oldest of Ireland's national parks, Killarney was established in 1932 when the **Muckross Estate** [see below] was donated to the public. Muckross now serves as the essential center of the park, a good jumping-off point since the **Killarney National Park Visitors' Centre** [see *need to know,* below] is located at Muckross House, and the little village of Muckross makes a good, if touristy, base for exploration.

The Upper, Middle (Muckross), and Lower Lakes comprise almost a quarter of the park's area. By far the largest at 19 square kilometers, the **Lower Lake,** called *Lough Leane,* or "Lake of Learning," harbors **Inisfallen Island** [see below], the site of important monastic remains. The Lower Lake is large and irregularly shaped, and toward the bottom it narrows where it connects with the **Middle** (or **Muckross**) **Lake.** The three lakes meet at a point known as the "Meeting of the Waters," a popular tourist hangout. From there the Upper Lake snakes downward into the area at the south end

pubs in the park

Sitting at the entrance to Killarney National Park, **Molly Darcy's** *(Muckross Village; Tel 064/34973)* unfortunately tends to cater to big boisterous tourist groups. But it's still a charming enough place with unusually good pub grub (there's no gristle in the lamb stew).

On the western side of the lakes and just outside the park, **Kate Kearney's** *(Gap of Dunloe; Tel 064/44146)* is a pub set in a traditional cottage hosting frenzied set dancing sessions every night during the summer months. But due to its all-too-convenient location at the Gap of Dunloe, the pub's just-too-quaint atmosphere is often marred by the presence of stinky poo-spewing jaunting cars.

of the park. The **Upper Lake** is the smallest, but perhaps the most scenic, of the three, set in the fantastic **Black Valley** region of the park.

Muckross House is located between the Lower and Middle (Muckross) Lakes; you'll probably enter from Killarney Town, which is near the northern end of the Lower Lake. Follow the lake's perimeter southward until you come to Muckross House.

You'll find a gate at the entrance from Killarney Town; there's no fee to get in, and it's always open. No cars are permitted inside the park, so it's best to park in Killarney and walk or bike in. It's around four kilometers from the center of town to the eastern edge of the park. Bikes are easy to come by [see *need to know,* below], and touring around Muckross Lake makes for excellent exercise. *Just make sure you're biking in the right direction*—bikers should only approach the route in a counterclockwise direction, heading from Muckross House to the Meeting of the Waters and not the other way around to avoid collision.

Of course you'll cover more territory on bike, but there are trails that are better taken by foot. Plenty of well-worn paths wind around the lakes and the surrounding areas, and up into the mountains. Easy hikes abound, especially in the Muckross area of the park; get maps or detailed directions from the **Visitors' Centre** at Muckross House [see *need to know,* below].

A lovely Victorian mansion now housing exhibits on rural life in County Kerry, **Muckross House and Gardens** *(Kenmare Rd.; Tel 064/31440; 9am-6pm daily mid-Mar to Jun/Sep-Oct; 9am-7pm daily Jul-Aug; 9am-5:30pm Nov to mid-Mar; Admission around £4)* is perfectly situated overlooking Muckross Lake, with the Park's **Torc** and **Mangerton Mountains** in the background. You ought to stop in at Muckross House to obtain park information and maps anyway, but there are other reasons to visit as well. You can watch traditional artisans at work in the craft shops in the basement, and check out all the old locally made furniture and artwork that are part of the exhibit upstairs. The much-ballyhooed Muckross gardens are certainly worth a look, but be forewarned: More than 250,000 people visit Muckross House every year, so you may well find yourself in the midst of the summer stampede.

Another reason to linger in Muckross would be nearby **Muckross Traditional Farms** *(Kenmare Rd.; Tel 064/31440; 1-7pm Mon-Fri May, 10am-7pm Mon-Fri Jun-Sep, 1-6pm Sat-Sun mid-Mar to Apr and Oct; Around £4 admission, discounted ticket for about £6 available for both house and farms),* which does an excellent job of simulating Irish rural life in the 1930s. You can watch farmers and housewives doing their thing, with all the traditional tools and surroundings—we're talking no electricity here. You'll wonder how they could ever stand life without hairdryers and television. It's worth a look, but on the other hand, the park in all its wild beauty awaits. Skip the farms if you're short on time.

One important monastic site in the park is the Franciscan **Muckross Abbey** *(1.5km north of Muckross House; Always open; Free admission),* founded in 1448 and ruined by none other than the nefarious Oliver Cromwell in 1652. The abbey received much abuse over the centuries, and the monks were said to have fled to a little spot known as "Friar's Glen" on Mangerton Mountain (several miles south, outside the Park) every time an assault was begun. The abbey is relatively well-preserved, for a bunch of ruins, although it's sadly lacking a roof. A yew tree resting gracefully in the old courtyard is said to be as old—or perhaps older—than the monastery itself.

Lazy, pressed for time, or both? Although you can't actually drive in the park, you can get pretty dang close. Take the Kenmare Road (N71)—you can pick it up just south of Muckross House and anywhere along the eastern shore of the Upper Lake—out towards **Moll's Gap.** This will get you past the Upper Lake and out to **Ladies' View**, one of the best spots to get a view of the whole park.

You'll soon reach 15th-century **Ross Castle** *(Ross Rd., off of Kenmare Rd.; Tel 064/35851; 11am-6pm Apr, 10am-6pm May and Sep, 9am-6:30pm daily Jun-Aug, 10am-5pm daily Oct, closed Nov-Mar; Admission £2.50 adults, £1 students),* on the shores of Lough Leane, or the Lower Lake. The castle is a *huge* tourist trap, especially during July and August, and as castles go this one's not all that special. So it's not really worth the entrance fee only to have to deal with the large, aggravating crowds.

Popular legend says the castle could never be taken by land, so in 1652 Cromwell's forces brought boats up from Kinsale to conduct an assault on the castle. It surrendered easily enough: By that late time it was obvious that Cromwell couldn't be defeated, so Lord Muskerry of Ross Castle was about to give it up anyway. About a half-kilometer southwest of the castle, on the misnamed **Ross Island** (it's actually a peninsula), you can see a prehistoric copper mine in addition to other well-preserved remains of bronze-age activity in Killarney.

The remarkably well-preserved ruins of seventh-century **Inisfallen Abbey** *(Inisfallen Island, Lough Leane, Killarney National Park; Always* *open; Free admission)* are definitely worth the ache you'll feel in your upper arms the morning after rowing out to their island site. The Abbey was founded by Saint Finian the Leper, and monks lived and labored here for 700 years, recording the history of Munster as it transpired in the *Annals of Inisfallen.* To this day, the *Annals* is one of the best sources of information regarding early Christian Ireland. (The manuscripts, as you'd expect, are no longer here but in a library in Oxford, England.) Reach Inisfallen Island by renting a boat from Ross Castle [see above], or hire someone to row you out for around £4 per person.

While you're in the neighborhood, take note that the **Knockreer Estate** *(Cathedral Place, off New St.; Tel 064/31440; Free admission to the grounds),* once the breeding ground of the Earls of Kenmare, now houses the field study center for the park—not open to the public—and offers stupendous views of the Lower Lake from its pathways and gardens.

Alright, so the **Gap of Dunloe** is technically outside Killarney National Park, but it still gets a flow of Killarney-bound tourists, who gape at the high cliffs, low valleys, and burbling little streams with cameras glued to their faces. The Gap is located 9.7 km(6 miles) southwest of Killarney; you can reach it by taking a path that begins at the Upper Lake within the Park and leads right through the Gap. The best way to take in this scenery is by bike, although you'll have plenty more of those horse-drawn car tours to contend with. In the summer, no cars or motorized vehicles of any kind are allowed in the Gap. Definitely set aside an entire day for biking out from Killarney and back.

Sounds like something some goon might shout in a high school locker room, but it's not: **Macgillicuddy's Reeks,** beyond the Gap of Dunloe, is Ireland's highest mountain range. Only serious hikers need apply for this challenge—if you take it on, your best bet might be to make the **Black Valley Hostel** [see *crashing,* below] your base and spend the following day lounging around, feet up, with a nice-smelling squeeze tube of muscle massage cream. Check with the **Killarney Tourist Office** [see *need to know,* below] for possible routes and practical information. This is definitely an all-day excursion; fit yourself with sturdy hiking boots and all the other requisite equipment for an all-out hike. The Black Valley Hostel is within a kilometer or so of the mountain range.

crashing

Although no camping is permitted in the park, you can stay at any of the hostels or B&Bs in Killarney. Or you could try one that puts you a bit closer to the action. There are plenty of excellent hostels to choose from, safely away from the tacky tourist hubbub.

Located just above the Upper Lake, **Aghadoe House Hostel** *(Killarney, 3 miles west of town on the Killorglin Rd.; Tel 064/31240; £7-8 dorms; V, MC)* offers free pickup service from the train or bus station in Killarney [see Killarney *need to know*]. This place is a real gem: Not only are you staying at a huge gorgeous old stone mansion in the middle of the forest, but you can enjoy barbecues, live music, history lectures, and cheap cafe food on the premises. Rent a bike here for 6 punts a day.

Highly recommended by all who pass through its doors, **Peacock Farm Hostel** *(Gortdromakerry, Muckross, Killarney; Tel 064/33557; Open Apr-Sept; £7-8 dorm; No credit cards)* offers excellent skylit rooms and comfortable facilities. To reach the hostel, take Muckross Road out of Killarney and turn left just before the Muckross Post Office. Follow the signposts along that road for 2 miles. Baggage too heavy and feet dragging? You can always call the hostel for a pickup. How amazing is this? Your dorm views encompass Lough Guitane, which you'll pass on the way to Muckross and the Middle Lake, and the surrounding hills, not to mention the family of peacocks who lent the hostel their name. Splendid.

Not quite as cool, but still totally adequate, **Black Valley Hostel** *(Beaufort, Killarney; Tel 064/34712; open Mar-Nov; £6-6.50 dorms; No credit cards)* is located about a kilometer or two from the Upper Lake in the National Park. Meals are provided, for an extra charge, of course. Basic meals are between £4 and £6, four courses around £10. There's a small store, so luckily there's no need for you to venture the 10 miles back into town to stock up on grub. Considering that there's no public transportation from here into Killarney, this isn't your best bet if you don't have wheels or the legs for pedaling. Black Valley is, however, situated a mere mile from the Gap of Dunloe and within (serious) hiking distance of Macgillycuddy's Reeks.

need to know

Hours/Days Open You can always get in and out of the park, but the hours are limited at the **Killarney National Park Visitors' Centre** *(Muckross House; Tel 064/31440; 9am-6pm daily Mar-June, Sept-Oct, 9am-7pm daily July-August, 9am-5:30pm daily the rest of the year; www.kerrygems.ie/muckross/, mucros@iol.ie).*

Tourist Information For information on hiking conditions in the surrounding mountains, check out the **Killarney Tourist Office** *(Beech St.; Tel 064/31633; 9am-8pm Mon-Sat, 9am-1pm and 2:15-6pm Sun Jul-Aug; 9am-6pm Mon-Sat, 10am-6pm Sun Jun and Sept; 9:15am-5:30pm Mon-Sat, 9:15am-1pm Sun Oct-May).*

Directions/Transportation For the carless, reaching Killarney by bus or train and then getting a ride from your hostel or hotel is the way to go. If you're only hanging around for the day, you could rent a bike [see *rental,* below] after you get off the bus or train and cover more ground than if you walk. To get to the park drivers should take N72 from Killorglin on the Iveragh Peninsula, N22 from Tralee or Limerick, or N22 from Cork to get to the park.

Rental Rent a bike from **Aghadoe House Hostel** [see *crashing,* above] for £6 per day; from **The Súgan Hostel** *(Killarney, Lewis Rd.; Tel 064/33104)* for a similar price; or from O'Sullivan's *(next to Neptune's Hostel in Killarney, Tel 064/31282; £6 a day).*

Ireland's hitmakers

For too long U2 and Sinead O'Connor have dominated our popular notion of Irish music. Hey, I'm not knocking either of them, but here are a few classics (some of them are gone, some will be around forever) that may often get neglected across the pond.

Thin Lizzy: Phil Lynott and the boys struck it big in 1976 with their ode to good times gone and good times yet to come, "The Boys are Back in Town." A one hit wonder to the unknowing, Thin Lizzy were in fact a much-adored hard-rocking pub band that represented both the exuberance and the sorrow of Ireland.

The Undertones: This Derry five-piece wrote pop-punk singles before upstarts like Blink-182 could even tell time. It was the quest for the perfect pop song that fueled the Undertones—that and the punk/new wave explosion that was occurring over in London. The tenacious longing for an unrequited crush may never be described better than on their classic "Teenage Kicks."

The Divine Comedy: One-man pop symphony Neil Hannon is indeed an original, writing some of the most lush, grandiose, melodramatic "rock" songs this side of Phil Spector. Often lumped in with 90s britpop faves, The Comedy are, shall we say, a bit different. An acquired taste? Pure genius? Absolute garbage? Who's to say. An Irish original? Definitely.

Kirsty Macoll: Perhaps best known for doing the original version of "They Don't Know," Tracy Ullman's theme song, Macoll was indeed a muse for many a rock performer. With as diverse a roster of collaborators as anyone (Talking Heads, Happy Mondays, Pogues), MacColl's voice worked with almost any genre. Killed in a motorboat accident in December, 2000, Kirsty's most lasting work is her classic duet with Shane McGowan, "Fairytale of New York."

The Pogues: Perhaps Ireland's most notorious musical outfit, The Pogues define the raucous spirit of Ireland. Formed in London, in 1982 and disbanded in 1996, the Pogues have been described as every thing from a cross between the Sex Pistols and the Chieftains, to a disgrace to the great tradition of Irish music. If trad-fueled and, no doubt, whiskey-fueled song's like "The Band Played Waltzing Matilda," and "Bottle of Smoke" don't get you in the proper mood, nothing will.

Shane MacGowan: The former lead singer of The Pogues and current lead singer of The Popes, not to mention Ireland's mad hatter #1, MacGowan sets back the stereotype of the drunken Irishman by about a hundred years. Nonetheless, MacGowan has been a bittersweet wellspring of Irish song for many years now and, pending the strength of his liver, many years to come.

ring of Kerry

Ring of Kerry

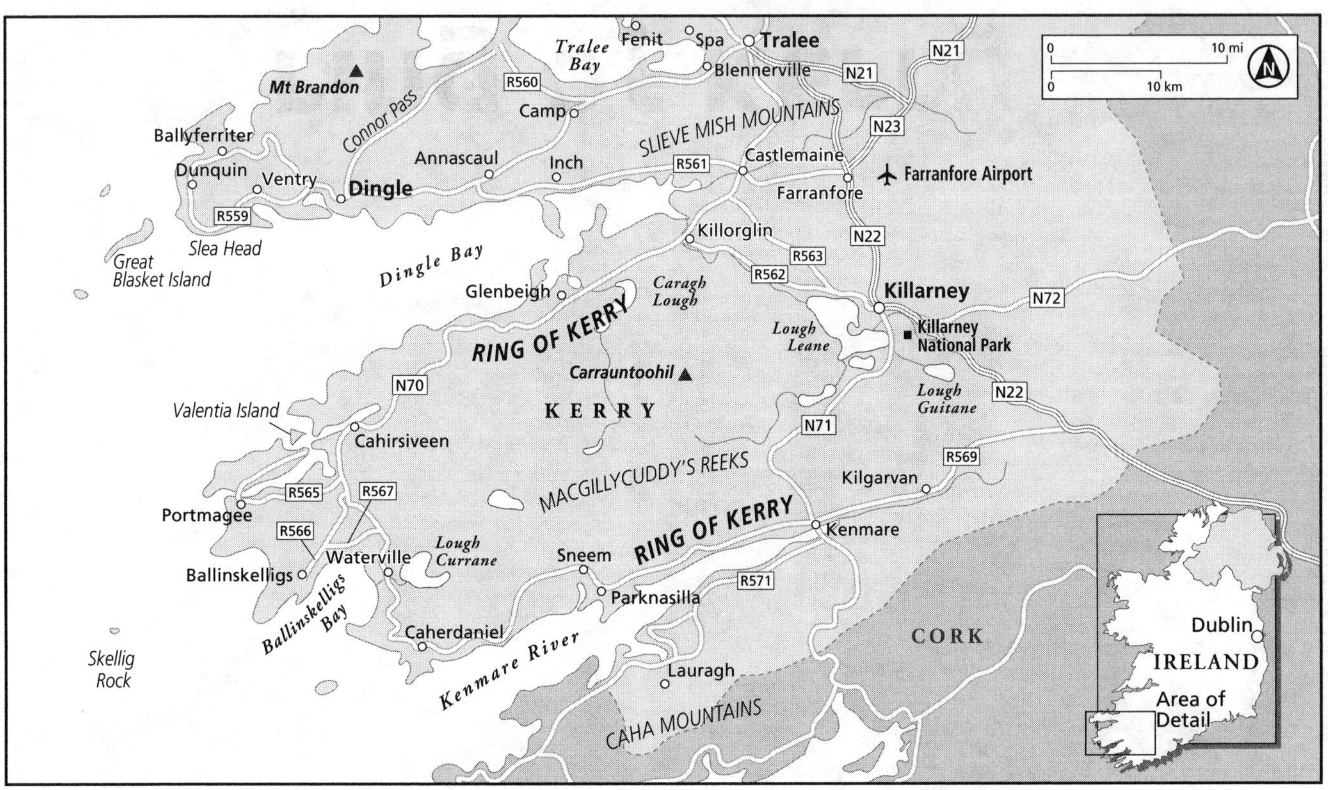

Without a doubt Ireland's most popular drive, the Ring of Kerry is a 110-mile panorama of seacoast, mountain, and lakeland vistas [see **southwest regional intro** for distances between towns]. Tiny villages line the route, so you are always within easy distance of a pint or pillow. And, yes, the tour bus crowd has discovered it already, so don't expect to be enjoying it alone. Still, there's enough beauty here to go around, from the lovely beaches to the midsection's gorgeous mountain range, **Macgillycuddy's Reeks.** Its glorious extremes go from the highest mountain in Ireland, snow-capped **Corrán Tuathail** at 3,414 feet (1,041meters), to a surprising effloresence of colorful sub-tropical plants throughout the countryside, evidence of a warm Gulf Stream presence.

For the most part, the Ring follows **N70** and circles the **Iveragh Peninsula** in lower County Kerry; it begins and ends at Killarney, but you can also use Kenmare as a base. You can drive in either direction, but counter-clockwise makes for better views.

You *could* buy a ticket for a coach bus that'll whip you 'round the Iveragh peninsula faster than you can sing "Oh, Danny boy." You could rent a car and drive around the whole thing in about a day. Or, if you're athletic and ambitious enough, you can rent a bike and cycle the perimeter of the peninsula, which will take you about three or four days, beginning and ending in Killarney—the longer it takes, the more you're sure to enjoy the experience. On the other hand, cyclists might prefer the Beara, Sheep's Head, or Mizen Head peninsulas of West Cork, where they aren't as likely to get run off the road by the Ring of Kerry tour buses.

That said, here's how you do it: Beginning in **Killarney,** proceed north-west to **Killorglin,** which doesn't have much going for it besides its annual Puck Festival, although it is near Caragh Lake and makes for a marvelous green hilly biking excursion. Then farther west, there's **Glenbeigh,** set at the foot of the Seefin Mountain, which is almost 500 meters high; there's nothing much in the way of nightlife or anything in Glenbeigh, either, but the beach there is consistently named one of Europe's very best.

The next town on the Ring is **Cahersiveen,** birthplace of Daniel O'Connell and one of the best stops on the Ring for lively traditional music, awesome "modern Irish" food , and a state-of-the-art Internet café if you're feeling homesick (or even if you want to play Nintendo). **Portmagee** and **Ballinskelligs,** two ferry ports for the **Skellig Islands,** are located towards the first tip of the peninsula (the coastline dips inward and then out for another mini-peninsula, where Caherdaniel is located). **Valentia Island,** reachable by bridge from **Portmagee,** is also a popular vacation spot and hosts the Skellig Experience museum.

Waterville, one of Charlie Chaplin's favorite haunts, is located on Ballinskelligs Bay, but again, there's not a whole lot to keep you here for more than an afternoon, although it is a possibility if you're planning a trip to the Skelligs; **Caherdaniel,** on the southwestern tip of the peninsula, makes an excellent diving spot. Turning around and coming back into Killarney, you'll reach **Sneem,** one of the cutest little towns in Ireland with its calendar-page rows of brightly colored buildings. The last town on the Ring is **Kenmare,** a quiet, picturesque little place that's only hopping in July and August. After Kenmare, the road leads back up into Killarney.

None of these towns have hot-'n-happenin' nightspots or anything; there's not so much of a commercially geared pub scene because most tourists choose to experience the Ring of Kerry via an afternoon-long bus tour. (The upside of this for you is that the hordes tend to clear out by evening, leaving these little towns quiet and unspoiled.) Otherwise, to avoid those tour buses, come in the early spring or the fall, because from May through September the coaches grind through constantly. And in April or October (or after that), the weather's not as nice (it gets cold enough in the summertime as it is).

shamrock shake

There's no question that the shamrock and Ireland are connected for eternity, but why? What is a shamrock and why has it become the internationsl symbol of Ireland?

Unless you've never left your house, you're aware that a shamrock is basically a three-leaved green clover. Historically though, it dates back as far as the Druids, who worshipped it as sacred plant because of its mystical three-pronged form. The best-known legend surrounding the shamrock, however, involves the most Irish of them all, Saint Patrick. It is said that ol' Patty used the leaf as a metaphor for the theory behind Christianity, no doubt banking on past fascinations with the shamrock.

As the first purveyor of "the word of the Lord" in Ireland, Saint Patrick used the shamrock to explain the idea of the inter-relationship of the Father, the Son, and the Holy Ghost: as each leaf of the clover is separate, so are the divisions of the holy trinity. However, all are connected as one, for the Shamrock it is through the stem, for the trinity, it is through God. Don't ask us what he would have made of those "lucky" 4-leafed clovers....

Killorglin

For most of the year, Killorglin is anything but a tourist trap; despite its location at the beginning of the Ring of Kerry, it's not an especially pleasant place to hang out. During the annual Puck Festival, though, the town springs into bacchanalian action [see *festivals and events,* below]. Held for three days in August to celebrate the Celtic god Pan, this claims to be the oldest festival in all of Europe. Goats and Guinness proliferate. Drinking, dancing, and carousing—sure, those crazy Irish do all that stuff *every* day, but you definitely haven't seen anything until you've seen this. The manliest—er, *goatliest*—he-goat in town is crowned "King Puck."

Just can't wait for that bus in the morning? Are you so super-psyched for that Skelligs trip early tomorrow morning that you can't waste time here? Ask in the tourist office [see *need to know,* below], a funny round little building just down the street from the bus stop, if there's any possibility of finding a ride out of town from a local; some of Killorglin's businesspeople live farther out on the Ring of Kerry.

bar and live music scene

Looking for the best pub in town? Try the **Old Forge Inn** *(Bridge St.; Tel 066/976-1231),* which has live music every night of the week: trad on Mondays, Tuesdays, and Wednesdays, and pop music every other night.

great outdoors

An ultra-scenic option four miles outside of Killorglin is **Caragh Lake,** surrounded by mountains and veiled in quiet beauty. Rent a bike from O'Shea's Cycle Centre [see *need to know,* below] and check it out.

If you're going to linger for a bit and you're feeling peppy enough, the **Cappanalea Outdoor Education Centre** *(North of Killorglin near Caragh Lake; Tel 066/976-9244)* offers a variety of adventure sports including canoeing, kayaking, and climbing. To get there, turn left off the main street onto Lower Bridge Street at the Bianconi Inn, then follow the signs to the adventure center.

eats

Pick up groceries at the **Supervalu** *(Tel 066/976–117; 9am-9pm Mon-Sat)* on the Main Street, adjacent to the police station.

The best value and the best food are found at **Nick's Seafood & Steak** *(Main Street; Tel 066/9761-219; main courses £10-£15; 5:30-11:30pm daily Apr-Oct; 5:30-11:30pm Wed-Sun Winter; AE, DC, MC, V).* A former veterinary surgeon, the owner and chef, Nick Foley, assisted by his wife Ann, offer fine dining from the sea and the hoof. Theirs is an old stone town house that is also one of the most popular bars in town. You can dine downstairs for more fun, but the more tranquil and formal dining area is one floor above. The name says it all—Nick's has the best of locally caught fresh fish and also the tenderest and juiciest of Irish steaks.

If you're visiting late in the year, you can order the special—a haunch of Kerry venison in a juniper berry-flavored red wine sauce. Nick's lies a 3-minute walk of the center.

crashing

Whether you're here for the festival or took the wrong bus by mistake (it's been known to happen), you'll probably need a place to stay. The **Laune Valley Farm Hostel** *(Banshagh; Tel 066/9761-488; £7-8 dorm, £18-20 double; No credit cards)* is a mile-and-a-half outside town on the Tralee Road. Here you'll receive a genuine taste of Irish farm life (not to mention the remote control for a satellite television, ironically enough). You can buy eggs and all sorts of other stuff produced on the farm from the owners, who also provide good meals. While Killorglin can be a bit dreary, the hostel is pleasant, welcoming, and rather unusual 'cause of all those chickens and pigs and cows poking around outside your dorm window. Look for the ruins of the 16th-century Ballymalis Castle nearby.

Other crashing options include **Riverside House** *(Killarney Rd.; Tel/Fax 066/9761-184; riversidehousebnd@eircom.net; Rooms with private bath £19, with shared bath £17, breakfast included; No credit cards);* **Hillcrest** *(Killarney; Tel 066/9761-552; Fax 066/9761-996; hillcrest_clifford@hotmail.com; Rooms £19/person, private baths, breakfast included; V, MC);* and **Hillview Farm** *(Tralee Rd.; Tel 066/9767-117, fax 066/9767-910; Rooms £21/person, private baths, breakfast included; V, AE),* 2 miles out of town, near the golf course.

need to know

Currency Exchange The **AIB** *(Bridge St.; Tel 066/9761-134; 10am-4pm Mon-Wed and Fri, 10am-5pm Tue)* has a bureau de change and an ATM, and the **Supervalu** [see *eats,* above] has an ATM as well.

Tourist Information The **Killorglin Tourist Office** *(Main St.; Tel 066/9761-451; 9:30am-5:30pm Mon-Fri, 9am-6pm Sat, 10am-3pm Sun, May-Sep)* is open for your tourist needs.

Buse Lines Out of Town Bus Éireann runs one bus from Killarney to Killorglin, and another twice each day in the summer through Killorglin to other towns further out on the Iveragh, including Cahirsiveen, Waterville, and Sneem.

Bike Rental If you want to take a spin around those rolling hills, try **O'Shea's Cycle Centre** *(Lower Bridge St.; Tel 066/9761-919; £7.50 per day, £40 per week).*

Laundry If you're stopping long enough, you can throw a couple of loads in at **Starlite Cleaners** *(Langford St.; Tel 066/9761-296; 9am-6pm Mon-Sat; £5 per load).*

Postal Send witty postcards to all your friends back home ("The weather is here; wish you were beautiful") from the **Killorglin Post Office** *(Main St.; Tel 066/9761-101; 9am-5:30pm Mon-Fri, 9am-1pm Sat).*

cahirsiveen

Cahersiveen? Cahirsiveen? Caherciveen? Cahirciveen? Any way it's spelled (there seems to be a bit of confusion about that), it's a charming little town amazingly unblighted by tourism and a perfect base for a trip to the Skellig Islands. The town consists of basically just one main street (called, of course, **"Main Street"**), where you'll find everything you need—pubs, net access, grocery shopping, and an excellent hostel. Best known as the birthplace of Daniel O'Connell, one of the foremost figures in all of Irish history, Cahirsiveen still bears the ruins of his home as well as the remains of a splendid 15th-century castle, Ballycarbery, where O'Connell's ancestors once lived.

bar, club, and live music scene

Visit early in the week and any pub will be quieter than usual: the locals are no doubt still recuperating from their weekend hangovers. Locals will make a point of informing you of this; while it seems like it would be true for any town in Ireland, it's especially the case here for some reason. Anyway, you know the drill: The pubs stop serving around 11:30pm.

The owner of **The Shebeen** *(East End, Main St.; Tel 066/9472-361)* is a great one to ask for local information. The pub itself is furnished com-

wired

Tucked away on a second floor across the street from the Old Oratory [see *stuff*, below] and decorated in bright jungle decor, **Javasite.ie** *(W. Main St.; Tel 066/9472-116; fortnite@iol.ie, www.java-site.ie; 9am-9pm; £5 per hour)* doesn't exactly seem ideally placed for a cybercafé. Most folks in Cahirsiveen haven't caught on to that whole new-fangled Internet thing yet, but those who have take full advantage of Lynn Weeks' speedy PCs, Nintendo and Playstation equipment, televisions, liberal candy stash, and brand new cappuccino-maker. (Lynn makes a great cup—sip away while checking your email.) Java's the perfect name for three reasons: the coffee, the business, and the name of the Indonesian island that inspired the colorful green computer stations and perky red wooden parrots. Sure, you can check your e-mail for free at the **Cahirsiveen Library** *(Church St.; Tel. 066/9472-287; 10am-5pm daily)*, but it's worth it to fork over the few punts you have for such a lively and comfortable atmosphere. It's perfect for an early-evening net fix, a cappuccino, and a bit of relaxation after an afternoon at the Skelligs.

fortably with booths, a pool table, and a dartboard, and you'll find trad here every night of the week in the summer and Wednesday through Sunday during the off-season.

Frank's Corner Bar *(Main St.; Tel 066/9472-217)* was, unfortunately, more interesting in the past than it is now. When the place was owned by a certain "Tessie," the old-style pub suffered from a defective chimney, and every time they started a fire in the fireplace the smoke went down instead of up, covering every glass, bottle, and counter—even Tessie herself. Now clean and modern, Frank's offers good pub food and live trad twice a week during the summer.

How many times do you come across a pub with a natural spring in a corner? **The Fertha** *(W. Main St.; Tel 066/9472-023)* has one behind a little glass window. Pretty cool, huh?

An Bodhrán *(E. Main St.; Tel 066/9473-023)* hosts live trad every night on the weekends, and the owners make it a point to encourage guests to join in. You'll find good pub grub and a much coveted pool table here too.

You can find great live music at the **East End Bar** *(East End, Main St.; No phone)*, where Ceann Eile, a trad group bearing fiddles, mandolin, guitar, whistle, and *bodhrán,* play on Friday nights beginning at quarter after nine; Ceann Eile also plays at the Shebeen on Wednesday night. At the **Sceilig Rock Bar** *(W. Main St.; Tel 066/9472-305)* the pretty-much-nightly live music alternates between trad and pop.

If telling your life story to a bunch of Irishmen you've known for just five minutes sounds like fun to you, head to **Mike Murts** *(East End; Tel 066/9472-396),* an exclusively local hangout and one of the oldest pubs in town, selling farming equipment on the side—or a farming equipment store pulling pints on the side, depending on how you look at it.

culture zoo

It's all about Daniel O'Connell in Cahirsiveen.

The Old Barracks Heritage Centre *(Main St.; Tel 066/9472-589; 10am-6pm Mon-Sat, 1-6pm Sun; £3):* The Old Barracks Heritage Centre celebrates "The Great Liberator." For all the fuss they make, you'd think he had invented Guinness. Nope, he only emancipated the Catholics and

festivals and events

Coming to Cahirsiveen during the first weekend in August? Lucky you! That's when the town hosts the **Celtic Music Weekend,** with free concerts, fireworks, street entertainment, and pumped-up pub sessions. Check it out at ***www.celticmusicfestival.com***

the great liberator

If you're an Irish Catholic, "Daniel O'Connell" ought to be a household name. Irish Catholics will tell you that nary a nobler figure graced the Irish history textbooks, and they could be right. He was the first Irish Catholic to win a seat in the British House of Commons—no small feat, mind you—and he served there from 1829 until his death in 1847. His persistence led first to the Catholic Association, which pushed the Catholic Emancipation Act successfully in 1829, a law which gave Catholic men the right to hold public office in Great Britain. O'Connell was also behind the passing of the Reform Act of 1832, which provided suffrage to middle class men. Ironically, he was convicted of plotting against the government after he supported a campaign to free Ireland from English rule in 1844 and spent three-and-a-half months in jail. Cahirsiveenians today are extremely proud of their most famous native son...and rightly so.

pressed for an independent Ireland as a member of Parliament [see *the great liberator,* above].

Ballycarbery Castle *(Make a left off the bridge by the Barracks, about a half-hour walk; Free admission):* This 15th-century castle was home to Daniel O'Connell's ancestors. If you retrace your steps back to the castle turn-off and walk 200 yards down the road, you'll find a couple of very well-preserved forts, **Cahergall** and **Leacanabuaile.**

O'Connell's Church *(Main St.; Free admission):* O'Connell's Church is the only church in Ireland named for a non-clergy member [see *the great liberator,* above].

great outdoors

Ballycarbery Castle [see *culture zoo,* above] and the nearby stone forts make a nice half-hour walk from the **Sive Hostel** on Main Street [see *crashing,* below]. Continue past the forts and you'll come upon the **Cuas Crom** beach, an ideal spot for swimming.

Otherwise, make sure to visit the Skellig Islands, which provide a strenuous uphill climb, captivating views, and a fascinating yet eerie taste of Irish medieval history (not to mention a rocky ferry trip that might just prompt you to taste breakfast twice).

Horse-lovers will want to check out **The Final Furlong Farmhouse Accommodation and Riding Stables** *(Glenbeigh Rd.; Tel 066/9472-810 or 066/947-3300; £19 per person in shared rooms; V, MC, AE),* about a mile outside town. Gallop along that pretty Cahirsiveen strand in slow motion like somebody out of a cheesy '70s movie. They'll also put you up for the night [see *crashing,* below).

stuff

The **Old Oratory Craft Shop** *(Main St.; Tel 066/9472-043 or 066/9472-996; 10am-7pm, Apr-Dec)* stocks crystal, books, sweaters, jewelry, and pottery. The shop serves coffee in the morning and light lunches and tea in the afternoon, which you can enjoy in a little garden out back.

eats

There are a few mediocre-to-good restaurants in Cahirsiveen, but if you're only staying one night it might make sense to stock up on basics at **The Market** *(Main St.; No phone; 8am-10pm daily),* right across the street from the Sive Hostel. For cheap breakfast or lunch, try **Aoife's Cupán Eile** *(Main St.; Tel 066/9473-200; 9am-6pm; under £5).* Aoife and her girlfriend once owned a café like this one—named An Cupán—together, but after they split she formed her own and named it, most appropriately, "Aoife's OTHER Cup." There's also good pub grub to be had at **The Shebeen** and **An Bodhrán** [see *bar scene,* above].

A vegetarian haven, **The Seahorse Restaurant** *(Main St.; Tel 066/9472-153; 5-10pm daily; Avg. entree £9; V, MC)* is unofficially the best restaurant in town. Relax to the strains of Billie Holiday and Louis Armstrong while you eat an incredibly savory vegetarian meatloaf, almost magically concocted with nuts, vegetables, and tomato sauce. The chef will even visit your table after dinner to ask if you enjoyed it. The pine nut roast is his specialty, and Cahirsiveenians just can't get enough of it. Coupled with the generous side salad, bread, and vegetables, it's more than enough to feed a mob of hungry Fenians. You'll find fish fresher than a Kerry sea breeze here as well. Try the banana boozy for dessert, a fantastically delectable sundae with vanilla and banana ice cream, whipped cream, almonds, banana slices, raisins, and a generous dash of rum. Too bad you can't take it home in a doggy bag, 'cause after all that food it won't be easy to finish.

crashing

You can sleep on one of the most comfortable beds anywhere in Ireland at the **Sive Hostel** *(15 East End, Main St.; Tel 066/9472-717; £8 dorm, £10 private; No credit cards),* where, as always, the three C's—comfy, clean, and convenient—spell a definite winner. An added plus is the arrangement the Sive Hostel owners have with Patrick Casey, a Skelligs ferry operator: He'll come by every night to ask how many people are going the next morning. Count yourself in and you're all set. The ferry launches from Portmagee, a 15-minute drive from Cahirsiveen, but Mr. Casey will pick you up at the hostel at 9:30am and drive you there himself; if he isn't able to take you back, he'll make other arrangements for you.

If you're doing the horseback riding thing, you can stay at **The Final Furlong Farmhouse Accommodation and Riding Stables**

(Glenbeigh Rd.; Tel 066/9472-810 or 066/9473-300; £18 Jul-Aug, £16 rest of the year; Private baths, full Irish breakfast included).

need to know

Currency Exchange The **AIB** *(Main St.; Tel 066/9472-022; 10am-5pm Mon, 10am-3pm Tue-Fri)* has an ATM.

Tourist Information You can find out about local trails, the Ring, and of course, Daniel O'Connell at the **Cahirsiveen Tourist Office** *(The Barracks, Main St.; Tel 066/9472-589; 10am-6pm Mon-Sat, 1-6pm Sun, May-mid Sept).*

Buses Bus Éireann runs one or two buses daily east to Killarney from Cahirsiveen as well as two daily in the summer around the Ring of Kerry to Waterville, Sneem, and Kenmare. The bus stop is outside the Cahirsiveen Library on Main Street.

Bike Rental You can pick up a bike at **Casey's** *(Main St.; Tel 066/9472-474; 9am-6pm daily; £7 per day, £35 per week).*

Postal Wouldn't your grandma just love a postcard from the Ring? Send it from the **Cahirsiveen Post Office** *(Main St.; Tel 066/9472-010; 9:30am-1pm/2-5:30pm Mon-Fri, 2-5:30pm Sat).*

Internet See *wired,* above.

valentia island

Just a short walk across the bridge from Portmagee is Valentia Island, which offers fantastic views of Dingle Bay and the Skellig Islands from an old lookout tower at Bray Head. A leisurely stroll will take you past megalithic burial chambers, monastic ruins, and the slate quarry, whose product was used in the early 1800s to build the British House of Commons.

You'll hear a lot about **The Skellig Experience** *(Skellig Heritage Centre; Tel 066/9476-306; 10am-6pm, Apr-Oct; £3 admission to exhibition),* just off the bridge on Valentia, which offers an audio-visual exhibition as well as boat cruises around—not *to*—the Skellig Islands. Don't bother. Spend three punts on a pint instead.

Other interesting Valentia tidbits: Selenium was discovered here in 1873 by Joseph May, making the invention of the television possible; in 1927, the island was the first piece of land seen by Charles Lindbergh on his round-the-world flight; and it's been said that St. Brendan the Navigator sailed from here to reach America in the 500s.

The best hostel on the island is part of a bed-and-breakfast, **Coome Bank House** *(Knightstown; Tel 066/9476-111; £10 dorm, £18 per person bed and breakfast, £4 continental breakfast),* an elegant old stone house. To get there, walk straight off the bridge and turn right at the Pitch and Putt. It's best to shop at a grocery store on the mainland before coming to Valentia. If you absolutely have to eat, (why you would, I'll never know), just over the bridge in Portmagee sits **The**

Bridge Bar *(Portmagee; Tel 66/77/108, Fax 66/77/220; 12:30-3pm/6 to 8pm daily).* They have good quality seafood, fresh from the ocean down the road, and a few beds upstairs in the adjoining **Moorings B & B** to boot.

need to know

Directions/Transportation Valentia Island is just across the bridge at Portmagee, off the Ring of Kerry road. There is no Bus Éireann service to Portmagee, unfortunately, but if you decide to stay here overnight after your Skellig trip, you might be able to catch a ride back to Cahirsiveen or Waterville to pick up bus service with one of the ferry operators. From April through September, people on foot, bicycle, or in a car can take a **ferry** *(Tel 066/9476-141; 7:30am-10:30pm Mon-Sat, 8:30am-10:30pm Sun; £3)* from Reenard Point, near Cahirsiveen, to the island. It's about a 10-minute ride.

the skellig islands

After visiting Skellig Michael, George Bernard Shaw described the Skellig Islands as "an incredible, impossible, mad place. I tell you the thing does not belong to any world that you and I have lived and worked in; it is part of our dream world."

And every word is absolutely true. You can't possibly imagine (until you've seen it) the literally breath-taking precariousness of the small island monastery on Skellig Michael, perched high atop a steep mountain 600 feet above the waves, with a long uphill ascent on true "stairway to heaven" rock steps that have stood in place for more than 1,400 years.

Oh, and see that other island that seems to be hosting one wild pillow fight? Those are feathers, all right, but they belong to birds, and tons of 'em. Small Skellig is inhabited only by birds.

The Skellig Islands, two crags rising from the sea, are situated eight miles off the coast of the Iveragh Peninsula; a ferry trip takes between 45 and 90 minutes depending on your port [see *need to know,* below]. It's best to prepare yourself for a rocky ride. Most operators don't supply raincoats and pants—although Patrick Casey does [see *need to know,* below]—so don't be surprised if you get totally soaked. Once ashore, you'll begin a long ascent of the island, climbing the same steps used by the monks for six centuries. The monastery consists of six beehive huts used for sleeping and living quarters, an oratory, and a very small graveyard, along with a fantastic high cross. Remember that none of this, not even the stairways, existed when the monks first arrived on Skellig Michael in the 600s A.D. Creating all this was certainly no easy task.

15,000 people will visit the island every year, yet only a dozen monks at a time lived here a millennium ago. How could they possibly have survived this way? And why did they come here in the first place? (For a solid and even entertaining exploration on that matter, read *Sun Dancing* by Geoffrey Moorhouse.) While the life the Skellig monks lived was arduous, it wasn't unbearable: the monks fished, gardened, and kept livestock. Rainwater was collected in cisterns under the courtyard, which you can even see now, although it's a little green and sludgy.

The monastery survived many attacks over the centuries. The monks finally left in the 12th century, but not because the rough, secluded island lifestyle became too difficult; the Normans were moving in, along with a more modern religious organization that had ever-lessening respect for ascetic ideals and the "spiritual warfare" the monks believed was necessary to preserve the souls of those on the mainland.

In the 19th century, lighthouse-keepers and their families lived on Skellig Michael and used the oratory as their church until around 1900, when it finally dawned on them that whitewashing its interior and using it constantly wasn't exactly preserving the original structure...

All ferries let you have about two or three hours on the island, which is plenty of time for the uphill hike, a lecture on the history of the monastery, a picnic lunch, and lots of picture-taking. A few hints: don't wear high heels (that sounds totally absurd, but it *has* been done). Bring at least a whole roll of film. Don't eat in the monastery (The guide will tell you this several times, but some people still pull out their lunches anyway. You can eat anywhere outside the monastery). If you can, try to come before the summer rush starts; even in May there are too many other visitors for one to imagine what a secluded place Skellig Michael once was.

Bottom line: Skellig Michael is a definite must-see. Start training now for that uphill climb.

need to know

Directions/Transportation: The only way you can get to Skellig Michael is by ferry. The price is £25 round-trip regardless of which ferry operator you pick. It might sound steep, but the price was £20 until very recently; it hadn't gone up in seven years. Nevertheless, a trip to Skellig Michael is definitely worth the money. Ferries to Skellig Michael leave from Portmagee, Ballingskelligs, and Derrynane. Try **Des Lavelle** *(Tel 066/9476-124; deslavelle@hotmail.com),* leaving from Valentia Island (just a short walk over a bridge from Portmagee), or **Patrick Casey** *(Tel 066/9472-347; caseyboats@tinet.ie),* leaving from Portmagee, who will pick you up from the Sive Hostel in Cahirsiveen. and arrange for your return after the trip. Portmagee isn't on the Bus Éireann schedule, so it's difficult to arrange a trip to the Skelligs without a car unless you can get a ferry operator to pick you up and take you back.

Other ferry operators who'll oblige include **Joe Roddy** *(Ballinskelligs; Tel 066/9474-268)* and **Michael O'Sullivan** *(Portmagee; Tel 066/9474-*

255), who will pick you up from Waterville. So, if you're traveling by bus and want to see the Skelligs, stay in Cahirsiveen or Waterville.

waterville

Wedged in between Lough Currane and Ballinskelligs Bay, Waterville makes an okay base for a trip to the Skelligs. The beach is decent, but it's by no means the coolest town on the Ring. Most people just stop for an hour or two.

In the past Waterville served primarily as a resort town for wealthy English, and it was known as one of Charlie Chaplin's favorite vacation spots. In fact, Waterville residents recently erected a statue to commemorate him (tacky, but they didn't ask our opinion).

eats

The Fisherman's Bar *(Butler Arms Hotel; Tel 066/9474-144; butarms@iol.ie, www.waterville-insight.com/butler-arms; Full-course meal in the restaurant £25-30, bar food £2-11)* offers good seafood dishes and was among Charlie Chaplin's fave hangouts.

crashing

You thought Pa at the Súgan Hostel in Killarney was a character? Wait till you meet Peter, owner of **Peter's Place** *(Waterville; Tel 066/9474-608; £7 6-bed dorm; No credit cards).* Of course the term "character" is used in the most affectionate way possible. Let's just call the staff...well...*frenetic....* You'll never suffer from a dull moment at Peter's Place—but that's what you wanted, right? The hostel offers to arrange Skellig trips, but ask the staff about it and they're bound to say a whole lot without actually saying much at all. (You can go from Portmagee and stay in Cahirsiveen instead, or stay here and call one of the ferry operators to pick you up.)

With a gorgeous view of Waterville's golf course and a big old lounge where you can relax, **Klonayke House** *(New Line Rd.; Tel 066/9474-119, Fax 066/9474-666; closed Nov-Mar; single £24.50, double £36; V, MC)* makes a nice home-away-from-home if you decide to make Waterville the base for your skellig explorations.

need to know

Tourist Information The **Waterville Tourist Office** *(Tel 066/9474-646; 9am-6pm daily; Jun-Sep)* is located right on the beach across from the Butler Arms Hotel.

Bus The **Bus Éireann** Ring of Kerry bus stops in Waterville in front of the Bay View Hotel on Main St. twice a day during the summer. The bus moves onward to Caherdaniel, Sneem, and Killarney, and there's a bus back to Cahirsiveen once per day.

caherdaniel & derrynane

Tourists usually overlook Caherdaniel, and that makes it the perfect spot to spend a nice, relaxing afternoon. A quiet, second-to-none beach and the easy accessibility of equipment for water sports make it one of the Ring of Kerry's coolest little secrets. Aside from the beach, there are other sites worth noting. Staigue Fort is thought to date from around 1,000 B.C., and Derrynane House was the long-time home of Daniel O'Connell.

bar scene

The absence of tourists in Caherdaniel makes a refreshing change, and nowhere is this more noticeable than in the pubs. **Freddy's Bar** *(Caherdaniel; Tel 066/9475-400)* offers groceries as well as pints. You might be able to catch one of the sporadic trad sessions at **The Blind Piper** *(Caherdaniel; Tel 066/9475-126),* which has outdoor tables by a little stream—we're defining the word "quaint" here, and loving every minute of it.

culture zoo

The two main points of interest in town are at opposite ends of the aerobics spectrum: a mammoth Flintstone-esque fort that requires a heart-pumping uphill hike and a quiet historic park that offers a sedentary stop for reading and videos.

Staigue Fort *(9.6 km (6 mi) west of Caherdaniel; Free admission):* The pre-Christian Staigue Fort requires a lot of uphill walking to reach, but the views of the sea from the largest fort in Ireland are well worth the exertion. And by large, we mean *large*—the walls are 13 feet thick at the base, and the diameter is about 90 feet.

Derrynane House National Historic Park *(Sign-posted from Derrynane Beach; Tel 066/9475-113; 9am-6pm Mon-Sat, 11am-7pm Sun, May-Sept; 1-5pm Tue-Sun, Apr and Oct; 1-5pm Sat-Sun, Nov-Mar; Admission £2 adults, £1 students):* On a 320-acre site between Waterville and Caherdaniel, you'll find the Derrynane House National Historic Park, where Daniel "The Great Liberator" O'Connell lived for most of his life. You can look at lots of memorabilia and watch an interesting half-hour video revealing the human behind the hero.

great outdoors

Caherdaniel's known for its excellent diving possibilities. Try **Skellig Aquatics Dive School** *(Across from the Caherdaniel Village Hostel, Tel 066/9475-277; half-day dive £30; Visa)* for a dip into the drink, or **Derrynane Watersports Centre** *(Tel 066/9475-266; Windsurfing: 3 2-hour classes £45, 2-hour intro course £15; £9/hr. equipment rental for experienced surfers; Sailing: 3 2-hour lessons £50; Water skiing: £15 beginner lesson, £12 for experienced water skiers; No credit cards)* for windsurfing, sailing, and water-skiing.

The lack of tourists on the **Derrynane Strand** only further heightens its loveliness, so swim away. The views at sunset are particularly thrilling, so be sure to stick around.

eats

You're not expecting much here, of course. Buy groceries at **Freddy's Bar** [see *bar scene,* above], or pick up some take-away at **Courthouse Café** *(Caherdaniel; Tel 066/9475-005; 5-11:30pm daily; Most items under £5)* and enjoy a romantic dinner on the strand as the sun sets. Within Derrynane National Park, **Anne's Tea Room** serves freshly made salads, homemade soups, well-stuffed sandwiches, and, of course, plenty of tea.

crashing

Caherdaniel has more than its fair share of good hostels. First, **The Travelers' Rest Hostel** *(Caherdaniel center; Tel 066/9475-175; £8 dorm, £10 single; V, MC)* boasts a better-than-average common room and dorms with plenty of breathing room.

Carrigbeg Hostel *(Derrynane, Caherdaniel; Tel 066/9475-229; £6.50-7 dorm, £14-15 double—only one available; No credit cards)* has a totally unbeatable location by the sea in Derrynane House National Park. Splendid views—and food—abound and the Carrigbeg folks will even pick you up from the bus stop. It's about two miles out of the town. There is a full kitchen which you can use to cook food bought at **Freddy's Food Market,** *(Tel 066/9475-400),* about a mile west of the hostel.

The advantage of **Caherdaniel Village Hostel** *(Tel 066/9475-227; Mar-Oct; skelliga@iol.ie, £8 dorm)* is that its staff organizes diving excursions and regular trips out into the Iveragh countryside. Both this hostel and Carrigbeg have only a handful of beds, so make sure to call ahead.

need to know

Currency Exchange There's a bureau de change at the **Wave Crest Caravan and Camping Site** *(1.6 km (1 mi) from Caherdaniel, overlooking Kenmare Bay; Tel 066/9475-188).*

Tourist Information The **Caherdaniel Tourist Office** *(No phone; 8am-10pm daily May-Sep)* is located a mile east of town. In town, the owner of **Mathius Adams Junk Shop** *(Caherdaniel center; Tel 066/9475-167; 10am-5pm)* also offers plenty of helpful information

sneem

Locals say that Sneem, known as Ireland's most colorful village, has been painted in bright and varied colors so that even Irishmen who are completely drunk can tell which house is theirs when the night is up. Sneem has postcard-perfect cuteness, all right—but it's sure selling too many postcards of itself these days.

george bernard shaw

George Bernard Shaw, winner of the Nobel Prize in literature and one of Ireland's most treasured playwrights, has never stopped making the rounds of the big-city theater circuits. Among his plays are *Mrs. Warren's Profession*, which criticized Victorian attitudes toward prostitution, *The Devil's Disciple*, about the American Revolution, which met with much success in New York City theaters, and *Pygmalion*, no doubt his most famous work, upon which the musical *My Fair Lady*, starring Rex Harrison and Audrey Hepburn, was based. Shaw also cranked out novels, nonfiction, and music criticism for several London newspapers. Shaw was the kind of man you couldn't help admiring—that is, unless you had a reason to hate him. Thoroughly tired of listening to an arrogant man at a dinner party one night, Shaw said, "Between the two of us, we know all there is to know. You seem to know everything there is to know except that you're a bore, and I know that."

It's worth noting that George Bernard Shaw wrote many of his plays at a hotel called the Parknasilla near Sneem. There's also a terrifically bizarre mix of works in the **Sneem Sculpture Park,** sometimes referred to as "The Pyramids," where the likenesses of past presidents and sporting heroes co-exist alongside those of the Egyptian goddess Isis. But if you're not crazy about Shaw or a fan of wacky monuments, there's really very little to do here—you'll probably spend an hour or two at most.

If you do decide to stay, you could opt for the **Harbour View Hostel** *(Kenmare Rd.; Tel 064/45276; £8 dorm, £10 per person double or twin, £15 single, £5 camping; No credit cards),* but it's sadly lacking in views and personality. Moving on to Kenmare for the night might be a better option.

If you'd like a little more comfort, and can pay for it, walk on over to **Bank House** *(North Sq.; Tel 064/45226; Single £24.50, double £36; V).* The couple who run the place are really really friendly and warm, above and beyond most Irish hosts (and that's saying a lot). Expect to be well taken care of.

As for food, if you're looking for something fast on the fly, you could try the fish and chips at **The Hungry Knight** *(Tel 064/45727).*

Bus Éireann routes cover Sneem only during the summer months, beginning in late June; take route 270 to Kenmare (excepting Sundays) and 280 to Killarney (both twice daily). If you stay at the Harbour View, you might be able to get a free bus ride to Kenmare in July, August, and September—be sure to ask.

need to know

Tourist Information Answers await at the **Sneem Tourist Office** *(Joli Coeur Shop; Tel 064/45270; 10:30am-5:30pm, mid-Mar-Nov).* The office is run out of the house of a local woman who essentially opens and closes when she feels like it. When things are up and running in full gear, by around mid-March or April, it's open 7 days a week.

Bike Rental If you need a bike while in Sneem, try **Burns' Bike Hire** *(North Sq.; Tel 064/45140; 9:30am-7pm Mon-Sat; £6 per day, £33 per week).*

Postal If it's stamp-licking you're looking for, try the **Sneem Post Office** *(Tel 064/45110; 9am-1pm/2-5:30pm Mon-Fri, 9am-1pm Sat).*

kenmare

The final town on the Ring of Kerry route, Kenmare, is by far the most enchanting. This is partly due to its location, snuggled between the River Roughdy and Kenmare Bay, but Kenmare's residents should also get credit for keeping the town so clean.

It's easy to get around Kenmare. The town is laid out like a big X, with **The Square** intersecting **Henry** and **Main Streets** in the middle; this junction, or nearby, is where you'll find most of the pubs, restaurants, and shopping.

Usually the Ring of Kerry tours go from Sneem to Moll's Gap and back into Killarney, but you can take the summer-only Bus Éireann bus from Sneem to Kenmare, and then a year-round bus through Moll's Gap into the Killarney Valley.

bar and live music scene

You're sure to hear a bit o' live trad any night of the week in Kenmare, at least at **The Square Pint** *(The Square; Tel 064/42356),* which takes the cake for the most picture-pretty pub in town. The pub food's better than average—pizzas, toasted sandwiches, and dishes like grilled breast of

wired

Get online at **Bean and Leaf** *(Rock St., off Main St.; Tel 064/42019; 9:30am-6:30pm Mon-Fri, 10am-6:30pm Sat-Sun, Mar-Nov; £6 per hour),* where you can also snack on some very good coffee and cake.

chicken with Parmesan are served at lunch between 12.30 and 5.30pm, and dinner's served between 7:30 and 10pm. You probably won't find music at **The Atlantic Bar** *(The Square; Tel 064/42072)*, but it's a lot less touristy and ever-popular with locals. **Crowley's** *(Henry St.; Tel 064/41472; No credit cards)* has that great hole-in-the-wall atmosphere and regular trad sessions almost every night. **Murty's** *(New Rd.; Tel 064/41453)* is one of the biggest pubs, featuring live bands shaking the beams every Wednesday, Friday, and Saturday night.

culture zoo

This town is a bit weak when it comes to major culture, to say the least, but you can get a good idea of what makes the town tick at the local heritage center.

Kenmare Heritage Centre *(The Square; Tel 064/41233; 9:15am-5:30pm April-Sep; Admission £2 adults, £1.50 students):* The centre offers exhibits concerning the town's history and has displays of locally made lace, since that's what the Kenmare peeps do best. Purchase a pint at any pub nearby and get more punch for your punt.

great outdoors

How about some windsurfing, kayaking, water-skiing, or maybe a tube ride? **Kenmare Bay Sea Sports Centre** *(5 km (3 mi) west on Sneem Rd. at the Dromquinna Manor Hotel; Tel 064/42255; £6-12 per person)* will set you up.

stuff

Pick up a souvenir for your grandma at **Nostalgia** *(27 Henry St.; Tel 064/41389; Open mid Mar-Dec)*, which carries new and antique lace, table linens, and old-fashioned teddy bears.

If you're driving from Kenmare back to Killarney (or the other way around), stop in for a browse around the **Avoca Handweavers** *(Moll's Gap, Ring of Kerry Road, N71; Tel 064/34720)* on a high mountain pass 293 meters (960 feet) above sea level. This shop's but one branch of the famous tweed-makers and hand-weavers of Avoca in County Wicklow, a business establishment founded in the early 18th century which still produces some of the softest, fuzziest, most touchable sweaters and blankets ever. You can find pottery, jewelry, and all other sorts of hand-woven items here as well, and the coffee shop sells far-beyond-average light meals.

▸▸BOUND

Not surprisingly, **Kenmare Bookshop** *(Shelbourne St.; Tel 064/41578; Mar-Dec)* specializes in books by and about the Irish. What's of special interest here is the exhibit on the Book of Kells, including a video, which makes for a worthwhile visit if you didn't get a chance to see the real thing on display at Trinity College in Dublin.

eats

The food's fine, but the lavender facade and funky art deco interior of **Café Indigo** *(The Square; Tel 064/42356; Food served 7-10:30pm, bar open until 1am every night but Saturday; Main courses under £10)* alone are worth the visit. Does the monkfish salad with crispy smoked bacon and poppy seeds in pesto dressing look good? (It is.) There's music every night at the adjoining pub, the smart-alecky-named **Square Pint** [see *bar scene,* above].

Excellent pastries and cakes abound at **Bean and Leaf** [see *need to know,* below], Kenmare's net café, or you could try **Mickey Ned's** *(Henry St.; Tel 064/41591; 9am-5:30pm Mon-Sat; No credit cards)* for cheap sandwiches and ice cream. If you're willing to spend a little more dough for dinner, check out **An Leath Phingin** *(35 Main St.; Tel 064/41559; 6-10pm Thu-Tue; Main courses £6-£12),* where you can find excellent homemade pizzas and pastas.

the twisted world of irish-celtic mythology

Celtic-Irish mythology is as intricate as that of its Roman or Greek counterparts, here are just of few of the more memorable figures of Ireland's magical past.

Aeval was a fairy queen who would, each midnight, put on trial those husbands who were accused of being bad lovers by their wives. The original Sally Jesse?

Belatu-Cadros was the biggest, the baddest, the Celtic god of war. He is he Irish equivalent of the Roman god Mars.

Cailleach Beara was an Irish woman who, unfortunately, turned to stone on the last day of April (Beltine) and was reborn every October 31 (Samhain, or as we Americans call it Halloween).

Dechtere

As the mother of Cuchulain, what makes this figure so interesting is more the circumstance around the birth of her son than any power she wielded. In a twisted precursor to the Immaculate Conception, the god Lugh is believed to have impregnated Dechtere by using only his soul. Soon after, Dechtere vomited her son into existence and, thus remained a virgin.

Emer

One of several hotties that existed in Celtic mythology, before Emer would allow her suitor, the hero Cuchulainn, (that's Dechtere's kid, remember?) to sleep with her, she demanded he perform several tasks of daring and danger in order to prove his worth in the face of

crashing

Kenmare's budget accommodation, the **Fáilte Hostel** *(Corner of Henry and Shelbourne Sts.; Tel 064/42333; £7.50 dorm, £20 double, £8.50 per person private rooms with at least 3 beds; No credit cards)* has furnishings á la *The Brady Bunch* and a 1am curfew. The decor is the loudest thing about this place, which is definitely a good thing if you're in dire need of a good night's sleep. Don't bum too much about the curfew—there's nothing to do that late at night in Kenmare anyway.

Other do-able options include **Greenville** *(Greenville; Tel 064/41769; £24/person; Private baths; Breakfast included; No credit cards)*, around the corner from the bus stop, only steps from the golf course; **Ard Na Mara** *(Pier Rd.; Tel/Fax 064/41399; Doubles £20/person, Singles, available Oct-Jun only, £25, private baths, breakfast included; V, MC)*; **Wander Inn** *(Henry St.; Tel 064/41038)*; and **Ardmore House** *(Killarney Rd.; Tel/Fax 064/41406; Rooms £20 per person, private baths, breakfast included; V, MC)*.

this most mesmerizing of mortals. Watch out fellas!

Fionnuala

This daughter of Lir, for displeasing the gods in some way, was turned in to a swan and forced to roam the lakes of Ireland, until Christianity made it's debut.

Goibniu

The man's-man of Celtic mythology's, Goibniu was not only the finest and most respected swordsmith in the land, he possessed the secrets of immortality, which came in the form of a life-giving batch of beer.

Macha

Macha basically cleans up after Morrigan the goddess of war: she devours the heads of the slaughtered.

Nuada

Seemingly a kinder gentler god, Nuada represents, life, youth, birth, beauty, the sun, and oddly enough, warfare. That must explain why he carries around a sword used for halving his enemies.

Oengus Mac Oc

Arguably Celtic mythology's most eligible bachelor, Oengus, or Aengus as he was known, represented love, beauty and youthfulness. He once loved a fair maiden so dearly he joined her in becoming a swan on the eve of Samhain.

Health nuts, you're in luck: **The Pantry** *(Henry St.; Tel 064/42233; 9:30am-6pm Mon-Sat)* is recommended especially for you. Non-health nuts can mosey over to the **Supervalu** *(Main St.; Tel 064/41037; 8am-8pm Mon-Thu, 8am-9pm Fri, 8am-7pm Sat, 9am-5pm Sun).*

need to know

Currency Exchange The **AIB** *(9 Main St.; Tel 064/41010; 10am-4pm Mon-Tue and Thu-Fri, 10am-5pm Wed)* has an ATM.

Tourist Information If you're starting the Ring from here, or just can't get enough info, stop by the **Kenmare Tourist Office** *(The Square; Tel 064/41233; 9am-5:30pm Mon-Sat Apr-Jun, Sep-Oct; 9am-7pm daily Jul-Aug).*

Health and Emergency **Garda Station** *(Shelbourne St.; Tel 064/41177).* **Kenmare Hospital** *(down Henry Street past the Square onto Old Killarney Rd.; Tel 064/41088)* provides medical care.

Pharmacies For pharmaceutical needs, try **Brosnan's** *(Henry St.; Tel 064/41318; 9:30am-6:30pm Mon-Sat, 12:30-1:15pm Sun).*

Bus Lines Out of the City **Bus Éireann** buses leave from outside Brennan's pub on Main Street. Two or three buses go to Killarney per day, and two head for Sneem in summertime. A bus goes to Schull, Skibbereen, and Bantry once or twice per day beginning in mid-May; route 282 goes to Castletownbere in West Cork once a day (except Sunday) beginning in late June.

Bike Rental If you'd like to see more of the delightful Kenmare countryside, you can rent a bike at **Finnegan's** *(Corner of Henry and Shelbourne Sts.; Tel 064/41083; 9:30am-6:30pm Mon-Sat; £8 per day, £40 per week).*

Laundry **O'Shea's** *(Main St.; Tel 064/41394; 8:30am-6pm Mon-Fri, 9am-6pm Sat; £5 wash and dry)* is conveniently located for your washing pleasure.

Postal That lace we mentioned above? Send it home from the **Kenmare Post Office** *(Henry St.; Tel 064/41490; 9am-1pm/2-5:30pm Mon-Fri, 9am-1pm Sat).*

Internet See *wired,* above.

dingle peninsula

dingle

Dingle is a fishing village with all the traditional architecture of the authentic Irish towns you find pretty much only in the west. Many of its inhabitants are former travelers themselves who loved the place so much they decided to extend their vacations for a while. Given the unparalleled beauty of the Dingle Peninsula's mountains, cliffs, and sea, it's no surprise that artists, writers, and musicians flock here to find their inspiration, and an inordinate number of celebrities come to the area in the off-season. You'll find their names on the sidewalk outside **Dick Mack's** pub on Green Street [see *bar scene,* below]. Dolores O'Riordan of Cranberries fame until recently had her summerhouse on Slea Head Drive as well. But it's Fungie, the friendly but egomaniacal dolphin who inhabits the waters of Dingle Bay, who is Dingle's most famous resident.

Tourism has only recently begun to infiltrate the peaceful sleepy-town atmosphere that makes Dingle itself so charming, so you won't feel oppressed by the hordes as you might when visiting Killarney or other heavily touristed areas. The exquisite landscape permeates every aspect of life in Dingle; as you walk through the streets or cycle out toward Slea Head you may feel that strangely quiet sense of awe yourself.

The town itself is pretty small and concentrated within just a few main streets—you'll know it like the back of your hand within an hour. Most of the pubs are located on either **Strand Street,** which runs along the water, or **Main Street,** which runs parallel to Strand a couple of blocks inland. **Green Street,** another road you'll likely find yourself on, runs between Strand and Main. The whole place has a postcard quaintness about it; the buildings are painted cheerfully, in tune with the people inhabiting them.

dingle

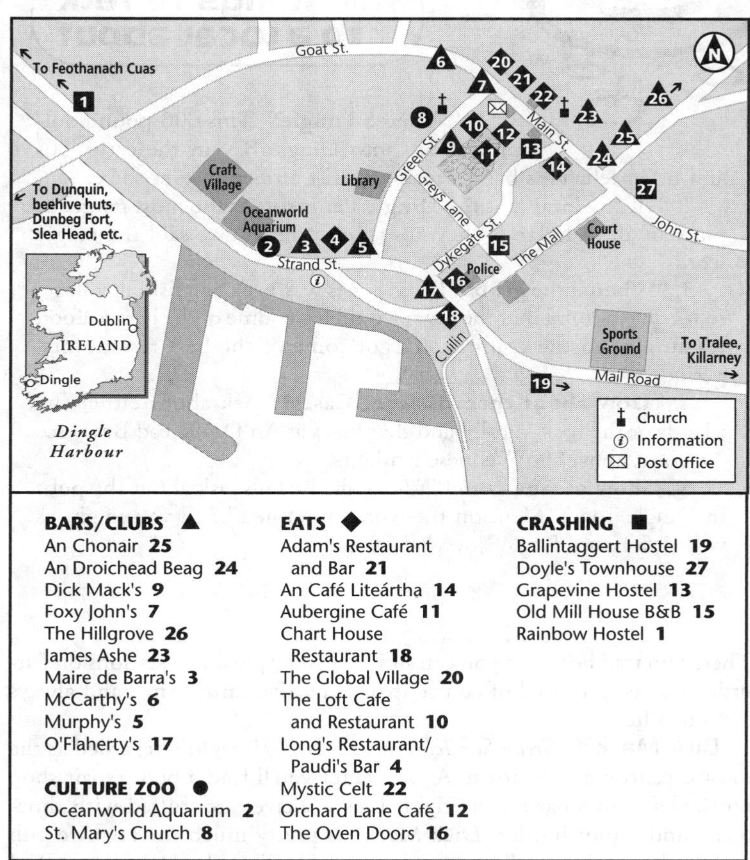

bar scene

Dingle pubs basically follow the same hours as every other pub in Ireland: they usually open at 10am, stop serving at 11:30pm in the summer and may be less than delicate in enforcing closing time. Many a bartender has been known to ask lingering patrons in no uncertain terms to leave the premises, but don't sweat it—none of the Dingle locals seemed to pay any attention, finishing their pints at quite a leisurely pace.

James Ashe *(Lower Main St.; Tel 066/915-1364)* has got to be the coziest place in town to soak up a pint. The back room, furnished with leather couches and a fireplace put to good use, resembles more of a family room than a pub. Even cooler, the owner is a cousin of Gregory Peck, so ask to see her family pictures and she'll talk for as long as you've got ears.

five things to talk to a local about

1. **"Where's Fungie?"** This 600-pound dolphin swam into Dingle Bay in the early '80s and never left. He's been a major tourist attraction ever since.

2. Tell any local that the **Dingle Peninsula** is the most gorgeous place in all of Ireland—hey, it's true!—and you've said the magic words.

3. **"Where's the grub?"** Dingle goes way back as a fishing village, so it's only natural that the town would have some of the best seafood restaurants in the country. It's got some of the best restaurants, period.

4. **"How about them Blasket Cases?"** Ask about either the islands or the rock 'n roll band that plays at An Droichead Beag [see *bar scene,* above] on Wednesday nights.

5. **"Show me the *craic!*"** When all else fails, ask about the pubs in Dingle Town. Mention the word "Guinness" and you might as well sit for a reading of Joyce's *Ulysses.*

There's no trad here, but you can sit in for some great jazz sessions on Saturday nights, provided of course that you arrive early—the band always plays to a full crowd.

Dick Mack's *(Green St.; Tel 066/915-1070)* is rightly regarded as the most eccentric pub in town. As you enter you'll find a boot repair shop on the left and a bar on the right. Dusty shelves are stuffed with shoeboxes and liquor bottles. Dick Mack's is pretty much the favorite pub among the locals as well as several celebrities: Timothy Dalton and Paul Simon are among past visitors (look for their names on stars on the sidewalk outside).

You'll find virtually no tourists at all at **Foxy John's** *(Main St.; Tel 066/915-1316; No credit cards),* another offbeat place with a bar on one side and a hardware store on the other. The atmosphere's haphazard, completely unpretentious, and therefore totally cool. This is the place to converse with the we-walked-ten-miles-to-school-uphill-both-ways-in-the-snow crowd.

An Droichead Beag *(Lower Main St.; Tel 066/915-1723)* is undoubtedly the most popular pub in town due to its warm, rustic, chummy atmosphere and lively trad sessions every night. Not surprisingly, "The Small Bridge," or sometimes just "The Droichead," has a higher tourist quotient than most of the other pubs in town, but the place is extremely popular with locals as well. Here the Irishmen are friendly. Very friendly. Perhaps even a bit *too* friendly.

The pints come served with history lessons at **O'Flaherty's** *(Bridge St.; Tel 066/915-1983)*, where the walls are covered in posters, pictures, newspaper clippings, and poems by local authors about—what else?—the Dingle peninsula. The warm and inviting atmosphere is heightened by the population-per-square-foot ratio: People pack themselves in tighter than sardines in a can. Hey, the trad's not *that* good.

McCarthy's *(Main St.; Tel 066/915-1205)* seems to attract the loud young footballing set as well as older, more weather-beaten types. There's a dartboard in the back, with comfy leather booths in the front, and plenty of people in between. Low ceilings and old photographs on the walls complete the quaint-but-fun ambience.

live music scene

Most pubs in Dingle offer live music almost every night, so if it's trad you're looking for, just follow your ears. Local musicians will be keeping their fingers nimble for the annual Dingle Music Festival in September [see *festivals and events,* below].

An Droichead Beag [see *bar scene,* above] boasts the best live trad in town, especially since it has more live sessions per year than there are days. The session never fails to inspire an impromptu set dance, and a rock band called the Blasket Cases plays here on Wednesday nights. Groan at the awful pun, but the music's actually quite good, although some nights are better than others.

An Conair *(Conor Pass Rd.; Tel 066/915-2011),* more modern and minimalist in decor than An Droichead Beag or Dick Mack's, boasts a vigorous nightly music schedule; with the exception of Tuesday, which is "sports night," there's always a session in full swing after 9:30pm. Set dancing is on Monday nights, accompanied by traditional music, of course; folk music on Wednesdays; more trad on Thursdays; the *uillean*

wired

For information on Dingle, surf ***www.dingleonline.com*** and ***www.iol.ie/~rainbow,*** which include helpful information on sporting and cultural activities in the Dingle area.

DingleWeb *(Lower Main St.; Tel 066/915-2477; 10am-late Mon-Sat, half-day Sun in summer; 10am-6pm Mon-Sat in winter; info@dingleweb.com, www.dingleweb.com; £5 per hour)* boasts of being the "most westerly Internet café in Europe." You can get special "early bird" rates before noon. If you're really trying to pinch, though, get to the **Dingle Library** *(Green St.; Tel 066/915-1499; 10:30am-1:30pm/2:30-5:30pm Tue-Sat),* sign up for a half-hour slot at one of the two library computers, and check your email for free.

pipes make a special appearance on Fridays; and you'll hear trad again with a twist on the weekends: the variety played here is called *sean nós,* an old unaccompanied singing style. It's easy to find, just around the corner from An Droichead Beag.

Not as traditional as some might prefer, **Murphy's** *(Strand St.; Tel 066/915-1450)* has live "entertainment" every night. The back room's a tangle of amps, microphones, and speakers as an enthusiastic band belts out "It's a Long Way to Tipperary" and plenty of weepy ballads in front of a full-to-brimming crowd.

O'Flaherty's [see *bar scene,* above] also has excellent live trad pretty much every night, but if you don't get there way before it starts you probably won't be able to find any breathing room after the music's begun.

The music sessions at **Máire de Barra's** [see *eats,* below] are rather sporadic, but stop in for the cheesy pasta bake and ask the bartender if you'll get lucky tonight. **James Ashe** doesn't do trad, but the jazz sessions on Saturday nights are always extremely popular. **McCarthy's** offers blues on Friday nights and traditional Irish music on Saturday nights [see *bar scene,* above, for both]

club scene

Please don't say you've come to Dingle looking for nightclubs. Good. In that case, the **Hillgrove Hotel** *(Spa Rd.; Tel 066/915-1131; 11pm-2am Fri-Sun, Cover £4),* down the street from An Conair, won't disappoint. All the Dingle teenyboppers arrive as soon as the pubs close, dance to chart tunes until 2am or so, and then congregate at a refreshment stand outside the pub until the cops arrive. It's a great place to sit around and laugh at the Irish guys dancing like caged monkeys on caffeine overload, and all for only £4 cover charge!

festivals and events

The **Dingle Music Festival** *(Sept; Tel 066/915-2477; www.iol.ie/~dingmus)* attracts famous musicians from every musical genre. It's reputed to be one of the coolest and most prestigious music festivals in the country, and with the fantastically beautiful Dingle peninsula as a backdrop, it's no wonder. Recent acts featured at the four-day festival included Luka Bloom and many other Euro-rock stars. Make sure to book well in advance (about 2 months) to get your pick of lodging in the area because of the explosion of tourism. Ticket prices vary, but £10 usually does it.

arts scene

Dingle doesn't have much in the way of art galleries, but you'll find plenty of craft workshops around town offering some of the most spectacular jewelry, ceramics, and weavings in the country.

Small but airy, the **Greenlane Gallery** *(Green St.; Tel 066/915-2018; 10am-9pm in summer; 11am-5pm daily in winter; info@greenlanegallery.com, www.greenlanegallery.com)* showcases contemporary Irish artists in every medium. Not surprisingly, the gallery is filled with fine renderings of the Dingle peninsula landscape, some of it vaguely Yeats-esque, as well as some neat abstract sculptures and offbeat portraits.

At **Niamh Utsch Goldsmith** *(Main St.; Tel 066/915-2217; 9:30am-7pm in summer, 9:30-6pm daily in winter; utschn@indigo.ie, www.nugoldsmith.com)* the prices might send you running the other way, but window-shopping is still fun. Niamh Utsch creates every piece by hand from original designs; you'll find no kitschy Celtic motifs here.

Brian de Staic *(Studio at the Wood, Strand St. shop on Green St.; Tel 066/915-1298; 9am-6pm Mon-Sat, Jun-late Autumn, usually Nov; info@brian-de-staic.iol.ie, www.iol.ie/brian-de-staic)* is the undisputed king of Irish jewelry. His Dingle workshop is brimming with intricate Celtic designs in gold and silver. Prices are steep, but worth a splurge if something particularly strikes your fancy and you can afford it.

Ceardlann na Coille, or **The Craft Village** *(The Wood, Strand St.; Tel 066/915-1778; 10am-6pm Mon-Sat)*, is made up of a ring of small cottages, each the workshop of a different artist. The jewelry, mosaics, sweaters, and ceramics are totally exquisite, especially since you can actually watch the stuff being made. Check out Gertrude Sampson's mysteriously soft—and amazingly expensive—fuzzy sweaters.

Lisbeth Mulcahy at **The Weaver's Shop** *(Green St.; Tel 066/915-1688; 9am-9pm Mon-Sat, 10am-6pm Sun, Jun-Sep; 9am-6pm Mon-Sat, Oct-May; lisbeth@mulcahy-pottery.ie; V, MC)* has a gallery with an assortment of hand-loomed scarves, weavings, rugs, framed prints, glassware, candles and tapestries in rich brilliant colors, as well as ceramics from Louis Mulcahy's pottery studio outside Dunquin. You might be able to see the loom in the corner of the shop in action if you come at the right time. The adjoining shop stocks delicious, if pricey, cashmere sweaters.

The crystal at **Dingle Crystal Ltd.** *(5 Orchard Lane; Tel 066/915-1550; www.dinglecrystal.ie)* sparkles like diamonds in the sunlight. Crystal connoisseurs will tell you that this kind is finer than the Waterford variety. You can watch pieces being made—by hand, naturally—in the workshop.

culture zoo

This peninsula's got the finest of everything, and the cultural attractions are no exception. Dingle has the highest concentration of archaeological sites in the country, mostly because it's so remote, fewer invaders and occupiers

nuala ni dhomhnaill

One of the coolest Irish poets around, Kerry-raised Nuala Ní Dhomhnaill ("NOO-lah knee YOU-nil") writes in Irish, and other renowned Irish writers, like Paul Muldoon, Ciaran Carson, and Eiléan Ní Chuilleanáin, do the translating. It's been said that she's among the most gifted poets to come along since Yeats, and that's no casual compliment. Her books are tough to find in the U.S.—you'll have to special order at most bookstores—but while you're in Ireland you can check 'em out. Her words, sharp as tacks, spare yet vividly descriptive, at times even blissfully and shockingly erotic, cut straight to the marrow of human instinct. You can find her work in any Irish bookstore worth its salt. **An Café Liteartha** [see *bound,* below] is sure to have it in stock.

(F.Y.I: when a woman's last name is prefaced by *Ní,* it means that name is her maiden name. If the name comes after *Uí,* the name is her married name.)

made it here to knock things down. The town itself was christened "An Daingean Uí Chuise" (that's "HOOSH!") in 1169, meaning "The Fort of the Hussey" (not hussy, though that might raise an interesting image).

Dingle Oceanworld Aquarium *(The Wood, Strand St.; Tel 066/915-2111; 9am-9pm daily, Jul-Aug; 9am-5pm Mon-Sat, Sept-Jun; marabeo@iol.ie, www.dingle-oceanworld.ie; Admission £5 adults, £4 students):* A bit cheesy, sure, but the aquarium is a pretty popular attraction in Dingle Town. People come looking for Fungie the dolphin and get interested in all stuff aquatic.

St. Mary's Church *(Green St.; No phone; Free):* Built in the 1860's, St. Mary's is strategically placed just across the street from Dick Mack's pub. Or is that the other way around? As the advertisement on Green Street reads, "Where is Dick Mack's? Opposite the church. Where is the church? Opposite Dick Mack's." Kind of a chicken-and-the-egg thing. At any rate, you can catch the 9am Sunday mass—in Irish—and spend the rest of the day drinking, if you're so inclined.

Gallarus Oratory *(Near Ballydavid; Tel 066/915-5333; 9:30am-8pm daily, Apr-Oct; Admission to visitor center £1.50 adults, £1 students; Free admission to oratory):* The Oratory, about a 15-minute drive west of the beginning of Slea Head, resembles an overturned boat and is an excellent example of 8th-century stonemasonry—it's totally watertight and perfectly preserved even after all this time.

Fahan Group *(Off Slea Head Dr.; £1):* Just beyond the oratory on Slea Head Drive, the Fahan Group of beehive huts, built by early monks and now fenced in by modern money-grubbers, aren't terribly impressive in comparison to, say, the Gallarus Oratory.

Dunbeg Fort *(Off Slea Head Dr.; £1 Adults, 80p Students):* The walls of this Iron Age fort, five miles beyond the Fahan Group, were once as thick as 22 feet, but most of the fort has long since fallen into the sea below.

Ballyferriter Museum *(Ballyferriter center; Tel 066/915-6100; 9:30am-6pm daily; Admission £1.50 adults, £1 students):* This museum (*"Chorca Dhuibhne"*), seven miles west of town on Slea Head, provides a good introduction to the history of the area, incorporating folklore and archaeology.

The nearby **Riasc Monastic Settlement** *(Ballyferriter; Free):* When the Riasc Monastic Settlement, begun in the 4th or 5th century, was thoroughly excavated in the 1970s, archaeologists discovered late Roman pottery on the site, a clear indication that the monasteries in Ireland weren't as isolated from the rest of Europe as previously thought. Here you'll find an oratory, a handful of cells, and a graveyard with engraved cross-slabs as well as much more recent headstones marking the resting spots of infants not baptized, and therefore not permitted burial in the regular cemetery.

Celtic and Prehistoric Museum *(Slea Head Dr., Ventry; Tel 066/915-9941; 10am-5pm, Jun-Sep, other times call ahead; celtmuseum@*

joyce in the making

Has the landscape inspired you to pick up that pen and paper? The directors of **Dingle Writing Courses** *(Ballintlea, Ventry; Tel 066/915-9052; dinglewc@iol.ie, www.iol.ie/~dinglewc)* hope so. They offer weekend, five-day or seven-day writing courses at a pretty little cottage at Inch, on the Dingle peninsula (east of Dingle Town) in the summer and autumn. Meals and lodging are included. Prices range from £250 for a fall weekend course to a bank-busting £900 for a weeklong course during the summer, but if you book three months ahead, you'll get a ten percent discount on any class you take. There's also a discount if you refer a friend. The teachers are mostly Irish and moderately successful, although most likely you haven't heard of any of them. (Don't let that discourage you, though; some of the best teachers aren't famous and famous writers don't always make good teachers.) Check out the full list of courses available on their website.

hotmail.com, www.kerryweb.ie; Admission £3): The folks at the Celtic and Prehistoric Museum to the west of Dingle Town will invite you to walk on floors of 300-million-year-old sea worms—don't worry, they're just fossils. The walls of this neat little museum are painted with as-accurate-as-possible reproductions of cave paintings, and there are some interesting examples of ancient Celtic jewelry and figurines and Iron Age tools. Afterwards you can have a cup of coffee in the museum cafe with windows overlooking the sea.

modification

You certainly won't find any tattoo parlors in Dingle, but there are some great new-agey places where you can treat yourself after a long day of cycling. **Lámh Iomláne Teo,** *(The Coast Guard Cottage, Cooleen; Tel 066/915-2474; £5-48 per treatment; No credit cards),* Dingle's Natural Therapy Centre, overlooks Dingle Harbour. The prospect of an hour-long full-body massage never fails to elicit a shudder of delight from any local who's ever been there. Reiki, yoga, shiatsu, aromatherapy, acupuncture, facials—you name it, they've got it.

If you're not just passing through for a day or two—and you're not scared of needles—you could also try the **Dingle Acupuncture Clinic** *(Green St.; Tel 087/274-4735 daytime, 066/915-9904 evening; 10am-5pm Wed-Fri; Appointment only, 10:30am-3pm Sat).*

The **Dingle Beauty Clinic** *(Main St.; Tel 066/915-2030; 10am-6pm Tue-Fri, 10am-4pm Sat; Appointment only Tue-Thu evenings)* is also popular and highly recommended. Facials go for £20-30, manicures or pedicures £15, and body massages £30.

great outdoors

Outdoor enthusiasts—and if you've made it this far west, that's probably what you are—have many thrills in store for them on the Dingle Peninsula. With beautiful beaches overlooking even lovelier seas, this is the place for walking, cycling, swimming, sailing, and diving. The best beaches are at **Brandon Bay,** on the northern part of the peninsula, and on the western side of **Tralee Bay.** To get there, take the Conor Pass Road by car, or by bike if you're up for some extremely strenuous pedaling. You can also try Bus Éireann: check the timetables outside Garvey's Supervalu for times. If you want something closer to Dingle, the beach at Ventry is perfectly good. You can also reach the lovely golden beaches at **Inch,** on the southern end of the peninsula, which is on the summer-only Dingle–Killarney route, or **Camp,** on the northeastern part of the peninsula, on the Dingle–Tralee route.

Serious hikers will want to try climbing **Mount Brandon,** which is 952 meters (3,123 feet) above sea level. The views from the eastern side, starting your climb at Cloghane, on Brandon Bay, are better, but attempting it from the western side will give you an easier climb. For directions and tips, check with the tourist office [see *need to know,* below].

The best way to see Dingle's stunning landscape is to cycle the **Slea Head Drive,** which will take you from Dingle Town through Ventry out to Dunquin and the Blasket Island Centre [see **Dunquin and the Blasket Islands**]. You'll pass the beehive huts and Dunbeg Fort on the way out to Slea Head; to get to the rest of the monastic sites or forts, pick up a map at the tourist office. *The Dingle Way Map Guide* will show you the route that begins in Tralee and covers 95 miles around the entire peninsula.

The perfect place to have a picnic lunch is well off the tourist track, and it only takes about an hour to cycle there. On Slea Head Drive, take the first left after the Celtic and Prehistoric Museum onto a gravel path that looks as though it leads only through open farmland. Take it anyway, and after about five minutes of walking your bike through the fields you'll hear waves crashing onto the rocks. Leave your bike, keep walking, and suddenly a gorgeous sea inlet with a totally awe-inspiring view is yours to enjoy for an hour or two. The only people you might come across would be a gaggle of schoolchildren out for a walk.

Rent a bike from **Paddy's Bike Shop** a few doors down from The Grapevine Hostel on Dykegate Street, **Foxy John's** on Main Street, or **Mountain Main** on Strand Street [see *need to know,* below for all].

If you'd rather let the horse do the pedaling, **Dingle Horse Riding** *(Ballinaboula, Dingle; Tel 066/915-2018; info@dinglehorseriding.com, www.dinglehorseriding.com)* has stables located in the hills overlooking Dingle Harbour.

If you're into that whole silly let's-swim-with-Fungie thing, you can rent a wetsuit from **Flannery's** *(Just east of Dingle on the Tralee Road; Tel 066/915-1967; £14 for 2 hours or £22 overnight),* so you can have your afternoon tea party with Ireland's most famous dolphin.

The **Dingle Marina Centre** *(Near the harbor; Tel 066/915-2422)* provides certification courses in addition to day-trip dives, which will set you back around £45. They also offer diving trips off the Blasket Islands.

The harbor is also ideal for sailing. The **Dingle Sailing Club** *(The Wood, Strand St.; Tel 066/915-1984; lfarrell@tinet.ie)* will set you up with boats and equipment. At Castlegregory on Tralee Bay, north of Dingle, **Jamie Knox Adventure Watersports** *(Tel 066/713-9411)* rents windsurfing and kayaking equipment.

stuff

You can find nice wool sweaters and blankets as well as some not-too-cheesy souvenirs at **Kerry Woolen Mills** *(Mail Rd.; Tel 066/915-2164; 9:30am-8pm daily in summer),* next to the Chart House Restaurant.

Commodum Art and Design *(Main St.; Tel 066/915-1380; 9am-10pm Mon-Fri, 9am-7pm Sat-Sun in summer; 9am-6pm daily in winter; shop@commodum.ie, www.commodum.ie; V, MC)* is decidedly the place to feed your shopping frenzy: Celtic jewelry, soft mohair wool blankets in sherbety colors from the Avoca Handweavers in Wicklow, wool sweaters and hats, fancy soap and perfume in pretty glass jars, books, wooden bowls and utensils, glassware—it's all here, so go ahead and pull out the plastic.

Annascaul Pottery *(Green St. Lane; Tel 066/915-7186; V, MC, AE),* next to the Loft Café and Restaurant, has a great stash of handmade pottery, scarves, candles, and prints.

▸▸TUNES

The Music House *(6 Orchard Lane; Tel 066/915-2633),* specializing in, not surprisingly, Irish music, declares itself to be "Dingle's largest record store." Not too hard to believe, since the only other one in town has all of about nine square feet of floor space.

▸▸BOUND

Though mouse-like in size, **An Café Liteártha** *(Dykegate St.; Tel 066/915-2204; 9am-6pm Mon-Sat, later in summer)* has a brilliant assortment of new and used Irish-interest books, with a special focus on County Kerry. The café in the back room [see *eats,* below] has good, cheap food and a handy information board. Another option for reading material, sans munchies, would be **Léigh Linn** *(Main St.; Tel 066/52433).*

eats

Good food? Uh-huh. *Excellent* food? Definitely, almost any place you go. There's hardly a bad joint in town.

▸▸CHEAP

The Loft Café *(Green St. Lane; Tel 066/915-2431; 10:30am-5:30pm daily, closed Sun in winter; V, MC),* complete with colored chalk and "doodleboards" on the walls and soft jazzy music, is the sort of small, friendly, laid-back place where you can chat with the locals or the girl behind the counter. You won't just find basic sandwich-and-coffee fare here; you can get a chicken sandwich with sun-dried tomato and pesto sauce for under £3 and tiramisu or Bailey's cheesecake for £2.50.

The **Orchard Lane Café** *(Orchard Lane; No phone; 8am-6pm Mon-Sat, 8am-2pm Sun; £1.60-6; No credit cards),* bright and sunny with price-tagged watercolor landscapes on the walls, is the perfect place for a full Irish breakfast or a light lunch, which could be sandwiches, burgers, steak, or chicken.

The **Aubergine Café** *(Orchard Lane; No phone; Dishes £2.50-4; No credit cards)* is pretty much the same as Orchard Lane: simple, quiet, with good food at change-purse prices. Have a sandwich and some of their tasty desserts, or pick up the ever-popular baked potato and salad.

An Café Liteártha *(Dykegate St.; Tel 066/915-2204; 9am-6pm Mon-Sat, later in summer; £1.50-5; No credit cards)* has more than good, cheap food going for it; the front-room bookstore is a great place to browse around, and while you're doing that you'll surely hear the owner conversing with patrons in Irish. Don't bring a ravenous appetite here, but the sandwiches are fresh, tasty, and easy on the purse.

You can pick up a delicious dinner for a scant £5 at **Máire de Barra's** *(Strand St.; Tel 066/915-1215; Pub hours; Avg. entree £5; V, MC).* The portions are generous, the staff is more than willing to give you sightseeing tips, and the pub itself has a warm comfortable atmosphere. Try the rhubarb pie for a perfect end to a perfectly delectable meal.

▸▸DO-ABLE

Whatever you do, don't pass up **The Loft Restaurant** *(Green St. Lane; Tel 066/915-2431; 12:30-2:30pm, Jun-Sep; 5:30-9:30pm Wed-Mon in summer, Wed-Sun in winter; main courses £7-12; V, MC).* If you're looking for authentic traditional Irish atmosphere, this is the place, and the food—seafood, pasta, and the best steak in town—is positively celestial as well. Owner and chef Nicola Aylward restored an old hayloft herself, and the cozy second-floor restaurant is furnished with pews taken from an old church in North Kerry, painted stone walls, 18th-century tables used during the Famine, and chairs handmade with *súgan* rope.

The Oven Doors *(The Holy Ground; Tel 066/915-1056; 9am-10:30pm daily, Mar-Dec; £3-7)* is the best place to grab a pizza in Dingle, which isn't saying a whole lot considering it's pretty much the *only* place to grab a pizza in Dingle. Nevertheless, the gourmet pizzas always get rave reviews and the desserts are delicious. They're still serving food long after the pubs have stopped, so you can pick up a pizza and sundae between pints.

If you need a break from pub fare, try **The Global Village** *(Upper Main St.; Tel 066/915-2325; martinbealin@hotmail.com; lunch £4-7, dinner £8-11).* It's aptly named for its delicious range of dishes from all over the world, and even cooler, the owner did the traveling to collect almost all of the recipes himself. The hot chicken sandwich with roasted peppers is especially recommended.

With its wide variety of domestic and foreign brews, **Long's Bar and Restaurant** *(Strand St.; Tel 066/915-1231)* could probably hold its own as a pub, but that's not it at all. As far as the local patrons are concerned (and they would know best) Long's has without a doubt the best seafood in town, caught fresh daily off the shores of the Atlantic. The pub menu next door at Paudie's Bar is pretty much the same; but whatever you order at either place, make sure you get Long's sticky toffee pudding for dessert.

Picture a steak marinated in red wine topped with fried onions on a toasted baguette, big enough to fill you up for the rest of the week. Sound good? Get yourself to **Adams Bar and Restaurant** *(Main St.; Tel 066/915-2133; £2-6),* a lovely place done in traditional decor on the main pub drag. The restaurant is open for dinner only in summertime.

▸▸SPLURGE

Just off the roundabout as you enter town, **The Chart House Restaurant** *(Mail Rd.; Tel 066/915-2255; 6:30-10:30pm; charthse@iol.ie; Dinners £9.50-15.50)* is quite popular, so make a reservation. The dining room is warm and inviting, the staff is always attentive, and tables are graced with the handmade pottery you'll find in craft shops. To use the word "delicious" would do the chef a grave injustice. The pasta is homemade, the seafood is fresh, and the portions are healthy. That's unfortunate, though, if you don't have room for dessert. If you're up for it, try the chocolate croissant bread pudding with blood orange ice cream (£4.25).

You know that chef Paul Smith's got the skills if *The Irish Times* made a big deal out of his opening **The Mystic Celt** *(Main St.; Tel 066/915-2117 or 087/699-8103; Opens 6pm daily, Jun-Sept, call for hours other times of the year; themysticcelt@oceanfree.net; Main courses £9-19; V, MC)* in Dingle Town. The menu posted outside is mouth-watering, and the food tastes every bit as scrumptious as it sounds: try the grilled filet steak, or a fancy pasta dish if you're trying to skimp.

Fenton's *(Green St.; Tel 066/915-1588; Noon—2:30pm/6-10pm Tue-Sun, closed Dec-Feb; Lunch £7, dinner £22; V, MC, AE, DC)* just keeps popping up over and over in Dingle's culinary conversation. It's one of the best seafood restaurants around, no doubt, so make a reservation before you go. The atmosphere is quiet and charming, with country furnishings, and there's a garden patio out back—take your hot-buttered lobster outside on a relatively warm evening. As always, the lunch is a better value than dinner, but the early bird menu from 6 to 7pm isn't a bad deal at £14.95.

crashing

You definitely can't go wrong when it comes to accommodations on the Dingle peninsula. The digs are some of the nicest in the country, and every single one has amazing seaside views, unless you're staying at the Grapevine, which is so perfect for pubbing that you won't even care.

▸▸CHEAP

The Grapevine Hostel *(Dykegate St.; Tel 066/915-1434; grapevine@dingleweb.com; £7-8.50 4- or 6-bed dorm; No credit cards)* is within a mere stone's throw of all the Dingle pubs. It's definitely the place to be if you're looking to do a late-night crawl, although the sitting room—complete with mellow music, big comfy sofas, and burning incense—is so alluring you might never make it out the door. The Grapevine's atmosphere and staff are so cool, many travelers pass on the ubiquitous nightly trad sessions to schmooze among themselves in the candlelight instead. Added bonus: a sizeable communal food stash.

For a great hippie vibe, check out the **Rainbow Hostel** *(Strand Rd.; Tel 066/915-1044; info@net-rainbow.com, www.iol.ie/~rainbow; £8 6-bed dorm, £10 per person double; No credit cards)*. A van, painted in bright rainbow colors, of course, will meet you at the bus stop in Dingle, although the hostel is situated less than a mile outside of town. The grounds are teeming with farm animals, the people are friendly, and the atmosphere is cheerful and laid-back. The hostel is situated at the beginning of the Slea Head route, and you can rent a bike here for £6 a day and head out.

Ballintaggart Hostel *(Mail Rd.; Tel 066/915-1454; info@dingleaccommodation.com, www.dingleaccommodation.com; £9-10 4-bed dorm, £8-9 8- and 10-bed dorm, £14-16 twin and double; V, MC)* is widely regarded as one of the best hostels in the area, if not in all of Ireland. The place is spotless, the staff couldn't be friendlier, and the building is sprawling and elegant. The house was built in 1703 as a hunting lodge for the Earl of Cork. Ballintaggart is a 20- or 30-minute walk outside of town, but the hostel provides free shuttle service back and forth five or six times daily. There is no curfew or lockout, as all guests are given the entry code. There is a big double kitchen for the use of the guests.

The beach at Ventry is within spitting distance of the **Ballybeag Hostel** *(Ventry; Tel 066/915-9876; ballybeag@iol.ie; £7.50-9 4-bed dorm; No credit cards)*. Chances are as soon as you get off the bus behind the Supervalu you'll find the Ballybeag minivan driver soliciting your business, providing a free shuttle to and from Dingle Town. Take him up on the offer and you won't be disappointed; the facilities are more than satisfactory, and all rooms come with private bath. It makes a good base for exploring the rest of the peninsula, and you can rent a bike here for around £5.

▸▸DO-ABLE

The Old Mill House B&B *(Dykegate St.; Tel 066/915-1434; verhoul@iol.ie, www.iol.ie/~verhoul; £15-22 single, £16 per person double; V, MC)* has a lot going for it: a central location (always a plus when planning that pub crawl), fantastic breakfasts (try the crepes) and some of the most comfortable beds in town. The owners have gone to great lengths to keep the place looking clean, quaint, and authentically Irish. Peat fires burn at night, the pine beds are handmade, and you can take your tea in the cheerful little garden out back.

Other do-able options include the **Marina Inn** *(Strand St.; Tel 066/915-1660; gogrady90@hotmail.com; Shared rooms £15/person, singles from £20, private baths; No credit cards)*, on the pier in the town center; and **Boland's** *(Main St.; Tel 066/915-1426; Rooms £20-£27.50/person; Private baths; Breakfast included; V, MC)*, a short walk from the town center.

▸▸SPLURGE

If you're going to splurge for a night, **Doyle's Townhouse** *(5 John St.; Tel 066/915-1174, or 800/223-6510 from the U.S.; cdoyle@iol.ie; £68 double, rate includes full breakfast; V, MC)* is definitely the place to do it. The especially comfortable rooms are furnished with antiques and the views, whether of the harbor in the front or the Slieve Mish mountain range in the back, are romantic and super-Kodak-friendly. The comfy sitting room boasts a Victorian fireplace and shelves filled with interesting old books.

need to know

Currency Exchange Improve your cash flow at **AIB** *(Main Street, 10am-12:30pm/1:30-5pm Mon, 10am-12:30pm/1:30-4pm Tue-Fri)* and **Bank of Ireland** *(Main Street, 10am-12:30pm/1:30-5pm Mon, 10am-12:30pm/1:30-4pm Tue-Fri)*. Both have bureaus de change as well as ATM machines.

Tourist Information Stop by the **Dingle Tourist Office** *(Strand St.; Tel 066/915-1188; 9am-6pm Mon-Sat, Jun-Aug; 10am-6pm Sun, 9am-5pm Mon-Sat, Sept-Oct and mid-Mar-May; closed the rest of the year)* for info on all things Dingle.

Public Transportation There's no local bus service, but **Bus Éireann** *(Tel 066/712-3566)* provides service to towns west of Dingle on Monday and Thursday, and daily to and from Tralee and Killarney, dropping passengers off by Garvey's Supervalu near the dock. For a cab, try **Paul Walker Taxi** *(Tel 087/686-9098 or 066/915-9923)* or **Seán O'Connor, Cooleen Cabs** *(Tel 087/248-0008),* the latter of which has 24-hour service. (Keep that number in your pocket if you're planning a night at the pubs and you're staying a ways out of town.)

Health and Emergency Emergency: *999,* no coins needed, **Garda Station** *(The Holy Ground, Tel 066/915-1522).* If your needs aren't quite so urgent, try the **Dingle Hospital** *(Upper Main St.; Tel 066/915-1455 or 066/915-1172).*

Pharmacies **O'Keefe's Pharmacy Ltd.** *(Main St.; Tel 066/915-1310; 9:30am-6pm Mon-Wed, Fri-Sat, 9:30am-1pm Thu, 9:30am-12:30pm Sun)* will serve your medicinal needs.

Bike Rental Cyclists have three options in Dingle: **Paddy's Bike Shop** *(Dykegate St.; Tel 066/915-2311; £7 per day, £6 per day for students, £30 per week)* or **Foxy John's** *(Main St.; Tel 066/915-1316; £6 per day, £30 per week).*

Laundry Scrub your duds at **Níolann an Daingin** *(Green St. Lane; Tel 066/915-1837; 9am-5:30pm Mon-Sat; Mon, Wed, Fri only, Nov-Apr; £6 wash and dry).*

Postal Mail those chain letters at **An Post** *(Upper Main St.; Tel 066/915-1661; 9am-1pm/2-5:30pm Mon-Fri, 9am-1pm Sat).*

Internet See *wired,* above.

everywhere else

Tralee

With a population of 20,000, Tralee may be County Kerry's economic hub and the Dingle peninsula's largest town, but apart from the notoriety of its roses (and the Rose of Tralee festival every August which includes a beauty pageant), there's very little of interest here. Frankly, Tralee's about as exciting as watching paint dry; the rather dreary streets and blah-inspiring industrial feel don't exactly spell "tourism." On the other hand, it's a necessary passing-through stop on the way out to the little towns on the peninsula, or back to Killarney.

There's always the chance you'll miss the last bus of the day and need a place to stay before hitting the road bright and early in the morning. You'll find almost anything you need along **The Mall** and **Castle** and **Denny streets,** about a 10-minute walk down Edward Street from the bus and train station.

bar and live music scene

There are a few solid choices for live trad with your pint in Tralee: Bustling **Bailey's Corner Pub** *(Ashe and Castle Streets; Tel 066/712-3230),* cozy **Paddy Mac's** *(The Mall; Tel 066/712-1572),* and old-fashioned **Seán Óg's** *(41 Bridge St.; Tel 066/712-8822).* Music nights can vary; check with the hostel owners to find out where to go.

culture zoo

Kerry the Kingdom *(Ashe Memorial Hall, Denny St; Tel 066/712-7777; 10am-6pm daily, Mar-Oct; Noon-4:30pm, Nov-Dec; £5.50 Adults, £4.75 Students):*Pretty much the only cultural attraction here is Kerry the Kingdom, the second largest museum in the country and definitely worth a visit, if you have time to kill. The exhibits cover basically every aspect of County Kerry from 8,000 B.C. to the present. Not surprisingly, a park across the street blooms with roses during the summer months.

wired

Get online at **Cyberpost** *(26 Castle St.; Tel 066/718-1284; 10am-10pm Mon-Sat, Jul-Sep; 10am-6pm Mon-Sat, Oct-Jun; £4.50 per hour).* To get there from the train station, at the corner where Oakpark Road and Edward Street meet, walk down Edward Street and continue on until you come to Castle Street running (sort of) perpendicular.

eats

There are a handful of places to eat in Tralee, but nothing particularly stands out. If you're of the vegetarian bent, you could try **The Skillet** *(Barrack Lane, near the Mall; Tel 066/712-4561; lunch entrees £5 or less)* or **Brat's Place** *(18 Milk Market Lane, near the Mall; £5).* They serve meat dishes too. If you want to grab some groceries and eat in, **Tesco** *(Tel 066/712-2788; 8:30am-8pm Mon-Wed, Sat; 8:30am-9:30pm Thur-Fri; 10am-6pm Sun)* has the largest stock of food.

crashing

If you do sleep over, try **Finnegan's Holiday Hostel** *(17 Denny St.; Tel 066/712-7610; £8-10 dorm, £12.50 per person double; V, MC).* It's right across from the tourist office [see *need to know,* below] and has a comfy, lived-in feel. Finnegan's is a short walk from the bus and train station, and it's the perfect location for catching whatever pub action, however scant, Tralee offers. From the station's entrance gate, walk straight ahead on North Circular Road and make a left onto Ashe Street, cross the Mall and proceed onto Denny Street.

The hostel closest to the train station, however, would be **Lisnagree Hostel** *(Ballinorig Rd.; Tel 066/712-7133; £8.50 dorm, £10 per person double; No credit cards),* which is ideal for an "I'm-heading-off-to-bed-at-ten-and-taking-the-first-bus-out-of-here-tomorrow" kind of night. Lisnagree also has more attractive single rooms than Finnegan's and an ample kitchen.

Another do-able option is **Sean Og's** *(41 Bridge St.; Tel 066/712-8822; Doubles £40, singles £20, twins/triples £16 per person, private baths, breakfast included; No credit cards),* near the town center.

need to know

Currency Exchange **Lisnagree Hostel** [see *crashing,* above] has a bureau de change; that's pretty much your best option after 5pm. Otherwise, there's the **Bank of Ireland** *(Castle St.; 10am-5pm Mon, 10am-4pm Tue-Fri)* and **AIB** *(Denny and Castle Sts.; 10am-5pm Mon, 10am-4pm Tue-Fri),* both of which have ATMs.

Tourist Information The **Tralee Tourist Office** *(Ashe Memorial Hall, Denny St.; Tel 066/712-12-88; 9am-7pm Mon-Sat, 9am-6pm Sun, Jul-Aug; 9am-6pm Mon-Sat, May-Jun, Sep; 9am-5pm Mon-Fri, Oct-Apr)* is a good place to find information on the Dingle Peninsula before you actually get out there. To reach it from the train station, make a left onto Edward Street, a right onto the Mall, and a left onto Denny Street.

Pharmacies Kelly's Chemist *(The Mall; Tel 066/712-1302; 9am-8pm Mon-Fri, 9am-6pm Sat)* is the only pharmacy in town. From the train station, make a left onto Edward Street and a right onto the Mall.

Health and Emergency Emergency: *999,* no coins required; **Garda Station** *(High St.; Tel 066/712-2022).* **Tralee County General Hospital** *(Off Killarney Rd.; Tel 066/712-6222)* is not centrally located; to get there, take John Joe Sheehy Road away from town (that is, make a left out of the train and bus station). When the street ends, make another left. Make a right at the roundabout and you'll be on Killarney Road.

Trains Trains from major cities arrive at the **Irish Rail Station** *(John Joe Sheehy Road; Tel 066/712-3522);* a train runs daily between Dublin and Tralee

Bus Lines out of the City Bus Eireann *(Bus Eireann Depot, John Joe Sheehy Road; Tel 066/712-3566)* departs daily for Dublin, as well as Rosslare via Killarney, Cork, and Waterford. If you're heading out to the peninsula, you can get a bus to Dingle or Dunquin about six times daily, in season (in the off-season that number is like 3-5). Other buses connect with Ennis, Shannon, and Derry.

Laundry Kate's Launderette *(Boherboy; Tel 066/712-7173; 9am-6pm Mon-Sat; £6 wash and dry; 10 percent off with student card)* is on Boherboy, the same street as the Mall and Castle Street, just with a different name. From the train station, make a left onto Edward Street and turn left onto Castle Street. This street will turn into Boherboy.

Postal The **Tralee Post Office** *(Edward St.; Tel 066/712-1013; 9am-5:30pm Mon and Wed-Sat, 9:30am-5:30pm Tue)* is in the middle of town. From the train station, make a left onto Edward Street. The Post Office is on the right.

Internet See *wired,* above.

dunquin and the blasket islands

If you've landed in the tiny village of Dunquin, chances are you've come to check out the Blasket Islands, are interested in Gaeltacht language and culture, or are short a few flapjacks.

Though Dunquin is a do-able day trip from Dingle, and offers its own charm, the best reason to come here is as a jumping-off point for the Blaskets. Just offshore lie the seven lonesome islands, connected by a ferry to the mainland May through September when the weather permits [see *need to know,* below]. The Blasket Centre, which celebrates the Blasket Islands and Gaeltacht language and culture, is in Dunquin, perched on the westerly tip of the Dingle Peninsula. It's worth a look if you can't get to the real deal. You can also wait for the weather to pass while enjoying a pint at Kruger's [see *crashing,* below].

Once hailed as the purest example of Irish culture, the Blasket Islands were evacuated in 1953 due to extreme—and we mean *extreme*—weather conditions that reduced the Islanders to a life of poverty and hardship. The Great Blasket was once an outpost of Irish civilization, nurturing a small group of great Irish-language writers. It's now inhabited only by staffers at a small cafe and hostel [see *eats and crashing,* below].

An afternoon exploring Great Blasket—you can take a magnificent 8-mile walk to the west end of the island and back—swimming on the beautiful Blasket beach, and visiting the old houses of the famous writers who lived here leaves travelers raving about these lonely but lovely islands. Be forewarned: the same brutal weather that cut the Islanders off from the mainland and eventually necessitated their permanent departure has been known to leave visitors stranded for weeks.

Before you go, you might want to acquaint yourself with the antiquated culture for which the Blaskets are renowned; many memoirs have been written lamenting its decline, including Maurice O'Sullivan's *Twenty Years A-Growing* and Peig Sayers' *Peig.* You can pick up these books at the **The Blasket Centre** *(Dunquin; Tel 066/915-6444; 10am-6pm Apr-Jun, Sept-Oct; 10am-7pm Jul-Aug; demordha@indigo.ie; £2.50 Adults, £1 Students).* The center also gives an excellent presentation of the lost lifestyle of the Blasket Islanders and the history and current status of the Irish language. A cafe at the Centre sports a view of the Blaskets.

crashing and eats

The recently opened **Great Blasket Island Hostel** *(Great Blasket; Tel 086/848-6687 or 086/852-2321; £10 dorm; Open Apr-Oct; No credit cards)* is outside the old village on Great Blasket. Don't take the hot showers, toilets, and kitchen facilities for granted; at a place like this they're all luxuries. There's no curfew, either, as the owners will make a point of noting, but where the heck *can* you party on this island, anyway? Camping is free, but you're *really* going to have to rough it.

If the weather keeps you from getting out to the islands, or if you prefer creature comforts, you can eat, sleep, and drink at Dunquin's social hub, **Kruger's Guest House and Bar** *(Ballinahara, Dunquin; Tel 066/915-6127; £36 double; No credit cards).* Kruger's offers *leaba agus bricfasta*—er, bed and breakfast—from March to September in the guest-house next door to the pub. And talk about a pub with stories to tell...Kruger's has plenty of them, mostly about the bar's colorful owner. The thoroughly un-Irish name began as the nickname of now-departed Maurice Kavanagh, Eamon de Valera's personal bodyguard and PR man for the Schubert Theater Company in New York City, among many other things. He was friendly with tons of politicians, gangsters, and Hollywood stars as well. *Ryan's Daughter* and *Far and Away* were both filmed within a few baby steps of Kruger's, and the latter's film crew, along with Tom Cruise and Nicole Kidman, hung out here constantly during the making of the film. It was also one of Brendan Behan's favored haunts. What makes the pub even more special is the area's untamed remoteness. You can find step-dancing and live trad on weekends, and *seán nós*— old Irish-style singing—every other night of the week.

You might also try the **Dunquin Hostel** *(Dunquin; Tel 066/915-6121; £6-8 dorm; No credit cards),* which is plain but serviceable. There's a midnight curfew and the lockout's between 10:15am and 5pm—so no sleeping in for you!

Kruger's Pub *(Main St.; Tel 066/915-6127; 10:30am-midnight daily; Meals £6-£9; Rooms £18 per person, breakfast included; No credit cards),* stands at the center of the hamlet and is loved by locals and visitors alike. From March to October Kruger's features the best trad in the area on weekends. The bar has a homey feel to it, with paintings on the walls of the locals, including the Kruger family themselves. Their pub grub is the town's best, and the inevitable fish and chips is a specialty. Kruger's will also house you for the night in one of its simple but well-maintained bedrooms upstairs.

If you want to cook for yourself, you'll have to bring your own groceries-Dunquin doesn't even have a grocery store.

need to know

Directions/Transportation **Dunquin Ferries** *(Tel 066/915-6455 or 066/915-6422; Every half-hour 10am-5pm during the summer, £10 return)* leave for the Blaskets daily from Dunquin, weather permitting. **Bus Éireann** *(Tel 066/712-3566)* provides service from Dingle to Dunquin Monday and Thursday; call for times, or stop by the Dingle tourist office for info [see **Dingle**, above].

the west

This is what you've been waiting for. Ever since you landed in Dublin or Shannon you've been hearing about the gorgeous West of Ireland: untamed, dramatic, inspiring, and *totally* worth the wait. Now you'll find out why.

Four counties—**Limerick, Clare, Galway,** and **Mayo**—lie between the almost tropical Kerry and the austere Northwest. There are so many fantastic things to see and do here, it'd take years to explore all the possibilities. In County Clare, you'll find the spectacular **Cliffs of Moher**—get there at dawn to beat the tour buses—and splendid little coastal towns like **Doolin** and **Miltown Malbay,** both centers of Irish traditional music, as well as the resort towns of **Kilkee** and **Lahinch,** favored by Irish families on holiday and travelers looking for especially good diving, sailing, swimming, and the like. But when it comes to sports, the Galway Coast is just as satisfying: At **Killary Harbour,** for example, you can take your pick of just about every adventure sport there is, from diving to kayaking to rock-climbing. Serious hikers and nature-lovers (except tree-huggers, because there aren't any trees here) head for **the Burren** (in County Clare), which is an unforgettable sight to see. One of Cromwell's men (or Cromwell himself, it's not certain) once stated that in the Burren region "there is not wood enough to hang a man, nor water enough to drown him in, nor earth enough to bury him in." That's not exactly true, but it does give you a slight idea of what the place looks like: barren and rocky, yet with beautiful wildflowers and prehistoric remains everywhere you look. If ancient ruins are your thing, you'll also want to check out the **Aran Islands,** off the southern Galway coast, which have preserved Stone Age dolmens and wedge tombs. As you pass a small traditional cottage alongside a weird maze of stones laid down thousands of years ago, you wouldn't be the first visitor to feel a shiver of awe at the sight of all the layers of history unfolding before you.

The West is definitely the place where that old Ireland-as-a-tiny-cottage thing is most highly developed. Don't be disappointed if you get to the Aran Islands and see that most of the residents of Inis Mór (the biggest and most popular island) now have shingled roofs and most modern conveniences just like the rest of the world; just hop on a bike and ride around a bit and you'll still see many a thatched-roof cottage. Inis Meáin and Inis Oírr, the two smaller islands, are much quieter and more authentic. You won't find any place to party there, but you will find a wee bit of Ireland that remains totally unspoiled by the base demands of the tourism industry. In Galway's **Connemara** area, old-style cottage industries are alive and well, while the northern coast of rural County Mayo offers impossibly picturesque seaside villages like **Enniscrone, Killala,** and **Ballycastle**—little more than a few streets with some old houses and maybe some docks or piers. Life is lived at a leisurely pace in this neck of the woods. If you're used to cities, you may feel a bit on edge in these tiny towns. Take your time and let the place's mellow spirit take hold of you, and you'll be rewarded.

If you're coming from the south or entering the country through Shannon Airport, you can get to Counties Clare and Galway through **Limerick,** a town with a deep-seated bad reputation that's been getting better in recent years. You may have been advised to skip Limerick altogether, but don't be too hasty. Awesome live music venues and contemporary art galleries, along with a pulsing youth vibe, may reward you for stopping here before pushing north.

Even more inviting is **Galway City,** which sparkles with a free-spirited, do-your-own-thing vibe. Creative types flock here, and though it doesn't have the remarkable performing or visual arts scenes of Dublin and other big European cities, Galway is the best city in Ireland for making art and living freely (freely at least by Irish standards). In fact this whole region is a magnet for boho types—the fantastically gorgeous scenery inspires even the most jaded artist, musician, or writer, and has ever since the days when William Butler Yeats bought a castle in Gort, in southern Galway, for £35 (property values have gone up a bit since then).

Near the bottom of County Mayo is **Westport,** a big holiday destination where people come to have a good time. It's a postcard-pretty little town in the Georgian style, but the streets bustle with a surprisingly urban feel for a town of only a few thousand people. Ever wonder what happens to resort towns when they fall out of fashion? Just visit sparsely populated **Achill Island,** once a major tourist destination and now an eerie ghost of its former self. Although scores of ugly white vacation cottages still dot the landscape, Achill's rugged cliffs, harsh seas, and pristine beaches (not to mention good budget accommodations) more than make it worth a visit.

Northern County Mayo is definitely, with the exception of Ballina, as rural as rural gets. Around the **Moy Valley, Killala Bay,** and to the west, there are ancient ruins, beautiful cliffs and ocean views, and inviting seaside villages. You can practically hear the strains of traditional Irish music as sweet-smelling blue smoke from burning peat floats from chimneys across the countryside, fading romantically into the still-lit evening skies. Bogs and mountains and heather and lakes—this is what you imagined Ireland would be like, and now you've found it.

getting around the region

Travel between the larger towns and attractions in the region is do-able as buses and trains come and go with frequency. If you're driving, you'll have no problem getting to the more remote parts of the region. If you're busing, you'll need to plan very carefully.

back to dublin

On your return from Galway to the pleasant urban jungle of Dublin—the common route of backpacker-types—there are some detours well worth a look in the Midlands.

In County Offaly, you can get a wild, ancient rush at **Clonmacnoise** *(Tel 0905/74195; 10am-5:30pm daily Nov to mid-Mar, 10am-6pm daily mid-Mar to mid-May and Sept-Oct, 9am-7pm mid-May to early Sept; Admission £3 adults, £1.25 students),* pronounced just like it looks. Meaning "Meadow of the sons of Nós," it's one of the most important monastic sites in the country. Built in the sixth century at an important crossroads (where the River Shannon and the Dublin-Galway road meet), Clonmacnoise was the center of scholarship and culture under many Irish kings—the illuminated manuscripts on view here are on par with the *Book of Kells.* The 12th-century church ruins show the effects of Viking attacks, among others, but the National Heritage Service is busy restoring the site properly. Scattered throughout the nearby area's green, isolated hills are also a museum with fantastic Celtic crosses, a large, dramatic cathedral, and several smaller churches, some still active. Unfortunately, a car is the only convenient way to get to Clonmacnoise, taking Route 457 north out of Shannonbridge for 4 miles. Otherwise you'll have to go to Athlone, about 96.6 km (60 mi) east of Galway and a stop on the Dublin-Galway Irish Rail route; from Athlone Castle, **Paddy Kavanagh** runs a daily bus to Clonmacnoise *(Tel 0902/74839; Departs 11am, returns 4pm; pkmail@eircom.net).*

Athlone is also a starting base for visiting the bucolic **Birr Castle Demesne** *(Rosse Row, Birr, County Offaly; Tel 0509/22154; 9am-6pm daily, Nov-Mar; www.birrcastle.com/birr/visitor/visitbirr.html; Admission*

In Mayo, the big towns like Westport and Ballina have buses coming and going several times a day, but getting around more rural areas like Killala, Ballycastle, and the whole of Achill Island can really suck. Buses come only once or twice a day to many small villages here, so make it a point to check the bus schedule before you make your next move.

▸▸ROUTES

To get the full effect of this magical area, you'll want to spend at least three or four days in the region, more if you expect to hang out in the villages along the coast. No matter what, be sure to stay over in Galway, the hottest town in the West.

To get out to the Clare coast from Limerick or Dublin-Heuston, take bus or rail to Ennis, and then bus to Doolin, Miltown Malbay, Kilkee, etc. A bus runs from Doolin to Galway two or three times a day. From Galway,

£4.75 adults, £3.20 students), pronounced "burr castle domain." From Athlone, you'll pass through Birr Castle Demesne on the bus or the Irish Rail train; **Busáras** *(Store St., Dublin 1; Tel 01/836-61-11),* will take you directly to Birr from Dublin. The adjacent area of Demesne boasts a 100-acre garden around a lovely lake and two rivers, with more than 1,000 species of plant life, plus an astronomy center with a 6-foot reflecting telescope built in 1845. You can use the telescope at noon and 3pm each day. Take a picnic lunch, hang out under the magnolias, and muse on your place in the great scheme of things.

The forests and boglands of the **Slieve Bloom Mountains** in Counties Offaly and Laois are perfect for a leisurely and secluded hike; this untouristed wooded region has spectacular views and sleepy little old settlements that look lost in time. Explore it by following the **Slieve Bloom Way**, a 50-km (31-mi) circular drive through the area, accessed from Mountmellick via R422. Start at the northern end of the route, at Glen Barrow's Car Park, and meander through ancient hills and valleys to **Cadamstown**, which features a classic pub. At the southeastern end of the route, the **Pine House Farm** *(Annaghmore; Tel 0509/37029; No credit cards)* is a comfy farmhouse that takes in boarders. The **Portlaoise Tourist Office** *(James Fintlan Lawlor Ave., Portlaoise, County Laois; Tel 0502/21178; 10am-6pm Mon-Sat),* served by **Bus Éireann** route 12 (every hour daily from Dublin), can help you plan a route and find the perfect cowshed.

Bus Éireann will take you out to the Connemara National Park and to any of the towns on the coast as well as Oughterard, on Lough Corrib, and Rossaveal, jumping-off point for the Aran Islands. (You could also take a ferry from Doolin to the islands, then take another ferry from Inis Mór to Rossaveal and a bus to Galway City.) Taking the southern half of Ireland in more or less of a U-shape lets you cover the punchiest attractions, all the must-sees, in a relatively efficient way. This method works with the bus and rail systems, involving the least amount of doubling-back and whatnot.

If precious little villages are your thing, take a day or two to do a tiny tour in Mayo: Start in Cong, then over to Keel, out on Achill Island, followed by seaside fave Killala, then finish up in Enniscrone. You may want to rent a car for this one, or pay especially close attention to your bus schedule.

Travel Times

* *By train*
** *Water-crossing required (by ferry usually)*
*** *By cable car*

	Dublin	Limerick	Bunratty	Ennis	Doolin	Balleyvaugn	The Burren	Fanore	Lahinch	Miltown	Kilkee	Galway City
Limerick	2:50	-	:15	:35	1:30	1:25	1:20	1:35	1:10	1:55	1:40	1:40
Bunratty	3:05	:15	-	:20	1:15	1:10	1	1:20	1	2:10	1:25	1:20
Ennis	3:25	:35	:20	-	:55	:50	:35	:40	:35	:45	1:10	1
Doolin	4:15	1:30	1:15	:55	-	:30	:15	:20	:25	:30	1:15	1:20
Balleyvaugn	3:25	1:25	1:10	:50	:30	-	:35	:40	:35	:45	1:30	:55
The Burren	4	1:20	1	:35	:15	:35	-	:20	:15	:30	1:05	1:20
Fanore	4:05	1:35	1:20	:40	:20	:40	:20	-	:35	:50	1:30	1:20
Lahinch	4	1:10	1	:35	:25	:35	:15	:35	-	:20	:50	1:35
Miltown	4:15	1:20	1	:45	:30	:45	:30	:50	:20	-	:40	1:40
Kilkee	4:30	1:40	1:25	1:10	:55	1:30	1:05	1:30	:50	:40	-	2:10
Galway City	3:20	1:40	1:20	1	:55	:55	1:20	1:20	1:35	1:40	2:10	-
Kinvara	4:15	2:40	2:20	2:05	2:20	1:55	2:20	2:15	2:35	2:30	3:15	1
Gort	3:05	1	:45	:30	1:10	:40	:50	1:10	1	1:10	1:40	:35
Aran Islands	4:50**	3:40**	3:20**	3**	2:20**	2:55**	3:20**	3:20**	3:35**	2:40**	4:10**	1**
Oughterard	3:50	2:10	1:55	1:35	1:55	1:30	1:50	1:50	2:05	2:20	2:45	:35
Clifden	4:50	3:10	2:55	2:35	3	2:30	2:50	2:50	3:05	3:20	3:45	1:35
Connemara National Park	5	3:20	3:05	2:50	2	2:40	3:05	3	3:20	3:35	4	1:50
Inishbofin Island	5:25**	3:45**	3:55**	3:55**	3:40**	3:30**	3:50**	3:50**	4:25**	4:25**	5:05**	2:55**
Roundstone	4:50	3:15	3	2:35	3	2:30	2:55	2:50	3:10	3:25	3:50	1:40
Killary Harbour	4:40	3	2:45	2:30	2:50	2:20	2:45	2:40	3	3:15	3:40	1:25
Westport	3:55	3:15	3	2:40	3	2:30	3	3	3:10	3:25	3:50	1:45
Murisk	4:05	3:20	3:15	2:50	3:15	2:45	3:10	3:05	3:25	3:40	4:05	2
Clare Island	5:25**	4:45**	4**	3:10**	4:30**	4**	4:20**	4:20**	4:40**	4:40**	5:05**	2:30**
Achill Island	5	4:20	4:05	3:45	4:05	3:40	4:05	4	4:20	4:30	4:55	3
Ballina	3:45	3:25	3:15	2:50	3:15	2:45	3:05	3:05	3:20	3:40	4	2
Ballycastle	4:20	4:05	3:50	3:30	3:55	3:20	3:45	3:45	3	4:10	4:40	2:40
Killala	4	3:45	3:30	3:10	3:30	3	3:25	3:25	3:40	3:50	4:20	2:20
Cong	4:05	2:30	2:15	1:50	2:15	1:45	2:10	2:05	2:25	2:40	3	:55
Knock	4:15	1:25	1:10	:50	1:35	1:40	1:20	1:40	1:05	:40	:30	1:50

Kinvara	Gort	Aran Islands	Oughterard	Clifden	Connemara National Park	Inishbofin Island	Roundstone	Killary Harbour	Westport	Murisk	Clare Island	Achill Island	Ballina	Ballycastle	Killala	Cong	Knock
2:40	1	3:10**	2:10	3:10	3:20	3:45**	3:15	3	3:15	3:20	4:45**	4:20	3:25	4:05	3:45	2:30	1:25
2:20	:45	3:50**	1:55	2:55	3:05	3:55**	3	2:45	3	3:15	4**	4:05	3:15	3:50	3:30	2:15	1:10
2:05	:30	2:30**	1:35	2:35	2:50	3:55**	2:35	2:30	2:40	2:50	3:10**	3:45	2:50	3:30	3:10	1:50	:50
2:20	1:10	2:50**	1:55	3	2	3:40**	3	2:50	3	3:15	4:30**	4:05	3:15	3:55	3:30	2:15	1:35
1:55	:40	3:25**	1:30	2:30	2:40	3:30**	2:30	2:20	2:30	2:45	4**	3:40	2:45	3:20	3	1:45	1:40
2:20	:50	3:20**	1:50	2:50	3:05	3:50**	2:55	2:45	3	3:05	4:20**	4:05	3:05	3:45	3:25	2:10	1:20
2:15	1:10	2:50**	1:50	2:50	3	3:50**	2:50	2:40	3	3:05	4:20**	4	3:05	3:45	3:25	2:05	1:40
2:35	1	3:05**	2:05	3:05	3:20	4:25**	3:10	2	3:10	3:25	4:40**	4:20	3:20	3	3:40	2:25	1:05
2:30	1:10	3:10**	2:20	3:20	3:35	4:25**	3:25	3:15	3:25	3:40	4:40**	4:30	3:40	4:10	3:50	2:40	:40
3:15	1:40	3:40**	2:45	3:45	4	5**	3:50	3:40	3:50	4:05	5**	4:55	4	4:40	4:20	3	:30
1	:35	1:30**	:35	1:35	1:50	2:55**	1:40	1:25	1:45	2	2:40**	3	2	2:40	2:20	:55	1:50
-	1:35	2:30**	:40	1	2:20	1:35**	:50	:50	1:30	1:30	2:40**	2:50	2:35	3:05	2:50	1:05	2:50
1:35	-	3:05**	1:10	2:10	2:20	2:45**	2:10	2	2:15	2:25	3:50**	3:20	2:25	3:05	2:40	1:25	1:15
2:30**	2:05**	-	2:05**	3:05**	3:20**	4:25**	3:10**	2:55**	3:15**	3:30**	4:10**	4:30**	3:30**	4:10**	3:50**	2:25**	3:20**
:40	1:10	2:05**	-	1	1:15	1:35**	1:05	:55	1:30	1:35	3:15**	2:50	2:25	3:05	2:50	1:05	2:25
1	2:10	3:05**	1	-	:10	:30**	:25	:40	1:20	1:20	3**	2:25	2:25	3	2:40	1:25	3:30
1:15	2:50	3:20**	1:15	:10	-	1**	:35	2	1:05	1:15	2:20**	2:30	2:10	2:45	2:30	1:20	3:35
1:35**	2:45**	4:25**	1:35**	:30**	1**	-	1:25**	:40**	1:40**	1:45**	2:40**	3**	2:45**	3:20**	3:05**	1:50**	4**
:50	2:10	3:10**	1:05	:25	:35	1:25**	-	1	1:45	1:50	3**	3	2:50	3:20	3:05	1:30	3:30
:55	2	2:55**	:55	:40	2	:40**	1	-	:40	:45	1:45**	2	1:45	2:15	2	:50	3:15
1:30	2:15	3:15**	1:30	1:20	1:05	1:40**	1:45	:40	-	:15	1:30**	1:15	1:05	1:35	1:20	:55	3:30
1:30	2:25	3:30**	1:35	1:20	1:15	1:45**	1:50	:45	:15	-	1:45**	1:30	1:20	1:50	1:35	1:10	3:45
2:40**	3:50**	4:10**	3:15**	3**	2:20**	2:40**	3**	1:45**	1:30**	1:45**	-	2:45**	2:35**	2:40**	2:50**	2:30**	4:50**
2:50	3:20	4:30**	2:45	2:35	2:25	3**	3	2	1:15	1:30	2:45**	-	2	2:20	2:15	2:10	4:35
2:25	2:25	3:30**	2:35	2:25	2:10	2:45**	2:50	1:45	1:05	1:20	2:35**	2	-	:35	:20	1:35	3:40
3:05	3:05	4:10**	3:05	3	2:45	3:20**	3:20	2:15	1:35	1:50	2:40**	2:20	:35	-	:20	2:10	4:20
2:50	2:40	3:50**	2:50	2:40	2:30	3:05**	3:05	2	1:20	1:35	2:50**	2:15	:20	:20	-	1:50	4
1:05	1:25	2:25**	1:05	1:25	1:20	1:50**	1:30	:50	:55	1:10	2:30**	2:10	1:35	2:10	1:50	-	2:45
2:50	1:15	3:20**	2:25	3:30	3:35	4**	3:30	3:15	3:30	3:45	4:50**	4:35	3:40	4:20	4	2:45	-

If you're heading straight to Galway from Dublin and have some time to burn, consider stopping off in County Offaly. There are a few cultural sites here that are definitely worth a day trip. Probably the best of them is Clonmacnoise [see *back to dublin,* above], with ruins dating to the 9th century overlooking the River Shannon. The ancient settlement has been called the most important monastic site in Ireland.

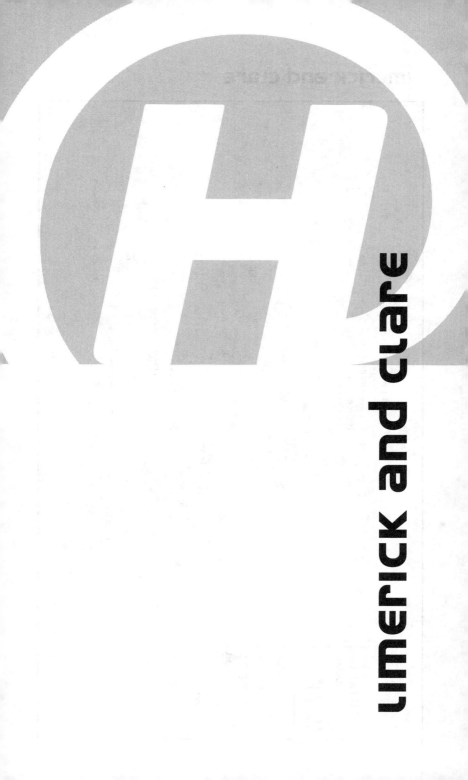

limerick and clare

Limerick and Clare

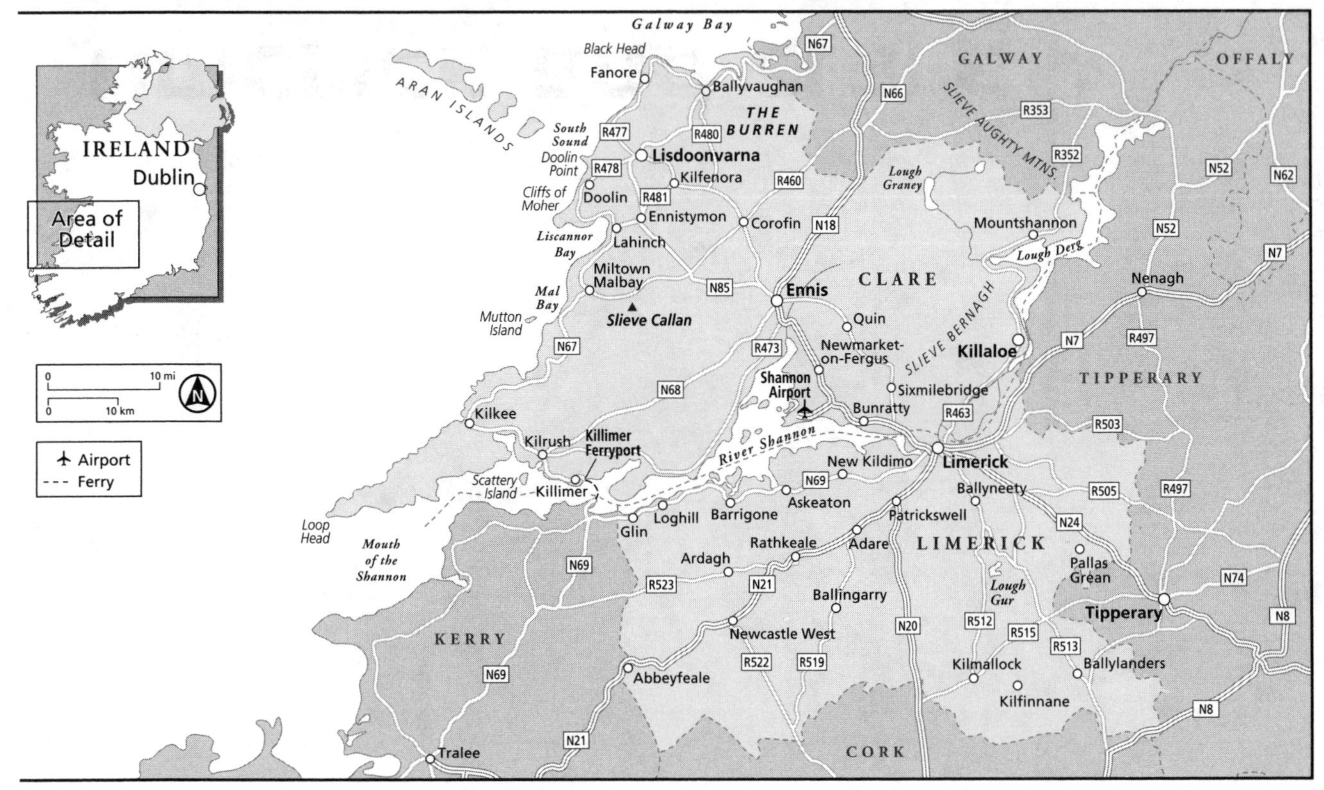

LIMERICK

So someone you met in a hostel last week told you that Limerick has a nasty reputation—"Stab City," it's sometimes called—and you've crossed it off your list. Not so fast—Limerick City might have gained a nasty reputation in past years, but you've gotta admire just how hard Limerick residents are working to shed that unfortunate nickname. Though still fairly dingy and blighted, with a populace that sometimes seems weighed down by it all, this city's making deliberate strides to brighten its dreary, forlorn, and even dangerous image. While we still wouldn't recommend strolling the streets alone at night with wads of cash, it's safe to say that Limerick's steadily improving.

Reconsidering? Good. For at least a day or two, anyway, Limerick's multitude of lively clubs and trad music pubs fueled by a college crowd are more than enough to keep you occupied. Limerick also has a couple of excellent art museums and a bunch of cool commercial galleries. Add to those the growing prestige of the Limerick School of Art and Design, which turns out some of Ireland's finest fashion designers, and you've got a city with definite assets that's still relatively undiscovered.

Of course Limerick's main claim to fame is as the setting for Frank McCourt's fabulously successful memoir, *Angela's Ashes* [see *frank mcCourt,* below], though **The Hunt Museum** in the Old Custom House on Rutland Street [see *arts scene,* below] is also renowned as *the* best place anywhere outside of Dublin to take in oh-so-fine art (including pieces by Picasso and Leonardo da Vinci, as well as some cool ancient Roman and Celtic stuff). Definitely make it a point to view the

five things to talk to a local about

1. **Irish Heroes:** Mention Irish hero Eamon de Valera, no doubt the county's most beloved resident.

2. **Limericks:** Make up a limerick inspired by your drunken stupor...*there once was a girl from New York....* You'll get a few groans, and the cornier you make it the more apt the bartender will be to pity you and give you a pint on the house. (Note, however, that limericks were actually *not* invented in Limerick, but grew out of an old Irish parlor game.)

3. **Suck up:** "Hey, this town's pretty damn cool after all!" Any Limerick resident will appreciate your commenting that the city doesn't deserve its dark "Stab City" image.

4. **Mention Dolan's:** "You going to Dolan's tonight?" Limerick's pubs host killer trad sessions, creating a perfectly festive getting-to-know-you atmosphere [see *live music scene,* below].

5. **Sports and Drinking:** You can always resort to the old standbys, if all else fails: sports or drinking.

self-portrait of Irish artist Robert Fagan and his pretty much totally naked wife, but don't bother looking for that one on a postcard in the museum gift shop (I already checked).

neighborhoods

Limerick City straddles the **River Shannon** and spreads out across the estuary in a big, industrial, and visibly underemployed sort of way. Its streets spread out in quite an orderly fashion, considering that it's an Irish city. The downtown area stretches across the eastern side of the muddy river, and you'll find the residential areas to the north and west. At the northern part of the city the Shannon forks, and in the divide stands the historic inner core, and such sights as **Saint Mary's Cathedral, City Hall,** and **King John's Castle**. As in any other city in this country, a street named **O'Connell,** running north and south, is one of the main drags, and most of the action takes place there or on the side streets. If not driving you'll likely arrive at **Colbert Bus and Rail Station** on **Parnell Street.** It is parallel to O'Connell and situated in the southern corner of the city, across from the **People's Park** [see *hanging out,* below]. The park itself is a pleasant enough green space in which to make plans of attack—if you can find an empty bench.

Limerick University is located 5 miles outside of Limerick City on the banks of the River Shannon, bordered by residential Castleroy district and the National Technological Park business area.

Though there are nice views from People's Park, nobody hangs out there. For some reason Limerick residents use it exclusively for dog walking. No picnics here. It could be all that rain that brings people inside and keeps them there even on sunny days. The favored pub for "just chillin'" would have to be **The Locke Bar** [see *bar scene,* below] with outdoor seating that Limerickians do make good use of—when the weather's nice. You'll probably have to wait awhile for a seat though—everybody else has got the same idea. Otherwise, try **Doc's** [see *live music scene,* below], which has a really nice beer garden bedecked with palm

frank mccourt

Born in New York and raised in Limerick, Frank McCourt returned to the Big Apple at age 19, attended New York University, and taught in the New York City school system for 30 years. His childhood memoir, *Angela's Ashes,* sent readers clamoring to the bookstores in search of one of the most popular and fantastically successful volumes in history, an achievement that culminated in the Pulitzer Prize (and probably more money than he knows what to do with). It was also made into a movie of the same name, starring Emily Watson. Citizens of Limerick have grumbled about the city's less-than-sparkling depiction in the book, but in reality the miserably negative role belonged to McCourt's drunken and reckless father. He writes, "When I look back on my childhood I wonder how I survived at all. It was, of course, a miserable childhood; the happy childhood is hardly worth your while. Worse than the ordinary miserable childhood is the miserable Irish childhood, and worse yet is the miserable Irish Catholic childhood." And there are tons more that would agree with whole hearts and big mouths.

At any rate, the city's grousing hasn't kept it from making tons of money off bus and walking tours catering to American readers eager to see the locations in Limerick that were mentioned in the book. Bottom line: *Angela's Ashes* is depressing and emotionally gut-wrenching, but it's extremely well-written, proving that the old Irish storytellers do indeed have their contemporary counterparts. Required reading.

wired

The eight PCs at **Webster's Internet Café** *(Thomas St.; Tel 061/312-066; 9am-9pm Mon-Sat, 1-9pm Sun; £6 per hour, £5 students; webster@iica.net; No credit cards)* aren't terribly fast, but they're adequate. Surprisingly, it's the only net cafe in Limerick. Don't forget to ask for your free tea or coffee if you've been surfing for an hour or more. For everything you ever wanted to know about Limerick, go to ***www.visitLimerick.com.***

trees and a waterfall. Members of Limerick's college crowd usually come here in the afternoons—and later, of course—for a pint or two and some laid-back conversation.

Good spots for sitting around for a couple of hours scoping out people and writing in your travel diary are **The Ice Café** and **Java's** [see *eats,* below]. Java's is open 'til 1am during the week and 3am on weekends, making it the unrivaled late-night Limerick hangout. (The food's pretty good, too.)

bar scene

There might not be any live music to speak of, but the **Old Quarter** *(Little Ellen St.; Tel 061/401-190; 10am-11:30pm; No credit cards)* is one of young, trendy Limerick's most popular pubs, thanks to pleasant outdoor seating, better-than-average pub food all day long, and a DJ most nights of the week. A spiffy modern design—complete with a horseshoe-shaped, marble-topped bar that bridges two rooms.

Sprawling and spacious with three different bars, **Riddler's** *(9 Sarsfield St.; Tel 061/414-149; 10am-11:30pm; V, MC, AE)* serves excellent bar food between noon and 4pm for only £5-6 for a full meal, even sirloin steak. A whole room has been set aside as a rugby shrine, and the walls are teeming with memorabilia. DJs spin Thursday-Saturday, and various live music shakes the floorboards on Friday, Sunday, and Monday (see *live music scene,* below).

Nestor's *(28 O'Connell St.; Tel 061/317-333; noon-3pm/5-10pm daily; V, MC, AE)* is another good choice for lunch or dinner, along with lively trad and folk music sessions most nights of the week. As always, lunch is a better value than dinner—be prepared to spend around £12 for a full meal after 5pm.

Renowned for its fine beer garden and rollicking trad sessions, **Nancy Blake's** *(19 Upper Denmark St.; Tel 061/416-443; 10am-11:30pm)* has that precious spit-and-sawdust-style atmosphere, complete with dim lighting, roaring open fires, fine pub grub, and plenty of local gossip.

On a dry day, it's virtually impossible to find a seat outside at **The Locke Bar** *(3 Georges Quay; Tel 061/413-773; 10am-11:30pm),* hands-down the best spot in the city for lounging around and doing nothing (besides guzzling down a pint or two, of course). The Locke was established in 1724, making it one of the oldest pubs in the city. The owner's a former rugby star who joins in on the live trad sessions twice a week; it's a shame there's not music every night, 'cause it's really, really good, and so's the pub grub.

live music scene

For all its grimness, or perhaps because of it, Limerick does deliver some of the hottest trad and folk jams around. One example is **Dolan's** *(3-4 Dock Rd.; Tel 061/314-483; 10am-11:30pm),* unrivaled as Limerick's tip-top, totally awesome, completely impressive venue for traditional Irish music and dance sessions. Both fun-loving locals and well-informed tourists make merry every night of the week.

The Warehouse *(Off Dock Rd.; Tel 061/314-483; Music Thur-Sat; £5-9, more for well-known acts),* run by Dolan's, brings both hot and just-getting-started musical talents from every genre to center stage for sweaty oh-so-enthusiastic young crowds. Check the free *Limerick Events Guide,* out every two weeks, for the lowdown.

A stage frequented by Limerick's best college bands, **Doc's** [see *club scene,* below] offers fantastic live rock, reggae, folk, and acoustic acts Tuesday, Thursday, and Sunday nights.

You'll hear similar stuff (minus the reggae, and add the trad) every Monday and Tuesday at **Molly Malone's** *(72 Catherine St.; Tel 061/411-680; No credit cards),* named for Ireland's most infamous fishmonger.

Friday, Sunday, and Monday nights, pub-goers at **Riddler's** [see *bar scene,* above] also enjoy a varied mix of live tunes. Here in Limerick, if you're put in **The Doghouse** *(19 Thomas St.; Tel 061/313-177; 11am-*

run, spot, run

Attempt to win back all the money you spent drinking last night while immersing yourself in a very Irish ritual at the **Limerick Greyhound Track** *(Market's Field, Mulgrave St.; Tel 061/415-170; Admission £3).* Pick up a brochure from the Tourist Office on Arthur's Quay [see *need to know,* above] and they'll knock a punt off the admission price. Races take place every Monday, Thursday, and Saturday at 8pm.

limerick city

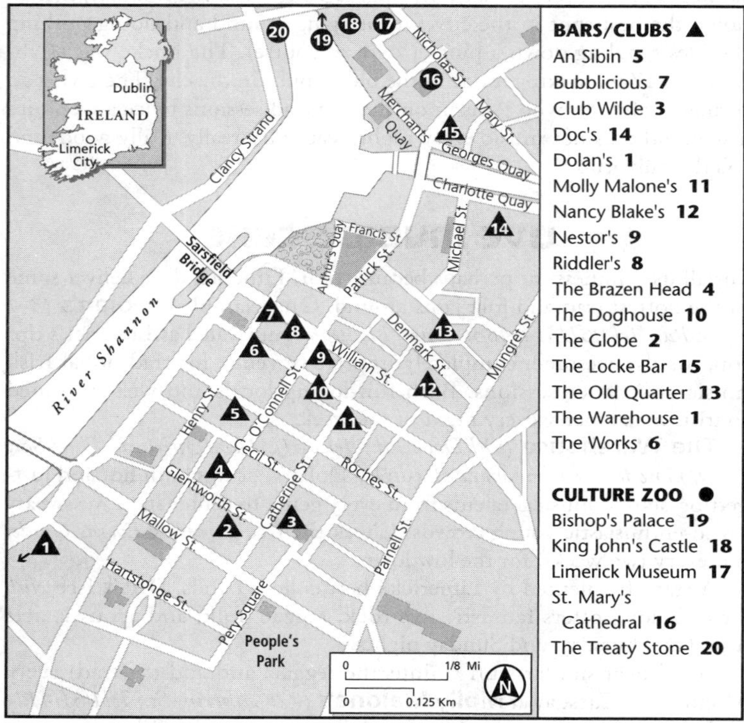

11pm daily) it's definitely no punishment, especially if you're a blues fan: Live sessions come virtually every night.

Second only to Dolan's, **An Sibìn** *(The Royal George Hotel, O'Connell St.; Tel 061/414-566; 11am-11pm daily)* has the trad thing going on every single night in the summer, aside from a few scattered country music nights. (Hope the night you're in town's not one of them.) Crowded and dim, the atmosphere inspires a deliciously warm and drowsy feeling to go along with the heavenly sounds of the fiddle and *bodhrán*—but then again, you could've just downed one too many pints.

You'll find more live trad sessions at **The Locke Bar** on Sundays and Tuesdays, at **Nancy Blake's** on Sunday through Wednesday nights; and at **Nestor's** on Wednesday through Sunday [see *bar scene,* above, for all]. As per usual, live music venues let the tunes commence between 9 and 9:30pm.

club scene

Like nightspots in any other Irish city, Limerick's clubs generally open their doors at 11pm, serve the booze 'til 1, and kick everybody out around

2am. FYI: You'll find that **Hanratty's Hotel** [see *crashing*, below] offers a nightclub as well, but you definitely won't find Limerick's coolest twenty-somethings present.

Undoubtedly the trendiest club in Limerick, **The Globe** *(Cecil St.; Tel 061/313-533; 11pm-2am daily; £5 cover)* serves fancy (and unbelievably expensive) drinks to Irish rock legends (like U2, for one—or four) at its members-only bar on the top floor. Downstairs, Limerick's hippest young things shake and groove amid tacky sexually explicit artwork 'til long after the cows have come home. Dress to impress or bring enough attitude to make even ratty jeans cool.

For those of us old enough to rent a car, there's always **The Works** *(Bedford Row; Tel 061/411-611; 11pm-2am daily; Cover approx. £6),* where bright flashing lights illuminate the skimpily clad and the totally schnockered. The music's mostly pop with a dash of indie mixed in. Pick up concessions, which are coupons for all manner of club freebies, at the **Sarsfield Bridge Inn** [see *crashing*, below], among other places around town.

Is there anything **Doc's** *(The Granary, Michael St.; Tel 061/318-466; Wed-Sun)* doesn't do? Yep, they've got a nightclub too, as popular in the wee morning hours with the UL (University of Limerick) and LCAD (Limerick College of Art and Design) students as it is during the day. Doc's would be your best bet if you're not yet old enough to drink at home. Expect the more driving variety of pop-rock tracks on the sound system.

Popular with Limerick's young professional crowd, **The Brazen Head,** known to locals as **Ted's** *(102 O'Connell Street; Tel 061/417-412; £5 weekday cover, £6 weekend cover)* offers two bars (one catering to sports freaks—er, fans) as well as a nightclub blasting popular music every night of the week. Ted's makes for a relatively generic clubbing experience, but after The Globe that might just be exactly what you're after.

arts scene

It might not rival Dublin—yet—but Limerick's got some great little galleries tucked away in its classy old Georgian-style structures.

▸▸VISUAL ARTS

The **Angela Woulfe Gallery** *(16 Pery Sq.; Tel 061/310-164; 11am-5pm Mon-Thur, open Fri-Sat by appointment; Free admission)* displays beautiful oil paintings by Irish and European painters, several of which hang in the University of Johannesburg as well as the European Parliament. (They *must* be good.)

Prints, prints, and more prints. This pretty much sums up **Chris Doswell's** *(Nicholas St., King's Island; Tel 061/318-29-92; 9am-5:30pm Mon-Fri, 10:30am-2:30pm Sat; Free admission),* which showcases the works of Irish printmakers working with etchings, engravings, and lithographs. Not cheap, but a cool investment if you've brought along a poster tube.

"Art for all" is the motto of **The '75' Gallery,** *(75 O'Connell St.; Tel 061/315-650; 10am-5:30pm Mon-Fri; Free admission)* a tiny gallery with

limerick city

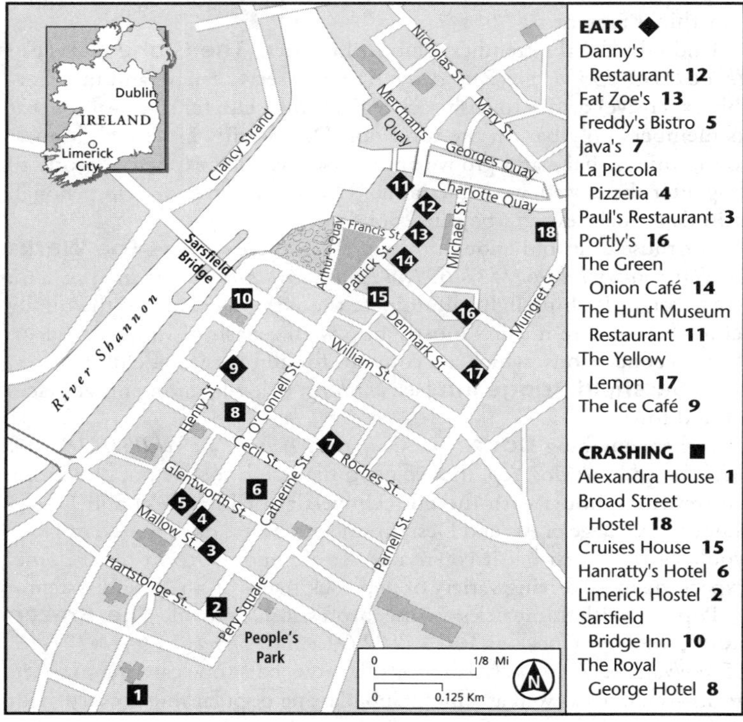

a ton of enthusiasm to make up for the lack of space. Edgy, 'Op'-y and outsider stuff in droves.

The **Limerick City Gallery of Art** *(Pery Sq.; Tel 061/310-633; 10am-1pm Mon-Sat, 2-6pm Mon-Fri, 2-7pm Thur; Free admission)* boasts an extensive permanent collection, a fraction of which is squished haphazardly into a solitary room in the back of the building. The other rooms in the gallery house visiting exhibitions; sometimes only a few works will be placed in an entire room. This leaves viewers wondering why more space isn't given to the permanent collection that's supposedly so marvelous. The Limerick City Gallery also has several notable pieces by Sean Keating and Jack Butler Yeats, so why not show 'em off? Don't pass this one up: The frequent visiting exhibitions are often wildly experimental and totally entertaining. (For example, one artist, Alan Keane, hung a series of very old school desktops upon which were scribbled universal and revolutionary ponderings as well as the usual crass "yo' mama" jokes, with an Irish twist, naturally. "If you had no feet would you still wear shoes?" or "If you had no mouth would you still talk shite?")

Even if you aren't a connoisseur of fine art, you'll appreciate **The Hunt Museum** *(The Old Custom House, Rutland St.; Tel 061/312-833; Mon-Sat 10am-5pm; £4.20 adults, £3.20 students)* which houses some of the most outstanding and exquisite ancient and medieval artifacts, paintings, and sculptures outside of Dublin. In fact, The Hunt is arguably *the* best art museum outside of Dublin in terms of breadth. Hey, they've a Picasso painting and a bronze horse crafted by none other than the original Renaissance Man himself, Leonardo da Vinci. The Hunt family collected all this stuff over several decades and enjoyed it in their own home before donating it to the city—imagine a wooden medieval icon on the table next to your remote control. The whole place is just chock-full of totally fascinating stuff. Don't miss it.

The **Belltable Arts Centre** [see *performing arts,* below] frequently houses temporary visual art exhibitions which showcase up-and-coming Limerick artists as well as more established Irish and international artists.

▸▸PERFORMING ARTS

Established a mere two decades ago, **Belltable Arts Centre** *(O'Connell St.; Tel 061/319-866; 9am-9pm Mon-Fri, 10am-9pm Sat)* offers ample facilities, including a relatively small-but-cozy theater, a space for frequent visiting art exhibitions, a film club, a coffee shop, and a bar. The theater hosts all the excellent brand-new plays traveling all over the country by Ireland's finest contemporary playwrights. The Belltable is often used for poetry readings, film screenings, lectures, and dance, opera, and music performances.

The grand **University Concert Hall** *(University of Limerick campus; Tel 061/331-549; Most performances begin at 8pm; Tickets £10-15)* hosts all kinds of musical entertainment, including a good measure of inspiring, edifying-type classical stuff. To find out what's on and when, pick up the free ***Limerick Events Guide,*** published every two weeks.

gay scene

If you're looking for support resources while you're in Limerick, unfortunately you'll have to do a bit of hunting around. The **Gay Switchboard**

festivals and events

No doubt one of the coolest, most talked-about events of the year, the **Limerick School of Art and Design Annual Fashion Show** *(Early June; Tel 061/208-208; Tickets around £12)* is the culmination of months of hard work on the part of aspiring designers. Don't miss it if you happen to be in the area in early June. The **Limerick Good Food Festival** *(early June; www.limerickgood food.com)* is another great way to kick off the Limerick summer; it's held at various times and locations around town.

Limerick *(P.O. Box 151, GPO, Limerick; Tel 061/310-101; 7:30-9:30pm Mon-Tue)* and the **Lesbian Line Limerick** *(Same; 7:30-9:30pm Thur)* aren't exactly available 24-7, but they're better than nothing. There's also a **Drop In Centre** *(29 Mallow St.; Same Tel; 2-4pm Sat),* sponsored by the Gay Switchboard, where anybody can stop in for tea and a nice long chat.

As for nightspots, **Bubblicious** *(Savoy Complex, Bedford Row; www.geocities.com/bubblicious_ie/bubblicious.html; Open Fri and Sun)* has been bumping and grinding since King John still inhabited his castle. (OK, maybe not, but it's been around for a good while anyway.) It's definitely a blissful disco gay joint but has a welcoming vibe for all.

If you're in town the first weekend of the month, **Club Wilde** *(Glentworth St.; First Sat of every month at 11pm)* holds a monthly fundraising social function benefiting the Gay Switchboard Limerick—things get wild here in the basement of the Glentworth Hotel with friendly beering, flirting, and friend-making. You'll find other Saturday nights at this venue gay-friendly as well. These are probably your best bets for seeing and being seen in the city. The club lies a 5-minute walk northeast of the Shannon Bridge, on the east bank of town, one block north of the City Gallery of Art.

culture zoo

Any grittiness to the city itself is more than balanced out by soaring, atmospheric fortresses, cathedrals, and musty museum exhibits on the private lives of 19th-century Limerickians.

Limerick Museum *(Castle Lane, Nicholas St.; Tel 061/417-826; 10am-1pm/2:15-5pm Tue-Sat; Free admission):* Since it's right next to the castle—and it's free—you might as well check out the Limerick Museum. Not that it's all *that* yawn-inspiring; there are a few cool things to look at. Check out the collections of really old furniture, clocks, silverware, and intricate lace patterns. Don't worry—it doesn't mean you're a frump if you get a kick out of 19th-century boudoir accessories and it's definitely worth a quick look at the old photographs, manuscripts, and other stuff redolent of Limerick's history.

King John's Castle *(Nicholas St.; Tel 061/411-201; 9:30am-5:30pm Apr-Oct daily; Admission £4.20 adults, £3.30 students):* Built somewhere around the year 1200, this castle should win an award for the ugliest castle in the whole country. Granted, it served as a strategic military center for hundreds of years, but definitely don't come here expecting something lonely, beautiful, and romantic and covered in ivy. They've sadly turned it into the typical touristy visitor's hub, with a 20-minute video detailing the castle's history, but a tour through dark tunnels beneath the floors does at least offer a frisson of creepiness.

St. Mary's Cathedral *(Bridge St.; Tel 061/416-238; 9am-5pm Mon-Sat June-Sept, 9am-1pm Mon-Sat Oct-May; £1 donation demanded):* The effect of St. Mary's Cathedral looming before you while the cold morning rain drenches you to your very bones is totally unforgettable. As was customary in the late 12th century, a Munster king donated the land to the Church and ever since this huge, awe-inspiring structure has occupied this spot overlooking the River Shannon. The interior is full of ancient and wonderfully ornamented tombs, as well as an incredible set of 15th-century misericords (the extensions of choir seats that supported tired choirboys when they stood) carved in black oak. It's old, cold, and creepy—and if you like Goth, try sneaking up the precariously narrow staircase at the back of the church that leads to the tower. The view of the interior from above ought to make you feel taller, but instead you end up feeling the size of a mouse just gazing down at it all.

Treaty Stone *(on the quay, opposite King John's Castle; Free admission):* Not much more than a big rock on a pedestal, Treaty Stone commemorates—what else?—the Treaty of Limerick, which promised protection to Irish Catholics from the English in 1691 but was almost immediately reneged on.

eamon de valera

So how'd a guy with a name like that end up one of the most important figures in Irish history? Limerick-bred Eamon de Valera was born in New York City to a Spanish father and an Irish mother. After his father died when de Valera was still a wee little thing, his mother sent him to Ireland to live with his uncle. As a young man, de Valera became involved with the Irish Volunteers working toward an independent Irish republic. During the Easter Uprising in 1916, his ambush resulted in the greatest Irish victory of the rebellion. When finally captured, de Valera's American citizenship saved him from the death penalty; granted amnesty in 1917, he served as president of Sinn Féin until 1926. When the British carved up Ireland in their 1921 treaty, de Valera headed the anti-treaty forces who refused to compromise, leading Ireland into the civil war in 1922. After his side was defeated, he formed a new political party, the Fianna Fáil, the "Soldiers of Destiny," and was elected to the Irish Parliament (the *Dáil*), serving despite his refusal to swear allegiance to the King of England. The Fianna Fáil party dominated Irish politics for a decade and a half; later, after the Irish republic was established in 1949, de Valera served two terms as its president. It's difficult to envision modern Irish politics without his influence.

take me out to the hurling match

You can watch the University of Limerick hurling team pull off amazing feats of grunting on the UL campus in Castleroy *(call 061/202-854 for information);* only problem is there's no public transportation and it's far enough that hitching or cabbing it will have to do.

Tollgate and **Bishop's Palace:** Both are located behind the castle, on the right side of the Shannon, in the vicinity of the Thomond Bridge at the northern end of the city, and both are pretty self-explanatory. Bishop's Palace was built in the 18th century.

great outdoors

You'll have to venture out of the city a bit, but there are plenty of opportunities for fresh air and exercise.

Situated on the outskirts of the city, **Coonagh Equestrian Centre** *(Coonagh, Ennis Rd., Limerick City; Tel 061/327-348)* offers treks through nearby forests, and all skill levels are accommodated. The only catch is, if you haven't got wheels, you'll have to cab it out to your mount.

Odd, but Shannonside **University of Limerick Activity and Sailing Centre** *(Killaloe, County Clare; Tel 061/376-622; £5-12 an hour)* isn't actually *in* County Limerick. To do some windsurfing, canoeing, or sailing, you first gotta catch Bus Éireann from the Limerick Bus Station to Killaloe (routes 323 or 345; one or two buses daily), which takes about 40 minutes. It's pretty much do-it-yourself sailing, though, so this is not the place for a guided tour of the waters.

Looking for secluded backcountry roads for bicycling or a nice long contemplative walk? County Limerick's got lots of 'em. Many cycling and walking routes across the Shannon region are signposted; just pick up a map or two at the **Limerick Tourist Office** [see *need to know,* below] and be on your merry way. One of these routes is the **Lough Derg Way,** stretching 58 km (36 mi) from Limerick City northward to Killaloe, where the UL Sailing Centre is located, and then uphill onto Dromineer, further along the banks of the Shannon. It makes a nice bike ride even if you aren't going to go for all of it (and you probably aren't).

Lough Gur *(Lough Gur, Limerick; Always open; Free admission),* one of Ireland's most important archaeological sites, makes for a perfect afternoon of cycling and exploring. Excavated and studied by John Hunt, benefactor of **The Hunt Museum** [see *arts scene,* above], the site was occupied continuously from Neolithic times. You'll see a 4,500-year-old wedge-shaped tomb serving as a communal grave, the Grange Stone Circle (Ireland's "Stonehenge"), and ruins of homes at least a thousand years old, —and in the middle of it all is a beautiful lake in a sylvan setting. Lough Gur's an excellent day trip out of Limerick City; rent a bike from any of several places in town [see *need to know,* below]. One tip: Don't bother with the **Lough Gur Visitor's Centre** *(Lough Gur, Limerick; Tel 061/361-511; 10am-6pm mid-May to Sept; Admission £3/£2.50 students),* except maybe to use the bathroom (if they'll let you). Like so many other "visitor centers" springing up around important (and some not-so-important) cultural attractions, this one's definitely not worth the admission fee. Biking to Lough Gur isn't for couch potatoes, though—it's 11.3 km (7 mi) southeast of Limerick on roads that aren't always flat.

stuff

Pick up some local craftsperson's creations, get a style makeover, or help fill out those loose clothes by eating gobs of fresh fudge. It's all here if you know where to shop.

▸▸MALL RATS

You can probably find whatever you're looking for at **Arthur's Quay Shopping Centre** *(Arthur's Quay; Tel 061/419-888; 9am-7pm Mon-Wed, 9am-9pm Fri-Sat; 9am-6pm Sun)* or **Cruises Street Shopping Centre** *(Cruises St., off Patrick St.; No phone; Various times).* These are the places to replace the walking shoes you've worn out, pick up standard-issue mall requisites or a souvenir that also looks and wears well.

▸▸CRAFTY

For all that craftsy souvenir stuff, try **C.C. Mirrors and Picture Boxes** *(Workspace, Michael St.; Tel 061/416-800)* for fancy mirrors and neat little picture boxes.

fashion

It's surprising that young Limerick residents haven't positioned themselves at the very cutting edge of fashion, considering that the well-respected School of Art and Design is located in this city. As in most other places, guys usually opt for rugby shirts, windpants, and the like, and girls dress in clingy, neon-colored duds from any of the popular chain clothing stores you'll find in the Arthur's Quay Shopping Centre.

The Garvey Enterprise Centre *(10 John's St.; Tel 061/400-488)* offers pretty papier mâché bowls and jugs (now how come we never learned to make stuff like this at the arts and crafts table at summer camp?)

For all things ceramic, try **Mary Gleeson** *(4 Denmark St.; Tel 061/319-533).*

eats

As in so many cities nowadays, Limerick offers more in the way of expensive restaurants perched on the rim of pretentiousness than laid-back, inexpensive little spots with plenty of personality and punch.

▸▸CHEAP

Limerick suffers from a lack of good cheap cafes, but there are still a few worth checking out. **Java's** *(5 Catherine St.; 061/418-077; 9am-1am Mon-Wed, 9am-3am Thur-Sat, 10:30am-1am Sun; No credit cards)* rules the late-night scene. (Maybe that's because it's the only place open that late.) Limerick's youngsters come here to feast on herbal teas and yummy sandwiches and salads, chat among themselves, and chill to the sounds of mellow jazz on the speakers 'til long after their curfews.

The Ice Café *(Henry St.; 061/319-790; 9am-8pm Mon-Wed, 9am-midnight Thur-Sun)* offers the same deal: basically—good cheap food and a great vibe, although it's not open as late.

For inexpensive breakfasts, try **Danny's Restaurant** *(3 Rutland St.; Tel 061/400-694; Mon-Fri 8:15am-5pm; No credit cards),* a comfortable little spot for a £3 full breakfast the morning after that late-night pub crawl.

The perfect little Italian place, with red-and-white-checked tablecloths and Chianti baskets hanging from the ceiling, is **La Piccola Pizzeria** *(O'Connell St.; 061/313-899; 12-3pm/5-10:30pm Mon-Fri, 5:30-10:30pm Sat, 6-10pm Sun; No credit cards).* You'll find sandwiches and salads here for under £3, pasta for 5 or 6 punts, and pizzas for less than £8.

You can get good pub grub that won't squeeze your wallet dry at most bars in town, including **Doc's** and **The Old Quarter** [see *bar scene,* above].

▸▸DO-ABLE

Sip tea and munch on a large plate of chicken or veggie loaf and vegetables at a table overlooking the River Shannon at **The Hunt Museum Restaurant** *(The Old Custom House, Rutland St.; Tel 061/312-662; 10am-5pm Mon-Sat, 2-5pm Sun; Main courses £5-12; V, MC).* It's self-service, so the food's served up fast, but it tastes just like something your grandmother (an expert cook, of course) would make you for dinner on a Sunday afternoon.

You'll find similar "contemporary Irish" fare at trendy **Portly's** *(Little Ellen St., off Denmark St.; Tel 061/313-388; 10am-6pm Mon-Sat; All items £4-10; V, MC, AE).*

The ever-popular **Green Onion Café** *(3 Ellen St.; Tel 061/400-710; 12-9:45pm Mon-Sat)* offers pasta dishes and the like, with more reasonable prices at lunch than during dinnertime. It's also a handy and comfortable spot for recharging.

irish coffee

Not to be confused with Bailey's coffee, which is just regular coffee with a shot of Bailey's Irish Cream, **Irish Coffee** was "invented" by Joe Sheridan, the head bartender at the Shannon Airport, just after World War II. To make some yourself (and impress your friends), put two teaspoons of brown sugar into a stemmed glass, fill the glass up a third with Irish whiskey, and two-thirds with very hot, very fresh black coffee, so that the mixture's about a half-inch below the top of the glass. Stir well, then spread light whipped cream over the top with the back of a spoon without stirring.

Craving a good pizza? **Fat Zoe's** *(Unit 1, Rutland St.; Tel 061/314-717; 5-10:30pm Mon-Sat)* serves 'em up right, along with pasta dishes and all that other good stuff—it's your typical candlelit sit-down pizzeria and family restaurant.

▸▸SPLURGE

One of the most well-established and well-respected places to eat in Limerick, **Freddy's Bistro** *(Theatre Lane, between Lower Mallow and Lower Glentworth Sts.; Tel 061/418-749; 5:30pm-late Tue-Sun)* serves the usual steaks, chicken, and seafood for around £13 but is at least handy and capable.

It might bear the most redundant name in town, but **The Yellow Lemon** *(Cornmarket Sq.; No phone; 12-4pm/6pm-late Tue-Sat; Dinner £10-15; V, MC)* is where the young and polished come to sip wine and chat effervescently over candlelit dinners. The decor is sleekly minimalist, the portions are generous, and the vibe is far from sour. Suitably enough, the ice cream and lemon tart (£3.95) are as delicious as the restaurant's yellow facade is bright.

Favored by locals for its clean, modern space and delicious dishes in an unpretentious atmosphere, **Paul's Restaurant** *(59 O'Connell St.; Tel 061/316-600; Lunch 12-2:30pm Mon-Fri, dinner 5:45-10:30pm Tue-Sat)* offers a three-course early bird menu from 5:45 to 7pm daily. For the main course, try the sautéed breast of chicken in a toasted sesame seed and coconut sauce, or perhaps the fillet of salmon topped with a roasted red pepper and almond pesto sauce. One word: Delish.

crashing

There used to be a ton of hostels to choose from in Limerick, but nearly all of them have been converted into living spaces for the economically disadvantaged, a major housing trend in Ireland these days. The two hostels in the city are comfortable enough, but they're by no means outstanding.

▸▸CHEAP

A solid choice, the **Broad Street Hostel** *(Broad St.; Tel 061/317-222; broadstreethostel@tinet.ie; £10.50 4-bed dorms, £15 singles, £15-17 doubles and twins per person; V, MC)* offers super-tight security, continental breakfast, excellent kitchen facilities, and spacious four-bed dorm rooms with desks. You'll find the place immaculate and the staff friendly, although the social vibe here's hovering somewhere around zero.

What really stinks about the An Öige **Limerick Hostel** *(1 Pery Sq.; Tel 061/314-672; £7.50-8.50 14-bed dorms; V, MC)* is the midnight curfew and often temperamental staff. Well, at least the place is clean and pleasant, with nice views of the People's Park, and it's right across from the main bus and train station—a sure plus if it's raining like mad when you arrive.

▸▸DO-ABLE

Two of the best bed-and-breakfast options in town are the brand-spanking-new **Cruises House** *(Denmark St.; Tel 061/315-320; £32 single, £48 double)* and Victorian **Alexandra House** *(O'Connell St.; Tel 061/318-472; £20 per person, £22.50 with bath)* both of which offer pleasant bedrooms and delicious Irish fry breakfasts.

At the **Sarsfield Bridge Inn** *(Sarsfield St.; Tel 061/317-179; rooms@sarsfield-bridge.com; £30 single, £35 deluxe; V, MC),* clean, spare, modern rooms, a light breakfast, and surprisingly helpful staff (considering that it's a hotel) make a perfectly good, but by no means fancy, option. Feel free to use the kitchen. Pick up passes for any of the nightclubs in town at the front desk, where you can also get good advice on the best pubs, clubs, and restaurants in town.

Limerick also sports the moderately priced **Clifton House** *(Ennis Rd.; Tel/Fax 061/451-224; Michaelpowell@eircom.com; £32 single, £50 double, all rooms have private bath; V, MC),* where there's a bus that pulls up right in front to take you into downtown Limerick.

▸▸SPLURGE

The oldest hotel in Limerick, **Hanratty's Hotel** *(5 Glentworth St.; Tel 061/410-999; £29-35 single, £55 double; V, MC, AE, DC)* has that cool old-world thing going on in every room. It's a favorite among corporate bigwigs on business trips, probably because Eamon de Valera used to stay here all the time [see *eamon de valera,* above].

Another option, if you can afford it, would be **The Royal George Hotel** *(O'Connell St.; Tel 061/414-566; Rates vary with availability, £39-59; V, MC, AE),* with comfortable rooms that can sleep up to three people for around £60 altogether. A good deal, if three's not a crowd. Bonus: An Sibìn [see *bar scene,* above], one of Limerick's coolest nightspots and a splendid venue for live trad, is just downstairs.

within 30 minutes

Adare is one of the prettiest little towns in the country, the quintessential postcard subject just 16 km (9.9 mi) southwest of Limerick City. Unfortunately, everybody knows it, and now the little town's bulging with fancy hotels, craft shops, and restaurants. It makes a fine afternoon for a picnic and a leisurely walk though: Take a 25-minute Bus Éireann ride (routes 13 or 14; at least 8 buses per day from Limerick's main station) [see *need to know,* below]. You'll find that the **Adare Heritage Centre** *(Main St.; Tel 061/396-666; 9am-7pm Mon-Fri, 9am-6pm Sat-Sun June-Oct, 9am-5pm Mon-Fri Nov-Dec and Mar-May)* is better than most of the useless visitor centers at historical sites.

need to know

Currency Exchange Bank of Ireland *(O'Connell St.; Tel 061/415-055)* and **AIB** *(O'Connell St.; Tel 061/414-388)* both have ATMs. The first is the better deal for exchanging money.

Tourist Information The Limerick Tourism Centre *(Arthur's Quay; Tel 061/317-522; 9:30am-5:30pm Mon-Fri, 9:30am-1pm Sat Nov-Apr, 9:30am-5:30pm Mon-Sat May-June, Sept-Oct, 9am-7pm Mon-Fri, 9am-6pm Sat-Sun July-Aug)* has loads of useful leads on accommodation and sites.

Public Transportation Walk: This city isn't that big. Otherwise, call **Top Cabs** *(Wickham St.; Tel 061/417-417)* for a ride. Public transport exists but is really not worth the long waits and complicated schedules.

Health and Emergency Dial 999 for emergencies, otherwise it's **St. John's Hospital** *(St. John's Sq.; Tel 061/415-822)*; **Garda Headquarters** *(Henry St.; Tel 061/414-222)* is the main police station.

Pharmacies Hogan's Pharmacy *(45 Upper William St.; Tel 061/415-195, 088/526-800 after hours)* or **Charlotte Quay Pharmacy** *(Charlotte Quay; Tel 061/400-722; 9am-9pm daily).*

Airlines The Shannon Airport *(Ennis Rd., N18; Tel 061/471-444)* is about 15 miles west of Limerick and accommodates flights to Europe and North America via **Aer Lingus** *(Tel 061/471-666).* **Bus Éireann** runs to the airport on its way to Ennis. Buses leave at least two dozen times a day, a dozen or more on Sundays, from the main station, Colbert.

Trains Colbert Station *(Parnell St.; Tel 061/315-555),* across from the People's Park, sends Irish Rail cars to Ennis and to Limerick Junction, where you'll have to make a transfer to get anyplace else.

Bus Lines Out of the City Bus Éireann, also at Colbert Station *(Tel 061/313-333)* runs buses to Ennis (seven a day), Waterford (five a day), Dublin (five to eight per day), Killarney (three to six), Cork (around six a day), and Sligo (six a day), among other destinations. Buses timed to meet the ferries at Rosslare Harbour leave four times a day. Pick up a timetable at the station.

Bike Rental Emerald Cycles *(1 Patrick St.; Tel 061/416-983; emarl dalp@tinet.ie; 9:15am-5:30pm Mon-Sat; £10 per day, £40 per week, £40 deposit),* offers one-way service for an extra £12. But you can also get bikes at **McMahon's Cycle World** *(25 Roches St.; Tel 061/415-202; 9am-6pm Mon-Sat; £7 per day, £30 per week).*

Laundry **Speediwash Laundrette & Dry Cleaners** *(11 St. Gerard St.; Tel 061/319-380)* will let you do your own or leave it, while **Laundrette** *(Mallow St.; Tel 061/312-712; Full service £5; 8am-6pm Mon-Fri, 8am-5pm Sat)* is strictly do-it-yourself.

Internet See *wired,* above.

everywhere else

bunratty

Two words: *tourist central.* (If you don't count Killarney, of course.) Bunratty attracts all of 'em, so if mass tourism isn't your thing, don't come here. That said, the nightly "medieval" banquets in the country's (supposedly) most authentically restored castle can be a lot of fun, if you've got deep enough pockets. A dinner (*sans* utensils—remember, it's "authentically medieval") and a show featuring young lasses dressed in garishly bright costumes will set you back around £35.

culture zoo

It's hard to say whether the main cultural attraction here is the castle or the phenomenal number of tourists who visit it as though it were a Disney World ride. **Bunratty Castle and Folk Park** *(Limerick-Ennis Rd., Bunratty; Tel 061/360-788; 9:30am-5:30pm Sept-May, 9am-6:30pm June-Aug, last admission to the castle at 4pm all year; Admission around £6/£4 students; V, MC, AE, DC)* consists of a sort of living history park and the completely restored castle, which dates to 1425 and is filled with authentic interiors and furnishings. You can take a castle tour during the day and partake of the feasts at night, as long as you've booked ahead; the banquets are held at 5:30pm and 8:45pm all year. (There's also a slightly cheaper—we're talking £5—plebeian version in a cottage on the premises.) As for the Folk Park, it was begun in the '60s when the guys building a new runway at Shannon Airport moved an old cottage out to Bunratty instead of tearing it down. Now it's the picture of a "typical" 19th-century Irish village—school, shops, cottages, grocery stores—and you can shop and browse around as you please. There's also a huge pub, **Durty Nelly's,** that accommodates the immense flow of tourists. The pub was founded in the early 1600s and got its name due to first-owner Nelly's, shall we say, *side* business.

Mead wine has always been the "drink of the high kings of Ireland," and for centuries even after the kings were gone it was a favorite tipple of the upper classes. (The rest of us drank plain old beer.) Mead is still brewed in the **Bunratty Winery** *(Bunratty; Tel 061/362-222; bunrattywinery@iegateway.net),* and you can buy a bottle anywhere in Ireland for £8-9, or you can get a glass of it at the **Bunratty Castle** banquet [see *culture zoo,* above]. (Don't buy a glass at a restaurant: If you go to the **Celtic Cauldron** in Killarney, for example, you'll pay £3 for a mere shotglass-full.) Mead is made with barley and honey, hence the name "honey wine," and it's intoxicating in a sweet, drowsy, delicious sort of way, especially since it's got a higher alcohol content than regular wine.

crashing

There aren't any hostels in Bunratty, but you could try **Bunratty Woods Country House** *(Low Rd., Bunratty; Tel 061/369-689; ireland.iol.ie/~bunratty; Approx. £45 double, includes full breakfast; V, MC),* which is gorgeously furnished and only a 10-minute walk from the Folk Park and a mere 10 km (6 mi) from Shannon Airport.

need to know

Buses To get to the Castle and Folk Park, which is located 12.9 km (8 mi) northwest of Limerick, you can take **Bus Éireann** (route 51) from Cork or Limerick; buses leave on the hour, but you've got to request Bunratty as a stop.

ennis

The town of Ennis has a vaguely dreary feel that'll leave you yearning for the Clare coast. Although it's Clare's principal town, the fact that it's landlocked and on the small side—a mere 16,000 people—probably won't spark much interest on your part.

In fact, there's really only one time of year when it makes sense to linger here, and that's during **Fleadh Nua.** This festival happens the last weekend of May [try the **Ennis Tourist Office** for info, see *need to*

ennis

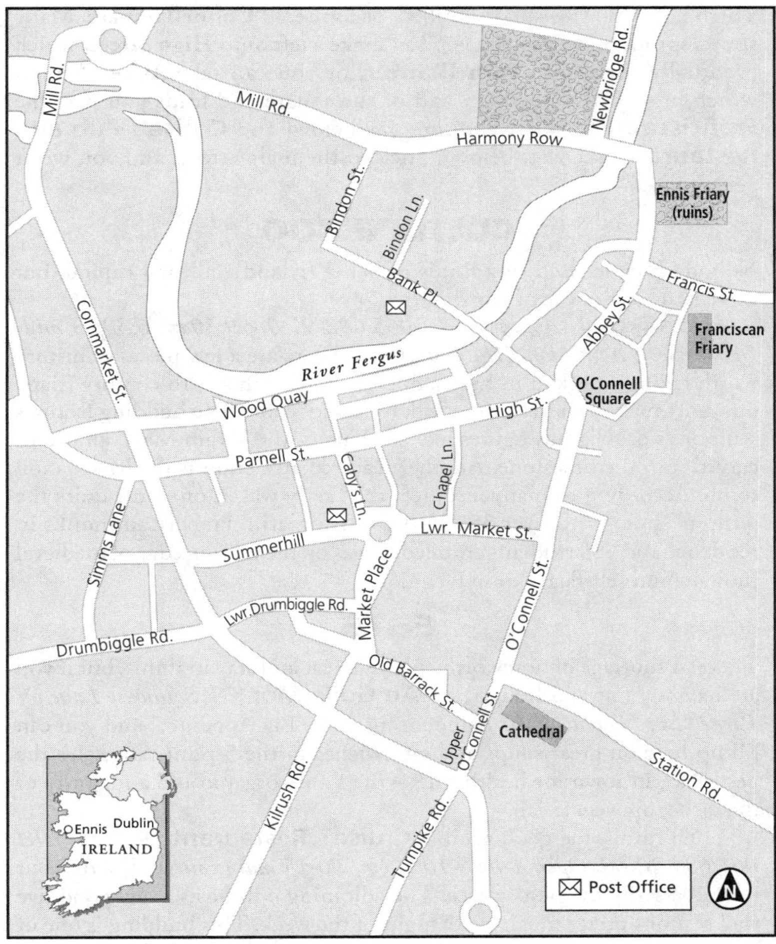

know, below, or check out ***www.c7r.com/fleadh/***] and features traditional music, dancing, and storytelling. Musicians often participate in concerts and seminars here before heading out to **Doolin** to join the regulars in the nightly trad sessions in the pubs. Otherwise, you've most likely found yourself in Ennis because you were just passing through on your way to somewhere more exciting.

Central Ennis is a rather confusing knot-work of narrow streets. If you're only spending the night and heading out early the next morning, though, it won't be hard to find your way around. To reach the town center from the bus and train station, walk down **Station Road** and then make a right onto **O'Connell Street.** You'll come to the town square, where a statue of "The Great Liberator" Daniel O'Connell stands atop a high pedestal. The square is called, of course, **O'Connell Square.** Many streets sprout off from here; you can make a left onto **High Street,** which eventually turns into **Parnell Street,** or you can take **Abbey Street,** which juts off the northern end of the square and leads you past the **Franciscan Friary** [see *culture zoo,* below] and **Cruise's Pub and Restaurant** [see *eats,* below]. Stick to the main streets and you won't get confused.

culture zoo

Nobody ever accused tiny Ennis of being Ireland's cultural capital, but there is at least one spot worth seeing.

Ennis Friary *(Abbey St.; Tel 065/682-91-00; 9:30am-6:30pm mid-May to Sept; Admission £1/40p students):* There are a few pieces of history worth taking a peek at in Ennis, one of which is this 13th-century friary, but don't make a special trip. (Still, it's pretty cool.) The building features sculptures of religious figures like St. Francis, the Virgin Mary, and Jesus carved into the limestone. Another featured attraction is the Macmahon tomb. According to many a source, the Friary was at one time quite the jumpin' spot. With over 350 burlap-sack-wearin' Franciscan monks in residence and 600 students enrolled, it was on the cutting edge of medieval thought and self-flagellation technique.

eats

There's a shortage of noteworthy places to eat and stay in Ennis, but if you are hanging out and hungry, try **An Goile Mór** *(17 Salthouse Lane off Parnell St.; No phone).* Its name means "The Big Appetite," and you can fill up here on great soups and sandwiches in the 5-punt range. It's the best place in town for health nuts—the food's organic and a majority of the dishes are vegetarian.

You'll find some good grub at **Cruise's Restaurant** *(Abbey St.; Tel 065/684-18-00; Open daily 6-10:30pm; £6-15 main courses; V, MC),* but not necessarily the best service. The adjoining pub hosts really good live trad sessions pretty much every night of the week. This building is one of the oldest in town, and the pub retains most of the original structure—cold and dim, but warmed with the enthusiasm of *craic* addicts and die-hard trad lovers.

crashing

Staying longer than you planned? There used to be two hostels in town, but they've both closed, so B&B it'll have to be. (And if you do find there's still a hostel open in town, be very wary.)

A good pick among the B&Bs would be **Derrynane House** *(O'Connell Sq.; Tel 065/682-84-64; £20 single; V, MC),* with en suite bedrooms and a vegetarian breakfast option. Despite the restaurant and bar downstairs, the rooms are surprisingly quiet.

A few more options that, while not dirt-cheap, certainly won't have you callin' home for cash include **Ardlea House** *(Clare Rd.; Tel 06/56-82-02-56, Fax 06/56-82-97-94; £19 single, £25 shared room, all rooms have private baths; V, MC),* a 10-minute walk from the town center; and the **Clare Manor House** *Clare Rd.; Tel 06/56-82-07, Fax 06/82-88-77; claremanor.ennis@eircom.ie; £28 single, £48 double; V, MC),* around 15-20 minutes outside the center of town.

need to know

Currency Exchange The **Bank of Ireland** *(O'Connell Sq.; Tel 065/682-86-15; 10am-4pm Mon-Tue and Thur-Fri, 10am-5pm Wed)* and **AIB** *(Bank Place, off O'Connell Sq.; Tel 065/682-80-89; Same hours)* both have ATMs.

Travel Information Find out about the Ennis walking trail at the **Ennis Tourist Office** *(O'Connell Sq.; Tel 065/28366; 9am-9pm June-Sept; 9am-6pm Mon-Sat, 10am-6pm Sun Oct-May).*

Health and Emergency Dial **999** or call the **Garda** *(Tel 065/682-82-05).*

Pharmacy Inside Dunnes Stores, you'll find **Michael McLoughlin** *(O'Connell St.; Tel 065/682-95-11; 9am-6pm Mon-Wed and Sat, 9am-9pm Fri-Sat).*

Airport The **Shannon Airport** *(Ennis Rd., N18; Tel 061/471-444)* is about 20 km (12.4 mi) south of Ennis and accommodates flights to Europe and North America via **Aer Lingus** *(Tel 061/471-666).* **Bus Éireann** runs to the airport on its way to Limerick; buses leave almost two dozen times a day, a dozen on Sundays.

Buses and Trains **Bus Éireann** *(Tel 065/682-41-77)* and **Irish Rail** *(Call the Limerick train station at 061/315-555 for information)* both operate out of **Ennis Station**; trains run to Limerick and on to Waterford, or you can change at Limerick Junction to reach Dublin, Killarney, Tralee, and other destinations, as well as Cork if you change again at Mallow. Buses leave for west Clare (Doolin, Kilkee, Lahinch, etc.), Limerick, the Shannon Airport, Galway, and Cork, in addition to Dublin via Limerick. Clearly posted signs outside the Bus Éireann office list the bus times for all destinations.

Bike Rental **Michael Tierney Cycles and Fishing** *(17 Abbey St.; Tel 065/682-94-33, after 6pm 065/682-12-93; 9:30am-6pm Mon-Sat; £4 per afternoon, £10 per day, £40 per week, deposit credit card or £40).*

Laundry Wash and dry for around £5 at **Parnell's** *(High St.; Tel 065/682-90-75; 9am-6pm Mon-Sat).*

Postal You'll find the **Ennis Post Office** off O'Connell Square *(Bank Place; Tel 065/682-10-54; 9am-5:30pm Mon-Fri, 9:30am-2:30pm Sat).*

doolin

It might be a teeny little town seemingly out in the middle of nowhere, occupied by scarcely more than 200 brogue-tongued *Homo sapiens* year-round, but Doolin's on the map just the same for one overwhelming reason: the music. It seems odd at first that such a small town—a village, really—with only three pubs could be so internationally renowned for its music scene, but it's true. Musicians are attracted from all over the world to play at sessions that resemble small orchestras to crowds that would rival those at any big-city concert hall. Call it the unofficial musical capital of Ireland.

This is *the* place for you guitar-strumming backpackers, if your idea of heaven is joining in at nightly trad sessions at **McDermott's, McGann's,** or **O'Connor's** [see *bar and live music scene,* below]. There's not a whole helluva lot to do in this town, but you could easily while away a few days in Doolin checking out the **Cliffs of Moher** [see *the cliffs of moher,* below]—a short drive or a leisurely hour-and-a-half's walk away—and all the other beautiful seaside scenery, and then spend all night paying jubilant homage to your musical muse.

In recent years Doolin's gotten a lot more touristy and commercialized; bed-and-breakfasts and a few extremely gaudy hotel resorts have sprouted up all over the countryside like weeds through concrete. Doolin's more established businesspeople may grumble about the influx and its (possibly) detrimental effect on the music, but everybody's profiting, and the way the music sounds nowadays, it doesn't seem to have been compromised any.

Doolin's layout consists of just a single street, **Fisherstreet,** running east-west through two clusters of buildings, one near the shore, called the **Lower Village,** where **Paddy Moloney's Doolin Hostel** [see *crashing,* below] and O'Connor's are located; and the **Upper Village** a bit inland, where the other two pubs, the **Rainbow Hostel** [see *crashing,* below], and **Bruach na hAille** [see *eats,* below] are positioned.

Don't bother hunting for an ATM; Doolin is so small, it doesn't even have its own bank. The nearest cluster of them is in Ennistymon, 16 km

outlaw music

Perhaps the traditional music is so extremely popular and pervasive today because it was outlawed during several periods in Ireland's troubled history. Elizabeth I once instructed that all Irish musicians should be hanged and their instruments burned.

bottoms up

"May your doctor never earn a penny out of you, may your heart never give out, may the ten toes of your feet steer you clear of all misfortune, and before you're much older, may you hear much better toasts than this."

(10 mi) southeast of here, so get all your banking business done before you come. Pretty much the only place in town that accepts credit cards is **O'Connor's** pub [see *bar and live music scene,* below].

bar and live music scene

Doolin's three pubs are essentially interchangeable; all three have excellent music every night of the week beginning around 9 or 9:30pm and lasting for two solid hours, as well as on Sunday afternoons.

Claustrophobics should avoid **O'Connor's** *(Lower Village; Tel 065/74168; V, MC, AE),* the most heavily touristed of the three pubs. You'll find far more people in this spacious establishment than there are residents in Doolin altogether, especially on bank holiday weekends when everybody and their uncle comes out here to escape the rush of the city. It's too crowded to be totally comfortable, but the out-of-this-world trad sessions, in which local musicians are joined by instrument-lugging travelers from all over the world, totally make up for the crunch. Find yourself a corner, sit back with that pint, and enjoy. Also note the international collection of police badges behind the bar.

Unfortunately neither **McGann's** *(Upper Village; Tel 056/707-41-33; No credit cards)* nor **McDermott's** *(Upper Village; Tel 065/707-43-28; No credit cards)* accepts plastic, so if you're hungry, thirsty, and hard-pressed for cash it'd be better to visit O'Connor's. That said, these latter two pubs are less touristy, and according to locals the music is even better at McGann's or McDermott's than at O'Connor's—which is hard to believe considering how amazing the sessions are there. Both O'Connor's and McGann's have won awards for the best live traditional music in the country, but McDermott's is no slouch: Nightly sessions in the summer are standing-room-only, and weekend winter sessions are popular as well. It's the bar favored by most locals.

culture zoo

Doolin's not exactly rich in all that cultural jazz, except for the outstanding music, of course.

Doonagore Castle *(On the coastal road, R478, 3 km south of Doolin):* This atmospheric fortress dates from the 15th century and consists of a

doolin

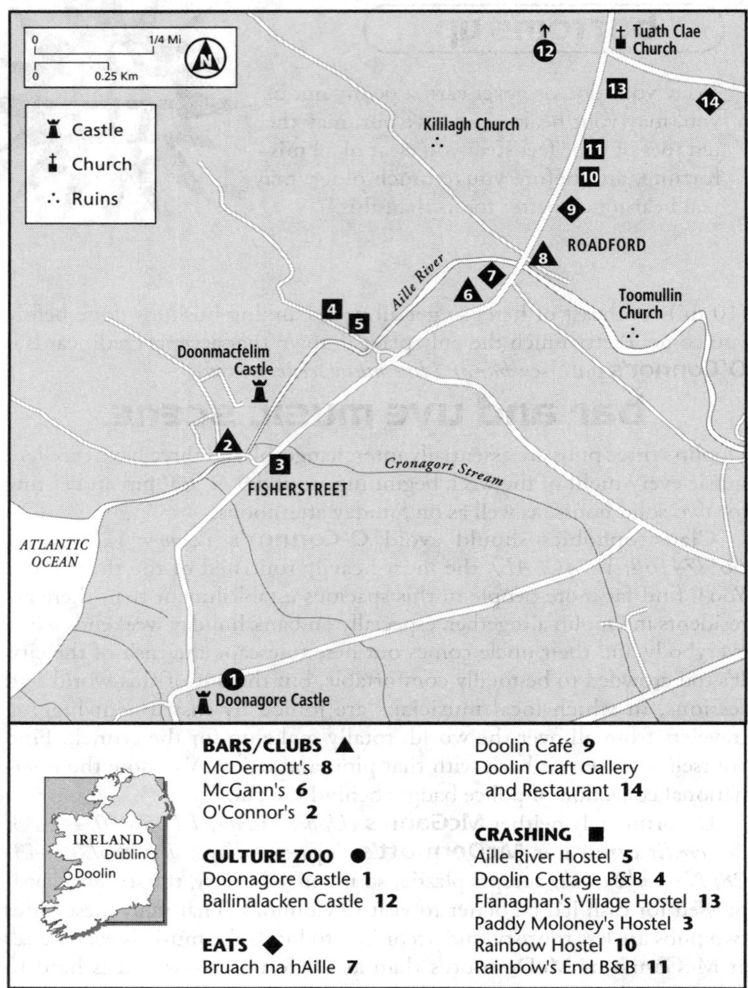

tower and a surrounding wall, all restored. It's not terribly impressive, but from here there's a great view of Doolin and the Aran Islands. The scenery's even nicer while the sun is setting.

Ballinalacken Castle *(On the road to Fanore, 5 km north of Doolin):* Perched on a small cliff, Ballinalacken is another tower house built during the same period. There are spectacular views of the Burren [see *below*] from up top. Admission to the castle is through the Ballinalacken Castle Hotel, which operates on site.

fiddles and pipes

Along with the drink, traditional music is totally inextricable from the rest of Irish culture, and if you want to immerse yourself completely in it you'd do well to brush up on the musical basics. Fiddles and guitars you've seen before, but what's that funny little drum-thing called? And how about that bagpipe-type job?

The *uilleann* ("ILL-uhn") pipes are a more complex instrument than Scottish bagpipes. They take more than a decade to master, and because of that you won't find this instrument present at trad sessions too often. It's a real treat when an *uilleann* player does sit in.

The *bodhrán* ("BOH-rawn") is the traditional drum—the *heartbeat* of Irish music, if you will. Made of wood and treated goatskin, the *bodhrán* is played with a double-headed stick called a "beater" or a *cipín.*

Other instruments used include tin whistles, as well as lutes, banjoes, and harps less frequently. You might also come across a singing style known as *seán nós,* an ancient form of unaccompanied singing that has been revived in recent years. A *céilí* is a traditional Irish dancing session; don't miss it if you get a chance at one.

great outdoors

The Burren Way is probably Doolin's greatest outdoor attraction; it links the town with the **Cliffs of Moher** [see *the cliffs of moher,* below] with an 8-km paved road, great for biking or walking. Of course the Way continues beyond this stretch; a map of its entirety sits in a case outside **Paddy Moloney's Hostel** [see *crashing,* below]; you can buy maps from the hostel or at any bookstore in the Burren area, or in Galway. Rent a bike from the **Doolin Bike Store** [see *need to know,* below]. Walking down the quiet roads overlooking the sea and the Aran Islands, especially at sunset, is a romantic and laid-back alternative to the noisy pub scene.

Don't try to go swimming at Doolin, though; it's just not safe.

stuff

Selection may not be the first word that springs to mind while shopping in Doolin—but hey, you came for the music, remember?

Of the limited gift shop options, **The Doolin Craft Gallery and Restaurant** *(Beside the cemetery, with the sea behind you, make a right off of Fisherstreet; Tel 065/74309; 9am-7pm; V, MC, AE)* at least has it all: soft,

the cliffs of moher

It's on everybody's travel itinerary: the fantastically breathtaking Cliffs of Moher. The Cliffs plunge over 700 feet into the waves and stretch for 8 km (5 mi) along Clare's rugged coastline. While deservedly popular, the wild pristine beauty of the cliffs is spoiled just a bit by all the oversized, smog-spewing coaches that arrive beginning around 9am every morning. You'll have to be an early riser to beat them; from Doolin, set your alarm for breakfast at daybreak and start off on an 8-km walk or bike ride. (It takes only 10 minutes by car.) O'Brien's Tower sits by the cliffs' parking lot, and you can go up for £2 (60p for students), but it's not necessary for the spectacular views, which you can get just as well at ground-level. The tower has that medieval look to it, but it was built for tourism purposes in 1835. If you're up for a bit of walking, there are marked paths along the cliffs; further information can be obtained from the **Tourist Office** [see *need to know,* below].

fuzzy sweaters, beautiful handmade pottery, glassware, and jewelry. It's also a good place to eat [see *eats,* below].

eats

The hippest spot in town, **Doolin Café** *(Fisherstreet, Upper Village, near McDermott's and McGann's; Tel 065/707-47-95; Under £5 for sandwiches, around £10 for dinner; No credit cards)* doesn't seem to have any sort of regular hours anymore. It used to be open all day from 10am to 10pm, but now you really need luck on your side to find it open. When it is, though, it's a great place for vegetarians and carnivores alike, with fresh and creatively prepared seafood, meat, and veggie dishes.

Bruach na hAille *(Fisherstreet; Tel 065/74120; 6-9:30pm mid-Mar to Oct; £10-18 main courses; No credit cards)* boasts an antique phonograph player and a front room with chairs around a crackling fire. You're given menus and invited to sit by the fireplace while you decide. The £12 three-course early bird menu, served between 6 and 7pm, is a good value, and the food is excellent, but with rather limited vegetarian options. The veggie dishes they do have, like "Mexican" tortillas, are even better than the real thing. Delicious desserts, too.

The Doolin Craft Gallery and Restaurant [see *stuff,* above] *(Restaurant open 10am-6pm; V, MC, AE)* is a 20- to 30-minute walk from the more popular hostels and pubs. The restaurant has a pleasant, airy atmosphere, and on nice days you can have lunch in a backyard garden: fresh seafood, salads, baked goods, and all that good stuff.

All the pubs serve food here, of course; at **O'Connor's** [see *bar and live music scene,* above] you can put a good steak-and-chips combo on the plastic for around £11, although the menu is mostly seafood. It's a good place for a late meal; at 9:30pm all the music—and the fun—is just beginning.

crashing

Doolin's not short on hostels, and it's all a toss-up: The standard is high and you'll be perfectly satisfied with any of them. Comfortable spaces and friendly staff abound; you can't go wrong.

The **Aille River Hostel** *(Just off Fisherstreet, across the bridge over the Aille River; Tel 065/707-42-60; £7-8 dorms, £16 doubles; Open mid-Mar to mid-Nov; No credit cards)* is a quaint little cottage with a roaring turf fire; it also has a campsite. The rooms are airy and comfortable, especially the private ones. Added perks include free—yes, free!—access to the laundry room and Internet access, on a real computer, no less, for £4 an hour, £5 if you're not staying there. For these reasons, in addition to clean facilities and a marvelously fun and laid-back atmosphere, Aille River has an edge over the other hostels in town. Not only that, but musicians are known to warm up here in the sitting room before heading off to nightly gigs at one of Doolin's three pubs. It's got the best vibe, no doubt.

how to catch a leprechaun

You know a lot about them already: They're 3 feet tall, they wear cute little green suits, and you know from watching that cheesy horror movie with Jennifer Aniston that they are often just a tad less than friendly. Most importantly, every leprechaun has a stash of gold hidden someplace, and if you can catch hold of one of the little fellows long enough to ask the right questions, it's yours for the taking. Easier said than done, though. The only time you can catch a leprechaun is if he's sitting down to mend his shoes. Should be easy enough. But keeping ahold of him is another matter. Don't take your eyes off him for an instant or he'll be gone like Carl Lewis in a track of dust. Ask where the gold is. He'll deny he has any. Keep asking, and a threatening tone of voice wouldn't hurt—y'know, put the ol' "fear of God" into 'im for a bit. And don't trust his word—make him show you *exactly* where it is. And if you ever get any of this to actually benefit you somehow, be sure to let me know.

clíodhna

Had a bad hair day? Cellulite getting you down? Leave a plate of cookies and milk out for Clíodhna (pronounced "CLEE-uh-nuh" or "clee-OH-nuh"), the ancient Irish goddess of beauty.

The newest hostel in town, **Flanaghan's** *(Fisherstreet, half-mile away, north of the Upper Village; Tel 065/74564; £7.50 dorm, £8.50-10 private room; No credit cards)* is a bit far away from the pubs, but it's still within easy walking distance. A second floor was recently added to the building, and all the rooms are bright and airy. Comfy leather couches and a fireplace furnish the sitting room, but perhaps the best feature of this cozy little place is its owners, who couldn't possibly be any friendlier or more welcoming.

Paddy Moloney's Doolin Hostel *(Fisherstreet, Lower Village; Tel 065/707-40-06; £7.50 dorm, £18 doubles; V, MC)* is the biggest one in town. Paddy's makes it oh-so-convenient: It offers a Bureau de Change and food for sale, sells bus tickets (the bus stops right outside!) and accepts credit cards. A cozy sitting room, a well-stocked kitchen, clean bedrooms (some with bathroom), and friendly staff make Paddy's yet another good choice while you're in Doolin.

Perhaps the greatest virtue of the **Rainbow Hostel** *(Fisherstreet, Upper Village; Tel 065/707-44-15; £7.50-8 dorm, £8.50 per person double; No credit cards)* is its close proximity to **McDermott's** and **McGann's** pubs [see *bar and live music scene,* above]. A wonderfully friendly, laid-back vibe, helpful staff, and free guided walking tours of the Burren [see *below*] make it even better.

Brand-spanking-new, **Rainbow's End B&B** *(Fisherstreet; Tel 065/707-44-15; £18 double; No credit cards)* is right next door to the Rainbow Hostel and is owned and run by the same friendly family. Not only is the place totally immaculate and cozily furnished, the woodwork—which can be seen in the ceiling beams and staircase—was all designed and furnished by the owner. Pretty impressive! Rainbow's End might remind you of a quaint little gingerbread house, but without the saccharine. It's a warm, relaxed, simple, and comfortable place to spend the night. Small too—only six rooms, so it'd be wise to book ahead.

There's also **Doolin Cottage** *(Behind the Aille River Hostel; Tel 065/707-47-62; £22 double, £24 with bath; Open Mar-Nov; No credit cards),* which welcomes drop-ins for breakfast along with its own guests.

Rooms are clean and brightly decorated, and the breakfast is excellent, with ample vegetarian choices. Cozy and small, so book your room ahead.

A few other options that won't drain the wallet include **Cullinan's** *(Doolin; Tel 065/707-4503; www.kingsway.ie/doonmacfelim; Rooms Summer season £23.50 per person, Low season £18 per person, all with private bath; V, MC)*, right in the center of Doolin; **Doonmacfelim** *(Doolin; Tel 065/707-4503, Fax 065/707-4129; www.kingsway.ie/doonmacfelim; Rooms summer season £23.50 per person, low season £18 per person, all with private bath; V, MC)*, also in the center of town; and **Atlantic View House** *(Doolin; Tel 06/57-07-418-9, Fax 06/57-07-49-14; atlanview@eircom.net; Rooms £25 per person, all rooms have a private bath; V, MC)*, a few minutes in either direction from the pier or downtown.

need to know

Currency Exchange At **Paddy Moloney's Doolin Hostel** [see *crashing*, above] and at **An Post** *(Tel 065/74209)* on the main street.

Tourist Information There's a **Tourist Office** at the **Cliffs of Moher** *(Tel 065/81171; 9:30am-5:30pm Apr-Oct)*. Hostel owners are a good source of information, too.

Bike Rental **Doolin Bike Store** *(Fisherstreet, next to the Aille River Hostel; Tel 065/707-42-82; Open 9am-8pm; £7 per day)*.

Laundry Do your laundry for free if you're staying at the **Aille River Hostel** [see *crashing*, above].

Bus Lines Out of the City: **Bus Éireann** *(Tel 01/836-61-11)* stops right outside **Paddy Moloney's Doolin Hostel** [see *crashing*, above], with direct service a couple times a day to Galway, Ennis, and neighboring towns like Lahinch, Lisdoonvarna, Ennistymon, and Ballyvaughan, as well as to the Cliffs of Moher. Indirect service to Dublin and Limerick via route 15.

Boats You can reach the Aran Islands from Doolin via **Doolin Ferries** [see **County Galway**].

Internet **Aille River Hostel,** £5/£4 residents [see *crashing*, above].

ballyvaughan

Another tiny town with a castle, a beach, and a couple of pubs, Ballyvaughan is 13 km (8 mi) east of **Fanore** and reachable from **Doolin** via **Bus Éireann** [see *need to know*, below].

the great outdoors

The beach is safe for swimming, but Ballyvaughan's biggest attraction for nature-freaks is the **Newtown Castle and Trail** *(N67 road, Ballyvaughan; Tel 065/77216; 10am-6pm Easter-Oct; Tours £2-3.50)*. The guided walk—which is 13 km (8 mi) long, starting from Newtown Castle—will give you an up-close-and-personal view of the Burren scenery [see *below*] as well as a look at a restored 16th-century home belonging to the "Princes of the Burren." You can also see an ancient cooking place on the higher ground above the trail. **Aillwee Cave** *(2 mi south of Ballyvaughan; Tel 065/77036; 10am-5:30pm mid-Mar to June and Sept-Nov, 10am-6:30pm July-Aug; www.nci.ie/aillwee; Admission £4.50 adults, £3.50 students),* reaches almost a mile into a mountain, and has waterfalls, weird rock formations, and hibernation chambers for brown bears. Relax, the big guys have been extinct in Ireland for quite some time.

crashing

The closest hostel is in Fanore, and there aren't too many choices here in Ballyvaughan for places to stay, but you might try **O'Brien's B&B** *(Main St.; Tel 065/707-70-03; £25 single, £35-40 double; V, MC),* which has a pub and restaurant downstairs. Even if you don't stay overnight, O'Brien's is one of the few places to eat in town, and the pub is as lively as the next.

need to know

Buses Ballyvaughan is 13 km (8 mi) from Doolin on **Bus Éireann** route 50, leaving Doolin Monday-Saturday at 1:30pm.

the burren

How'd you like to spend the day on another planet? The Burren—from the Irish *bhoireann,* meaning "a rocky place"—is a limestone plateau that stretches for 300 square kilometers across the northwestern Clare countryside and out to the coast. This rocky region has few trees and little vis-

ahhh

Tired and stiff after a day of hiking in the Burren? **Clare's Rock Hostel** [see *crashing,* below] offers a full-body aromatherapy massage to residents for £20. You should anticipate that you're really going to need one and book a massage when you call to make your room reservation. You can also get a back-and-shoulders massage for £10. Even cooler, you can drink fresh spring water from a 500-foot-deep well nearby for free.

the story of a potato

Did you know that the potato isn't actually indigenous to Ireland? The Spanish explorers brought the now-ubiquitous tuber from South America to Europe in the 16th century, and almost immediately the potato became an Irish staple food because it grew so well on the island, and soon the entire population was completely dependent on it.

Beginning in 1845, Ireland's potato crop failed, causing widespread starvation. The Famine saw the deaths of more than a million Irish, and another 1.25 million emigrated between 1845 and 1849. Fortunately, the Irish enjoy a much more diversified diet today, but potatoes will always be inextricably linked to Irish culture.

ible soil. But look closer: Sprinkled everywhere are brilliant-hued wildflowers, and spectacular views lie in all directions.

Nature-lovers, archaeology buffs, and outdoorsy types will all relish long hikes in the Burren. A good place to make your base for exploring is the town of Carron, if only because that's where you'll find **Clare's Rock Hostel** [see *crashing,* below]. If you're at all interested in hiking, consider walking the **Burren Way,** which runs for 35 km (22.7 mi) along the dramatic Cliffs of Moher near Doolin out toward Ballyvaughan to the north. Even if you don't want to do the whole route, take time to explore the Burren's prehistoric ruins, some of the most amazing megalithic tombs in Ireland, if not in all Western Europe. The most famous is the huge dolmen at **Poulnabrone,** about 6.44 km (4 mi) northwest of Carron. It has literally tons of wedge tombs, ring forts, and other ancient stone structures. Another fascinating site is the **Aillwee Caves**, which lay undiscovered for thousands of years until a farmer accidentally came across them while tending his sheep.

Best of all, here in the Burren you'll have the place (almost) to yourself. You have to be more adventurous than the average tourist to make a trek out here, but rest assured, it'll be totally worth it. It may be the closest you'll ever get to walking on the moon.

For information about the Burren, check out **The Burren Centre** *(Kilfenora; Tel 065/708-80-30; 10am-5pm Mar-Oct, 9:30am-6pm June-Sept; burrencenter@tinet.ie, homepage.tinet.ie/~burrencenter; Admission £2.50/£1.50 students),* which is within (long) walking distance of Carron. It's also reachable by bus from Ennis, Galway, or Doolin using **Bus Éireann** (route 337). You can stop in Kilfenora from any of those places before taking the next bus to Corofin, where the **Clare's Rock**

the burren

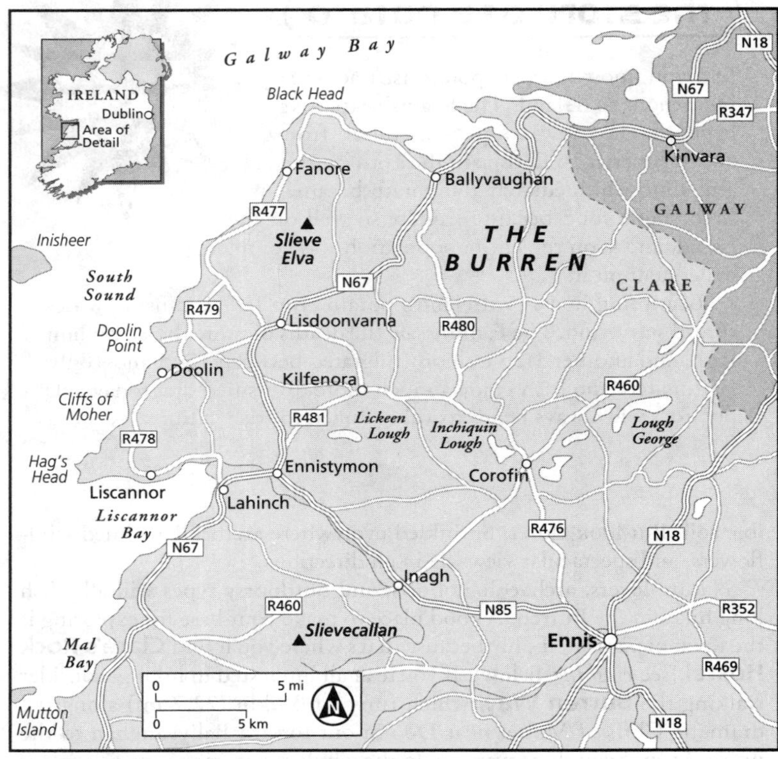

Hostel [see *crashing*, below] people will pick you up. Or try **Burren Exposure** *(Whitethorn, Ballyvaughan; Tel 065/707-72-77; 10am-5pm; Admission £3.50).*

If you want to explore the Burren, the easiest thing to do is to make **Clare's Rock Hostel** [see *crashing*, below]—which accurately describes itself as located in the very "heart of the Burren"—your base camp and go exploring from there. Public transportation to the Burren is limited, but definitely do-able. If you go, plan to stay for a few days, since the bus service can be rather infrequent. Guided walking tours of the Burren are available; check with the hostel when you arrive. They'll hook you up with maps and the info for any sporting or cultural activity possible in the area. Another option is to stay in Doolin, rent a bike, and pedal inland.

crashing

Clare's Rock Hostel *(Carron; Tel 065/708-91-29; Open May-Oct; claresrockhostel@tinet.ie, www.claresrock.com; £8 dorms, £9-11 per person private rooms; No credit cards)* makes an excellent choice—well, it's the only choice out here, come to think of it. This hostel employs half the town's population, and it makes an excellent base for exploring the Burren, because you're right smack in the middle of it. The hostel has amazing views over a "disappearing lake." There are other hostels at the edge of the Burren, like in Doolin, Lahinch, etc., but if you're serious about exploring the Burren, this is really the way to go.

need to know

Directions and Transportation No car? No problem! **Barratt Coach Tours** *(Tel 061/384-800 or 087/237-59-86, 24-hour booking line; £5 one-way)* drops you near the hostel from Limerick and Ennis. The bus route operates on Thursdays and Saturdays only, leaving the Limerick Tourist Office at Arthur's Quay at 9am, departing the Ennis Tourist Office at 10:10am, and arriving at Shesamore Cross, which is 1.60 km (3 mi) from Clare's Rock Hostel, at 10:30am. When you call to make a reservation, be sure to ask the hostel bus to pick you up (for free, of course). If you're coming from Galway, **Bus Éireann** *(Tel 091/562-000)* buses leave from the Galway Bus and Train Station for Bellharbour, the closest stop to Carron. Buses leave three times a day (at 8:50am, 11am, and 6pm, approximately), and once per day (at 10am) in the off-season (i.e., before May 20). Again, the hostel will pick you up, but inform them of your travel plans when you make your reservation.

Bike Rental You can rent a bike from **Clare's Rock Hostel** [see *crashing,* above], although most people opt to explore by foot instead.

fanore

If you want a village *completely* untouched by a speck of tourism, it's gotta be Fanore, 17 km (10 mi) north of **Doolin.** "Village" isn't really the right word for it; there's only one shop, **Fitzpatrick's** (4 km [2.5 mi] south of the Fanore beach, on the sea-side of the road), which serves as a small grocery store, post office, newsstand, and fishing tackle shop. The only problem with finding a spot so untainted is that there's really no way to get there other than by car, unless you request a stop on the **Bus Éireann** route [see *need to know,* below]. If you're lucky enough to have a set of wheels, though, it's a good place for an afternoon picnic. The beach at Fanore is the only "safe" one for miles around.

eats

There are no restaurants in Fanore, so you should plan on bringing a sandwich in your backpack, picking up a wee snack at **Fitzpatrick's** (see above), or stopping in for whatever paltry pub snacks are to be had at the local pub, **O'Donoghue's** *(Just outside of Fanore; Tel 065/76104; Free trad music sessions Tue and Sat nights throughout the summer).* Tourist alert: Even though it is mostly a local hangout during the off-season (October-

April), O'Donoghue's is bursting at the seams with tourists during the summer. There's literally nowhere else to go in Fanore.

crashing

If you want to stay the night, try the **Bridge Hostel** *(Fanore, a few hundred yards inland from the river crossing on the main road; Tel 065/76134; around £7 dorm, £17 double; Open Mar to end Oct; No credit cards),* which used to be a police station. (This place is so remote, the idea of having a police station here *does* seem a little silly.) The riverside location—overlooking some great Burren scenery—along with friendly staff and hearty dinners (for a mere £4!), make this a good choice even if it *is* in the middle of nowhere. You can also camp out for the night.

If none of these strike your fancy you've always got the moderately priced **Admiral's Rest Seafood Restaurant** *(Fanore; Tel 06/57-07-61-05, Fax 06/57-07-61-61; jdmn@iol.ie; £15 per person, all rooms have private baths; V, MC, AE), right near a new nature preserve.*

need to know

Currency Exchange The closest Bureau de Change is in **Lahinch** *(Main St.; Tel 065/708-17-43; 9am-10pm Mon-Sat).*

Tourist Information Nearest tourist office's at Lisdoonvarna, in the **Burren Smokehouse Visitor Centre** *(Doolin Rd., N67; Tel 065/707-44-32; 10am-6pm daily, open later in summer).*

Public Transportation Bus Éireann route 423 *(Ennis bus station; Tel 065/682-41-77; Summer only, usually May 20-Sept 17)* leaves Doolin at 8:45am and takes 40 minutes to reach Fanore and another from Galway passes through Fanore on its way to Doolin around 7:30pm. There's no Fanore stop on Sundays.

lahinch

Reachable by bus from Doolin, Lahinch offers good beaches, amusement arcades, and plentiful B&Bs. It's considered the country's surfing headquarters. There are a bunch of surf shops on the waterfront that rent boards and wetsuits. If you wimp out at the thought of cold water, there's always the **Lahinch Seaworld Leisure Centre** *(The Promenade; Tel 065/708-19-00),* which offers a pleasant way to spend an afternoon. Among its many activities is a large swimming pool (heated) open seven days from noon to 6pm. There's also a steam room and sauna, as well as an aquarium with both tropical and domestic fish on parade. The on-site cafe supplies sandwiches and chips for about £4. Individual tickets cost £6.50, family tickets go for £16.95. You can find it 5 minutes south of the heart of town.

The **Spinnaker Restaurant** *(The Promenade; Tel 065/81933; noon-9pm daily; AE, MC, V)* is a pretty touristy spot—but then so is Lahinch—

with a relaxed white brick interior and the ever-popular "Modern Irish" menu on tap. Think a lighter side of "fry." Dress: what you have on.

A pleasant surprise here is **Raphael's Internet and Ice Cream Café** *(Main St.; Tel 065/708-10-20; £3 per hour),* which serves more than just stale coffee! Who'd have thought you'd find such a thing, and among Clare's far reaches, of all places?

If you want to spend the night, try **Lahinch Hostel** *(Church St.; Tel 065/708-10-40; £8-9 dorms, £24 doubles; V, MC, 5 percent surcharge to use credit cards),* with clean, comfortable rooms and a location right by the water. The hostel also rents bikes for £7 a day.

need to know

Buses Bus Éireann route 15 serves Lahinch, leaving twice a day from Doolin. The trip takes about a half-hour.

miltown malbay

Midway between Kilkee and Doolin on the County Clare coast, Miltown Malbay is said by music lovers to be what Doolin was once: A totally uncommercialized haven for traditional Irish music. Music, music, music, all for music's sake; if you found yourself irritated by Doolin's proliferation of tour buses and tacky B&Bs, you'll find Miltown Malbay a refreshing change. And the music's getting even better as more artists move to this little town, while an infrequent Bus Éireann route [see *need to know,* below] and a lack of hostels keep it well off the beaten tourist path. The highlight of the year, **"Willie Week,"** sponsored by the Willie Clancy School of Traditional Music *(mid-July; Tel 065/84148),* brings musicians, instrument-makers, and die-hard trad fans to Miltown Malbay for a weeklong series of seminars, lessons, and concerts with a mere £50 price tag. (Never heard of Willie Clancy? You will.) Finding a great trad session any time of year in Miltown is as easy as seeing green.

eats

Try **An Sceallain** *(Town Center; Tel 065/708-44-98; Items £2-7),* whose name—"The Potato Skin"—isn't terribly appropriate when you consider that the place is known for its pizzas.

There's also a **Spar Supermarket** *(Main St.; Tel 065/708-40-93; 9am-9pm Mon-Sat, 9am-1:30pm Sun)* if you're thinking do-it-yourself.

crashing

For logistical reasons, you'll want to spend at least one night in town; try **O'Loughlin's Ocean View B&B** *(Town center; Tel 065/708-42-49; £17 per person; V, MC),* featuring clean comfortable rooms and a staircase

heroes and villains

The fight for independence is an integral part of understanding the culture and people of Ireland. The following men and women, whether they are revered or reviled, are an essential part of 20th century Irish history because of the role they played in the fight for independence.

MICHAEL COLLINS (1890-1922)

Michael Collins was born and raised in West Cork, the son of a farmer. At age 15 he emigrated to London, where he joined Sinn Fein, the Irish Republican Brotherhood (IRB), and in 1914 the Irish Volunteers. Two years later, he returned to Ireland to avoid British conscription. Within several months, at age 26, Collins found himself in the General Post Office fighting a losing revolution, and subsequently returned to Britain in irons. Before the year was out, however, he was back in Dublin, on the supreme council of the IRB. In the war for independence, Collins was the legendary commander-in-chief of the IRA, everywhere and nowhere, striking and eluding the British like a phantom. Having brought the British to the negotiating table, he accepted the division of Ireland with great reluctance. He knew and said, at the same time, that the treaty would prove to be his death warrant. He was right. On August 22, 5 days before he would have turned 31, he was ambushed and assassinated.

JAMES CONNOLLY (1868-1913)

Born of poor Irish Catholic parents in Edinburgh, Connolly worked from age 11, and at 14 falsified his age to enlist in the British army. After being posted in Dublin, he deserted and returned to Scotland. He eventually made his way back to Ireland, where he founded the Irish Socialist Republican Party. Unable to support a family in Dublin, Connolly emigrated to America, where he founded the Irish Socialist Federation in New York City. Several years later, however, he was back at it in Ireland, closing the port of Dublin to bring about the release of James "Big Jim" Larkin. In 1916, Connolly was appointed commandant-general of the Dublin forces and led the assault on the General Post Office. Wounded and unable to stand for his own execution, he was strapped to a chair when brought before the Kilmainham firing squad.

EAMON DE VALERA (1882-1975)

The Irish nationalist politician was born in New York of an Irish mother and a Spanish father. When his father died in 1885, de Valera's mother sent the boy to Ireland, and his grandmother raised him in County Limerick. He joined the Irish Volunteers in 1913 and commanded the Boland's Mills garrison in the 1916 Easter Rising, for which he received the death sentence. It was eventually commuted on account of his American citizenship. After fiercely opposing the Anglo-Irish Treaty and serving with the IRA in the Irish civil war, de Valera formed Fianna Faiíl. He went on to become the first president of Dáil Eireann, the Irish Parliament, and the first Taoiseach (prime minister). From 1959 to 1973, he served as president of the Republic.

MAUD GONNE (1865-1953)

Born in England and educated on the French Riviera, Gonne spent several years in Ireland when her father, a colonel in the British army, was posted to Dublin Castle. Moved by the Irish cause, she pledged herself to the struggle. Although she turned down a proposal of marriage from W. B. Yeats, Gonne founded with him the Association Irlandaise in Paris. She was a member of the secret Irish Republican Brotherhood and later established two organizations: *Inghinidhe Na he ireann* (Daughters of Ireland) and the Women's Prisoner's Defense League. Imprisoned in 1923, she was released after beginning a hunger strike.

BOBBY SANDS (1954-1981)

Practically a saint to Republican freedom fighters, Sands joined the movement in 1972 after seeing his Catholic Republican family become the victims of continued harassment and abuse at the hands of Northern Ireland Loyalists. An advocate of local politics and neighborhood improvement, Sands had an immediate impact on those around him. Arrested and imprisoned in 1977 on a trumped-up handgun charge, Bobby became a leader behind bars as well as outside. In early 1981 Sands began his second hunger strike in protest of the British authorities decision to strip IRA prisoners of their "political prisoner" status. On the 31st day of his hunger strike, Sands was informed that he been elected to the British House of Parliament. Two months later, Bobby Sands MP died of starvation in Long Kesh prison, a hero to all who knew him.

fashioned by the infamous Willie Clancy himself, who was both a master carpenter and a brilliant musician.

need to know

Currency Exchange **Bank of Ireland** *(Next to O'Friels; Tel 065/ 708-40-18; 10am-12:30pm and 1:30-4pm Mon-Wed and Fri; 10am-12:30pm and 1:30-5pm Thur).*

Pharmacy **Marie Kelly's** *(Main St.; Tel 065/84440; 9:30am-6:30pm Mon-Tue and Thur-Sat, 9:30am-7pm Sun).*

Buses **Bus Éireann** *(route 15; call the Ennis bus depot at 065/682-41-77 for information)* has no direct links from Doolin to Miltown Malbay, but buses go from Ennis to Miltown Malbay at around 10:20pm on Friday nights; a daily Ennis-bound bus (337) leaves from Miltown at 4:50pm. Route 333 leaves from Miltown (to Ennis) at 8:25am. There's also a Kilkee-bound bus at 10:20am on Fridays only.

climbing up the family tree

So your mother is always saying you look like Great Uncle Mickey from Bunratty, lovely fellow, had a heart of gold, never did make it over to the States though. Well, if you ever get the urge to learn more about Uncle Mickey, Aunt Maggie, or whomever it is, most tourist offices throughout Ireland either run, or can refer you to a genealogical center that will trace your roots right back to the Celts (well almost).

Equipped with computerized versions of almost every public record that has survived over the years (particular attention is paid to church, land, and civil records), the kind folks at the local center, for a fee ranging from as little as £5 up to a whopping £200, can tell you everything from what parish your family belonged to and what kind of job they had, to what kind of whiskey they drank and who their grammar school sweethearts were.

This is an extremely popular activity among tourists, therefore, there are usually a great many family histories on back order; the folks that run the centers will do everything they can to fulfill your request, but there's always a chance they'll have to mail it to you after you leave.

Here are a few good ones that service the Limerick, Clare and Galway areas:

Clare Heritage & Genealogical Centre *(Corofin; Tel 065/683-7955, Fax 065/683-7955; contact Antoinette O' Brien; clareheritage @eircom.net; www.clareroots.com; V, MC).*

KILKEE

Located on the southern part of the Clare coast, Kilkee might be a little too crowded with hotels and amusements catering mostly to Clare and Limerick families on holiday, but you'll absolutely love it here if you're into diving. Kilkee has been called Ireland's diving center because of its limestone caverns perfect for exploring, and the beaches make for fine swimming as well. Stop by **Kilkee Diving and Watersports Centre** *(At Kilkee Harbour; Tel 065/905-67-07; www.diveireland.com)* for equipment rental. Or try the **Kilkee Pony Trekking and Riding Centre** *(Kilkee; Tel 065/906-00-71; Rides around £25)* if you want to travel by land. This town is pretty much a crossroads that exists to service the beachcombers, but it does offer superb coasts to wander, even for landlubbers, with its stunning sea and rock face interaction.

Limerick Archives & Ancestry *(The Granary, Michael St.; Tel 061/415-125, Fax 061/312-985; contact Margaret MacBride www.mayo-ireland.ie; No credit cards).*

Galway Family History Society West *(Unit 3 Venture Centre, Liosbaun Estate, Tuam Road; phone: 091-756737, fax: 091-756737; contact Marie Mannion; £20 initial registration fee).*

Keep in mind the above sites are for those parts of Ireland only, just about every county has their own equivalent. So if the person you're looking for ends up being from an area not serviced by one of the above, your search is far from over.

Note:
If your family hails from County Dublin, try either of the following options, (the county actually divides itself into three areas for genealogical research, only two are currently offering services) **Fingal Heritage Group** *(Carnegie Library, North Street, Swords; Tel 084-03629; Open daily Mon-Fri)*, for northern Dublin or **Dun Laoghaire Rathdown Heritage Society** *(Moran Park House, Dublin; Tel 280-6961 Extension 238, Fax 280-6969), for southern Dublin and the city.*

eats

The best restaurants in Kilkee specialize in seafood, just as you'd expect from a town situated on the Atlantic Ocean. And "seafood" often means "expensive." But there are ways to enjoy the fresh local catch without spending much money. Stop in at **The Strand** *(Overlooking the ocean on the Strand; Tel 065/905-61-77; Open daily 6:30-11pm Apr-Oct; entrees £10-20; V, MC, AE, DC),* Kilkee's finest dining house, at dinnertime, and you can get a bowl of creamy homemade seafood chowder for £2.75. Add a side salad or an order of fries for another £2 and you'll have a great meal for less than a fiver. There are plenty of other yummy options for under £5 if you stick with the appetizers and side orders.

crashing

There's one hostel in town, **Kilkee Hostel** *(O'Curry St.; Tel 065/905-62-09; Open Feb-Nov; Around £8 dorm; No credit cards),* which has everything you'll need: clean facilities, bike rental, Bureau de Change, a coffee shop, and a location within spitting distance of the water.

There are also a few decently priced hotels in town like **Duneam** *(West End; Tel 065/905-6545; £25 single, £20 per person shared, all rooms have private bath; No credit cards),* with a beautiful view overlooking the cliffs; or **Harbour Lodge** *(6 Marine Parade; Tel 06/59-05-60-90; £19 per person, all rooms have private baths; No credit cards),* also on the sea near the town center.

need to know

Currency Exchange There is a Bureau de Change at the **Kilkee Hostel** [see *crashing,* above].

Trains and Buses To reach Kilkee from Ennis, take **Bus Éireann** route 15, leaving three times a day Monday-Saturday and twice a day on Sunday. That's also the route to take if you're coming from Galway or Limerick. Buses leave for Kilkee three or four times daily and once or twice on Sunday. A bus to nearby Miltown Malbay leaves once a day, and an infrequent bus service links Miltown Malbay with other coastal towns to the north. If you want to get to Doolin from Kilkee, it'd be easier to go back to Ennis and take another bus out to Doolin.

Bike Rental You can rent some wheels at the **Kilkee Hostel** [see *crashing,* above].

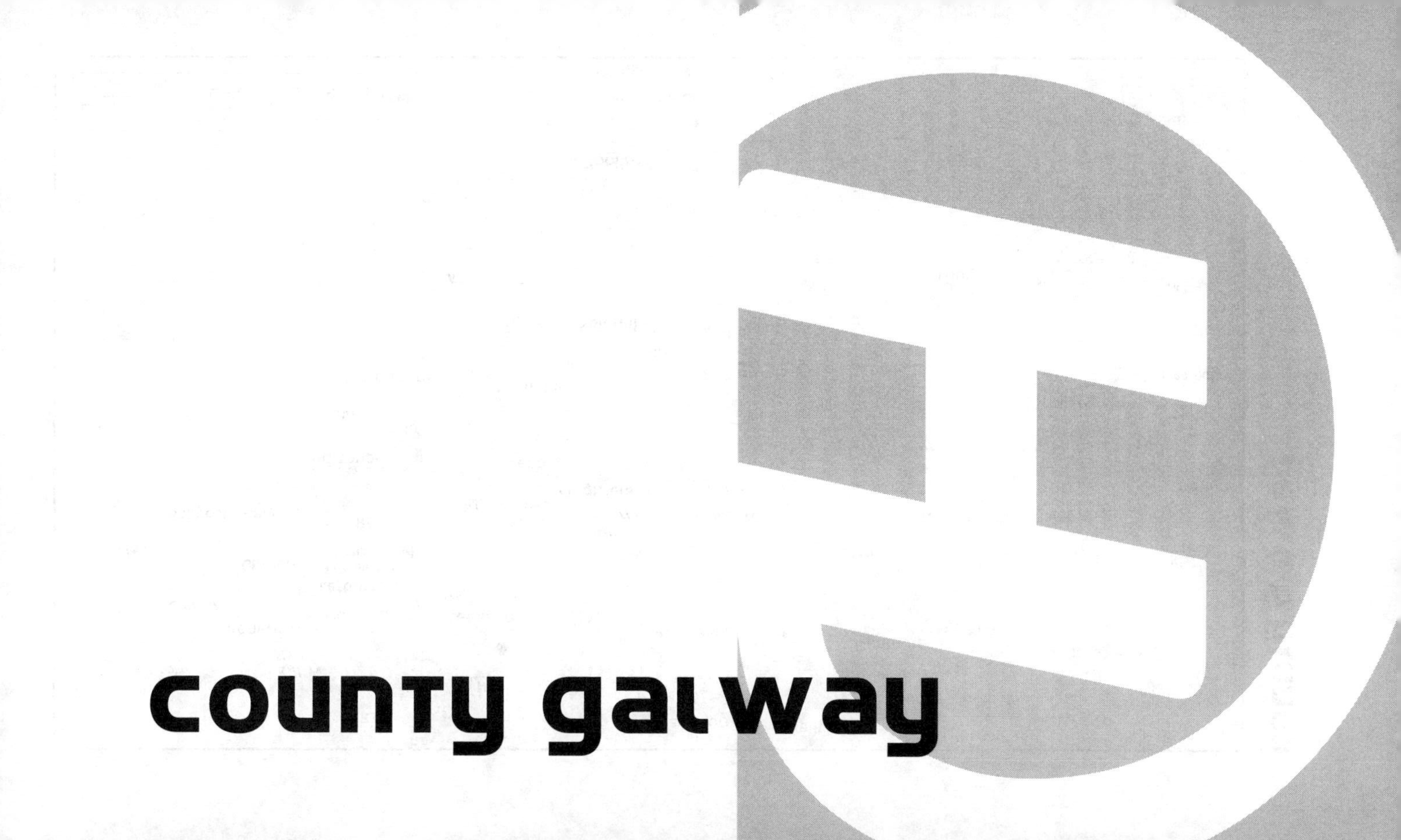
county galway

county galway

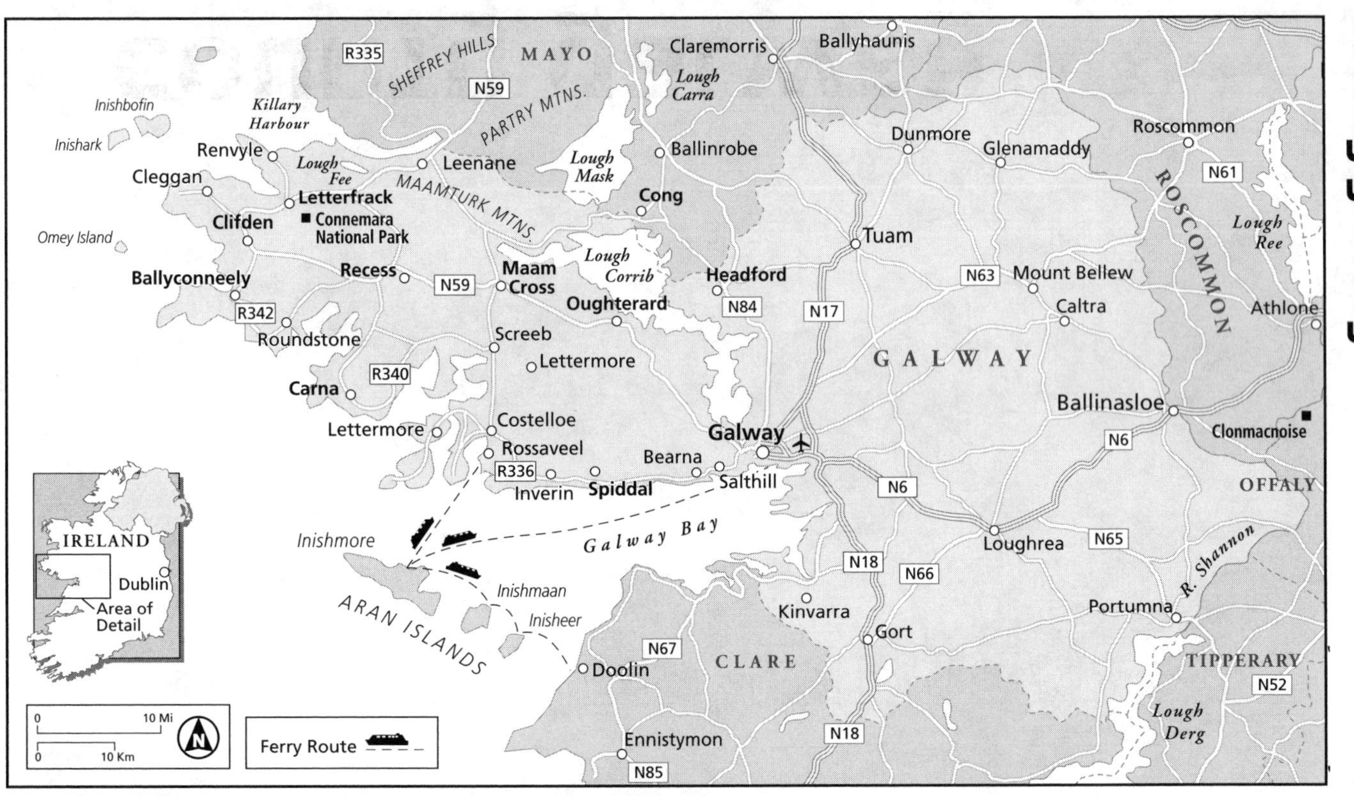

galway

Galway is to Ireland what California is to the States: the wild and beautiful west where the disaffected free thinkers from the east came to start over. By the early '80s, the influx of artists and other boho types, combined with the presence of a major university, had transformed this once-grand medieval port of derelict buildings into the most happening hotbed of the arts in Ireland: Experimentation is the norm, partying is a serious occupation, and the cast of local characters is a lot wilder, more diverse, and a helluva lot more fun than you'd expect from a little town of 60,000 souls.

With stunning surroundings, scores of bars and cafes, tons of live music, packed clubs, internationally renowned theater, plus a summer-long schedule of kick-ass festivals, Galway's not lacking much. The pubs are the heart of this city, and you'll find them full of former travelers who came here for a weekend, loved the vibe, and never left. The general welcome for young globe-trotters goes something like this: "You're from out of town? That's nice. Let's party." It's more than likely you won't want to leave, either.

neighborhoods

Most everything in Galway is centered around two parks: **Eyre Square,** by the train station in the east end of the city, and **Spanish Parade,** to the west of Eyre Square by **Galway Bay.** The parks are connected by a half-mile of the pedestrian-only **Shop Street** (as per usual in Ireland, this street changes names five times, but we'll stick with this one). The maze of medieval streets to either side of Shop Street is where you'll find the more tourist-oriented cafes and pubs. Just west of the Spanish Parade, you'll cross the **River Corrib,** which, in this stretch, is a spectacular network of stonework canals, bridges, and waterfalls, full of hundreds of gliding swans, crisscrossed by footpaths and bordered by banks of flower gardens. The other side of the Corrib is slightly less touristic, more student-ish.

portrait of the artist

James Joyce has long been hailed as one of Ireland's finest writers, possibly *the* finest of them all; critics say Joyce is Shakespeare's sole rival when it comes to a mastery of the English language. But although every story he wrote took place in Ireland, he left Ireland in his early twenties and only came back twice—both times to see Nora Barnacle, the Galway woman he later married; you can read their love letters at the Barnacle family house on Bowling Green [see *culture zoo,* below]. Joyce made no secret of his quarrels with his native land, yet Ireland was always at the very heart of his novels, short stories, and poems.

With spells in Paris, Rome, Trieste, and Zurich, Joyce's life reads like an exciting, romantic adventure. In reality, he was plagued by rotten health, money troubles, censorship, and family strife throughout his now much-celebrated life.

Joyce's most famous works include *Dubliners, Finnegan's Wake,* and *A Portrait of the Artist as a Young Man.* But it was the notorious 1922 publication of *Ulysses* that catapulted him into the international literary spotlight, principally because the novel was sensationally banned from the United States on grounds of obscenity. (There, that got your attention, didn't it?) But before you lasciviously plunge in, be forewarned that Joyce's dense, allusive, wordy writing is hard to crack (many's the college student who's dismissed it as mere drink-inspired gobbledygook). Don't give up, though: Joyce's subtle plots, psychologically vivid characters, and stream-of-consciousness narrative style, all radical in their day, get to the heart of human reality in a way no mere fiction ever had before. Highbrow academics now fight over who can come up with the "deepest" analyses of the many hidden meanings and complex symbolism in James Joyce's work, and Joyce himself once said that a reader could easily spend a lifetime studying only *Finnegan's Wake.* But on another day, and in another mood, Joyce also said, "I'm afraid I'm more interested in Dublin street names than in the riddle of the universe." Contradictions, ambiguities, and sly Irish humor—that's James Joyce for you.

five things to talk to a local about

1. **"Know any cute hoors?"** The word is pronounced scandalously, like "whores," but has nothing to do with the world's oldest profession. Rather, it's an expression better left to the Irish for explanation.

2. **"What's up with this town's obsession with JFK and Ché Guevara?"** [see *by foot,* below].

3. **"Who's this Ming character?"** (A minor local celeb/politician. Look for the guy who's the spitting image of Ming the Merciless.)

4. **"Do fairies really exist?"** Late one night outside a chip shop, a perfectly lovely, and otherwise sane, worldly, and intelligent undergrad spent an hour and a half trying to convince me of the existence of the wee little people.

5. As per usual, anything touching on the subject of **drinking** will get you along like a house on fire.

Things peter out quickly here, into a big housing development on the bay side, and the university campus upriver.

Since Galway is so small, the best public transit is your feet and a good map: You'll definitely need one to find your way around here. For info on local happenings, pick up the free bi-weekly ***Galway List,*** scattered around most cafes, or the west country's monthly arts and culture mag, ***Magpie (£1.50),*** on sale at any newsstand. Another good one, with more "real news," is the weekly ***Galway Advertiser.***

hanging out

Hands down the best gathering place in town is **Eyre Square** (aka JFK Park). On a sunny afternoon, droves of merry Galwegians join the usual cast of resident winos and stretch out on nature's goodness. You can almost always count on a good vibe and a spontaneous guitar or drum session.

The multitudes gathered at the riverside park and plaza by the **Spanish Arch** usually seem deeply mellowed, perhaps lulled by the drifting swans, swirling seagulls, and beautiful view of Galway Bay.

Just out of town, **South Park** is the favorite spot for kite flyers, with lots of beachfront grass; it's never crowded, and often gusting like a wind tunnel.

Disheveled students, wayfaring street performers, or bermudas-and-baseball-cap tourists all drop in at people-watching central outside **Tigh Neachtain** [see *bar scene,* below], one of the best pubs in Galway. **Café du Journal** *(The Halls, Quay St.; Tel 091/568-426; 8:45am-9:30pm*

galway city

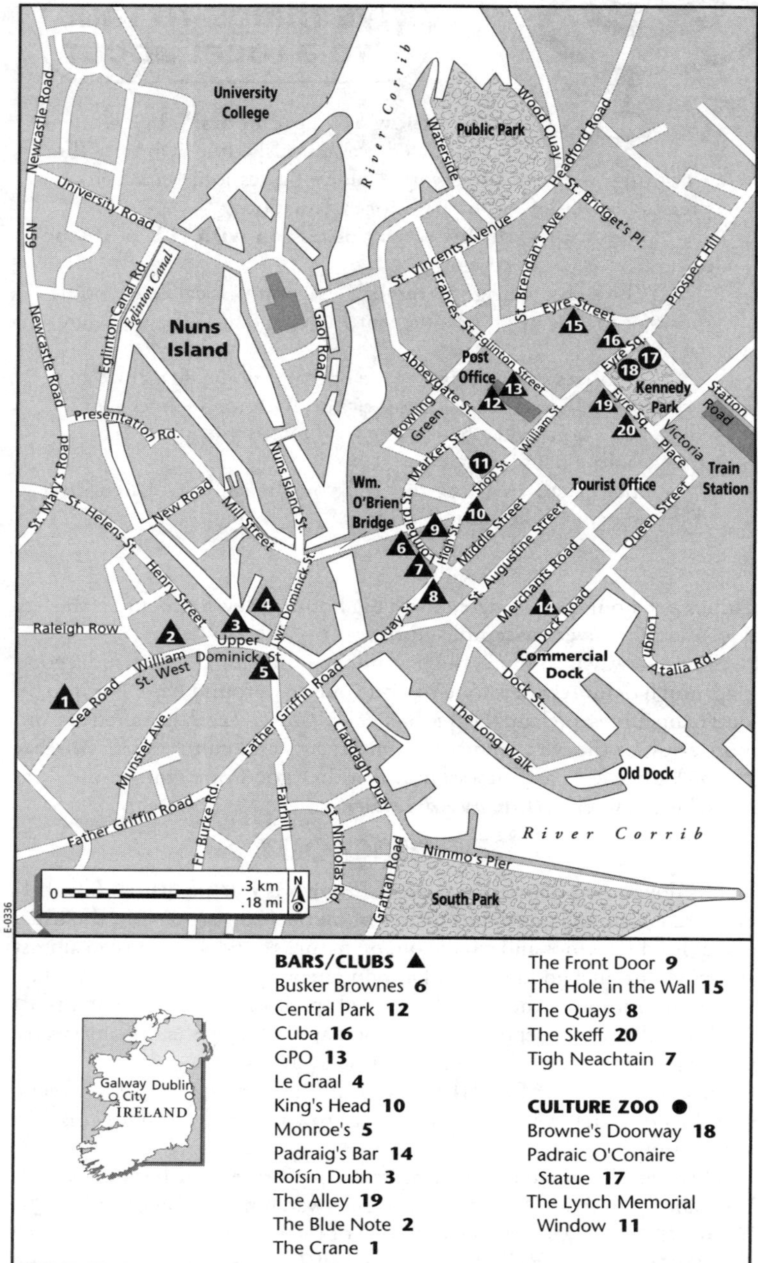
University College
River Corrib
Public Park
Waterside
Wood Quay
Headford Road
Newcastle Road
University Road
N59
St. Bridget's Pl.
St. Brendan's Ave.
St. Vincents Avenue
Prospect Hill
Eglinton Canal Rd.
Eglinton Canal
Nuns Island
Gaol Road
Frances St.
Eyre Street
Eyre Sq.
Post Office
Eglinton Street
Abbeygate St.
Kennedy Park
Station Road
Presentation Rd.
Bowling Green
Market St.
William St.
Victoria Place
Train Station
Nuns Island St.
Wm. O'Brien Bridge
Shop St.
Tourist Office
St. Mary's Road
St. Helens St.
New Road
Mill Street
Lombard St.
High St.
Middle Street
St. Augustine Street
Queen Street
Henry Street
Lwr. Dominick St.
Quay St.
Merchants Road
Dock Road
Raleigh Row
Upper Dominick St.
William St. West
Lough Atalia Rd.
Commercial Dock
Sea Road
Father Griffin Road
Dock St.
The Long Walk
Munster Ave.
Claddagh Quay
Old Dock
Fr. Burke Rd.
Fairhill
St. Nicholas Rd.
Grattan Road
Nimmo's Pier
South Park
0 .3 km .18 mi
N
E-0336
Galway City
Dublin
IRELAND
BARS/CLUBS ▲
Busker Brownes 6
Central Park 12
Cuba 16
GPO 13
Le Graal 4
King's Head 10
Monroe's 5
Padraig's Bar 14
Roísín Dubh 3
The Alley 19
The Blue Note 2
The Crane 1
The Front Door 9
The Hole in the Wall 15
The Quays 8
The Skeff 20
Tigh Neachtain 7
CULTURE ZOO ●
Browne's Doorway 18
Padraic O'Conaire Statue 17
The Lynch Memorial Window 11

daily; No credit cards) features stone-topped cafe tables and wooden church pews under chaotic piles of books and the daily papers. As the name suggests, it's a bit of a literary intellectual/journalist hangout, but everyone goes—and goes by—here.

Two cafes reign over Galway's late-night scene. Both serve good cafe food, with soundtrack, to a student/backpacker crowd. **Apostasy** *(56 Lower Dominick St.; Tel 091/561-478; 10am-4am daily; No credit cards)* is a funky little chamber with a wall shrine to the genius of espresso and other incarnations of the divine bean. **Java** *(17 Upper Abbey St.; Tel 091/567-400; 10am-4am Mon-Sat, noon-4am Sun; No credit cards)* takes up two floors. The long kitchen-style tables upstairs are great if you're doing the late shift with posse in tow. Last time I was here, a soft-spoken guy wearing a spiked dog collar served me chamomile tea.

For late-night wine, candles, and weirdness, try **O'Ché's** (*3 Francis St.; Tel 091/585-126; Noon-4am daily; info@e-maginet.com, www.e-maginet.com/jazz; £2 after 11pm; No credit cards),* a landmark of Galway's bizarre Ché obsession [see *by foot,* below]. Check out the cosmic-erotic entrance mural starring that darling "Commie Christ," his pal Fidel, and dancing showgirls, then submerge yourself in the slightly eerie underground atmosphere of this up-all-night wine bar. The two candlelit rooms won't fill up with the usual revolutionary leftists until well after midnight. Glasses of house wine run £2.20, pitchers of sangria keep the crowd happy, and the little stage hosts live acts almost every night, starting around midnight.

bar scene

Sure, and the Irish love the drink—and the music. There's no such thing as a dead night out, or a night without music. Seems every pub in town hosts nightly gigs, usually trad sessions or cover bands [see *live music scene,* below]. Most young travelers in Galway gravitate toward the tourist-oriented "superpubs" of Shop and Quay streets. Sardine-packed with drunken hordes of university students in winter months and drunken

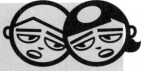

lad meets lassie

Galway's a college town, so if you're young, comely, and nocturnal, you shouldn't have any trouble getting the affection you (perhaps) so richly deserve. For the locals, hookups mostly happen at the clubs, while the touristy "superpubs" fill the bill for the backpacker set. Crossover is frequent and not a problem. Mating here remains in the classic collegiate style: It's just as likely the object of your lust will end the night by barfing all over your shoes or hopping into bed with you (or both).

hordes of tourists in summer, they're definitely a blast, in that beer-blast kind of way. For a more mellow, local feel, try the cluster of bars around Dominick Street, on the west side of the River Corrib.

Galway's drink prices are country-cheap, compared with Dublin. The general price for a pint in a pub hovers around £2.20, or £1.85 for a shot. Drink prices at clubs are around 20p higher across the board. Pub hours are the same as in the rest of Ireland *(10:30am-11pm Mon-Sat or till 11:30pm in summer, and 12:30-2pm/4-11pm Sun year-round),* but it's standard publican practice in "the country" to shut the front doors at the prescribed closing time, then let the party roll on inside for another hour or so. You won't get in off the street anywhere after legal closing, so if you're still doing the crawl at 11pm, give it up quick and settle into your favorite pub.

Despite its ground-zero location in Galway's teeming tourist hub, the scrappy little **Tigh Neachtain** *(17 Cross St.; Tel 091/568-820; No credit cards)* maintains an old-timey, wooden snugs-and-stools character. The crowd is a mix of locals and scruffy beatnik travelers. Allen Ginsberg was known to enjoy a pint (and maybe a joint) here, when in town. On sunny afternoons, drinkers take to the tables outside, resting their chair backs against the cool blue of "Knocktan's" wall.

The Hole in the Wall *(9 Eyre St.; Tel 091/586-146; No credit cards),* right on Eyre Square, is the kind of chill, friendly pub where you wish you could be a regular: Low-beamed ceiling, a jukebox with the standard rock classics, a sunny beer garden out to the side, and just enough off the beaten track so you can always find a seat. The Hole ain't too fashionable, but it fits. One warning: The owner is big into horses, so madness reigns during the late July races.

Just to confuse you, the **Front Door** *(Cross St.; No phone; 10:30am-11:45pm Mon-Sat, 4-11:30pm Sun; No credit cards)* presents itself as "Tomás ó Riada: Draper, Grocer, Matchmaker" over its other entrance on High Street (which turns into Shop Street). The best bar in town for playing hide-and-seek with its maze-like layout, it's also the mellowest of the superpubs, catering to an unpretentious post-university crowd.

fashion

The fashion in Galway? Grunge is dominant. Really, nobody cares what you're wearing. Relax.

The other, interchangeable "superpubs" include **The Quays** *(Quay St.; Tel 091/568-347; V, MC)* done in "seagoing church" decor; the **King's Head** [see *live music scene,* below]; **The Skeff** *(Eyre Sq.; Tel 091/563-173; V, MC)* with six different bars on two floors, and **Busker Brownes** *(Cross St.; Tel 091/563-377; www.failte.com/king-buskers; V, MC)* featuring an impressive, medieval "Hall of Tribes" on the third floor that's definitely worth a look. These are the pubs with the highest pickup potential. Come'n git it!

On the alternative side of town, there's the **Le Graal** *(38 Lower Dominick St.; Tel 091/567-614; 6pm-12:30am daily, plus extra summer hours of noon-3pm Mon-Fri, 9am-12:30am Sat, Sun; V, MC),* whose motto is "atmosphere in action." Popular with Galway's international and gay crowds, who come to drink wine and lounge about on the red felt couches while candelabras flicker against the rough stone walls. Dance to sounds of Latin, jazz, salsa, and world music, or grab a bite—the tropically relaxed staff also serve up food until last call. Sometimes there's a cover of two to three punts.

In the same neighborhood, the **Blue Note** *(William St. West; Tel 091/568-347; 5-11:50pm Mon-Thur, 3-11:50pm Fri, Sat, 4-11:30pm Sun; No credit cards)* is the committed clubber's pre-club hangout. Here, in the murky blue shadows, you'll find the town's greatest density of green hair. Local DJs spin hip-hop, house, and techno on weekends. Go for the great BBQ deal on Tuesday nights in the summer: Buy a Heineken, get a free burger, repeat.

Padraigs Bar *(The Docks; Tel 091/563-696; 7:30am-11:30pm Mon-Sat; No credit cards)* defines the classic Irish "early": right on the docks, maybe a little sketchy, and always full of hearty, salt-of-the-earth types exuding 80-proof perfume from every pore. Best on a weekend morning, when all walks of life can be seen crawling in for "just the one more" under the smoke-stained collection of classic film posters. There's a pool table in the back and a spinning ceiling fan to help patrons further lose their bearings.

live music scene

For the most part, trad rules the night in Galway. Other than that, your standard rock cover bands fill the bills at pubs all around town. Sort of like college parties all over again—which makes sense, given the overwhelming university crowd in Galway. No matter what's playing, everyone's out for a good time. One exception to the cover-band rule is **Roísín Dubh** [see below], a live joint with enough character (and incoming talent) to stand out in any city. **BarCuba*** [see *eats,* below] spices up the week with jazz on Saturdays and occasional imported Latin-flavored bands.

You can hear tourist-trap trad almost anywhere in town, but the place to go for the real stuff is **The Crane** *(2 Sea Rd.; Tel 091/567-419; No cover; No credit cards).* It's an old man's pub a little out on the west side of town, so the dress code is a lot of old tweed and a weather-beaten face

galway city

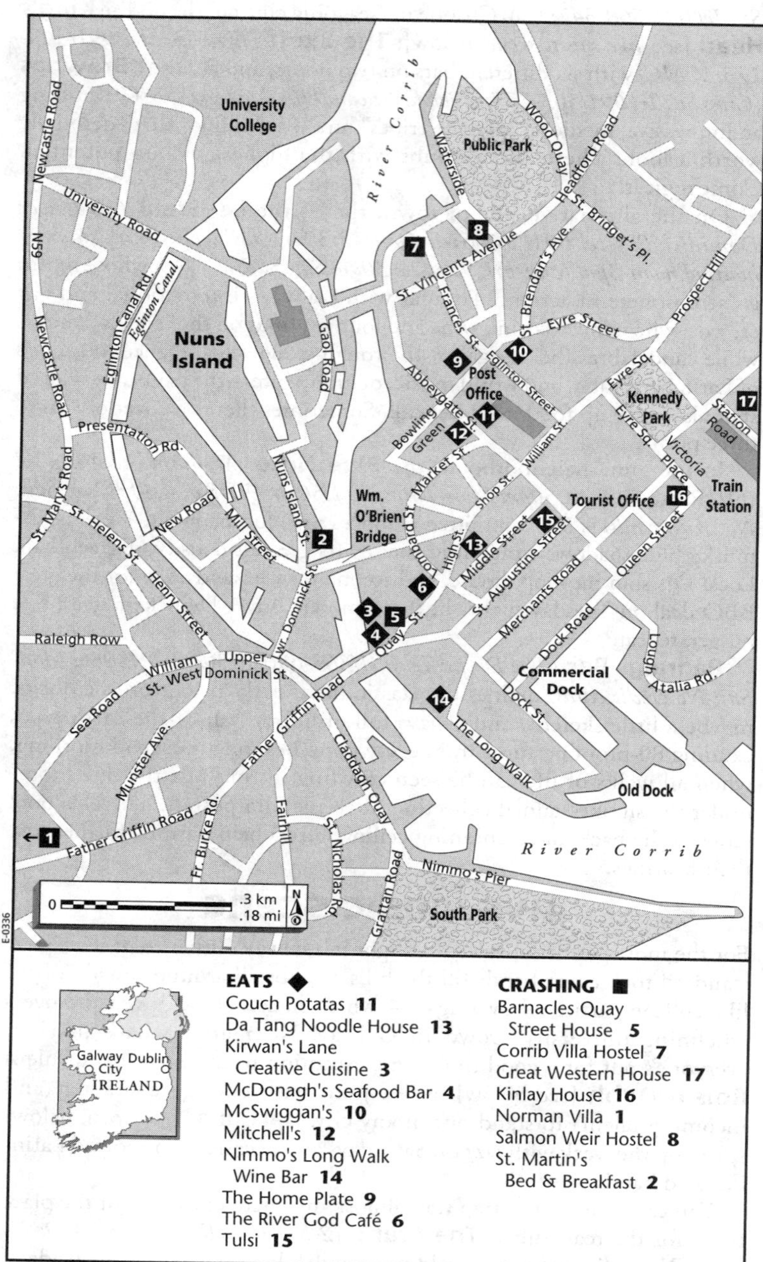
University College
River Corrib
Waterside
Public Park
Wood Quay
Headford Road
St. Bridget's Pl.
Newcastle Road
University Road
N59
St. Vincents Avenue
St. Brendan's Ave.
Prospect Hill
Eglinton Canal Rd.
Eglinton Canal
Nuns Island
Gaol Road
Frances St.
Eyre Street
Post Office
Eglinton Street
Abbeygate St.
Eyre Sq.
Kennedy Park
Station Road
Presentation Rd.
Bowling Green
Market St.
William St.
Victoria Place
Train Station
St. Mary's Road
Nuns Island St.
Wm. O'Brien Bridge
Shop St.
Tourist Office
St. Helens St.
New Road
Mill Street
Lombard St.
High St.
Middle Street
St. Augustine Street
Queen Street
Henry Street
Lwr. Dominick St.
Quay St.
Merchants Road
Dock Road
Raleigh Row
Upper
William St. West Dominick St.
Lough
Atalia Rd.
Commercial Dock
Sea Road
Father Griffin Road
Claddagh Quay
Dock St.
The Long Walk
Munster Ave.
Old Dock
Fr. Burke Rd.
Fairhill
St. Nicholas Rd.
Father Griffin Road
River Corrib
Grattan Road
Nimmo's Pier
South Park
0 .3 km .18 mi
N
E-0336
Galway City
Dublin
IRELAND
EATS
Couch Potatas 11
Da Tang Noodle House 13
Kirwan's Lane Creative Cuisine 3
McDonagh's Seafood Bar 4
McSwiggan's 10
Mitchell's 12
Nimmo's Long Walk Wine Bar 14
The Home Plate 9
The River God Café 6
Tulsi 15
CRASHING
Barnacles Quay Street House 5
Corrib Villa Hostel 7
Great Western House 17
Kinlay House 16
Norman Villa 1
Salmon Weir Hostel 8
St. Martin's Bed & Breakfast 2

behind a scruffy beard. A session could occur at any time, but a good bet is the one casually "scheduled" nightly at 9:30pm. The Sunday afternoon session here can be a religious experience.

The wood-lined pub **Roísín Dubh** *(Dominick St.; Tel 091/586-540; Free-£10; info@roisindubh.net, www.roisindubh.net; No credit cards)*—that's "rawsheen dove" to you—happens to be one of the best places in Ireland for all that other music, hosting local and international names in rock, folk, R&B, blues—and trad—on the little stage in back. Definitely a musicians' hangout, the bar fills with what one local rocker called "a good, healthy bohemian blend." The all-fun house band Full Trousers jams with reggae and ska every Sunday; no cover.

The King's Head *(High St.; Tel 091/566-630; No cover; No credit cards)* is elbow-to-elbow most nights with the young and drunk, all staggering along to the daily parade of (actually, pretty good) cover bands. Summer meat market provided by weekly package bus tour shipments of eager young backpackers. Their chill Dixieland jazz session, Sunday afternoons at 12:30pm, has become a local institution.

Catch an excellent (and very well attended) set-dancing session at **Monroe's** *(Upper Dominick St.; Tel 091/583-397; Mon-Sat from 9:30am, Sun from 12pm; No credit cards)* every Tuesday night. And you can hear trad, trad, and more trad every night of the week, beginning at 9:30pm Irish time, which is to say "very approximately." Although relatively spacious for a pub (and charming, too, with murals of the countryside gracing the walls), there's almost never any room to sit down when the music starts, so get here early, around 8-9pm, for a prime seat. Monroe's also serves good pub grub during breakfast and lunch times, and you can get above-average pizzas beginning at 4pm at the little hole-in-the-wall pizzeria they operate next door. Aside from a few well-informed hostellers, the crowd here's exclusively local.

club scene

As you might expect in such a laid-back town, Galway clubs are a no-stress affair. Some fashion victims don the full get-up, but the guy in Birks just behind them gets in just the same. With a little straightening, your grungy travel gear might even pass muster. Sounds too good to be true, but bouncers are (relatively) mellow, and the mainly undergrad clubbers are out to drink, dance, drink some more, then hook up—not pose or critique. The size of these places may surprise you—there's no shortage of floor space here. For a night-by-night breakdown, pick up the ever-present *Galway List.* Covers run from £4 mid-week to £6 weekends. Clubs are open from 11pm till 2am, but the crowds, and the lines, arrive after the pubs clear out at midnight. Make an early dash out of the pub on weekends, or take the chance of waiting in line half the night.

GPO *(Eglinton St.; Tel 091/563-073)* does its best to keep the western flame of trendiness alive, trying just a little harder than the rest to be hip. Wear black to match the inky dark interior and the rest of the patrons. The "Drum Bar" is downstairs, a dance space the size of a four-car garage

rules of the game

Public drinking, locally called "bushing," doesn't seem to get anyone *too* nervous in Galway. Still, it's best to keep it mellow, and in a paper bag. Favorite spots include Eyre Square and along the banks of the Corrib, preferably on the down-low. As with the rest of Ireland, the drinking age is 18, all recreational drugs are illegal, and walking down the street with a joint will likely get you in big trouble.

is upstairs. Home of local heroes, the Disconauts duo, spinning soul and funk-infused house to loving crowds, GPO also regularly hosts hip-hop and drum 'n' bass nights. Daytime barstaff often have free passes hidden behind the jungle-gym piping—just ask sweetly.

Big and blue and three stories high, **Cuba** *(Eyre Sq.; Tel 091/565-991)* has a lounge bar on one, DJs on two, and live bands on three. Indie Mondays, Latin jazz, funk, and soul Saturdays, and a healthy mix of chart, disco, and dance for the rest of the week. This place is relatively new on the scene, so no niche crowd yet, but the smurfy lighting and Latin rhythms seem to get the co-eds en fuego. Public displays of lust abound. Passes behind the bar during daytime hours; ask the bartender to give you a few.

The Alley *(Ball Alley Lane, off Williamsgate St.; Tel 091/563-173)* is youthquake central in a converted warehouse. They claim to be over-21-only at the door, but the dance floor and three bars are packed with the youngest club crowd in town—seems to be a don't-ask-don't-tell policy. Once in, you don't have to be off your face, but it would definitely help you blend....Mostly college pop tunes, with the dance stuff coming on later in the night. To sum up: The theme to "Friends" played in here one night, and the crowd loved it. Yikes!

Rumor has it that **Central Park** *(Upper Abbeygate St.; Tel 091/565-974; www.indigo.ie/~cpbran)* is a big ol' meat market for dirty old clubbers over 23, which in this town means over the hill. The standard diet of chart and dance applies under space-age molded plywood and tin. You may want to get here early: It's pretty big, but fills up fast.

arts scene

▸▸VISUAL ARTS

Like the little government-funded bohemian paradise that it is, Galway is home to a number of established artists, and a few contemporary galleries. As you would expect from a city set between two national parks, local art tends towards landscapes, but the constant influx of art pilgrims can bring all sorts of unexpected global variety.

A quiet little gallery on a quiet little lane, the **Logan Gallery** *(4a St. Anthony's Place; Tel 091/563-635; 9am-6pm Mon-Sat; No credit cards)* is *the* commercial gallery for contemporary fine art in Galway (which might be because it's the only one...). There's no predominant style or medium here, but the work is of a uniformly high standard. The friendly, laid-back owner is always up for a chat about the Irish art scene.

The **Galway Arts Centre** *(47 Dominick St.; Tel 091/565-886; 10am-9:30pm Mon-Sat; gac@indigo.ie)* has two galleries on two floors of an airy restored mansion. Government-funded and committee-run, the GAC shows about 24 exhibitions a year of what they call "leading and emerging Irish artists," as well as some international stuff. This is the only space in town for installation-piece artists with giant seesaws made from railroad ties.

You can also take your hungry artist's soul to the restaurants and cafes in town hanging regular exhibitions of local work. If you dig around, maybe you'll find that fabled diamond in the rough at **Kirwan's Lane Creative Cuisine** or **Le Graal** [see *eats,* below]; **Apostasy** or **Kenny's Book Shop and Gallery** [see *stuff,* below].

For an eyeful of the big names in contemporary Irish design and fashion, try **Design Concourse Ireland** *(Kirwan's Lane; Tel 091/566-016; 9am-6pm Mon-Thur, Sat, 9am-7pm Fri; V, MC, AE, DC).* This place is pricey, but it's fun just to drool over the jewelry, clothing, furniture, sculpture, and prints.

▸▸PERFORMING ARTS

For such a small town, Galway's theater scene is kickin'. Some of Ireland's finest have come out of this artistic hotbed. If you're lucky enough to be in Galway when the **Druid Theatre Company** *(Chapel Lane; Tel 091/568-617; Box office noon-8pm, shows 8pm; druid_@iol.ie; Tickets £8-10; V, MC, AE)* is here, go to a show. They're old hands in London and on Broadway, have recently won several Tonys, and are considered by many to be the best theater company in Ireland. Their own theater is pretty small, so the Town Hall Theatre on Courthouse Square usually hosts their larger productions.

Based in Galway but traveling worldwide, **Macnas** *(Fisheries Field, Salmon Weir Bridge; Tel 091/561-462; macnas@iol.ie, www.failte.com/macnas; No credit cards)* is another company you should catch if they're in town when you are. Known for mind-blowing costumes and sets, these are the people who put on the surreal parade at **Galway Arts Fest** [see *festivals and events,* below].

Town Hall Theatre *(Courthouse Sq.; Tel 091/569-777; Box office 10am-7:30pm Mon-Sat, shows 8pm Mon-Sat; tht@tinet.ie, home_page.tinet.ie.~tht; Tickets £5-13; V, MC)* is the big new theater in town, just across from the courthouse. Hosts anything that fills seats: Irish or international theater, dance, opera, music, and readings, and serves as main venue for the **Cúirt** [see *festivals and events,* below]. The Town Hall people also run the **Studio** (on the same site), for smaller productions, and the **Black Box** *(Dyke Rd.; Tel 091/568-151)* which does everything from theater to music to comedy to circus in a big school gymnasium–looking space.

gay scene

Galway's no gay mecca, but it does have a small scene. Your best bet for a comfortable place to check out the local talent, or just be yourself, is probably **Le Graal** [see *bar scene,* above]. Keepers of the faith often congregate in other hip spots, such as **Café du Journal** and **Apostasy** [see *hanging out,* above], and **Nimmo's** [see *eats,* below].

The **Galway Gay Help Line** *(Tel 091/566-134)* and **Galway Lesbian Line** *(Tel 091/564-611)* are good resources, or check out the monthly freesheet, *GCN (Gay Community News)* and look for listings on Galway in the back.

Friday and Saturday nights, Club Mix in The Attic at **Liquid** *(Salthill; Tel 088/269-14-12; Doors open 10:30pm; £4 cover)* draws every lonely farm boy and maybe an incognito village priest or two from the homophobically oppressed western hinterlands.

Jazz Juice brings a mixed crowd of hipsters, trendy folks, and gay and straight undergrad bohos to **GPO** [see *club scene,* above].

culture zoo

As you might have guessed, there are no cavernous art museums tucked into Galway's quaint little streets. But there are a few gorgeous churches and other neat old structures.

Galway Cathedral *(University and Gaol Rds.; Tel 091/563-577; 8am-6pm daily; Free admission):* A 1960s-vintage cathedral with saintly mosaic of JFK, obscured in darkness since those shocking revelations of his lecherous character. The hopelessly tacky mishmash of architectural styles make for an art history student's worst nightmare.

Cathedral of Our Lady Assumed in Heaven and Saint Nicholas *(Lombard St.; Tel 091/564-648; 9am-5:45pm Mon-Sat, 1-5:45pm Sun Apr-Sept, 10am-4pm Mon-Sat, 1-5pm Sun Oct-Mar; Free admission):* This 14th-century Protestant church features a crusader's tomb with Norman inscription. Cromwell kept his horses here and destroyed every other church in Galway. It's the largest still-used medieval church in Ireland.

Galway City Museum *(Next to Spanish Arch; Tel 091/567-641; 10am-1pm/2:15-5:15pm daily Apr-Sept, Tue-Thur only Oct-Mar; Admission £1):* A walk around this tiny museum is sure to inspire a nap in the park out front.

Nora Barnacle House *(8 Bowling Green; Tel 091/564-743; 10am-1pm/2-5pm Mon-Sat mid-May to mid-Sept; Admission £1):* Ireland's westernmost outpost of James Joyce worship, being the former home of the Great One's in-laws [see *portrait of the artist,* above].

Lynch's Castle *(Allied Irish Bank; Corner of Abbeygate St. and Shop St.; 10am-4pm Mon-Wed, Fri, till 5pm Thur; Free admission):* Witness the march of civilization: Intricately carved medieval stones once harboring Galway's richest clan now house ATMs supplying booze money to pub crawlers.

calling all yeats fans

Poetry lovers won't want to miss a visit to **Thoor Ballylee** *(N18, Gort; Tel 091/631-436; 10am-6pm Easter-Sept; Admission around £3.50),* the 16th-century residence that William Butler Yeats purchased in the 1920s for a mere £35. Usually referred to as a castle, although it's really more of a tower house, Thoor Ballylee provided inspiration for much of Yeats's finest poetry, such as *The Winding Stair* and *The Tower.*

The price of admission entitles you to the run of the house, which offers some fine views of the surrounding countryside—the tower is a lot taller than it looks from the outside. There is also a short audio-visual presentation on Yeats's life and work. Gort is right on the Bus Éireann line (routes 51 and 55) between Ennis and Galway (37 km from Galway) and buses pass through literally dozens of times a day, so you'll have no trouble getting here. Call the **Galway Bus Station** *(Tel 091/562-000)* for information.

Spanish Arch *(End of Quay St.; Free admission):* Once part of the city wall through which Spanish ships bearing exotic spirits could unload. In short: Sexy name, uninteresting structure.

Padraic O'Conaire Statue *(Eyre Sq.):* This monument commemorates one of Ireland's most revered writers, a Galway native controversial for his thoroughly grim depictions of "realistic" everyday Irish life. Though O'Conaire is acknowledged as an initiator of the Gaelic Revival, most folks pass right by the western end of this public square without acknowledging the debt owed, so pause a moment for Paddy.

Browne's Doorway *(Eyre Sq.):* Right next to O'Conaire's statue stands this imposing example of a townhouse of the once-powerful shipping classes of Galway. It's an elaborate and rather creepy structure, decorated with family seals and hand-carved stonework, dating from the early 17th century.

Lynch Memorial Window *(Market St., north of St. Nicholas's Cathedral):* The story goes that a man named Lynch, mayor of Galway in the late 1400s, condemned his own son to death—and when no one else in the city would serve as executioner, he personally followed through on his order. The Window supposedly marks the spot where the gallows stood.

The most important part of this walk is to somehow find a way to announce to anyone who will listen that you are either of "Clan Kennedy" or descended from the mighty Ché, or both. How and where you do this is entirely up to you. It's only fitting that two of the most charismatic ideological enemies of the cold war should be united in the geography of friendly, neutral Galway. (Of course, we all know it was Ché's idea to assassinate Kennedy for trying to assassinate Castro, and Kennedy's successors in Washington repaid the favor.) May old foes rest in peace, and may we get to drinking, please?

First, we must start at JFK's *Freeman of the City* monument next to the fountain at **Eyre Square.** This special honor was granted (on this very spot) by the publicans of Galway, involving a promise to supply lifelong "free" pints to our young Prez. Feels historic, no? Now, for a drink: Walk south across the square, past the **Tourist Office** [see *need to know,* below], and take a right onto **Queen Street** (becoming **Dock Road**), where you'll find **Padraigs Bar** [see *bar scene,* above]. Legend has it ol' Jack and Co. stopped in here the morning after the "Freeman" ceremony for one last free pint before catching an early Air Force One back to D.C. Can you spot his special friend Marilyn among the movie posters? Next, take a right out the door, a right again onto **New Dock Street,** then a left on **Flood Street,** which brings us to Jury's Inn at **Wolfe Tone Bridge.** Take in the view, and the swans, and the fresh sea air, then continue north by the path running along the riverside just on

great outdoors

For a nice place to run, try the path along the Corrib starting beside Jury's Hotel in front of the Spanish Arch, going up to the **Salmon Weir Bridge** [see *by foot,* above], or cross the Wolfe Tone bridge and head out along the coast to Salthill, via **South Park** [see *hanging out,* above].

If paddling away up the River Corrib in a little wooden boat to picnic in the ruins of an old castle surrounded by fields of grazing horses sounds like good exercise to you, drop by **Corrib Boat Hire** *(Brando Screen Printing, Waterside St. across from the old Galway Rowing Club; No phone; 9am-8pm daily; Rowboats £4 per hour, £25 per day; No credit cards).* The whole trip, including about 45 minutes for a picnic, takes about 2 hours.

For everything else, you really ought to get out of the city. If beaches good for prancing and showing off your nonexistent tan will satisfy, you

by foot

the left of Jury's. Continue up past **William O'Brien Bridge,** looking for fish in the clear waters, then take a left onto the **Salmon Weir Bridge** and up into **Galway Cathedral** [see *culture zoo,* above]. Once inside, look for Saint Kennedy's mosaic. (Hint: It's hidden, and to your left as you face the altar.) Can you identify the other two men pictured with him on the wall? Exit and re-cross the bridge, jogging right before turning left onto **Saint Vincent's Avenue,** then your first right onto **Francis Street.** Drop into **O'Ché's** [see *hanging out,* above] for the new-age Guevara mural and a pitcher of sangria in an underground atmosphere fit for conspiring to overthrow the parasitic ruling class. Next, take a left out the door and your first left at **McSwiggan's** [see *eats,* below] onto **Eyre Street.** Continue to the **Hole in the Wall** [see *bar scene,* above] for another pint, of course. Here, hidden among the celebrity photos on the wall is one very interesting picture: bar owner Stephen J. Fahy holding a youthful Jack and smiling Ché under each arm, taken during the memorable '52 **Galway Races** [see *festivals and events,* below]. Stay here for a good long while. Feel the love. Turn right up the street and continue to the taxi rank at Eyre Square, turn left and enter **BarCuba*** [see *eats,* below] a veritable shrine to the patron saint of communism, overlooking our starting point, a monument to the greatest son-of-a-bootlegger there ever was. That's full circle. Have a fine Cuban cigar with a whiskey and ponder the whimsy of history, my friend.

can take a 20-minute walk out to **Salthill,** a hotel- and amusement-gorged suburb west of the city center and across the bridge, home to Galway's closest beach. It's almost always teeming with humanity's ritzier half. That said, you can probably find nicer strands among Galway's outermost reaches [see **Connemara,** below], or try the beach at **Spiddal,** a short Bus Éireann (route 424) ride west of Galway, past Salthill. It's actually nicer than Salthill's beach: clean, sandy, and perfect for swimming.

You can also take the bus to the **Aille Cross Equitation Centre** *(Aille Cross, Loughrea; Tel 091/841-216; Approx. £12 per hour),* positioned 32 km (20 mi) east of Galway. This is one of the largest horseback riding centers in the country, with 50 mounts and 20 Connemara ponies available; you can ride down forest trails, through farm lands, and over mountains. Week-long riding trips throughout Connemara are conducted regularly. Take Bus Éireann (route 70) from the Galway Bus and Train Station to Loughrea; it's about a half-hour ride.

festivals and events

The schedules on these festivals vary, so call for exact dates.

Cúirt International Festival of Literature *(Apr, flexible dates; Most events in Town Hall Theatre, Courthouse Sq.; Tel 091/569-777):* An eclectic migration of world-renowned scribblers letting it all hang out, literally. Past greats have included Seamus Heaney and Allen Ginsberg, presumably stoking the flames of culture, creativity, and lust.

Galway Early Music Festival *(Three days in mid-May; Tel 091/846-366):* Pageantry, theater, and music from those vibrant Dark Ages.

Galway Film Fleadh *(Early July; Tel 091/569-777):* Your standard film festival, with past appearances by famous Irish actors, including Gabriel Byrne.

Galway Arts Festival *(Mid-July; Tel 091/562-480; info@gaf.iol.ie; www.galwayartsfestival.ie):* The Big One. Famous for its street carnival, music, theater, and much more. Could be the best summer festival in Europe.

Galway Races *(Late July; Tel 091/753-870):* A Bukowski-like horse-racing bacchanal that utterly transforms the town. Many businesses shut down for the week as everybody goes to the track and/or pub. You won't find a vacancy in a Limerick broom closet, let alone in Galway.

Galway International Oyster Festival *(Late Sept; Tel 091/527-282):* Besides lots of oyster-eating, this festival includes, among other things, a golf tournament and yacht race to celebrate Ireland's favorite bottom-feeding mollusk.

stuff

Galway ain't your shopper's mecca. We're talking a town of 60,000 folks. If you gotta have that shopping fix, check out a few of the 50 shops in **Eyre Square Centre** *(Eyre Sq.; Tel 091/568-302; 9am-6:30pm Mon-Wed, Sun, 9am-9pm Fri, Sat).* This mall features a real scratch 'n' sniff medieval wall.

▸▸VINTAGE

For funky vintage '70s stuff, mostly for women, climb the stairs to **Idol Angel** *(24 Upper Abbeygate St.; Tel 091/562-240; 12-6pm Mon-Sat; £2-30 price range; No credit cards).*

▸▸BAZAAR

Try the **Galway Market** *(Market St.; 9am-5pm Sat)* for stands of fruit, organic veggies, pottery, clothes, jewelry, and trinkets. They've got good eats here: Look for the famous "Curryman" and the stand selling sweet and savory crêpes.

In the taxi rank area at the top of Eyre Square, stalls sell clothes, jewelry, and even horse and bridle stuff from 9am till 5pm every Monday through Saturday.

▸▸BOUND

Don't let the slightly precious exterior fool you, 'cause **Kenny's Book Shop and Gallery** *(Corner Middle and High Sts.; Tel 091/562-507; 9am-6pm Mon-Sat; www.kennys.ie, queries@kennys.ie; V, MC, AE)* is the grand old man of Galway books. The three floors are packed with all sorts of subjects and titles, both rare and budget-bin, with a specialty in (what else?) Irish literature.

Conveniently opposite the back door of Kenny's, there's **Charlie Byrne's Bookshop** *(The Cornstore, Middle St.; Tel 091/561-766; 9am-6pm Mon-Thur, 9am-8pm Sat; chabyrne@iol.ie; No credit cards)*. Just a big, comfy ol' horde of used, remaindered, and discounted books. Books,

surf's up

Since Ireland hosted the European surfing championship in '98, word's gotten around about the good Irish surf. The Atlantic swells come year-round, but the best are in April/May and September/October. Sampling Ireland's tubular bounty is easy in Galway: Just call Bryan Redmond at **Outback Ireland Surf Tours** *(Tel 091/84001, 086/814-26-61; £30 per person; No credit cards)*. For beginners, usually in groups of five, Bryan and his staff will pick you up at 8:30am, transport you to the slow-rolling beach break at Lahinch, County Clare, provide board, wetsuit, and an hour and a half of individual instruction followed by a full day of surfing. The tour includes a beach barbecue lunch and a scenic return through the desolately beautiful landscape of the Burren. Of course, a pub stop or two is always an option before returning to Galway in the evening. Bryan offers more experienced surfers a choice of breaks from Dingle to Donegal, and will arrange custom tours of one to three days for surfers of any level.

For the lowdown on surfing from Galway locals, talk to the staff at **Great Outdoors Sports Centre** *(Eglington St.; Tel 091/562-609)* or contact the **Irish Surfing Association** *(Tel 096/49428)*. For gear, check out the **Lahinch Surf Shop** *(The Promenade, Lahinch; Tel 065/708-15-43; 11am-6pm Tue-Sun; V, MC)*. Owners Tom and Rosemarie Buckley rent beginner surfboards, boogie boards, and full-length wetsuits all for £5 per 2 hours each, and offer instruction for £5 per hour.

books, and more books, from Behan to Dewey, line every inch of wall space. This is the one in town with that stay-all-day vibe. Mmm...it even smells like a good bookshop.

For rock-bottom pulp fiction, it's gotta be **Book Exchange** *(23 Lower Abbeygate St; Tel 091/562-225; 10am-6pm Mon-Sat; No credit cards),* a tiny hole-in-the-wall used bookshop full of those cheap, trashy novels and spy thrillers you just need on a trip through Europe.

Your best bet to find out what's up here in a literary way is to check in with local author **Fred Johnston** *(Upstairs at Galway Center for the Unemployed, Canavan House, Nun's Island St.; Tel 091/567-438; 9am-5pm Mon-Fri).* Fred founded the **Cúirt** festival [see *festivals and events,* above] back in '86 and currently works in community literary arts development. You could also check for literary news in Markings and Bookview West, Fred's pages in the weekly *Galway Advertiser.*

▸▸TUNES

Besides being the only place in town where you can score secondhand vinyl, **Mulligan** *(5 Middle St. Court, Middle St.; Tel 091/564-961; 10am-7pm Mon-Thur, till 9pm Fri, till 6pm Sat, 2-6pm Sun; mulligan@indigo.ie, indigo.ie/~mulligan; V, MC, AE)* boasts of having "everything" in Irish and Scottish trad, along with respectable collections of jazz, blues, soul, and ethnic music. Tickets for Roísín Dubh [see *live music scene,* above] shows, other biggish local gigs, and charity events are all on sale here.

Half-looking like yet another cheesy tourist-drag souvenir shop, **Zhivago** *(5 Shop St.; Tel 091/509-960; 9am-6pm Mon-Wed, Sat, till 9pm Thur, Fri, 10am-6pm Sun; www.musicireland.com, info@musicireland._com; V, MC, AE)* has the Ticketmaster outlet for all major shows nationwide. And you can pick up a "Guinness Is Good For You" T-shirt while you're getting your tix.

eats

For a small town, Galway has an impressive number of cafes and restaurants. Unfortunately, like most of Ireland, the wait service here is uniformly bad, which verges on spoiling your meal, no matter how good it tastes. The cafes and restaurants listed below are usually pretty good with the service, among other things.

▸▸CHEAP

The Home Plate *(13 Mary St.; Tel 091/561-475; Noon-9:30pm daily; £1.95-4.95 per entree lunch, £4.75-6.95 per entree dinner; No credit cards)* is possibly the best place for lunch in Galway. Huge, fresh, tasty helpings of pasta, curry, or sandwiches for next to nothing in a homey little place across from the post office with checked tablecloths, friendly staff, and good service.

McSwiggan's *(3 Eyre St., Woodquay; Tel 091/568-917; Normal pub hours, Carvery lunch noon-3pm; £4.50; V, MC, AE, DC)* is a little off the tourist path, in the Eyre Square area, but the meat-and-potatoes food is plentiful, tasty, and reasonably priced. Plus, you can eat your grub under the looming presence of a huge, shellacked, indoor tree. Get here before 1pm, and beat the hordes.

Also on Eyre Square, **BarCuba*** *(Eyre Sq.; Tel 091/565-991; 10:30am-11pm Mon-Sat, or till 11:30pm in summer, 12:30-2pm/4-11pm Sun; £5 or under per entree; V, MC)* has tasty Caribbean food, killer coffee, and folks toking on fat stogies of a kind embargoed in the States. Just what you expected from an Irish pub, right? This spacious, loungey bar may well have Ireland's finest collection of wall-sized photos, Ché memorabilia, and potted shrubbery. They've definitely got good eats, and possibly the strongest cup of joe in Galway.

You want some fish and chips with your grease? **McDonagh's Seafood Bar** *(22 Quay St.; Tel 091/565-001; Noon-12am Mon-Sat, 5-11pm Sun; £5-14 per entree; V, MC, AE, DC)* serves it up right, over by the William O'Brien Bridge. There's eats outside on picnic tables come sunny days. The lunch is a better value than dinner.

A languorous and well-endowed mermaid on the first-floor mural points you to **The River God Café** *(2 Quay St.; Tel 091/565-811; 12:30-10pm; therivergod@eircom.net, www.therivergod.com; £4.95 two-course lunch; V, MC),* as does the menu board outside proclaiming that a delicious two-course lunch is available for just £4.95 until 4pm. Sound good? Dude, it's *more* than good! This chow nearly merits the "divine" description the restaurant gives it—and it'll feed you for dinner as well. Try the roasted aubergine and red lentil soup, followed by salmon and lemon rice fajitas with a side salad. Dinner main courses here go for £6.50 to £12.50, and of course they're equally mouth-watering, but as usual the lunch is a better value. All in all a splendid afternoon hangout with fantastic service, a classy yet casual atmosphere, and great views overlooking Galway's eccentrics doing what they do best on Quay Street.

More than any other place in town, the relatively new **Mitchell's** *(Lower Abbeygate St.; Tel 091/66441; Hours vary; All items under £8, most under £5; No credit cards)* resembles a typical American diner. The menu's similar too, with nice hefty Irish breakfasts for around £3.50, a veggie option for a mere £2.50, sandwiches for well under £2, and cheap main courses. The hours are still rather erratic; at some point the owner aims to be open 24-7, but a lack of help makes that goal a tad difficult to achieve. At any rate, the place'll stay open for as long as you choose to hang out, which means that if you're still alert and hungry after closing time at **Java's** or **Apostasy** [see *hanging out,* above], and you don't feel badly about further darkening the bags under the poor proprietor's eyes, it's the perfect place.

And here's what you've been waiting for: an homage to Ireland's favorite tuber. The folks at **Couch Potatas** *(Upper Abbeygate St.; Tel 091/561-664; Noon-10pm Mon-Sat, 1-10pm Sun; All items under £5; No credit cards)* offer nice big spuds with a ton of different fillings. (But don't come here if you don't like potatoes.) Try the Hawaii 5-0, with ham, onion, pineapple, peppers, and melted cheddar cheese. Every 'tater comes with a generous side salad, as well. It's a great spot for lunch, although it does get quite crowded at midday.

▸▸DO-ABLE

A tiny place on a quiet street off Shop Street, **Da Tang Noodle House** *(2 Middle St.; Tel 091/561-443; Noon-3pm/5:30-10pm Mon-Thur, till 10:30pm Fri, Sat, 5:30-10pm Sun; £5-10 per entree; V, MC)* has just a few tables inside, but it's got that great hole-in-the-wall atmosphere. And great noodles.

Also in the Shop Street area, **Tulsi** *(3 Buttermilk Walk, off Middle St.; Tel 091/564-831; £5.95-12.95 per entree, 20 percent discount on takeout; V, MC)* is your standard Indian restaurant: lots of dark tapestry and rattan, and lots of excellent vegetarian options. Go for the takeout and save a bunch.

▸▸SPLURGE

Set on the river in an old stone house just behind the Spanish Arch, **Nimmo's Long Walk Wine Bar** *(Spanish Arch; Tel 091/561-114; Winebar: lunch 12:30-3pm, dinner 6:30-10pm, open till 11:30pm; Restaurant: 7-10pm Tue-Sat, 5-11:30pm Sun; £6-13 per entree; No credit cards)* is the little romantic bistro all the others wish they could be. Local fishermen bring in the daily catch for your wine-soaked soirée in a cozy alcove. If this place don't set fire to your love life, give it up.

How 'bout some balsamic roasted duck with sweet pear and sage dressing, or perhaps a couple of pan-seared lamb's kidneys in honey and black pepper? Chef Padraic Kielty, who has the helm at the famous **Kirwan's Lane Creative Cuisine** *(Kirwan's Lane; Tel 091/568-266; 12:30-2:30pm/6:30-10:30pm Mon-Sat; £6.95-16.95 per entree; V, MC, AE)* won't disappoint. Enjoy the extensive wine list in this stylish space by the William O'Brien Bridge.

crashing

Being the festival capital of Ireland, Galway naturally has a wide range of good digs, from super-cheap to absolutely opulent. Still, you definitely need to book ahead for weekends, during festivals [see *festivals and events,* above], or anytime in the summer, or you might end up in some dingy dive. If you do find yourself bedless on a packed weekend, give your feet a rest and try the reservations center upstairs at the **Tourist Office** [see *need to know,* below]. For a measly punt, they'll call around until they find you something.

▸▸CHEAP

For the most part, the hostels in Galway are clean and well-run. The ones listed here all have laundry services, comfy TV lounges, and well-equipped kitchens.

Directly opposite the train station, **Great Western House** *(Frenchville Lane, Eyre Sq.; Tel 091/561-139; shaungwh@iol.ie, www.iol._ie/~shaungwh; £8.50-9.50 large dorm, £11.50-12.50 4- and 6-bed dorm, £26-32 double, £36 triple, £45-60 3-bed quad; V, MC)* has to be one of the best-equipped hostels in Ireland. Get this: In addition to the spacious and immaculate kitchen, dining room, TV lounge, laundry service, billiard room, and access for disabled travelers, they've got a sauna. Price includes a small breakfast and discount entrance to **The Alley** [see *club scene,* above], but the staff here can be a little cold, and there's not much of a social vibe.

Like a black hole of fun, like a soap opera with a laugh track, the **Salmon Weir Hostel** *(3 St. Vincent's Ave., Woodquay; Tel 091/561-133; £7.50-8 10-bed, £8-8.50 6-bed, £8.50-9 4-bed, £20-22 double/twin; No credit cards)* has that welcoming, party-loving atmosphere. Up near the Public Park, this place has such a good vibe, one-time guests long since settled into Galway regularly come by just to hang out. A clean and cozy converted house, the "Sadly Weird" features B.J. McKay shower curtains, a Scott Baio shrine, free-flowing tea and coffee, and mucho mayhem. The whole place, including the slacker-paradise TV room with VCR, is totally nonsmoking. Not for introverts.

Barnacles Quay Street House *(10 Quay St.; Tel 091/568-644; qshostel@barnacles.iol.ie, www.iol.ie/~lalco; £8-9.50 dorm, £10.50-13 4-bed, £13-16 twin/double; V, MC)* takes the prize for bravest paint job in town. Something in "Radioactive Tang" covers the facade, entrance hallway, and reception area of this clean, well-managed hostel right on the main

12 hours in galway

This town ain't so big. No need to rush.

1. Chill.
2. Call your mother. She'll be relieved you're in such a safe, happy little village instead of one of those big, bad European mega-metropolises full of strange people who can't speak English and rip the roofs off McDonald's with their tractors.
3. Hang out outside **Tigh Neachtain's,** and check out the human circus [see *bar scene,* above].
4. Find the Corrib River's alpha swan, and pick a fight with him. Legend has it the hero who defeats this mighty swan will break an evil spell and raise the merry medieval Iberian sailors from their slumber under the Spanish Arch, who will in turn show their gratitude by delivering up the lost treasure of Lynch's Castle (now a bank). A thousand years of peace and prosperity will follow.
5. Do a pub crawl and try not to crawl by the end of it [see *by foot,* above].
6. Walk the beautiful banks of the Corrib and fine-tune your soul.
7. Keeping with the soulful, but livening it up a bit, go hear some good trad [see *live music scene,* above].
8. Chill some more.

pub drag. Most rooms are bright, white, and airy, and come with the added ambience of busker music drifting up from the street. There's bike storage, and the price of a bed includes a small breakfast.

By far the coolest hostel in town, by general consensus, is **Corrib Villa** *(4 Waterside; Tel 091/562-892; Open 24 hours; 6-bed dorms £8.50; No credit cards),* which epitomizes the fun, laid-back, boho lifestyle for which Galway is renowned. A Georgian townhouse with festively painted walls, cool artwork, a cozy atmosphere, and an ultra-friendly staff, Corrib Villa is located right on the river, convenient for boat rental and just across the street from the **Town Hall Theatre** [see *arts scene,* above]. This is the hostel where all backpackers eventually end up after enduring bad—or at least lukewarm—experiences at almost every other hostel in town. It's the kind of place you'll hate to leave when your sojourn in Galway has ended.

Still not interested? There's also the pretty cheap **Kinlay House** *(Merchant's Rd.; Tel 091/565-244, Fax 09/15-65-245; kinlay.galway@usitworld.com; Nov-Feb £10-17, March-Oct £11-18, some rooms have private baths, while others are shared; V, MC, AE),* in the heart of the city, a mere 2-minute walk from the bus station.

▶▶DO-ABLE

St. Martin's Bed & Breakfast *(2 Nun's Island St.; Tel 091/568-286; £20 single, £36 double; No credit cards)* is your fantasy B&B made reality. With a house set in a flower garden overlooking the river just 5 minutes out from the center of town, super-friendly owners Mary and Donie Sexton have a real gem here. You'll fall asleep to the sound of little waterfalls, and awake to freshly squeezed OJ, Mary's homemade brown bread, and a full Irish breakfast, made to order. Sounds good, no? Just remember this is a family home, so it won't be robo-pound in the breakfast room at 4am, but you may be able to talk Donie into going out for a pint.

Some other reasonably priced spots include **Roncalli House** *(24 Whitestrand Ave.; Tel 091/584-159, Fax 091/584-159; £20-29.50, all rooms include private baths and complimentary breakfast; V, MC),* a 10-minute walk from the city center, **Knockrea B&B** *(55 Lower Salthill Rd.; Tel 091/520-145, Fax 091/529-985; www.galway.net/pages/knockrea/, knockrea@eircom.net; £20-25 single, £25-30 double, all rooms have private baths; V, MC),* a nice 10-minute walk from the city center; and the **Adare Guesthouse** *(9 Father Griffin Place; Tel 091/582-638, Fax 091/583-963; adare@iol.ie; July-Sept £45 single, £30 per person double, £37.50 per person suite, Oct-June £27.50 single, £25 per person double, £27.50 per person suite, all rooms have private baths; V, MC),* 5 minutes from the city center and only a 15-minute walk from the bus station.

▶▶SPLURGE

For a crash course on the best in contemporary Irish art, check into **Norman Villa** *(86 Lower Salthill; Tel 091/521-131; £37 single, £64-70 double; V, MC).* Only 10 minutes' walk from downtown, Dee and Mark Keogh's impressive Victorian is pure class, with pine floors, flagstone dining room, and art pieces hung over the brass beds in every room. Made-to-order breakfast is included. You want smoked salmon, kippers, and poached eggs? No problem. On a sunny morning, take it in the beautiful, quiet garden out back.

Looking for another place to blow all of your money? Try **Great Southern Hotel** *(Eyre Sq.; Tel 091/564-041, Fax 091/566-704; res@galway.gsh.ie; www.gsh.ie; Summer £117 single, £170 double, rest of the year £105 single, £190 double, all rooms have private baths; V, MC, AE),* located right downtown.

within 30 minutes

All right, so it's gonna take you longer than a half-hour to get out to **Connemara National Park** or some of the cool little towns on the coast that make perfect sporting spots, but they still make excellent trips out of Galway City. **Oughterard** is a 35-minute bus ride (via Bus Éireann routes 416 or 419); this little town is usually just a passing-through spot on the way out to Connemara, but there's actually plenty to do here: canoeing on **Lough Corrib,** hiking in the **Maam Turk Mountains,** and visiting **Inchagoill Island,** with its incredible ancient ruins [see *everywhere else,* below, for both]. And, of course, there's always **Salthill** [see *great outdoors,* above].

need to know

Currency Exchange A Bureau de Change within any bank will have the best rates.

Tourist Information **Ireland West Tourism** *(Victoria Place, off Eyre Sq.; Tel 091/563-081; 9am-5:45pm daily, till 7:45pm July, Aug).*

Public Transportation Buses to Salthill and other suburbs depart from the **Bus Éireann Travel Centre** *(Tel 091/562-000)* in Ceannt Station (get your bus maps here) and Eyre Square. The flat rate is 70p. Within the city, you really don't need public transportation.

Bike Rental **Mountain Trail Bike Shop** *(St. Augustine St.; Tel 091/569-888)* or **Celtic Cycles** *(Queen St., Victoria Place; Tel 091/566-606)* are good options.

American Express Northwest side of Eyre Square *(Tel 091/562-316).*

Health and Emergency Emergency: *999.* **Galway University College Hospital** *(Newcastle Rd.; Tel 091/580-580),* **Merlin Park Regional Hospital** *(Merlin Park; Tel 091/757-631).*

Pharmacies **Flanagan's Pharmacy** *(32 Shop St.; Tel 091/562-924; 9am-6pm Mon-Sat; V, MC)* or **Whelan's Chemist** *(Williamsgate St.; Tel 091/562-291; 9am-6pm Mon-Sat; V, MC, AE).*

Telephone City code: *091;* information: *1190;* international operator: *114.* International and local phone cards can be purchased in almost any shop. The green-and-pink "Spirit" cards have the best international rates.

Airports Galway Airport *(Tel 091/755-569)* is out in Carnmore, just 6 km from the city center; cabs to Galway cost around £12; the bus is £2.50.

Airlines Aer Lingus *(Tel 018/868-888)* offers service into Galway Airport.

Trains Irish Rail *(Tel 091/562-000)* trains run into **Ceannt Station** *(Tel 091/562-000),* just off Eyre Square in the city center.

Bus Lines Out of the City Bus Éireann *(Bus Éireann Travel Centre, Ceannt Station; Tel 091/562-000)* or **CityLink** *(Forster Court; Tel 091/564-163).*

wired

For web access, try **Net@ccess Cyber Café** *(The Olde Malte Arcade, High St.; Tel 091/569-772; 10am-10pm Mon-Fri, 10am-7pm Sat, noon-6pm Sun; www.netaccess.ie; £5 per hour, £4 students),* and don't forget to ask for your free coffee! Star Trekish murals spout interstellar wisdom above the 14 fast PCs. Equipped with friendly staff, scanner, fax, and printer. A lesser-known late-night option, just over the Corrib, is **Jamie Starlights** *(Upper Dominick St.; Tel 091/588-710; 9am-12am Mon-Sat, noon-midnight Sun; £2.50 per half-hour, £2 students).* Five PC carrels line one side of this video library-cum-cybercafe. They don't sell "real" food anymore, but there's plenty of candy store rotgut for your munchies. Monitors here spew a constant stream of those action movie explosions so beloved by video clerks the world over. Neither of these places has much of a social vibe.

everywhere else

kinvara and dunguaire castle

This quiet, lovely little town overlooking Galway Bay south of Galway City lends a dramatic setting to the 16th-century **Dunguaire Castle** *(On N67, just east of Kinvara; Tel 061/360-788 for info, 061/361-511 for dinner reservations; Banquets £30 per person nightly in summertime; V, MC, AE)*. Built on the site of a seventh-century fortress of a certain Guaire, a Connaught king, Dunguaire offers "traditional" dinner banquets similar to those at **Bunratty** in County Clare. True, it's a tourist magnet, but it's great fun as long as you're not traveling on a shoestring. You'll find traditional Celtic music and food, mead wine, and no eating utensils, along with literary tributes to William Butler Yeats, George Bernard Shaw, and John Millington Synge, and all those other Irish Literary Renaissance types, who met here when the castle was a popular retreat for writers and artists.

If it's a lower-key vibe you're looking for, you're on. Kinvara is also a great starting point for hikes around the surrounding Burren [see **County Clare,** above]. The map and guide *Kinvara: A Rambler's Map and Guide* will keep you on some beautiful trails.

live music scene

The prime spot to foot-stomp the night away to trad fiddlers is **The Pier Head,** easy to find right on the Kinvara quay. Pubs in the surrounding blocks also feature an assortment of the usual fine blend of Guinness and folk. Best strategy is to follow your nose—or your ears.

eats

The whole reason to go to Kinvara is to see **Dunguaire Castle** *(Tel 061/361511 for dinner reservations; Banquets £30 per person nightly in summertime; V, MC, AE)* and, if you can afford it, to *eat* there. Banquets are held twice nightly in the summer. Otherwise, classic "olde Ireland" atmosphere is the draw at the **Merriman Inn and Restaurant** *(Mainstreet; Closed Jan; Tel 091/638-222; dinner £8-18; V, MC, AE),* where you dine in a cottage on hearty staples like beef, roast potatoes, and salmon.

crashing

The **Cois Cuain B&B** *(Tel 091/637-119)* is a good option for a stay, with relatively cheap rooms and a brilliant waterside view.

need to know

Buses Dunguaire Castle is located only a half-hour's drive or bus ride south of Galway City; take **Bus Éireann** *(Tel 091/562-000)* routes 50 or 423 out of Galway. Be advised that the last buses leave Kinvara for a return to Galway around 8:30pm, so if you don't plan to sleep over here, make reservations for the earlier dinner seating.

the aran islands

Looking like three skipping stones thrown across the waves of Galway Bay by a giant, the Aran Islands are among those rugged, mystical, and serene Irish places you'll never forget. Fully two-thirds of the islands' landscape is bare limestone, fissured and sculpted into bizarre patterns by millions of years of erosion. Jagged-edged cliffs, some rising 300 feet above the Atlantic, run along the entire southern edge of the main island, **Inis Mór** ("Inishmore"). Here, on a precipice 300 feet above the waves, sits **Dún Aengus** [see *culture zoo,* below], one of the most dramatic ancient ruins in Europe.

Among other things, these stunning, sparsely populated islands are absolutely among the finest spots in the world for a picnic with your honey. What could be more romantic than a long walk along sea cliffs, through fields of wildflowers and ancient stone walls, with a spectacular view across the water to the Irish coast?

The Aran Islands are an easy trip from Galway, and many folks go for only an afternoon. Another possibility is to chug across via **Doolin Ferries** from Doolin, County Clare [see *need to know,* below].

Chances are that if you have time for only one of the islands, you'll be visiting Inis Mór, and it's definitely got the most going on. But if you do have time, consider visiting **Inis Oírr** ("Inisheer"), which could be even more romantic for those long walks because it hasn't yielded to tourism as thoroughly as Inis Mór has. There are enough B&Bs (and one well-above-average hostel) to choose from [see *crashing,* below], and they're all within a horseshoe's toss of the pier. You can easily walk from one end of the island to the other (it's only 3 miles long), through mazes of ancient stone walls fencing in a few petulant cows. You may not see a single soul all afternoon, and when you do, it'll be a farmer driving by in his tractor or a young mother hanging her laundry out to dry. Plop yourself down on the large rocks—perfect for sunbathing, were this the Mediterranean—and watch the tide rush in and the sun set. You could easily fool yourself into believing you were the tiny island's sole inhabitant. If you were looking to do a little soul-sifting, there's no better place.

As for **Inis Meáin** ("Inishmaan"), the middle and least-visited of the three islands, the scenery isn't as fantastic and those pressed for time end up skipping it. There are several noteworthy diversions here for an afternoon visit, including the hang-out spots of **John Millington Synge,** the renowned Irish playwright and poet who wrote about his experiences in *The Aran Islands* [see *john millington synge,* below]. Be forewarned, however: The locals on this island aren't used to visitors, and they aren't exactly welcoming. Don't expect warm and friendly greetings waiting for you in the island's only pub—a complete anomaly given the Irish people's famous hospitality. Consider staying on Inis Mór, visiting Inis Meáin for an afternoon, and taking an afternoon ferry [see *need to know,* below] to Inis Oírr for a romantic walk in the twilight. And have a pint in one of its three pubs afterwards, where the people *are* friendly enough to cancel out Inis Meáin's chilliness.

The renowned rustic traditional life of the Aran Islanders has faded somewhat; the young people here aren't too interested in such a life anymore, and whitewashed, thatched-roof stone cottages are becoming less common. Oddly enough, the most popular place for hanging out on Inis Mór seems to be in the lot outside the Spar Supermarket in **Kilronan,** the port village. The village of **Killeany** is to the south, on the eastern edge of the island, and **Kilmurvey** is several miles west.

Although everything is within walking distance, it's easier and faster to rent a bike on Inis Mór [see *need to know,* below]. As for Inis Meáin and Inis Oírr, bikes aren't necessary. You can cover the whole of each island in a matter of a couple of hours by foot. Bring a picnic lunch, sturdy shoes, and an open pair of eyes, and you're all set for a lovely afternoon.

bar and live music scene

The shortage of rollicking trad sessions on the islands is a bit disappointing. Sure, there's live music, but it seems a bit half-hearted compared to the trad played in other places in Ireland—Doolin, Galway, Kilkenny, wherever. Most pubs open around 10am, and close around 11pm.

On the offhand chance you came to Inis Mór specifically to hear Irish guys singing Garth Brooks and Goo Goo Dolls tunes, **Joe Watty's** *(Kilronan, main road, left side, past the post office and bank; No phone; No credit cards)* is just the place for you. Watty's isn't your typical Irish pub; it's brightly lit and may remind you of a makeshift bar in someone's basement game room. The music's nightly, and this bar stays open later than normal, till 1:30am. The two-man band stops playing sometime around half-past midnight, but if you beg for an encore they'll play another song or two before packing it in. Watty's serves good pub grub, until 8pm in summertime.

The American Bar *(Kilronan, Inis Mór, at the pier, behind Bayview House; Tel 099/61130 or 099/61338; american_bar@esatclear.ie; No credit*

you are now entering the gaeltacht

Don't dare call it "dead"; Irish may still be a minority language, but this hauntingly melodic tongue is becoming more and more popular every day. Just about all Irish-speaking Irishmen or -women, even in the Gaeltacht (areas in which Irish is the primary language spoken), also speak English, but still it would definitely score points if you could speak a few words in Irish. Who knows? You might even get a free pint out of the deal.

Call the old language "Irish" rather than "Gaelic," because the latter term is too vague—there's Scottish Gaelic, too. (Both languages have the same roots but aren't super-similar.) There are three main Irish dialects—an Irish speaker in Donegal will sound significantly different from a Cork speaker—but speak loudly and clearly and they should still be able to understand you. And now for your first language lesson:

- *Go raibh maith agat* ("go row my ah-gut"): Thank you; when spoken to more than one person, replace *agat* with *agaibh* ("ah-give"). You can also use it to mean "please."
- *Dia duit* ("gee-ya ditch"): The traditional greeting, preferable to "hey you." To more than one person, it's *dia daoibh* ("gee-ya yee-iv").
- There isn't a more romantic way to say "I love you" than in Irish; *Tá mo chroi istigh ionat* ("ta mo hree ISS-tee YUH-nat"), literally, "My heart is inside you." Aww....
- You've seen *fáilte* ("FALL-cheh") around; it means "welcome."

cards) is so named simply because it has a pool table in the back room and rock music playing on the loudspeaker. It's got more of a "real pub" feel than Joe Watty's, and there's live trad music here most nights in the summer, and no cover.

Unless you'd rather hear those rocking cover tunes, the action is at **Tí Joe Mac** *(At the pier, Kilronan, Inis Mór; No phone; No credit cards).* Just below the **Kilronan Hostel** [see *crashing,* below], it's usually the most crowded pub on Inis Mór on chilly moonlit nights. So crowded, in fact, that the musicians barely have room to play. Tí Joe Mac is also the most touristy of the three Kilronan pubs, since the hostel is right upstairs and there are so many B&Bs nearby. There's a good mix of locals here, as well as Irish people on their holidays.

Care to dance the night away on Inis Mór? Every Friday, Saturday, and Sunday night a *céilí*—that's a traditional dancing session—is held at the **dance hall** [for specific information, check with the tourist office, see *need to know,* below] beginning at midnight. Admission is £3; storytelling and ballads precede the dance. Ask any of the locals at the bars around closing time; chances are a lot of them are heading to the *céilí.* (In the winter, the sessions are held only on Saturdays.)

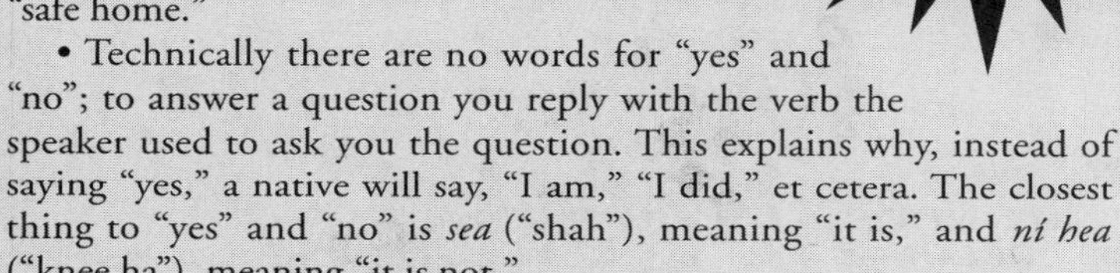

There's a bunch of ways to say good-bye: *Slán* ("slahn"), literally "safe," *sláinte* ("SLAWN-cheh"), literally "health" (it's also used to mean "cheers"), or *slán abhaile* ("slahn ah-wall-eh") for "safe home."

• Technically there are no words for "yes" and "no"; to answer a question you reply with the verb the speaker used to ask you the question. This explains why, instead of saying "yes," a native will say, "I am," "I did," et cetera. The closest thing to "yes" and "no" is *sea* ("shah"), meaning "it is," and *ní hea* ("knee ha"), meaning "it is not."

• *Bá mhaith liom pionta eile* ("Bah why lum pyon-ta el-leh"): "I would like another pint."

• Emotions and illnesses are always said to be "on you." *Beidh áthas orainn* ("bay ah-hass or-in"): There will be joy on us; *bhí imní orthu* ("vee im-knee or-hoo"): There was worry on them; *tá poit orm* ("tah poych a-rum"): There is a hangover on me. (That one's likely to be the most useful.)

• *Cá bhfuil an seomra folctha?* ("cah will an show-mra fulc-ha?"): Where is the bathroom?

• And if anybody makes an unwanted advance, you can always say, *"Pog mo thoin"* ("pohg mo hoe-in")—that is, "Kiss me arse."

Inis Meáin's got only one pub, **Teach Ósta Inis Meáin** *(About a half-mile straight on away from the pier; No phone; No cover; No credit cards),* but don't go in there expecting a party. You'll have a hard enough time eliciting a single grunt from the weather-beaten locals at the bar.

Tigh Ruairí *(The Strand Rd., Inis Oírr; Tel 099/75002; No cover; V, MC)* is a cozy little place for a pint and a bit of Irish gab [see *you are now entering the gaeltacht,* above]. The food's excellent [see *eats,* below], and there are trad sessions most nights in summer, although there's no established schedule. The sea winds will chill you at sunset, so after that romantic stroll to the other end of Inis Oírr and back, get yourself a delicious steaming mug of Bailey's coffee at Tigh Ruairí.

The pub at **Hotel Inis Oírr** [see *crashing,* below], **O'Flaherty's** *(On the Strand Rd. leading to Tigh Ruairí, Inis Oírr; Tel 099/75020; No cover; V, MC),* is much more spacious than the other two bars on the island, but there's not too much going on here besides a few musicians engaged in a too-casual-to-be-entertaining jam session. It's not the best pub on the island, but okay for a pint before heading to Tigh Ned's. Note the trophy and American license plate collections above the bar.

Were O'Flaherty's and Tigh Ruairí a wee bit quiet for you? Wondering

aran islands

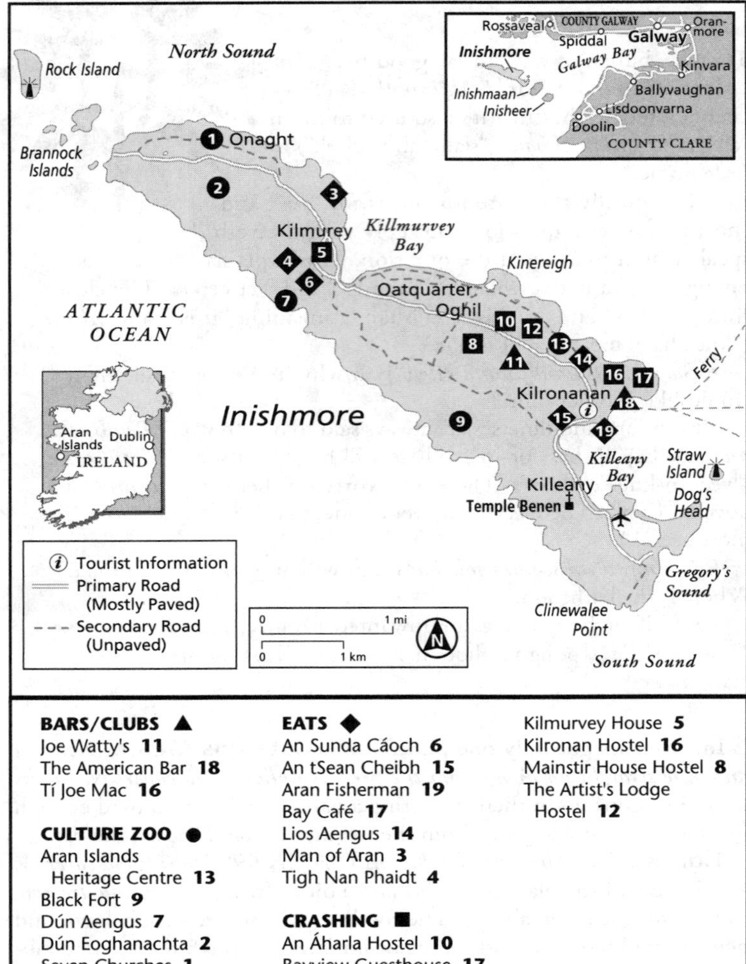
North Sound
Rock Island
Brannock Islands
Onaght
Kilmurey
Killmurvey Bay
Kinereigh
Oatquarter
Oghil
ATLANTIC OCEAN
Inishmore
Kilronanan
Killeany Bay
Killeany
Temple Benen
Straw Island
Dog's Head
Gregory's Sound
Clinewalee Point
South Sound
Ferry
Rossaveal
COUNTY GALWAY
Spiddal
Galway
Oranmore
Galway Bay
Kinvara
Inishmore
Inishmaan
Inisheer
Ballyvaughan
Lisdoonvarna
Doolin
COUNTY CLARE
Aran Islands
Dublin
IRELAND
Tourist Information
Primary Road (Mostly Paved)
Secondary Road (Unpaved)
0 1 mi
0 1 km
N
BARS/CLUBS
Joe Watty's 11
The American Bar 18
Tí Joe Mac 16
CULTURE ZOO
Aran Islands Heritage Centre 13
Black Fort 9
Dún Aengus 7
Dún Eoghanachta 2
Seven Churches 1
EATS
An Sunda Cáoch 6
An tSean Cheibh 15
Aran Fisherman 19
Bay Café 17
Lios Aengus 14
Man of Aran 3
Tigh Nan Phaidt 4
CRASHING
An Áharla Hostel 10
Bayview Guesthouse 17
Kilmurvey House 5
Kilronan Hostel 16
Mainstir House Hostel 8
The Artist's Lodge Hostel 12

where everybody went? Try **Tigh Ned** *(Inis Oírr, on the Strand Rd., a short walk from the pier, next door to Brú Radharc Na Mara [see* crashing, *below]; No phone; No credit cards).* Everyone and their brother's here, and everybody's young—and surprisingly hip, too, for such a seemingly out-of-the-way place. You'll find comfy booths, walls covered with old photographs and the like, and truckloads of rugby boys swarming around the dartboard. Tigh Ned has traditional music most nights in the summer (beginning around 9:30pm, as is customary in Irish pubs); there is no definite schedule, though. These sessions are more impromptu than average.

culture zoo

The Aran Islands are loaded with history and folklore; you'll find everything from Paleolithic stone forts to famous Irish writers' rustic hideaways on these three small rocks in the Atlantic.

▸▸INIS MÓR

Aran Islands Heritage Centre (Ionad Árann) *(On the right of the main road, Kilronan; Tel 099/61355; 10am-7pm Apr-Oct; Admission £2 adults, £1.50 students):* The center makes a good introduction to the history, archaeology, and everyday life of the Aran Islands. You might start out with the stirring 1937 movie *Man of Aran,* which they screen pretty much continuously at this brand-new center. It's well worth a visit, and hey, if it happens to be raining too hard to make that bike trip to Dún Aengus, you can always sit and watch the movie over and over and over....

Dún Aengus *(Take the main road from Kilronan, about two-thirds of the way down the island, signs marked from Kilmurvey; Tel 099/61010; 10am-6pm mid-Mar through Oct, 11am-3:30pm Nov to mid-Mar; Admission £1 adults, 40p students):* Hailing from the first century B.C., Dún Aengus is the largest and most impressive of the prehistoric stone forts on the Aran Islands. Why Dún Aengus was built, whether for defensive or religious purposes, is still a matter of debate. It's a bit of a walk up a rocky hill to reach the top, but when you reach the crest, prepare to be amazed. Be *very careful,* too, because you won't find that dramatic cliff so amazing if you fall off (it has happened). The drop's a good 300 feet, there's no railing, and winds are strong.

Black Fort, or **Dún Dúchathair** *(On the southern edge of Inis Mór, 2 km southwest of Kilronan; Free admission):* This is another ringed fort, 1,000 years older than Dún Aengus. It's not nearly as popular as Dún Aengus, but it's definitely worth a visit for the dramatic effect of its precarious setting.

The Seven Churches *(Signposted on the right off the main road approx. 1 km past Kilmurvey; Free admission):* This lovely little spot with the haunting remains of a few early Christian churches and a graveyard with more recent headstones also offers a picturesque view of the sea. This is a good spot to sit and engage in a little quiet contemplation—that is, if you manage to elude the mini-tour buses, which won't be easy.

Dún Eoghanachta *(On the main road past Kilmurvey; Free admission):* Just up the road from The Seven Churches, on the opposite side, is a large and perfectly circular fort with walls 16-foot thick and a pleasant

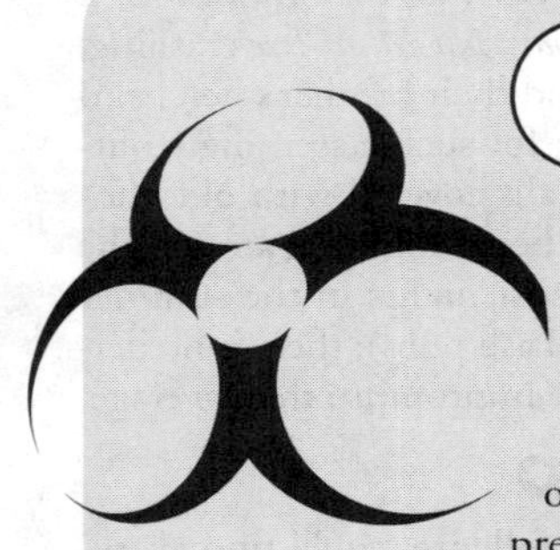

what the heck are those dots, anyway

You see signs all over Ireland with dots over some consonants. You know the accent is a *fada,* or long mark, but what's the dot? Since there wasn't an "h" in the Old Irish alphabet, a *buailte* ("BOOL-chuh"), meaning "struck" or "beaten," was placed over the consonant preceding where the "h" would have gone.

view of the Connemara Mountains on the mainland to the north. Seldom-traveled paths join it to Dún Aengus, but if you haven't picked up a really detailed map of the island (the Richardson map, for £5, is a good one) from the Tourist Office [see *need to know,* below], it would be wiser to get back onto the main road and follow it west for about a mile, where you may or may not see a barely visible signpost.

▸▸INIS MEÁIN

Dún Chonchúir *(On the left of the winding main road; Free admission):* Similar to Dún Aengus but situated inland on Inis Meáin, Dún Chonchúir has good views of the whole island. Near the turnoff for the fort is a thatched-roof cottage where **John Millington Synge** [see *john millington synge,* below] spent his summers over a period of four years at the turn of the last century. His hangout, called "Synge's Chair," is a sheltered spot along the path leading to the sheer cliff overlooking Gregory's Sound, at the far end of the island. Walk too much farther on that path and you'll drop right into the sea.

Other sites of note on Inis Meáin include **Cill Cheannannach** *(Close to the pier, on the left; Free admission),* and **Dún Fearbhaigh** *(Just a little further out from Cill Cheannannach; Free admission).* Cill Cheannannach is a church more than 1,100 years old; Dún Fearbhaigh is another fort, remarkably intact, which dates from about the same time.

▸▸INIS OÍRR

O'Brien's Castle *(Facing the island, turn left on The Strand; Free admission):* Easily seen from the pier at Inis Oírr, this castle dates from the 15th century, but the ruins you see around it are those of a fort probably built in the first century A.D. The castle itself isn't terribly spectacular, but the views of the island and harbor are nice.

There are other ruins nearby as well on Inis Oírr, but don't worry yourself hunting them out: There's the 10th-century **Church of St. Kevin,** on the Strand; **Cill Ghobnait** (Church of St. Gobnait), the most interesting feature of which is its odd name; and the **Well of St. Enda,** on the western end of the island *(Turn right on the Strand and follow the road out to reach it).* There's also the **Inis Oírr Heritage House** west of the Pier, but the most substantial thing about it is the cafe inside.

great outdoors

It might be tempting not to budge from that comfy old chair by the fire if you're staying at **An Áharla** or **The Artist's Lodge Hostels** [see *crashing,* below] on Inis Mór, especially if the weather's looking formidable, but don't indulge yourself for too long. There's so much to see, and although biking several miles while it's spitting outside might not sound terribly appealing, you'll get the most out of your visit to Inis Mór if you visit the prehistoric and monastic ruins scattered all over the island.

Renting a bike couldn't be easier. Two shops right on the pier will solicit your service as soon as you step off the boat; rates are 5 or 6 punts per day. It'll take about five or six hours to bike to the end of the island and back. Keep in mind the bike rental places aren't open past 7pm, even 5pm if business is slow. Pick up a map of the prehistoric and early monastic sites from the **Tourist Office** [see *need to know,* below] and you're ready to see **Dún Aengus, The Black Fort, The Seven Churches, Dún Eoghanachta,** and everything else there is to see [see *culture zoo,* above].

Inis Mór has a few sandy beaches for strolling or (if the weather's unusually cooperative) swimming and sunbathing. At **Kilmurvey Bay,** 4 miles west of Kilronan, you can see the Connemara Mountains in the

john millington synge

J. M. Synge (1871-1909; pronounced "sing"), Irish poet and dramatist, spent much time in reflection on the Aran Islands, notably in a little cottage overlooking the sea on **Inis Meáin** [see *culture zoo,* above]. For a great introduction to the islands, read his book *The Aran Islands,* in which he observes the customs and everyday life of the locals—not a whole lot has changed since then. His one-act play, *Riders to the Sea,* also set in the Arans, has been called one of the greatest tragedies ever written. Along with William Butler Yeats, Sean O'Casey, and Lady Augusta Gregory, Synge helped to spark the Irish Literary Renaissance, a turn-of-the-century movement pushing for the revival of ancient Irish folklore and traditions in contemporary works. He also helped to found the renowned Abbey Theatre in Dublin, where his comedy *The Playboy of the Western World* caused quite a stir in its 1907 premiere for mentioning the word "shift" (we're talking women's underwear). And you thought people in Ireland *today* are prudish....

distance. Take the main road and you can't miss it on the right. Near Killeany, the village south of the Pier at Kilronan, there's **Cockle Strand,** which is safe for swimming. If you continue another mile south toward the airstrip, though, you'll find a strand that *looks* safe but has sinking sand and rough tides. To find safe beaches on the eastern end of the island, take the main road past the airstrip eastward until it ends, then walk north.

stuff

The Aran Islands are most famous for the wonderful hand-knitted **sweaters** commonly known as "fisherman's" sweaters because the local ladies used to knit them to keep their menfolk warm when they were out to sea. But Irish women are a practical lot, and they certainly didn't spend all that time on those intricate patterns just for fun; each sweater had a unique cable-knit family design that was used to identify a fisherman if he died at sea. Today's machine-loomed imitations, some of which look and feel almost as good as the real thing, cost much less at the duty-free airport shops, but they'll never be a true Aran Island sweater and they don't come with the great stories you get from the ladies who still hold the knitting needles in their hands.

Snámara Árainn Teo *(On the main road in Kilronan, on the left by the post office as you're walking away from the pier, Kilronan, Inis Mór; Tel 099/61359; V, MC, AE)* is one of the best places on the island to pick up a genuine hand-knitted Aran sweater; colors are bright and varied, and each one bears a tag signed by the person who made it [see *the aran sweater,* below]. There's also a really nice selection of Celtic-style jewelry, hats, pottery, handbags, and backpacks that look like they were made from patches of your grandfather's tweed coats.

Yes, there are a few cheesy souvenirs as well. Even if you aren't going to buy anything, it's fun just to listen to the owner and her daughter switching from Irish to English to Irish again as though they've been speaking one language all along.

queen of the forest

Feel like doing some tree-hugging? You can thank Danu, the ancient Irish mother earth goddess, for all that gorgeous (and even almost *otherworldly* at times) Irish scenery.

the anatomy of a fairy

Fairies, it is said, are really fallen angels. At the beginning of time, or so the legend goes, during the battle between God and Satan, some angels remained neutral, willing to go along with whomever won. When it was all over, Satan and his followers were banished to Hell and God cast the neutral angels, who had committed a sin of omission, to the Earth as fairies. They occasionally accompany departed souls to heaven, but they can never enter through the gates.

Fairies are supposed to live in old ruined castles and churches, deserted graveyards, and secluded mountain glens, lakes, and caves, especially on the west coast. Translucent and usually the size of a human finger, they can assume any conceivable form or become invisible at whim. The question of whether or not they have wings is still open to debate—witnesses are usually too schnockered to tell for sure. Sociable and mischievous, fairies are known to be as helpful as they can be nasty; it all depends on how they're treated. A few pointers, should you ever come across one:

1. Don't talk about Yeats. Fairies despise all academic pursuits and cannot be found anywhere near a school.

2. Be respectful. Even if they drink your last bottle of whiskey, don't complain—it's not worth the trouble they'd cause you afterward.

3. If you're ever invited to a fairy ball, count your lucky stars. Their music and dancing far surpass anything you'll see in the human realm. Don't speak though, or the scene will immediately vanish and you'll wake up lying in the middle of the road in the morning with a headache the size of Montana.

4. Hold onto your baby. Fairies are known baby-snatchers—they can't help it, they just love those cute, pudgy, googly-eyed little things so much.

5. Don't speak of the fairies to *anyone*. They do not like being talked about, and besides, silence is your best bet for preserving your illusion of perfect sanity.

the aran sweater

Sure, you can buy one anyplace in Ireland, but most of them are machine-knit, and they just aren't as nice as the ones you'll find *hand-made* here on the islands, and you know just by looking at one that it'll last you for years and years, if not forever. You can tell the difference easily: Hand-knit sweaters have a thicker, coarser feel. These truly authentic sweaters can be found mostly only on the Aran Islands or in the Connemara region of Galway, where the cottage industry is still alive and well. Look for a tag signed by the woman who knitted it—the best sweaters will have one attached. It's hands-down the finest souvenir you can buy; a really good sweater could set you back £85, but you're making a wise investment, not to mention that you're promoting a traditional Irish way of life.

The **Aran Sweater Market** *(At the pier, Kilronan, Inis Mór; Tel 099/61140; www.aransweatermarket.com)* usually has higher prices than Snámara Árainn Teo, and somehow the sweaters just don't seem quite so authentic without the autographed tag. The quality at **Carraig Donn** *(At the pier, Kilronan; Tel 099/61123)* next door isn't as good, either.

You can find beautiful sweaters in one of the cottages, like **Tíg Sarah,** at the turnoff to Dún Aengus. Even better, you can often see the knitters at work, when they're not helping customers to find the perfect sweater.

Cniotáil Inis Meáin *(Tel 099/73009),* on Inis Meáin, exports really nice sweaters and other items from here to upscale shops all over the world, but you can get the goods from this factory shop for around half of the retail prices.

eats

If you'd rather do your own cooking it won't be easy to find a supermarket, at least not on the two smaller islands. On Inis Mór, **Spar Supermarket** *(Tel 099/61203; 9am-8pm Mon-Sat, 10am-6pm Sun)* is on the beaten path, though. Just take the main road from the pier out toward the far reaches of the island and it'll be on the right (give yourself 5 minutes). Stock up on groceries if you're heading out to the other islands later on. As for Inis Oírr, **Tigh Ruairí** [see *crashing,* below, and *bar scene,* above], along with providing a pub and B&B, has a small convenience store *(Open 9am-8:30pm July-Aug, 9am-7:30pm Mon-Sat and 10:45am-12:30pm Sun Sept-June).*

There are several simply decorated little cafes on Inis Mór, all pretty much interchangeable. Each offers sandwiches, soups, and other light fare for around £2, as well as meat or fish dishes for around £5. There's **Lios**

Aengus, next to the Spar supermarket, **An tSean Cheibh,** across the street and right behind the **Aran Sweater Market** [see *stuff,* above], and a few farther out on the island. **An Sunda Cáoch** *(Tel 099/61218; No credit cards)* or "The Blind Sound," is the cafe and coffee shop outside the entrance to Dún Aengus; it serves coffee, sandwiches, and cake, all under £2. **Tigh Nan Phaidt** *(Just off the main road, at the turnoff to Dún Aengus; Tel 099/61330; 10am-9pm July-Aug, 10am-5pm Sept-Dec and Mar-June; All items under £6; No credit cards),* in a little thatched-roof cottage, has good smoked salmon sandwiches and homemade bread.

At **Man of Aran** *(Past Kilmurvey Beach, on the right of the main road, Inis Mór; Tel 099/61301; Lunch daily 12:30-3:30pm; Sandwiches under £5; No credit cards),* a small traditional cottage where the movie of the same name was filmed back in 1937, you can fill 'er up with tea and tasty organic lunches. Man of Aran also offers B&B; while the atmosphere is charmingly authentic, the location is a bit out of the way.

Less rustic is the **Bay Café** *(At the pier, Kilronan; 8:30am-9:30pm daily),* part of the brightly painted **Bayview Guesthouse** [see *crashing,* below] overlooking the pier at Kilronan. Prices and menus are the same as Man of Aran's, but the decor's a bit spiffier, with bright orange and blue walls that somehow manage to keep from looking gaudy.

For dinner on Inis Mór, there are several good choices. The organic vegetarian meals at **Mainstir House Hostel** [see *crashing,* below] always receive glowing reports. Bring a bottle of wine from the supermarket and you're all set. At the **Aran Fisherman** *(Near the pier, Kilronan, Inis Mór; Tel 099/61104; 11am-9pm; £5-15; V, MC)* the menu's got—you guessed it—seafood, so fresh you might want to check first to make sure the lobster's not still snapping before you take a bite. This restaurant has pizza, burgers, and vegetarian dishes, as well.

On Inis Oírr, one of the best places for dinner is **Tigh Ruairí** [see *bar and live music scene,* above]. Yeah, it's pub grub, but it's extremely good pub grub. The chef's special recipe for making fish and chips (£6.50 for a

the quintessential irish blessing

"May the road rise up to meet you.
May the wind always be at your back.
May the sun shine warm upon your face,
and rains fall soft upon your fields.
And until we meet again,
May God hold you in the palm of His hand."

huge portion) is so delectable, he's been solicited by *Bon Appetit* magazine for the top-secret info. The soups are excellent as well: Try the tomato basil or clam chowder. Steak or salmon dishes go for around £10.

crashing

Not all hostels on Inis Mór are made equal. The ones you hear about most often are adequate, but they aren't actually the nicest ones. On Inis Oírr, **Brú Radharc Na Mara** [see below] is the only hostel, but it's a good one. There are plenty of B&Bs on Inis Mór as well, but there are only a few places to spend the night on Inis Meáin (we'll say it again, you'll probably enjoy yourself more if you stay on Inis Oírr for the night). On all the islands, even the higher-end accommodation doesn't quite reach the splurge category.

▸▸CHEAP

It doesn't get any more convenient than the fluorescent green **Kilronan Hostel** *(At the pier, Kilronan, Inis Mór; Tel 099/61255; £9-10 dorms; No credit cards)*. Not only is it located right on the pier, but there's a pub, **Tí Joe Mac's** [see *bar and live music scene,* above], on the floor below it. That said, this one shouldn't be your top choice. Reception is chilly and so's the atmosphere. At least the place is clean, and it's big enough that you're pretty much guaranteed a bed. Should you arrive in Inis Mór deadbeat tired in the pouring rain, it'll serve your purposes quite well.

The other popular place is the **Mainstir House Hostel** *(On the main road, Inis Mór; Tel 099/61169; mainstir@galway.net, www.galwayguide.com/pages/mainstir; £8-15 single, £20 double, breakfast included, £8 for dinner; V, MC),* about a 15-minute walk from the pier, on the left side. While it has a reputation as being a haven for artists, writers, musicians, and backpackers alike, there have been complaints about unfriendly staff and less-than-clean facilities. What really gives Mainstir House its international renown is the unique talent of resident chef and DJ Joel D'Anjou, who cooks up organic vegetarian feasts for a laid-back dining room of happy eaters. He's not exactly known for his sunny demeanor, so be sure to stay on his good side. You can have dinner even if you're not staying there; it costs £1 more. Be sure to make a reservation; the food is popular, and deservedly so. As for the hostel itself, well—let's just say we've been to better.

Like twin angels glowing in the sylvan Aran darkness, **An Áharla Hostel** *(Off the main road, signposted; St. Rónáins Rd., Kilronan, Inis Mór; Tel 099/61305; £7 dorm; No credit cards)* and **The Artist's Lodge Hostel** *(Off the main road, signposted; St. Rónáins Rd., Kilronan, Inis Mór; Tel 099/61457; £7 dorm; No credit cards)* are without a doubt the friendliest, most comfortable places to stay on Inis Mór. Ironically, they're also the cheapest. We just can't say enough about The Artist's Lodge: There are only 10 beds in the whole place, a cozy little cottage with a fantastic sitting room, lovely views, and a fire going all afternoon and long into the night. Residents from all over the island come to borrow from the sitting-room bookshelves, and naturally the selection of books about the Aran

Islands is especially good. Owner Marion Hughes makes you feel even more comfortable than you would in your own home; if you write your address in the guest book she'll even mail you a Christmas card. The price includes toast and tea for breakfast (and anything else around the kitchen that you can get your hands on). On top of all that, the beds are incredibly comfortable; you'll remember them longingly for the rest of your stay in Ireland. Hostelling just doesn't get any better than this.

Pretty much the same can be said for **An Áharla:** roaring fires, comfy rooms, and a friendly and colorful owner, Colm Conneely, who will tell stories and crack jokes by the fireside at night. The super-cozy atmosphere brings one-time lodgers back again and again. Book well ahead during the summer months just as you would anywhere else that's especially small. Although these gems are overshadowed by the larger, more impersonal Kilronan and Mainstir House Hostels, it's only a matter of time before everybody catches on to just how wonderful both these hostels are—especially The Artist's Lodge.

On Inis Oírr, **Brú Radharc Na Mara** *(Strand Rd., short walk from the pier, to the right, Inis Oírr; Tel 099/75024; £7.50 4- and 6-bed dorms, £10 singles, £11 with bath; V, MC)* is an excellent choice—so what if it's the *only* choice for a hostel on the island, it's a very good one just the same. There's a nice big kitchen, a cozy sitting room with fireplace overlooking the ocean, and the skylit rooms on the upper floor are perfect for bedtime stargazing. "Brú" also serves meals: continental breakfast for £2, Irish breakfast for £4, and dinner for £10.

▸▸DO-ABLE

The purple-and-white **Bayview Guesthouse** *(At the pier, Kilronan, Inis Mór; Tel 099/61260; Open Mar to mid-Nov; £18 single, £34 double; V, MC)* is central to all the Kilronan action. Hands-down the best place to stay, though, is the friendly, immaculate **Kilmurvey House** *(Kilmurvey, Inis Mór; Tel 099/61218; Closed Nov-Easter; £44 double, rate includes full breakfast; V, MC),* which is widely regarded as the finest accommodation on the island. Situated in an 18th-century stone house and near **Dún Aengus** [see *culture zoo,* above], Kilmurvey House serves delicious breakfasts as well as a four-course dinner at 7pm; reservations necessary.

There aren't any hostels on Inis Meáin, but for B&B try **Créig Mór** *(Creigmore, 500 meters northwest of the pier; Tel 099/73012; £14 per person; Open Mar-Dec; No credit cards),* one of the friendliest, most comfortable B&Bs on the island, or **Mrs. Faherty's** *(Ard Alainn, Inis Meáin, follow signs from the pier; Tel 099/73012; Open mid-Mar to Nov; £28 doubles; No credit cards),* the *other* friendly, comfortable place to stay, in a lovely old Aran farmhouse. Mrs. Faherty also serves a huge dinner for £11.

Is there anything the folks at **Tigh Ruairí** *(The Strand, Inis Oírr; Tel 099/75002; V, MC)* don't do? In addition to great dinners, a cozy little pub, and a convenience store, there's a B&B *(leaba agus bricfeasta)* option. All rooms have their own bathroom, and the whole place is clean and airy. It's much quieter than the typical B&B-over-a-pub, too. Nearby **Hotel Inis Óirr** *(The Strand, Inis Oírr; Tel 099/75020; Open Apr-Sept; £25* *single, £46 double; V, MC)* is another option for bed-and-breakfast, with clean, modern rooms; main courses at the hotel restaurant go for around £10.

need to know

Currency Exchange There's a Bureau de Change at **An Post** *(On the main road, Kilronan, just past the Spar, Inis Mór; Tel 099/61101; 9am-5pm Mon-Fri, 9am-1pm Sat),* and a small **Bank of Ireland,** open Wednesday and Thursday only. The **Tourist Office,** farther down the road on the left, changes money as well. There are no ATMs.

Tourist Information On Inis Mór, there's the **Tourist Office** *(On the pier, Kilronan; Tel 099/61263; 10am to 5pm from Apr to mid-Sept).* You can also call the **Inis Mór Island Cooperative** *(Tel 099/61354; year-round)* for information. The **Inis Meáin Island Cooperative** *(Tel 099/73010)* is located inland from the pier, across from the post office. On Inis Oírr, the **Tourist Office** *(Tel 099/75008; 10am-6pm July-Aug)* is located in a little hut right on the pier; you can also call the **Inisheer Island Cooperative** *(Tel 099/75008)* for information.

Health and Emergency Emergency: *999.*

Airports You can fly from Galway to the airport on Inis Mór (hence the name "Aer Arann"). **Aer Arann** *(Connemara Regional Airport, Inverin; Tel 091/593-034; Daily departures at 9am, 10:30am, 4pm, 5pm, or anytime there are five or more passengers; aerarann@iol.ie, www.aerarann.ie; £35/£29 students round-trip; V, MC)* also provides free bus service between Eyre Square, Galway, and the Galway airport.

Buses There are plenty of buses, both tour and transport, all over Inis Mór, lots parked right at the pier (they aren't shy about soliciting your business, either); cost £5 return to Dún Aengus. One of these bus lines is **Noel Mahon Mini Bus** *(Tel 099/61213 or 099/61386, mobile 086/877-37-66),* offering tours and taxi service.

Boats From Doolin or Galway your options include **Doolin Ferries/O'Brien Shipping** *(Tel 065/74455, after hours 065/71710, Galway 091/567-283; Service year-round; £20 round-trip Doolin to Inis Mór, £18 round-trip to Inis Meáin, £15 round-trip to Inis Oírr, £25 Galway-Inis Mór-Doolin, £15 round-trip Galway to any island; £3 discount with International Student ID; V, MC),* and island-hopping from Doolin is included in the price; from Galway, inter-island stops are £5 each. **Aran Island Ferries** *(Victoria Place, off Eyre Sq., Galway; Tel 091/568-903; £15/£12 students round-trip, £3 round-trip for bus connection to Rossaveal; £6 inter-island; Departs Rossaveal 10:30am, 1:30pm, 6:30pm daily Apr-Oct, 10:30am, 5:30pm daily Nov-Mar; V, MC)* also operates between Galway and the islands. It has a return bus to Rossaveal departing 90 minutes before ferry time in front of the Tourist Office in Galway City.

Bike Rental You can't miss the bike shops at the pier in Kilronin; among them is **Aran Bike Hire** *(At the pier, Kilronan, Inis Mór; Tel 099/61132; 9am-5pm Mar-Nov; £5 per day, £21 per week, £9 deposit).*

oughterard

You could be forgiven for wanting to rush on to Clifden, traditional jumping-off point for the wild beauty of Connemara. But if you do, you'll likely pass right on by Oughterard, just as most visitors do, on the Bus Éireann [see *need to know,* below] route out from Galway into Connemara. And sure, that'd be a pity. This little town on Lough Corrib, a half-hour by bus from Galway, is well worth a stop, at least for a day trip.

The dramatic 16th-century **Aughnanure Castle** *(Off N59; Tel 091/82214; 9:30am-6:30pm mid-June to mid-Sept; Admission £2/£1 students)* is located 2 miles south of Oughterard. Check out the "murder hole" above the front entrance—and don't try to get in without forking over your punt or you're dead meat. It's all deliciously ghost story–worthy, complete with a secret room off the main living room and a trap door in the banquet hall that once dropped unsuspecting scoundrels into the peat-filled river below. Brrr!

There's plenty of nature around Oughterard to keep you occupied for at least a day: Canoeing on **Lough Corrib,** hiking in the nearby **Maam Turk Mountains**, and ferrying to **Inchagoill Island,** with some of the oldest early Christian structures in Europe. The **Oughterard Tourist Office** [see *need to know,* below], though not affiliated with Bórd Fáilte, will provide you with all the information, trail maps and tickets you need; make a quick stop there and you're all set.

Lough Corrib, the largest lake in Ireland, is mostly noted for its angling possibilities. There are plenty of people willing to take you on cruises, but the best thing to do is to hire a fisherman to row you out to Inchagoill Island to hunt around in the mysterious early monastic ruins for an hour or two. Otherwise, the Tourist Office [see *need to know,* below] will happily sell you a boat ticket to the island for about £8. The Guinness family (of brewing fame, naturally), who once owned Inchagoill, restored one of the old churches and created walking paths through the woods all over the island.

great outdoors

The **Maam Turk Mountain** chain, one of the most beautiful in Ireland, is usually explored from a base at Oughterard. From Oughterard, drive 10 miles east on N59 to Maam Cross. At this fork in the road, bear right for another 5 miles to Western Way where parking is available. From here, it is a 30-minute walk along a trail that leads to the base of the mountains. Public transportation is not available from Oughterard.

The mountains are covered with a green, mossy base, with more of a jagged, rocky appearance as you get closer to the peaks. In all, Maam Turk has 15 peaks, rising to a height of only 1,000 feet, which make them walkable. Nonetheless, climbing all the way to the top of any of these peaks can be tricky, so unless you're experienced, it's best to have a guide (seriously). For a reliable guide, contact Michael Gibbons who is the head of

beyond bizarre

Just 14 km (9 miles) outside northwest of Oughterard you'll find a spot called the **Hill of Doon,** off the Glann Road. Way *way* back, before even the Celts were around, a bunch of pagans used to get a kick out of sacrificing virgins to their fave goddess up on this hill. Sure, stuff like that's happened all over the world all throughout history, but it's been rumored that a bunch of neopagans kept the practice up here until pretty recently—meaning sometime in the 1960s. Whoa. The Hill of Doon's a bit of a stretch by bike unless you're in reasonably good shape, but you'll find the views overlooking Lough Corrib definitely worth the extra exertion. Bring a picnic lunch and stay awhile, but be sure to save some energy and time to pedal your way back.

the **Maam Turk & Western Walking Club** *(£20 per person, with fees starting at £20).* Walks vary from 1 hour for novices to 5 hours for more experienced hikers who cross some pretty rugged terrain. Once you reach the summit of any of the 15 peaks, you're rewarded with spectacular views of the country and the surrounding lakes.

eats

This is the kind of town where you buy your own groceries and have picnic lunches by day and spaghetti-o's by night. **O'Fatharta's** *(Main St.; Tel 091/552-697)* is just about the only option, but thankfully it's a good one, with hearty local cuisine—main courses run about £10. But why waste time indoors when you could be eating your cheese and potato bread in the midst of some of the loveliest scenery in County Galway? Which makes **Keogh's Grocery** *(The Square; Tel 091/552-583; 8am-10pm Mon-Sat, 9am-9pm Sun; Open till 8pm in winter)* a very attractive choice. It might not have the selection of SuperValu, but the hours sure are convenient.

crashing

There are two good hostels in Oughterard: **Lough Corrib Hostel** *(Camp St.; Tel 091/552-866; Around £8 dorm beds, £4 to camp),* which offers camping, bike and canoe rentals, and **Cranrawer House** *(Station Rd.; Tel 091/552-388; Around £8-9 dorm beds),* which is the slightly more comfortable, nonsmoker's hostel of choice around these parts.

As far as hotels go, you've got two decent choices, **Forest Hill** *(Glann Rd.; Tel 091/552-549; lakeshoreroad@eircom.net; www.forresthillbb.com;*

£19 per person, special student rate £16, all rooms have private baths; V, MC), right near the Western Way; or **Glann House** *(Glann Rd.; Tel 091/552-127; £32 single, £50 double, all rooms include breakfast and private baths; V, MC),* around 15 minutes outside of town in the lovely Oughterard countryside.

need to know

Currency Exchange **Bank of Ireland** *(Main St.; Tel 091/552-123; 10am-4pm Mon-Wed and Fri, 10am-5pm Thur)* has an ATM.

Tourist Information **Oughterard Tourist Office** *(Main St.; Tel 091/552-866; 9am-5:30pm Mon-Sat, 10am-2pm Sun July-Aug, 9am-5:30pm Mon-Fri Sept-Apr)* can give you the information needed for all your outdoor activities.

Bus Lines in and Out of Town **Bus Éireann** routes 61, 416 and 419 pass through Oughterard on the way to Clifden from Galway City, and on the return route, several times a day (only once or twice on Sundays).

Bike, Canoe Rental At **Lough Corrib Hostel** *(Camp St., Oughterard; Tel 091/552-866; Around £8 per day).*

Pharmacy **Geoghegan's** *(Main St.; Tel 091/552-348; 9:30am-1:30pm and 2:15-6pm Mon-Tue and Thur-Sat, 9:30am-1pm Wed).*

Postal **Oughterard Post Office** *(Main St.; Tel 091/552-201; 9am-1pm and 2-5:30pm Mon-Fri, 9am-1pm Sat).*

clifden

Clifden is the largest—and thus the most congested and tourist-ridden—town in the Connemara region, though it doesn't take a crossroads of much size to win that honor. You'll find more amenities here than anyplace else in the region, and it's a picturesque little town, surrounded by the spectacular, rocky Connemara Mountains. But if you're set on digging beneath the surface of Ireland's picturesque Western seacoast, you won't want to linger here too long. A telltale sign of its commercialism is that Clifden is an English-speaking town, which is rare in the *Gaeltacht,* or Irish-language, region of Connemara. On the upside, the pub scene here is the liveliest outside of Galway.

Orient yourself at **The Square** (typically creatively named); the main streets—**Main Street, Market Street,** and **Church Hill**—spread out from there. From town, you can take the N59 in a northeasterly direction 5 km (3 mi) to Cleggan, where you catch the ferry out to **Inishbofin Island,** or continue further to **Letterfrack** and the entrance to **Connemara National Park.**

bar and live music scene

For (relatively) cheap yet delicious pub grub and a jolly, if tourist-infused, atmosphere, the prescription is **E.J. King's** *(The Square; Tel 095/21330;*

Food served noon-9pm daily; Regular pub hours); live trad as well as occasional rock or modern folk sessions occur pretty spontaneously.

The most reliable place for live traditional music is **Mannion's** *(Market St.; Tel 095/21780),* which offers up the *bodhrán* and fiddle nightly in the summertime and on Friday and Saturday nights in the winter.

culture zoo

Clifden Castle *(Sky Rd.; Free admission):* Er...there's not too much to be seen here, other than the ruins once inhabited by Clifden's founder, John D'Arcy. The town was founded only in 1812—not a whole lot of history behind it, as compared with the rest of Ireland—and the Famine ruined the D'Arcy family a few decades later.

great outdoors

The scenery of Clifden itself is not breathtaking, but if you venture westward out of town on Sky Road you'll find a precarious cliff or two and some truly spectacular coastal landscapes. Better yet, sign up for a guided walk at the **Connemara Walking Centre** *(Market St.; Tel 095/21379; 10am-6pm Mon-Sat Mar-Oct; Walks around £10-20),* which offers either half- or full-day tours of the surrounding bogs and mountains.

Horse-lovers can rent a Connemara pony, famous for their hardiness and mild temperament, at the **Errislannan Manor** *(3.5 km, or about 2 mi, south of town on the Ballyconneely Rd., or R341; Tel 095/21134; Closed Sun; conamara@indigo.ie; Around £15 an hour)* and go for a lovely little trek in the hills or along the Galway coastline.

eats

Unfortunately, it's rather hard to find inexpensive places to eat in Clifden. Try picking up groceries at **O'Connor's SuperValu** *(Market St.; 8:30am-8pm Mon-Sat, 9am-7pm Sun)* and getting creative in the hostel kitchen. Otherwise, there are a few places that serve good lunches for around £5 or less. Try the pub food at **E.J. King's** *(The Square; Tel 095/21330; Food served noon-9pm daily).* Order the old fish and chips standby for £5, then congratulate yourself for not having gone to the restaurant upstairs, which offers the exact same food at higher prices. There's also **Walsh's** *(The Square; Tel 095/21283; 8am-9pm Mon-Fri, 8am-6:30pm Sat, 9am-6:30pm Sun, open later in July and August),* a bustling little bakery serving sandwiches, soups, and salads for around 2 or 3 punts each. Check out the lunch specials at **Derryclare Restaurant** *(The Square; Tel 095/21440; 8am-10:30pm daily; No credit cards);* a plate of oysters (around £5) or a pasta dish (around £7) thankfully won't bust your wallet either.

crashing

There are tons of hostels, B&Bs, and fancy hotels here, but as usual, book way ahead in summertime! All the hostels adhere to a relatively high standard necessitated by stiff competition; there's not a bad pick in town. You could try the many-virtued **Clifden Town Hostel** *(Market St.; Tel 095/21076; £8 dorms, £10/£9 per person triples/quads, £12 per person doubles; No credit cards);* its close proximity to the Clifden pubs, clean quiet rooms, bike rental, a kitchen, no curfew or lockout, and a very friendly and helpful owner make it a solid choice.

There's also the **Brookside Hostel** *(Hulk St.; Tel 095/21812; £8 dorms, £9 private rooms; £4 laundry; V only, 5 percent surcharge),* in a pretty and quiet little spot by the Owenglin River. It offers super-clean and relatively spacious dorm rooms, cooking facilities, and handicapped toilet/shower; there is no curfew or lockout.

As for bed-and-breakfasts, you can't go wrong with **Kingstown House** *(Bridge St.; Tel 095/21470; dunri@anu.ie; £20 single, £34-36 double; V, MC):* Mrs. King takes excellent care of her guests, providing comfortable, elegant rooms, friendly service, and a huge and enthusiastically recommended breakfast, and all for quite a reasonable price.

If you're not interested in any of the above, try **Mallmore House** *(Ardbear; Tel 095/21460; mallmore@indigo.ie; £21 per person, all rooms have private bath; No credit cards),* about 20 minutes from town, but quaint in that "countryside" way; or **Ben View House** *(Bridge St; Tel 095/21256, Fax 095/21226; benviewhouse@ireland.com; £18.50-£24, all rooms have private baths; V, MC),* in the heart of the city center.

need to know

Currency Exchange **AIB** *(The Square; Tel 095/21129; 10am-12:30pm and 1:30-4pm Mon-Tue and Thur-Fri, 10am-5pm Wed),* with an ATM, and **Bank of Ireland** *(Sea View; Tel 095/21111; 10am-12:30pm and 1:30-5pm Mon-Fri).*

Tourist Information **Clifden Tourist Office** *(Market St.; Tel 095/21163; 9:45am-5:45pm Mon-Sat and noon-4pm Sun July-Aug, 9:30am-5:30pm Mon-Sat May, June, Sept),* is a good source of information about anyplace at all in the Connemara region.

Public Transportation No inner-city buses; Clifden's obviously not big enough. For a taxi, call **Joyce's** *(Tel 095/21076).*

Health and Emergency **Garda** *(Tel 095/21021);* **Clifden Hospital** *(Galway-Clifden Rd.; Tel 095/21301 or 095/21302).*

Pharmacy **Clifden Pharmacy** *(Main St., Clifden; Tel 095/21821; 9:30am-6:30pm Mon-Fri, 9:30am-6pm Sat).*

Bus Lines Out of the City **Bus Éireann** *(Call the Galway City office at 091/562-000 for information)* runs routes back to Galway via Oughterard (route 419, five buses per day in summer and two on Sundays, one per day otherwise), which may or may not go on north to Letterfrack, and Cleggan (also route 419, with service once or twice per day June through September, twice a week the rest of the year). The bus stops outside the Clifden Library on Market Street.

Bike Rental **Mannion's** *(Bridge St.; Tel 095/21160 or 095/21155 after hours; 9:30am-6:30pm Mon-Sat, 10am-1pm and 5-7pm Sun; £7 per* *day, £40 per week, £10 deposit required).* Also try **The Clifden Town Hostel** [see *crashing,* above].

Laundry **The Shamrock Washeteria** *(The Square; Tel 095/21348; 9:30am-6pm Mon-Sat; Around £4 wash and dry).*

Postal **Clifden Post Office** *(Main St.; Tel 095/21156; 9:30am-5:30pm Mon-Fri, 9:30am-1:30pm Sat).*

connemara national park

Like the **Burren** in County Clare, the Connemara region of western Galway is known for its sparse population, desolation, and always breathtaking, wild beauty. Here you'll find wet blanket bogs and heath land, dramatic mountain ranges (the greatest of which is known as the "Twelve Bens"), shimmering lakes, rare flowers and fauna, and glimpses of old-time Irish life—peat fires, thatched roofs, the whole nine yards. Cottage industry (supplying those gorgeous hand-knits for all the Irish Shoppes across the States) is still alive and well here, as is traditional folk music. Donkeys and Connemara ponies are still used on the farms (unfortunately for us, those donkeys are infinitely more reliable than the Irish public transportation systems!).

Though Clifden is the gateway town for Connemara, you'll need to get beyond it to really get a feel for the region. Its dramatic landscapes are shown off at their best in the **Connemara National Park.** The park is beautiful, but not huge: It covers only about 13 square kilometers (8 square miles). And be advised: This place is *extremely* wet. (Don't be like those featherbrained tourists who wear high heels on Skellig Michael: You need boots. *Waterproof* boots.) Still, there are plenty of easy hikes and guided nature walks in the park—just ask at the **Visitor's Centre** [see *need to know,* below]. For experienced hikers only, the **Twelve Bens** on the southern side of the National Park reach as high as 2,400 feet. Unfortunately, no trails are marked, so you'll have to depend on a guidebook, which you can get at the Visitor's Centre.

Letterfrack, at the park's northern end, makes the ideal base for exploring the Connemara National Park. There's not much here—just three pubs and a general store, basically—but the hostel's a splendid one [see *crashing,* below] and the park and the Visitor's Centre are close at hand.

need to know

Tourist Information All the dope on Connemara is available at the Ireland West Tourist Office in Galway *(Victoria Place, off Eyre Sq.; Tel 091/563-081; Open 8:30am-5:45pm May-June, Sept, 8:30am-7:45pm July-Aug, 9am-5:45pm Mon-Fri, 9am-12:45pm Sat Oct-Apr; info@western-tourism.ie),* or if you're already touring around Galway, try the **Oughterard Tourist Office** *(Main St.; Tel 091/8280; Open*

9am-5:30pm Mon-Fri, extended hours in summer). Closer to the Park itself, **Clifden** [see above] has a seasonal office *(Tel 095/21161; Open May-Sept).*

Buses Bus Éireann *(Tel 091/562-000)* route 419 heads out for the Galway coast at least once a day; pick up a connection to Letterfrack from **Clifden** [see above]. If you're driving, pick up the N59 road, which leads from Galway to Oughterard, then runs 40 km (23 mi) west through Connemara to Clifden, then swings north from Clifden to Letterfrack.

Bike Rental The best place to rent a bike is the **Old Monastery Hostel** [see below] for around £7 per day.

Eats The best place to eat is also the best place to stay: **Old Monastery Hostel** *(Letterfrack; Tel 095/41132)* [see *crashing,* below]. If you're staying overnight there, breakfast is included. If not, you can still enjoy a good, very reasonably priced meal. Bonus: It caters to vegetarians, a welcome and uncommon pleasure in Ireland.

Crashing The **Old Monastery Hostel** *(Letterfrack; Tel 095/41132; £8 8-bed dorms, £9 6-bed dorms, £10 4-bed dorms; Breakfast included; V, MC, AE)* makes the perfect base for exploring the Connemara National Park. It's not only convenient, but it's also among the finest hostels in the country, with spacious rooms, authentic peat fires burning in the common room, and great food catering mostly to vegetarians. If you're a committed hiker trying for the Twelve Bens, you might want to stay instead at the **Ben Lettery Hostel** *(Ballinafad, off N95, 8 miles east of Clifden; Tel 095/51136; Open Easter-Sept; Around £6 dorm).*

inishbofin island

There's a buzz among mainland Irish locals that Inishbofin Island makes a splendid, if rather uneventful, getaway spot. It has all the rough, wind-tossed, otherworldly beauty of the Aran Islands, with fewer people and stone walls but more seals, sheep, and wild birds. Inishbofin offers picturesque walking excursions and lovely beaches, and, perhaps best of all, very few tourists. It's the perfect spot for a long quiet stroll and a bit of introspection—inspired, of course, by everything around you. Ferries [see *need to know,* below] leave regularly for Inishbofin from the pretty little village of **Cleggan,** about 10 miles northwest of Clifden, though there's only one per day off-season, November through April.

eats

It'd be best to load up on groceries at **Cleggan's Spar** *(Near the pier; Tel 095/44750; 9am-10pm)* before you leave, but in case you don't, on the island try **Day's Bofin House** *(Tel 095/45809),* a friendly little joint with the freshest seafood around as well as solid Irish staples.

crashing

The greatest asset of the **Inishbofin Island Hostel** *(Uphill after a right at the pier; Tel 095/45855; around £7 dorms, Around £10 per person private rooms, £4 per person camping)* is indisputably the tremendous view. The place itself wins praise, too, especially for its conservatory. How many hostels have one of *those?* There's also a self-catering kitchen where you can do your own cooking.

need to know

Tourist Information For background on the island and walking tour routes, contact the **Island House** *(Tel 095/21379; Closed Sept-Apr. Open Mon-Sun 9am-6pm May-June and 8:30am-9pm July-Aug).*

Directions and Transportation Take **Bus Éireann** from Clifden to Cleggan, leaving Clifden at 8am Tuesdays and Fridays, June-August, then either take the **Island Discovery** ferry *(Tel 095/44642; Three ferries per day July-Aug, two per day Apr-June and Sept-Oct; £12),* the faster, larger, more expensive option, or sail with **Paddy O'Halloran** *(Tel 095/45806; Three ferries per day July-Aug, two per day Apr-June and Sept-Oct, one per day Nov-Apr; £10),* who, as you would suspect, has been operating his ferry since before Moses was born. Many people prefer to take Paddy's ferry rather than patronize the ferry people who operate purely for profit. (Besides, Paddy doesn't charge as much, and a trip taking 10 or 15 minutes longer doesn't matter unless you've got a really weak stomach.)

Bike Rental Rent a bike at the **Inishbofin Pier** for around £6 to £8 per day, or you can bring your bike onto either ferry for no extra charge.

roundstone

Trad music, it should be apparent by now, is everywhere in Ireland, but Roundstone truly stands out. The heavenly strains of fiddle, flute, and drum drifting on the evening air out of the pubs around here are enough to win over even the tone-deaf. And just in case you can't resist the urge to join in the music jams, the town bills itself as the world capital of that ancient goathide drum, the *bodhrán* [see *stuff,* below]. Roundstone also delivers an "olde Irish" rush just by virtue of being a pretty seaside fishing village with little in the way of tourism. It makes a splendid spot for a laid-back afternoon of beach-frolicking and a night full of pints, music, and lively conversation after the stars come out.

There's no tourist office, but you can learn all you need to by asking any of the Roundstone shopkeepers, who are a well-informed and helpful bunch. This town checks in at fewer than 300 souls, so it'd be best to buy groceries and change money before you get here. Roundstone makes a good base for hiking **Errisbeg Mountain,** one of the **Twelve Bens** [see

Connemara National Park, above], very do-able at just 300 meters (984 feet) high. The hike up to the top takes approximately two hours and the views of Connemara are magnificent. And little over a mile west of Roundstone, the clean, quiet, lovely **Gurteen Strand** is perfect for swimming.

pub scene

There are only a couple major spots here, both of which offer some combination of food, drink, and music. The music is good at **Beola** *(Roundstone Harbour; Tel 095/35871; Noon-1:30pm/6:30-9:30pm daily, Easter to mid-Oct; V, MC, AE),* but the food is *great.* It's located in Eldon's Hotel, where the owners do everything from making their own tables and chairs to cooking the evening meals—even the art displayed on the walls is created by the family owners. They offer live traditional every Wednesday and occasionally on Saturday. The drums will beat and the flutes hum until 9:30pm. The dinner menu ranges from vegetarian plates to juicy Irish steaks, but local seafood dominates. Just across the way is **Shamrock's** *(Main St.; Tel 095/35010; noon-9:30pm daily),* owned by the same family (see above). They feature more pub grub–type food than Beola, which is a more fully rounded restaurant. Shamrock's is the best place to go if you want to fill up cheaply on homemade Irish soups and well-stuffed sandwiches. From Thursday to Sunday they sponsor live Irish groups here playing trad. A nostalgic aura prevails as patrons sit in front of a crackling fireplace listening to cyclic melodies that have been passed down through generations of musicians. It's surprising—and disappointing—that here in the best town in the world for buying a *bodhrán,* most of the sessions you'll hear don't incorporate it much, at least not on any given night. The crowds are mostly local and traveling musicians, though, so this is a great place to pick up the line on what's going on in trad around the country.

stuff

You can pick up a *bodhrán* of your very own at **Roundstone Musical Instruments** *(The Monastery, Michael Killeen Park; Tel 095/35875; www.bodhran.com; 9am-6pm May-Oct, 9am-6pm Mon-Sat Nov-Apr).* This place transcends cool: Malachy Kearns makes *bodhráns* for many of Ireland's finest musicians, including those of *Riverdance* fame. His contributions to the Irish music industry (which it technically is, although somehow it seems like the wrong word) have even earned him a cameo on the 32p postal stamp. You can buy other Irish instruments here as well, like harps and tin and wooden flutes. Even cooler: You can buy a *bodhrán* and have it personalized with the Celtic design of your choice. This place is a must-see for all music enthusiasts. Attached to the workshop and store is a cozy cafe and the **Folk Instrument Museum** with loads of interesting blarney on the history of ancient Celtic music. If you don't have time to make it out to Roundstone, but you're stuck on buying a *bodhrán,* the Kearnses offer a mail-order catalog. (Just check out the website for more information.)

If you're still not shopped out after all this, there are several great craft shops in Roundstone worth checking out—many of them part of the Industrial Development Agency craft complex in Michael Killeen Park. Stop by **Síla Mag Aoide Designs** *(The Monastery, Michael Killeen Park; Tel 095/35912; 9am-9pm May-Sept, shorter hours in low season),* offering unique, Celtic-inspired, handmade jewelry, paintings, and the like.

On the harbor, the excellent **Sheepchandler Gallery** showcases totally drool-worthy and inspiring examples of top-notch contemporary Irish art—loads of evocative landscapes.

crashing

There aren't any hostels in Roundstone, but you can camp out at the **Gurteen Beach Caravan and Camping Park** *(2 km west of Roundstone at Gurteen Beach; Tel 095/35882; £7 per person),* although the price does seem just a tad exorbitant for not much more than a well-located plot of ground.

Not much for sleeping in the dirt 'neath a skyful of stars? The best B&B in town, no doubt, would have to be **Saint Joseph's** *(Main St.; Tel 095/35865; Around £25 single, £36 double),* with friendly service, great seaside views, and an excellent, traditional evening meal costing about £12, summertime only. The rooms do the job but wouldn't be mistaken for your second home.

need to know

Trains and Buses Roundstone is reachable via **Bus Éireann** *(Tel 091/562-000)* route 419 between Galway and Clifden, which pretty much operates only once a day Wednesday-Friday all year; route 61, also running between Galway and Clifden, covers Roundstone July-August, about five times daily (twice on Sundays).

killary harbour

For outdoor-thrill-seekers, Killary Harbour's a prime destination. A once-thriving area that was devastated by the Famine, Killary now feels remote (read "tourist-free"); driving down the N59 motorway to the Harbour, you'll see green, rocky landscapes and abandoned farmhouses now in ruins. If you're looking for sports activities, what really matters is that here the **Devilsmother Mountains**—known more for being the setting of the 1990 Richard Harris film *The Field* than for its less-than-daunting 800-foot peaks—meet Ireland's only fjord, creating the perfect place for stretching your physical limits: Water trips around the fjord, hikes along the wild and romantic coast, and climbs on the rocks above are all available at this one incredible spot. Try to arrive early to spend at least one whole invigorating day outdoors.

Driving here is your best bet; otherwise you'll have to hike or bike 11 km (7 mi) from Leenane, the nearest town served by Bus Éireann. But hey, since you're coming here to get physical, what's a measly 7-mile hike? The Harbour hosts the **Killary Adventure Company** [see *need to know,* below] and **Delphi Adventure Centre,** both of which offer loads of options. They'll outfit you for an amazing range of sports, many of which you can't find elsewhere in Ireland: Hobie-cat sailing, wind-surfing, water-skiing, canoeing, wake-boarding, knee-boarding, speedboat trips, diving, mountain biking, gorge walking, hill walking, rock-climbing, abseiling, rope-climbing, archery, orienteering, clay-pigeon shooting, "survival experience," or horseback riding. Whew. Killary Adventure Centre is particularly proud of its zip-wire.

eats

You have three choices; Bring your own grub, eat at the **Killary Harbour Hostel** *(Tel 095/43417)* [see *crashing,* below], or head back to Leenane, a town (if you could call it that) 11 km (7 mi) to the east.

architecture

The fortification walls surviving at least in part around many Irish towns and cities can be credited to the Normans, who also built great churches and cathedrals but are best remembered for their castles. Many Norman castles are still occupied today. Others recline, moss-covered, more or less as ruins, some with rectangular keeps, lichened towers, and timeworn turrets making mute gestures into the empty air above.

The British left their own unique architectural legacy, from the Georgian avenues, squares, and public buildings of Dublin, Limerick, and Armagh to the sprawling "big houses" of the countryside. Built by the Anglo-Irish aristocracy and absentee landlords, these manor homes date from the 17th and 18th centuries and reflect a spirit of "spare no expense." More than 40 of these great houses, originally occupied by the rich and powerful, are open to the public as museums. Others have been converted into hotels.

Also dotting the rural landscape are simple whitewashed, thatched-roof stone cottages. They're traditionally the homes of farming people, many of whom have traded in their cottages for modern bungalows and two-story stucco homes.

Modern Irish architecture tends toward glass-and-concrete construction, but many newer buildings are designed to blend harmoniously with nearby Georgian, Edwardian, and Victorian landmarks. In recent years, the work of contemporary Irish architects has gained increasing international notice and praise.

crashing

Killary Adventure Company makes it very easy: They run the **Killary Harbour Hostel** *(Tel 095/43417; Open Jan-Nov; £7 dorm),* which actually sports a rather stunning view of the surrounding scenery. If that doesn't suit your fancy, it's out to Leenane again.

need to know

Tourist Information Er, call one of the adventure centers [see above]. There's really nothing else out here.

Public Transportation Unfortunately, it's nearly impossible to get here if you're relying on public transportation (and if you refuse to resort to hitchhiking, which isn't a great idea even if you *are* in Ireland). The nearest **Bus Éireann** *(Tel 091/562-000)* stop is at least 11 km (7 mi) away in Leenane (are you surprised?), served by bus route 61, leaving Clifden Monday-Saturday at 11:15am. If you're driving, take the N59 west from Oughterard; it's about 64 km (40 mi) and will take you about an hour to get here.

Rental **Killary Adventure Company** *(Tel 095/43411, adventure@killary.com)* rents just about anything you'd need for outdoor sports.

county mayo

county mayo

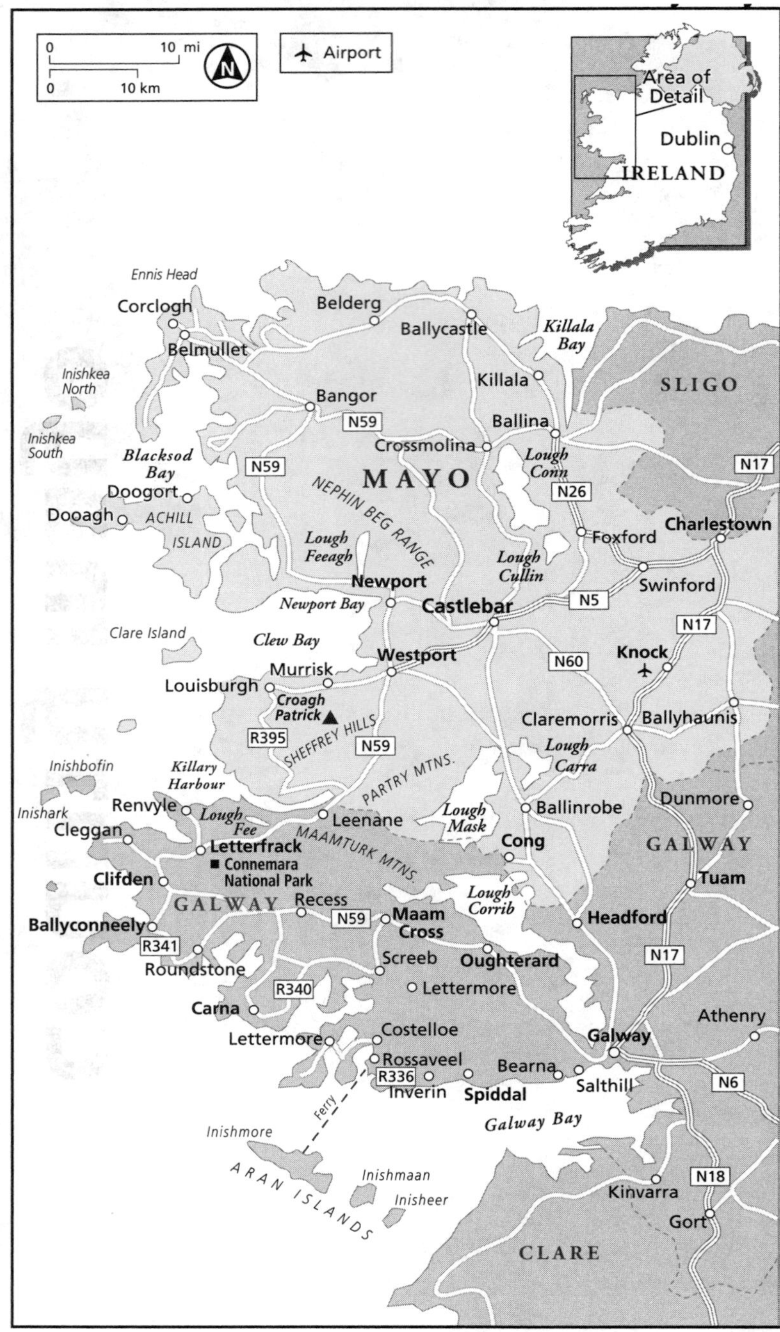

0 10 mi
0 10 km
N
Airport
Area of Detail
Dublin
IRELAND
Ennis Head
Corclogh
Belmullet
Belderg
Ballycastle
Killala Bay
Killala
SLIGO
Inishkea North
Inishkea South
Bangor
N59
Ballina
Crossmolina
Lough Conn
N17
Blacksod Bay
N59
MAYO
N26
Doogort
Dooagh
ACHILL ISLAND
NEPHIN BEG RANGE
Foxford
Charlestown
Lough Feeagh
Lough Cullin
Swinford
Newport
Newport Bay
Castlebar
N5
Clare Island
Clew Bay
N17
Westport
N60
Knock
Murrisk
Louisburgh
Croagh Patrick
Claremorris
Ballyhaunis
R395
SHEFFREY HILLS
N59
Lough Carra
Inishbofin
Killary Harbour
PARTRY MTNS.
Inishark
Renvyle
Lough Fee
Leenane
Lough Mask
Ballinrobe
Dunmore
Cleggan
Letterfrack
MAAMTURK MTNS.
Cong
GALWAY
Connemara National Park
Clifden
Tuam
Lough Corrib
GALWAY
Recess
Ballyconneely
N59
Maam Cross
Headford
R341
Roundstone
Screeb
Oughterard
N17
R340
Lettermore
Carna
Athenry
Costelloe
Lettermore
Galway
Rossaveel
Bearna
R336
Inverin
Spiddal
Salthill
N6
Ferry
Galway Bay
Inishmore
ARAN ISLANDS
Inishmaan
Inisheer
N18
Kinvarra
Gort
CLARE

westport

Westport is a hell of a cute little place. It's one of the few planned towns in Ireland, designed in the 18th century by James Wyatt with Georgian streets, beautiful row houses, and a leafy mall that makes it postcard-pretty. Even more amazing is the fact that Westport has avoided the kitschy excesses of so many other major vacation spots in Ireland. It's got a refreshing feistiness to it, but still remains—and prides itself on being—sophisticated, charming, and relaxing. That doesn't mean it isn't still a resort town, though; there's definitely an emphasis on enjoying oneself, eating well, and drinking aplenty. The crowd is generally older, although there are a good number of younger people who come here. You'll find a nice mix of styles, dress, and income brackets.

With its proximity to the Atlantic, Westport is a natural destination for water-sports lovers. If you're into surfing, you'll be impressed to know that this area has produced some world-class *stand-ups* (surfers) and *spongers* (boogie boarders), who honed their craft in the chilly Atlantic at the excellent nearby surfing spots [see *city sports,* below]. But even if your *Jaws* flashbacks keep you a landlubber, don't stay away—it's worth visiting for the town itself.

Spend an afternoon shopping in some of the cute shops on the main streets or sipping tea and reading a book at a cafe, then head down to a pub in the evening and sing along to some incredible traditional music. (How good is the music scene here? Matt Malloy's eponymous pub is owned by the flutist of the internationally renowned group the Chieftains. How's that for credibility?) On your way back to your B&B or hostel, take a walk down along Carrowbergh River and be enchanted by the moonlight glistening off the water as it meanders slowly through the canal.

neighborhoods

Westport is really a tiny town; all of its downtown streets, of which there are about 10, can be walked in under 2 minutes if you're under the age of 90 and have no serious injuries. Westport's gentle sprawl emanates from the **Octagon,** a roundabout in the town center. At its center stands a statue of a beardless St. Patrick, one of the few depictions of the saint in his youth. From here, dozens of pubs, shops, restaurants, cafes, and more pubs are an easy walk away. Head north on **James Street,** past St. Mary's Church, and wind up at the west end of **The Mall,** a handsome tree-lined street on either side of the canal of the **Carrowbergh River. Quay Road** leads out of town toward the coast.

bar, club, and live music scene

For a town of only 4,500, there sure are a lot of places to drink in Westport, and their vibe is celebratory. Even off-season when there are no tourists around, Westport's pubs are full of life and often full in the middle of the afternoon. Clubs are usually bars with dance floors and DJ booths and are only marginally less casual than the pubs. Pub hours are generally from early afternoon, around 1-3pm, till 11:30pm.

By day **Matt Malloy's** *(Bridge St.; Tel 098/26665)* is a cozy pub with a coal fireplace in the back and an enclosed beer garden beyond that. At night it's elbow-to-elbow and a bit of a pain in the ass to get a pint from the clogged bar. Because this place is owned by world-renowned, Mayo-born millionaire/musician Matt Malloy of the Chieftains, you probably won't be surprised to hear that it's absolutely packed almost every night of the week with both visitors and locals proud of their home slice. Some superlative trad sessions happen here several times a week, so it's definitely worth checking out. You'll find the pub halfway down Bridge Street and on your left as you walk toward the water.

O'Malley's *(Bridge St. a couple doors off Shop St.; Tel 098/27308; V, MC)* is an atmospheric pub and restaurant in the traditional style. The bar is absolutely packed with wines, and they even do cocktails. There's a definite American sense of presentation here in Irish pub surroundings (picture a TGI Friday's with soul). Burgers are delicious but pricey at £8; seafood is superb and goes for around £12-13. The space is intimate and caters to an older crowd, but it's a fun place to meet locals.

They don't make any pansy cocktails at **P. Dunning's** *(The Octagon, attached to Dunning's B&B; Tel 098/25161, Fax 098/27203; dunnings@anu.ie, http://dunnings.irishbiz.com),* an old-school pub on the Octagon. The room's bright, unfinished pine look is both invigorating and relaxing. An older crowd hangs out here, sipping drinks slowly while they talk about old times. When the visitors come—and, with the pub being attached to a B&B, they do come—the bar disappears in a sea of polo shirts and baseball caps.

Right on the river, **The West** *(Bridge St.; Tel 098/25886)* is dark, smoky and packed with kids. The crowd is *very* young—the average age is probably somewhere around 19. They've got live music, mostly rock and/or roll, on Fridays and Saturdays, more often in the summer.

Next door you'll find **Geraghty** *(The Octagon),* an old-timer affair that's brilliant in the daytime when you just want to have a drink, hold the chit-chat. It's quiet, and the woodwork inside is warm and slightly more welcoming than the sometimes-cantankerous bartender.

If you're dying to catch a game of Gaelic hurling or football on TV, or are the sportin' type yourself, head to **John Maughan's** *(High St.; Tel 098/28494).* They've got a big-screen TV, a pool table, and a dartboard, which you can play with the thick-necked regulars. Women, be prepared to be hit on by guys who are about as good at flirting as Michael Jordan was at baseball.

Henehans *(Bridge St.; Tel 098/25561)* is a rustic, back-to-basics, check-your-guns-at-the-door type of pub. The crowd varies depending on time of day and year, but is usually older. There's music throughout the week: trad sessions Monday, Thursday, and Sunday, live rock Friday and Saturday. The Sunday night trad sessions are a good way to bid farewell to the weekend.

If you're itching to shake your butt to some live music, come on down to the **Wits Westport Inn** *(Mill St.; Tel 098/29200).* Some nights you'll actually hear ska/punk stuff; most nights it's straight-ahead rock. The bar is open late, thank the Lord, till about 1 or 2am, depending on how big the crowds are.

Youngsters congregate amid laser lights and theatrical smoke to dance and drink at **The Castle** *(Castlebar St., at the Castlecourt Hotel; Tel 098/25444, Fax 098/286-222; Disco nights usually 9pm-1am, Fri-Sun only; Cover £5),* one of the few dance spots in town. The atmosphere is a bit like that of a high school dance: lights and pleasant hotel-lounge surroundings. You may occasionally smell illicit smoke in the air.

Cosy Joe's *(Bridge St.; Tel 098/28004)* is one of the more cheesed-up disco spots in town, but hell, everyone has fun. This is a prime place to mack on the opposite sex, and the pub food ain't bad either. There are two levels in this pub—upstairs is the dancing, downstairs is the grub—and there's usually no cover, ya' cheap bastard. If you're south of the river, take Bridge Street across the river and head up to the corner of Distillery Road and Castlebar Street.

culture zoo

The big cultural attraction in town is a mansion, but the best way to enjoy it is to stay in the yard—an expanse that is actually more of a park—and have a wee picnic.

Westport House *(Take Quay Rd. a mile outside of town; Tel 098/25430; 1:30-5:30pm Mon-Sat, 1:30-5:30pm Sun May-June; 11:30am-5:30pm weekdays, 1:30-5:30pm Sat, Sun, July-Aug; 2-5pm daily, Sept; closed Oct-Apr; Admission £6 adults, £3 students):* Westport House is

festivals and events

In late September, Westport celebrates its annual **Arts Festival** *(Contact either the tourist office at Tel 098/25711 or Mary Phelan at 090/544-132; http://mayo.local.ie/content/44354.shtml/westport/entertainment)*, a weeklong orgy of artistic endeavors. Poetry, music, art, drama, and drinking are all well represented. Shunning the coming of the crisp autumn chill, the festival heats up the streets with unbridled *craic.*

a beautiful 18th-century mansion built on the site of Grace O'Malley's castle [see **clare island,** below], surrounded by acres of lovely green. A river runs by the house, and manicured grounds and forest surround it. A word to the wise: Skip the pricey tour of the house—and the especially lame petting zoo—and just enjoy the beautiful parkland around it. Bring a picnic lunch and spend the afternoon watching all the tourists blow their cash at the absurd "Gifte Shoppe" whilst thou savest thine monies.

city sports

There is a good amount of surfing in the Westport area, with prime spots like Louisburgh, Killary, Easky, and Bondoran all within a half-hour drive. The place to get info on where to catch the best waves is **The Portwest Outdoor Shop** *(Bridge St., a couple of doors up from O'Malley's; Tel 098/25177; 9:30am-6pm; V, MC, AE).* They can hook you up with people who can meet you for lessons, rides, and tips. They also rent equipment.

If you don't feel like hanging ten, the **Delphi Adventure Center** *(In nearby Leenane; Tel 095/42232; 9:30am-5:45pm Mon-Sat)* offers water-skiing and horseback riding for £16 and £12, respectively. Delphi's staff can arrange shuttles from Westport that will take you to the nearby lakes, ocean, and countryside for a variety of outdoor stuff.

stuff

Because Westport is a major destination for those seeking Irishness, the shops downtown tend to sell goods loaded with Irishness. With tons of shops in town, you'll also find the goods to satisfy almost any shopping jones, Irish or otherwise.

▸▸TUNES

Downtown Records *(The Octagon; Tel 098/26811; 10am-6pm Mon-Sat, open late July-Aug)* has mostly Irish trad music and assorted, rather out-of-place pop cheese for sale. You can buy concert tix for any venue in Ireland here as well, through the evil Ticketmaster system.

▸▸BOUND

Do you like interesting books? Well, **Young's Interesting Books** *(Lime Court off James St.; 10am-5pm Mon-Sat)* is, obviously, the place to buy them. Young's has a good collection of secondhand and antiquarian books.

Besides being one of the few shops open on Sunday year-round, **The Bookshop** *(Bridge St.; Tel 098/26816; 10am-6pm daily)* has a fairly comprehensive selection of Irish literature.

▸▸IRISH STUFF

There is generally excellent handmade work stocked in the many local craft shops, but if you're about to shell out serious money for a cool pot or *bodhrán* (traditional Irish drum), make sure you check to see that it's *really* handmade. Most works reflect a traditional Irish aesthetic imbued with modern sensibilities. **Richard Weston Pottery** *(Main St.; Tel 098/41353; 10am-5:30pm Mon-Sat),* **Absolute Pottery** *(Quay St.; Tel 098/25416; 9:45am-5:45pm Mon-Sat),* the **Lower Deck Café** *(The Quay; Tel 098/28555; 10am-5pm, Mon-Sat),* and the **Andrew Stone Gallery** *(Bridge St.; Tel 098/25619; 10am-5pm Mon-Sat; No credit cards)* are some of the better—and more reputable—shops.

eats

Thai, Italian, cafe and pub food, excellent surf and turf—Westport has a tremendous variety of food for a town of its size. All of these cuisines can be found within a few blocks of the Octagon. All the hostels have kitchens, too, so budgeteers can always cook in and save their pence for the pubs. **Supervalu** *(Shop St. off the Octagon; 8:30am-7:30pm Mon-Sat, open till 9pm Thur, off-license store open till 10pm daily)* has super groceries.

For a cafe that's attached to a supermarket, **O'Cee's** *(Shop St. off the Octagon, attached to Supervalu; 8:30am-7pm Mon-Sat, 10am-6pm Sun)* is surprisingly cool. They have great fry-ups (eggs, bacon, sausage, more sausage, tomatoes, mushrooms, toast, tea, beans) for a dirt-cheap £3. And it's located conveniently on the Octagon.

The prices are high at **Urchin Restaurant** *(Lower Bridge St.; Tel 098/27532; Open daily in summer, closed Tue and Wed off-season; Seafood entrees £9-12; V, MC, AE, Laser),* but after you taste the delicious nouveau *fruits de mer* dishes, you'll be coming back for more. Featuring a tasteful, minimalist decor, the Urchin is located on Bridge Street, a few doors from O'Malley's [see *bar, club, and live music scene,* above].

Brooding poets come and soak in the atmosphere at the dimly lit and cozy **High St. Café** *(High St.; Tel 098/29171; 9am-10pm daily; Breakfast £3, lunch £5.50, dinner £7.50).* The tortured souls eat up the smoky atmosphere, great fry-ups, yummy and filling lasagna lunches, and Guinness and beef casserole dinners.

Antigua Roma *(At the south end of Bridge St.; Noon-7pm Mon-Sat; £3-6)* is a cheap but good dive for dinner grub. It's basically fast food Italian, but very tasty. Join the young folk who come here for the personal pizzas, cheap wine, and greasy but oh-so-delicious burgers and fries.

crashing

Westport is packed in the summer months with backpackers, old people, yuppies, etc. You name 'em, they sleep here. Book a week or more in advance for a hostel bed on a weekend, four to five days ahead for weekday stays. The tourist office [see *need to know,* below] can help you out, but you'll probably pay less if you book yourself.

The best hostel in town is the **Old Mill Hostel** *(James St.; Tel 098/27045, Fax 098/26644; £7 dorm, £1 sleep sheet, call for rates on doubles; £3 laundry).* Only a 2-minute walk from the Octagon, it's housed in—you guessed it—an old mill. Stone walls and a gravel courtyard create a unique, antique atmosphere. The dorms are pleasingly spacious and have big, comfortable duvets. The common area and kitchen form one big room, where guests sit and talk till all hours.

When you first walk into the big **Club Atlantic Hostel** *(Altamont St.; Tel 098/26644; March-Oct only; £6.50-8 dorm, £10 per person double)* you may start having intense summer-camp flashbacks. All the walls are made of cinder blocks, giving it a sort of camp rec hall feeling. Also, because of its size, this hostel attracts a lot of big tour bus groups, so there may be two or three dozen 12-year-olds whipping wet towels at each other in the bathroom. But don't run screaming yet—there is a lot of good here. They've got a handy shop that sells pasta, batteries, and all sorts of travel goodies. The big rec room—complete with ping-pong, pool, and upright piano—really *is* fun. The hostel is only about a 10-minute walk from downtown: From the east end of the Mall where it

full moon fever

A strange custom has developed among young visitors who stay in hostels in Westport. Depending on how you look at it, it's either crass and insensitive or good old-fashioned fun. Basically, it goes like this: At the end of a night of drinking, you walk to the Mall with a group of fellow travelers, pull down your pants, and bend over the walls of the canal. One member of the group, usually the most modest, takes everyone's picture, and then you continue home. Sure it's childish, but it's something you'll never forget. If you decide to partake in this unique ritual, make sure you're not too loud. The people who live in the neighborhood don't like to awaken to a bunch of bare asses at one in the morning.

hits Mill Street, take Altamont Street due east (it's a gradually sloping hill upward all the way). It's about a half-mile.

You can't beat the central location of **Dunning's B&B** *(The Octagon; Tel 098/25161, Fax 098/27203; dunnings@anu.ie, http://dunnings.irishbiz.com; £20 single, £32 double),* which offers a cozy bed and breakfast, with meals served at Dunning's restaurant downstairs. The Dunning's empire also includes the popular P. Dunning's [see *bar, club, and live music scene,* above], and Dunning's Cyberpup [see *need to know,* below], both attached to the B&B.

The swank **Central Hotel** *(The Octagon; Tel 098/25027; £45-55 single, £70-100 double; V, MC)* has a rustic, country-style feel but doesn't skimp on comfort. The plush rooms all have bath, TVs, and direct-dial phones. The lively pub downstairs is more modern, but finished in warm tones of wood.

You'll also have good luck at a few other moderately priced spots like **Plougatel House** *(Distillery Rd.; Tel 098/25198; £20 single, £25 double per person, all rooms have private baths; No credit cards),* right in the town center; **Woodside** *(Golf Course Rd.; Tel 098/26436; Rooms £20; V, MC),* a 5-minute walk from downtown; or **The Anchorage** *(7A Altamont St.; Tel 098/25448; £20 per person, all rooms have private baths; V, MC),* in the center of town.

need to know

Currency Exchange You can deal with your dough at the **Bank of Ireland** *(North Mall; Tel 098/25522; 10am-4pm Mon-Wed and Fri, 10am-5pm Thur)* or **Allied Irish Bank** *(Shop St.; Tel 098/25466; 10am-4pm Mon-Wed and Fri, 10am-5pm Thur).* Both feature 24-hour ATMs and Bureaus de Change.

Tourist Information The ever-helpful **Westport Tourist Office** *(James St.; Tel 098/25711; 9am-12:45pm/2-5:45pm Mon-Sat Apr-Oct, open Sun 10am-6pm July-Aug)* is conveniently located for your pleasure.

Health and Emergency Emergency: *999,* Police (Garda): *Tel 098/25555.* If you need a hospital, call 999 and they'll whisk you to the hospital in nearby **Castlebar** *(Tel 094/21454).*

Pharmacies If you've cut your finger surfing, you can pick up bandages and the like at **O'Donnell's** *(Bridge St.; Tel 098/25163, after hours 098/27347; 9am-6:30pm Mon-Sat).*

Trains Trains leave from **Altamont Station** *(Altamont St.; Tel 098/25253)* and run to Dublin three times a day Monday through Saturday, twice on Sunday.

Bus Lines Out of the City Buses leave from the Octagon, near the Central Hotel. From Westport, you can go to Dublin (five per day, two on Sunday), Sligo (two per day), Belfast (three per day, two on Sunday), and Galway (seven per day, two on Sunday). The tourist office can give you schedule information, or call **Bus Éireann** *(Tel 01/830-22-22; www.buseireann.ie).*

westport

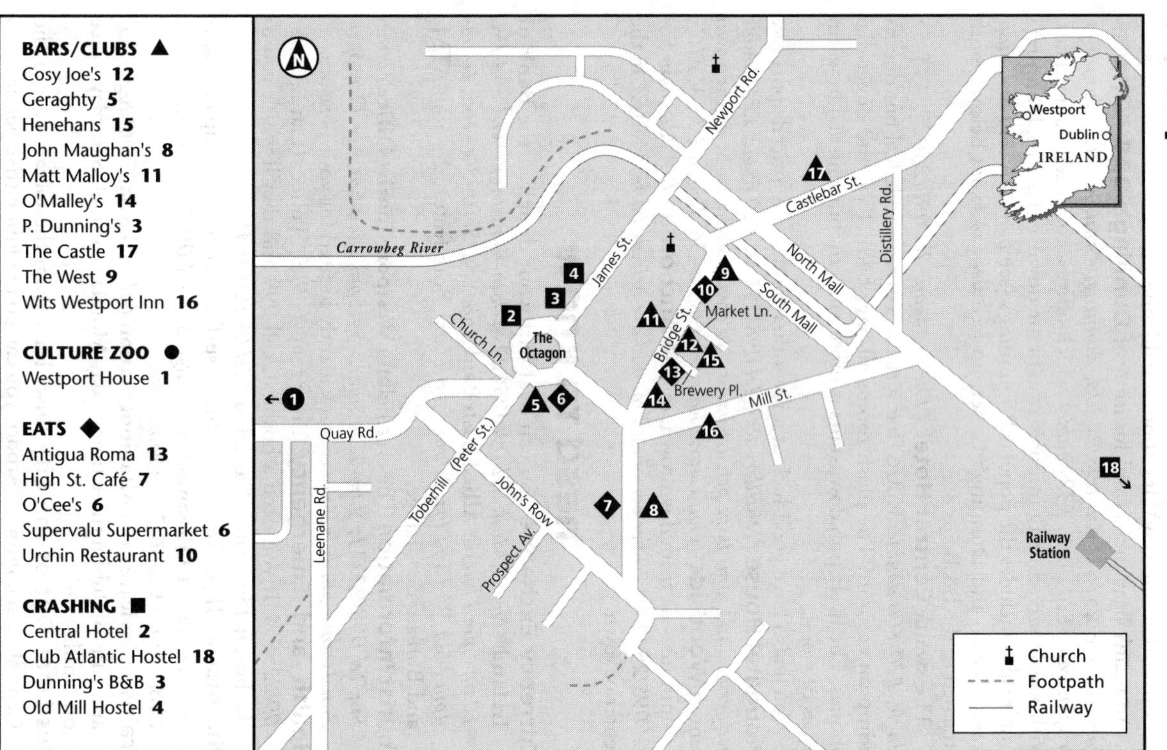
BARS/CLUBS ▲
Cosy Joe's 12
Geraghty 5
Henehans 15
John Maughan's 8
Matt Malloy's 11
O'Malley's 14
P. Dunning's 3
The Castle 17
The West 9
Wits Westport Inn 16
CULTURE ZOO ●
Westport House 1
EATS ◆
Antigua Roma 13
High St. Café 7
O'Cee's 6
Supervalu Supermarket 6
Urchin Restaurant 10
CRASHING ■
Central Hotel 2
Club Atlantic Hostel 18
Dunning's B&B 3
Old Mill Hostel 4
Westport
Dublin
IRELAND
Carrowbeg River
Newport Rd.
James St.
Castlebar St.
Distillery Rd.
North Mall
South Mall
Market Ln.
Bridge St.
Brewery Pl.
Mill St.
The Octagon
Church Ln.
Quay Rd.
Leenane Rd.
Toberhill (Peter St.)
John's Row
Prospect Av.
Railway Station
Church
Footpath
Railway

Boats O'Malley's Ferries *(Roonagh Pier, west toward Westport on R335; Tel 098/25045, Fax 098/26976; Ferries leave several times a day in summer, less often in winter; £10 return)* will take you to Clare Island. Buses departing the tourist office at 10am and 5pm daily will take you to the pier.

Bike Rental J.P. Breheny and Sons *(Castlebar St.; Tel 098/25020; £7 per day, £30 per week)* will get you mobile. You can arrange to bike to Galway and leave your bike there. Stop by for details.

Laundry Bring your soiled goods to **The Washeteria** *(Mill St.; Tel 098/25261; 9am-3:30pm Mon-Sat; £2.50 wash and dry).*

Postal You can mail your packages and whatnot from the **Westport Post Office** *(North Mall; Tel 098/25475; 9am-noon/2-5:30pm Mon-Sat; No credit cards).*

Internet Dunning's Cyberpub *(Inside Dunning's Bed and Breakfast, on the Octagon; Tel 098/25161, Fax 098/27203; dunning@anu.ie, www.dunningspub.com; £5 per hour)* has full Internet access on iMacs.

everywhere else

murrisk

The biggest attraction in the little town of Murrisk, just south of Westport, is **Croagh Patrick**, where the devout come to climb. This 2,510-foot (765-meter) mountain has been a pilgrimage site since St. Patrick climbed atop its rocky peak back in the 5th century to drive the snakes out of Ireland. Thousands of pilgrims—including the elderly, crippled, and ill—make this arduous ascent every year, many of them *barefoot* (but don't you get carried away: Sturdy shoes or boots are definitely recommended). It's a true struggle—steep and humbling, as a religious quest should be.

To start your climb, go behind **Campbell's Pub** *(On R335 at the foot of Croagh Patrick)*—where you'll want to stop for refreshments after the hike—and walk along the gravel path about a half-mile until you hit a gate at the foot of the mountain. The climb takes 1 to 3 hours, depending on your endurance. The last few hundred meters are so steep and rocky you'll probably wind up crawling part of the way on your hands and knees. There's a little stone chapel at the summit that looks like no more than a speck of white when seen from the ground; there's also a w.c. but no running water, so bring your own to drink. On a clear day, you'll get great views over Clew Bay. Warning: It's busiest on the last Sunday in July, when thousands of people make the climb.

Back down the hill, across the street from Campbell's, is the **National Famine Memorial,** a sobering metal sculpture of a ship covered in skeletons. It's meant to represent one of the rickety, barely seaworthy ships used during the Potato Famine. Thousands of Irish boarded these "coffin ships," hoping to reach America or Australia but often instead sailing to their deaths. If you follow the path past the memorial, you'll reach **Murrisk Abbey,** a ruined 15th-century site. As ruined abbeys go, it's not spectacular.

need to know

Tourist Information Go to the **Westport tourist office** for info about Croagh Patrick.

Directions and Transportation To get here from Westport, head west on R335 for about 8 km (5 mi) till you hit Murrisk. You'll see Croagh Patrick dominating the skyline. Continue on for another mile west and you'll see signs for the National Famine monument. On your left will be Campbell's Pub. You can easily bike out in this direction from Westport, but make sure you have enough energy to bike back after climbing the peak. Climbers might want to take a taxi from Westport *(Tel 053/25529; 50p per mi, roughly £10 round-trip).*

Eats You can get a bag of chips or a cup of soup at **Campbell's** [see above].

Crashing The nearest place to find a room for the night is in Westport.

clare island

The tourist brochure hits this place right on the nose—this really is a "miniature paradise." Beaches, hills, and spectacular views make this island chock-full of cool stuff. Floating a mere 3.5 miles off the Mayo coast just beyond Clew Bay, Clare Island is roughly 40 square miles of unspoiled splendor. Inhabited for 5,000 years and once quite populous—

portrait of the 16th-century entrepreneur as a young woman

Thelma and Louise were nothing compared to the 16th-century pirate chick Grace O'Malley. Clare Island was Grace's home base; from here, she would board passing ships, levy heavy duties on them, or else wreak havoc on the crew and steal cargo. Fans of Grace, pirating, or debauchery in general can go to the 14th-century **Clare Island Abbey,** where a stone is inscribed with the O'Malley family motto: "Invincible on land and sea"—a philosophy Grace clearly embraced with gusto.

with 1,700 pre-Famine residents—Clare is now home to 150 year-round islanders, and perhaps as many sheep. **Grace O'Malley's castle** [see *portrait of the 16th-century entrepreneur as a young woman,* above], and the partially restored **Cistercian Abbey** where she is buried are among the island's few attractions.

The real attraction is the island's remote natural beauty—the sea cliffs on the north side of the island are truly spectacular. The short but still impressive **Mt. Knockmore** rises 461 meters to dominate the island, and there are plenty of areas to hike around as well. Stop by the **Bay View Hotel** [see *crashing,* below] for more information.

The great thing about Clare Island is that it's not a built-up tourist trap. It remains an isolated spot where you can get away from civilization and get in touch with Mother Nature. There is only one pub, in the **Bay View Hotel** *(Tel 098/26307),* but it's open till the unusually late hour of 2am. There's also a scattering of shops, B&Bs, and restaurants on the island.

You might also want to try the affordable **Cois Abhainn** *(Tomore; Tel 098/26216; £18 per person, only one room has a private bath, price includes breakfast; No credit cards),* in the countryside on the west side of the island; or, if you're looking to drop some fast cash, try **Clare Island Lighthouse** *(Clare Island; Tel 098/45120, Fax 098/45122; £50 single, £60 double per person, price includes dinner; V, MC),* with a beautiful view overlooking the sea and cliffs.

need to know

Tourist Information Although there's no tourist office, information can be found at the **Bay View Hotel** [see below].

Directions and Transportation To get out here, you need to take **O'Malley's Ferries** *(Roonagh Pier, west of Westport on R335; Tel 098/25045, Fax 098/26976; £10 return);* ferries leave several times a day in summer, less often in winter. Buses depart the **Westport Tourist Office** at 10am and 5pm daily and take you to the pier. From there, it's a pleasant 15-minute cruise to the island. A special bonus: they'll give you a bike to ride for free when you get to the island. Call ahead for other times without connections.

Eats Your food selections are limited. A small pub grub menu is available at the **Bay View Hotel** [see above]. **O'Malley's** *(Harbor Rd.; Tel 098/26987; Open daily)* has a small grocery selection. You can also get dinner at most of the B&Bs in town for around £10.

Crashing If you want to stay on the island, the **Bay View Hotel** *(Tel 098/26307; June-Sept only, £25 single, £40 double; V, MC, AE)* and the inexpensive **Seabreeze B&B** *(Tel 098/26746, Fax 098/25649; £16 per person sharing, £19 single occupancy; No credit cards)* are good options.

achill island

If you're heading north from Westport or south from Sligo, you owe it to yourself to take a day and spend it on Achill Island. Rugged cliffs, pristine beaches, and friendly pubs dot the island's shores, while bleak bogs blanket its interior in an almost supernatural emptiness. Tax incentives in the '60s and '70s made Achill a prime resort area for moneyed folk from Ireland and England. It also led people to build ugly white houses everywhere like a crop of sore thumbs, marring the otherwise beautiful landscape. These little houses look totally out of place, but even they cannot ruin the overwhelming beauty of Achill.

These days, Achill is a seldom-visited place, almost forgotten by the rest of Ireland. This works to your advantage—accommodations are cheap, and beaches and scenic roads aren't cluttered with people. This is true even in the summer. There is plenty of space for quiet contemplation, walking, and relaxation. Achill sees a lot of rain, and it can be miserable when the weather sucks. On a sunny day, though, or during a sunny period in an otherwise dismal day, the island offers stunning views of the sea as the bright sunlight dramatically etches detail into the craggy cliffs and mountains.

The first two weeks of August, during the **Soil Acla Na Milaoise** (Achill School) festival, is an especially good time to come here [see *festivals and events*, below]. Another fun time to be here, although the weather will be crap, is St. Patrick's Day, when pipes and drummers ring in the feast day in full traditional regalia.

neighborhoods

A string of villages stretches along the island's 20-km breadth. Because they're all so small, it's better to think of the island as a whole, and each village as a neighborhood. From east to west, you pass through **Achill Sound, Cashel, Keel,** and **Dooagh,** finally running out of land and hitting the ocean at **Keem Bay.** You can also visit the weird **Deserted Village** [see *culture zoo,* below]. Achill Island is reached via a bridge that runs from the mainland over to the village of **Achill Sound,** but after

wired

Surf to ***www.achill-island.com*** for general information about the island. The only way to get online on the island is if you stay at the Rich View Hostel [see *crashing,* below]. They may let you use their Internet TV if you ask nicely.

achill island

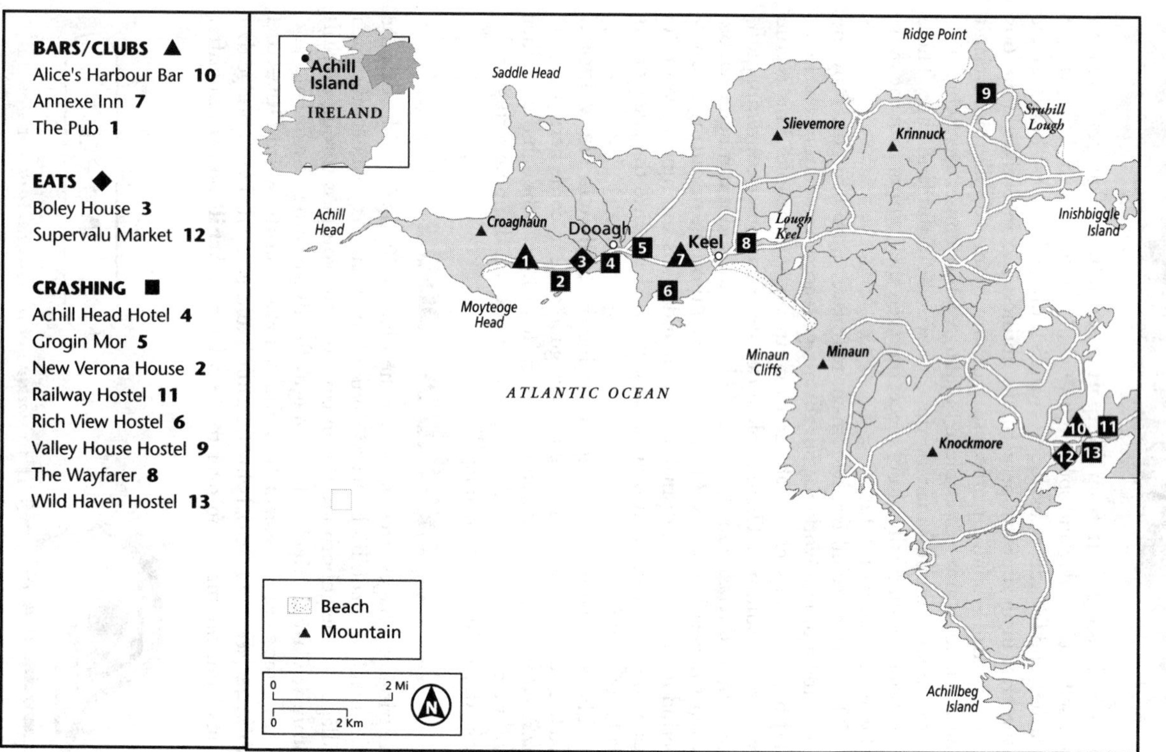

that the best way to see the rest of the island, if you don't have a car, is to rent a bike [see *need to know,* below].

You'll find a tourist office [see *need to know,* below] in Achill Sound where you can grab a map of the island. There is a post office, gas station, and food shop here as well, so it's best to stock up with whatever you need if you're headed out on the island for the night.

The most scenic route on the island is the **Atlantic Way,** a series of roads that take you around the coast. You can hop on it in Achill Sound, or even before you get on the island in **Mulrany.** This route gives you maximum views of the ocean and the rugged terrain of Achill. It also takes you through most of the minute villages on the island. From Mulrany, follow signs for the Atlantic Way.

Passing through **Cashel** (not much happening here), you'll eventually hit **Keel,** the Times Square of Achill Island. A highlight here is the friendly **Annexe** pub [see *bar scene,* below.] As you drive west along the island and come to Keel, take the first right you see. You'll soon arrive in **Dugort,** near the Deserted Village. Continue along the road for another couple of miles and you'll hit Dooagh (pronounce it like Al Pacino would, *DOO-ah*), home of **The Pub** [see *bar scene,* below].

Continue on for another 2.5 miles down the winding road until you hit the astoundingly beautiful Keem Bay. Biking here is an absolute bitch—be ready to face serious uphill and narrow roads, with sheer cliffs to one side. *Be careful.* The scenery is worth the journey, though. On a clear day, the waters are still and blue, protected by the imposing cliffs surrounding the beach. Keem was once the center of activity of the Achill Basking Shark Fisheries; basking sharks—big, gnarly, 5-ton suckers—were netted and harpooned, then towed away by boat, and their livers extracted for oil. The fins were sun-dried and shipped abroad. If you're into it, you can see the head and photographs of a 365-lb. porbeagle shark caught in these very waters at the Achill Head Hotel in Keel [see *crashing,* below].

bar scene

Achill Island's nightlife is pretty much the same as its day life—laid-back and quiet. The best pub on the island is **The Annexe** *(Tel 098/43268; Open till 11:30pm most nights, but may close early on quiet nights),* in Keel, a long, rustic establishment with friendly proprietors and an earthy crowd. Trad music plays every Saturday, and every day in July and August. This is a great place to sip a whiskey or nurse a pint when the weather turns on you. They also do bed and breakfast in the adjoining room in the summer. Call ahead for rates and info.

Dooagh's **The Pub** *(Main St.; Tel 098/43120)* is another good bet. They have trad here on weekends year-round, and all the time in the summer during the festival.

In Achill Sound, **Alice's Harbour Bar** *(Tel 098/45138)* is a little closer to civilization and has a nautical theme, a great view, and good pub food for around £5.

culture zoo

If you've never been to a ghost town before, you might be a bit put off by the abandoned village just outside of town.

Deserted Village *(Take a right onto the road that veers off the main road as you approach Keel from the east):* This eerie settlement was home to cattle ranchers until the mid-1800s. No one is really sure why the inhabitants left; some say the Famine had something to do with it, others say aliens landed and abducted everyone and took them and their sheep into outer space (generally this theory is put forward by someone who's been watching too many episodes of *The X-Files*). The village consists simply of a bunch of stone houses falling into ruin. The whole thing is spooky, even a little depressing—more of a bike-through than an all-day excursion.

great outdoors

Keel has the windswept **Trawmore Strand,** a 5-km stretch of beach, and the dramatic **Minawn Cliffs** and **Cathedral Rocks.**

Surfing is great here and the beaches are blue-flagged, which means the water off shore is not polluted (red-flagged beaches, of course, are dangerous). The water even in summer may be too cold for you if you're from Florida.

For experienced hikers, Achill offers the daunting challenge of **Mount Slievemore** at 2,204 feet—it takes almost 12 hours to reach the summit and return. Begin at the Slievemore Deserted Village car park. Along the way you'll encounter panoramic vistas of **Mullet** and **Blacksod Bay.** You can also climb **Mount Croaghaun** at 2,182 feet. It lies on the west side of the island. The approach is from **Keem Bay** where you head north to **Corrymore Lough.** From here some of the most precipitous cliffs in Northern Europe drop down to the sea. Unlike Mount Slievemore, Croaghaun takes about 6 hours for a return journey. Before attempting either of these climbs, head out with good maps, which can be purchased in town or from the tourist office [see *need to know,* below].

festivals and events

During the **Soil Acla Na Milaoise (Achill School) festival** *(The first two weeks of Aug),* Achill becomes a music and arts retreat, offering performances, workshops, and overflowing *craic.* You can learn to play the *uilleann* (elbow) pipes, take a painting course, or learn the jig. Or you can just go to the pubs and listen to music. Trad sessions happen everywhere every night, with all students and teachers participating. The atmosphere is great, and everyone spends all night jamming, talking, and drinking.

eats

There are chip shops in Achill Sound and Keel. If you want something more refined, head for Dooagh and the **Boley House Restaurant** *(Main St.; Tel 098/43147; £6-12)* for some excellent home-style cookin'. Chicken, beef—it's all fresh and delicious. There's also a **Supervalu** *(Main St.; 9am-7pm daily)* in Achill Sound for groceries.

Keel's superb **Beehive Handcrafts and Coffee Shop** *(Village of Keel; Open Spring to Winter; Tel 098/43134 or 098/43018; Approx. £5)* sells both traditional crafts and great food. Would you like cream with your sweater?

crashing

Achill has a wide selection of hostels. In Achill Sound, **The Wild Haven Hostel** *(Behind the church; Tel 098/45392; £7.50 dorm)* is your best bet for its friendly staff, nice furniture, and comfy bar.

Also in Achill Sound, **The Railway Hostel** *(Tel 098/45187; £6 dorm, £1 linen)* provides basic accommodations in, you guessed it, a converted railway station.

Arguably the best place to sleep on the island is **The Rich View Hostel** *(Tel 098/43264; richview@unison.ie; £7),* in Keel. The husband, wife, and cat are all ultra-friendly. Shay, the man of the house, plays trad at **The Annexe** [see *bar scene,* above] on Saturdays. There are musical instruments and small brightly painted rooms, as well as a fireplace and Internet access.

The Wayfarer *(Tel 098/43266; mid-Mar to mid-Oct only; £6.50 dorm, £7.50 per person double),* also in Keel, is big and cheap and has great views.

Housed in a cool old home, Dugort's **Valley House Hostel** *(Tel 098/47204; Apr-Oct only; £7 dorm)* is kind of in the middle of nowhere, but it is within walking distance of the beaches. Plus there's a full bar, which makes things fun and sociable when crowded in the summer.

For B&B, head to Dooagh and check in to the **New Verona House** *(Dooagh; Tel 098/43160; £20 single, £18 per person double; All rooms have bath).* The rooms are basic but spotless. Some even have a spectacular view of Keem Bay; they say on a good day you can see dolphins.

Grogin Mor *(Keel; Tel 098/43385; £20 single, £18 per person double)* does the basic B&B thing.

If you want a hotel, head for **The Achill Head Hotel** *(Tel 098/43108; £60-75 depending on season)* in Keel. The main thing going for it is its bar and nightclub, which is one of the more lively spots on the island.

need to know

Currency Exchange Go to the **post office** in Achill Sound. Make sure to get money there, as there are no banks anywhere on the island. No one takes credit cards either, so if you're cashless, you're gonna wind up washing dishes to pay off that tuna melt and lemonade.

Tourist Information There are **tourist offices** in Achill Sound *(Next to Alice Harbour Bar; Tel 098/45384; 10am-6pm Mon-Sat, summers only)* and in Keel *(Next to the Esso station on the road into town; Tel 098/47353; 9am-5pm Mon-Fri).*

Pharmacies The island's lone **pharmacy** is in Achill Sound *(Tel 098/45248; 9:30am-6pm Mon-Sat, closed Mon Sept-June).*

Buses You can get to Westport, Sligo, Galway and other destinations from the island three-five times a day in summer, two-three in winter. There is a bus that runs the length of the island and makes many a stop along the way (including Dooagh, Dugort, Keel, and Achill Sound). You can pick up the bus outbound at any of the stops. Inbound buses generally go to the end of the island and wind up in Keel. If you want to stop before Keel, ask the driver and he'll gladly let you off.

Bike Rental In Achill Sound, you can rent a bike at the **Achill Sound Hotel** *(Tel 098/45245; £6 per day).* In Keel, get your wheels at **O'Malley's Island Sports** *(Tel 098/43125; £7 per day, £40 per week).*

Postal The lone **post office** is in Achill Sound *(Tel 098/45141; 9am-12:30pm/1:30-5:30pm Mon-Fri, 9am-1pm Sat).* It also has a Bureau de Change.

Internet See *wired,* above.

ballina

Ballina has a bustling, distinctly urban mentality that stands out in this otherwise rural part of Ireland. Its streets are crowded all day long, and its pubs are crowded through the night. It's a perfect base for exploring County Mayo, close to scenic villages like Killala, Ballycastle, and Enniscrone, and the town itself has a down-to-earth charm about it. The people here are cool; they're not used to seeing a lot of tourists, but nonetheless are very accommodating. Ballina does a better job of reflecting modern Ireland than say, Westport, in that it's just a place where people live and work, and doesn't make its living from tourism. Nearby towns—like Castlebar, for instance—are outwardly quite similar to Ballina, but lack the same vitality in their nightlife.

There is no university or college in Ballina, and young people seem a bit pissed that more doesn't go on—though they do manage to have a jolly good time when they're out enjoying the few options that the town has to offer. For them, it's probably a case of going to the same pubs, seeing the same people, and shopping in the same stores every day for the past 25 years. All the more reason why they will welcome you as a drop of fresh blood. You'll find it quite easy to engage people at pubs or shops, and, maybe because it's not a tourist town, people take a genuine interest in where you're from and why you're here.

neighborhoods

There isn't that much to see in Ballina and you can pretty much get a feeling for the place in one afternoon. Ballina's 8,000 people exist comfortably along the **River Moy,** which is responsible for the chief influx of visitors here, who come for the fishing—the River Moy boasts one of the highest salmon-to-rod ratios in the world. The downtown area is traversed by the **Upper Bridge,** but you'll likely want to stick to the west side of the river, where almost all commerce and nightlife happens. Downtown, **Pearse Street** is the main street. Perpendicular streets run off it; most of the pubs are on these streets. **Emmet Street** runs along the west bank of the Moy; **Cathedral Road** runs along the east bank; the tourist office, St. Muredach's Cathedral, and the ruins of an Augustinian abbey are all on Cathedral Road. Don't worry; there are no East Side vs. West Side gang rivalries between the ladies running the B&Bs and the shopkeepers downtown.

bar, club, and live music scene

Ballina's pubs pack a surprising punch for a town its size. Pubs are generally open till around 11:30pm or midnight every day. Most of them also have pub grub in the day from around noon until 3pm. There are something like 50 pubs around town, not all of them worth visiting. Several are hard-core drinking spots packed with guys sucking beer out of cans and smoking cigarettes that seem to have extra tar. Most of the pubs you want are right downtown, on or nearby Pearse Street. On weekends, things get really crazy at these spots.

Dancing is a little harder to come by, but you can still get your groove on at a few places on weekends. The cool thing about Ballina on weekends is that everyone comes from the surrounding towns, creating a festive, everybody-dance-now feeling.

Enough talk, here is the definitive list of Ballina watering holes:

The Bard *(Garden St.; Tel 096/21894; No credit cards)* is a splendid mix of classic pub and contemporary bar. Celtic stained-glass insets in the walls are illuminated from behind, and recessed lighting all over gives the place a loungy feel. A beautiful, shiny copper-and-brass bar winds around the front room, while tables full of chatty youths and middle-aged folks fill up the back room. The music is a bubbly mix of techno-pop and the crowd is multigenerational with a lean toward the yuppie persuasion. You can order pub food as well, or hit the **Bard Restaurant** [see *eats,* below], upstairs. It's pretty packed weekday or weekend.

A vast traditional pub spread out over two levels, **The Broken Jug** *(O'Rahilly St. beside the post office; Tel 096/21655; No credit cards)* is comfortable, with a warmly furnished interior that offers several different rooms to choose from. The crowd is a mixture of old and young and is especially relaxed and friendly. There's trad music here on occasion; call ahead for details. The Broken Jug also has the best lunch special in all of

Ireland [see *eats,* below]. **The Pulse,** next door, is a popular nightclub where the young folk go.

Eclectic is the word at **The Loft** *(Pearse St.; Tel 096/21881; Open till 11:30 daily; No credit cards),* where Victorian glass mixes with kitschy '50s tables and chairs and slick dancing lights. The pub is a roomy, three-level affair that gets packed on the flirty, popular Saturday club nights, but there's always a dark little corner someplace to hide out with your pals if you need to escape the fairly mundane dance music. Live music plays Tuesday-Friday and sometimes on Sunday, usually rock or trad.

They must have five dozen types of whiskey at **Murphy Brothers** *(Clare St., past the tourist office on the way out of town),* a huge cave of a pub whose striking, saloon-like appearance is matched by its equally impressive collection of spirits. They also serve delicious meals [see *eats,* below]. The crowd is generally older and more touristy than in other places in town, but it's still fun. Murphy's is attached to **Longneck's,** a crowded club that serves heaping helpings of top 40 and techno-pop. It's open on weekends only, and draws a younger crowd.

culture zoo

There isn't much to see in Ballina itself, but within a few kilometers there are some minor sights to attract history buffs or fans of ruins.

North Mayo Sculpture Trail: The North Mayo Sculpture Trail is a route of 15 outdoor sculptures celebrating the 5,000-year history of Mayo. Sculptors from around the world were commissioned to create work for the project. The trail begins in Ballina, off R314, and runs through Killala, Ballycastle, Belderriig, Belmullet, and finally into Blacksod Point. Besides all the cool sculptures, you'll also get to enjoy the views of and from this stretch of rugged coastline.

Rosserk Abbey *(Take R314 north for 6.5 km (4 mi), turn right at sign, take first left at the crossroads; continue for 1 km (0.6 mi), then look for signs):* It seems that the 16th-century English governor of Connacht, Sir Richard Bingham, made it a point to burn just about every Irish religious site he saw, and Rosserk Abbey is no exception. But despite the arson, Rosserk, the finest Franciscan abbey in the country, is remarkably well preserved. The double piscine (stone water basin) has an intricate round

festivals and events

The **Salmon Festival** *(Tel 096/70905),* a music, fish, arts, theater, parade, fish, fireworks, and fish extravaganza, happens here. It's very cool, and usually runs the second week in July. Live music fills the streets, people in crazy costumes walk around entertaining the kids, and the pubs, of course, are packed.

ballina

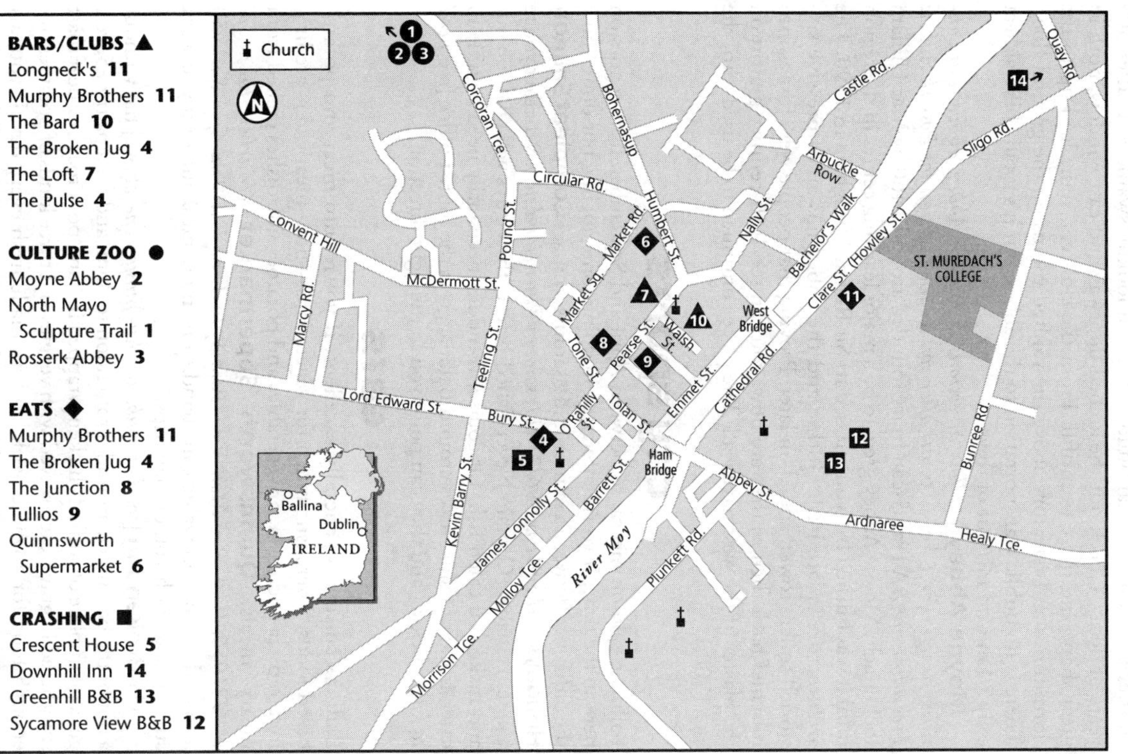
BARS/CLUBS ▲
Longneck's 11
Murphy Brothers 11
The Bard 10
The Broken Jug 4
The Loft 7
The Pulse 4
CULTURE ZOO ●
Moyne Abbey 2
North Mayo Sculpture Trail 1
Rosserk Abbey 3
EATS ◆
Murphy Brothers 11
The Broken Jug 4
The Junction 8
Tullios 9
Quinnsworth Supermarket 6
CRASHING ■
Crescent House 5
Downhill Inn 14
Greenhill B&B 13
Sycamore View B&B 12
Church
Corcoran Tce.
Bohernasup
Castle Rd.
Quay Rd.
Sligo Rd.
Arbuckle Row
Circular Rd.
Humbert St.
Nally St.
Bachelor's Walk
Clare St. (Howley St.)
ST. MUREDACH'S COLLEGE
Convent Hill
Pound St.
Market Rd.
Market Sq.
McDermott St.
Marcy Rd.
West Bridge
Walsh St.
Pearse St.
Tone St.
Teeling St.
Emmet St.
Cathedral Rd.
Lord Edward St.
Bury St.
O'Rahilly St.
Tolan St.
Ham Bridge
Barrett St.
Abbey St.
Bunree Rd.
Kevin Barry St.
James Connolly St.
Ardnaree
Healy Tce.
River Moy
Plunkett Rd.
Molloy Tce.
Morrison Tce.
Ballina
Dublin
IRELAND

tower carved into its shaft. The square tower, nave, chancel, south transept cloister and conventional buildings are all lookin' swank even after 500 years of decay. Check out the arched doorway and east window, both in great shape and quite beautiful. From the cloisters, stairs lead up to the dormitories and refectory above the vaulted rooms on the ground floor. There is no public transportation to the abbey, but it's totally bike-able at only 7 km (4.3 mi) out of town.

Moyne Abbey *(Follow directions to Rosserk Abbey, above, but continue straight for 1 km (0.6 mi) after you see the last sign for Rosserk Abbey; Free admission):* A Franciscan friary founded around 1460 by Mac Uilliam Iochtarach, Moyne Abbey grew to be a major learning center in the region until it was burned by (you guessed it) Sir Richard Bingham in 1590. The architecture is late Irish Gothic and the abbey has an impressive six-storied square tower, added on later. Proving that people were just as into mischief back then as they are now, you can see 16th-century graffiti on the plaster of the west nave wall. The place continued to be used until the late 1700s.

city sports

Ballina is salmon mecca, so between April and September, fishing goes on here all the time. If you're interested in doing some angling but don't know the difference between a salmon and a sardine, contact **Compleat Salmon Holidays** *(Tel and Fax 096/31011; salmon@in-ireland.net)*. Whether you're Captain Ahab or Captain Never-fished-before, these guys will take you out and make you catch fish. Of course, you don't necessarily need a guide to catch fish. For fishin' holes around Ballina, go to the tourist office [see *need to know,* below] and they can point you in the right direction.

eats

Ballina's cuisine is generally excellent, if you're into meat-and-potato-based foods. There isn't much for vegetarians—non–meat eaters are limited to pizza and pasta, or vegetables and potatoes side dishes picked from meaty meals. **Quinnsworth Supermarket** *(Market Rd.; Tel 096/21056; 9am-7pm Mon-Wed, 9am-9pm Thur-Fri, 9am-6pm Sat)* will also feed you if your wallet can't handle one more meal out, or if you want stuff to take with you on day trips.

The **Broken Jug** [see *bar, club, and live music scene,* above] has without a doubt the best lunch around. From noon to 3pm, and for a paltry £5, you get a giant plate of stuffed chicken wrapped in ham, pork roast, or beef roast smothered in gravy, each served with veggies and three kinds of potatoes. It's enough food for a whole week, and it's made fresh every day. If you're a vegetarian, you can get everything but the meat and still be full for the rest of your life.

You can pack in delicious steaks, seafood, and pastas at **Murphy Brothers** [see *bar, club, and live music scene,* above]. It's pricey, with sandwiches going for £8 and entrees upwards of £12. If you're looking to splurge, this is the place to do it.

The word around town is that **Tullios** *(Pearse St.; Tel 096/21890; Noon-3pm/6-10pm; £5-8; No credit cards)* is the best restaurant in town. It's hard to disagree, with yummy pizza, pasta, and bistro dishes coming at you for a surprisingly cheap £5-8.

The Junction *(Pearse St. at Tone St.; Noon-midnight; Under £4)* serves greasy-but-good fried stuff for less than £4. Go crazy.

crashing

Further proving the theory that Ballina is not a tourist destination, there is no hostel here (there used to be, but it closed). B&Bs are the lifeline of the cheap and poor visitors. There are some swanky hotels if you like your sheets starched and your breakfast served with fresh squeezed OJ—and can lay down the bucks for it. The B&Bs are just lovely, though, and they're more apt to give you the lowdown on Ballina's nightlife—they're usually run by women whose kids have grown and left the nest, and sometimes there are little relatives or neighbor kids hanging around to add to the home-style experience. Like everyone else in town, B&B proprietors are friendly, interesting, and welcoming.

Sycamore View *(Cathedral Close, right behind the Cathedral on the east side of the River Moy; Tel 096/21495; £12 per bed in new bunkhouse, £20 per person for B&B)* has a super-friendly proprietor and a brand-new bunkhouse in the backyard, the closest thing to a hostel in Ballina. The main house is clean and welcoming, with a bright yellow glass entrance that's bathed in golden light at dusk. Rooms with bath are a couple punts more; otherwise you shower down the hall. The street is extremely quiet but still close to downtown. If they're all booked up here, they'll gladly phone around town until they find you something.

You'll have a similar experience at **Greenhill** *(Next door to Sycamore View; Tel 096/22767; £20 per person for B&B)*, minus the golden light. Most of the rooms have TV, and some have their own bath (again for a few more punts).

Another option right in town is the **Crescent House** *(O'Rahilly St.; Tel 096/70932; £20-25 per person, depending on season)*, at the top of O'Rahilly Street, next to the post office. The location is perfect for stumbling home when you're faced, but be sure to respect the other guests. Like all the other B&Bs, it's friendly, comfortable, and not too expensive.

The Downhill Inn *(1 km (0.6 mi) outside of Ballina on the N59 Sligo Rd.; Tel 096/73444, Fax 096/43411; £45-55 for up to 3 people, 2 nights with dinner and B&B for £62-80)* is a standard, chain-type hotel. It's clean and relatively cheap for a three-star place, and you get a bathroom and TV in your room. Its Terrace Restaurant has a bar and good food too.

need to know

Currency Exchange Head to the **Bank of Ireland** *(Pearse St.; Tel 096/21144; 10am-4pm Mon-Wed and Fri, 10am-5pm Thur)* if your cash flow is low. They've also got a 24-hour ATM outside.

Tourist Information The **Tourist Office** *(Cathedral Rd.; Tel*

096/70848; 10am-1pm/2-5:30pm Mon-Sat) has a good map of Ballina and other towns in County Mayo and the recommended *Mayo Magazine*, an annual tourist glossy. **Keohane's Bookstore** *(Arran St.; Tel 096/21475; 8am-6:30pm Mon-Sat, 8am-1:30pm Sun)* also has info on local attractions.

Public Transportation **Mulherin Taxi** *(Tel 096/22583)* has 24-hour service.

Health and Emergency Emergency: *999;* Garda (police): *Tel 096/21422.* **Ballina District Hospital** *(Cherry St; Tel 096/21166)* offers medical attention.

Pharmacies For all things pharmaceutical, get thee to **Quinn's Chemist** *(Pearse St.; Tel 096/21144; 9am-6pm Mon-Sat).*

Trains Trains run to Dublin (three times a day except Sunday, when there are no trains) from the **Train Station** *(Kevin Barry Street at James Connolly Street; Tel 096/71818).*

Bus Lines Out of the City You can get to Galway, Westport, Donegal, and Sligo by bus from Ballina. Routes run one to three times a day from the **Bus Station** *(next door to the Train Station; Tel 096/71800).*

Bike Rental If it's a two-wheeler you seek, check out **Gerry's Cycle Centre** *(6 Lord Edward St.; Tel 096/70455; 9am-7pm Mon-Sat; £7 per day, £30 per week).*

Laundry Wash your grubby duds at **Moy Launderette** *(Cathedral Rd.; Tel 096/22358; 9am-6pm Mon-Sat; £4.50 for wash and dry).*

Postal The **post office** is on Casement Street, at the top of the hill *(Tel 096/21498; 10am-1pm/2-5:30pm Mon-Sat).*

ballycastle

A single street going downhill is about all there is to Mayo's Ballycastle (not to be confused with the Ballycastle on the Antrim Coast in the North). What you're coming here for, though, is outside the town: the prehistoric excavations at Ceide Fields and the awe-inspiring views at Downpatrick Head.

You may never forget the feeling of the grass underfoot at **Downpatrick Head** *(Look for signs on R314 between Ballycastle and Killala, it's about 4 km (2.5 mi) away).* Soft and resilient, it's like walking on a big mattress. Downpatrick Head is a rugged indentation of sea-pounded cliffs, offering spectacular views of the ocean and white waves pounding against Ireland. See that weird little island of rock where all the gulls roost? It's a *sea stack;* this one in particular is called **Dun Briste.** There's also a blowhole a couple hundred yards from the edge of the cliffs that's fenced off. When the seas are really raging, water sprays out of the hole—seeing the water shooting up from the surface of the earth can be an otherworldly sensation.

To reach Ballycastle's other main attraction, take R314 west of town for about 10 km (6.2 mi) as it winds along the coast and up Maumakeogh

Mountain. This trip would make an epic 3- or 4-hour walk—it's long and steep—so you may want to make the trip by car. You'll get spectacular views of Downpatrick Head and the Atlantic as you approach a large mound of earth with a big glass pyramid on the side of the mountain. This is **Ceide Fields,** a Stone Age excavation site 6,000 years old (the glass pyramid was built a little more recently, by 20th-century researchers). The formerly fertile site is now a desolate bogland, so waterlogged and oxygen-deprived that no life can be sustained under the soil; only a thin layer of heather grows on top. Prehistoric settlers, however, once cultivated this land, raised animals here—and cut down all the trees that grew. This, along with changes in weather patterns, ruined the natural drainage of the soil and turned it into bog.

The stone-agers, realizing that things were going bust, split the scene, leaving behind the remains of their settlement. How, you may ask, could this ancient settlement still be preserved after all this time? Well, the bogs, in addition to not supporting plant life, are also too wet to support microscopic life. When a tree branch or a piece of animal hide is immersed in a bog, there are no microorganisms to break it down, so the object will remain in perfect condition almost indefinitely—people have found dead human bodies still in perfect condition after resting in bogs for 50 years. Tons of objects in the National Museum in Dublin were dug up from bogs by farmers around Ireland. So watch your step....

You'll learn fascinating facts like these, and more, at the **Ceide Fields Interpretive Center** *(Tel 096/43325; 9:30am-6:30pm daily June-Sept; 10am-4:30pm daily Mar-May and Oct-Nov; Admission £2.50 adults, £1 students).* The guided tour at Ceide Fields, included with the price of admission, takes you outside to the stone walls and animal corrals, and even lets you take a shot at archaeology by poking at soon-to-be-unearthed fences and walls with a long metal rod. Inside the interpretive center are some clever exhibits. Overall, the place is an archaeology buff's dream; it's amazing what you can learn from some rocks and broken pottery. The tearoom is far less bleak than the bogs, and has good soup and sandwiches for £3-4.

Ballycastle has a handful of accommodations and watering holes. Everything is on the **R314,** which is the closest thing to Main Street Ballycastle has.

need to know

Directions and Transportation If you're driving, take R314 west from Ballina toward Killala about 15 km (9.3 mi). Continue past the Ross Beach turn-off and you'll arrive in downtown Ballycastle. **Bus Éireann** runs one-two times daily from Ballina to Ballycastle Monday-Saturday. Check the schedule for times.

Eats If you decide against **Ceide House** [see *crashing,* above], there are a couple of other options on the main street. An ancient little pub with a bright beer garden in the back, **Katie Mac's** *(Tel 096/43031; Open from early afternoon till 11:30pm daily)* does pub food for around £5.

Mary's Bakery *(Tel 096/43361; 10am-5pm Mon-Sat)* has okay sandwiches and sweets for under £5.

Crashing For one-stop shopping, stay, eat, and drink at the **Ceide House** *(Tel 096/43105; £20 single, £35 double)*. They've got rooms and a pub, and serve good food in friendly environs. For the same prices, you can stay in slightly more refined digs at the **Suantai B&B** *(On the Killal Rd.; Tel 096/43040; £20 single, £35 double)*. Another rather affordable option is **The Hawthorns** *(Beldrigg; Tel 096/43148, Fax 096/43148; camurphy@indigo.ie; £18 per person with bath, £16 without bath; No credit cards)*, in the countryside just outside of town.

killala

Wee Killala is one of the wee-est places you've ever been. A 75-foot round tower is the dominant feature of the village's minimalist skyline. Nothing really goes on in Killala. Now and then, a person will come out of a house, take a look in both directions and decide to cross the street. Once across the street, she will probably take a long look at where she just came from, then another long look at where she is now. Then maybe she'll hear a dog bark from behind a fence or around a corner. Does she know that dog? A car will drive by; she'll wave hello to the driver. Then maybe she sees someone she knows coming out of his house; she'll wave, he'll wave back. The woman will take one last look at the place where she crossed the street, then—since it's been a busy day—she hits a pub for a pint, then retires to her home.

When you think about it, though, a place this tiny and slow-paced may be just what you need to complete your memories of Ireland. Three intersecting streets make up the village, with a handful of pubs, a post office, and no bank. There is also a waterfront area that's kinda pretty too. Down the road a bit is the secluded **Ross Strand** beach, a lovely place to loll about in the sun. Killala makes for a tranquil vacation from your vacation.

bar scene

A colorful cast of regulars decorates the bar at **The Anchor Inn** *(Ballycastle Rd.; No phone)*, a local favorite. In summer, they have live trad on weekends. It's the kind of place you go for a game of snooker at noon on a Wednesday.

eats

The **Country Kitchen Restaurant** *(Down the street from the Anchor Inn; No phone; £5)* besides being one of the only options in town, is rustic and friendly. You can even get a veggie burger here.

crashing

The closest place to Killala is **Kevin Munnelly's** *(1 km (0.3 mi) out of town on the Crossmolina Rd.; Tel 096/32331; £30-35 double, single rooms* *negotiable; No credit cards).* Rooms are basic and comfortable. No mints on your pillows or anything, but it's a place to rest your weary bones.

need to know

Buses **Bus Éireann** *(Tel 074/21309)* goes from Ballina to Killala once per day, stopping near the post office. You can buy your ticket on the bus.

Postal Blink and you'll miss the **post office** *(Market St.; Tel 096/32022; 9am-1pm/2-5:30pm Mon-Fri, 9am-1pm Sat).*

cong

Wee Cong, a village of only a few hundred people and a handful of streets, sits prettily along the Cong River in the southernmost part of County Mayo, making it a good stop if you're traveling up to Westport from points south. At first glance, it's like any other cute little village in the region: quiet, isolated, and picturesque. Stay for an afternoon, though, and you'll discover this sweet little village's strange obsession. For the last 50 years, it has been solely devoted to the memory of the movie *The Quiet Man.*

For six weeks in the summer of 1951, Irish émigré film director John Ford shot exterior locations here for *The Quiet Man,* starring John Wayne and Maureen O'Hara. Local newspapers were filled with headlines about Cong's conversion into a Hollywood soundstage. Fair enough. But ever since then, the village has made its living off tourist punts generated from the film's legacy, and has directed all its efforts toward promoting itself as a shrine for fans of the movie.

Ironically, the movie stuff isn't even the best part about Cong. The tiny town itself—with cunning little rows of houses, a handful of streets, and a lazy pace—is the main reason to come. Although it certainly is weirdly

top o the mornin, pilgrim

Cong-ites have decided that it's not nearly enough to commemorate John Wayne's visit to their village 50 years ago by putting his picture up all over town: They've decided to resurrect him in the flesh and award prizes for the effort. During the **Cong Midsummer Ball,** lads and lasses from far and wide gather for the chance to compete in the John Wayne and Maureen O'Hara Lookalike Contest. Are you big enough to swagger like the star of *Big Jake, Big Jim McLain, Big Stampede,* and *The Big Trail*?

fun to see the movie-related attractions in Cong, the truth is that it gets old real quick. In tourist season, July and August, Cong gets awfully crowded. Sure, it can create a fun and festive atmosphere, but it can also be irritating as hell, given the minute size of the place.

Luckily, within the greater metropolitan region of Cong there are a couple of other smashing things to see. A few miles outside of Cong, the incredible **Ashford Castle** [see *culture zoo,* below] is something you really must check out. Once home to Lord and Lady Ardilaun, the heirs to the Guinness fortune, it is now a luxury resort hotel. You'll also find some cool caves around Cong in which you can explore the dark underground of the village.

The **Cong River** marks the western boundary of the village. There are three main roads in town, **Main Street, Abbey Street,** and **Circular Road;** together they roughly form a square—Abbey Street to the south, Main Street along the eastern edge of town, and Circular Road forming the west border along the river, then curving to the north. You'll find a scattering of restaurants and accommodations here, as well as the main *Quiet Man* attractions in town.

bar scene

Nightlife here is a quiet affair, although it can get very crowded in the summer when the tourists come. Cong has a couple of friendly pubs. Most highly recommended is the **Carlisle Arms Pub** *(Circular Rd. across from the salmon hatchery; No phone),* which has live trad some nights and decent pub food. **The Rising of the Waters** *(Next to the Esso station on Main St.; No phone)* is also a good bet. Both pubs get full in the summer, when plenty of backpackers and other visitors come and drink till they can drink no more. In the winter, it's likely to be just you and the bartender.

culture zoo

Quiet Man Heritage Cottage *(Circular Rd.; Tel 092/46809; 10am-6pm daily; quiet.man.cong@aol.ie; Admission £2.50 adults, £2 students):* This truly bizarre museum pays tribute to the film in a postmodern sort of way. The cottage is a reproduction of the "White-o-Mornin" cottage from the film, which was itself a reproduction of traditional Irish thatched-roof cottages that once existed in Cong. The interior is a painstaking replica of the sets built and filmed not in Ireland, but on a Hollywood sound stage—they shot only exteriors in Cong. If you ask nicely, you can try on costumes and have your picture taken by the fireplace in the cottage. In one part of the cottage, newspaper clippings about the filming from local papers in the 1950s tell how it all happened. The upstairs of the cottage is the **Cong Archaeological & Historical Interpretive Center** *(Included in the price of admission),* a small exhibit with stone chips, illustrations, and a video, detailing the physical history of the region from 7000 B.C. to the 19th century. All in all, not a breathtaking exhibit.

Ashford Castle *(From Cong, take R346 toward Cross; Tel 092/46003, Fax 092/469-260; www.ashford.ie; ashford@ashford.ie):* Sitting about two miles outside of Cong on a beautifully manicured, 450-acre estate on the shores of Lough Corrib is this majestic manor, now a hotel. Parts of this mammoth, rambling castle date from the 13th century, and a walk around its turrets and towers is a feast for the eyes. You can't actually go inside unless you're willing to pay the £200 room rates, but you can hang out in the gardens, walk along the shore of the Lough, and ramble on its lawns for £3. It's sort of stupid that you have to pay to just walk around, but it's worth it.

Cong Abbey *(Abbey St.; Open 24 hours; Free):* Dating back to the early 12th century, this Augustinian ruin was founded by the High King of Ireland, Turlough O'Connor, the last monarch to rule a united Ireland. The abbey, a short walk south on Main Street from downtown, is quite large and was once a major center of learning, with over 3,000 aspiring men of God living and studying here. It was partially rebuilt in 1860, and many of the intricate stone carvings on the archways and in the cloister are in great shape, making it worth a visit. Unfortunately, the **Cross of Cong**—a gold cross believed to have once contained a piece of the True Cross—is no longer here; it's now in the National Museum in Dublin. (Could be worse—it could have been carted off to the British Museum.)

great outdoors

If you want to get lost in the dark, Cong has some extremely cool caves. To get to the **Pigeon Hole Cave,** cross the river on the path south of the southwest corner of Abbey Street and Circular Road and walk northwest once you've crossed the water. In front of you, you'll see some stone steps that go down to the cave. Be careful; it's dark and wet down there—it's probably a good idea to bring a flashlight. Or head out of town east on R346, right past the school, and you'll see a sign for **Captain Webb's Hole;** a bit beyond that is **Kelly's Cave,** a couple hundred yards off the road on the dirt path. The key to the gate at Kelly's Cave is at the Quiet Man Coffee Shop [see *eats,* below]. Just ask and they'll give it to you.

eats

There are enough good food spots to keep you satisfied in Cong. Most pubs do lunches for under £4. For a cheap lunch in the spirit of Hollywood, go to **The Quiet Man Coffee Shop** *(Main St.; Tel 092/46034; 10am-6:30pm daily Mar-Oct; closed Nov-Feb; sandwiches £2-3).* You can park your behind at the counter and admire the black-and-white glossies from the film hanging on the walls, go to the dining room in the back to look out at the river, or admire the black-and-white glossies from the film hanging on the walls.

Danagher's Hotel [see *crashing,* below], serves up filling meat-and-potatoes dishes for £6-8. The best meal in town is had at **Echoes** *(Main St.; Tel 092/46059; 6:30-10pm Tue-Sat Mar-Oct; Entrees £12).* They've got scrumptious seafood, lamb, steak, and some vegetarian options.

If you'd rather do your own cooking, head to **O'Connor's Supermarket** *(Main St.; Tel 092/46008; 8am-9pm daily)* for groceries.

crashing

Cong does budget travelers right with its fine selection of hostels and B&Bs.

The **Cong Travel Inn** *(Abbey St.; Tel 092/46310; £10 per bed in 6- to 8-bed dorms; No credit cards)* is clean and comfortable. All rooms have an attached bath.

The Quiet Man Tourist Hostel *(Abbey St.; Tel 092/46089; £7.50 per bed, £18 double; V, MC)* is the more sociable hostel in town, and has the best rates. All the rooms are named after characters in the movie. This hostel is sometimes booked for large groups, so call ahead before you come.

If The Quiet Man Tourist Hostel is booked, they'll refer you to the fun **Cong Hostel** *(0.3 km (1 mi) out of Cong on the Galway Rd.; Tel 092/46089; £7.50 per bed; V, MC)*, run by the same owners, where every bright room has a skylight. There's also a piano and game room.

Finally, a few miles out of town is the peaceful **Courtyard Hostel** *(In Cross, call ahead for pickup; Tel 092/46203; £7 per bed; £5 campsite; V, MC)*, where the dorms are actually converted stables. They can also rent you a bike for £5 per day.

Lydon's Lodge *(Attached to the Carlisle Arms Pub; Tel 092/46053; £25 per person; V, MC)* does B&B in a basic setting.

If you are a son or daughter of the insanely rich, or just made your first million on an internet IPO, stay where John Wayne, Maureen O'Hara, and later, Ronald Reagan did: **Ashford Castle** [see *culture zoo,* above], the ultimate in luxury. Oak paneling, oil paintings, and suits of armor adorn this incredible hotel. All this—plus complimentary hard-court tennis-court access—can be yours for a mere £200-300.

There are a few other solid choices around town like the very presidential **White House** *(Abbey St.; Tel 09/24-63-58; £20 single, £17 per person shared, all rooms have private baths, the price includes breakfast; No credit cards)*, right in the city center; or **Villa Pio** *(Gurtacurra Cross; Tel 09/24-64-03, Fax 09/24-64-03; villapio@hotmail.com; £19 per person, all rooms have private baths; No credit cards)*, about 20 minutes from town.

need to know

Currency Exchange The nice folks at the **post office** *(Main St.; Tel 092/46001; 9am-1pm/2-5:30pm Mon-Tue, Thur-Sat)* will change your money.

Tourist Information If you need more information on *The Quiet Man*, or anything else about Cong, get along to the **Cong Tourist Office** *(Abbey St; Tel 092/46542; 9:30am-6pm daily Mar-Oct, closed Nov-Feb)*.

Pharmacies If you've taken a fall off your horse, head over to **Daly's Pharmacy** *(Abbey St.; Tel 092/46119; 10am-6pm Mon-Fri)*.

Bus Lines Out of the City Buses go to Galway (two per day), Westport (one per day), and Clifden (one per day) from **Ryan's Hotel.** For times, call **Bus Éireann** *(Tel 096/71800).*

Boats You can take a boat tour of Lough Corrib on **Corrib Cruises** *(On the grounds of Ashford Castle; Tel 092/46029; £8).* The boat will take you out to Inchagoill Island, giving you beautiful vistas of the lake and countryside. Pretty as a picture.

Bike Rental Renting a bike is an excellent way to see the Cong area. **O'Connor's** *(The Esso station on Main St.; Tel 092/46008)* or the **Courtyard Hostel** [see *crashing,* above] will rent you wheels.

Postal Mail that John Wayne postcard from the centrally located **post office** *(Main St.; Tel 092/46001; 9am-1pm/2-5:30pm Mon-Tue, Thur-Sat).*

knock

If it's divine intervention you seek, come to Knock, in the eastern part of County Mayo. Back in August 1879, the Virgin Mary, her hubby Joseph, and St. John the Evangelist were said to have appeared here before two women. More than a dozen others witnessed the apparition, which lasted over two hours. It was immediately pronounced a miracle, and Knock's future was assured as a site of pilgrimage, tacky tourist shops and all. Around 1.5 million people now come here each year to see the site and to go Knock, Knock, Knockin' on heaven's door.

The tiny town is held together by a huge complex dedicated to the Apparition, **The National Shrine of Our Lady of Knock.** On the grounds, which are open year-round, you'll find a museum, the church where the apparition appeared, and the enormous **Basilica of Our Lady, Queen of Ireland**, which could hold a crowd for a Springsteen concert. It's about as big, and as ugly, as Madison Square Garden. Stop by and settle into one of its 12,000 seats for one of its four daily masses. The **Knock Folk Museum** *(Next to the basilica; Tel 094/88100; 10am-7pm July-Aug; 10am-6pm May–June and Sept-Oct; £2)* expands the complex's scope somewhat, displaying a large collection of artifacts related to life in rural Ireland during the 19th and early 20th centuries (including, of course, eyewitness testimonies given at the Commission of Enquiry in 1879, as well as modern-day accounts of the apparition and details of "cures").

There are no youth hostels here, so B&Bs and hotels are your only options; unless you're staying over, you should bring your own eats. Stay at **The Knock International Hotel** *(Main St.; Tel 094/88466; £20-25 per person; V),* which has rooms right in town, or **Mervue Guest House** *(Main St.; Tel 094/88127; £20-25 per person; No credit cards)* where all rooms come with private baths. In July and August, you're about as likely to find a room without calling ahead as you are to see a busload of Buddhist monks kneeling before the Blessed Virgin, so call ahead.

Some other very inexpensive options include **Byrne Craft Shop** *Main St.; Tel 094/88184, Fax 094/88184; Open Easter-Oct; £18 per person, most rooms have private baths; No credit cards),* right in the village center; and **Aisling House** *(Ballyhaunis; Tel 094/88558; £25 single, £19 per person double, price includes breakfast, all rooms have private baths; No credit cards),* just a short (10 minute) walk outside the town center.

need to know

Currency Exchange The **Bank of Ireland** *(10:15am-12:15pm Mon and Thur May-Oct; Mon only Nov-Apr)* has an ATM.

Tourist Information Just north of the shrine is the **Knock Tourist Office** *(Tel 094/88193; 10am-6pm daily May-Oct).*

Airports The **Horan Cutril Airport** *(Charleston, 15 km (8 mi) from Knock on the N17 road; Tel 094/67222)* has direct flights to Dublin every day.

Bus Lines Out of the City **Bus Éireann** *(Tel 094/88150)* goes to Galway, Sligo, and Westport daily from Lennon's on Airport Road; buses to Dublin leave from a stop 100 yards down the road from Lennon's.

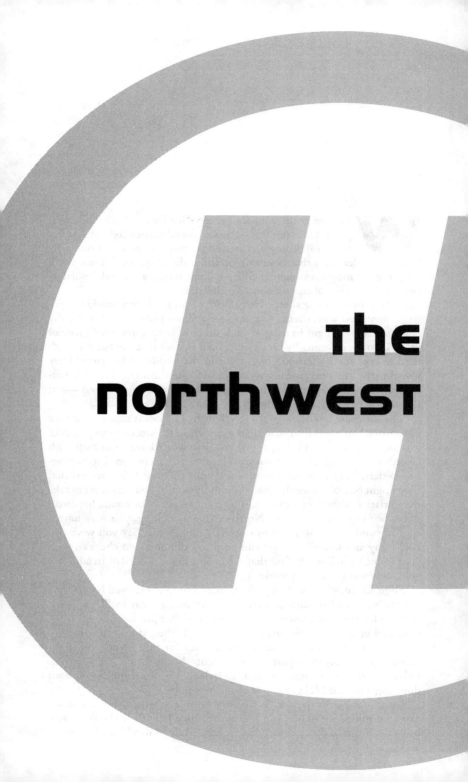

the northwest

Welcome to the wild and woolly Northwest. If it's wilderness you're after, this is it—the rough and rugged Ireland that has been mythologized in songs, movies, and in poems by William Butler Yeats that have immortalized the Sligo coast. Here you'll find some of most breathtaking cliffs, majestic mountains, and desolately beautiful stretches of coastline in all of Ireland.

And then there are the sheep. Every field, farm, road, and hillside seems to be peppered with them. You may see a sheep giving birth to a baby lamb, or two of them baa-ing at each other over an unchewed piece of grass. If you're traveling by car or bus, you'll also see that our fuzzy friends tend to take their afternoon naps right in the middle of the road. They love the pavement because it stays warm well into the night. This wee natural phenomenon is great for the sheep—who have the right of way—but it can be very frustrating for motorists. *Waaa-aaatch out.*

The sheep are just one sign that the Northwest doesn't exist for the sake of tourists. You won't find road signs everywhere to direct you to points of interest (definitely get a map), but you also won't have to put up with crowds at every sight. In some towns, locals aren't accustomed to throngs of travelers, but that doesn't mean they aren't friendly. It just means that they might be a bit more shy than folks in the south. You may have to take the initiative when it comes to starting a conversation or asking for directions, but once you get these Northwesterners talking, you may have a spot of trouble getting them to stop. (Be diplomatic. Say you wish you could stay and talk all day but you need to call home and check in with your mum.) You'll surely find that the people here, as in all of Ireland, are genuinely warm and hospitable.

Sligo County is Yeats Country, plain and simple. He lived here, wrote poems here, and is buried here. You can't swing a cat in **Sligo Town** without hitting a monument to the great poet. But just because the town is all tied up in poetry doesn't mean the people there don't know how to party. It's a surprisingly action-packed place for pub lovers and night crawlers, especially in August, when students throng for the Yeats festival. Pub alert: A trip to Sligo—indeed, to Ireland—is not complete without downing a pint at McLynn's, one of the best pubs anywhere.

Just a stone's throw away is **County Donegal,** where the geography can be summed up in one word: extreme. **Tory Island,** to the far north, bears the brunt of the Atlantic Ocean's fury, while **Malin Head** juts out as the northernmost point in the country. **Horn Head,** near the town of Dunfanaghy, an incredible region where vertigo-inducing cliffs overlook the ocean—it's terrific for cycling. Bogs, too wet to sustain life beyond small shrubs, blanket much of the inland Donegal region. Mount Errigal, the highest peak in Donegal, slopes gently in to **Glenveagh National Park,** home to even more spectacular beauty: mountains, lakes, valleys, and a 19th century castle.

Donegal Town is the busy seat of the county, and the largest population center with a whopping 3,000 residents (you read that right: three thousand). Its friendly vibe, relaxed pace, and proximity to even more of nature's coastal splendor deserve some of your time. Donegal is also one of the Gaeltacht (traditional Irish-Gaelic speaking) centers of the country. Don't be surprised to hear people speaking their native Irish language in a small village pub, or to see road signs only in Old Irish. Hint: If someone asks you, "An bhfuil Gaeilge agat?" (Un will gayga ugut?), they want to know if you speak Gaelic. Your answer will probably be, "Ni maith," (Nee mah), which means, "No, I do not."

To the west of Donegal are the highest cliffs in Europe, **Slieve League,** and the tiny villages of **Glencolumbkille,** a center of Gaelic culture, and **Killybegs,** one of the biggest—and smelliest—fishing ports in Ireland. You'll also find Trabane Strand, one of the best beaches in the galaxy, near **Malin Beg.**

Donegal is a place where you'll want to stay in hostels, even if you've been splurging on hotels or B&B's thus far. They're often in unique, old buildings and have exceptionally friendly atmospheres amidst gorgeous natural surroundings. A night with fellow travelers at Donegal Hostel with a few cans of beer, a guitar, and a roaring fire, can be more fun than a night out in Dublin, plus it won't break your bank. The Corcereggan

drunk, drunker, drunkest

The Irish, reknowned for their love of spirits, consider drinking a fine art and drunkenness a matter of opinion. The Irish language, in fact, has many phrases to distinguish between specific degrees of inebriation. Here are five, one for each finger of your sober hand:

súgach *(soo-gakh)* tipsy
ar meisce *(air maysh-ka)* drunk
ar deargmheisce *(air jar-egg-vaysh-ka)* quite drunk
ólta *(awlta)* very drunk indeed
caoch ólta *(kay-oakh awlta)* blind drunk

Travel Times

* By train
** Water-crossing required (by ferry usually)
*** By cable car

	Dublin	Sligo	Enniscrone	Donegal Town	Lough Derg	Lough Eske
Sligo	3:15	-	1:05	1	1:20	1:15
Enniscrone	3:50	1:05	-	2:05	2:30	2:20
Donegal Town	4	1	2:05	-	:45	:15
Lough Derg	3:40	1:20	2:30	:45	-	:50
Lough Eske	4:15	1:15	2:20	:15	:50	-
Killybegs	4:45	1:35	2:40	:35	1:20	:50
Kilcar	4:50	1:50	2:55	:50	1:30	1:05
Glencolumcille	5:15	2:10	3:15	1:10	1:55	1:25
Slieve League	5:10	2:10	3:15	1:10	1:40	1:25
Dunlewey	4:40	2:45	3:50	1:45	2:05	1:55
Tory Island	6:20*	4:10*	5:10*	5:10*	3:30*	5*
Dunfanaghy	4:30	2:35	3:40	1:35	2;20	1:45
Horn Head	5	3:05	4:10	2:05	2:50	1:55
Mailn Head	4:55	3:35	4:30	2:30	3:10	3:15

Killybegs	Kilcar	Glencolumcille	Slieve League	Dunlewey	Tory Island	Dunfanaghy	Horn Head	Mailn Head
1:35	1:50	2:10	2:10	2:45	4:10	2:35	3:05	3:35
2:40	2:55	3:15	3:15	3:50	5:10*	3:40	4:10	4:30
:35	:50	1:10	1:10	1:45	5:10*	1:35	2:05	2:30
1:20	1:30	1:55	1:40	2:05	3:50*	2:20	2:50	3:10
:50	1:05	1:25	1:25	1:55	5*	1:45	1:55	2:15
-	:15	:20	:15	1:55	3	2:20	2:50	3
:15	-	:20	:15	1:55	3:15*	2;20	2:50	3:15
:20	:20	-	:20	1:35	3:10*	2:10	2:40	3:35
:15	:15	:20	-	2	3:20*	2:25	2:55	3:40
1:55	1:55	1:45	2	-	1:50*	:40	1:10	2:45
3*	3:15*	3:10*	3:20*	1:50*	-	2:10*	2:40*	4:30*
2;20	2:20	2:10	2:25	:40	2;10*	-	:30	2:25
2:50	2:50	2:40	2:55	1:10	2:40*	:30	-	2:55
3	3:15	3:35	3:40	2:45	4:30	2:25	2:55	-

Mill Cottage Hostel, where you can sleep in a converted train car or a loft of a kiln house, is up north near Dunfanaghy, The Ball Hill Hostel, outside of Donegal Town, has a pop culture graveyard and a view of a lake.

Soaking up the Northwest's abundant natural beauty, with one breathtaking site after another, you run the risk of growing numb to them. So take it easy. That's what the Northwest is for. Spend time in the minute villages, hang out with the locals at a pub, let the Guinness inspire you to write a poem or two of your own about this rural land.

A final word of advice: Donegal is Ireland's rainiest county, so there's a good chance your sightseeing will be interrupted by bouts of seemingly endless gray wetness. Don't let it get you down. On a sunny day, or even on one of those many days where it will be raining and sunny at the same time (what the Irish call "a soft day"), it's an incredible place.

getting around the region

The main problem you're likely to encounter when touring around Donegal is that there aren't a whole lot of ways to get around, especially if you're on a budget. Buses are infrequent and trains are non-existent for most of Sligo (Sligo Town has train service to Dublin), and all of Donegal, where roads are a nightmare. Narrow, poorly marked, and filled with sleeping sheep, tractors, and speeding automobiles, they present real perils for people on bikes, in rental cars, or hitchhiking. If you're driving in this country, be careful–the roads rarely, if ever, have shoulders, are often barely two lanes wide, and are filled with blind curves. Remember that the people who whiz by you have been driving these roads all their lives and know every twist and turn; don't try to keep up with them. Hitchhiking is a major mode of transportation for backpackers in Donegal, and often it's the only way to get short distances between small villages without waiting all day for a bus. Biking, aside from the perils of the road, is a good option as it will allow you to hop from village to village and make detours to scenic spots.

▸▸ROUTES

Unless you are a hard-core Yeats fan or just want some down time on the coast, you'll probably pass through Sligo Town on your way to Westport to the south or Donegal Town to the north.

To be honest, the best route around Donegal is any route around Donegal–there is so much scenery to behold here, it's almost too much for one lifetime, let alone one vacation. If you had to pick the best of the best, it'd be hard to beat the Horn Head Drive, a 20km circuit of some of the most incredible coastal scenery in the country. If you've only got a day or two, you'll probably be best off basing yourself in Donegal Town, the center of human activity, and heading out to the Slieve League Cliffs for your dose of nature at its boldest. The Town has great pubs, two of the best hostels in Ireland and a welcoming vibe. If you're seeking solitude and quiet, head north to either Dunfanaghy/Horn Head or Malin Head. Things in these parts are isolated and, again, beautiful. If you've got a few

Know your castles

Ireland, as even the most casual visitor will notice, has no shortage of stones. When the first Irish farmers began to turn over the soil, the stones merely got in their way. Eventually, they put the stones to use, to build walls. The first walls were built to keep out animals and the elements. Eventually, however, what had to be kept out were other humans. In the intricate world of walls, you can't miss the difference between walls raised to deter wolves and those raised to deter warriors.

The earliest stone fortifications in Ireland round forts, often on hilltops, date from the Iron Age, sometime after 500 B.C Dun Aengus on the Aran Islands, Staigue Fort in County Kerry, and the newly restored Lisnagun Ring Fort are among the survivors of as many as 30,000 stone forts that once protected the Irish from each other. On a smaller scale, individual families seem to have fortified their homes with mud and stone bulwarks. Another form of fortification was the crannog, a stone and mud island, complete with palisades.

Later, in the early Christian period, the centers of Irish civilization, those poor helpless monastic communities, came under attack from those bloodthirsty tough guys the Vikings. Round towers that often climbed to nearly 100 feet in height were constructed to lift life, limb, and everything else precious out of harm's reach. This strategy, however, depended on the enemy's going away, like when you climb the tree and wait for the bully to get bored and find some other kid to wail on. Vikings, however, preferred to stay, and smoke or burn or starve the monks down from their towers.

With the Normans came the first Irish castles constructed with massive rectangular keeps. Trim Castle in County Meath and Carrickfergus Castle in County Antrim are impressive reminders of Norman clout. Next came the tower house, a fortified residence. Needless to say, these were residences worthy of a little architectural back-up. Bunratty Castle in County Clare and Dunguaire Castle in County Galway are splendidly restored examples of this kind of "safe house," which remained in vogue for several centuries. Wealthy merchants and others with less to protect built semifortified mansions, of which a well-preserved example is Rothe House in Kilkenny. Nearly all of the above might loosely be called "castles." After all, a man's (or woman's) house is reputedly his or her castle. a point made then, as now, by walls, towers, dead bolts, motion detectors, and alarm systems.

extra days, don't miss driving through the Glengesh pass, hit both Horn Head and Malin Head, and check out the inlands of Glenveagh National Park. With a car, you can drive through all of this in a couple of days. Oh, and it's better to skip Letterkenny. While it looks potentially exciting/big on the map, it's really a bore.

Also keep in mind that the northern reaches of Donegal are mere miles away from Derry (see Northern Ireland), so if you're basing yourself there, consider a day trip to Malin Head.

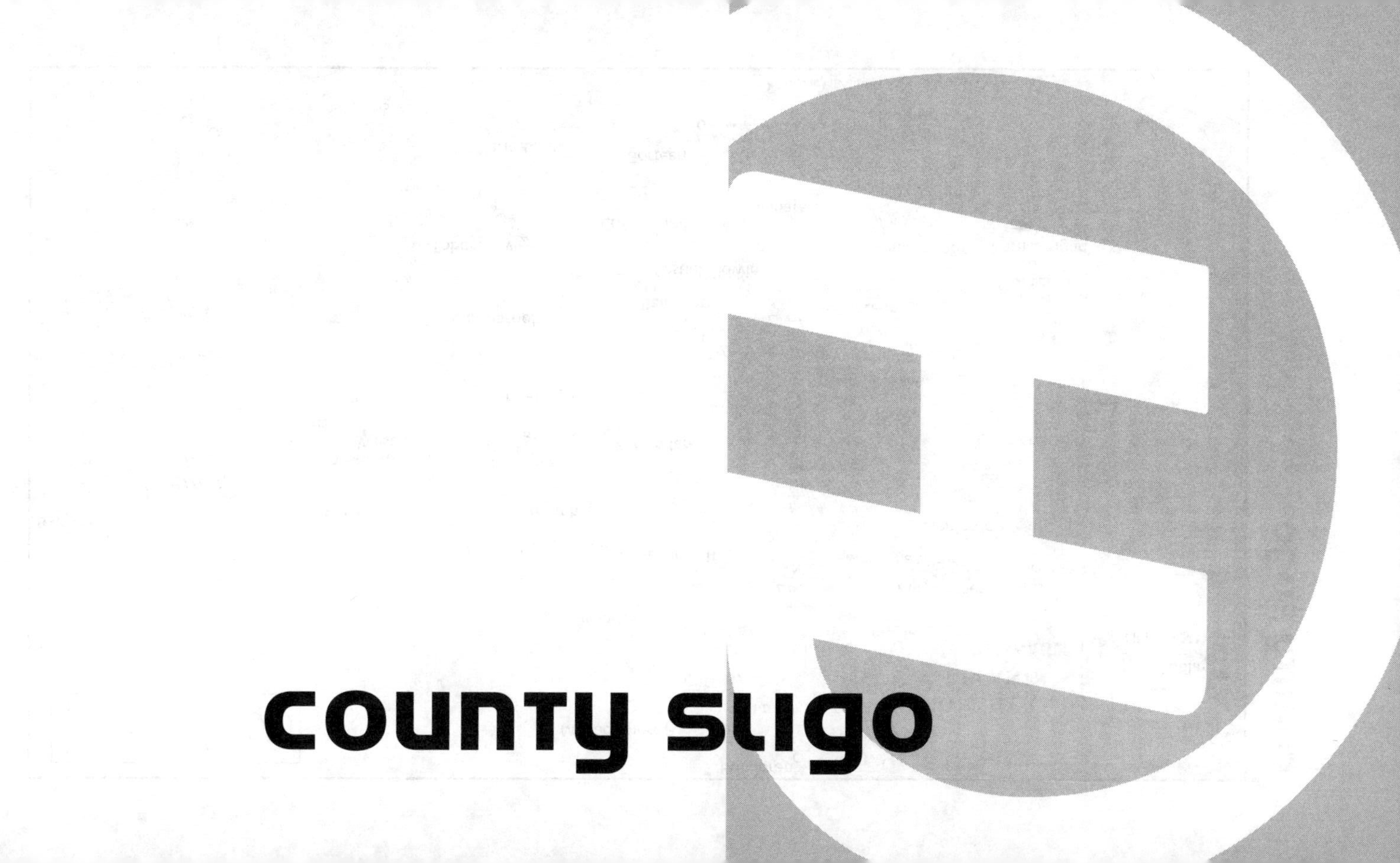
county sligo

COUNTY SLIGO

sligo

Bustling and gritty Sligo makes no pretense of being a quaint Irish village. It is what it is, a thriving center of commerce in the west of Ireland. Don't come here looking for the sort of strictly tourist attractions that places like Westport or Donegal offer. What you will get here is a sense of authentic *modern* Irish life, which in some ways is more valuable an experience than all those precious Celtic relics served up elsewhere. What's more, Sligo's smack-in-the-middle-of-the-mountains-and-beaches location makes it a perfect home base for exploring the region.

Sligo is also a home to celebrities. First and foremost, it is Yeats Country—the great Irish poet wrote about, lived in, and is buried a couple of miles outside of Sligo, a fact you'll be reminded of by many a street sign, monument, statue, plaque, restaurant, hotel, bar, and theme sandwich. Second, Sligo has the honor of being hometown to two members of the Irish heartthrob boy band Westlife who, at last count, had five (count 'em, *five*) number one hits in Ireland. This is a fact locals don't seem all that proud of, so it's fun to tease them about it.

The town has a kick-ass nightlife, holding the crown as the best in the northwest, and second only to Galway in the whole of the west. People here take partying seriously, and on the weekends, girls and boys get gussied up for the festivities that erupt in the local pubs, clubs, and restaurants. Just about anything the party animal could be on the hunt for can be found here in Sligo. Check the ***Sligo Champion*** for info about live music and other nightlife happenings; you can find it at any bookstore, clothing store, or record store, as well as in most pubs.

12 hours in sligo

If you're in Sligo for only a short period, don't miss Yeats' grave, if for no other reason than so you can say you saw it. Other than that, Sligo isn't particularly a sightseeing city. Our advice: come late in the day, head for the pubs, then leave early the next morning for the beautiful surrounding countryside (where you may run into some of the same Sligoans you met at the pub last night...).

neighborhoods

There are 18,000 people in town, and they all seem to be in the same vicinity, outside by day and in the pubs by night. Sligo is compact and easy to figure out, with everything of interest in its busy **city center,** only about a half-mile square. **The River Garavogue** bisects Sligo with an L-shaped bend. West and south of the river are the **bus** and **train stations** [see *need to know,* below, for both], and the busy intersection of **Wine Street, O'Connell Street, Hyde Bridge** and **Fish Quay**. Also south of the river you'll find **High Street,** a cinema and a theater [see *arts scene,* below, for both], **The Abbey** [see *culture zoo,* below], several restaurants, most of the pubs and shops, and a host of B&B's. North of the river is the mall. More restaurants and pubs line the bank.

If you head west on Wine Street and drive or bike for 7 km (4.3 mi), you will come to **Strandhill,** a fun little resort village on the ocean. **Knocknarea Mountain** and the airport are also out here. Head north along the coast and you'll end up in **Rosses Point** [see *great outdoors,* below], another resort town with its own Coney Island (minus the dilapidated roller-coasters and garbage) and a great beach.

hanging out

The one thing Sligo lacks is a nice park. That said, the city center streets, cafes, and bars are good places to while away the days that you don't spend communing with nature. Ground zero for the young and bohemian crowd is **Bar Bazaar** *(Market St. at Gratton St.; Tel 071/44749; 9am-6pm Mon-Fri, 10am-6pm Sat).* At this delicious little café, you can check out fliers on Buddhist meditation, browse through secondhand philosophy books and encounter unwashed French philosophers, all the while sipping a cappuccino. It's also one of the few places open on Sunday. **Eurobar** *(Stephen St., north side of the river; 7am-7pm daily; No credit cards)* is a slicker café that lacks the cozy charm of Bar Bazaar but is also popular with locals, as is the nearby **Hy-Breasil**

five things to talk to a local about

1. **Nicky Byrne**
2. **Bryan McFadden**
3. **Kian Egan**
4. **Mark Feehily**
5. **Shane Filan**

These are the members of the boy band **Westlife.** People love to hate them and hate to love them. Either way, you can have fun goading people about them. Other topics, of course, include **Yeats, Yeats,** and **Yeats,** and if you're at the Yeats County Hostel [see *crashing,* above], the **Kennedy clan.** One more topic which you may want to avoid, or not, is the long-held joke that Sligo's people are to Ireland what people from Tasmania are to Australia—backwoods types in the middle of the wild and woolly west. Ironically, Sligo's really a hipper place than most towns where this joke is told.

(Bridge St., north side of the river; Tel 071/61180; 8:30am-6:30pm Mon-Sat; No credit cards), which offers a more basic and new-agey feel. **The Winding Stair Bookshop** [see *stuff,* below] attracts the egghead crowd and has great food and a relaxed atmosphere.

If you're here on Sunday the town will be dead, so head for the outdoors, or see a matinee at the **Gaeity Cinema** [see *arts scene,* below] and bide your time till sundown when the pubs start to fill up.

bar, club, and live music scene

Sligo's cardinal virtue is its nightlife. The pubs crank especially hard on the weekends, but you'll find a great scene any night of the week. Whether you're looking for trad, folk, blues, or techno, hippies, or hipsters, Sligo can accommodate you. High Street and the banks of the River Garavogue

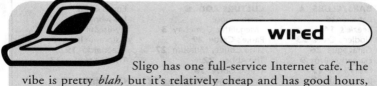

wired

Sligo has one full-service Internet cafe. The vibe is pretty *blah,* but it's relatively cheap and has good hours, which'll make you say *yah!* To get online, go to **Cygo Internet Café** *(19 O'Connell St.; Tel 071/40082, Fax 071/40081;.10am-7pm Mon-Sat; £5 per hour, £4 per hour with student I.D.)*

sligo

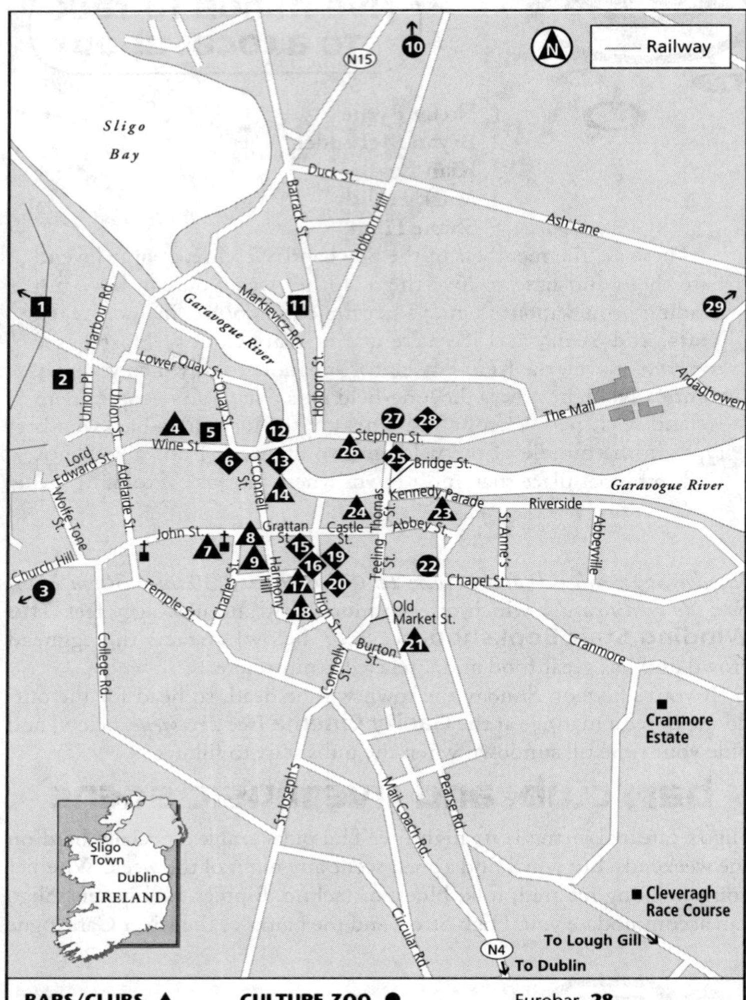

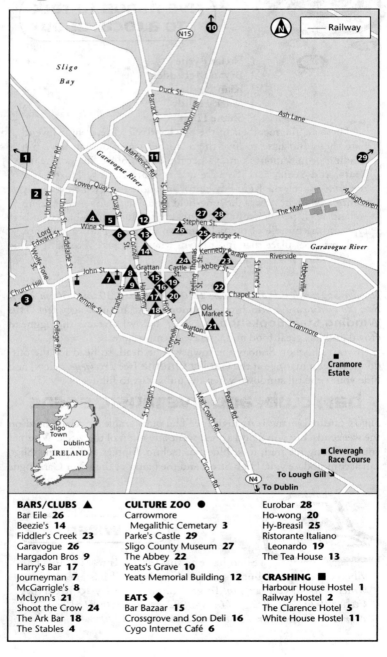

BARS/CLUBS ▲
Bar Eile **26**
Beezie's **14**
Fiddler's Creek **23**
Garavogue **26**
Hargadon Bros **9**
Harry's Bar **17**
Journeyman **7**
McGarrigle's **8**
McLynn's **21**
Shoot the Crow **24**
The Ark Bar **18**
The Stables **4**

CULTURE ZOO ●
Carrowmore Megalithic Cemetary **3**
Parke's Castle **29**
Sligo County Museum **27**
The Abbey **22**
Yeats's Grave **10**
Yeats Memorial Building **12**

EATS ◆
Bar Bazaar **15**
Crossgrove and Son Deli **16**
Cygo Internet Café **6**
Eurobar **28**
Ho-wong **20**
Hy-Breasil **25**
Ristorante Italiano Leonardo **19**
The Tea House **13**

CRASHING ■
Harbour House Hostel **1**
Railway Hostel **2**
The Clarence Hotel **5**
White House Hostel **11**

have the biggest glut of pubs, but there are many good spots in other places. Explore and don't settle for one that doesn't suit you. Pubs in Sligo, unless otherwise noted, keep traditional pub hours.

A trip to Sligo is not complete without a night at **McLynn's** *(Old Market Street, near the courthouse; Tel 071/44209; No credit cards),* one of the best pubs in the world. You can count on great live music every night, but the best nights are those when Shane, the wild, white-haired owner, jumps up on the bar with his guitar and leads the whole back room in a sing-along. The crowd then takes turns singing favorites to Shane's accompaniment. Arrive at about 8 or 8:30pm and grab a table in the back. It may be empty, but within the hour you'll have the best seat in the house for one of the best nights of your trip. You may also get coerced into singing lead on a number or two, so come prepared.

Oozing laid-back atmosphere, **Shoot the Crow** *(Castle St. near Market St.; Open daily)* is full every night. Décor is a kooky mix of red copper ceilings, African wood objects, little hobgoblin sculptures, and dust. Every square inch of bar, wall and shelf is covered with cool stuff, and not in a scary TGI Friday's kind of way. The CD collection is awesome; you're likely to hear Miles Davis, the Velvet Underground or Tom Waits on the stereo. Ladies, come here to meet your ice cream man as this is where the hip, educated boys are (or at least those that appear as such). Fellas, order a Guinness and ponder the meaning of your goatee.

For that "everyone-puts-down-their-pint-and-stares-at-you-when-you-come-in" experience, head to **Harry's Bar** *(High St. next to the Ark Bar; Open daily; No credit cards).* Each night, the place is filled with red-faced regulars, all men, drinking cans and pints. A perennial happy hour and more cigarette smoke than the Philip Morris laboratories makes Harry's either drinker's heaven or drinker's hell. There's also an off-license (liquor store) around back if you didn't get enough at the bar.

Next to Harry's is **The Ark Bar** *(High St.; Tel 071/42014; Open daily; No credit cards),* an old wood and brass pub with great booths. The good restaurant next door, also called Ark's Bar, makes it an ideal lunchtime pub, serving up simple but tasty food like burgers and chicken with potatoes.

Maybe the most atmospheric pub in town, **Hargadon Bros.** *(4 O'Connell St.; Tel 071/70933; Open daily; open till 1am Thu-Sat; No credit cards)* is made special by its dark wood and maze-like interior. With all of the snugs and corners everywhere, you could play hide-and-seek here for hours.

Beezie's *(Tobbergal Lane, off O'Connell Street; Tel 071/45030; No credit cards)* tries too hard. Futuristic blue light fixtures, crystal balls, and weird water sculptures don't quite make up for the fact that the place looks like a very nice TGI Friday's dressed up for an after-prom party. Beezie's is very popular, though, and gets boisterous and loud on weekends. It's also the best place in town to scope for nookie [see *lad meets lass,* below]. DJ's spin uninspired techno and pop remixes on Thursdays through Saturdays. The **Penthouse Restaurant** [see *eats,* below]

lad meets lass

A pick-up town Sligo is not. Of course, you've got a decent chance of meeting a random snog partner here on a drunken Saturday night, but by and large, people seem to be relatively conservative about one-offs. People in the more mingling-type places seem a little too preoccupied with appearance, but as they say, love is like a potato, it sprouts from the eyes. Hit **Beezie's** [see *bar, club, and live music scene,* above] or any other crowded place on a Saturday night if you want to get your schwerve on.

upstairs, which also has a bar, is much preferred over Beezie's for an elegant cocktail.

A local favorite, **Fiddler's Creek** *(Rockwood Parade aka JFK Parade, by the river; Tel 071/41866)* is traditional without being stodgy. A fun place with atmosphere to spare, it caters mainly to a thirty- and fortysomething crowd, but there's a speckling of youngsters. The best thing about Fiddler's is the space itself—stone archways, tin ceilings and peat fireplace. The attached restaurant of the same name offers food that's good and filling [see *eats,* below].

The open, plant-filled space that is **Garavogue** *(15-16 Stephen's St.; Tel 071/40100, Fax 071/40104; V, MC)* feels a little like a Frank Lloyd Wright building that serves booze. Skylights, couches, and lots of green are the main features here, along with 20-foot high ceilings that capture all the light that peeks through the gray clouds in the sky. The polo-shirted crowd mingles over beer and the whole place has a busy-but-carefree vibe. Drinks are 30-50p more expensive here than at most other places, but the space is 30-50 percent more impressive than at most other places. Separated only by a door, the **Bar Eile** is part of the Garavogue complex but with a much different flavor. Live DJ's spin soul, funk and house Thursday through Saturday for a grungier crowd. The milieu is dark and slightly futuristic, and there are lots of windows overlooking the river.

Big bald bouncer Fuzz is the man in charge at **McGarrigle's** *(O'Connell St; Tel 071/41667; No credit cards),* a fun, smoky, hippie hangout crossbred with a honky-tonk joint. The bar is too brightly lit, and the crowd seems a gently misanthropic set, but they're all friendly. Grab a pint, settle into a booth and groom your love bride's hair for bugs as you listen to live acoustic blues (or rock on some nights). They also have soup, sandwiches, and coffee by day for under £4. BYO patchouli.

Cavernous, dark, and full of young people, **Journeyman** *(22 Chaplan St.; Tel 071/42030)* is at its best on the weekends when DJ's make the place throb. There's no sign out front (so you know it's got to be cool...)—it's next to a place called Abakebabra, just look for that. Even on off nights, the music on the stereo is excellent dance/electronica stuff. The crowd is more made up than at most places, but in a messy-chic sort of way.

arts scene

▸▸VISUAL ARTS

The **Sligo Art Gallery** *(Lower Knox and O'Connell St. in the Yeats Memorial Building; Tel 071/45847; 10am-5pm Mon-Fri, 2-5pm Sat; Free)* exhibits a variety of modern work. You may not see anything stellar in this gallery, but it's interesting to see what's up with the almost exclusively Irish artists whose work passes through here.

▸▸PERFORMING ARTS

Hawk's Well Theater *(Temple St.; Tel 071/61518; Call for info),* although small, gets pretty much everything that goes on the road from Dublin or Galway—from opera to drama to dance. The **Gaiety Cinema** *(Wine St.; Tel 071/62651; £5 admission, £3 matinees)* plays mainstream mostly American flicks at night, with matinees on the weekend.

culture zoo

The Abbey *(Abbey St. at Charlotte St; Tel 071/46406; 9:30am-6:30pm daily, Jun-Sep; Admission £1.50 adults, 60p students):* Sligo's only remaining medieval building, founded in 1252 by Dominican monks, the Abbey is in pretty good shape considering all it's been through. During the Ulster Rebellion of 1642, Sir Fredrick Hamilton and company attacked Sligo and, as the plaque out front reads, "fell upon the abbey, set fire to everything they could, within and without the church and conventual buildings, and burned altars, altar ornaments, vestments, and various articles of value committed by the townspeople for safekeeping to the friars." Ouch. Of particular interest is the 15th-century altar, one of the few intact medieval altars in Ireland.

festivals and events

The major festival in Sligo is the **Yeats International Summer School,** *(Late Jul-early Aug.; Tel 071/42693 for information)* which attracts thousands of scholars, students, and tourists here to celebrate the poet and drink alcohol. This event usually brings out the big guns in Irish literature (Edna O'Brien gave opening remarks in 2000). Readings, lectures, and drinking are all to be expected.

Sligo County Museum *(Stephen St.; Tel. 071/47190 10:30am-12:30pm/2:30-4:30pm, Mon-Sat, Jun-Sep; 10:30am-12:30pm, Apr-May and Oct; Free):* This small museum stocks photographs, letters, and other goodies of interest primarily to Yeats freaks.

Yeats Memorial Building *(Lower Knox and O'Connell St; Tel 071/45847; 10am-5pm Mon-Fri, 2-5pm Sat; Free):* Well, it is what is says it is: a building dedicated to the memory of the poet. It's a lovely red brick building that was completed in 1895. Inside, there's a library full of Yeats-related material poured over by scholars and PhD candidates. In August, the building is the headquarters of the Yeats International Summer School [see *festivals and events,* above].

Yeats's Grave *(Drumcliff, take the N15 road north from Sligo or take the 8:45am bus from Sligo to Drumcliff):* Five miles north of Sligo Town is Drumcliff, site of the Church of Ireland cemetery where W.B. Yeats is buried. He died in France, but in accordance with his wishes, returned to Sligo for burial beneath the slopes of Ben Bulben, a mountain rising 1,730 feet in the Sligo countryside. His grave is a somber yet

amaze your friends with your knowledge of sligo's favorite son

Because you're on the road and your attention span probably isn't what it could be, what with all of the drinking, sleeping, and map reading, we're giving you Yeats 101, a handy collection of bon mots to drop at the next party:

William Butler Yeats was born in Dublin in 1865 but spent his early years shuttling between Dublin, London, and Sligo, his mother's hometown. Sligo was the home of his imagination—his early poems draw from the Sligo countryside and its people.

Yeats fell in love with Irish nationalist revolutionary Maud Gonne, a total babe, but, alas, she did not reciprocate. So in 1917 he married a medium, George Hyde-Lees, who revealed to Yeats the powers of "automatic writing": Pen in hand, you let go of your consciousness and let your unconscious—or thoughts of a spirit communicating through you—spill onto the page. Yeats thought this was da bomb, and produced a 3,600-page tome, rich with inchoate symbolism, that eventually yielded many of his later works.

In 1922, he became a member of the Irish Senate; in 1923, he won the Nobel Prize for Literature. He died in Italy in 1939, where he had fallen under the lure of fascism. His body was later returned to Ireland, and is buried at Drumcliff [see *culture zoo,* above].

tranquil site from which not even the nearby gift shop can detract. You can easily find the poet's tombstone bearing the epitaph from his poem "Under Ben Bulben":

"Cast a cold eye
On life, on death.
Horseman, pass by!"

Carrowmore Megalithic Cemetery *(Head out of town on John St.(N4); Tel 071/61534; 9:30am-6:30pm daily, May-Sep; Admission £1.50 adults, 60p students):* Located on Sligo's Coolera Peninsula, Carrowmore's Stone Age cemetery is one of the great sacred landscapes of the ancient world. The giant's tomb, a massive passage grave, is the centerpiece. As many as 100 to 200 passage graves circled it, each of them also circled in stone. Tomb 52A, excavated in August 1998, is estimated to be 7,400 years old, making it the earliest known piece of free-standing architecture in the world. Unfortunately, about a third of the rocks have been carried away over the years to be used in fences, buildings, and other rock piles. You'll take John St, which turns to Church Hill, out of Sligo. From there, you'll see signs to the site. Follow them.

great outdoors

Rosses Point is a tiny peninsula jutting out into the Atlantic about four miles northwest of Sligo, and it's got the best beach around town. When temps are warm it's unbeatable. The sands are soft, the view of the bay breathtaking, and the Irish crowd so pasty and white you're sure to need sunglasses. To get here, take the N15 north out of town and take a left after about a mile onto R291; or take Bus Eireann 473 from the Sligo Bus Station.

If you decide to stay out here, near the beach is the nondescript and clean **Yeats Country Hotel** *(Tel 071/77211; £25-35 per person for bed and breakfast).* There's a pub on the road to the beach called the **Nifty Bunker** *(Open daily till 11:30pm),* where you can swill a pint and grab some pub grub too.

The 24-mile road running around **Lough Gill** *(Take N16 northeast out of town and make a right on the R285; follow signs to Lough Gill, about 3 miles)* is a pretty little path that makes an excellent cycling excursion for an afternoon. Besides the pleasant environs, highlights include a handful of microscopic villages and **Parke's Castle** *(Tel 071/64149; 9:30am-6:30pm daily, Jun-Sep; 10am-5pm Tue-Sun, Apr-May, Oct; £2 Adults, £1 Students),* a 17th-century construction on the lake's northeast shore that was once used to protect greedy landowner Anglo Parks from his starving tenant farmers.

stuff

The intersection of John, O'Connell, and Grattan streets is the radiation point for all commerce. Generally, the selection of clothes and music is good but nothing special, but bookworms are in luck.

▸▸DUDS

For all your trendy clothing needs, head to **Addam** *(10 Gratton Street;*

Tel 071/42977; 9:30am-6pm Mon-Sat; V, MC). They offer a wide selection for lads and lasses alike.

▸▸TUNES

The Record Room *(Gratton Street; Tel 071/43748, Fax 071/46811; 9:30am-6pm Mon-Sat; V, MC)* sells a good range of Irish music and a small selection of vinyl, mostly new techno and pop for local DJ consumption. They also give good advice on what's playing around town.

▸▸BOUND

No question, the best bookstore in town is **The Winding Stair Bookshop and Café** *(Corner of Lower Knox and O'Connell St; Tel 071/41244, Fax 071/42144; 10am-6pm Mon-Sat),* named after a famous volume of poetry by, yes, W. B. Yeats. The café upstairs serves great soup and homemade bread and sandwiches for £2-5, and is a hangout for the Sligo intelligentsia.

eats

If you just want to get by, most of the pubs in town can rustle you up some grub for under £5. Spending a little more will get you good, though non-adventurous, dinners. There is a definite lack of culinary innovation in Sligo, so it doesn't make sense to spend £15 on a dinner that won't knock your socks off.

▸▸CHEAP

The large dining room at **The Tea House** *(34 O'Connell St.; Tel 071/43999; 10am-6pm Mon-Sat)* reminds you of a library reading room: very spacious and peaceful, with dark oak furniture. Even during the extremely busy lunch hour, when crowds of young diners pour in, there's something eminently relaxing about eating here. Although the food is only average—think chicken noodle soup and an egg salad sandwich—it's a great place to see a cross-section of Sligo's inhabitants.

The Winding Stair [see *stuff,* above] has great lunches of homemade soup and sandwiches at dirt-cheap prices. You can eat from the time they open up till they lock the doors.

Sligo doesn't disappoint in the cheap-and-greasy department either: Cheap Chinese take-out can be had from **Ho-wong** *(High St.; Tel 071/45718; Open till 12:30am daily, till 1:30am Fri-Sat)* for under £5. If you're in a pinch for late-night food, there's a kabob chain and a burger chain on John Street and Grattan Street, both near the **Journeyman,** [see *bar scene,* above]. Both stay open till after the pubs close.

Then there are cafes that, besides being cool places to hang out, serve up some worthy cafe fare. **Hy-Breasil** has a veggie breakfast with fresh squeezed o.j., sandwiches, and lots of sun. **Eurobar** has cakes and capps and **Bar Bazaar** has herbal tea, coffee, and muffins. Everything is in the £1-5 range [see *hanging out,* above, for all].

▸▸DO-ABLE

Fiddler's Creek [see *bar scene,* above] serves slightly exotic food in a traditional pub setting. The Portuguese chicken piri-piri (light, delicately

TO MARKET

If you're looking for healthy groceries, hit **Cossgrove and Son Deli** *(Market St., 2 doors up from Bar Bazzar; Tel 071/42809; 9:30am-8pm Mon-Sat, 10am-2pm Sun).* They've got an awesome selection of gourmet fruits, grains, health food, meats and groceries, and an eccentric proprietor.

seasoned, and amply portioned) is excellent, while the veggie fajitas are passable. Entrees run £8-10.

Attached to **Beezie's** [see *bar, club, and live music scene,* above], the **Penthouse Restaurant** *(6 pm-10:15 pm Wed-Sun)* is one of the better places in town for dinner. The decor is minimal, done in an arid, slightly surreal desert palate. Entrees run about £10 for decent meat, fowl, and seafood dishes. The Penthouse bar has oversized brass candlesticks and offers a sophisticated setting to sip a martini before dinner.

You can grab a light dinner—think club sandwiches and Greek salads—for about £8-10 at **Garavogue** [see *bar, club, and live music scene,* above].

Ristorante Italiano Leonardo *(Market St.; Entrees £7-10; V, MC)* is decorated with so much muted beige that it's almost annoying. Order a colorful entrée to increase brain stimulation. The standard Italian entrees like ravioli and fettuccini alfredo are excellent, and are complemented by a strong wine list.

crashing

There are plenty of hostels in Sligo, and all of them are pretty small, which makes them primo places for socializing, swapping information, and rounding up drinking buddies.

▸▸CHEAP

The **White House Hostel** *(Markievicz Road, north of town center; Tel 071/45160; £7 dorm in 8-12-bed rooms; £1.50 key deposit; No credit cards)* has a full kitchen, fireplace, and smoking porch. The crowd tends to lean toward aloof, and the dorms are nothing to write home about, but the location is great. Beware of the lukewarm trickle machines, er...showers. This is, on good nights, the best *party* hostel in town. People tend to loosen up once the booze starts flowing (go figure).

And then there's the lovely **Railway Hostel** *(1 Union Place; Tel 071/44530; 10 beds, all £8; No credit cards).* More like a B&B than a hostel, this small, cozy lodging place is an old house that's newly remodeled. Rooms are brightly colored, with hardwood floors and central heat, and some are en suite with electric showers. There are no more than four beds in a room; most of them have a double bed with a top bunk. The one drawback is that there's not a full kitchen, but a microwave, toaster oven, sink, and tea and coffee machines are all available for your cooking pleasure. You probably won't find a big party happening here, but it can't be beat for relaxation, cleanliness, or location. From the bus station, turn onto Union Street, take a left around the corner, and thar she is.

The **Harbor House Hostel** *(Finisklin Road, northwest of city center; Tel 071/71547; £8 dorm; No credit cards)* is so immaculate that it almost makes up for the completely anal attitude of the proprietors. The dorms have great beds, some have TV's *in the room*—a major rarity for hostels—and all have clean bathrooms. The downstairs has a complete and fully functional kitchen, an adjacent dining area and a comfortable TV room that looks way too nice to be in a hostel. Avoid making loud noises late at night or daring to ask to use the kitchen after 11pm. Another drawback: The Harbor House is a 15-minute walk from downtown, which can feel much, much longer after a big night out. To get there from rail and bus stations, take Lord Edward Street east and make a left onto Union Street. Take your second left onto Lynn's Place, which turns into Finisklin Road.

Staying at the **Yeats County Hostel** *(12 Lord Edward St., near the train and bus stations; Tel 071/46876; £7 dorm; No credit cards)* is an experience unto itself. Liam, the manager, will give you an earful about Sligo, ask you about yourself, and tell you about his years in America as the butler to Rose Kennedy (you've never met a nicer woman), Barbra Streisand (a bit of a nut) and other who's-who's of 20th-century Americana. The TV room gets *smoky,* so asthmatics be advised. The beds are average, the dorms are a bit dark and dank, but the location is good, and the atmosphere is welcoming and fun.

▸▸DO-ABLE

Halfway between the bus station and the bars sits **The Clarence Hotel** *(Wine Street; Tel 071/42211; £36 single, £66 double, includes full breakfast; MC, V, Eurocard),* offering a step up from a B&B. Rooms are basic and clean with all the little soaps and shampoo bottles you can stuff in your backpack. The bar/restaurant here has nightclub-ish parties on weekends that draw the local youths [see *bar, club, and live music scene,* above].

The **Renate House** *(Upper John St.; Tel 071/62014; £20-30 per person per night; No credit cards)* offers basic and comfortable B&B. Perfect if you want a little privacy but don't want to kill your wallet.

need to know

Currency Exchange The major bank branches in town will give you the best rates. **Bank of Ireland** *(Stephen St.; Tel 071/6162; 9:30am-4pm Mon-Fri)* and **AIB** *(Stephen St.; Tel 071/42157; 9:30am-4pm Mon-Fri)* both have bureaus de change, with ATMs outside for 24-hour access.

five-o

The police don't have much of a presence in Sligo, but it still ain't the kind of place that you can smoke crack with a prostitute in front of the Yeats statue on a Wednesday afternoon. Word on the street is that there are more plainclothes police than actual Garda walking around; it's rumored that you can tell a vice guy from his clean haircut and new shoes. This city loves to puff—even The Man tokes, say the locals—but be *careful.* People drink indoors, smoke at home, and save their pharmaceuticals for the dark corners of crowded clubs.

Tourist Information The gleaming and modern **Tourist Information Office** *(Temple Street at the Lungy; Tel 071/61201; 9am-5pm Mon-Fri, 9am-1pm Sat; open till 8pm all days Jun-Aug)* is located a couple blocks outside of downtown. The best of show among their propaganda is the **Walking Tour** brochure, which will help you get around the historic buildings in town in a couple hours' time. Walk up Charles Street as it turns into the Lungy. The office is on the corner of Temple Street and the Lungy.

Pharmacies There are pharmacies scattered all around town, including centrally located **Toher's Chemists** *(O'Connell St.; 9am-7pm Mon-Wed, 9am-9pm Thu-Fri, 9am-6pm Sat; V, MC).* Various chemists rotate being open on Sundays from 11:30am-1pm, and a sign on the door of any pharmacy will tell you which one in on duty.

Airports **Sligo Airport** is about 8 km (5 mi) west of town, and can be reached by cab for £9. There are daily flights to Belfast, Shannon and Dublin.

Trains The bus and train stations are right next to each other west of downtown on Lord Edward St., so it's easy to take the train in and transfer to a bus for destinations south. The **Train Station** *(Lord Edward St.; Tel 071/69888)* has trains leaving three times daily for Dublin.

Bus Lines Out of the City **Bus Eireann** *(Lord Edward St.; Tel 071/60066)* runs to Dublin, Galway, and Derry three times daily.

Bike Rental **Gary's Cycles** *(Lower Quay St., west end of town near river; Tel 071/45418; 10am-6pm Mon-Sat)* rents for a pricey £10-40 for daily or weekly rentals.

enniscrone

This popular summer resort is a place where people go to get away from it all. Smooth-sanded Enniscrone Strand stretches out down the hill from the main road through town, **the R297.** Situated on the eastern shore of Killala Bay, the beach provides calm waters and incredible sunsets. The town itself is busy in the summer, but never overrun with tourists, and most visitors come to Enniscrone with a fun, relaxed mindset. You could spend all day watching the gentle ocean waves lap against the sand, broken by the snug crescent of Killala Bay. At dusk, frolic along the water, running from the waves as the tide rolls in, then make out with your sweetie in the sand.

A cool thing to do while you're here is to hit **Kilcullen's Bath House** *(Tel 096/26238; 11am-9pm daily, May-Oct; 10am-10pm daily, Jul-Aug; Noon-8pm Sat-Sun, Nov-May),* where you'll learn the virtues of hot seawater and seaweed. For about £10, you can relax in a tub covered in seaweed, immersing yourself in hot iodine-rich salt water. It's good for what *eels* you.

If you take a liking to Enniscrone and want to stick around, crash at the **Gowan House B&B** *(Pier Rd.; Tel 096/36396; £17 per person; V, MC, AE),* just a two-minute walk from the pier. There are five rooms available, all en suite. At only £17 per person, it's a real deal. Have a drink at **Walsh's Pub** *(Main St.; Tel 096/36137),* where you can also get good grub of the pub persuasion. They have live music once or twice a week, more often in the summer.

need to know

Directions/Transportation Enniscrone is serviced by **Bus Eireann** *(Tel 074/21309)* one-two times daily to and from Ballina. If you're driving, take R297 out of Ballina about eight miles and you'll reach Enniscrone.

Bike Rental West Coast Cycles, *([Quigabar, Enniscrone] Tel 096/36593; £7 per day, £30 per week)* will hook you up with wheels.

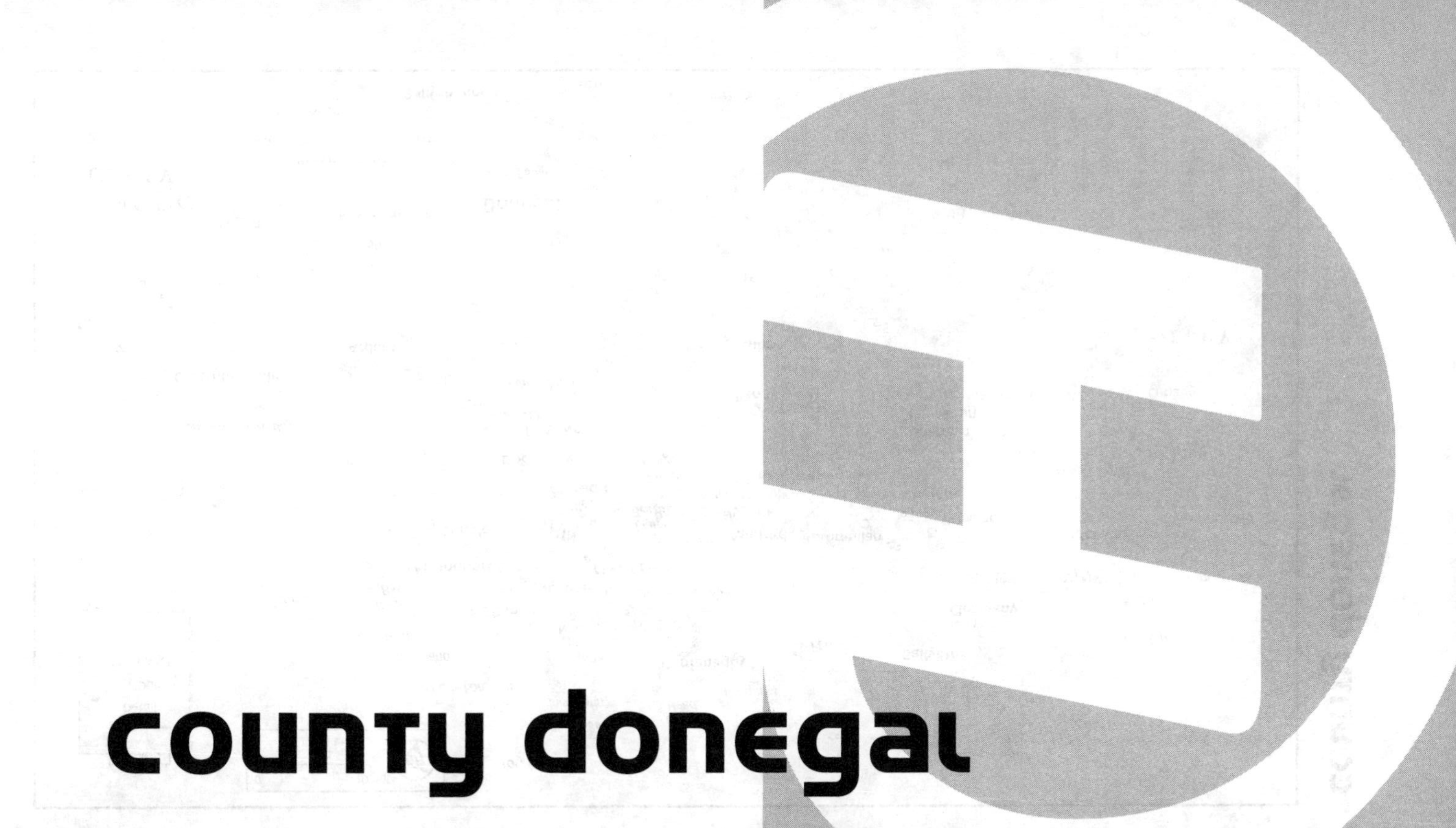
county donegal

county donegal

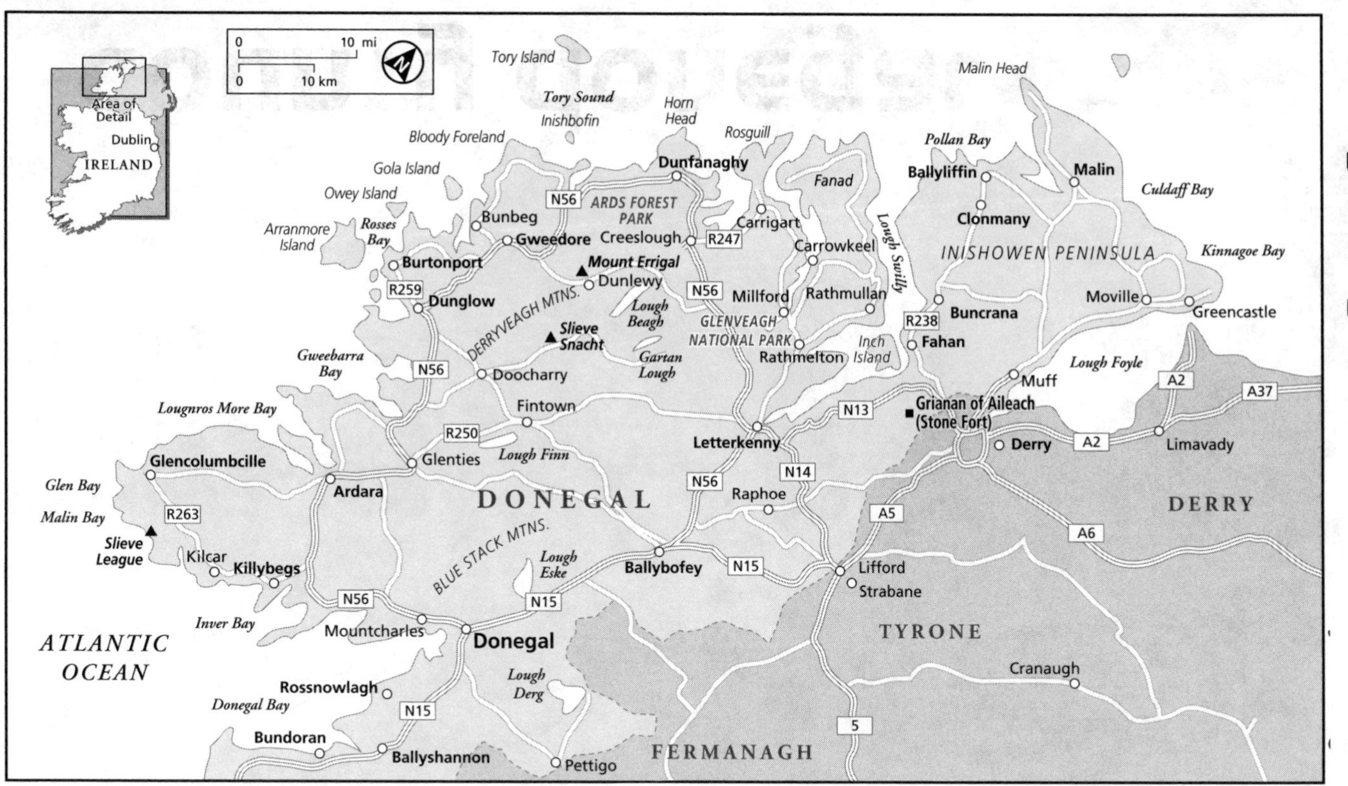

donegal

Set peacefully in Donegal Bay at the edge of the Atlantic, Donegal Town is a little blip of bustle in an otherwise isolated region. It's a place to stop before you set off for adventures in the wilderness that begins as soon as you step outside the town's borders. But there are other reasons to come to Donegal Town besides its proximity to the wilds and woolies of the northern country. The hostels are quirky and extremely social, there are delicious little restaurants like the **Blueberry Tea Room** [see *eats,* below], and friendly people and fantastic traditional music flourish at **Murphy's Riverside Pub** [see *bar, club and live music scene,* below].

You may find yourself completely confounded at the local usage of the word "Donegal." Maybe you have to grow up here to understand, but for newcomers the whole thing is confusing. Donegal County and Donegal Town are both referred to as "Donegal". Even in mid-sentence, locals use the term multiple times to refer to both County and Town without any confusion whatsoever. It could be the inflection of the word. It could be the context of the conversation, or it could be an elaborate hoax played on tourists to identify them as dorks. It's up to you to uncover the truth.

The town gets pretty crowded and busy on weekdays, but it's so small—only 3,000 people live here—that it's a pleasant sort of congestion. Donegal is also the transportation hub for the region, so you'll find buses to take you almost anywhere you want to go—if you're willing to wait for them. Although it's not recommended, it's also easy to get a hitch heading out of town to places like Slieve League and Glencolumbkille.

After a day or so in Donegal, you'll inevitably want to start heading out into the wilderness. If you don't have a car or bike and don't want to risk

wired

The main tourist sites are ***www.donegal.ie*** and ***www.donegaltown.ie.*** For access to the web at £5 per hour, go to the upstairs cybercafe at **The Blueberry Tea Room** [see *eats,* above].

hitching or waiting all day for a bus, there are organized tours you can take to the surrounding areas. Check with the tourist office. In the meantime, though, enjoy the mellow 'tude that Donegal exudes from every nook and cranny.

neighborhoods

This town is on the small side, maybe a ten-minute walk from one end to the other, and is centered around **The Diamond.** This little roundabout is the commercial heart of Donegal. Three main streets branch off the Diamond. Head south and you'll be on **Quay Street,** which leads you to the very helpful tourist office [see *need to know,* below] and then, eventually, to Sligo. East is **Main Street,** and west is **Bridge Street.** The **River Eske** flows north alongside the western edge of Donegal, then takes a sharp bend east and cuts across the top of town. By day, the Diamond is where people are. You'll see school kids, adults, and tourists alike wandering around in tweed jackets and skirts bought from local shops. There are also plenty of places to grab a bite. Food runs the gamut from fish and chips to more expensive hotel prix fixes on the Diamond or nearby. The impressive **Donegal Castle** [see *culture zoo,* below] stands at the elbow of the River Eske, right off Bridge Street to the north of the Diamond. Continuing on, you'll cross a little bridge on Bridge St, then go through a roundabout and onto the **N56 Killybegs Road** and out toward the two best hostels in these parts, 15- and 45-minute walks away, respectively.

bar, club, and live music scene

Let's face it, young people here are not in overabundance. Most people who grow up here leave when they graduate from secondary school, so there's a big gulf between 18 and 30. The biggest crowd of twentysomethings you're likely to find will be fellow travelers. Donegal draws a different kind of young globetrotter than those who flock to Dublin or Galway. More laid-back and earthy, the travelers here will be happy to go out for a pint, listen to some music, and talk the night away. Cocktails are pretty much unheard of in these parts, and Guinness is, as always, the drink of choice. This fits perfectly with Donegal's attitude towards nightlife: relaxed, friendly, and fun. The best place in town for music and great local crowds peacefully coexisting with out-of-towners is Murphy's Riverside Pub. The Coach House is a good bet for trad music and great local *craic.* The Star Bar and The Voyage are good bets to meet that elusive young local crowd.

Murphy's Riverside Pub *(Bridge St.; No phone; Open till 11:30pm, later on weekends; No credit cards)* is a simple, rather poorly lit bar, dressed mainly with white walls and cigarette smoke. You'd never guess at first glance that you had stumbled upon the epicenter of good times in Donegal. Friendly bartenders serve up excellent pints of the Black Stuff, and locals of all ages gather to hear tremendous trad sessions. The music is spontaneous—the occasional Oldie Olsen-type character will get up and dance with a chair, and aspiring trad masters are generally welcome to sing a song. Bring your *uilean* pipes, fiddle, banjo, or guitar if you think you've got what it takes. It's currently undergoing a transition in name from the Riverside Pub to Murphy's Pub; no one's sure when the sign out front will change, so keep an eye out for it.

The downstairs at **The Coach House** *(Main St.; Tel 073/22855; No credit cards)* hosts nightly trad sessions and has a liberal open mike policy. Bring your gee-tar and blow 'em away with your rendition of "American Pie."

Like the pied piper, **The Star Bar** *(Main St.; Tel 073/21671; No credit cards)* attracts most of Donegal's youth with its musical atmosphere. Thursday through Sunday you'll hear live rock, blues, and the occasional trad set. The vibe is fun, if a little immature.

Schooner's *(Main St.; Tel 073/21671; No credit cards)* has great trad sessions every night and good pub grub in the daytime. If it weren't for the friendly patrons, a mix of locals and tourists, you'd feel like you were on a pirate ship. Ahoy, matey!

The most popular club night in town is in the downstairs lounge of the **Abbey Hotel** *(The Diamond; Tel 073/21014; Cover £5)* on Sundays. It's nothing big, but it's lively and the mood is happy.

culture zoo

Donegal Castle *(Castle St.; No phone; 9:30am-4:30pm Mon-Sat, May-Oct; £2 for guided tour):* It's not the biggest or most dramatic castle in Ireland, but it has a certain *je ne sais quoi* that makes it one of the most enjoyable to visit. The highlight of the excellent guided tour is the manor, two beautifully furnished wooden floors on the side of the castle grounds. It's strangely reminiscent of a really nice New York City loft apartment—albeit one that's full of centuries-old furniture.

stuff

Donegal sells all kinds of cool traditional Irish crafts. If you're looking for a bong shop or a place to pierce your nipples, catch the first bus for Galway. Otherwise, explore the virtues of shopping in a traditional Irish vein.

▸▸TWEED

Ah yes, legendary Donegal tweed. This world-famous fabric is a coarse blend of dyed wool woven into jackets and skirts worn by college professors and their admirers worldwide. The drape is luxurious, the durability

donegal

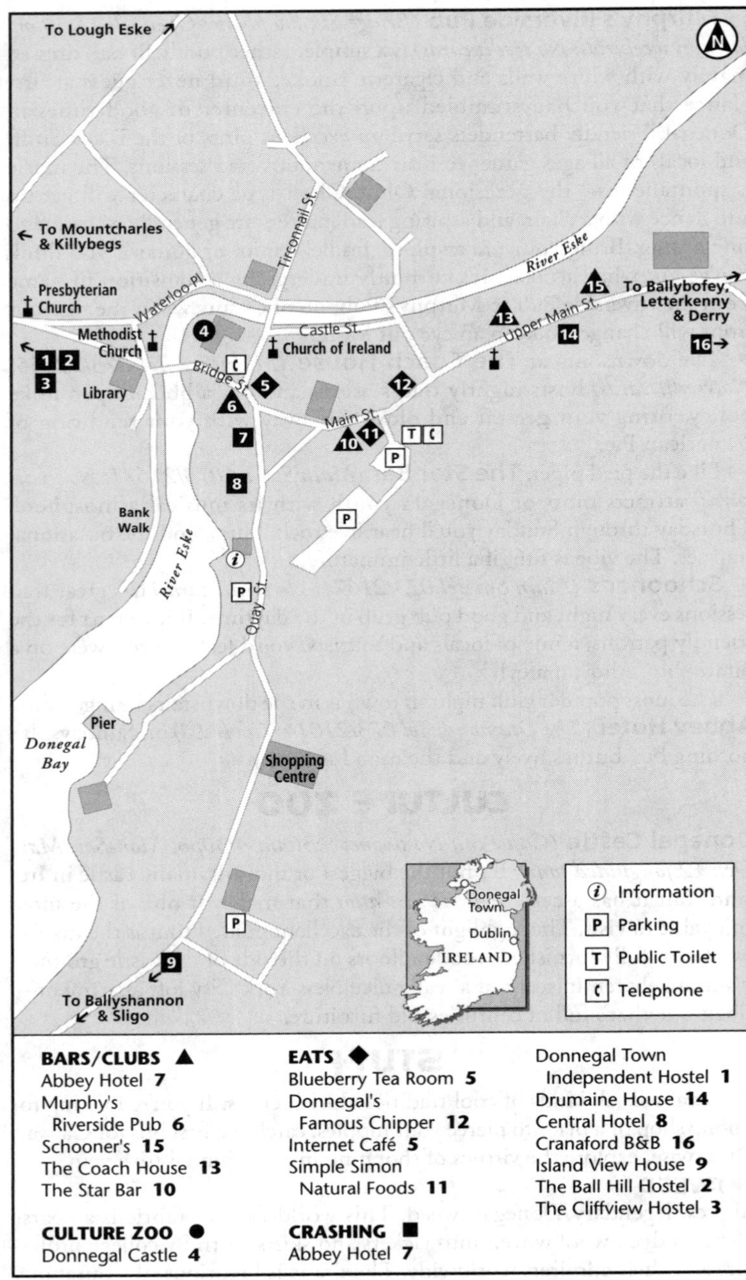
To Lough Eske
N
To Mountcharles & Killybegs
Presbyterian Church
Methodist Church
Library
Waterloo Pl.
Tirconnail St.
River Eske
Castle St.
Church of Ireland
Bridge St.
Main St.
Upper Main St.
To Ballybofey, Letterkenny & Derry
Bank Walk
River Eske
Quay St.
Pier
Donegal Bay
Shopping Centre
To Ballyshannon & Sligo
Donegal Town
Dublin
IRELAND
Information
Parking
Public Toilet
Telephone
BARS/CLUBS
Abbey Hotel 7
Murphy's Riverside Pub 6
Schooner's 15
The Coach House 13
The Star Bar 10
CULTURE ZOO
Donnegal Castle 4
EATS
Blueberry Tea Room 5
Donnegal's Famous Chipper 12
Internet Café 5
Simple Simon Natural Foods 11
CRASHING
Abbey Hotel 7
Donnegal Town Independent Hostel 1
Drumaine House 14
Central Hotel 8
Cranaford B&B 16
Island View House 9
The Ball Hill Hostel 2
The Cliffview Hostel 3

unmatched by anything this side of Kevlar. Both high class and down to earth, tweed makes a statement of relaxed luxury without the slightest hint of ostentation. Are you sold yet? If you want to get something tweed, it won't be cheap, but Donegal is definitely the place to do it. A decent jacket will go for around £100-150, and a tweed skirt will cost around £60. The best place to find some phat-dope-mac-daddy tweeds is **John Molloy's Genuine Donegal Tweed** *(The Diamond; Tel 075/41133; 9am-6pm Mon-Sat).* They've got a brilliant selection of tweed jackets, scarves, hats, skirts, and shawls. Tweed underwear? If you're nice maybe they can make you a pair. They've also got wool sweaters and mittens. Do what you want but don't step on their blue tweed shoes.

▸▸CRAFTS

The crafts are generally of exceptional quality at the **Donegal Craft Village** *(Take the N15 Ballyshannon Road toward Sligo 1.6 km (1 mi) out of Donegal; Tel 073/22228; 9am-6pm Mon-Sat, 11am-6pm Sun, Jul-Aug),* a cute little cluster of shops selling *uilean* pipes, jewelry, pottery, and batik—anything you could want—at good prices.

eats

Donegal does well for the hungry traveler. Most of the fare is simple, straightforward and delicious.

The best food in town is served at the **Blueberry Tea Room/Internet Café** *(Castle St. right off the Diamond; Tel 073/22933; 9am-6pm Mon-Sat; Sandwiches £5; Internet £5 per hour; No credit cards).* You could have a different delicious meal here seven days a week. Great fry-ups start off the morning, and incredible, inventive sandwiches and delicious soups with homemade brown bread are served all afternoon. The Internet cafe upstairs is an added bonus [see *wired,* above].

Donegal's Famous Chipper *(Main St; Tel 073/21428; 4:15-11:30pm Mon-Thu, 12:30-11pm Fri-Sat, 4-11pm Sun; under £5)* is the

to market

If you'd rather cook than eat out, head for the excellent **Supervalu** *(Sligo Road at the Donegal Town Shopping Center; 9am-7pm Mon-Wed, Sat, 9am-9pm Thu-Fri)*

Go to **Simple Simon Natural Foods** *(The Diamond; Tel 073/22687; 9:30am-6pm Mon-Sat, No credit cards)* for the usual health food store selection of organic grains, vitamins, oils, and handmade soaps; stay for the delicious organic breads and cakes.

best greasy take-away in town. Chips deserve their moniker, and fish actually tastes like fish.

The decor at **Abbey Restaurant** *(The Diamond; 10am-6pm Mon-Sat; lunch £5; No credit cards)* is nondescript, but the pub grub lunches are delicious.

crashing

The owners of the **Donegal Town Independent Hostel** *(A half-mile out of town on the Killybegs Road, on the right side and up a little hill; Tel 073/22805; £7 dorm, £17 double, £4 camping)* introduce you to everyone else in the hostel, make you a cup of tea, and generally make you feel like one of their family, all within about 10 minutes of your arrival. If you don't leave here best friends with half-a-dozen travelers, you're a hopeless case. The kids of the management are little geniuses and complete cut-ups. Barely ten years old, they've been known to run the hostel when their parents go away, and kick start conversations if the common room gets too quiet for their liking. The rooms are fairly clean and spacious as far as bunkrooms go, and have funky murals painted in bright colors on the walls. Full kitchen and hot showers are included. This place gets our highest recommendation. The Paddywagon bus, a 20-seater group tour coach, rolls through here once a week, filling up a good portion of their beds, so call ahead to book.

Housed in a former Coast Guard Station, **The Ball Hill Hostel** *(Follow directions to the Independent Hostel, but continue on for another mile. Turn left at the Opel Garage. If you pass the Texaco station, you've gone too far; Tel 073/21174, Fax 073/22604; £7.50 dorm)* perches right on the shores of Donegal Bay. There's a great view everywhere you look, especially from the Coast Guard lookout balcony on the second floor. But the beautiful immediate surroundings are only one aspect of the coolness of this hostel. The comfy "uncommon" room, quirky owners, and a bizarre, hilarious graveyard-ish shrine of pop culture and Irish history all set a convivial mood. You can tell the owners love what they do—they even arrange walking, fishing, and sea trips for all us crazy kids.

If all you need is privacy and giant fry-ups in the morning, head to the **Drumaine House** *(Upper Main St.; Tel 073/21516; £20 single, £35 double)* The location is great, right in the middle of town, allowing for easy access after a night at the pubs or a long day out in the wilderness. Bonus: all rooms have their own bath.

Close to downtown, the **Cranaford B&B** *(Take Main St. away from the Diamond and make a right past the school, across from the hospital; Tel 073/21455; £20 single, £35 double)* is totally unremarkable, but offers a great night's sleep at a good price.

Located a little ways outside of town, the **Island View House** *(On the Ballyshannon Road outside of Donegal; Tel 073/22411; £20 single, £30-35 double)* does the basic B&B thing. All rooms are clean, plain, and comfortable, with TVs and baths. Credit cards are accepted only between June and September; the proprietor explained it's not really worth her while in the off-season.

If you enjoy the finer things in life—and can afford to pay for them—take your pampered butt to the **Central Hotel** *(The Diamond; Tel 073/21027; £35-55 depending on season).* Pleasant and clean, the rooms all have baths, TVs, and beds (har har).

need to know

Currency Exchange **Bank of Ireland** *(The Diamond; Tel 073/21079; 10am-4pm Mon-Fri),* **Ulster Bank** *(The Diamond; Tel 073/21064; 10am-4pm Mon-Fri),* and **AIB** *(The Diamond; Tel 073/21016; 10am-4pm Mon-Fri)* all on have bureaus de change and 24-hour ATMs.

Tourist Information The **tourist office** *(Quay St., 1 block south of the Diamond; Tel 073/21148; 9am-8pm Mon-Fri, 9am-6pm Sat; 9am-5pm Sun Jul-Aug; www.donegaltown.ie)* has lots of good info on the whole county—and is one of the more helpful tourist offices you'll come across in Ireland.

Health and Emergency Emergency: *999;* Garda: *(Tel 073/21021).* **The Donegal Community Hospital** *(Tel 073/21019)* is on the main Donegal-Ballybofey Road.

Pharmacies Your best bets are **McSharry's Pharmacy** *(Donegal Town Shopping Center, up Quay St. past the tourist office and up the hill; Tel 073/21112, Fax 073/21560; 9am-7pm Mon-Sat, open till 8pm Thu-Fri, 2-6pm on bank holidays.)* or **Begley's Chemist** *(The Diamond; Tel 073/21232; 9:15am-6pm Mon-Fri, 9:30am-6:30pm Sat),* which is more central, but open fewer hours.

Bus Lines Out of the City Buses go to Sligo (seven per day, three on weekends), Dublin (one per day), Galway(three per day, two on Sunday). All buses stop in front of the Abbey Hotel on the north side of the Diamond. You can buy tickets on the bus and inquire about schedules at the Hotel desk, or at the tourist office.

Boats There's a little pier at the bay in nearby **Teelin,** You can find a boat there *(Tel 073/628-4688)* that offers tours around the coast, where you can see Slieve League Cliffs from the water. It's a spectacular ride. Call to negotiate prices based on how many people you have; rides can be arranged from Donegal

Bike Rental Unless you've rented a car, you'll need a bike to *really* explore the regions surrounding Donegal. **The Bike Shop** *(Cross the river on Bridge St., take the first right and wind around Waterloo St.; Tel 073/22515; £7 per day, £40 per week, £40 deposit)* will hook you up.

Laundry Get yer duds clean at **Derma's Launderette** *(Millcourt Shopping Mews off the Diamond; Tel 073/22255; £7 for each 25 lbs.; drop off wash, dry, and fold; No self service).*

Postal From the Diamond, head north up Tirchonnail Street. You'll cross over a little bridge. The **post office** *(Tel 073/21074; 9:30am-noon/3:30-4:30pm Mon-Fri)* will be on your left.

Internet See *wired,* above.

lough derg

Lough Derg is an important pilgrimage site, open to anyone serious about their religious devotion and willing to test it through physical hardship. St. Patrick is believed to have fasted for 40 days and 40 nights in the middle of this holy lake on **Station Island**. For decades, thousands of pilgrims have gathered here from June 1 to August 15 to show their devotion and to repeat Patrick's actions. If you desire, you too can spend three days eating black tea and dry toast once a day, walking barefoot, and contemplating your faith.

Although the purpose of the Station Island pilgrimage is to reaffirm Christian faith, there is no reason a non-Christian shouldn't go. The experience can be purifying and very powerful, regardless of faith.

need to know

Hours/Days Open If you want to go on the pilgrimage, contact the **The Priory** *(7km south of the Lough in Pettigo; Tel 073/61546; lochderg@iol.ie; Accomodations provided)*. They'll hook you up.

Tourist Information If you want to experience it without going through the actual rigors of the pilgrimage, check out the **Lough Derg Visitor's Center** *(Main Street, Pettigo; 10am-5pm Mon-Sat, noon-5 Sun; £2)*

Directions/Transportation From Donegal, take R232 about 16 km(10 miles) to Pettigoe, then turn onto R233. As there isn't much around here in the way of civilization, better to call the Priory ahead of time if you want to do the pilgrimage. You can also take a bus from Enniskillen or Ballyshannon once a day.

lough eske

Come to Lough Eske, about three miles northeast of Donegal, for a little respite. Overgrown vegetation and buildings in ruin give the place a serene, post-apocalyptic-Eden feel. This inland lake stretches about 6 miles across and is known for its year-round trout and salmon fishing—its name translates as "fish lake." Even in summer, it's no good for swimming (unless you're a fish) because of its bitterly cold temperatures.

In the middle of the lake stands **O'Donnell Tower,** a haven over the centuries during times of war. Legend has it the Tower's underground passage stretches eight kilometers to **O'Donnell Castle.** You can take a scenic 2 to 3-hour hike around the lake, beginning at a signposted trail along Killybegs Road. Along the way you'll pass the ruins of **Lough Eske Castle,** constructed in Victoria's heyday in the 1860s. Chances are you'll encounter picnickers here as it's one of the area's most scenic places for a bite, providing you remembered to bring provisions.

The lake's proximity to Donegal makes it a great day trip by bike or on foot.

need to know

Directions Take the N56 Killybegs road from the Diamond in Donegal Town. After you cross the bridge, turn right and follow the signs for "Harvey's Point." You'll join the N15 Road, which will take you all the way out to the lake, about 2.5 miles from here.

killybegs

Coming in to Killybegs, the first thing that catches your eye is the big clump of masts sticking out of the water. As this sight may lead you to suspect, Killybegs is the fishing capital of the Northwest. One whiff and you'll know it's true. There isn't too much here to detain the traveler, but Killybegs makes a nice little stop-over as you explore the coast of Donegal—and if you come at the right time, you can watch the fishing boats come in and unload their catch, a pretty cool, if odiferous, sight.

The pubs here all have late licenses to accommodate the notorious appetites of local fishermen for food, drink, and music; things usually begin to clear out by 1:30am. And of course you can find a plate of fish and chips, if that is your desire. **The Sail Inn** *(Tel 073/31130)* on Main Street has some inspired traditional sessions almost every night of the week, as well as some great pub grub. **The Pier Bar** *(Across the parking lot from the Sail Inn; Tel 073/31045)* is the place to see local fishermen drink like their catch.

Stay at the **Tullycullion House** *(About a mile out of town south on N56; Tel 073/31842; tullys@gofree.indigo.ie; £15-20 per person depending on season; V, MC)*. The rooms are basic and clean and all have baths. The views of the harbor are delicious, and the hospitality hospitable. And you can play with their pet donkeys. Really.

need to know

Currency Exchange The **Bank of Ireland** *(On the west end of town; 10am-4pm Mon-Wed and Fri)* has an ATM and bureau de change.

Pharmacies McGee's Pharmacy *(Main St.; Tel 073/31009; 9:30am-6pm Mon-Sat)* is also (surprise!) on Main Street.

Buses Bus Eireann *(Tel 074/21309)* comes through three times a day. A bus leaves Killybegs for Donegal Monday-Friday at 8:20am. Buses from Donegal arrive once in the morning and twice in the afternoon. **McGee's Coaches** *(Tel 075/46150)* runs from Dublin to Glencolumbkille via Killybegs daily.

Postal The **post office** *(Main St.; Tel 073/31060; 10am-noon/3:30pm-5:30pm, Mon-Wed, 11am-noon/3:30pm-5:30pm Thu, 11am-noon/4pm-5pm Fri, 10am-noon Sat)* will sell you a stamp during its erratic business hours.

kilcar

Kilcar's main attractions are its pleasant minuteness and its concentration of tweed factories. It also makes a fine base for exploring the coast, including the amazing cliffs of Slieve League [see below].

You can buy tweed here at **Studio Donegal** *(Tel 073/38914; 9am-5:30pm Mon-Fri, 9am-5:30pm Sat, Jun-Sep)*. When you're through shopping, head to the **Piper's Pub** *(Main St.; Tel 073/38205)* for traditional music and pub grub. Musical instruments hang on the walls, enticing all who play to spark up a tune.

If you decide to spend the night, stay at The **Derrylahan Hostel** *(3 km (1.8 mi) west of town on R263; Tel 073/38079; derrylahan@tinet.ie; £7 dorm; No credit cards)*. Originally a 200-year-old church, it's now a favorite of travelers who are in the know. This is a friendly place to rest in a beautiful stretch of country.

need to know

Buses Bus Eireann *(Tel 074/21309)* runs the 490 line from Kilcar to Killybegs once a day. To get here from Donegal, take N56 west to the turn-off for the R263 Killybegs Road. It's about 15 miles to the turn-off, then another ten to Kilcar.

glencolumbkille

Glencolumbkille has fewer than 300 people and is a mere speck on the map, but it's a great place to find some small-town charm and soak in a rural setting on the Atlantic coast. It sits in the heart of Gaeltech country, so you'll hear plenty of Gaelic speakers and see plenty of signs written in a language you can't understand (hats off to you if you can...). In this part of the country, you're likely to see a sign for a destination that reads, for example, "7 km to Graffy." A few kilometers down the road, you may see a sign that says "8 km to Graffy." This is strange and pretty much inexplicable, so be ready and armed with a good road map—and a sense of humor.

The main attraction in Glencolumbkille, besides the wee town itself, is the **Folk Village** *(Tel 073/30017; 10am-6pm Mon-Sat, noon-6pm Sun, Apr-Sep; £2),* a cluster of old, weather-beaten cottages replicated from the 18th and 19th centuries. They're outfitted with period furniture and artifacts that reflect life in this remote corner of Ireland over the last few centuries. Another cool attraction at the Folk Village is the homemade wine they sell, made from seaweed. If you've ever wanted to drink alcoholic ocean foliage, you've come to the right place!

eats

Biddy's Pub *(Carrick Rd; Tel 073/30016; Open till 11:30pm)* has trad a couple of times a week and a lot of Gaelic-speaking clientele. A more down-to-earth spot you could not find in all of Ireland. The **An Christan** at the **Ulster Cultural Institute** *(Tel 073/30213; 10am-6pm Mon-Sat, noon-6pm Sun; Lunch £5)* serves up cheap seafood, and you can rub elbows with students immersed in Gaelic culture.

crashing

The oldest independent hostel in Ireland, the fantastic **Dooey Hostel** *(About a mile out of town, make a left-hand turn at the Glendhead Tavern, then up the hill; Tel 073/30130; £6 dorm; Wheelchair access; No credit cards)* has six kitchens, friendly people, and great views. They can give you information about hiking, beaches, and walks in the area. If they're full, the comfortable **Atlantic Scene B&B** *(Tel 073/30186; May-Sep only; £15 per person; No credit cards)* is next door.

need to know

Currency Exchange Change your money at the **post office** [see below].

Tourist Info The **tourist office** *(Cashel St.; Tel 073/30116; 9:30am-9pm Mon-Sat, noon-6pm, Sun, Jul-Aug; 10am-6pm Mon-Sat, 1-5pm Sun,*

Apr-Jun and Sep-Nov) can give you information on the town and coastal activities.

Directions/Transportation **Bus Eireann** comes through here one-two times daily. Call the tourist office or go to ***www.buseireann.ie*** for schedule info. To get to Glencolumbkille from Donegal, take the N56 to Killybegs, then continue on the R263 past the Slieve League Cliffs, and you'll hit the village. It's about a 20-mile drive.

Postal Mail your clever postcards from the **post office** *(Main St.; 7:30am-1pm/2-5:30pm Mon-Fri, 9am-1pm Sat).*

slieve league

One of the most beautiful stretches of coast in the country, the Slieve League Cliffs are just a hop and a skip from Donegal. A bumpy, windy mountain road takes you all the way up to **Bunglass,** the rock formation that makes up the lower side of the cliffs. The view is incredible from here, and you'll need to decide whether you want to merely gaze at their 1,000-foot splendor as the rough Atlantic pounds away at the cliffs, or get up close and personal on the wind-buffeted walk along the ridge (only the fearless and fit need apply).

You can hike from the Bunglass lookout point all the way to **Tramane Strand** in Malin Beg, a few miles southwest of Glencolumbkille. This walk involves crossing the infamous "One Man's Pass," a narrow ridge with steep drops on both sides that should not be attempted by the acrophobic, nor those wearing high heels. It's a nine-mile walk, and you'll have to arrange a pick-up at the end. The summits of Slieve League are often capped in clouds—think twice about this escapade if there is danger of losing visibility along the way.

need to know

Directions/Transportation It's about an 18-mile stretch of road from Donegal Town to the cliffs, so a car is your best option. To get here, follow Slieve League road signs from Donegal on the R263 Killybegs Road past Kilcar. Here, turn off to Teelin and follow signs for the Bunglass viewing point, about a mile away. There are also various bus tours of Slieve League that leave from Donegal. Check with the tourist office in Donegal for details.

dunlewey

Not even a village, Dunlewey is basically a strip of road with a few houses on it. The reason people come here is because of its proximity to Mt. Errigal—the stunning peak rising up from otherwise flat terrain—and Glenveagh National Park.

Mt. Errigal reminds you of a squat Mt. Fuji, with its symmetrically pointed peak, rocky surface, and complete dominance of the surrounding landscape. The second-highest peak in Ireland at 752 meters (2,467 feet), it's a difficult climb, not for the wimpy outdoorsman. You'll be rewarded, weather permitting, with great views of this lonesome countryside. Leave yourself at least four-five hours for the climb, a rest at the top, and the descent. At the top, there are two summits, about 30 yards apart; they're connected by the dangerous "One Man's Pass." It's narrow and sheer, so be careful.

Near Mt. Errigal is the **Poison Glen,** a little splash of water on the shore of which is an abandoned church. It's quite a scenic spot, with big hills rising up from the far edge of the glen. It's called Poison Glen because of the legend of the Formorian giant Balor, who reputedly could turn people to dirt just by lookin' at 'em. One day Balor fought with Lugh (rhymes with "Hugh") at Dun Lugh (the name of the town Dunlewey is an anglicized version of *Dun Lugh,* or *Lugh's Fort,* a fort that may or may not have existed at one time). Lugh shot an arrow into Balor's eye and his poisoned eye sack spilled into the lake. So think twice before taking a dip.... Actually, the lake isn't poisonous, but it's pretty murky, so you wouldn't want to swim in it anyway. To get here, take R251 a mile west of the Youth Hostel and you'll see a turn-off with a sign that says "Poison Glen."

Glenveagh National Park *(Head east on R251 out of Dunlewey for about 10 km (6.2 mi) until you see signs for the Visitor's Center; Tel 074/37090; 10am-6:30pm daily; £2 Adults, £1 Students)* has 16,500 hectares of mountains, glens, forests, and lakes for you to ramble around, along with plenty of red deer and birds (stop by the visitor's center to fiddle with the cool interactive machines where you guess what the calls of local indigenous birds mean). From the visitor's center, you can take walks out into the park, or take a free shuttle bus to **Glenveagh Castle** *(Follow directions for the park, above; Buses leave every 30 minutes; £2 for tour),* built around 1870 by local tenant farmer, landlord and general son of a bitch John Adiar. This guy was reputedly crooked in business dealings, stole from orphans, evicted 244 tenants off his land, and generally made many people suffer, so maybe it's fitting that the tour of his castle is brutally boring (do you really care what type of china or bedsheets this tyrannical monster wanted for his house?). It's worth it to see the castle from the outside, and to walk around the beautiful gardens, but to pay an extra couple of pounds to get inside is a waste.

One thing to note: The national park, especially on humid days, is absolutely infested with midge bugs. So small that it's impossible to swat—or see—them, they're an unfortunate but inevitable part of your visit. Passing through a swarm of these little guys will leave you playing connect-the-bites on your arms. Avoid wearing perfumes or scented anything when visiting and you'll save yourself a lot of itchiness later on.

Stop by the **Lakeside Center** *(Head west of the Youth Hostel about 300 yards, then turn off R251; Tel 075/61699; 10:30am-6pm daily, Jun-Sep; weekends only Apr-May; closed Oct-Mar)* for info on routes to the top of Mt. Errigal, or to check out the reconstructed cottage of Manus Ferry, the last local weaver (he died in 1975). You can also pet the farm animals and walk around the lovely grounds. In the summer, folk/trad concerts are held on certain days (call ahead to find out what's up). There's also a small cafe here that has good, cheap sandwiches.

crashing

If you're staying the night, stay at the **Backpackers Ireland Lakeside Hostel** in the **Old Dunlewey Hotel** *(Dunlewey, Tel 075/32133; Open year-round; £8 bunk, £10 per person single and double)* a 3 km (1.9 mi) walk to the mountain. The hostel is clean and spacious; there's even a great porch out back where you can barbecue. **McGerdy Shap,** right across the street from the hotel, sells sausages, bacon, eggs, hamburgers, and various meats you can throw on the grill.

need to know

Tourist Information Stop by the **Lakeside Center** [see above] or **Glenveagh National Park Visitor Center** [see above].

Directions/Transportation As you head up the coastal main road, the N56, from Donegal Town, it eventually takes a turn inland at Gweedore. A couple of kilometers (a little over a mile) past Gweedore, you can turn off onto R251, a minor road, and you'll soon see Mt. Errigal. It's about five kilometers (three miles) from the turn onto R251 to Dunlewey.

Postal Yes, there is a **post office** in Dunlewey *(Tel 075/31217; 9am-1pm/2pm-5:30pm Mon-Fri, 9am-1pm Sat).*

tory island

A trip to Tory Island is certainly a weird sociological experience. The mostly Gaelic-speaking locals in this burg of 160 people have created their own little country: They elect a king of the island to a lifetime post, pay no Irish taxes, and refer to mainland Ireland as "the country." The Tory Islanders are an independent lot but not unfriendly to visitors—just sort of oblivious to their presence. Eight miles across the Atlantic from "the country," tiny Tory Island (five kilometers long, one-two kilometers wide) gets a constant pounding by Mother Nature. With no landmasses around it to break the chilling, harsh wind—and but one lonely tree on the whole island—it's certainly a bleak spot. But a climb up the sloping bird cliffs, high above the pounding sea, is an

If you see someone walking around with a little plastic baggie full of dirt, it's probably a mainlander bringing some Tory soil back to wherever they came from. Legend has it that St. Colmcille came here 1,400 years ago and drove all the rats away. People gather the earth to take back to their rat-infested towns in hopes of repeating Colmcille's miracle.

unforgettable experience. If you've never seen puffins in action, this is your chance.

Tory Island has two tiny villages. **West Town** has one street and is the center of Tory life. **East Town** is the other little town and also has one street.

Club Soisialta Thoraigh *(West Town, Tory Social Club; Tel 074/65121; Open till 11:30 pm daily)* is the best pub on the island, often featuring unique Tory trad music sessions here—imagine John Lee Hooker playing trad. A few doors down is **Ostan Thoraigh** *(Tel 074/65121)*, the other pub in West Town, which has reasonably priced pub food day and night.

The nearby **Gailearai Dixon** *(Dixon Gallery, near the harbor)* features the work of the Tory Primitives, a painting collective whose work reflects the rugged nature of life on the island.

Are you stranded due to the weather, or have you taken a liking to Tory? In either case, you can rest your head at the **Radhard na Mara Hostel** *(West Town; Tel 074/65145; Apr-Oct only; £7 dorm)*.

need to know

Boats The only way to get to Tory Island is by boat, and if the weather is bad, you could get stuck out here. The weather is unpredictable, so it's better to come only if you have at least a moderately flexible schedule. **Donnegal Costal Cruises, aka Turasmara** *(Tel 075/31230, Fax 075/31665)* runs ferries between Bunbeg and Tory *(Take the R 258 from Gweedore to Bunbeg; Tel 075/31991)* with one ferry per day in spring and summer, fewer in winter. They also offer ferries from Magheraroarty to Tory *(Off the N56 between Gweedore and Dunfanaghy; look for signs; Tel 074/35061)*, with two per day, June-August only. Most ferries run about £12 round trip.

dunfanaghy

Right on the calm waters of Sheep Haven Bay, the little strip of land and people known as Dunfanaghy isn't much, but it offers a little civilization in this wild countryside. With a cluster of good hostels and pubs, not to mention decent beaches, it could make a great place to plant yourself for a couple of days to let Donegal seep into your soul The town is roughly centered around **Market Square,** a tiny patch of pedestrianized concrete surrounding by shops off **N56,** the main road running east-west through town. Behind the main road lies the bay and the sandy shores of **Killahoey Strand** beach. From here you can see the angling boats sitting in Sheep Haven Bay. About a mile west of town is the turn-off for Horn Head [see below]. This peninsula juts out into the rough Atlantic and provides arguably the most scenic drive/bike/hike in the north. Farther east, heading out of town, look for the signs to **Marble Hill Beach,** a blue flag (an important stamp of approval for Irish beaches) stretch of sand where you can go crazy with the water sports.

bar scene

Best in the summertime, Dunfanaghy's handful of pubs is surprisingly lively for a town this small. Things stay open till around 11:30pm, later on weekends. Pints run £2-2.50.

McGalloway's Pub *(Across from Market Sq. and east about 100 yards; Tel 074/36438)* is hands down the best bar in town. Hand-drawn portraits of Tom Waits, Bob Dylan, Van the Man, and other musical favorites adorn the walls along with old tubas, baritones, and jugs. Live music is offered nightly in the summer. Tuesdays are trad nights and Saturdays are full-out rock 'n' roll. They've also got a projection screen TV for big matches and a peat fireplace to warm your tootsies on a wet afternoon. It's the fun-lovin'-est place in town.

They've got live music in the summer—mostly trad sessions—at **Danny Collins** *(Next-door to McGalloway's; Tel 073/36502),* and cozy snugs (little Irish pub booth-type seating areas) where you can spend your entire evening in snug comfort. Pub food is available noon-3pm for around £5.

The **Highwayman Bar** *(Tel 074/36133)* inside the **Carrig Rua Hotel** [see *crashing,* below], serves pints to a slightly more moneyed crowd that has seen a few more moons than the youngsters who ramble into town looking for youngster-type fun. It's a classy place with polished wood everywhere and a dark, spacious atmosphere.

culture zoo

The Workhouse *(About a half-mile west of town; Tel 073/36540; 10am-5pm Mon-Fri, noon-5pm Sat-Sun, Mar-Oct; £2):* A reason to come to Dunfanaghy in itself, this museum exhibit tells the ugly history of County Donegal during famine times. Life-sized animatronic "Wee

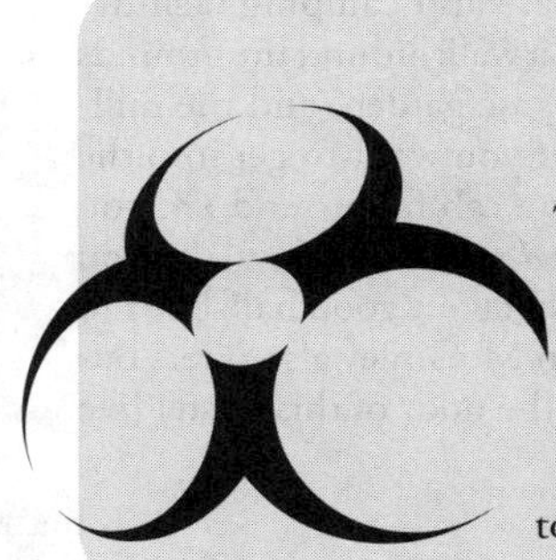

TO MARKET

The **Market House,** on Market Square, has a farmer's market every Saturday from 11am to noon. That's right, just one hour. You can get fresh eggs, fruits, veggies, jams, and delicious sweets, all made by locals. Mmm. Everything is cheap too. Come early to get the best stuff.

Hanna" is your guide as she takes you through the hardships of her childhood, from the horrors of the famine to her internment at the Workhouse, which became half-prison, half-sanctuary for the suffering famine victims.

city sports

If your idea of enjoying the gorgeous waters of Sheephaven Bay is to skim over them at top speed, call **Marble Hill Windsurfing** *(Across from Market Sq.; Tel 074/36231; 10am-7pm Mon-Sat, 11am-7pm Sun, Jul-Aug).* For £25, they'll give you a lesson and a wetsuit.

eats

The staff is young and cool at **Much-n-Muffin** *(Market Sq.; Tel 074/36780; 10am-6pm daily),* a cute little upstairs cafe right in the middle of town. The place has a colorful, red-toned aesthetic, with an exhibition of local, hand-thrown pottery downstairs. Backpackers get a discount on the delicious sandwiches and sweets.

The **Red Rock Café** *(Carrig Rua Hotel; Tel. 074/36133; lunch £5-7 12:30-9pm daily; Visa)* at the **Carrig Rua Hotel** [see *crashing,* below] has lunches amidst a moderately classy setting. There's a lot of wood on the walls and the sandwiches are served with little sprigs of parsley on the side.

crashing

The Corcreggan Mill Hostel *(3 km (1.9 mi) west of Dunfanaghy on the N56; Tel 074/36409; £7-9 dorm, depending on season; £10-11 per person private rooms; No credit cards)* is yet another brilliant Donegal hostel. Converted from an old corn mill, it's one of the most comfortable retreats in the region. The kiln house is a big dormitory with high ceilings. The station house is a 120-year-old mahogany railway carriage that's been renovated into small, private bedrooms. The only sleeper cars in Ireland, these rooms are adorable. The common room has a great old peat fire-place, a guitar, and comfortable couches and chairs. There are two well equipped kitchens and a dining room. There are also camping facilities with separate kitchen and shower facilities. Take a walk around the grounds and check out the other old buildings, the organic garden, and the mill-stream. It's rustic comfort at its absolute best. If you want to get into the pubs, round up some fellow hostelers and split a cab for around £3. You can get here from Dunfanaghy by taxi [see *need to know,* below], or you can make the hike yourself, though it'll probably take a good half-hour to an hour, depending on how drunk you are. John McGinley also offers bus service from Dublin that will take you right to the door of this hostel [see *need to know,* below].

whiskey in the jar

With intepretors running the gamut from Thin Lizzy and the Pogues to the Chieftans and trad legends Metallica, *Whiskey in the Jar* is arguably the drinkin' man's national anthem over here in Ireland, so if you want to hang, take a look below.

As I was going over the far fam'd Kerry mountain,
I met with Captain Farrell, and his money he was countin'
I first produced my pistol, and I then produced my rapier
Sayin': "Stand and deliver fo you are my bold deceiver."

Musha ring dum a doo dum a da,
Whack fol de daddy o
Whack fol de daddyo
There's whiskey in the jar

He counted out his money, and it made a pretty penny,
I put it in my pocket, and gave it to my Jenny,
She sighed, and she swore that she would never betray me,
But the devil take the women for they never can be easy.

Musha ring dum a doo dum a da,
Whack fol de daddy o
Whack fol de daddyo
There's whiskey in the jar

I went into my chamber all for to take a slumber,
I dreamt of gold and jewels and for sure it was no wonder,
But Jenny drew my charges, and she filled them up with water,
An' she sent for Captain Farrell, to be ready for the slaughter.

The three-star **Carrig Rua Hotel** *(A couple of houses east of Market Sq.; Tel 074/36133, Fax 074/36277; carrigruahotel@eircom.com; £100 and up for double occupancy; V)* is for those whose idea of roughing it involves essential amenities like little shampoo bottles and tea makers. It's a lovely little hotel with clean, spacious rooms, and has a bar and restaurant downstairs [see *bar scene* and *eats,* above].

Rosman House B&B *(On N56 east of Market Sq.; Tel 074/36273; £15-20 per person depending on season; Visa)* is a cool little bungalow. All rooms have baths. Eating your breakfast while looking out onto Horn Head will make you want to jump up and scream "Look at how beautiful

Musha ring dum a doo dum a da,
Whack fol de daddy o
Whack fol de daddyo
There's whiskey in the jar

And 'twas early in the morning before I rose to travel,
Up comes a band of footmen and likewise, Captain Farrell
I then produced my pistol for she stole away my rapier,
But I couldn't shoot the water, so a prisoner I was taken.

Musha ring dum a doo dum a da,
Whack fol de daddy o
Whack fol de daddyo
There's whiskey in the jar

If anyone can aid me 'tis my brother in the army,
If I could learn his station, in Cork or in Killarney,
And if he'd come and join me we'd go roving in Kilkenny,
I'll engage he'd treat me fairer than my darling sporting Jenny.

Musha ring dum a doo dum a da,
Whack fol de daddy o
Whack fol de daddyo
There's whiskey in the jar

the world is!" Restrain yourself, though, as you may be asked to leave if you don't.

need to know

Currency Exchange If you're having trouble with cash flow, try the **AIB** *(Across from Market Square; 10am-12:30pm/1:30pm-4pm Mon-Fri, Thu till 5pm.).*

Public Transportation: Need a cab? Call **Hornhead Taxi** *(Tel 074/363620; 24-hour service)* or **Dunfanaghy Cabs** *(Tel 074/36365; 24-hour service).*

Bus Lines Out of the City It's a little tricky to get to Dunfanaghy, but not impossible. Bus Eireann does not come here, but there are three private bus lines that do: **John McGinley bus service** *(Tel 074/35201 or 01/451-3804)* goes from Dublin, Glasgow, or Belfast to the front door of the **Corcreggan Mill** [see *crashing,* above]. **Feda O'Donnel's bus** *(Tel 091/761656 or 075/48114)* goes to and from Galway. **Lough Swilly's bus** *(Tel 071/262017, or 074/22863)* goes from Derry to Dunfanaghy three times daily on weekdays, once on Saturday. All three companies are small and privately owned, so they're likely to change schedules or routes, so *call ahead.*

Bike Rental Okay, pay close attention. Up the hill (there's only one hill, the one due west of Market Square) and across the street from Market Square, four buildings up from the Community Playhouse, there is an archway. To the immediate right, there is a white door in the stone-faced building there. Knock on that door during the day and you can rent a bike for about £7 per day.

Postal Send a letter from the lovely **Dunfanaghy Post Office** *(Market Square; Tel 074/36112; 9am-1pm/2pm-5:30pm Mon-Fri, 9am-1pm Sat)*

horn head

Incredible coastal scenery is synonymous with Horn Head, a small peninsula that juts out into the fury of the Atlantic Ocean. It's about a 3- or 4-hour hike from Dunfanaghy to the tip of Horn Head, but it's worth the trek. There are several scenic viewpoints and car parks along the way, and the road is well marked and not treacherous for walkers or bikers alike. Of course, common sense is still the rule here. If you're walking, don't be so swept away with the view that you don't notice that truck about to run you over. From the Head, you can see ocean, cliffs, the village below, and sailing vessels on the horizon. Truly breathtaking.

need to know

Tourist Information You can buy a map of Horn Head and Dunfanaghy at the Post Office in Dunfanaghy.

Directions/Transportation At the western edge of Dunfanaghy, there is a turn-off marked with a sign for "Horn Head Drive." This is the only way to get to the Head. Continue past the sign and it will take you all the way to the head.

malin head

The farthest point north on the Ireland map, Malin Head tops off the beautiful Inishowen Peninsula with its rugged and beautiful land and seascapes, punctuated by giant sand dunes. Few travelers make the trek up this far; Malin Head is slowly becoming a popular backpacker destination, but it remains pristine.

If you've got a bike—or if you rent one at the Malin Head Hostel [see *need to know,* below]—you can spend a day pedaling up the coast. From Malin village, head north out of town on Inish Eoghin 100 (this is a road name) and you'll hit Malin Head proper after about eight miles. The scenery is terrific, replete with rocky coast and rough ocean, all the way up.

A triangle-shaped green is the center of Malin Village. Trad and tackle are available—in addition to plenty of beer and whiskey—at **Farren's Pub** *(Noon till 11:30pm daily),* the northernmost watering hole in the land.

need to know

Directions/Transportation The easiest way to get here by bus is from Derry on **Lough Swilly Buses** *(Derry; Tel 028/7126-20-17, or Letterkenny; Tel 074/22863),* which runs one-four times a day Monday-Saturday, with no bus on Sunday. If you're behind the wheel, head up R238/242 from Carndonagh.

Crashing Malin Head Hostel *(Tel 077/70309; Mar-Oct only; £6-8 dorm, £17 double, £3 for laundry;)* provides comfortable accommodations and much more. Organic vegetables, culled from the on-site garden, a roaring peat fire, and reflexology treatments are among the services available at this bohemian hostel. They can also give you tips on great walks or biking routes to take in the region, and they'll even rent you a bike for £6 per day. The small and simple **Malin Hotel** *(Tel 077/70645; £30 and up)* is a more private option. All rooms have private baths.

northern ireland

A trip to Northern Ireland, Ulster, or The Six Counties, as it is variously known, is not on top of most tourists' lists. Mostly we've all heard the bad things: Protestants killing Catholics, Catholics killing Protestants, IRA and paramilitary assassinations, car bombs, hunger strikes, riots, marches. Sure, all that has happened here. Northern Ireland was—and is—a volatile region. But what you rarely hear is the fact that Belfast, the North's largest urban center, is one of the safest major cities in Europe. And not only is it safe, it's a blast. In fact, the whole region is really fun, no matter where you go. There are hot nightclubs in **Belfast,** cool surf spots from **Portrush** to **Castlerock,** miles of hiking trails in the **Mourne Mountains,** and fewer tourists than in the rest of Ireland.

Although the media has completely fixated on "The Troubles" and what has gone wrong in the North for the past 30 years, major progress has been made toward securing peace. Ironically, the media's distorted image of the place actually has helped make it one of the best places to visit in Europe by making it totally unappealing as a tourist destination. So go there now, before it becomes overrun with camera-toters like every other cool place in Europe.

But before you go, you should try to get at least a vague idea of the area's history, because it has so vitally shaped what you'll see there today. Northern Ireland has for thousands of years been a land apart. Bits and pieces of ancient walls in the region are visual reminders of early division and hostility. These walls have been built and rebuilt, deepened and reinforced over and over again.

Pre-Christian sites are scattered throughout the North, some dating from 4000 BC In the fifth century, St. Patrick lived in County Down, where he was first a slave, then converted his first followers, and was later rumored to die here—a stone marks the spot in **Downpatrick.** St. Columba built his first monastery in **Derry** in 546 AD. Then the Vikings passed through, followed by the Normans, who left castles along the coast.

The early 17th century marks the beginning of modern day divisions between the North and South. The problem began with the Planters, Protestants from Scotland and England transplanted to the region by England to establish a loyal following. As you might imagine, England set up a government that greatly aided the Protestant planters and their descendents while discriminating against Catholics. The Planters were given land, aid, and support by the British military. Suffrage was determined largely by land ownership, giving minority Protestants—who had become majority landowners—a huge advantage over Catholic tenant farmers. So naturally Protestant officials were elected, and established discriminatory policies that gave Protestants first dibs on good jobs and social welfare aid, continued unfair voting policies, and basically discriminated against Catholics any way they could. Politicians favored laws that separated the Catholics and Protestants, creating two separate societies. This had the understandable effect of arousing suspicion and misunderstanding between the two groups, which has led to so much of the violence that has occurred here. It's important to note, however, that there were plenty of poor Protestants in the mix. They weren't all wealthy landowners looking for political power and cheap labor.

At the time of the Plantation the city of London sent builders to reconstruct Derry, and the name became, for some of its inhabitants, Londonderry. The city's great walls, about a mile in circumference and 18 feet thick, are a legacy from that era. In the 1960s and 1970s, the North's civil rights movement began here in earnest. These days, Derry—which has reclaimed its original name—is helping lead the way to a new North, as the majority of Irish people, in the North and the South, want peace above all else.

So, back to the present, what's there to do? Start in Belfast. Nearly half a million people reside within the city limits, so the place is buzzin'. Queen's

five things to talk to a local about

In Belfast, it's important to not talk about the wrong things. Don't talk about the "Troubles" unless someone talks about it first. If you do, better to ask questions than to be overly opinionated. Other than that, the top five things would be:

1. **Where to drink:** Everyone has his or her favorite place to get hammered, or to quietly sip.
2. **How to meet a person of the opposite sex:** Another big winner. What person living in a city where it's rainy nine months out of the year doesn't think about sex?
3. **American tourists:** People like to poke fun at Americans. If you're American, it can be a self-deprecating way to lubricate a conversation.
4. **Knock-knock jokes:** Everybody's got one.
5. **IT:** Or Internet Technology to the cyber-impaired. People are nuts about it. It's the future.

Travel Times

** By train*
*** Water-crossing required (by ferry usually)*
**** By cable car*

	Dublin	Belfast	Derry	Portrush	Bushmills	Ballintroy
Belfast	2* or 3	-	1:30	1:30	1:45	2
Derry	4:30	1:30	-	1:10	1:25	1:40
Portrush	4:30	1:30	1:10	-	:15	:30
Bushmills	4:45	1:45	1:25	:15	-	:15
Ballintroy	5	2	1:40	:30	:15	-
Ballycastle	5	2	1:55	:45	:30	:15
Giant's Causeway	4:55	1:55	2	:25	:10	:15
Ards Peninsula	3:55	:55	3	2:20	2:40	2:55
Armagh	3	1:25	2:10	2	2:15	2:25
Newcastle	2:50	1:45	3:40	2:50	3:05	3:20
Downpatrick	3:05	:40	3	2:30	2:45	3
Mourne Mountains	2:40	1:55	3	3	3:15	3:30

Ballycastle	Giant's Causeway	Ards Peninsula	Armagh	Newcastle	Downpatrick	Mourne Mountains
2	1:55	:55	1:25	1:45	:40	1:55
1:55	2	3	2:10	3:40	3	3:15
:45	:25	2:20	2	2:50	2:30	2:35
:30	:10	2:40	2:15	3:05	2:25	2:50
:15	:15	2:55	2:25	3:20	2:40	2:55
-	:40	3:05	2:45	2:45	2:35	3:10
:40	-	3:45	2:30	2:50	2:30	3:05
3:05	3:45	-	2:55	1:55	1:35	2:10
2:45	2:30	2:55	-	1:20	1:35	1:20
2:45	2:50	1:55	1:20	-	:15	:10
2:35	2:30	1:35	1:35	1:45	-	:25
2:55	3	2:10	1:20	:10	:25	-

University brings out the bohemian temperament of its inhabitants, and there are great places to eat, shop, and shake your groove thang along the town's Golden Mile. Belfast also sports fab pubs, and clubs where you can break a sweat. So unpack that number you haven't worn since Dublin and rave on, brothers and sisters. After you've recovered, check out the Murals in West Belfast. A visual crash course in The Troubles, these public artworks are a must-see. The biggest city outside of Belfast is Derry, and it's one of the coolest places in the North. Although Bloody Sunday may ring a bell, there is more to Derry than the Troubles. That was then, this is now, and Derry is moving on. Stroll through the Walled City, the four hundred-year-old heart of town, and you'll find a cosmopolitan mix of bars, cafes, and galleries. Big enough to hold several clubs, but close to many of the outdoorsy highlights of the North, Derry is a happenin' spot.

A short distance from both Belfast and Derry, the Antrim coast offers clean, sandy beaches, chalky cliffs, and perky Cornish-style villages. The coastal road meanders under bridges and arches, passing bays, beaches, harbors, and huge rock formations, including the Giant's Causeway, roughly 40,000 tightly packed basalt columns that extend for 3 miles along the coast. Speaking of the coast, you may want to check out the surf—it's a fine place to hang ten, particularly near party central Portrush.

County Armagh is a real treat if you come around apple blossom time. The town of **Armagh** is one of Ireland's most historic cities. Legendary pagan queen Macha is said to have built a fortress here in the middle of the first millenium BC, and St. Patrick chose this place as a base from which to spread the Christian word.

County Down is one of sunniest and driest spots in the North. The **Ards Peninsula** curls around lovely **Strangford Lough,** and has some good beaches and an excellent windmill. **Newcastle** is worth a trip if you need to pick up a cheesy souvenir, or better yet, are heading into the **Mourne Mountains.** They are the highest mountains in Northern Ireland, with a dozen of nearly 50 summits rising over 2,000 feet. You can hike like crazy in these parts—it's a ramblin' man's (or woman's) dream.

getting around the region

Most of Northern Ireland benefits from a solid transportation infrastructure. Derry, Belfast, and much of the Antrim Coast are served by trains, while buses run frequently to Armagh and Newcastle. The Ards Peninsula is served a little less frequently, but still several times a day by bus.

▸▸ROUTES

If you've only got a couple of days in the North, head for Belfast, spend a full day there, tour the murals, then head for the Antrim Coast. You can take the long route, a train from Belfast to Portrush then a bus from Portrush to the Giant's Causeway, or simplify things and take an arranged tour, which you can book at any hostel in Belfast. It may cost a few pounds more, but it'll save you three or four hours of down time. If you've got

Easter 1916

As one of Ireland's most treasured poets, W. B. Yeats is arguably the finest literary illustrator of Irish culture and countryside. His famous phrase "terrible beauty" has commonly been mistakenly quoted as a description of the stark yet magnificent landscape in the Northwest, where he lived and died. But those words were actually used in his poem "Easter 1916," in which he watches Ireland struggle to enter a proud new era. The final penetrating verse is excerpted below.

Too long a sacrifice
Can make a stone of the heart.
O when may it suffice?
That is Heaven's part, our part
To murmur name upon name,
As a mother names her child
When sleep at last has come
On limbs that had run wild.
What is it but nightfall?
No, no, not night but death;
Was it needless death after all?
For England may keep faith
For all that is done and said.
We know their dream; enough
To know they dreamed and are dead;
And what if excess of love
Bewildered them till they died?
I write it out in a verse -
MacDonagh and MacBride
And Connolly and pearse
Now and in time to be,
Wherever green is worn,
Are changed, changed utterly:
A terrible beauty is born.

only a short time but want to see some remote beauty, go for a hike in the Mourne Mountains on day 1, then move on to Belfast and the Antrim Coast for days 2 and 3.

If you've got more like five days, start out in the Ards Peninsula for a day and a night, do the Belfast thing for two days and really revel in the nightlife, then head up to the Antrim coast. If it's history and beauty you're after, spend your last day in Armagh. If you want a little more urban grit, head to Derry. From Derry you can easily go on to Donegal, Galway, or Dublin.

If you're interested in understanding the politics of the North, this would involve a tour of the murals in Belfast and a trip to Derry and the Bloody Sunday tribunals.

belfast

Despite the best attempts of dozens of paramilitary groups, armed militias, splinter political factions, splinters of splinters, and an unforgiving international media, Belfast is emerging from the rubble of its history as a vibrant, international city rich in culture and nightlife—and it's pretty safe, too. Northern Ireland has the second lowest crime rate of any European country (right behind prudish Finland). Beyond the occasional armored transport rolling down a boulevard, you hardly see a military presence in Belfast these days. There are no checkpoints, passport inspections, or any such intrigue. A tenuous balance of peace has been established between Unionist Protestants and Republican Catholics and relative order has been maintained in the notorious **Falls** and **Shankill** areas of West Belfast, where most of the city's violence has occurred over the past 30 years of the "Troubles."

The presence of a major university and heavy investment in city center shops, restaurants, and pubs means that having fun is becoming a priority in Belfast, home to a half-million people. Tourists have rarely, if ever, faced dangers anymore than in any other big city. Now, with a booming economy all over the island, Belfast revels in it's own affluence and invites you to partake of the new economy's bounty. It seems that the overwhelming desire for life and peace may finally overcome the hatred and discord of the past. For information on what's going on culturally, musically or alcoholically, check out **The List,** Belfast's local freebie paper. In addition to pub, club, movie, and art listings, it has excellent reviews and witty commentary about what's happening around the greater Belfast area. You can pick it up in most bars, record shops, or bookstores.

belfast

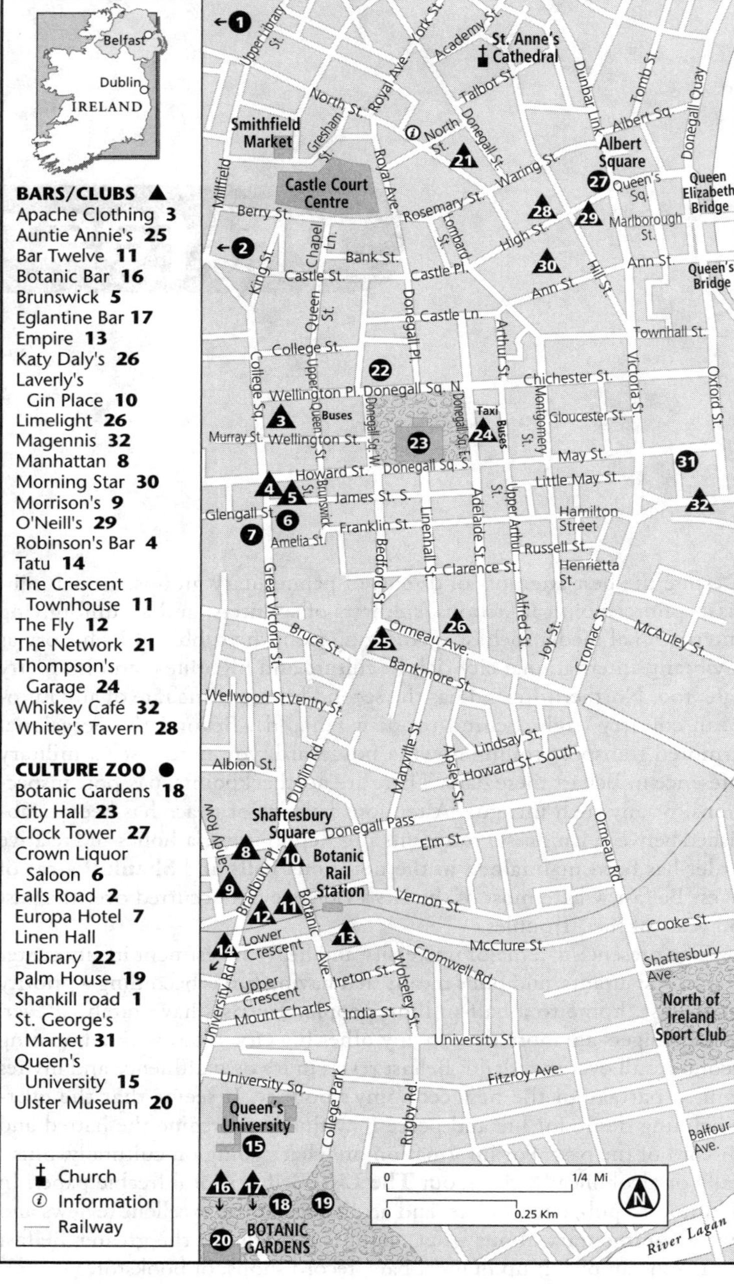
Belfast
Dublin
IRELAND
BARS/CLUBS
Apache Clothing 3
Auntie Annie's 25
Bar Twelve 11
Botanic Bar 16
Brunswick 5
Eglantine Bar 17
Empire 13
Katy Daly's 26
Laverly's Gin Place 10
Limelight 26
Magennis 32
Manhattan 8
Morning Star 30
Morrison's 9
O'Neill's 29
Robinson's Bar 4
Tatu 14
The Crescent Townhouse 11
The Fly 12
The Network 21
Thompson's Garage 24
Whiskey Café 32
Whitey's Tavern 28
CULTURE ZOO
Botanic Gardens 18
City Hall 23
Clock Tower 27
Crown Liquor Saloon 6
Falls Road 2
Europa Hotel 7
Linen Hall Library 22
Palm House 19
Shankill road 1
St. George's Market 31
Queen's University 15
Ulster Museum 20
Church
Information
Railway
St. Anne's Cathedral
Smithfield Market
Castle Court Centre
Albert Square
Queen Elizabeth Bridge
Queen's Bridge
Shaftesbury Square
Botanic Rail Station
North of Ireland Sport Club
Queen's University
BOTANIC GARDENS
River Lagan
Upper Library St.
York St.
Academy St.
Talbot St.
Dunbar Link
Tomb St.
Albert Sq.
Donegall Quay
North St.
Royal Ave.
Gresham St.
North St.
Donegall St.
Waring St.
Queen's Sq.
Millfield
Berry St.
Rosemary St.
Lombard St.
High St.
Marlborough St.
Chapel Ln.
Bank St.
King St.
Castle St.
Castle Pl.
Ann St.
Hill St.
Queen St.
Donegall Pl.
Castle Ln.
Townhall St.
College St.
Arthur St.
Chichester St.
Victoria St.
Oxford St.
College Sq.
Upper Queen St.
Wellington Pl.
Donegall Sq. N.
Montgomery St.
Gloucester St.
Taxi
Buses
Donegall Sq. W.
Donegall Sq. E.
Murray St.
Wellington St.
May St.
Howard St.
Donegall Sq. S.
Little May St.
Brunswick St.
James St. S.
Upper Arthur St.
Hamilton Street
Glengall St.
Franklin St.
Linenhall St.
Adelaide St.
Amelia St.
Russell St.
Bedford St.
Henrietta St.
Great Victoria St.
Clarence St.
Alfred St.
Joy St.
Cromac St.
McAuley St.
Bruce St.
Ormeau Ave.
Bankmore St.
Wellwood St.
Ventry St.
Lindsay St.
Albion St.
Dublin Rd.
Maryville St.
Apsley St.
Howard St. South
Ormeau Rd.
Sandy Row
Donegall Pass
Elm St.
Bradbury Pl.
Vernon St.
Botanic Ave.
Cooke St.
Lower Crescent
McClure St.
Cromwell Rd.
Shaftesbury Ave.
University Rd.
Upper Crescent
Ireton St.
Wolseley St.
Mount Charles
India St.
University St.
Fitzroy Ave.
University Sq.
College Park
Rugby Rd.
Balfour Ave.
1/4 Mi
0.25 Km
N

Studies of other war-torn regions—Beirut, Jerusalem, South Africa—show that three full years have to pass after a major outbreak of violence before tourism starts to rise. Belfast is in its second year (the last major bombing in nearby Omagh killed 28 people in 1998) without a big hit in the area, and is waiting, as is all the north, for the tourists to start coming. For now though, things remain largely un-mobbed by visitors, and even the biggest tourist draws like the **Crown Liquor Saloon** [see *bar scene,* below] retain an authentic flare that you'd never find in, say, Temple Bar in Dublin.

Something else you may notice about Belfast is that it feels, well...British. Say this around a staunch Catholic Republican and you'll probably get into an argument, but you can't deny the British influence here. Belfast uses pound sterling, talks on British Telecom, watches the BBC, and performs ritual sacrifices honoring the queen every morning on the green at City Hall (kidding).

neighborhoods

Belfast is big, but it's walkable. Most of what you'll want to see can be traversed in under an hour. The vast majority of places you'll want to see sit on a 3.22 km (2-mile) stretch from the area north of City Hall to the University area. **City Hall** [see *culture zoo,* below] is the main landmark of the city center and is surrounded on all sides by the commercial heart of Belfast. Above City Hall, on **Donegal Place, Royal Avenue,** and **High Street,** you'll see that shopping has become a way of life here as big name chain shops like the Virgin Megastore have moved in as well as a large number of independent book and clothing shops. This area is known as the **Cornmarket.** There are also a number of old-style pubs in this neighborhood that are generally busy during lunch hours and weekends, but dead on weeknights. Things shut down here around 5:30pm and downtown turns into a ghost town.

five-o

Belfast's police, the Royal Ulster Constabulary, have long been controversial. They've been criticized for brutality and discrimination against Catholics and are now undergoing a major overhaul, attempting to adjust the makeup of the overwhelmingly Protestant squad. When it comes to tourists, they're pretty easy going, but they are harsh when it comes to maintaining order in the streets. There is a visible police presence in Belfast, though nothing like it used to be. At night, if you're drunk and screaming like a loony or get in a scuffle, expect to get treated roughly. You may not be arrested, but you definitely won't look back fondly on the experience.

East of the city center is the waterfront on the **River Lagan.** The Lagan is nothing to write home about, and a lot of it actually travels underground through the city via a big pipe. Regardless, there are places of note in the area like **St. George's Market** [see *culture zoo,* below], a big clock tower, and a soon-to-be-opened $50 million science center/hockey rink. Budgeted at $22 million, it will be interesting to see if this strange mix of education and entertainment will draw them in enough to recoup massive over expenditure.

South of City Hall lies the **Golden Mile,** aka **Great Victoria Street.** Filled with nightlife spots, trendy restaurants, and shops, including the many-times-bombed **Europa Hotel** and the beautiful **Crown Liquor Saloon** [see *bar scene,* below], this is a place you'll definitely want to hit. Further south lies **Queen's University.** This is by far the best area in all of Belfast, with numerous cheap and funky eating options, small bookshops, record shops, and clothing shops, a couple of small theaters, and a bunch of great bars. Also, the sprawling **Ulster Museum** and beautiful **Botanic Gardens** are enclosed within Queen's University [see *culture zoo,* below, for both].

If you head out of the city center a mile or so along **Lisburn Road,** you'll run into a lot of good little places to eat and drink. The definite hot spot of the moment is the recently opened **Tatu** [see *bar scene,* below], perhaps the most stylish place in Belfast. A brand new club, **Milk** (got any?), promises to give Tatu some stiff competition, and another party option for the fashionable local or tourist.

West of city center is (surprise!) **West Belfast,** a neighborhood that is absolutely worth seeing. This is the place where most of the violence in Belfast has occurred; it's also the area you've probably seen on TV. You'll find the bulk of murals and plaques here, too. Things are very stable in town these days, and walking around here by day is generally a safe endeavor. To get here, you need to head north of City Hall, and head west along Castle Street or North Street. The best way to see it is in a Black Taxi Tour [see *need to know,* below] which you can book at any youth hostel in the city.

Citybus [see *need to know,* below] is the citywide transportation system. You don't really need city buses to tour Belfast if you stick to the city center and university area, but they're there if you want them, are exhausted, or don't feel like walking more than a few miles. The best way to get a handle on the buses is to hit the **Tourist Office** [see *need to know,* below] and get one of their excellent city maps, which include a list of where all the buses go. Belfast has been spiffing up its bus schedule, so double-check any listings for routes before you get on.

hanging out

Belfast's large student population makes it a vital and young city. Amid the throngs of busy business people bustling around the City Hall area, and down the large boulevards of Great Victoria Street and Donegal Place, Belfast is bustling and cosmopolitan. As you head farther downtown toward the University, Belfast's large student population brings out the bohemian elements of the city. Smaller side streets overflow with students studying, partying, or lying outside on their blankets on the few sunny days of late spring.

During the day, you'll see tons of people sprawled out on the wide-open and green **City Hall lawn,** unadorned save the masses eating their lunches on the surrounding benches. Even more mellow is the **Botanic Garden** [see *culture zoo,* below] where couples, studious types, and others seeking quiet convene amid its winding, abundant, and colorful biomass.

The young people hang out is the University area, where the streets and cafes teem with life day and night. Head to a cafe on Botanic Avenue like **Vincent's** [see *eats,* below] and soak in the peppy bohemia.

bar scene

Oh, can they party here. A big student population and a booming economy mean there's plenty to do well into the wee hours. Belfast's Golden Mile and the area around Queen's University contain enough pubs and clubs to crawl home from for a solid week. Many are open late, until 1am and beyond, and are indicated as such by the words "open late," whereas city center pubs often close before 11pm. Otherwise, you can expect things to shut down around 11:30pm-12:30am.

In addition to the traditional, old school Irish pubs like **The Crown Saloon** and **Robinson's,** there is a new crop of fun, loungy-type places like **The Fly** that manage to be cool without copping major attitudes. You may feel that the kids in Belfast don't quite know how to pose in these swank places, but that makes for less attitude and more relaxed fun. If you're a raver girl or boy, Belfast will not disappoint. There is a constant influx of international DJ's coming through town, or nearby **Portrush** [see **counties derry & antrim**]. There are several live venues for trad, rock, and jazz as well.

Funny thing about Belfast— you'll often see people proudly drinking "exotic" beers like Coors Light and Budweiser. This is good for visitors who want to sample what locals have to offer as it keeps Guinness in the range of £2 per pint. Mixed drinks go for £2.50-3. Cocktails are a rarity and are priced as such, usually exceeding £3.

Because there are so damn many pubs in Belfast, it makes sense to divide them into groups: student, traditional, and trendy. Student pubs feature (big surprise) lots of students, a loud and friendly atmosphere, and drinks that are 20-30p cheaper than elsewhere. They're usually not big on fancy decor as they cater to casual.

The best student pubs are down in the **University Quarter,** while several new, ultra-slick trendy places have opened up a couple of miles out on the Lisburn Road and also are speckled along the Golden Mile. Trendy pubs cater to a younger, affluent crowd, sometimes wearing clothing that typically costs more than the gross domestic product of a small country. The crowds are slick, but very few pubs are downright snobbish. Cocktails are available at these places, and they often have DJ's, sometimes have

belfast

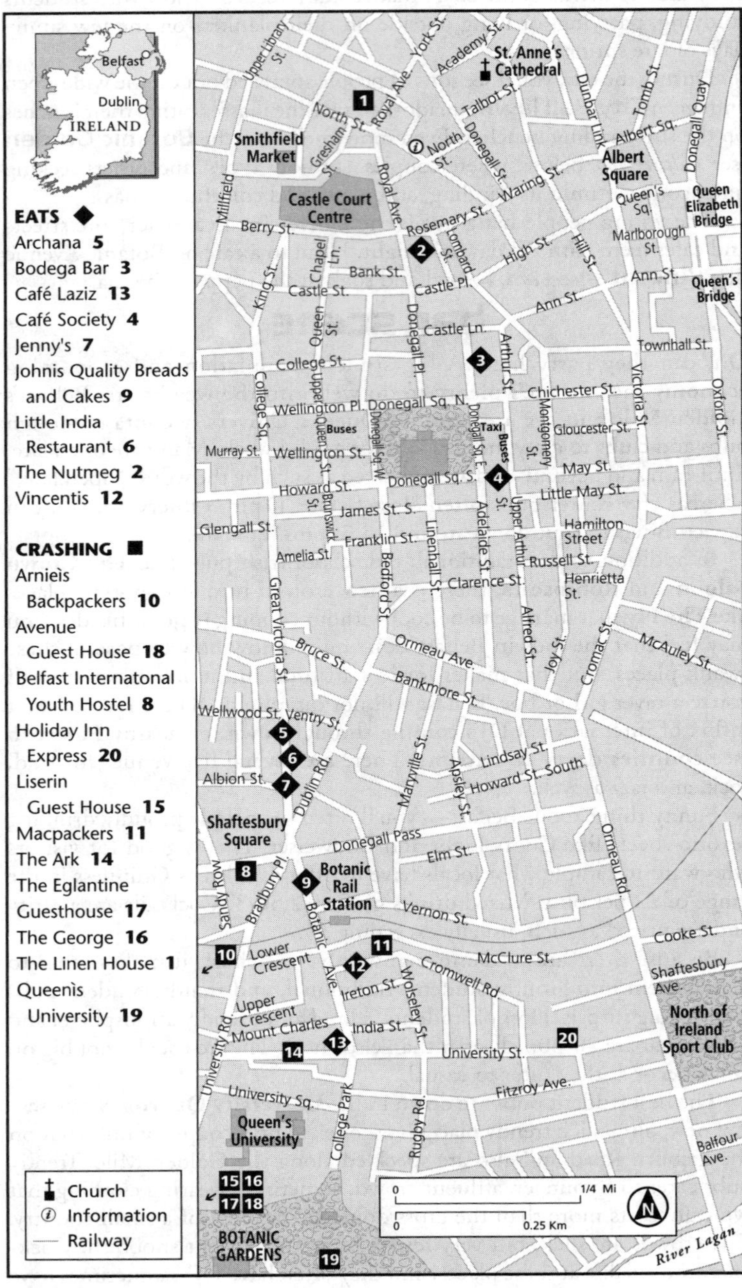
Belfast
Dublin
IRELAND
EATS
Archana 5
Bodega Bar 3
Café Laziz 13
Café Society 4
Jenny's 7
Johnis Quality Breads and Cakes 9
Little India Restaurant 6
The Nutmeg 2
Vincentis 12
CRASHING
Arnieis Backpackers 10
Avenue Guest House 18
Belfast Internatonal Youth Hostel 8
Holiday Inn Express 20
Liserin Guest House 15
Macpackers 11
The Ark 14
The Eglantine Guesthouse 17
The George 16
The Linen House 1
Queenis University 19
Church
Information
Railway
St. Anne's Cathedral
Smithfield Market
Castle Court Centre
Albert Square
Queen Elizabeth Bridge
Queen's Bridge
Shaftesbury Square
Botanic Rail Station
North of Ireland Sport Club
Queen's University
BOTANIC GARDENS
River Lagan
Upper Library St.
York St.
Academy St.
Royal Ave.
North St.
Gresham St.
Talbot St.
Donegall St.
Dunbar Link
Tomb St.
Albert Sq.
Donegall Quay
Waring St.
Queen's Sq.
Marlborough St.
Millfield
Berry St.
Rosemary St.
Lombard St.
High St.
Hill St.
Ann St.
Chapel Ln.
Bank St.
Castle Pl.
King St.
Castle St.
Queen St.
Donegall Pl.
Castle Ln.
Arthur St.
Townhall St.
College St.
Chichester St.
Victoria St.
Oxford St.
College Sq.
Upper Queen St.
Wellington Pl.
Donegall Sq. N.
Buses
Taxi
Donegall Sq. W.
Donegall Sq. E.
Montgomery St.
Gloucester St.
Murray St.
Wellington St.
May St.
Howard St.
Donegall Sq. S.
Little May St.
Brunswick St.
James St. S.
Adelaide St.
Upper Arthur St.
Glengall St.
Franklin St.
Linenhall St.
Hamilton Street
Amelia St.
Bedford St.
Russell St.
Clarence St.
Henrietta St.
Great Victoria St.
Alfred St.
Joy St.
Cromac St.
McAuley St.
Bruce St.
Ormeau Ave.
Bankmore St.
Wellwood St.
Ventry St.
Maryville St.
Apsley St.
Lindsay St.
Albion St.
Dublin Rd.
Howard St. South
Ormeau Rd.
Donegall Pass
Elm St.
Sandy Row
Bradbury Pl.
Botanic Ave.
Vernon St.
Cooke St.
Lower Crescent
McClure St.
Cromwell Rd.
Shaftesbury Ave.
Ireton St.
Wolseley St.
Upper Crescent
Mount Charles
India St.
University Rd.
University St.
Fitzroy Ave.
University Sq.
College Park
Rugby Rd.
Balfour Ave.
0
1/4 Mi
0.25 Km
N

dancing, and go all out on decor. After all, image is the key to success of such a place. Two places in particular to look out for are **Milk** and **Tatu.** Both are new and trendy beyond belief.

Traditional pubs, which generally (though by no means exclusively) cater to an older crowd, are identified by their cozy, wood-paneled decor, mellow vibe, and dim lighting. In other words, they're great for an afternoon pint or a night of conversation with friends. Many of the traditional pubs in Belfast are in the city center. They fill up during lunchtime and afternoons before emptying out around 5:30, filling up again in the evening before closing early, sometimes by 10pm. The early close may strike you as odd, but consider this: These pubs *were* good night spots until they all got firebombed. As the violence continued, people retreated into their own neighborhoods to drink and the city center became a late-night no-man's land. Things are starting to pick up. Places like O'Neill's can get packed, but you'd never know it by the surrounding streets. The best traditional pubs in the city include The Crown Liquor Saloon, Robinson's, and the city center's Morning Star, and White's Tavern.

A busy, large pub next door to St. George's Market, the **Magennis/Whiskey Café** *(May St. at Victoria St.; Tel 02890/230295; No credit cards)* hums on market days (Tuesdays and Fridays). You can grab a good pub lunch for under £4. There is another room off the main room, the Whiskey, which opens at night mostly, and offers a lounge replete with leather couches and a DJ spinning mainly R&B. Cover bands play at Magennis on the weekends.

Although it may not be as beautiful as its famous neighbor, The Crown, **Robinson's Bar** *(38-40 Great Victoria St.; Tel 0123/902-4477; No credit cards)* is arguably more fun. It's huge, with a big front room that gets busy on weekends and a smaller back room filled with old bottles and *objet d'art* of times long gone. The back room hosts trad and rock sessions several times a week. The crowd is lively and there are often sporadic outbreaks of dancing.

The Crown Bar *(46 Great Victoria St.; Tel 0123/9024-9476; No credit card)* is the granddaddy of Belfast pubs. This Victorian masterpiece is obscenely ornate, almost gaudy, and charming as all hell. Hand-blown glass, plaster, brass, and wood all are illuminated softly by warm lights that still burn gas. It's often filled with tourists, but is so beautiful that it doesn't matter. The Crown's other big plus are its *snugs:* large booths with doors that drown out the din of the bar and add intimacy to the experience. There are little bells in each snug that you ring to order more pints, but there isn't wait service here anymore, so ringing them will do little more than irritate your bartender. There is also a pub camera broadcasting live feed images of the bar on the Internet: ***www.belfasttelegraph.co.uk/crown.***

One of the oldest pubs in the world, the 350-year-old **White's Tavern** *(Wine Cellar Entry; Tel 0123/9024-3080; No credit cards)* has atmosphere to burn. Ancient wood juts out at odd angles, creating enticing nooks and crannies. Chunky wood tables and dim lighting add to the rustic appeal.

drinking by numbers

You'll probably find yourself doing a lot of drinking in Ireland. Fortunately, there are a lot of great homegrown brews to choose from. Try them all and find your favorite. To get you started, here's a handy guide to the Irish brews and their alcohol content.

Guinness: 4.2 percent. Black, heavy, creamy, bitter, like a full meal. You can float a matchstick or a bottle cap on top.

Caffry's: 4.3 percent. Like milk it's so creamy. Medium-bodied and dark amber color. Easy to drink and smooth as silk.

Smithwick's: 3.8 percent. Brassy, a tad bitter with a strong taste. Most say it's an acquired taste, for others it's love at first sip.

Kilkenny: a whopping 4.8 percent. More bitter and darker than Caffry's but equally smooth. That extra .5 percent. alcohol really makes a difference over the course of an evening.

Harp: 4 percent. Lightweight, golden lager. Crisp and refreshing, it's a good place to start for those unaccustomed to the heavy Irish brews.

Tennents: 4 percent. A new edition. Like an Irish version of Honey Brown. What teenagers drink out of paper bags. Still worth a try. Its main virtue is that it's usually the cheapest beer in a pub and often served as a drink special during happy hours or special promo nights.

Bru (aka **White Guinness)** 4.5 percent. A misfire from the usually reliable Guinness corporation. Not yet but soon to be available in every pub, it's the Guinness version of wheat beer. Light in color and cloudy, it's unfiltered and has a slight sweetness to it. Piss-water or delicious drink? You decide.

Strongbow Cider: 4.5 percent. Fruity and sweet, crisp, and lots of bubbles. Great for afternoons or if you're not in the mood for a heavy beer. Deadly if you drink too much of it.

It's the kind of place where you'd expect to see sawdust on the floor. As with most city center pubs, it can close early or be very dead on weeknights. But by day, it's full of people grabbing a quick pint on their lunch break. At night, the crowd is surprisingly young and punk-bohemian.

Set in a relaxed and dimly lit interior with a Spanish flavor, the **Bodega Bar** *(4 Callendra Street; Tel 0123/9024-3177; No credit cards)* hosts a crowd as mellow as the weathered brick on the walls. The sun's rays accent your beer's frothy head through stained glass windows. You can also get a mean plate of fries here [see *eats,* below].

A busy, centrally located pub, **The Morning Star** *(Pottingers Entry; Tel 0123/9032-3976; No credit cards)* embodies the traditional pub feel. It has dark wood on the walls and leather booths that are so comfortable you could wile away years here before you know it. This pub attracts a mix of people from kids to pensioners, students to business people. It's a busy, noisy, and fun place to enjoy a midweek pint.

Further downtown, **The Crescent Townhouse/Bar Twelve** *(13 Lower Crescent; Tel 02890/323349)* is a relaxed, older person's pub. The big draw here is the enormously popular Great Music Quiz, a rousing test of music trivia. What is Van Morrison's weight in kebabs? Come here to find out.

A university institution, the **Botanic Bar** *(23 Malone Rd.; Tel 02890/ 660460; Open late)* is usually chock full of students. The upstairs has been remodeled into a disco that pumps that crazy disco beat Thurs-Sat, but the music scene is trad on some nights, modern on others. The large downstairs bar itself is nothing spectacular, but the vibe is familiar, everyone is chatty, and you can play Who Want's to be a Millionaire with questions about the U.K. you'll probably never be able to answer. Dress is extremely casual on weeknights; on weekends people try a bit harder.

Right across the street from the "Bot," you'll find the "Egg," **Eglantine Bar** *(32 Malone Road; Tel 02890/381994; Open late)*. Equally popular with students around here, it's similar to the Bot, but a little more flashy. The vibe is more glamour, and you're likely to see sequined midriff tops and hair with lots of petroleum products in it. Still, not the least bit pretentious.

Morrison's *(21 Bedford St.; Tel 02890/24-8458; No credit cards)* is a brilliant pub remodeled to look old. The new/old design makes the vibe as relaxed as at a traditional pub, but draws a very sophisticated clientele. Big and comfortable, it's surprisingly dead on weeknights: Come on a Friday or Saturday for excellent live rock and trad. The crowd is a mix of students and young urban professionals who are cool but not cold. On Saturday nights, the upstairs area is transformed into a hip-hop/R+B party known as the "Beat Suite."

The rough and eclectic crowd, coupled with the rustic interior makes **Laverly's Gin Place** *(12 Bradbury Place; Tel 02890/327159; No credit cards)* seem more like a saloon than a pub. Bikers, students, business-people, and all other forms of drinker gather here nightly. Come here and judge for yourself whether it's a beautiful mosaic of drinking culture or a cluttered mess.

The place to see and be seen in Belfast is **Tatu** *(701 Lisburn Road; Tel 02890/380818)*. Slick, pretentious, and expensive, Tatu is located in the trendy Lisburn Road strip. It has a modern interior, great lighting (you'll look marvelous), and beautiful people. Dress to impress or you may not get in. Warning: Queues are looooong on weekends.

Milk *(Tomb St.; Tel 02890/278876; www.clubmilk.com; £3-£8 cover weeknights, £10 Fri & Sat)* is rumored to be the coolest new club and bar in town. "Milk 54," a disco-laden recreation of the legendary NYC nightspot, is held on Thursday nights. On weekends, expect to hear a pulsing mix of garage and R&B. Check out their web site to find out what's going on.

live music scene

The live music scene in Belfast is great. It's not uncommon to see indie rock heroes like Yo La Tengo and Belle and Sebastian pass through town, and the local bands know how to rock. Trad is also well represented, as is jazz to a lesser extent. If you want a good take on U.K. music culture, check out ***The Fly,*** a free monthly mag reviewing albums, bands, gigs, and rock and roll philosophy. (No relation to The Fly bar.) Pick up a copy at any record store, many pubs, and many bookstores. Check their web page at www.channelfly.com.

For live, loud rock and roll music, you can't beat the **Empire** *(42 Botanic Ave.; Tel 02890/249276; £3-5 cover).* Once a church, it's now a multi-floor rock and roll temple. Empire pulls in big-name indie bands and the best of local rockers. They also have comedy night [see *performing arts,* below] on Tuesdays and trad sessions on Thursday. The crowd is grungy, dedicated, and definitely knows what's happening. People of all ages come here in their leather jackets and jeans. Indie rock and low-fi are the staples of the Empire's repertoire.

Featuring mostly live rock and roll, **Katy Daly's,** *(17 Ormeau Ave.; Tel 02890/325942; £3-5 cover)* can go neck and neck with the Empire. Trad and folk sessions also happen here once in a blue moon—check for specifics before you come. Katy has the added bonus of being connected to **Limelight** [see *club scene,* below], one of the best dance spots in Belfast. Katy's also hosts *Iration,* a soul-dub party every other Sunday. Call for info.

Auntie Annie's *(Dublin Road; Tel 02890/501660; Call 01232/325942 for open mike info; Doors open 9-10pm; £3-4 cover)* is a sweet little dive with two floors of live music every night. Everything from sensitive, singer/songwriters to angry goth, punk, and metal bands perform here. Monday night is open mike night, so bring your acoustic and your original songs.

rules of the game

Some people say that drugs like Ecstasy and ketamine have done a lot to calm Belfast down from its hard-drinking, hard-fighting former self. Nevertheless, it's all illegal and you don't want to just start puffing away on a crowded street. You'll see and hear people snorting stuff in bathrooms at some of the hipper spots. This is something you're better off not doing. Watch out in general, as getting caught will mean rough treatment from the guys in the armored paddy wagons that cruise the party boulevards on weekends.

club scene

Belfast's best and most popular club nights are Saturdays. When walking around town, look for flyers at any record or trendy clothing shop in the city center or university area. Keep an eye out for what suits your fancy.

If you are remotely interested in clubbing, music, or any other sort of urban debauchery, we strongly suggest you stop by **Apache Clothing** [see *duds,* below]. Sort of a DJ's collective that sells clothes, it has in-house DJ's passing through every day (as well as stocking the shelves with clothes). Apache hosts some of the best parties at local clubs including *Beat Suite* on Saturdays at **Morrison's Bar** [see *bar scene,* above]. It's also the best place to get info on what's happening. If you spin, call ahead and they'll let you have a go at the turntables for a few hours right in the shop. This shop is thoroughly committed to making Belfast the youth mecca it ought to be.

Connected to **Katy Daly's** [see *live music scene,* above], **Limelight** *(till 2am Thur-Sat, usually; No phone; £5 or less)* deserves a separate mention. Some of the best, most attitude-free dancing in Northern Ireland happens here. The scene is undeniably cool without being pretentious. Music runs the spectrum of electronic beats to DJ remixes, but it's always excellent.

If you're lookin' for action with the opposite sex, you might just find it at **The Fly** *(Lower Crescent Street; Tel 02890/235666; No cover).* It's definitely not your father's Irish pub. Decked out in their Saturday best, local hipsters congregate here for drinks, dancing, and so-so music. The club is adorned with metal-worked flies with inset stained glass eyes and has a generally buggy feeling. You'll find the main bar on the first floor. The second floor has a DJ, but the super-cool "Absolut Vodka lounge" on the third level is definitely the place to see and be seen. Its recessed lighting and curved couches, tables, and bar have a Korova Milk Bar feel (there, now all you New Yorkers feel at home, and all you non-New Yorkers don't—just how we like it....). It's the place to prowl.

The Brunswick *(10 Brunswick St.; Tel 02890/581222)* is a mammoth, five-level club with a downstairs bar playing jazzy stuff, a pizza parlor around the corner, and upper floors devoted to eclectic music, from hip-hop to hard house. Look for flyers announcing parties here. The best one is *Vigos,* featuring hard techno and bouncing hip hop.

As you approach Joy's Alley on a Saturday night, you may think someone has given you bad directions as High Street will be dead as disco. Once you get inside **O'Neill's** *(Joy's Alley off of High Street, No phone),* you'll be engulfed in a wave of hundreds of sweaty bodies dancing to hip hop, acid jazz, or funk under pulsating lights and very live DJ's. There may be users of alternative substances enjoying the sounds, but the bouncers are real assholes, so watch yourself. And dress to impress.

Manhattan *(Bradbury Place; Tel 02890/233131; £4)* is a big cheesy disco and also a major pickup joint. Get dressed up in your flashiest clothes, order a bottle of imported beer, and start scopin'. Those who prefer pills to punch, glowsticks to glitter, and baggy t-shirts to spandex halters would

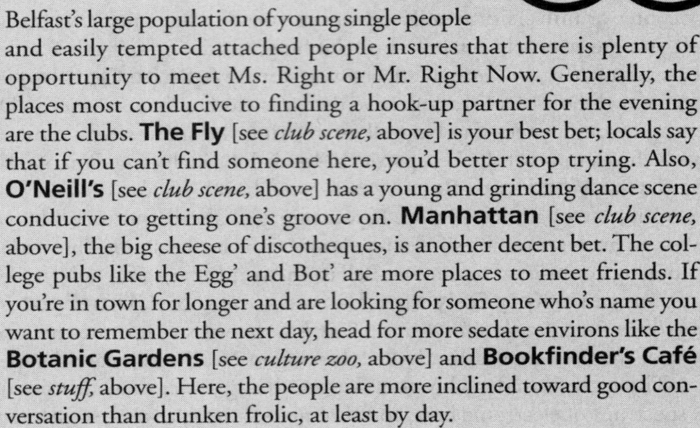

lad meets lass

Belfast's large population of young single people and easily tempted attached people insures that there is plenty of opportunity to meet Ms. Right or Mr. Right Now. Generally, the places most conducive to finding a hook-up partner for the evening are the clubs. **The Fly** [see *club scene,* above] is your best bet; locals say that if you can't find someone here, you'd better stop trying. Also, **O'Neill's** [see *club scene,* above] has a young and grinding dance scene conducive to getting one's groove on. **Manhattan** [see *club scene,* above], the big cheese of discotheques, is another decent bet. The college pubs like the Egg' and Bot' are more places to meet friends. If you're in town for longer and are looking for someone who's name you want to remember the next day, head for more sedate environs like the **Botanic Gardens** [see *culture zoo,* above] and **Bookfinder's Café** [see *stuff,* above]. Here, the people are more inclined toward good conversation than drunken frolic, at least by day.

thumb their noses at this place, but you shouldn't let that stop you from having fun. There are three giant floors, all with flashy lights and good sound. If you're low on cash or suck at dancing, just go to the first floor bar (no cover) and hit on people on their way out. If you want to dance, go upstairs, pay the man, and cut loose 'cuz you're a stud muffin superstar.

▸▸PARTIES

Belfast has a number of weekly or biweekly parties to suit every taste. Bouncers are pretty easygoing around town but they can smell trouble, so don't mess with them. Dress codes vary depending on venue.

First, there are the **early parties,** to get you revved up for the night out. One of the most popular early parties in town is *Strutt (8:30pm Sat; £2),* a pre-club event at the **Empire** [see *live music,* above]. Jazz, deep house, funk, drum and bass and electronica are all spun in a funky, get-your-energy-up mix.

Fuel features "4-star quality house music." It takes place at **Strike Four** *(Bedford St.; Tel 02890/238238; 8pm-1am).* Cheap drink specials include £1 vodka and cokes or the deadly £1.95 Fuel Cocktail, a sweet, peppy mix of spirits. It's also free, so major props there.

And let's not forget *Clubversive,* Boy George's (of Culture Club fame) radio club show from 6 to 8pm on 96.7 FM. This is the traveling poor alternative: You can have a pre-party for free between the headphones of your Walkman.

Then there are the **prime time parties.** *Shine (in the Student Union at Queen's University, off of University Road; Tel 02890/324803; Doors open at 8pm; £10)* is one of the best parties in Belfast. Located in the Student

Union of Queen's University, this Saturday night treat offers the best crowds, DJs, and atmosphere anywhere in town. It's one of the most expensive places to dance, but well worth it if you love great dancing. You're technically supposed to be a student to come here, but it's doubtful that they'll give you trouble getting in.

If you're into garage and house with a distinctly west of the Atlantic feel, check out *Congress (Thompson's Garage; 3 Patterson Place; Tel 02890/323762; 9pm-3am; £10).*

Roots (Thur biweekly; Venue changes; £3) is a funk, soul, jazz, Latin, reggae party with the Beat Suite DJ's creating a laid-back atmosphere and some seriously soulful grooves. The Belfast Drum Circle, a loose collective of local percussionists, often makes an appearance. Keep a look out for fliers or check out **Apache Clothing** [see *duds,* above] for details.

And just when you thought you'd had enough, there are the **after-hours parties.** Looking to dance till the cows come home? *Network (11a Lower North St.; Tel 02890/237486; Midnight to 6am; No denim jeans; £10)* is a good late-night option, featuring resident DJ's Dan Jericho and Jamek. This party may change locations, so look for fliers at record stores and pubs.

arts scene

Belfast has an active and growing arts scene. Whatever you fancy, you can find it here. In the past few years, indie art has gotten big, and each week there are a number of alternative theater, art, and film events all over the city. Graffiti art is making a showing these days; check out **Apache Clothing** [see *duds,* below] for info. Most of the modern art in Belfast is, like everywhere in Ireland, restricted to dark, earthy pallets, and features abstract, subtle brushstrokes.

▸▸VISUAL ARTS SCENE

In addition to the **Ulster Museum** [see *culture zoo,* below], which has a decent collection of international, mostly modern, work, there are a number of other spots to see art.

Home to four spacious galleries on two levels, the **Ormeau Baths Gallery** *(18a Ormea Avenue; Tel 02890/321402; Mon-Sat 10am-6pm; Free)* displays contemporary art from both sides of the Atlantic. Exhibitions change all the time, so call and find out wuzzup'. The gallery is in an old Victorian bathhouse that closed 14 years ago and was made into the present gallery in '95.

The smaller **Frendersky Art Gallery** *(At the Crescent Art Center; University Road; Tel 02890/242338; Mon-Sat 10am-5pm; Free)* displays modern art as well. Exhibitions change frequently, and lean more toward the avant-garde.

For photography, check out **Belfast Exposed** *(48 King St.; Tel 02890/230965, Fax 02890/314551; 10am-6pm weekdays, 10 am-10pm Thur-Fri, noon-6pm Sat; belfastexposed@hotmail.com; Free)* a multi-purpose space for photography exhibition and education. As the name suggests, the work displayed explores life in Belfast. A new collection of more

festivals and events

Among the highlights of the Belfast festival year is the **Belfast Summerfest.** During Summerfest, the streets of the city center come alive with music, parades, street performers, and general good will toward humankind. Runs from around May 20 to June 4. *(Tel. 90/270345; www.belfastcity.gov.uk/summerfest)*

July 12 brings the **Orange Parades** when various Protestant groups flaunt their victory over Catholics in the 1690 Battle of the Boyne. It's often a time of turbulence, bringing arrests, riots and all sorts of trouble. Probably a good time to *not* be in town.

From around Oct. 27 to Nov 12, the **Belfast Festival at Queen's** brings in performing artists from around the world for a series of shows in and around Queen's University. Check it out at www.belfastfestival.com.

than 400,000 images documenting the last 18 years in the city was underway when we were in town. The collection will be displayed on a rotating basis, exploring different aspects of the city's turbulent past. Other exhibits explore the vision of the city through individual artists. The coffee shop downstairs has live acoustic music on Thursdays from 8 to 10pm.

▸▸PERFORMING ARTS

One of the most pleasant surprises of Belfast's performing arts scene is its lively comedy scene. It's a good way to get a feel for the resilient sense of humor Belfast has about its turbulent place in the world. The comedy stage seems to give both comedian and audience a forum to let off steam. After a night of listening to people on all sides of the spectrum get thoroughly roasted, you're likely to appreciate this place a lot more. Of course, it's not all heavy stuff—comedians still make plenty of sex and poop jokes. The best venues for comedy are Tuesday nights at the **Empire Bar** [see *live music,* above] and **The Laughter Loft** *(Great Victoria St.; Tel 02890/247447; Shows Thurs-Sat; Cover £5).*

Next to the Europa Hotel, the **Grand Opera House** *(Great Victoria St.; Tel 02890/240041; Tickets available at Booking Office, 17 Wellington Place; Tel 02890/241919; Concession tickets start at £10)* is a beautiful old Victorian building. It shows everything from modern Irish dramas by Martin McDonnough to cult screenings of *The Sound of Music,* where nuns and transvestites gather to sing the songs, drink beer, and scream out their favorite lines (like a European *Rocky Horror Picture Show*). The house itself first opened in 1895, designed as a diversion for the Victorian people of the city, wealthy and otherwise. The boxes to the left and right of the stage give a better view of the audience than of the stage, which was the whole point of paying what in today's money would be £500 for a seat. The design elements were intended to evoke the "east"; to 19th-century audiences, that meant most anything east of the Lagan, so the range of symbolism and decoration is truly eclectic. A Star of David decorates a window in the upper balcony, several elephants grace the walls, and pineapples, a very rare commodity in those days and a symbol of hospitality to rich folk, speckle the ornate panels around the upper deck of the place. The architect was only consulted twice during the project, once at the outset of construction and once on opening night, and you can tell. It's still a great room to see theater. Seats for plays run about £8-16. Call or visit the ticket office across the street to find out what's playing or to buy tickets.

At the **Arts Theater** *(41 Botanic Ave.; Inquiries 02890/316900, box office 02890/316900; £5-10 for tickets)* the resident company most commonly performs here, though the theater features a wide range of productions, from one man or woman shows to stuff from out of town. Call the inquiry line to find out what's on.

The **Lyric Theater** *(55 Ridgeway St.; Tel 02890/381081; Show times 8pm and 2:30pm matinee on Saturday; £7.50-10 for tickets, weekday student discounts of £2)* performs mostly serious drama. Ibsen, Chekov, as well as modern Irish playwrights all play here. Local hero Liam Neeson got his first serious gigs here.

The **Group Theater** *(Bedford St.; Tel 02890/9323900; Call for prices and show times)* is a good place to see small, local productions, ranging from avant-garde to traditional. You may luck out and catch some undiscovered genius here. Call and find out what's on.

For film, **Queen's Film Theater** *(Off Botanic Ave. near the college; Tel 0800-328-2811; www.qub.ac.uk/qft; £4.20, nightly £3.20 concession; £3.20 matinees, £2.80 concession)* is the art house cinema in town. Showing a mix of classics and new "art" films, it's a pleasant alternative to Hollywood fodder.

If you're into Hollywood fodder, get thee to **Virgin Cinemas** *(14 Dublin Road; Tel 02890/245700, Book by credit card at 0541-55-5176; £4.50, £3.50 concession).*

gay scene

Belfast's gay scene is definitely happening, but you may not realize it walking down the street. It's a don't-walk-too-close-to-each-other kind of place. It's likely that you'll get funny looks and the occasional verbal harassment if you walk hand in hand with your partner. Most people probably wouldn't have a problem, but the occasional jerk might. The clubs and bars are cool, though, so check them out.

For information on services and all things gay and lesbian, contact the **Rainbow Project N.I.** *(33 Church St.; Tel 02890/319030; Mon-Fri 10am-4pm)* or the **Lesbian Line** *(Tel 02890/238668; Thur 7:30-10pm).*

Belfast's gay scene offers a decent range of places to go. For bars, **Queen's Bar** *(Queen's Arcade off of Fountain St.; 02890/321347)* is a mixed and friendly watering hole.

down and out

There are a number of spendy things to do in Belfast, but it doesn't cost a dime to walk around. You can see the murals in **West Belfast** [see *wall of trouble,* above]. Then check out the **Ormeau Baths Gallery** [see *visual arts scene,* above], splay out on the grass in **Donegal Place** [see *culture zoo,* above]. At night, see an art flick at the **Queen's Film Theater** [see *visual arts scene* above] for a paltry £2.80. For food, hit any **Boots Pharmacy** (they're everywhere) and grab a sandwich, soda, and crisps for £2.50. End your evening over club soda and live jazz at the **Europa Hotel Lounge** (bottom floor of the Europa Hotel; see *crashing,* below]

Karaoke, anyone? **The Crow's Nest** *(26 Skipper St.; Tel 02890/325491)* is frequented by an older crowd—thirty and fortysomethings—and has popular quiz nights, drag shows, and musical entertainment.

You'll find something happening every night of the week at **Kremlin** *(96 Donegal St.; Tel 02890/809700; Fax 02890/809701; www.kremlinbelfast.com),* the biggest gay club in town, where DJs spin glammy house and techno to a gay and lesbian crowd. From bingo to the famous **Bang Cock** party, an Asian-themed meat market on Saturday nights, there is something to suit every taste.

Another club/bar is **The Parliament Bar** *(2 Dunbar St.; Tel 02890/234520).* The crowd is free-wheelin', diverse, and fun; expect gay and lesbian, both young and old. The bar turns into a disco on Saturday night. On Mondays, things are more subdued, with classical music, dinner, and chess matches.

culture zoo

It's not Dublin, but this city of Queen's University is a center of art and culture—not just bombings—and you can easily spend a full day exploring its attractions. If time is running out, opt at least for the Botanic Gardens, the Ulster Museum, and maybe the magnificent City Hall. The city center is the cultural hub so it's easy to walk to all the most intriguing places. After a decade of everyone going into hiding at night, cultural Belfast is thriving once again, as fears diminish. Some of the world's leading artists are showing up once more to perform to large audiences who now attend theater, concerts, and the visual arts without fear of harm. If you want to pick one area to concentrate your sight-seeing on, the **Queen's University Area** [see *neighborhoods,* above] is a good choice.

Queen's University Belfast *(visitor's center: Lanyon Room, University Road; Tel 02890/325252; 10-4pm Mon-Sat, closed Sat Oct-Apr. The University grounds are, of course, open 24/7):* The buildings of the North's best university are brilliant examples of Tudor architecture. There is a great vibe generated by all the students here, and a walk around the campus is well worth your time. Pick up a map of the grounds in the visitors center, study it on the sly, then conceal it well so you might pass for a student.

Botanic Gardens *(Stranmillis Road; Tel 02890/324902; 8am-dusk daily; 9am-noon/1-5pm Mon-Fri, 1-5pm Sat; Free):* In the middle of Queen's University are these peaceful, immaculately maintained gardens filled with pasty students on sunny days. It's a great place for a picnic. Bright flowers of every size and shape, winding corridors of fragrant greens, reds, and yellows make you forget you're in a city. Don't forget the Botanic Gardens' beautiful **Palm House** *(10-noon/1-5pm Mon-Fri, 1-5pm Sat-Sun Apr-Sep; 10-noon/1-4pm Mon-Fri, 1-4pm Sat-Sun Oct-Mar; Free),* filled with exotic flora. Bring your romantic partner here and discuss pollination.

Ulster Museum *(Stranmillis Rd.; Tel 02890/383000; 10am-5pm Mon-Fri, 1-5pm Sat, 2-5pm Sun; Free):* Also on the grounds of the university is this sprawling, multi-dimensional museum that is ultimately too garbled, too diverse, to keep you riveted to anything for very long. Ranging from Native American and ancient Irish to Arabic and Egyptian to a wildlife and undersea exhibit to coins and the history of the post office, the museum covers too many topics too briefly for any one of them to be truly informative. The steam engine exhibit is great, though. It's got tons of big gears and old metal hunks. Heck, it's at least worth the price of admission.

City Hall *(Donegal Square; Tours 10:30am/11:30am/2:30pm Mon-Fri July-Sept; 2:30pm Mon, Tue, Thur-Sat Oct-June only; Free):* An impressive neoclassical building seen by some as a reminder of British imperialism—

the fool on the hill

Legend has it that Catholic priests moved their parishes out of Belfast central during times of persecution and hid out in the caves in what is now **Cave Hill Country Park** [see *great outdoors,* above]. They supposedly conducted mass and offered their services to local Catholics forbidden to practice their faith. Driving out of town on the northbound A6, you'll question this myth. The caves are perfectly visible from the ground, making Cave Hill perhaps the worst possible place in Belfast to hide. Stone-agers found the hills much more habitable: the caves fit in quite nicely with their stone-age lifestyle, making perfect sanctuaries from wild beasts and giving great vantage points from which to spy would-be invaders.

wall of trouble

West Belfast, home to **murals** depicting the Troubles, is a neighborhood that's been through hell and is, unfortunately, Belfast's most famous "attraction." Although the mural tradition dates back almost 100 years, most of the murals started appearing in the '60s, when conflict in Belfast and Derry heated up. Although a tour of West Belfast will probably not make you feel good about the world, make sure you do make it here—you'll leave a changed person. It's not particularly dangerous to walk around here during the day, but you may get funny looks or mildly offensive comments made in your direction from the locals if you're snapping pictures at every turn. At night, don't even think of coming here. While the peace process seems to be progressing smoothly and violence is down from past years, there are still abductions, killings, and other assorted violent crimes that happen here.

By far the best way to experience this incredible neighborhood is in a **Black Taxi Tour** (arrange at any youth hostel in town). Black Taxi provides safe transportation, and excellent commentary. They take you to these disturbingly beautiful expressions of sectarian conflict, and offer insights into the history of the neighborhoods and the Troubles. Any time you want to take a picture of a mural, just ask and they'll stop for you.

West Belfast's two neighborhoods surround Catholic **Falls Road** and the Protestant **Shankill Road.** Dividing them is the ironically named **Peace Wall,** an ugly slab of industrial metal that attempts to keep both sides to themselves. Originally installed to deter troublemakers from starting shit and then running back to their neighborhood, it's now become more of a Berlin Wall, a symbolic reminder of the differences on both sides. There are several gates in the wall that close at night to deter would-be hooligans.

The murals incorporate several recurrent themes of either Nationalist/Republican (Catholic) or Loyalist/Unionist (Protestant) sentiment. In both neighborhoods, martyrdom, militancy, and vigilance are the main themes. On the Falls Road, one recurring icon is **Bobby Sands.** Sands, a leader of the Nationalist resistance movement, led more than 300 prisoners in a hunger strike in 1981. Sands and many

one look at the creepy statue of Queen Victoria out front may convince you of the same—City Hall is now a place of uneasy coalition between Catholics and Protestants. The tour takes you through the various chambers, murals, and portraits inside. The **council chamber,** where government happens, is the best part of the tour.

Linen Hall Library *(On the northwest corner of Donegal Square across from City Hall; Tel 02890/321707; 9:30am-5:30pm; Mon-Wed, Fri, open till 8:30pm Thur, Sat till 4pm, closed Sun):* Perfect for a lazy day, this is a great others had been thrown in jail and held without trial, as was the procedure of Britain then. They were not given political prisoner status and so starved themselves in protest. While in prison, Sands was elected as an MP (member of Parliament). He died 66 days later. By the end of the strike, 10 were dead. This act, combined with the hard-line attitude of Margaret Thatcher's government, solidified support for the resistance movement and the IRA.

In both the Protestant and Catholic neighborhoods, murals depict fallen leaders of the "struggle," innocent victims of its violence, and depictions of various paramilitary/terrorist groups. On the Falls Road, the IRA, the Real IRA, and the Provisional IRA are all represented. On Shankill Road, the UVF (Ulster Volunteer Force) and numerous other splinter factions are represented. On both sides of the Peace Wall, these "heroes" are represented in a surprisingly similar way. Men clad in black suits and masks tote automatic rifles, depicting both Catholic and Protestant paramilitary/terrorist groups.

In viewing the often glorified depictions of these paramilitary groups, it is important to not let the romantic portrayals of the "struggle" of either side obscure the fact that innumerable lives have been destroyed by parties on all sides of the conflict. Talk to most Belfast residents, especially the young ones, and they'll agree that they're sick of the violence and want peace more than anything else.

You'll also see the **Divas Flats,** a hideous low-income high-rise that once was a hole up for paramilitaries; today its top two floors are a base for the British Army. Helicopters still land on the roof of the flat, and security cameras seem to stick out of every crevice of the building. This is a side of Belfast that you should under no circumstances miss out on; you'll come away with a better knowledge of the divergent attitudes that coexist here. Yet in the end you may find that rather than clarify things, a trip to West Belfast just makes the whole thing even more incomprehensible.

place to get your learn on. Grab a seat by the window on the second floor (the first floor is for members only), and check out the view. The library has a great, worn-in feel to it, more like a second-hand bookshop than a library.

The Ulster Folk and Transportation Museum *(Take Ulsterbus 1 from the Laganside Bus Center or take the A2 road east for about 7 miles to the town of Hollywood; Tel 02890/428428; 10:30am-6pm Mon-Fri, 10:30-6pm Sat, noon-6pm Sun Apr, Jun, Sept 10:30-6pm Mon-Sat, noon-6pm Sun; July-Aug; 9:30-4pm Mon-Fri, 12:30-4:30pm Sat-Sun Oct-March;*

£4): The best museum in Belfast is actually outside of Belfast, but it is cool enough to warrant a full day's visit. The highlight of the museum is the "folk" section, where the "museum village" re-creates life in old Ulster with around 30 actual buildings from all around the region, some dating back to the 18th century. Staff members hang out unobtrusively to answer questions. One of the coolest history exhibits anywhere, the entire complex is a treat, with everything from buggies to trains to a Titanic exhibition (oh yeah, the Titanic was built in Belfast). History buffs and laymen should all make it out here.

great outdoors

To see some green, you don't have to go far. The **Botanic Gardens** [see *culture zoo,* above] is a good bet for chilling out without making a big journey. Several miles north of the city lies the **Lagan Valley Regional Park** *(Citybus 69 or 71 out of the city; Tel 02890/491922; Free)* which

12 hours in belfast

1. First things first, book a Black Taxi Tour of West Belfast and its **murals** [see *culture zoo,* below]. The guides have firsthand knowledge of what's gone on here and provide an invaluable glimpse into the "Troubles." You may feel depressed by the end of the tour, but it's something you owe yourself to see.

2. After the tour, calm your nerves at the **Botanic Gardens** at **Queen's University** [see *culture zoo,* above]. It's a floral wonderland.

3. For a delicious and cheap veggie lunch grab something at **Little India Restaurant** [see *eats,* above].

4. Stroll up the **Golden Mile,** aka Great Victorian Street, home to trendy restaurants, shops, and nightlife spots.

5. Check out the beautiful **City Hall** [see *culture zoo,* above] to splay out on the grass and watch Belfast's youth bask in the sun.

6. Stop into the authentic **Crown Liquor Saloon** [see *bar scene,* above] for a pint. It's one of the most popular tourist bars in the city.

7. Sing along with nuns, transvestites, and other fans of the Von Trapps at a screening of *The Sound of Music* at the **Grand Opera House** [see *performing arts scene,* above].

8. After the show, head down to Crescent Street and have a drink at the trendy **Fly Bar** [see *bar scene,* above]. From there, you can call it a night or crawl your way back to the city center by way of innumerable pubs and clubs.

straddles the River Lagan for 20.92 km (13 miles) and offers pleasant walks through splendid parks, canal paths, trees, birds, bees, and people, all in their natural habitats.

Closer to the city center is **Cave Hill Country Park** *(Off Antrim Rd., Citybus 45 or 51 or drive out on the A2; Tel 02890/776925; Free).* This grassy expanse has caves and hills that stone-aged settlers once called home. But what do you *do* here? Well, you can walk off your beer gut with a hike up to **Cave Hill.** At 1,182-feet high, it's a challenging little climb and offers cool caves to explore and a view of the Mourne Mountains to the southwest. There is also **Belfast Castle,** a charming old mansion that has a great little garden outside. On the third floor, ask to see the long-range camera. It allows you to spy on pretty much anything in Belfast. You too can be Big Brother!

stuff

As in most big cities, shopping is a preoccupation of many Belfast residents. Beyond the usual chain stores in the **Cornmarket,** the area north of Donegal Square, there are cool shops around the university area selling African trinkets, metal objects, and other things that couldn't really fit in your suitcase, but are worth checking out. There are several cool boutiques for clubbers, skaters, and others looking for trendy clothes, shoes, and accessories around the city center that won't break your bank, the best of which we list here.

▸▸HOW BAZAAR

St. George's Market *(Corner of Oxford and May streets; No phone; Open all day Tuesdays and Friday)* is capitalism at its stinkiest. Step through the front gates and the first thing you'll be accosted with is the overwhelming stench of tons of raw fish lying out on tables to your left. If you don't gag, you can continue on and buy fresh fruit, £4 sandals, or even a cheap radio in a brand that sounds like one you've heard of. Worth seeing more for the spectacle of it than for the crap for sale, St. George's Market is a true testament to humanity's love of a bargain.

▸▸CRAFTS

Craftworks *(Bedford St., right off of City Hall; Tel 02890/244465; Mon-Sat 9:30-5:30pm, open till 8:30pm on Thur)* offers a great selection of local crafts. The best examples of handmade jewelry, pottery, textiles, and leather are all for sale.

▸▸DUDS

Apache Clothing *(60 Wellington Place; Tel 02890/32905; 10am-6pm daily; www.apache-tribe.com; No credit cards)* sells club duds, has live DJ's, and is THE place to find out what's happening. Just look for the store on the corner with graffiti art on the front.

For retro styles, check out **Liberty Blue** *(9 Lombard St.; Tel 02890/597555; Visa/MC/Amex).* Funky tunes play as you browse jeans, cords, and pillboxes. No vintage, but the new stuff they sell here isn't that expensive anyway. It's also another good place to get info about clubs in and around the city.

fashion

Belfast fashion is pretty varied and not cut-throat in the least. As in any big city, there are all kinds of people who dress differently. If you're gothic, preppie, clubby, or geeky, you'll fit in. When you're out at slick discos, people dress in tight, glammy clothes—girls wear a lot of flashy, midriff-bearing stuff, while guys go for slacks and tucked in shirts. Guys get off a little easier and girls generally make more of an effort to look good. At college pubs like the **Bot'** and **Egg'** [see *bar scene,* above], people usually look like they've just gotten back from an all-day exam.

Project Clothing *(Pottinger's Entry; Tel 02890/325295; 10-5:30pm Mon-Sat; No credit cards)* sells cool new and used stuff. Not quite as plastic as other young people's clothing shops in town, they have a soulful mix of trendy and classically cool duds.

If you're looking for super swank duds so you can be majorly impressive wherever you go, head to **The Bureau** *(1-4 Wellington Street; Tel 02890/311110; 9:30-5:30pm Mon-Sat).* Staffed by well-dressed young men, it has designer shit, very expensive, but cool as hell.

▸▸SUDS

It's a strange thing to want to eat giant tubs of soap and mud masks, but that's exactly what happens when you walk into **Lush** *(7 Castle Lane; Tel 02890/438672; 10am-5:30pm Mon-Sat).* Henna hair dye is sold by the ladle-full from what looks like a hot and cold buffet. Soap is cut from big slabs that resemble cheese wheels. Lush is easy to find. Just keep your nose up for the perfumey clean smell that wafts through the city center.

▸▸BOUND

For secondhand readables and a snack, swing by **Bookfinder's Café** *(47 University Rd.; Tel 02890/328269; 10am-5:30pm, Mon-Sat; No credit cards).* You'll find a decent selection of used books and a great little cafe in the back that serves up fresh sweets and sandwiches daily. It's vegetarian-friendly. Don't forget to try a cake baked by the owner's grandmother. Mmm.

Ulidia Books *(Shaftsbury Sq.; Tel 02890/597684; 10am-6pm, Mon-Sat)* is a small storefront absolutely crammed with secondhand books, including excellent literature, poetry, and history selections. For your browsing pleasure, two comfy leather armchairs sit amid the stacks on the floor.

Mystery buffs, go to the university quarter's **No Alibis Bookstore** *(83 Botanic Ave.; Tel 90/31-9607; 10am-5:30pm, Mon-Sat; david@noalibis.com)* for an excellent selection of all the classic guys and gals mystery writers, as well as current and local writers like Colin Bateman. There are couches in the back, and free tea and coffee will keep you upright while you peruse the merchandise.

▶▶THRIFT

There isn't much of a vintage clothing market in Belfast, but **Rusty Zip** *(28 Botanic Ave.; 10am-6pm Mon-Sat, till 8pm on Thurs)* sells your basic vintageware. A lot of the stock is on the kitschy side, but there are good finds if you dig.

▶▶TUNES

One of the cooler record shops in Belfast is **Backbeat Music Exchange** *(121 Great Victoria St.; Tel 02890/200397; 10am-6pm Mon-Sat, open till 8pm on Thur; No credit cards).* The most laid-back proprietor in the world will guide you through his delicious vinyl and CD collection. He's got a list of upcoming rock shows in town. Fliers for local clubs and shows are available at the door or at the counter.

A good place for used CD's in the university area is **Knight Records** *(33 Botanic Ave.; Tel 02890/322925; 9:30am-5:30pm Mon-Sat; No credit cards).* A knowledgeable staff knows their way around the crowded shelves.

eats

Belfast cuisine is arguably the finest in Ireland. In a country not known for the variety or delectability of its food, Belfast is a welcome place for gourmands. Indian, Thai, Italian, French, and bistro food are all well represented. There are also tons of bistros, cafes, and takeout stands that serve cheap and generally excellent food. Little-known fact: The best kebabs in the world are in a tiny no-name storefront across from the **Manhattan** disco on Bradbury Place.

▶▶CHEAP

In the mood for a little curry? One of the only completely vegetarian restaurants in Ireland, the **Little India Restaurant** *(55 Dublin Rd.; Tel 02890/583040; Entrees run about £5-7, with rice add £1.50; No credit cards)* offers cheap eats on a student-infested block. The interior is colorful and casual.

Vincent's *(78-80 Botanic Ave.; Tel 02890/242020; Open for breakfast thru dinner; Sandwiches in the £3.25-3.45 range, design a pizza for £5-8)* is a funky, faux arty environment that serves up artistic sandwiches. Try the Gaughin, chicken and hummus, or if you prefer, the Monet, smoked cheese, tomato, and mustard mayo. Or you can opt to design your own masterpiece, a personal pizza. They serve breakfast, too. Check out the veggie fry, with eggs, tomato, soda and potato bread, mushrooms, OJ, and hash browns (£3.25).

When hippies need lentils and brewer's yeast, they go to **The Nutmeg** *(9a Lombard St.; Tel 02890/249984; 10am-5pm Mon-Sat; V, MC).* It's got a good selection of soy products, organic grains, and delicious sweets. No meals, just ingredients for meals.

Imbued with a Spanish flavor, the **Bodega Bar** *(4 Callendra St.; Tel 02890/243177; Sandwiches are £5 and up, dinners £7-10; No credit cards)* does some of the best pub grub in the city. Try the stellar French fries and the astronomically good tuna melt. The comfy restaurant is upstairs, with a spacious bar downstairs.

John's Quality Breads and Cakes *(21 Botanic Ave.; Tel 90-24-7568; Mon-Sat 10-5pm; Sandwiches start at £2)* is a little university-area bakery that serves up cheap and delicious take-away soup for a mere 99p; the sandwiches are a deal, too.

For another excellent lunch option, check out **Bookfinders Café** [see *bound,* above].

If you're looking for food like your mama makes, **Jenny's** *(81 Dublin Rd.; Tel 02890/249282; 8am-4:45pm, Mon-Sat; Lunch items in the £2.50 range)* could be the ticket. It's a great little luncheonette that feels like a small-town diner, with soft green and earth tones making the place nice and mellow. Cheap, hot lunches include lasagna and quiche.

▸▸DO-ABLE

Archana *(53 Dublin Rd.; Tel 02890/323713; Generally open daily 4-11pm, but hours vary; Entrees run £8-10; No credit cards)* is one of a few completely vegetarian restaurants in Ireland. It's delicious and pricier than its downstairs neighbor, Little India, but its décor is a tad more elegant, and the service is more...well, elegant. Despite the more expensive food, dinner here is still a casual affair. Students, yuppies, and businesspeople all eat here.

For that Continental feeling that you've been dying for, try **Café Society** *(3 Donegal Square East; Tel 02890/439525; Prices range from about £4.95 for lunch to £7-10 for dinner)*. It's a cute little place that does a pretty good job of evoking the feeling of a French café, from the wrought iron railings leading up the staircase to the rack of wine bottles behind the bar. The downstairs bistro is open for lunch, the upstairs for lunch and dinner. You can get a good sandwich for lunch; dinners mainly consist of excellent chicken and meat dishes.

Café Laziz *(99 Botanic Ave.; Tel 02890/234888; Entrees £9-11, Lunch £5)* serves good Moroccan cuisine. Lots of lamb and chicken with garlic, mushrooms, and saffron. Décor is tasteful with lots of white and red.

Nick's Warehouse *(35/39 Hill Street; tel. 028/9043-9690; lunches £8; dinner main courses £5.20-£9.60; noon-3pm Mon-Fri; 6-9:30pm Tues-Sat; AE, DC, MC, V)*, changes its menu daily to take advantage of the best local produce. This former warehouse has been transformed into a popular wine bar-cum-restaurant with wrought-iron culinary sculptures, an open kitchen, and brick walls. "We're trendy and tasty," the chef assures us. You'll believe him as you dip into a casserole of local venison with a red wine and pearl barley sauce; penne pasta with roasted sweet peppers; or especially a fennel and leek risotto with Cambazola and sweet pepper compote. The baked lemon tart with crème fraîche is reason enough to save room for one of the chef's nightly "puddings," as they say here.

crashing

Belfast has five hostels, not a lot considering the dozens in Dublin and Galway, and the city's size. Beds fill up fast year-round so book ahead. All of

wired

Belfast is serviced by several Internet cafes. The best and most central are in Shaftsbury Square. **Revelations** *(27 Shaftsbury Sq.; Tel 02890/320337; 10am-10pm Mon-Fri, 10am-6pm Sat, 11am-7pm Sun; £3/hour for students and hostellers (bring your isic card), £4 for everyone else)* has decent snacks like nachos and a bustling, friendly atmosphere. As a special courtesy, they'll scan in a photo for free so you can e-mail it to your pals back home. Also a good way to let your mom know you're still alive. (She'll appreciate that.)

Belfast's hostels are at least passably clean but not all of them are particularly fun or friendly. All the B&B's listed here are good quality and pretty similar—clean rooms, decent breakfasts, and nice people. Pay a few more pounds and you'll get a bathroom attached to your room and a fancier set of silverware, but unless you're a stickler for that stuff, the cheaper places are just as good as the expensive ones. Hotels range in quality from clean and comfortable to luxurious. If you have money to spend, you can live it up. Prices are often lower on the weekend for hotels as most cater to business travelers.

▸▸CHEAP

What **Arnie's Backpackers** *(63 Fitzwilliam St.; Tel 02890/242867; Bus 71 from Donegal Square; Dorms £7.50 in 3-6 bed rooms; No credit cards)* lacks in tidiness it makes up for in character. This place defines independent hostel spirit with its jovial owner, fun-loving guests, and relaxed surroundings. Its small size makes it a welcome port in a big city. The common room and kitchen are adjacent and create a social atmosphere. There are even two Jack Russell Terriers (Snowy and Rosy) for you to play with. It gets hot and crowded to the point of cramped in the summer, so if you're the private type, it may not be the place for you. Call ahead at least a week in the summer, as it's the most popular hostel in Belfast. From the Europa Bus Terminal, head south on Great Victoria Street and continue through Bradbury Place to University Road. Take your fourth right onto Fitzwilliam and you'll be at Arnie's. You can also book a **Black Taxi Tour** here [see *culture zoo,* above].

The Ark *(18 University St.; Tel 02890/329626; Bus 71 from Donegal Square; £6.50 6-bed dorms, £7.50 4-bed dorms, £30 doubles, long-term stays can be negotiated; No credit cards)* has a fantastic location right in the university area and is well-equipped. The Ark is a good place to go if you're looking to work in Belfast. There is a job bulletin board with good advice about where to go for jobs. The dorms are decent; the beds are too. The one drawback is 2am curfew. Otherwise it's a pleasant spot. Follow directions for Arnie's to University Road, then take your fourth *left* onto University Street.

Macpackers *(1 Cameron St.; Tel 02890/220485; Bus 71 from Donegal Sq.; £7.50 for bed in 4-6 bed dorm; No credit cards)* is the latest addition to

Belfast's hostel scene. It was closed for remodeling at the time of writing, but judging from Steve's other hostel in Derry, Steve's Backpackers, it's a good bet. Stay four nights and get the fifth free here or in Derry. From the Europa Hotel, go south on Great Victoria Street. At Shaftsbury Square, take Botanic Avenue and take the third left at the **Empire** club [see *club scene,* abve] onto Cameron Street.

Huge, austere, and sans kitchen, the **Belfast International Youth Hostel** *(22 Donegal Rd.; Tel 02890/324733; Bus 71 from Donegal Square; £8-10 for bed in 4-6 bed dorms, £40 doubles; V, M, Switch)* caters to large groups. It has an enormous common room, so the vibe is not that intimate. The rooms, however, are clean and have wash basins. Showers down the hall are quite hot and powerful. Breakfast will set you back a couple of pounds for eggs, cereal, bacon, and toast. Located on the outskirts of the Sandy Row neighborhood, a notoriously sketchy Protestant enclave, it's recommended that you do not stray east of the hostel at night. From Europa Bus Terminal, take Great Victoria Street south and turn left at Shaftsbury Square onto Donegal Road.

The largest independent hostel in Ireland, **The Linen House** *(18 Kent St.; Tel/Fax 02890/586400; Beds £6.50, £7.50 or £8.50 for 18-, 8-, or 6-bed dorm with bath; No credit cards),* is housed in an old linen factory. Although fine during the day, the neighborhood is completely dead and can be dangerous at night due to its proximity to the Falls/Shankill neighborhoods. Walking home alone at night is not recommended. It's also about a million miles from the University and the Golden Mile. There is a cool common room in the basement with snooker game and couches. The beds and rooms are okay, but the showers can be temperamental with heat. Internet access is cheap at 50p/10 minutes. From Europa Bus Station, head north on Great Victoria, turn right at Howard Street, left onto Donegal Square West, swing around to the right to the front side of Donegal Square and cross the street onto Donegal Place. It turns into Royal Avenue, and then take a left onto Kent Street.

Queen's University *(78 Malone Rd.; Tel 02890/381608; Bus 71 from Donegal Square; £9.40/11.75 for student/non-student rooms, singles and doubles only; V, MC, AE, Switch)* houses travelers from June to September and on Christmas and Easter breaks. The setting is institutional and sterile, but you get a big, clean room cheap. From the Europa Hotel, follow directions to Arnie's until you get to University Road. Continue on University until it turns into Malone Road. About a 30-minute walk from Europa or take the bus.

▸▸DO-ABLE

In the University area on Eglantine Avenue, **Liserin Guest House** *(17 Eglantine Ave.; Tel 02890/660769; £20 per person),* **The George** *(9 Eglantine Ave.; Tel 02890/683212; £20 per person; V, MC)* and **The Eglantine Guesthouse** *(21 Eglantine Ave.; Tel 02890/667584; £20 per person, No credit cards)* all provide comfortable B&B's at an excellent value. All of these places have big Irish breakfasts and comfortable beds for reasonable prices.

The sheets are a bit whiter, the china a bit fancier, and the price a bit higher at the **Avenue Guest House** *(23 Eglantine Ave.; Tel 02890/665904; £35 per person; All rooms have bath; No credit cards).*

The Holiday Inn Express *(106a University St.; Tel 02890/311909, Fax 02890/311910; £32.50 mid-week per person, £27.50 weekend per person; express@holidayinn-ireland.com; www.holidayinn-ireland.com V, MC, AE, D)* offers reasonable rates for clean, plain, comfortable hotel rooms in a good location.

Other do-able options include **Botanic Lodge Guesthouse** *(87 Botanic Ave.; Tel. 02890/327682)* and **Helga Lodge** *(7 Cromwell Rd.; Tel. 02890/324820).*

▶▶SPLURGE

Because it was once the place international journalists stayed when they came to town, **The Europa** *(Great Victoria St.; Tel 02890/327000; Fax 02890/327800; res@eur.hastingshotels.com; www.hastingshotels.com; £95 mid-week, £45 weekend; V, MC, AE, DC, Switch)* was the most bombed hotel in the world (32 times at last count). But it is still a beautiful place to stay, with plush rooms, comfortable beds, room service, and little mints on your pillow. Once a place to plant a bomb, now a place that is da' bomb. The Europa is worth seeing for its history (Bill Clinton and friends slept here, too), and just outside the Europa Bus Station, it's close to everything.

Another splurge is **McCausland Hotel** *(34-38 Victoria St.; Tel. 02890/220200).*

need to know

Currency Exchange **Thomas Cook** *(22-24 Lombard St.; Tel 02890/883800),* **Ulster Bank** *(Donegal Square West; Tel 02890/270909),* **Bank of Ireland** *(54 Donegal Pl.; Tel 02890/244901),* and **Northern Bank** *(Donegal Square West; Tel 02890/245277)* all have 24-hour ATM's and *Bureax de Change.* All the banks are open 9am-4:30pm.

Tourist Information The **Tourist Office** *(59 North St. at St. Anne's Court; Tel 02890/246609; 9am-7pm Mon-Fri, 9am-5:15pm Sat, noon-4pm Sun July-Aug; 9:30am-5:15pm Mon, 9am-5:15pm Tue-Sat Sept-June)* has an excellent free map of the city with bus lines and accommodation listings. There's a 24-hour computer info kiosk out front that's usually broken. The **Board Failte** *(52 Castle St.; Tel 02890/327888; 9am-5pm Mon-Fri, 9am-12:30pm Sat Apr-Sept; 9am-5:15pm Mon-Fri Oct-Mar)* office has info on the Republic of Ireland.

Public Transportation **Citybus** *(Donegal Square; Tel 02890/246485)* is the citywide transportation system. (**Ulsterbus** is the long-distance, town-to-town system.) The main bus hub is around **Donegal Square.** Northbound buses depart Donegal Square North, southbound depart Donegal Square South, ditto for eastbound and westbound. Grab a map at the **Tourist Office** [see above]. It will tell you where the buses go. Remember, Belfast is completely overhauling their bus schedule, so double-check listings before you hop on. Cabs run all around town. You can usually flag one down at any time of the day or night but if you can't, call **City Cab** *(Tel 02890/242000)*, or **Diamond Taxi Service** *(Tel 02890/646666)*. There is a £2 minimum charge, and £5 will take you anywhere around the city center.

Health and Emergency Emergency, fire, ambulance or police: *999*. The most centrally located hospital is **Shaftesbury Square Hospital** *(16-20 Great Victoria St.; Tel 02890/329808)*; farther south is **Belfast City Hospital** *(9 Lisburn Rd.; Tel 02890/329241)*. There is also a Rape Crisis Center in Belfast *(Tel 02890/326803)*.

Pharmacies: There are pharmacies all over the city center and University area. They are generally open from 9-9:30am to 5:30-6pm. In the mall complex attached to the Europa Bus Station, there is a **Boots** *(35-47 Donegal Pl.; Tel 02890/242332; 8:30am-6pm Mon-Wed, Fri, 8:30am-9am Thur, 1pm-5pm Sat and Sun)*.

Telephone: Country code: *02890;* City code: *90*. The phones here are British Telecom and take coins 10p and up.

Airports: **Belfast International Airport** *(Aldergrove; Tel 02890/422888)* serves the U.K., U.S., and destinations in Europe. Belfast has a pretty efficient **train service** (30 per day) running from the airport to Belfast Central Station, and a **bus service** from the airport to the Europa Hotel and from Central Station to the Europa Hotel *(one every hour, 50p)*, making connections easy.

Trains Trains leave Belfast from **Central Station** *(East Bridge St.; Tel 02890/899411)*, or **Great Victoria Station** *(Next to the Europa Bus Station; Tel 02890/434424)*, and sometimes **Botanic Station** *(Botanic Ave. near the University; No phone.)* for **Dublin** *(8 daily, 2 hours)*, **Derry** *(7 daily; 2hr 40 min)*, **Coleraine** *(9 daily; 2 hr)*, and **Portrush** *(7 per day; 2 hr)*. You can pick up a schedule at any of these stations.

Bus Lines Out of the City Both **Ulsterbus** and **Bus Éireann** leave **Europa Bus Station** *(Behind the Europa Hotel on Great Victoria St.; Tel 02890/333000, phones open 7:30am-8:30pm Mon-Sat, 9am-7:30pm Sun)* and go pretty much everywhere, including **Dublin** *(8 per day, 3 on Sun; 3 hours)*, **Armagh** *(11 daily, 1hr 30 min)*, and **Downpatrick** *(20 times daily, 1hr 30 min)*. Call for other times. Connections are available through Bus Eireann to destinations in the south. **Laganside Bus Terminal** *(Donegal Quay, east of the Albert Clock Tower; 90-33-3000)* has buses going to **Antrim** *(All day, 40 min)*, **Portaferry** *(4 daily, 1 hour 30 min)*, **Portrush** *(11 daily, 2hr 30 min)*, and numerous other towns.

Bike Rental You can rent a bike at **McConvey Cycles** *(10 Pottinger's Entry, also at 467 Ormeau Rd.; Tel 02890/491163; 10-6pm Mon-Sat; £7/day or £30/week; V/MC)*. You can *only pay by credit card*. They take your number so if you run away with it they can charge you.

▸▸LAUNDRY

Laundry is best done at **Duds-n-Suds** *(Botanic Ave.; Tel 02890/243956; 8am-9pm Mon-Fri, 8am-6pm Sat, noon-6pm Sun; £4 wash/dry)*.

▸▸POSTAL

The **General Post Office** *(25 Castle Pl.; Tel 02890/323740; 9am-5:30pm Mon-Sat)* is at the intersection of Royal Avenue and Donegal Place.

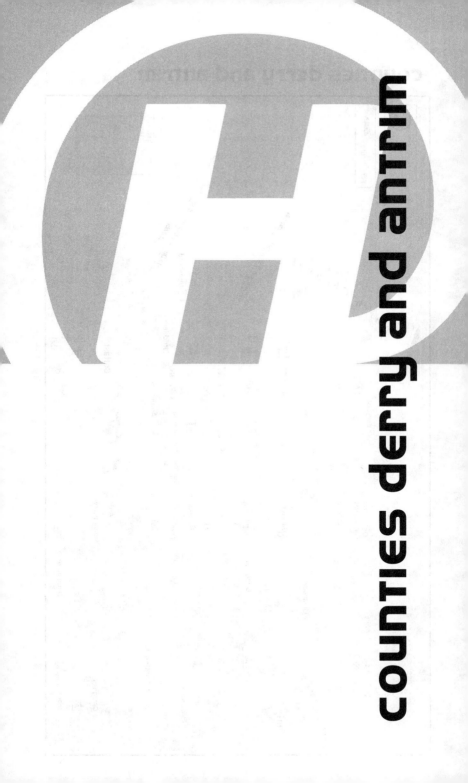

counties derry and antrim

counties derry and antrim

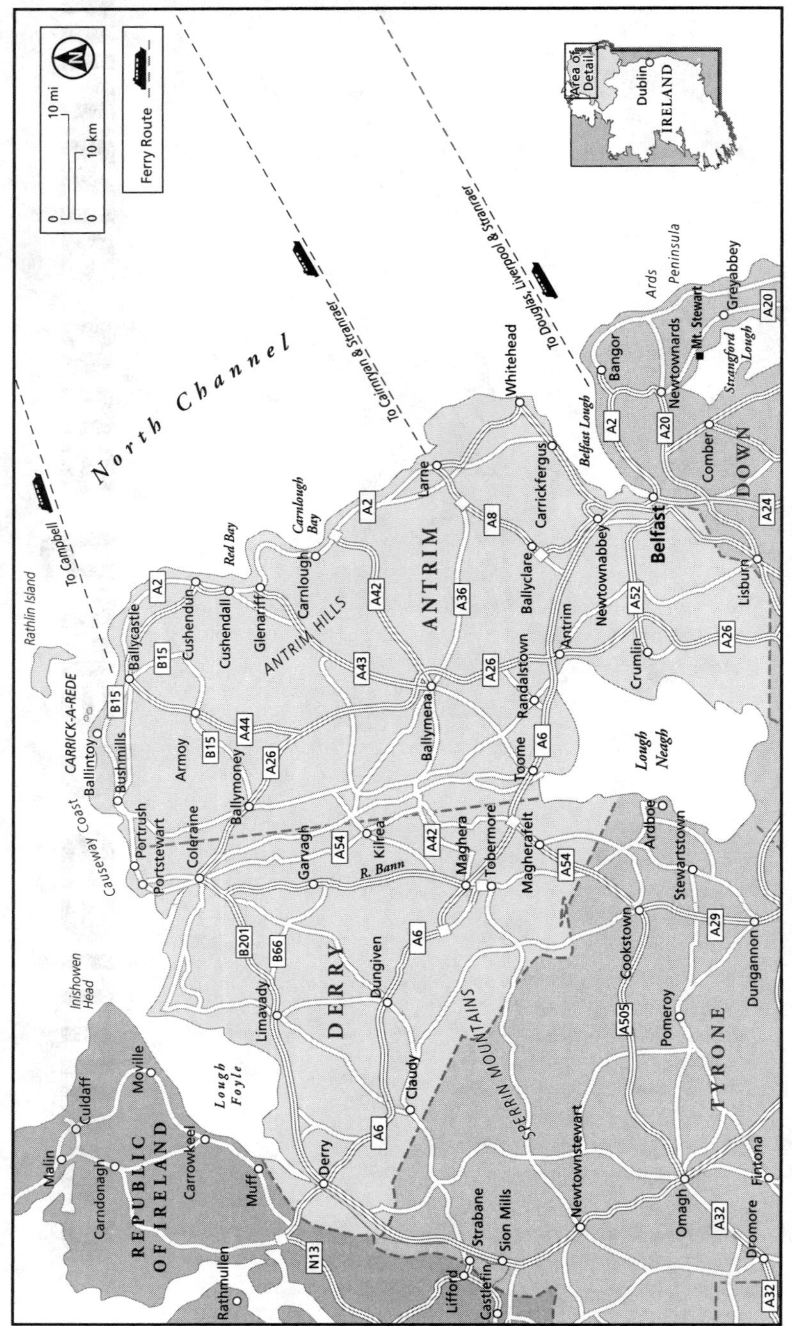

derry

Derry is one of the coolest places to visit in Northern Ireland. It's so steeped in history and so willing to have a good time in the present, it's unfortunate that it's not a major tourist destination. No doubt 30 years of violence from "The Troubles" have scared away many would-be visitors. This used to be a legitimate concern, as the city was the center of much of the sectarian strife. If you've ever seen any coverage on TV news about violence in Northern Ireland, chances are you've seen pictures of this place. The biggest flashpoint of it all was 1972's Bloody Sunday [see *culture zoo,* below], which left 14 dead and boosted IRA membership.

Nowadays, with a fervor much greater than that of other towns in the North, Derry is moving on and trying hard to embrace an enlightened, heterogeneous future. Walking through the Walled City, the 400-year-old heart of Derry, you'll see slick bars, cafes, and galleries that have an international feel that would fit right in on the European mainland. Spend a night in one of Derry's modern pub/clubs and you'll realize that the last thing on the minds of most young people here is the past. When it comes to partying and the arts and music, you get the sense that people here know they live in a place that's been isolated from the mainstream and are working twice as hard to prove to everyone that they know what's up. Be prepared to have great fun, see cool stuff, and encounter a bit of attitude.

A lot of people who pass through Derry make the mistake of doing just that—passing through. While your initial response to a walk around downtown while waiting for a bus transfer may not be one of rapture, chances are that if you stay for a day or two, you won't want to leave. Derry is the fourth-largest city in Ireland and has a population of over

12 hours in derry

If you're just passing through Derry and refuse to give yourself over to its charm for longer than a day, you're missing out. Here's what you should do: Check out the **murals** first thing before it starts raining [see *culture zoo, below]. Then grab lunch at* **Indigo** [see *eats,* below]. *Take an evening walk around the walls to work off your meal, then forego the pleasantries and start drinking. Go to* **Pedar O'Donnel's** for some trad [see *bar scene,* below], then hit the **Nerve Center** [see *club scene,* below], where there's bound to be a great performance or band or club night happening.

100,000, but is often written off the tourist map. This obscurity is what gives it its unique feeling—so much to offer and so few to share in it. Come. Revel.

neighborhoods

Derry has three major areas, each geographically separated.

The one where you'll hang out most is the historically important **Walled City** and the areas immediately to the north, east and south. They're attractive, they're the center of culture, and they make up the throbbing heart of the city west of the **River Foyle.** Here are all the trendy cafes, beautiful old buildings, bookstores, clothiers, and pubs ranging from traditional to posh to Planet Hollywood-esque. As for the Wall itself, it's old, big, thick and all encompassing—and the focal point of the Derry universe. Most things cultural exist inside it, in the Walled City proper. Live music can be found here seven nights a week and club nights happen from Thursday onward. At the middle of the Walled City is **The Diamond** (actually more of a public square) and at the center of the Diamond is the War Memorial. From the Diamond, four streets, **Bishop, Butcher, Shipquay** and **Ferryquay** go outward in roughly the four cardinal directions. Each of these streets leads to a gate in the wall of the same name—i.e. Shipquay Gate—and these are the impressive ways in and out of this ancient heart. In olden days, of course, most great cities were walled to keep out invaders, but in Derry, where the walls still stand, you can get a feeling for just how formidable a target this place used to be.

Outside the walled city area to the west is the **Bogside,** still a Catholic stronghold and once the center for much of the city's violent past. Free Derry, nearly autonomous and rife with firepower, was set up by the IRA in this neighborhood in the 1970s. A huge, ominous security tower rises from behind a wall to preside over Bogside, loaded with dozens of cameras and microphones. Free Derry folk say that the police can see and hear for up to two miles with the high-tech equipment. Even vibrations coming off windshield glass are enough for them to hear what you're saying. Creepy.

Take the double-decker **Craigavon Bridge** across the River Foyle and you're in the **Waterside,** a predominantly Protestant and residential area that makes up the western half of town. The **train station** is here, as are some ghastly loyalist murals and the **Workhouse Museum** [see *culture zoo,* below].

hanging out

By day, **The Diamond** is the center of all action. You'll see school kids window-shopping on their lunch breaks, babes smoking cigarettes outside of boutiques, and businesspeople talking frantically on their cell phones.

Outside the city walls, you can see club-goers forming modern plans of attack for entering—or just orbiting in the surrounding streets. Youngsters congregate after 1am in **Waterloo Place,** at the intersection of Strand Road, Waterloo Road, and the Wall to figure out where to go next and who to take with them. You'll see the good, the bad, and the ugly of Derry youth here. Fights, laughter, declarations of love, public displays of affection, and plenty of drinking can be witnessed any night of the week. It's a beautiful thing in a weird way. Derry people are known to party until the obscene hours of the morning, so this is the place to go to find after-hours action of all sorts.

Derry lacks a nice park, but if you're looking to walk on a grassy patch, cross the Craigavon Bridge and walk south along the Foyle; there's a scenic river walk trail there. Any of the cafes and many of the pubs around the Diamond teem with activity around lunchtime. **Fitzroy's** [see *eats,* below] is a good place to see and be seen.

Everything around the Walled City is easily walkable, and the best hanging-out options are in mild summer months—that is, when it's not

five-o

Let's put it this way: don't try shit here. Derry has seen enough troubles over the last 30 years for them to be a bit, ah, sensitive to disturbances. If there is a bomb scare anywhere in Ireland or the UK, there's a good chance security will be beefed up in Derry as a precautionary measure. Not to say that it's dangerous to walk the streets (it's not), but it is definitely idiotic to be a punk here. Graffiti, fighting, and other asshole-ish behavior could get you beat down or thrown in jail for a few days, which is perfectly legal to do. Think Singapore. Think caning. If you steal anything, you'll be cuffed faster than you can say, "Book 'em, Danny Boy."

wired

Internet access is the cheapest at the **Central Library** *(35 Foyle St.; Tel 02871/371-747; 9:15am-5:30pm daily, till 8pm Mon and Thu; £2.50 per hour),* but it's also cheap at **Steve's Backpacker's Hostel** [see *crashing,* above], which charges £3 per hour.

pouring, of course. As for the Derry-ites, they're a tough breed, as you'd expect (and they party appropriately hard), but this is also a big enough city for a somewhat cosmopolitan, and increasingly fashionable, mix.

bar scene

Derry has a million bars and pubs to suit whatever sort of clientele, music, or drink you're looking for. Very generally speaking, pubs lean toward either *trendy* or *traditional,* though many of the trendy pubs have a traditional feel—lots of wood and cozy snugs—but are jazzed up with fancy lights, trippy decorations, and primo sound systems. A lot of Derry's trendy bars are theatrical (Mullan's, for instance) and sometimes you may feel like you're on stage. People tend to dress up, guys in jackets or at least slick clubby shirts, and girls in little black dresses.

▸▸TRENDY PUBS

The Strand *(35-38 Strand Rd.; Tel 02871/260-494)* is the mainstay of all young partying in Derry. Packed every night of the week, the Strand has everything from disco night to an immensely popular karaoke thang on Tuesdays. The decor is traditional pub updated with colored lights and booming speakers. If you walk in and it appears dead, head downstairs and it's probably crammed with people. Funky rock dominates the tracks and high drink prices tend to reflect the trendiness here.

On Shipquay Street, inside the walled city, **Townsman Bar** *(33-35 Shipquay St.; Tel 02871/260-820; Cover £6 for Fri-Sat disco; MC, V)* is the dominant force in bar and club life. You'd never guess from the outside, but you could spend an entire night here and not see half of it. Boasting half-a-dozen bars, dancing, games, food and endless nooks and crannies, Townsman is like a giant funhouse for post-adolescents. Pulsing music and high-tech lighting abounds. Just two Townsman offerings: cocktails and dancing's available in **Vibe** [see *club scene,* below], while Pool Works has top-quality American-style pool tables, a bar and theatrical lighting. The place is so big that crowd, music and drink of choice all depend on what room you're in. They have a little bit of everything.

There are two great pubs in the **Trinity Hotel** [see *crashing,* below]. Businessmen from out of town dot **Porter's Café** *(22-24 Strand Rd.; Tel 02871/271-272, Fax 02871/271-271)* by day, while a young crowd comes at night. It's got an elegant, art-deco feeling with leather-upholstered booths, brownstone pillars, and a beautiful dark wood bar. On weekends, DJs bring in hordes of people and spotlights crawl along the walls and ceilings. Next-door is the cozy **Nolan's Snug**. Here the motif is pub-*elegante* and the crowd is generally a generation older than next-door. Feel like a cultured grown-up and sip a Bushmills and soda as you talk about the Great War.

What would happen if you turned loose the art director for Club MTV in an Irish pub? You'll find out at **Mullan's** *(13 Little James St.;)*. Everything in this incredible pub is at once unpretentious and stylish as hell. From giant bronze lions to LCD TV monitors in the cocktail tables to the swing bands that frequent the stage, everything clicks perfectly. Also, it's one of the best lit bars anywhere, with evocative halos, recesses and strategic spots. Even if you don't drink, come here to appreciate the craft. The main floor has a bar, stage, and tables. The second and third floors are balconies ringing the bottom floor and also have bars, where the bartenders aren't half-bad at cocktail mixing.

Other classy places to get a drink and mingle with a cool crowd include the blue heaven **Indigo** [see *eats,* below] and the loungy **Sandino's** [see *gay scene,* below].

▸▸TRADITIONAL PUBS

Derry was a major point of exit during the Famine of the 19th century, and each pub along Waterloo Street carried a name to identify it with a specific town so that people emigrating would have a place to stay and drink before they left for North America or Australia. So every pub owner along Waterloo Street has a story about his place; just ask them to tell you.

Pedar O'Donnel's *(53 Waterloo St.; Tel 02871/372-318)* is the heart of traditional music in Derry. The pub itself is covered with flags from Ireland and all over the world, acknowledging its role as watering hole to the foreign masses. Pedar's also draws great local crowds that seem to take no notice of the busloads of tourists among them. The musicians are excellent, specializing in wistful, bittersweet tunes about leaving home, lost love, and drinking (though you're likely to hear the occasional Neil Young song thrown into the mix).

Next door is the **Gweedor Bar** *(53 Waterloo St.; Tel 02871/372-318)*, a comparatively atmospheric and homey pub. You're more likely to hear rock or blues here than trad, and the crowd is a bit younger. There is a door in the back connecting it to Pedar's.

Bound For Boston *(27-31 Waterloo St.; Tel 02871/374-343)*, also known as "The Bound For," is a grungy little pub that gets packed on weekends. The crowd is young; the music is rollicking rock 'n' roll. The decor is standard-issue Irish pub. Tell your friends to watch as you get pissed. During the Famine exodus, the Bound for Boston was a major stopover for that last Irish quaff, so that gives you an idea how old it is. Originally called the Rosses, the pub drew people from the Rosses region of Ireland, a wild, Gaelic-speaking region in the northwest. Upstairs, **Club Q** *(Tel 02871/374-343; Noon-1am; £5 per hour for pool,*

derry city

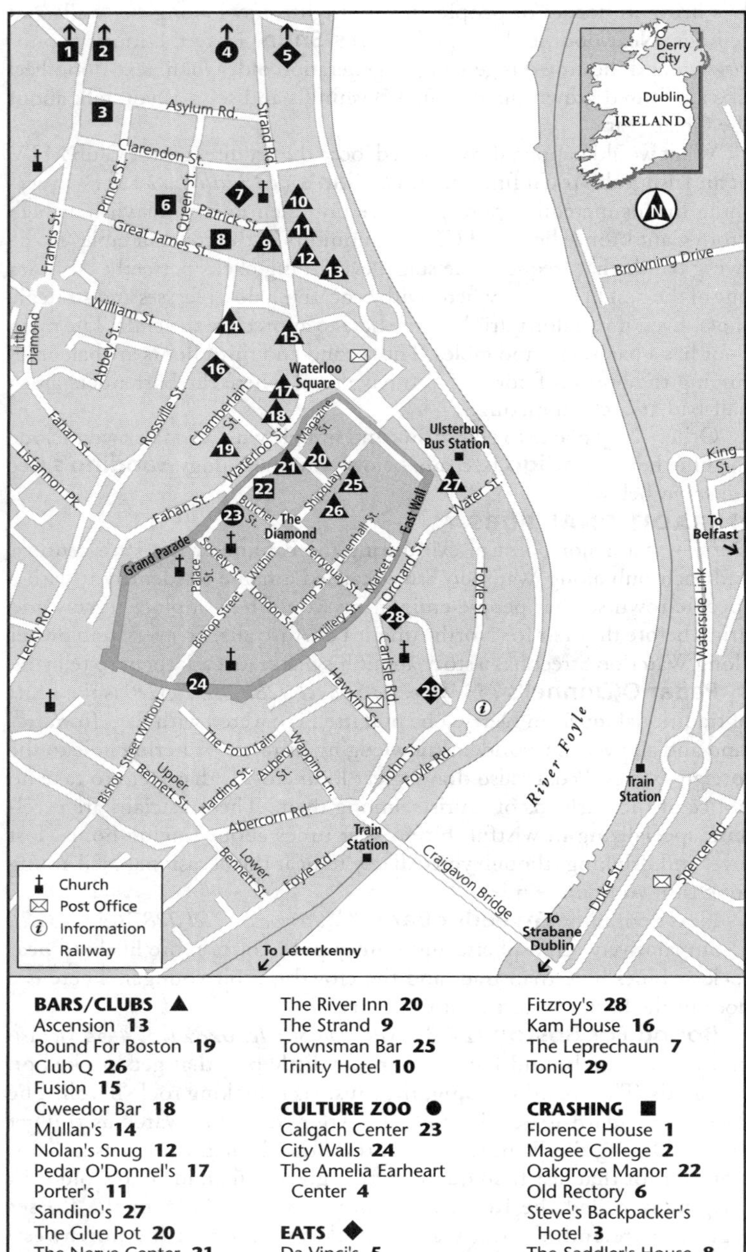

BARS/CLUBS ▲
Ascension **13**
Bound For Boston **19**
Club Q **26**
Fusion **15**
Gweedor Bar **18**
Mullan's **14**
Nolan's Snug **12**
Pedar O'Donnel's **17**
Porter's **11**
Sandino's **27**
The Glue Pot **20**
The Nerve Center **21**
The River Inn **20**
The Strand **9**
Townsman Bar **25**
Trinity Hotel **10**

CULTURE ZOO ●
Calgach Center **23**
City Walls **24**
The Amelia Earheart Center **4**

EATS ◆
Da Vinci's **5**
Fitzroy's **28**
Kam House **16**
The Leprechaun **7**
Toniq **29**

CRASHING ■
Florence House **1**
Magee College **2**
Oakgrove Manor **22**
Old Rectory **6**
Steve's Backpacker's Hotel **3**
The Saddler's House **8**

£3 per hour before 7pm) boasts six American pool tables and assorted game machines, and 90 percent male clientele—not gay either, just really macho.

The River Inn and **The Glue Pot** *(Tel 02871/371-965)* are stuck together on Shipquay Street. The River Inn dates from 1684 and is in the basement. The Glue Pot is upstairs, and has cocktails but less charm than its atmospheric downstairs neighbor.

live music scene

Live music is well integrated into most of Derry's pubs and clubs. You'll find live everything almost any night of the week. **Pedar O'Donnels** is the best bet for trad, while **Mullan's** [see *bar scene,* above, for both] or **Sandino's** [see *gay scene,* below] are live jazz hot spots where locals and touring players jam. **The Nerve Center** [see *club scene,* below] is the most happening venue for underground rock, while **Bound for Boston, The Gweedor,** [see *bar scene,* above, for both] and **The Dungloe** *(41-43 Waterloo St.; Tel 02871/267-529)* feature rock and blues. Many pubs will play *mostly* one kind of music and occasionally slip into other genres. Mullan's, for instance, will have trad or a top-40 DJ when it doesn't have jazz. Check the pages of *The Derry Journal* to see who's up tonight.

club scene

You know how every city has one of those places that isn't the coolest, where the decor is a little bit cheesy, and the music kind of sucks, but everyone has a great time? Well, in Derry, **Fusion** *(Waterloo Square; Tel 02871/267-600; www.clubfusion.co.uk, fusion@clubfusion.co.uk)* is that place. It's where you admit that you like that Billy Ocean song from 1985, that you enjoy dancing like a dork, and that you're proud to hit on someone while a sweatshirt's tied around your waist. The club sports purple carpet, lava lamps, and Gaudi-esque stucco walls. Don't listen to the snobs who'll tell you to avoid this place like the plague, it's pretty darn fun. If you're looking to find a random snog or hook-up partner,

lad meets lass

If you want to get some nookie in town, head for **Fusion** [see *club scene,* above], the biggest pick-up game this side of a Brooklyn b-ball court. Or gather in Waterloo Square after the pubs close and you'll find someone to do stuff with. Derry is perfectly fine with random sexual encounters. The rule seems to be have a couple drinks with your friends, make eye contact with someone of the opposite sex, have a couple drinks with them, then go for it. People grab life by the balls here, and they just might do the same to you.

this is a good place to probe [see *lad meets lass,* above]. If you want to test your trivia knowledge, go Thursday night for the popular music quiz. You won't find the drinks any more exceptional than anything else. **Level 1,** upstairs at Fusion, offers a slightly more sophisticated atmosphere, for which you're likely to pay a £5 entry on weekends. The crowd is a bit more serious about their music, mostly house and occasional trance, and the DJ's are proficient.

Is there *anything* **The Nerve Center** *(7/8 Magazine St.; Tel 02871/260-562, Fax 02871/371-738; info@nerve-centre.org.uk; prices and times vary depending on what's happening, so definitely call ahead)* doesn't have? As if movies, theater, art, and live music are not enough, they also host the best club night in town, *Praise,* which draws the Prodigys as well as some fantastic unknowns. An evening and morning of sweaty fun are sure to be had. Check **Cool Discs** [see *tunes,* below] for nights and times, or look for fliers at cafes and clothing shops, as *Praise* is on a sporadic schedule. Dress to impress.

Vibe, part of the mammoth Townsman Bar complex [see *bar scene,* above], is a slick super-club. Plush couches and an excellent sound system are among its attributes. They have an extensive (and expensive) cocktail menu, which is a rarity anywhere in Ireland. Good idea to suss out where the exits are before you start putting chemicals in your body, as the building is huge, gets packed, and is built like a maze. Or just follow the exit signs and hope for the best.

The Strand also has club nights Thursday-Saturday, as does **The Gweedor** [see *bar scene,* above for both]. Many pubs have irregular DJ nights, with covers in the £5 range, so keep your ear to the ground, buddy.

arts scene

▸▸VISUAL ARTS

Orchard Gallery *(Orchard St.; Tel 02871/269-675; 10am-6pm Tue-Sat; Free)* is an impressive little gallery, the finest in the city, showing works of contemporary painters, photographers, and multi-media artists. Similar but not quite as innovative is the **Context Gallery** *(5 Artillery St.; Tel 02871/373-538; 10am-5:30pm Tue-Fri, 10am-4:30pm Sat; Free).* Both feature interesting contemporary local and international artists' work.

▸▸PERFORMING ARTS

Derry isn't a theater city like Dublin, but it does get a goodly allotment of major tours and hosts small but vital independent dance and theater scenes. While not in use as the seat of the city council, the **Guildhall** *(Guildhall Sq.; Tel 02871/377-335; 9am-5pm Mon-Fri; Free)* serves as a public theater for music, dance and theater. The Bloody Sunday Tribunals [see *culture zoo,* below] will probably pre-empt a fair amount of scheduled performances here for the next year or two, but keep your eyes peeled for other events. The **Foyle Arts Center** *(Lawrence Hill; Tel 02871/266-657)* has a 100-seat auditorium that puts on various performances now and then as well. **The Playhouse** *(5-7 Artillery St.; Tel 02871/268-027;)* is a good place to see the works of innovative theater and dance, while the

sculptures in derry

Let it never be said that Derry has not had its fair share of tough times. From the Famine to the Troubles, they've suffered through it all. Derry's residents have made big efforts to commemorate and understand their history through museums, murals, and these fascinating sculptures.

The best known, called *Hands Across the Divide*, sits on the little square on the west side of the Craigavon Bridge. Two winding paths slant upward and end in ledges. There is a gulf between the ledges, and atop each path is a man, representing both sides of the sectarian strife. The image is at first an icon of hope. Each man has his arm extended at the end of a long journey, seemingly ready for reconciliation. Take a second look, though, and notice the indifference in their expressions and posture. Their hands extend weakly, offered more cautiously than enthusiastically, indicating that both sides have come a long way but could lose a chance for peace if they just wait passively for the other side to make all the effort.

On Waterloo Place, three blocks north, the Emigration Statues depict another traumatic event in Derry history, the mass exodus during the Potato Famine in the 19th century. A family walks toward a boat that will take them away from home. The father is stoic, the girl looks forward with hope, the mom is sad, and the boy looks back in the knowledge that he will return.

glammy **Rialto Entertainment Centre** (5 Market St.; Tel 02871/260-516; www.derrytheatre.com) is the biggest venue in town, and hosts major touring plays, ballet, musicals, rock shows, operas and orchestras as well as community productions.

Go to the **Orchard Theater** *(Orchard St.; Tel 02871/267-789; £3.50 Adults, £2.50 Students)* right next to the Orchard Gallery, to experience a night at the movies the way it's supposed to be. The only problem with the Orchard, a great old cinema showing art house and revivals films, is that there is no incline from the back of the house to the front. This can be a source of duress for shorter people. Often, when the movie starts, people jump up and change seats to get a better view, creating a game of cinematic musical chairs. It's quite amusing. There's also a great lounge to the right of the box office where you can park your behind on a comfortable old couch and enjoy a beer (I ain't talkin' no paper cup either, I'm talkin' about a *glass* of beer) before the show. Ah, it's the little things. If you're more the Meg Ryan meets Tom Hanks type, head for the **Strand Multiplex** in the Quayside Shopping Centre.

In addition to a million other cool things, **The Nerve Center** [see *club scene,* above] has a small theater which holds screenings periodically. Student films, shorts, or animation may be playing on any given week. You never can tell what will be here next. Check the listings section of the local paper *The Derry Journal* for what's on the program.

gay scene

The gay scene in Derry is not quite a scene, but there are a couple of pubs that cater to at least a significant minority of gay and lesbian clientele. There is a certain irritating machismo element present in Derry's male population, so gay people still run the risk of getting harassed by small-minded idiots. Most people you talk to don't condemn gays and lesbians in a theoretical sense, but that doesn't seem to stop them from casting a disapproving eye on public displays of affection. However, club nights at the **Nerve Center** [see *club scene,* above] are likely to be gay-friendly, and generally, the pubs along Waterloo street are not unfriendly. There is no gay/lesbian paper in town, but check out ***www.iol.ie/~nwgay/support.htm*** for a comprehensive list of services for gay and lesbians in Derry.

The atmosphere at **Ascension** *(64 Strand Road; open till 1am, till 2:30 am on Fridays and Saturdays; usually free, or £3 when not free)* is friendly but gets meat-market-like when crowded on Saturday night (what bar doesn't on a Saturday night?). They've got disco nights on Tuesdays, Thursdays and Fridays, and Karaoke on Sunday evenings, plus a weekly drag show, *Drag Acts & Frolics Clubnite,* that features slammin' DJ Steadman.

Sandino's *(Water St.; Tel 02871/309-297)* has a great jazz brunch on Sunday with a big, real Irish fry. It does the regular bar thing the rest of the week.

cellular development

In Ireland, you may find it odd that what looks like every man, woman, and child has a cell phone. In fact, Ireland has one of the highest rates of cell phone usage in the world, with more than one in three people toting what is as much a fashion accessory as it is a way to keep in touch. Surprisingly, Ireland is also the most expensive country in Europe in which to use a cell phone. It seems that living in what was for generations a poor, technologically backward country has created an urge to embrace technology with a vengeance at whatever cost. Are cell phones endemic, or have they revolutionized the way Irish people communicate? You decide.

I'm too sexy for this parapet

Bet you didn't know Derry was once the epicenter of Victorian style. It's true. Back when Derry's elite lived inside the city walls and everyone else lived outside, a popular activity for the well-to-do ladies was to get dolled up in the latest fashions from London and parade around the walls all day, showing off their new duds. The disgruntled poor people down in the Bogside found this custom particularly offensive and got so fed up with it that they wrote to London newspapers, complaining about the shameless "cats" parading along the wall. The term stuck, the area around the wall became known as a "cat walk," and soon the expression became synonymous with fashion.

culture zoo

If you have any interest in the Troubles, Derry is the place to be. The town's murals alone are as good as any history lesson you'll ever get.

The City Wall: A half-hour walking trip around the Walled City when you first arrive will acquaint you with the city's history and give you a good view of modern-day Derry.

Derry murals: Colorful, spooky city walls have been painted to commemorate the fallen from both sides of the Troubles. They're another fascinating, and heavily mythologized, way to connect with what's happened here. You'll notice them just walking around, looming over shops in the hardcore Protestant and Republican pockets of town.

Bogside murals: These are scattered around Rossville Square, also known as Free Derry Corner. It was here that Nationalists declared themselves an autonomous nation in the seventies. The most famous mural is on a reconstructed wall of a house and is simply composed of big block letters stating, "You are now entering Free Derry." Other murals pay tribute to vendetta martyrs and to the victims of Bloody Sunday. Across the Foyle in the Waterside, grizzly Loyalist murals depict the other side of the coin. There are murals scattered around the Rossdowney Roundabout and along the Glendermott Road. The murals started appearing in the 1960's, when sectarian strife started pushing people to violence. They are painted by people who are either Nationalists (those who want to be united with the Republic of Ireland) or Unionists (those who want to remain part of the U.K.) to remember those who have died, to rally support for their cause, or to villify the other side. A walk around the city is

sunday, bloody sunday

In the late sixties and early seventies, Derry was the epicenter for the worst of things and, on Bloody Sunday, became the catalyst for the Troubles over the next three decades. On January 30, 1972 20,000 civil rights protesters marched through Derry to oppose discrimination in housing, and employment, and demand an end to the British policy of internment without trial for political prisoners. As the crowd moved through town, small scuffles developed before the First Battalion of the Parachute Regiment opened fire on the crowd. At the end of the day, 14 unarmed men, mostly teenagers, were dead and many were wounded. The army's position was that they were fired upon, even though there was no hard evidence and none of the dead or wounded were found with guns or bombs. The Widgery Commission, created to investigate the incident, was seen by many as a whitewash to cover up the army's irresponsible actions toward the protesters. Many citizens saw this as a call to arms against a government that had fired on its own people, membership in the IRA rose dramatically, and the real Troubles soon began.

These days, the peace process seems to be approaching some semblance of stability. Efforts like the Bloody Sunday Tribunals, an ongoing series of investigations happening right downtown in the Guild Hall are representative.

For more info on all these places, go to ***www.derry.net.***

the best way to see the murals, and people will often come up to you and tell you about them (usually with a decidedly biased point-of-view).

Tower Museum: *(at Magazine Gate; 02871/37-2411; 10am-5pm Mon-Sat, 2pm-5pm Sun July-Aug, 10am-5pm Tue-Sat Sept-June; £3.75/1.25 for adults/students):* Housed in O'Doherty's Tower, this place gives you a comprehensive and informative history of Derry, the North, and a lot of good information about the Troubles. Some of the audiovisual elements paint a too-rosy portrait of Derry and try so hard not to take sides or condemn anyone that they end up being ineffectual. However, there is a better display at the end of the tour, plus more historical artifacts like a 1,500-year-old log boat. You also get to walk through centuries-old tunnels that were once used by pedestrians to get around town but are now part of the museum. There's a guided tour you can take for a small extra fee, which does a lot to contextualize the masses of information you get here. Leave time after that to linger over what you've seen and let it all sink in.

Calgach Center *(4-22 Butcher St. within the Walled City; Tel 02871/37-3177; 9am-5pm Mon-Fri; free, £1 for Fifth Province exhibit):* If you want to find out about Derry history in a slightly Disney-fied way, head here. In the Fifth Province exhibit, you get to walk through the five stages of Derry history and explore the Fifth Province, a mythical part of Ireland that some say is akin to Atlantis—while others insist it's a sort of mystical Irish diaspora and consists of the traditions and cultures all Irish around the world carry with them. The coolest part of the show is the second part, where you step into an Irish time machine/spaceship that rattles and shakes and takes you from ancient Ireland to outer space. By the end of the tour, you'll be thoroughly convinced that every Irish emigrant became a world leader, famous athlete, or historical figure. The tour is a little long (allow yourself a whole morning or afternoon), but it's fun in a cheesy kind of way.

Amelia Earheart Centre *(From the city center, take the Strand Rd. to the Colmore Roundabout, take Madam's Rd. to Ballyarnett Roundabout, follow signs to Ballyarnett; Tel 02871/354-040; 10am-4pm Mon-Fri; Free):* This cool museum commemorates the landing of the famous flyer on her historic solo flight across the Atlantic. Just too bad she thought she was landing in Paris....

city sports

There isn't terribly much to do for outdoor activity in Derry other than walking. But Derry-ites love football, Gaelic football (similar to rugby) and hurling. Football fans can check out a match at **Brandywell Stadium** *(Lone Moor Rd.; Tel 02871/281-333)* while Gaelic die-hards can go to **Celtic Park** *(Lone Moor Rd.; Tel 02871/267-142)* to catch games from mid-February on. Seasons for the NFL, the National Football League, run throughout the fall. Best way to find out what's what is in a big newspaper like the *Belfast Telgraph,* which has complete listings for all national teams. If you want to get buff in Derry, you can do it for free. **Stress X** *(14 the Diamond; Tel 02871/269-298; 9am-10pm Mon, 7am-10pm Tue-Thu, 9am-8pm Fri-Sat, 11am-3pm Sun; £5 per day, £15 per week, first visit free)* gives you a chance to try out their facilities at no cost or obligation to you, dear customer. Two treadmills, half-a-dozen Stairmasters, and a small but sufficient free weight area fill the main room. There's also a studio where you can try out one of those newfangled tae-bo classes all the kids are talking about. If you're more traditional, you can stick to dumbbells.

stuff

Derry probably has whatever you're looking for. Most of the shops are in the Walled City and around Bridge Street and Orchard Street. There are two main shopping centers in Derry, the **Foyleside Shopping Center** *(Orchard and Bridge St.)* and the **Richmond Centre** *(On the Diamond*

fashion

The kids in Derry are fashion-conscious and fairly uniform in their tastes. A pair of Diesel jeans is mandatory, and baggy cargo/clubber pants are popular with both sexes. You'll be amazed at how the girls get dressed up in tight clubber clothes and heels to go out to Tuesday karaoke at the Strand Bar. It seems that every night is an opportunity to strut one's stuff and compete for fashion queen. Guys seem to catch a break on dressing up, and are often wearing just a T-shirt or polo shirt and jeans. If you go see a rock show at the Nerve Center or happen by Cool Discs, you'll encounter a classic rock aesthetic.

at Shipquay and Ferryquay St.). One unique aspect of Derry commerce is the **Craft Village** *(Enter off Shipquay or Magazine St., about halfway up),* a square within the old city walls that's lined with little shops selling glassware, woolens, and handmade woodsy-craftsy sorts of souvenirs. It's like stepping back in time into a 300-year-old strip mall. The whole scene is more for the graying-at-the-temples set, but if you're looking for gifts, check it out. **Austin & Co., Ltd.** *(The Diamond; Tel 02871/261-817)* is Ireland's oldest department store, dating from 1839. If you want to buy some china for Aunt Minnie, this is the place.

▸▸DUDS

Clothes in Derry are available all through and around the Walled City. In the Foyleside Shopping Center and the Richmond Center are the bigger chain stores, like **Diesel,** while on Shipquay Street, you'll find smaller boutiques. There are no fantastic or unique places, and nothing that really screams "Derry," but you'll find plenty of quality clothes and shoes all over the place.

▸▸BOUND

The best bookstore in town is **Bookworm Bookshop** *(Bishop St. at London St; Tel 02871/261-616; 9:30am-5:30pm Mon-Sat),* which has the biggest stock of used books, Irish literature, and other things with words printed on them. This is a good place to pick up *The Derry Journal,* with listings of what's happening in town. There is also a big chain bookstore in the Foyleside Shopping Center.

▸▸TUNES

Cool Discs *(Foyle St.; Tel 02871/260-770; 9am-6pm Mon-Thu, 9am-9pm Sun, Fri; www.cool/discs.com; MC, V)* is one of the better record stores in Ireland, with a great selection of all kinds of techno and electronica 12-inch singles and LP's, as well as the usual pop stuff on CD.

They even have turntables where you can try out the vinyl. Check out their website for info on local musical happenings. They also promote parties at the **Nerve Center** [see *club scene,* above] and other venues around town.

eats

▸▸CHEAP

The blue couches, candles, and chill-out music at **Indigo** *(27 Shipquay St.; Tel 02871/271-011; Noon-11pm, Mon-Sat, noon-10pm Sun; around £4; No credit cards)* make it seem like midnight even if you're there at noon. Lounging feels mandatory, and you can pass hours drinking wine and admiring the modernist decor. It serves delicious and cheap lunch food, like toasted sandwiches and salads from noon to 6pm and dinner and bar bites the rest of the night.

Java *(Artillery St. at Ferryquay St.; Tel 02871/362-100; 9am-5:30pm Mon-Thu, 9am-6:30pm Fri-Sat, 11am-5pm Sun.; around £3; No credit cards)* caters to working stiffs in the city center, offering espresso, smoothies and sandwiches. The big windows that wrap around the front make for excellent people-watching.

The Leprechaun *(21-23 Strand Rd.; Tel 02871/363-606; 9am-6pm Mon-Sat.; around £2; No credit cards)* is a big and comfy place to get fresh baked bread and sandwiches for around £2.

▸▸DO-ABLE

A bit more expensive, **Fitzroy's** *(3 Carlisle Rd./2-4 Bridge St; Tel 02871/266-211; 10am-11pm daily; lunch £4, dinner £6-10)* is a smart, modern cafe with innovative lunchtime cuisine. A blue croissant—poached pear or melted blue cheese over toasted croissant—is quite yummy. Sit at the bar downstairs and sip espresso, wine, or beer or ascend the green neon steps to the second floor dining room and watch passers-by on Carlisle Road. Good food and service, and a giant peppermill on each table. Dinner is served till 11pm, and features entrees like salmon, stir-fry vegetables and gourmet tortilla dishes.

Kam House *(William St.; Tel 02871/372-166; entrees £8-10),* right around the corner from Pedar O'Donnel's, has excellent Chinese food.

to market

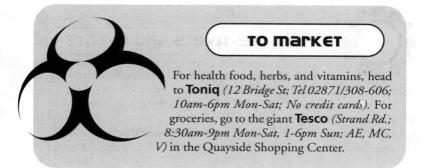

For health food, herbs, and vitamins, head to **Toniq** *(12 Bridge St; Tel 02871/308-606; 10am-6pm Mon-Sat; No credit cards).* For groceries, go to the giant **Tesco** *(Strand Rd.; 8:30am-9pm Mon-Sat, 1-6pm Sun; AE, MC, V)* in the Quayside Shopping Center.

The interior is red, red, and more red. Kam also has a cheap take-away only menu with most stuff for around a fiver.

▸▸SPLURGE

Worth the trek outside of the city walls is **Da Vinci's** *(15 Culmore Rd., a five-minute drive outside of Derry; Tel 02871/264-507; 5:30-9:30pm Mon, 5:30-10pm Tue-Fri, 5:30-10:30pm Sat, 5:30-9pm Sun; entrees £8-15, prix fix £11.95 before 7:30pm and £13.95 after; AE, MC, V).* This restaurant is a romantic and stunningly beautiful setting for some of the best food in the city. Stone walls, arched doorways, and candles all help set the mood. Try the sumptuous sun-dried tomato-stuffed chicken breast with pesto cream. To get there, take the A2 Culmore road out of town; it's about five minutes by car.

crashing

Derry's accommodations are cheap and excellent, including one of the coolest hostels in Ireland. There are several inexpensive and excellent B&B's, and beautiful hotels that cost a fraction of what they would in other regions, all the more reason to stay an extra day or two.

▸▸CHEAP

Judging from the lack of hostels, you sometimes get the feeling that the powers that be don't want young tourists in Derry. This is unfortunate because it could easily become a hot spot for twentysomething travelers. **Steve's Backpacker's Hostel** *(4 Asylum Rd., take Strand Rd. past the Tesco and turn left; Tel 02871/377-989; £7.50 per person, 2-3-bed room, or 6-bed dorm)* is where you should go first, though it's a bit out of the center, a ten-minute walk north of the Walled City. It's like a college apartment but cleaner. It's so casual and fun that you may get caught in the "Derry Vortex" and never want to leave. There's a comfy lounge room with TV, VCR, couches, and a cool dining/social room complete with a stereo and tapes. Bring your CD's for Steve to dub and add to the fun. It's also information central—find out what to do, where to go, and how to have great *craic* Derry-style. Steve's also has a kitchen, laundry (£3 for a wash and dry) and Internet access for £3 per hour. If you stay four nights, you get a fifth night free, either here or in Steve's other hostel, Macpackers, in Belfast.

festivals and events

In June, the **Walled City Festival,** a music/food/drinking street carnival takes place for 3 days.

July brings the **Foyle Cup Car Rally,** where people drive very fast to win money.

November is time for the **Foyle Film Festival,** where independent works from Ireland and abroad are screened around town.

Derry's other hostel, **Oakgrove Manor** *(4-6 Magazine St.; Tel 02871/284-100; £7.50 per person 8-10-bed dorm, £8.50 per bed 3-6 bed dorm)* is right inside the city walls, making it a great location, but it's impersonal and otherwise nondescript. Well, at least you can do your laundry here for £3.50. **Magee College** *(Corner of Northland and Rock Rd.; Tel 02871/575-283; mid-May-Sept; £15 single)* offers rooms in their student flats.

▸▸DO-ABLE

Two B&Bs that offer excellent prices in an old-fashioned Victorian setting are **The Saddler's House** and **The Merchant's House** *(36 Great James St. and 16 Queen St.; Tel 02871/268-093; Singles without bath £20, with bath £25; doubles without bath £40, with bath £45; saddlershouseb&b@binternet.com; V, MC)*. Enormous breakfasts include homemade jam and fresh fruit at both places. Definitely the first two B&Bs to call. The musical **Florence House** *(16 Northland Rd.; Tel 02871/268-093; £17-20 per person; No credit cards.)* seems to have a piano everywhere you turn. Rooms are comfortable and bright, and you're just six blocks north of the Walled City.

▸▸SPLURGE

The Trinity Hotel *(22-24 Strand Rd.; Tel 02871/271-271, Fax 02871/271-277; £70 en suite, call about luxury suites; AE, D, MC, V)* caters mainly to businesspeople, but its comfort level, attached pubs and restaurant, and location just north of the Walled City make it perfect for the well endowed tourist as well. Rooms are spotless and modern, with satellite TV, tea and coffee facilities, direct dial phones, Internet access, and a trouser press. The luxury suites have fireplaces and king-sized beds.

need to know

Currency Exchange The local currency is pounds sterling, *not* Irish punts. It's worth noting that many shops, pubs, and restaurants in town *will accept* punts as well as sterling at close to the current rate, so if you roll into town after the banks close, you'll probably be able to find places that will take your funny money. The **Bank of Ireland** *(Shipquay St.; Tel 02871/262-211; 9:30am-4:30pm Mon-Fri)* and **Ulsterbank** *(Waterloo Place; Tel 02871/261-882; 9:30am-4:30pm Mon-Fri)* both have bureaus de change, as does **Thomas Cook** *(In the Quayside Center; Tel 02871/374-174; 9am-5:30pm Mon-Fri).*

Tourist Information The **Derry Visitor and Convention Bureau** *(44 Foyle St.; 9am-7pm Mon-Fri, 10am-6pm Sat, 10am-5pm Sun, Jul-Sep, 9am-5:15pm Mon-Fri, 10am-5pm Sat, Apr and May)* has both Bord Failte and Northern Ireland Tourist Board desks. From the main bus station just east of the Walled City, go outside, take a left, and walk a block-and-a-half to find the bureau. Other than booking accommodations for B&Bs and hotels, though, they're really not that helpful. Do, however, be sure to pick up their very good free map.

Tourist Info USIT Travel *(Ferryquay St.; Tel 02871/371-888; 9:30am-5:30pm Mon-Fri, 10am-1pm Sat)* is the student travel office, where you can get discounted airfare or change your return dates if your ticket is from any USIT office worldwide.

Public Transportation You can get a lift from **Co-op Taxis** *(Tel 02871/371-666)* or the **Derry Taxi Association** *(Tel 02871/260-247).*

Health and Emergency Emergency: *999;* Police: **RUC Police Station** *(Strand Row; Tel 02871/367-337).* **Altnagelvin** *(Belfast Rd.; Tel 02871/345-171)* has emergency service.

Pharmacies There are two **Boots Pharmacies,** one just north of the Walled City *(3 Strand Rd. at Waterloo Place; Tel 02871/264-502; 9am-5:30pm Mon-Sat; AE, MC, V)* and one in the Foyleside Shopping Center *(Orchard and Bridge St.; Tel 02871/260-432; 9am-6pm Mon-Tue, Sun, 9am-9pm Wed-Fri; AE, MC, V).* There are numerous other pharmacies scattered around town as well.

Airports Derry Airport is 20 minutes east of town, with regular bus service connections to the main bus and train stations.

Trains The **Main Station** *(Duke St., on the east side of the Foyle; Tel 02871/342-228)* has connections to Belfast seven times daily for £6.40. Connect there to Dublin and points south.

Bus Lines Out of the City Ulsterbus goes virtually everywhere you'll want to go in the north, with 15 Belfast connections Monday-Saturday and eight Sunday, for £6.80. There are also five daily connections to Dublin Monday-Saturday, with two Sunday, for £10.50. The center of Derry is completely walkable and can be reached in minutes from the bus and train stations.

Bike Rental Hire two-wheeled manual powered cycling transportation at **An Mouintean B&B and Cycle Hire** *(245 Lone Moore Rd.; Tel 02871/287-128; £7 per day, £30 per week).*

Laundry Duds-n-Suds *(141 Strand Rd.; Tel 02871/266-006; 8am-9pm Mon-Fri, 8am-8pm Sat; £4 per wash and dry)* makes this most monotonous of tasks almost fun, with a pool table, video games and a snack bar. **Steve's Backpacker's Hostel** [see *crashing,* above] also does laundry for £3 a load.

Postal You can send your postcards from the **main post office** *(3 Custom House St.; Tel 02871/362-563; 8:30am-5:30pm Mon, 9am-5:30pm Tue-Fri, 9am-12:30pm Sat).*

Internet See *wired,* above.

everywhere else

portrush

Somewhere between glitz and gloomy weather, Portrush is like a family-oriented Las Vegas. It's a party town for kids of all ages. For the youngsters, it's got roller coasters, arcades, bumper cars, and cotton candy. For people who consider themselves mature, Portrush has classy places to wine and dine, and plenty of beautiful serene beaches. But if you fall between those two extremes, you're in luck, because what Portrush *really* excels at is being an orgiastic center of post-adolescent partying. If you're young, like to dance and pour substances in your body that make you feel funny, or want to check out some world-class surfing, this is the place to be. People here don't seem to acknowledge that it never gets much above 20° Celsius here. You'll see kids partying with their shirts off around bonfires at the beach in the middle of the chilly summer, and crazy surfers sealed tight inside rubber suits and masks in the middle of freakin' January going absolutely apeshit on their boards.

On the down side, there is a gritty kitschiness that pervades, reminiscent of a fairgrounds the day after the circus leaves town—the stench of greasy fried food, litter collecting in corners, etc. The town is completely set up to cater to the tourist mobs, in fact. It's tacky as hell, but you've got to love it. Because of its proximity to the big city, Portrush is a major party destination for university students from Belfast—and young people from every other town in the region—so the crowd here is much younger and more rockin' than in other mega-touristy Northern towns like, say, Newcastle. Come here during high season and you'll have a blast. Come here in low season and, well, you'll have a blast too. Whenever you're here, make sure you go to **Kelly's** [see *bar and club scene,* below], a giant estate of a club attracting all the international big guns to its multiple DJ stages.

neighborhoods

The layout of Portrush is easy. There is water all around the town, as it's basically a short peninsula jutting out northward into the surf-crazy waters of the chilly Atlantic. **Eglinton Street** is where the trains roll in, just on the southern, or landed, end of the town. The station area is home to tons of fast-food stands and arcades. Eglinton intersects with **Causeway Road** and from here three main streets run parallel from east to west through the town. It's an easy walk to **Kerr St., Mark St.,** and **Main St.** All three have B&B's up the yin-yang.

Natural beauty abounds outside of the tourist tack of downtown. Walk down the beach a couple of miles and you'll want to faint at the splendor. You'll see **Dunluce Castle** [see *culture zoo,* below], maybe the funkiest castle in Ireland. A couple miles more and you'll be at the Giant's Causeway, the weirdest damn natural wonder you've ever seen [see **The Giant's Causeway**]. Surf, sand, scenic splendor, and souped-up sonic booms all await you in this groovy region.

bar and club scene

The shores of Portrush are hopping with beach parties in the summer months, sort of like a refrigerated "MTV Spring Break". When the weather gets cold enough to drive even the heartiest partier indoors, don't fret: the pubs stay open late in this town. Closing time is officially 1am, but it's not uncommon to see people staggering home at 4am. If police roll up, Portrush pub staff can clear every drop of liquor off the tables in under a minute to avoid a beefy fine. It's quite a sight to see. As soon as the fuzz rolls on, the fun begins again. There are also several clubs here that stay open all night—they're always full of kids from Belfast. Unlike the pubs, these places are *allowed* to stay open.

You are so fabulous. You've been looking around for a club that's big enough to contain your raging party fury, one that has eleven different bars because your appetite for fun is so great. No mere club with four-five bars could possibly contain it. You want big-time DJ's with funny names like Digweed to blow your mind with all-night grooves. Officially known as Beetles Bar and Disco, **Kelly's Nightclub** *(Bushmill's Rd., right outside of town; Tel 02870/823-539; Cover £10 on Sat.)* is your salvation. All the major blokes, from London to Ibiza to "Madchester," show up at Kelly's. Thousands of kids pack the place every weekend for *Lush!*—the biggest party in Ireland. Every kind of person, all ages, comes here to get down. Just one rule, and it's a biggie: no sneakers. Otherwise, it's easy to get in, you can dress however you want and probably find dozens of people to hang with while you're here. The music is everything you could imagine depending on which end of the club you're in. The biggest parties are usually the trance/rave ones, though. Not to be missed.

It'll seem a step down by comparison, but **The Harbour Bar** *(5 Harbour Rd.; Tel 02870/822-430)* attracts a diverse crowd of locals and tourists and is a solid place to drink till late.

Rogues *(54 Kerr St.; Tel 02870/822 076; No credit cards)* has more locals than other pubs in town, but that doesn't mean that they don't like talking to out-of-towners. Across the way from the Harbour Bar, it's a great place to witness peaceful coexistence of natives and tourists. Right.

The scene at the **Trocado Lounge** *(Main St.; Tel 02870/823-693)* is a vodka-filled orgy in the heart of downtown. With close to 40 types of the clear firewater to choose from, people get buzzed early and dance to DJ's or live bands till late. It's a bar-cum-club with room for a couple hundred people. Crowds are touristy and studenty and young.

Jump around to oodles of techno pumped out every night in one convenient location: **Traks** *(In the bus station on the Promenade; Tel 02870/822-946).* Bring your baggie pants and sun visor.

culture zoo

Yes, there is culture even in such a hedonistic party town. You just have to hike a bit to find it.

Dunluce Castle *(On the A2, 5 km (3 mi) east of town; 10am-7pm Mon-Sat, 11am-7pm Sun, Apr-Aug; 10am-4pm Mon-Sat, Oct-Mar; £1.50):* The castle is best reached by a beautiful five-kilometer (three-mile) walk up the beach from Portrush (then take the winding road that'll bring you right here). As the tourist brochure says, "Like something out of a Tolkien fantasy, the ruins of Dunluce Castle have a desolate, awe-inspiring grandeur as they rise dramatically from a precipitous basaltic rock standing over a hundred-foot sheer above the wild and chill northern sea." Precipitous who? Anyway, the ruins are great. One night in 1639 in the middle of a dinner party at the castle, the kitchen fell off into the sea, proving that too many cooks in the kitchen spoil the broth.... Skip the boring crap in the information center and make for the ruins. There are some great, still intact archways and intricate carvings in the windows. After the grounds close, you can still get into the castle and have a private look around by hopping the wall on the east side. There's a little railing that enables you to spring up onto the wall and hop over. You can pull the ladder lying in the ground to the wall and help your friends over. Saves a couple pounds, yo. Of course this misbehavior is at your own, albeit minimal, risk. The law probably wouldn't haul you into jail or anything, just kick you out. But you never know.

great outdoors

Surfing is huge in Portrush. There are great waves to be had all around the area along the coast in both directions. Your one-stop shop for advice, rentals, lessons, and gear is **Troggs** *(88 Main St.; Tel 02870/825-476; 10am-5:30pm daily; £5 for surfboards, £5 for wetsuits),* owned by the six-time national surf champion of Ireland, Andy Hill. He also runs the Surf Hostel [see *crashing,* below] right downtown. These crazy guys will get you surfing in the middle of January if you're bold enough.

eats

Most of the food here is cheap and greasy, but a few places are expensive and good. Let your food mirror your fun.

For gloriously greasy take-away that'll have you coming back for more, look no further than the **Savoy** *(Eglinton St., kitty-corner to the bus stop;*

Tel 02870/824-113; 11am-7pm daily; under £5). **Don Giovann's** *(9-13 Causeway St.; Tel 02870/825-516; 3pm-11pm; entrees £5-7)* may sound like an expensive Italian place in Little Italy, but it's actually a quite reasonably priced pasta house in Portrush. Their noodle plates are the most filling dishes in town.

Spinnacher *(25 Main St.; Tel 02870/822-348; noon-9:30pm daily; entrees £7-12; AE, MC, V)* has both entrees at dinnertime and great, great, *great* sandwiches in unusual and enticing permutations all afternoon. If you dine here at night, have some wine from their excellent list.

You'll find basic and tasty little sandwich combinations at **Bread Shop** *(21 Eglinton St.; Tel 02870/823-722; 8:30am-6:30pm daily; under £4),* as well as greasy and delicious cod and chips. And it's easy to find, right next to the post office [see *need to know,* below].

Hey, nobody's saying they serve the greatest food in the world at **Lucky House Chinese** *(53 Eglinton Ave.; Tel 02870/823-855; 5pm-midnight Mon-Wed, 5pm-2am Thu-Sat; entrees £3-8),* but it's on the south end of downtown, open late, and there's nothing like eating fried wontons at two in the morning on a Saturday after a night of debauchery at a local pub or club.

Sure, **Ramore's** *(On the Harbor, off Kerr St.; Tel 02870/824-313; 12:15-2:15pm/5-10pm Mon-Sat, 5pm-9pm Sun; entrees £10 and up; MC)* is pricey, but it's the best food in town—and the wine bar overlooks the harbor with gorgeous views. A generally older crowd gathers to eat, drink wine, and act sophisticated. The Char-sui chicken breast in a mango/peanut sauce with Asian salad is unbeatable. If you aren't packing a lot of cash, stop in for unbelievable burgers for a mere £4 at lunch.

crashing

Crashing on the cheap in Portrush is easy. There are only two hostels, both small, but dozens of B&B's line the streets along the peninsula. Even so, reserve in the summer and on weekends to avoid being shut out or paying a lot of dough.

TO market

A fun local attraction as well as a place to get groceries, the weekly **Country Market** *(The Market House, the Square, Portaferry; 10am-1pm Sat)* features locally grown plants, produce and, *mmm-mm,* fresh baked goodies.

Run by a delightful husband and wife team, **Macools Portrush Youth Hostel** *(5 Causeway View Terrace; Tel 02870/824-845; scilley@portrush-hostel.totalserve.co.uk; dorm beds £7, one double room £16; Internet £4 per hour, bike hire and laundry service also available; No credit cards)* is small and friendly and a real treat. The husband's philosophy on life is worth experiencing for the sheer conviction of his beliefs. We won't spoil it by giving you specifics, but sit down and talk with him about WWOOF. Dorms are small and a bit cramped, but the beds(there are 25) are noticeably bigger and more comfortable than most hostels'. Bathrooms and common areas are clean and exceedingly comfortable. It feels more like staying at a friend's house than a hostel. The kitchen is spotless, and big jars of curry, oregano and other spices make cooking here a real pleasure. Macools can also give you great information on what to see in the area, plus a complete history of the various ruins, myths, and attractions. You'll find it at the northern tip of the peninsula. At the intersection of Main and Mark streets, turn onto Causeway Terrace.

The latest addition to the Portrush hostel scene, the **Surf Hostel** *(6 Bath St.; Tel 02870/825-476; £10 per bed; No credit cards)* is run by the owners of **Troggs Surf Shop** [see *great outdoors,* above]. There are only a handful of beds, but the place is spacious and the atmosphere definitely leans toward party mode. Since it just opened in May 2000, they haven't quite figured out their policy on renting to non-surfers, so call ahead and make sure they can accommodate you. They give deals on surfing lessons and rentals if you stay here. There's a full kitchen, some bachelor-pad leather couches in the lounge, and surfing posters on the walls. And it's all right downtown.

Kerr Street, on the west side of the peninsula, along the water, is packed with B&Bs, all virtually identical: clean, pretty cheap, and close to the water. A place unknown to most budget travelers, the **Alexander House B&B** *(23 Kerr St.; Tel 02870/824-566; £10 per bed 4-bed room; £32 double, breakfast included)* is the only B&B in town with hostel-priced accommodations. The place is clean and basic, nothing fancy, but totally comfy and friendly. Another good Kerr Street option, **Brae Mar B&B** *(28 Kerr St.; Tel 02870/825-224; £20 single, £30 double)* is as basic and clean as the Alexander, but a bit smaller and more intimate. **A Rest a-While B&B** *(Atlantic Ave., past Main St. toward the ocean; Tel 02870/822-827; £20 single, £30 double)* gives good bed: clean, simple, and cheap.

Other do-able options include **Clarence** *(7 Bath Terrace; Tel. 02870/823575),* **Beulah House** *(16 Causeway St.; Tel. 02870/822413),* **Seamara** *(26 Mark St.; Tel. 02870/822541),* and **Old Manse** *(3 Main St.; Tel. 02870/824118).*

need to know

Currency Exchange Get your cash at **Northern Bank** *(60 Main St.; Tel 02870/822-327; 9:30am-12:30pm/1:30-5pm Mon-Fri)* or **Ulster Bank** *(33 Eglinton St.; Tel 02870/822-726; 9:30am-12:30pm/1:30-*

5pm Mon-Fri). The tourist office at **Dunluce Center** [see below] also has a bureau de change with horrible rates; stick to the bank unless they're already closed.

Tourist Information You got questions? **Dunluce Center** *(Sandhill Rd.; Tel 02870/823-333; 9am-7pm daily Jun-Aug; 9am-5pm Mon-Fri, noon-5pm Sat-Sun Apr-May, Sept; noon-5pm Sat-Sun Oct-Mar)* has answers.

Public Transportation Call **Portrush Taxis** *(Tel 02870/823-483)* for a lift.

Health and Emergency Emergency: *999;* Police: *02870/822-721.* There are no hospitals in Portrush.

Pharmacies **Heron Chemists** *(5/9 Main St.; Tel 02870/822-324; 9am-6pm daily, till 10:30pm, Jul-Aug)* is right downtown.

Trains Catch a big steel ride out of town at the **Eglinton St. Station** *(Eglinton St.; Tel 02870/822-395)* with connections to Belfast and Derry by way of Coleraine, five-nine times a day.

Bus Lines Out of the City You can get to Bushmills, Giant's Causeway and Ballycastle via bus from the station on Dunluce Street at the south end of downtown.

Bike Rental **Bicycle Doctor** *(104 Lower Main St.; Tel 02870/824-340; £7 per day, £30 per week)* is located conveniently downtown.

Postal The **post office** *(23 Eglinton St.; Tel 02870/823-700; 9am-12:30pm/1:30-5:30pm Mon-Fri, 9am-12:30pm Sat)* is at the intersection of Eglinton Street and Causeway Road downtown.

Internet The best place to get online is at **Macool's Portrush Youth Hostel** [see *crashing,* above]. Unfortunately, you do have to be a guest to take advantage of it. Nowhere else in Portrush offers access, so better plan accordingly.

bushmills

This little town is primarily a Protestant enclave, but you'll likely come here to worship at a different altar: the **Bushmill's Whiskey Distillery** *(Tel 02820/731-521; Mon-Sat 9:30am-5:30pm, tour every hour, last tour at 4pm; £3.50 Adults, £3 Students).* It's the one highlight in this otherwise un-fantastic little town. You get a tour of the old distillery and a much coveted sample of this smooth, blended whiskey. At the end of the tour, they'll ask you who wants to taste five different flavors of Scotch. Don't raise your hand! It's a trick question. We're in Ireland, not Scotland, remember? Wait till all the rubes are found out, then raise your hand when they ask who wants proper *Irish* whiskey and have five free samples. Yee-haw!

If you need a place to pad your tummy for the whiskey, try **Valerie's Pantry** *(125 Main St.),* which does sandwiches and burgers.

If you get stuck here for the night, don't just pass out in the street—try **Ardeevin** *(145 Main St.; Tel. 02890/731661).*

need to know

Directions/Transportation Buses go from Portrush or Ballycastle to Bushmills only a couple of times a day, so plan ahead. Call **Ulsterbus** *(Tel 02890/351-201)* for schedule info. Bushmills is a 15-minute ride from Portrush, even closer to the Giant's Causeway.

ballintoy/carrick-a-rede island

Between Ballycastle and Portrush sits the village of Ballintoy, and another must-see Antrim attraction, the Carrick-a-Rede Island. This little speck of an island sticks out in the ocean connected to the mainland only by a swaying rope bridge over a 100-foot drop into the drink. It's not as sketchy as it sounds: the bridge is heavily reinforced with nylon cords and sturdy planks. It jumps up and down a bit when more than one person walks on it, though, and looking down can make the faint of heart a bit uneasy. This is a big draw for all who pass through; it's something you owe it to yourself to do. Lines can be long, but it's never crowded on the bridge itself.

crashing

There is also a little hostel in Ballintoy, the **Sheep Island View Hostel** *(42 Main St.; Tel 02820/762-470; £9 en suite dorm)* which is pretty much standard issue hostel fare. Another option is **Ballintoy House** *(9 Main St.; Tel. 02820/762317; £14/person with shared bath and continental breakfast; £16/person with private bath and full Irish breakfast; No credit cards).*

eats

A **teahouse** *(Tel 02821/761-437; 10am-6pm daily Apr-Jun, early Sep; 10am-8pm Jul-Aug)* operates at the bridge in spring and summer, offering decent scones and warm drinks.

need to know

Directions/Transportation If you're driving or biking to Ballintroy, take the A2 onto the B15 between Portrush and Ballycastle. From Ballycastle, head west on the A2 and turn right onto B15 about 3.2 km (2 mi) out of town then continue on for 8 km (5 mi).

ballycastle

Not as rowdy as its die-hard party-town cousin, Portrush, this cute little seaside town offers more relaxed charm. It's close to all the major attractions of the region, has some fine pubs, and is overall a pleasant place to spend a day.

Ballycastle is centered around one main street that runs southwest away from **Ballycastle Bay,** changing names a few times along the way. Starting at the water, it is **Quay Road,** then **Ann Street,** then **Castle Street.** Most of what you'll visit in Ballycastle is along this stretch. Along the shore, **Mary Road** runs out to the southeast from the main street, while **North Street** goes to the northeast. **The Diamond,** a square formed at the end of Ann Street by the intersection of several roads, acts as the tiny town's center.

bar scene

Pubs are not in overabundance in Ballycastle, but there are good times to be had. Pubs shut down around midnight, but you can usually hang out for an hour more. In the summer, they'll be open longer.

McCarrols *(7 Ann St.; Tel 02820/762-123)* is a good, basic pub serving properly poured pints of Guinness to tourists, locals, old and young alike in a rustic setting.

There's trad and folk music at the **House of McDonnell** *(Castle St.; Tel 02820/762-975)* almost every day of the week, and sessions can be brilliant. It's a rather touristy spot, but it's got the biggest concentration of people under 30 in town.

Wysner's *(16 Ann St.; Tel 02820/762-372; lunch £5)* serves up basic, pub grub-esque food, good and cheap, in a small diner-type milieu.

crashing

The most popular hostel in town is the **Castle Hostel** *(Tel 02820/762-337; 62 Quay Rd.; £7 dorm).* It's big and bright and right in the middle of things, down by the bay.

Ballycastle Backpackers *(4 North St.; Tel 02820/763-612; £7 dorm)* is another decent hostel option. It's also right on the water, and some rooms have a view of the sea. Dorms are a bit tiny for full-grown people, but comfortable enough.

Also handy to the waterfront, **Hilsea B&B** *(28 North St.; Tel 02820/762-385; £20 single, £35 double)* will give you sea views, and very comfortable accommodations for a modest price.

Other do-able options include **Fair Head View** *(26 North St.; Tel. 20/769376),* **Glenluce** *(42 Quay Rd.; Tel. 20/762914),* **Fragens** *(34 Quay Rd.; Tel. 20/762168),* and **Antrim Arms Hotel** *(75 Castle St.; Tel. 20762284).*

need to know

Currency Exchange **Northern Bank** *(Ann St.; Tel 02820/762-238; 10am-12:30pm/1:30-3:30pm Mon-Fri)* has both an ATM and bureau de change.

Tourist Information The **tourist information office** *(7 Mary St.; Tel 02810/762-024; 9:30am-7pm Mon-Fri, 10am-6pm Sat, 2-6pm Sun, Jul-Aug; 9:30am-5pm Mon-Fri, Sep-Jun)* has all the maps and info on town you'll want.

Public Transportation **Ballycastle Taxi** *(Tel 02820/762-822; 24-hour service)* is there if you need it, and handy in the absence of buses, but everything's walkable here.

Emergency **Dalriada Hospital** *(Coraine Rd.; Ballycastle; Tel 02870/762-666)* is the local care facility.

Pharmacies **McMichael's** *(10 Ann St; Tel 02820/763-342; 9am-1pm/2-6pm Mon-Sat)* is about the only pill source in town.

Bus Lines Out of the City **Ulsterbus** *(Tel. 02890/351201* goes to Portrush and Belfast several times a day.

Bike Rental **Northern Auto** *(41 Castle St.; Tel 02810/763-748; £6 per day, £30 per week)* will rent you wheels for exploring.

Postal The **post office** *(3 Ann St.; Tel 02820/762-519; 9am-1pm/2-5:30pm Mon-Tue, Thu-Fri; 9am-12:30pm Wed)* is there whatever the weather.

the giant's causeway

The title "The Eighth Wonder of the World" has been bestowed upon such enormities as America's "World's Largest Ball of Twine," and wrestling legend Andre the Giant. But the Giant's Causeway, another enormity that has often been conferred this title, is by far the most deserving. Thousands of hexagonal pillars of basalt jut out from the sea all along the shoreline, making a big plane of geometrically pleasing steps. The scientific explanation for the pillars is that they were caused by the unusually even cooling of the molten igneous basalt rock as it rose from a shallow fissure millions of years ago. The cooling allowed its natural crystalline shape to emerge unadulterated. Got all that?

The mythic—and much more fun—explanation is that the legendary Irish giant Finn McCool wanted to see his Scottish girlfriend, and built these stepping stones so he could get over to Scotland's Staffa Island (the only other place where these kinds of pillars exist). Why he'd need 37,000 steps is beyond modern explanation.

need to know

Tourist Information The **Causeway Visitor's Center** *(At the car park at the entrance to the Causeway Trail; Tel 02820/731-855; 10am-6pm* *daily, Jun; 10am-7pm daily, Jul-Aug; 10am-5pm daily Mar-May, Sep; £3 parking, Free admission)* does the whole question-answer thing. Though the original building burned down in April 2000, temporary facilities are now in place.

Directions/Transportation Take **Ulsterbus** *(Tel 090/351-201)* from Portrush or Ballycastle. Buses leave twice a day from both of these places and take you a stone's throw from the entrance. Belfast and Derry also have tourist buses making trips here several times a day. Check with the tourist offices in those cities or at any youth hostel for more info.

Crashing If you want to stay here, your only option is the **Causeway Hotel** *(Causeway car park; Tel 20/731-226; Restaurant open 11am-6pm; £40-70 double).* Otherwise, we recommend you make the commute to Portrush or Ballycastle.

Eats If you want a bite, head for the **Causeway Hotel** [see above], where you can get chips and chicken or fish for around £5—but do it before 6pm. You can also grab a light meal at the **Tea Room** in the Causeway Visitor's Center [see above].

the ards peninsula

Traveling down the Ards Peninsula from Belfast, you'll eventually run out of road and hit water at **Portaferry,** a sleepy little waterside village set magnificently on **Strangford Lough,** a 20-mile long, serene little body of water with pristine shores that runs into the turbulent Irish Sea via the narrow channel between Portaferry and **Strangford.** Portaferry wakes up in June with the Galway Hooker Festival [see *festivals and events,* below]. Contrary to the expectations of many a randy back-packer, these hookers are sailing and fishing boats with big sails. Never-

festivals and events

The **Galway Hooker Festival and Boat Regatta** is a unique Portaferry event. In the last week of June, sailing ships slip into port for a week of drinking, games and song. Regatta (rowing) competitions are also held. The mood is festive, Ferris wheels are set up, the tiny town is packed with people, and the *craic* is almost too much to handle. Book early if you're coming during the event and bring some extra pounds for drinking as leaving a pub without quaffing your fair share is viewed as sacrilege.

theless, the partying during the festival is non-stop and the place gets crowded, so book what scarce accommodations there are in town early if you're gonna come. Across the lough is the tiny little village of Strangford, which is little more than a couple of streets, but it's cute as heck. If you've got nothing planned, spend an afternoon here sitting on the waterfront and wandering around Strangford's handful of picturesque streets.

neighborhoods

Portaferry and Strangford are *tiny,* so if you get lost, you're a hopeless case. Both towns revolve around their own respective **Squares,** though they feel like two sides of the same coin. Many people traverse the lough daily to eat, shop, or visit friends. Everything worth doing and seeing in Portaferry (except for the windmill) is based around the Square and the waterfront area. To get from the shores of the lough to the Square, walk uphill on **Castle Street** about 200 meters. You travel between the two towns by ferry. On the Strangford side you'll be dropped right in front of the Square; in Portaferry you'll be let off at **The Strand,** the usual Irish town name for the waterfront. Even if you only want to hit one of these cute little villages briefly, take the ferry crossing for the beautiful views of the lough and the countryside surrounding it. The crossing takes about 15 minutes.

bar scene

The nightspots on the Ards Peninsula are few, but they are of excellent quality. There are a couple of pubs around Portaferry's Square, the best being **Fiddler's Green** *(Church St.; Open till 11:30pm),* about eight houses up the street from Adair's B&B [see *crashing,* below]. It's a relaxed, multi-generational atmosphere chock full of old jugs, road signs and people. They have great trad music on weekends and some weeknights, and the place is always packed at night. In Strangford, **The Hole in the Wall** *(Downpatrick Rd., right off the Square; Tel 02844/881-301)* and the bar at the **Cuan** [see *crashing,* below] are the only options in town. The Hole in the Wall is a standard-issue traditional pub, and the Cuan is similar, if a little more upscale, and has trad some nights.

culture zoo

Exploris Aquarium *(Castle Lane, Portaferry; Tel 02842/728-062; 10am-6pm Mon-Fri, 11am-6pm Sat, 1-6pm Sun, Apr-Aug; 10am-5pm Mon-Fri, 11am-5pm Sat, 1pm-6pm Sun, Sep-Mar; Admission £3.75):* Portaferry's biggest "attraction" is this modern aquarium, the only one in the North, which has excellent exhibits about the marine life in the Irish Sea and the lough. Don't miss the "touching tanks," underwater petting zoos containing starfish and other bottom-feeding cuties. Watch little kids as their eyes light up at their first experience with deepsea life.

Portaferry Castle: These ruins are next-door to the aquarium. They're adequate as ruins go, but nothing more.

Windmill: The one single thing you should do when you're in Portaferry is make the short hike up Windmill Hill Road to the old windmill (you can't miss it). Once you're up the hill, the views of the lough are so beautiful and serene, they'll likely melt your heart. You can climb up the tower, but the vista is much more panoramic from downstairs on the grass. If you happen to have someone acquiescent handy, take them up the tower at sunset for a good snog.

great outdoors

Diving is possible in Portaferry, and there are chartered diving boats that go out on the deep and exploration-worthy lough. Call **Desmond Rogers** *(Tel 02842/728-297)* to make arrangements. You can also inquire at the Barholm Youth Hostel [see *crashing,* below] or the tourist office [see *need to know,* below] for information about diving, sightseeing and fishing excursions. Call ahead, though, as things could be completely full in high season or non-operational in low season.

eats

For food, there are not many budget options. There are a couple of ultra-greasy take-away shops around the Square in Portaferry (to list them here would be to actively promote heart disease), but otherwise your best bet if you're staying at the hostel is to just buy groceries and cook for yourself. **The Shambles** *(Castle St.; 10am-6pm Mon-Sat; sandwiches £2; No credit cards)* has good, basic, non-heart-attack-inducing lunches and soups for a cheap price. The **Portaferry Hotel** *(10 the Strand, Portaferry; Tel 02842/728-412; £6-15; V, MC, AE, D, Switch)* serves decent lunches and pricey upscale dinners that incorporate lots of delectable fresh seafood. Across the lough in Strangford, **The Cuan** [see *crashing,* below] does pub food in both sit-down and take-out forms (about £8), and offers a more pricey dinner menu in a relaxed, country-elegant atmosphere. Think heavy meat dishes and pasta with rich sauces.

crashing

The 45-bed **Barholm Youth Hostel** *(11 the Strand, Portaferry; Tel 02842/729-598; £10.95 per person single, double, and 6-8-bed dorm; No credit cards)* is clean, well maintained, has laundry facilities for £3, as well as a kitchen, and is a stone's throw from the lough—which is all gravy, considering it's the only hostel in these parts! Reservations are recommended. Fishermen who work in Strangford Lough are allowed to come in and take a shower for £1, so watch for scales under your bare tootsies. **Mrs. Adair's B&B** *(22 The Square, Portaferry; Tel 02842/728-412; £20 single, £30 double; No credit cards)* is a great budget option as well, comfortable and convenient, if basic.

If you want to sleep in luxury, take the ferry to Strangford to **The Cuan** *(The Square, Strangford; Tel 02844/881-222; £35 single, £60 double; MC, V).* The Cuan exudes charm, has cozy en suite rooms with TV and

old ireland

Despite being written well over a century ago, Walt Whitman's words in "Old Ireland" resonate with a new hope and new power as the people of Ulster attempt to escape the horrors of The Troubles and begin a new day in what is truly a new nation.

"Far hence amid an isle of wondrous beauty,
Crouching over a grave an ancient sorrowful mother,
Once a queen, now lean and tattered seated on the ground,
Her old white hair drooping disheveled round her shoulders,
At her feet fallen an unused royal harp,
Long silent, she too long silent, mourning her shrouded
  hope and heir,
Of all the earth her heart most full of sorrow because most
  full of love.

Yet a word ancient mother,
You need crouch there no longer on the cold ground with
  forehead between your knees,
O you need not sit there veiled in your old white hair so
  disheveled,
For know you the one you mourn is not in that grave,
It was an illusion, the son you love was not really dead,
The Lord is not dead, he is risen again young and strong in
  another country,
Even while you wept there by your fallen harp by the grave,
What you wept for was translated, passed from the grave,
The winds favoured and the sea sailed it,
And now with rosy and new blood,
Moves today in a new country."

tea-making facilities, and the staff is exceptionally friendly. There's also a nice pub downstairs [see *bar scene,* above] and a take-away restaurant [see *eats,* above].

need to know

Currency Exchange: **Northern Bank** *(The Square, Portaferry; Tel 02842/728-208; Mon 10am-5pm, Tue-Wed, Fri 10am-3:30pm, Thu 9:30am-3:30pm)* has a 24-hour ATM.

Tourist Information: The **tourist office** *(Inside the Portaferry Castle* *grounds; Tel 02842/729-882; 10am-5:30pm Mon-Sat, noon-6pm Sun, Jul-Aug; 10am-5:30pm Mon-Sat, 2-6pm Sun, Easter-Jun, Sep)* is in Portaferry.

Bus Lines Out of the City **Ulsterbus** *(The Square, Portaferry; tel. 028 90/351201; £3.50 single)* makes the 90-minute trip from the Peninsula to Belfast 18 times a day Monday-Saturday, eight times a day on Sunday.

Boats A **ferry** runs between Portaferry and Strangford every half-hour *(The Strand, Portaferry and the Square, Strangford; 7:45am-10:45pm Mon-Fri, 8:15am-11:15pm Sat, 9:45-10:45pm Sun; 85p).*

Postal The **post office** *(The Square, Portaferry; Tel 02842/728-201; 9am-5:30pm Mon-Wed, Fri, 9am-1pm Thu, 9am-12:30pm Sat)* is where to drop those postcards.

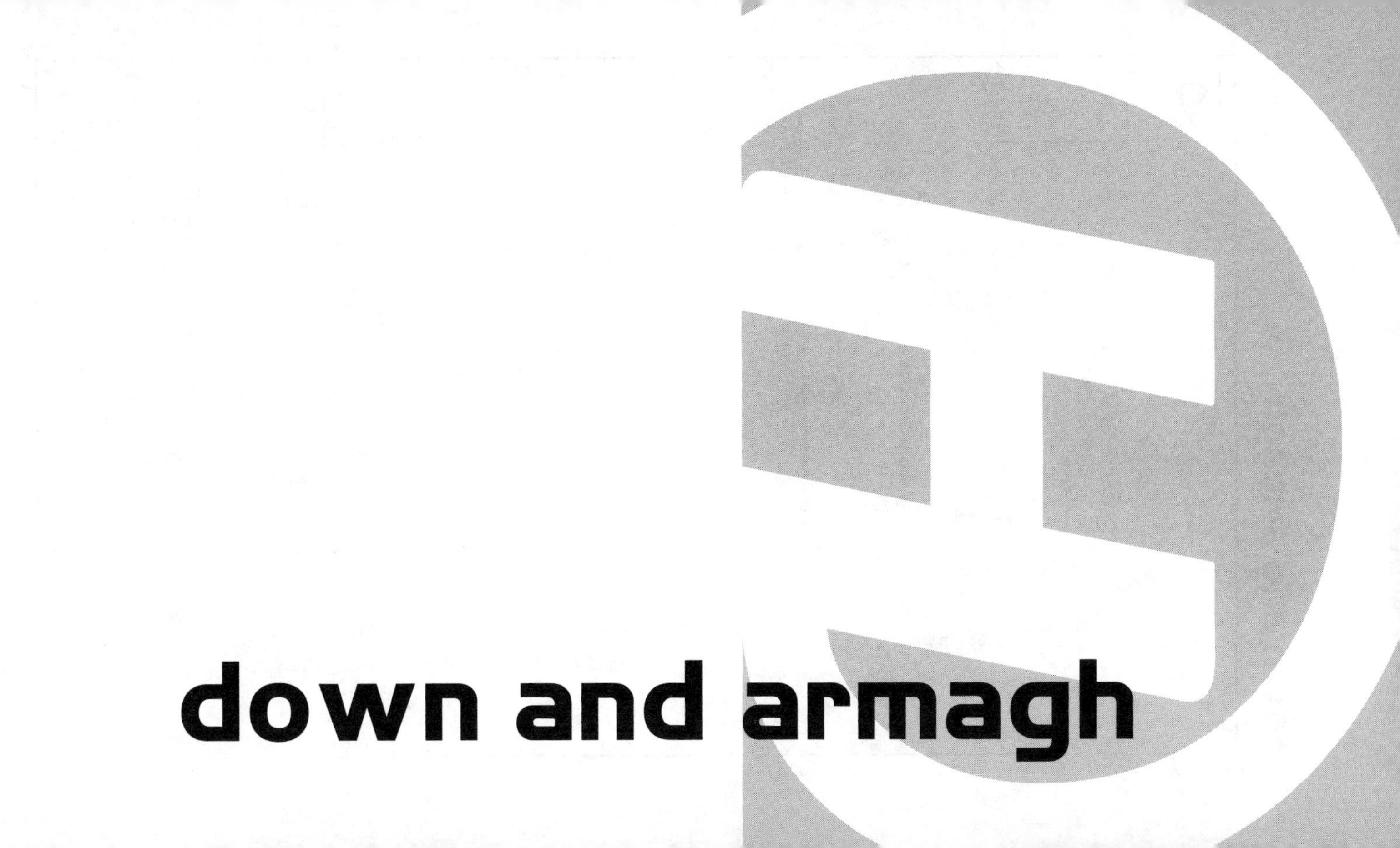
down and armagh

down and armagh

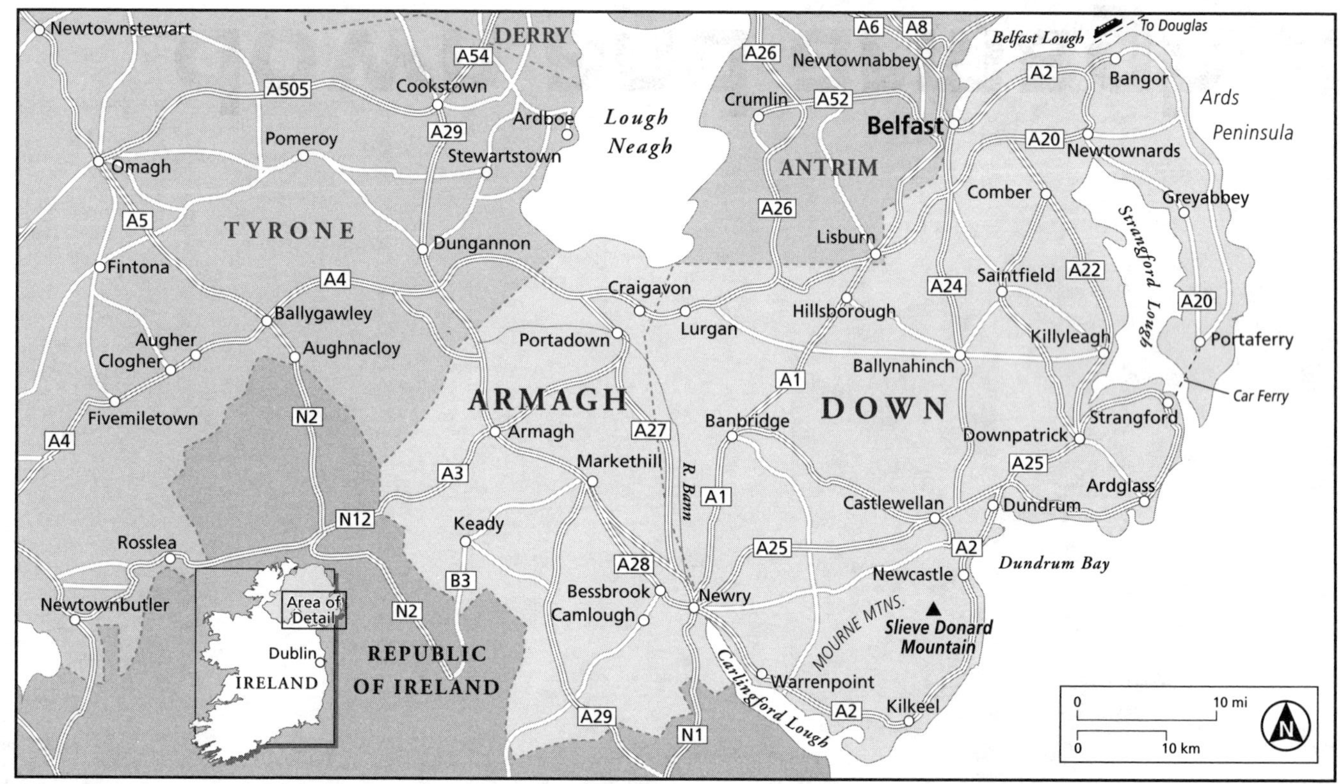

armagh

The town of Armagh feels a bit pensive, as if it's waiting with baited breath for a tourist onslaught that never quite fully comes. County Armagh is among the hardest hit by the Troubles; previously plagued by violence, and now suffering from the lingering effects of all the bad press. Nevertheless, Armagh has emerged like a phoenix from the ashes as a beautiful and engaging town. You'd be hard pressed to find a place as significant to Irish religious history, or one quite as pretty on a spring or summer day.

In a couple years, as word spreads, Armagh could become a hot destination for travelers, overrun with screaming babies and whining yuppies. But for now, it awaits you as an unadulterated and peaceful place to explore.

History buffs will feel like pigs in slop here. One of the oldest settlements in Ireland, legend has it that Armagh was supposedly founded by the mythical Queen Macha 600 years after Noah raised anchor in the Flood. Armagh is the "Christian capital" of Ireland, and on Árd Macha (Macha's Hill), St. Patrick built a church in 445. One has stood here ever since. Over the next few centuries, the town flourished as a center of culture and learning. It also excelled at attracting invaders. During the 9th and 10th centuries, the city was sacked by the dastardly Vikings more times than a rookie quarterback in the Pro Bowl. Irish kings took control again in 1014, but sure enough, the Normans invaded in the 12th century. In later centuries, the Reformation and "planters" (English and Scottish settlers shipped in by England) again changed the face of the town, creating a religious, and increasingly tribal, tension that exists to this day [see *marching season,* below].

marching season

You may have heard people say "Don't come to Armagh during marching season." Indeed, it may *not* be wise to come to town on, or a few weeks before, July 12, the day when various Protestant Orange organizations—the biggest being the Loyal Orange Institution, aka The Orange Order—march through town commemorating King William III of Orange's defeat of James II at the Battle of the Boyne in 1690. There may be scuffles, an increased police presence, and a few arrests. The Orange Order goes back to 1795, and has been hugely influential in the Unionist political structure and in determining the course of Protestant-Catholic relations. As the negotiation process steps cautiously toward a lasting and real peace, it seems that the potential for violence is lessening. 1999 saw a peaceful marching season, but in future years it will be difficult to tell if the promise of peace brings out the best or the worst in these hardline Loyalists. Fortunately, most of the young people you talk to in Armagh seem to be sick of the violence and the ill will. Don't let this sort of thing deter you from visiting Armagh, though, as it's generally safe any other time of the year.

The modern city of Armagh embraces its complex and important history, some would say to the detriment of its present. Young people in town will tell you, in much the same vein as kids from American suburbia, that there's just "nothing to do". Indeed, a none-too-vibrant youth culture and nightlife may be the only remaining obstacles to this beautiful town becoming a truly incredible place to visit.

The best time to come here is in May, during apple blossom season, when the countryside is in full bloom and everything is covered in white blossoms. It may be all a sinner will ever know of heaven. The worst time to be in Armagh is any Sunday of the year, when everything except the plumbing shuts down.

neighborhoods

Armagh is a small city or large town, depending on whom you ask. There are 14,000 people here. At the center of town stands the impressive **St. Patrick's Roman Catholic Cathedral,** and up on Ard Macha, the big hill north of the center, is the **St. Patrick's Church of Ireland Cathedral** [see *culture zoo,* below, for both]. These are the major landmarks in town; if you don't know where you are, look up for their impressive spires to get your bearings straight. Also, the grounds outside the Roman Catholic cathedral are an excellent place to get a panoramic view of town and set the layout in your head.

During the day, people tend to congregate on **Market Square,** south of Protestant St. Patrick's. On the square you'll find some cool haunts like the **Basement Café** [see *eats,* below] and the chic **Marketplace** [see *arts scene,* below] with its bars, art gallery and theater, and a number of pubs. From Market Square, head north on **English Street,** take your first right onto **Russell Street** and you'll hit **The Mall,** a beautiful patch of green ringed with trees and surrounded by Georgian houses. You're likely to see sunbathing cuties, picnicking families, and cricket matches [see *city sports,* below]. Head south from the Mall toward the edge of the city proper and you'll run into the **Palace Demesne** [see *culture zoo,* below], an enormous stretch of green that holds the ruins of a Franciscan friary, the beautiful palace stables, and a golf course on its acres of land.

Armagh's major drawback for young travelers, and for its young inhabitants, is its limited nightlife. There *are* places to go, but there is no gay scene whatsoever, little diversity in the crowds from place to place and not much good music to be heard. So come here for the beauty and the history, but don't expect to get too jiggy.

bar, club, and live music scene

Pub life in Armagh is not extremely swinging. Many of Armagh's local young folk feel pretty alienated by the town's interest in promoting its past and unwillingness to liven up its present, but it is possible to have a fun night out here. The biggest concentration of pubs is on English Street and the surrounding blocks.

The best pub in town, **Hughe's Northern Bar** *(100 Railway St.; Tel 02837/527315; Noon-11:30pm Mon-Thu, Sun, noon-1am Fri-Sat; No credit cards),* is a few blocks north from English Street on Railway Street. Pronounced "Hughe-zes," this is the best place to meet young people that are cool. The bar is full of traditional pub elements—a fireplace, wooden booths, stained glass in the windows—yet it manages to be modern. Upstairs they have live rock music on Friday and Saturday; Sunday features local trad.

McKenna's *(21 English St.; Tel 02837/568437; Noon-11:30pm Mon-Thu, Sun, noon-1am Fri-Sat; No credit cards)* exudes a lively, fun feeling, and on weekends, it's possible to have a great time. The setting is basic if not a little rustic. There isn't much to look at here, but the people, everyone from old codgers at the bar to 18-year-olds giggling in the booths, seem intent on conversing with anyone and everyone in sight.

The chic bar/cafe—actually two bars and a restaurant—at the brand new, modernist **Market Place Café** *(Market Square; Tel 02837/521820; coffee house opens at noon for lunch, cocktail bar opens for performances, usually in the evening from around 7pm till around 11pm)* buzzes on theater nights. It's worth a look in the daytime for a snack, a burger, or a glass of

armagh

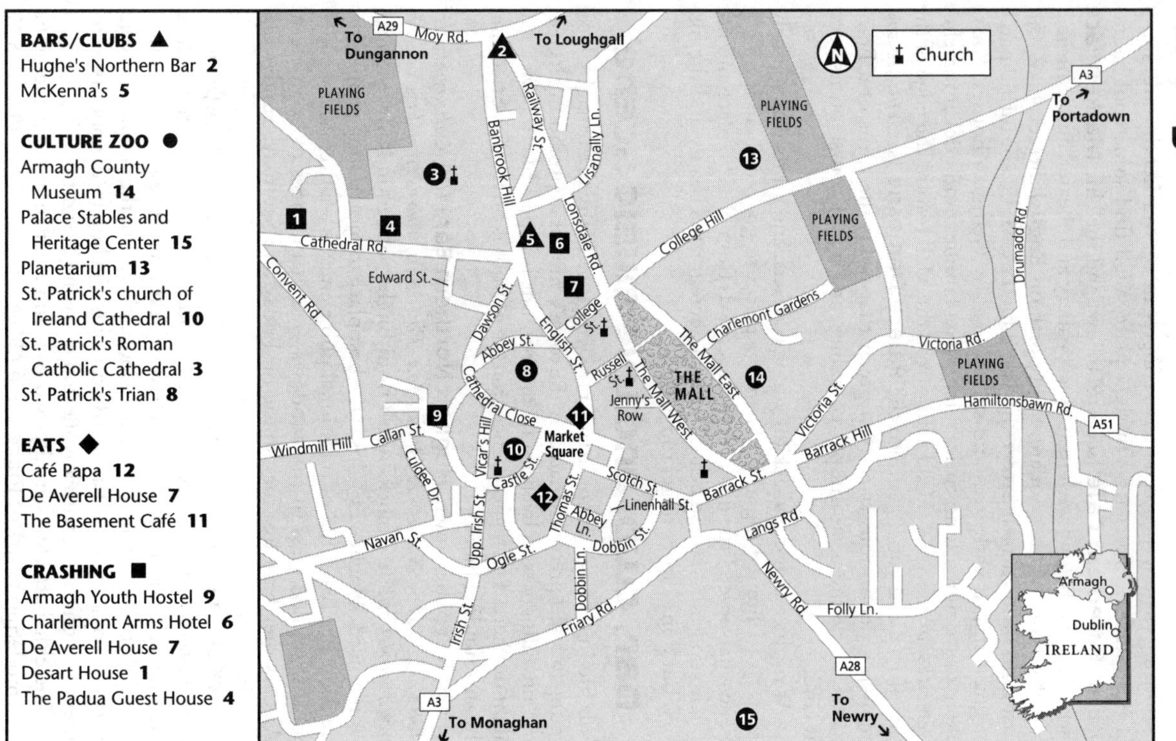

BARS/CLUBS ▲
Hughe's Northern Bar 2
McKenna's 5
CULTURE ZOO ●
Armagh County Museum 14
Palace Stables and Heritage Center 15
Planetarium 13
St. Patrick's church of Ireland Cathedral 10
St. Patrick's Roman Catholic Cathedral 3
St. Patrick's Trian 8
EATS ◆
Café Papa 12
De Averell House 7
The Basement Café 11
CRASHING ■
Armagh Youth Hostel 9
Charlemont Arms Hotel 6
De Averell House 7
Desart House 1
The Padua Guest House 4
Church
To Dungannon
A29
Moy Rd.
To Loughgall
Railway St.
Banbrook Hill
Lisanally Ln.
Lonsdale Rd.
College Hill
To Portadown
A3
Drumadd Rd.
Victoria Rd.
Hamiltonsbawn Rd.
A51
PLAYING FIELDS
Charlemont Gardens
The Mall East
THE MALL
The Mall West
Victoria St.
Barrack Hill
Barrack St.
Langs Rd.
Newry Rd.
Folly Ln.
A28
To Newry
Armagh
Dublin
IRELAND
Cathedral Rd.
Edward St.
Dawson St.
Abbey St.
English St.
College St.
Russell St.
Jenny's Row
Scotch St.
Linenhall St.
Market Square
Thomas St.
Abbey Ln.
Dobbin St.
Dobbin Ln.
Friary Rd.
Cathedral Close
Castle St.
Vicar's Hill
Upp. Irish St.
Irish St.
Ogle St.
Callan St.
Culdee Dr.
Navan St.
Convent Rd.
Windmill Hill
To Monaghan

festivals and events

In May, the town gets hoppin' for the **Apple Blossom Festival,** which features everything from blues music to tours of blossom country to the Apple Blossom Fashion Show. Stop by the tourist office [see *need to know,* below] and pick up a brochure for all the happenings.

wine. The crowd is older, moneyed folk and their young offspring. It's a good place to schmooze with the upper crust of Armagh society; expect people in blazers and long skirts and dresses.

arts scene

Armagh's arts scene is small but growing, and is centered at Market Square. The newly opened **Market Place Arts Center** *(Market Sq.; Tel 02837/521820; Performances usually at 8pm, call for info)* has a spacious gallery spread out over two levels of modern white walls and glass floors. Most of the work is contemporary Irish: lots of earth tones on minimalist milieus. You can also catch plays, opera, and dance here. The large theater hosts big-name acts like the Chieftains and the Irish Tenors. There is also a 150-seat black-box theater that hosts stand-up comedy nights, "The Empire Laughs Back" (monthly, call for details).

The **Armagh City Film House** *(Market St.; Tel 02837/524311; tickets £5),* down the hill from Market Square, is a decent theater with four screens playing mostly mainstream American films. Catching a show here is one of the few things to do in town after dark besides drinking....

culture zoo

Palace Stables and Heritage Center *(From the Friary Rd, look for signs for "Palace Stables" and follow them; Tel 02837/529629; 10am-7pm Mon-Sat, 1-7pm Sun, Apr-Sep; 10am-5pm Mon-Sat, 2-5pm Sun, Oct-Mar; Admission £3 adults, £2 students):* Few things are more fulfilling in a Zen sort of way than a trip to these impressive grounds. It's basically a huge park or "demesne," with a number of different attractions in it. From the main entrance off the Friary Road, the first sight is the Franciscan Friary Ruin, a large, ruined 13th-century abbey, the longest Friary church in Ireland, of which a few impressive arches remain. Its pastoral setting—trees and lush grass everywhere—make it one of the more atmospheric settings for an abbey in the North. On the land, there are a number of old buildings, trees, and flowers. Farther up the path is the courtyard, which is surrounded by various rooms made up in period decor like the coachman's kitchen, and the stables. Then there is the Victorian conser-

road bowling

If, on a Sunday in County Armagh, you happen to see two guys hurling heavy balls of steel down a rural road surrounded by cheering onlookers, you aren't witnessing a group of mental patients on a weekend furlough. What you're watching is probably a road bowling match. A local favorite, this sport is a true oddity. The object is to get the heavy metal ball to the end of a stretch of road in the least amount of tosses. Matches take place mostly in the springtime and rarely receive official sanction from town or county, so ask around and see where you can watch one of these games. The only other place to see these matches is down south in County Cork, so if there's a match happening, it may be your only chance to see what it's all about.

vatory, an ornate 19th-century glasshouse full of flowers, and the beautiful ornamental garden. Also recommended is the Eco Trail, a pleasant path through the demesne filled with local flora and fauna. You can also catch walking tours among the apple blossoms here in May [see *festivals & events,* below]. You can get info on these and other walks at the heritage center or at the tourist office downtown [see *need to know,* below].

St. Patrick's Roman Catholic Cathedral *(Cathedral Rd.; 9am-6pm daily; Free):* Though not as old or steeped in history as other big cathedrals in Europe, St. Patrick's is still mighty impressive. The foundation was laid in 1840, but the Famine (1845-1849) brought further building to a standstill. Construction resumed on Easter, 1854, and the cathedral was finally dedicated in 1873. Outside, the 210-foot Gothic Revival twin spires dominate the church, while inside the Italian marble mosaic work is brilliant both in color and impact, yielding an almost psychedelic effect. You might detect a Byzantine influence similar to that of St. Marco's Cathedral in Venice. You could spend hours gazing at the swirling patterns, or the impressive roof paintings, and the view of the city from the front lawn is spectacular.

St. Patrick's Church of Ireland Cathedral *(Cathedral Close; Tel 02837/523142; 10:30am-5pm, Apr-Sep; 10:30am-4pm, Oct-Mar):* This bad boy isn't too shabby either. The design and lineage of the church dates back to St. Patrick's 5th-century efforts here. One of the highlights of a trip inside is an 11th-century Celtic cross.

The Armagh Planetarium *(College Hill; Tel 02837/523689; 10am-4:45pm Mon-Fri, 1:15-4:45pm Sat; Admission £3.75):* A trip here will probably remind you of a planetarium you visited on a 6th grade field trip, right down to the Atari 520st interactive media display and the 1980's space documentary playing on one of the monitors. The planetarium looks a little rundown, like one too many kids has spun the solar wheel and fondled the fossils. Nevertheless, there's something fun about seeing the universe portrayed in such accessible, innocent terms. Various exhibits take you through our universe, culminating in the way cool show in the Star Theater. Here, you are taken through a few billion years of cosmic history in only a half-hour. It's majorly trippy stuff, although the lights are a bit dim, so hopefully they will have changed the light bulb in the projector by now. Outside is almost better than inside. In the Astropark, you really get a sense of the scale of the solar system as all the planets are represented, as well as a hill of infinity, a big logarithmic cube, and other goodies. On the same grounds is the Observatory, which is unfortunately closed to the public. The Planetarium also has a huge telescope, which is opened up to the public twice a month from September to April. Call ahead for details. There's also a little cafe on site, and a cheesy gift shop as well.

St. Patrick's Trian *(40 English St.; Tel 02837/521801; 10am-5pm Mon-Sat, 2-5pm Sun, Sep-Jun; 1-6pm daily, Jul-Aug; Admission £3.35 adults, £2.50 students):* St. Patrick's Trian is a nifty little exhibition using wax people to document the life of St. Patrick, as well as the histories of Christianity in Armagh and faith around the world. A 20-foot giant recounts the adventures of Gulliver from *Gulliver's Travels,* whose author, Jonathan Swift, spent time here way back when.

Armagh County Museum *(The Mall East; Tel 02837/523070; 10am-5pm Mon-Fri, 10am-1pm/2pm-5pm Sat; Free):* The oldest county museum in Ireland, this place looks something like a Greek temple and holds a decent collection of artifacts pertaining to Armagh's history. They range from ancient, prehistoric stones to axe-heads, to more recent costumes, clothing, and ceramics.

eats

Armagh eats are definitely on the yummy end of the food-quality spectrum, but unfortunately they are not wonderfully diverse. That being said, if you like rich meat and fowl dishes, you'll love it here. Vegetarians, be prepared to eat a cheese sandwich or two.

Tucked underneath the Armagh City Film House [see *arts scene,* above], **The Basement Café** *(Market St.; Tel 02837/524311; 9am-5:30pm Mon-Sat; £4 entrees, £1.50 soup)* is a cool hideaway for an afternoon coffee, sandwich or pre-movie snack. 1950s American ads and pop-culture paraphernalia adorn the walls of this popular youth hangout.

Easily identifiable by its red awning, the cozy little Italian **Café Papa** *(15 Thomas St.; Tel 02837/511205; 9am-5pm Mon-Sat; lunch £4.50; No credit cards)* serves up a mean espresso. You can get a great little homemade soup and sandwich lunch, or skip straight to dessert and dig in to their fresh-baked and majorly delicious cakes.

to market

Budget-minded eaters should go to **Emerson's Supermarket** *(55-57 Scotch St.; Tel 02837/522846; 8:45am-5:30pm Mon-Wed, 9am-9pm Thu-Fri, 8:45am-6pm Sat; No credit cards).*

The cafe at **The Market Place Arts compound** [see *bar, club, and live music scene,* above] is swanky and modern—you'll feel like an Armagh high roller as you rub elbows with prominent citizens, patrons of the arts, and ordinary folk gussied up in their Sunday best. Lunch is around £5; dinner will set you back £8-10.

The **De Averell House** *(47 Upper English St.; Tel 02837/511213; dinner served from 5-10pm; entrees £8-10; V, MC)* is, hands down, the best bet for dinner in town. Tony, the head chef and owner of the hotel, serves up a marvelous fusion of Indian, Mexican, Italian, and traditional Irish meat and fowl dishes. This is *the* place in Armagh to get a dinner with flava. The space, in the basement of the hotel, is warmly lit and has an unfinished wood bar, stone fireplace, and homey, old fashioned bric-a-brac on mantle and wall. Couples wax romantic, their eyes sparkling from the light reflected off their Chianti. The attitude is casual, but the food is sophisticated.

crashing

In the past couple of years, Armagh has done a lot to welcome the budget traveler. Even if you don't want to stay at a hostel, there are other relatively inexpensive options that'll give you more privacy and/or luxury. Overall, accommodations at any price here are excellent: clean, welcoming and friendly.

Neat freaks who spend most of their travels cringing from the grime that coats so many hostels can rest easy at the **Armagh Youth Hostel** *(39 Abbey St.; Tel 02837/511801; £11.50 dorm, £13 double (hostel members receive £1 off), towel rental £1; breakfast £2.20; laundry £3; No credit cards),* possibly the cleanest hostel you'll ever come across. Rooms are all relatively new, and many of the doubles have TV and tea facilities. That said, it doesn't have a tremendous amount of character and feels a little impersonal, like a Motel 6. Still, it's great for the money, has a large, full kitchen, a TV room—and did we mention how *clean* it is?

The Padua Guest House *(63 Cathedral Rd., near the Catholic Cathedral; Tel 02837/522039; £16-20 per person; No credit cards)* is a good B&B option, if you don't mind being surrounded by glassy-eyed toys—the owners have a thing for dolls, which perch all over the place. They're kind of charming in a "Twilight Zone" sort of way. Rooms are clean and comfy, and breakfast is enormous and delicious.

Desart House *(99 Cathedral Rd., past the cathedral heading out of town; Tel 02837/522387; £15-20; No credit cards)* is similar—but minus the doll collection.

The friendly and funky **De Averell House** *(47 Upper English St.; Tel 02837/511213; £20 single, £55 double; V, MC)* is a five-minute walk from most pubs, restaurants, and attractions in Armagh. Bright, unique color schemes and brand new bathrooms are standard in each room, giving this elegant 18th-century house a fresh feeling. All rooms have private baths, and the price includes a full Irish breakfast, with sumptuous fresh fruit, at the downstairs restaurant [see *eats,* above]. There is an ultra-comfy living room on the first floor where you may get to take a crack at the Sony Playstation belonging to the owners' kids.

Other do-able options include **Dean's Hill** *(College Hill; Tel 02837/5 24923)* and **Hillview Lodge** *(33 Newtownhamilton Rd.; Tel 02837/522000).*

The more traditional—and more pricey—**Charlemont Arms Hotel** *(57-65 English St.; Tel 02837/522028; £40 single, £70 twin; V, MC)* has an old-time family feeling as moms, daughters, aunts and uncles all seem to help out. The rooms are nothing special, but they are comfortable. The restaurant downstairs [see *eats,* above] is a local favorite and offers delicious and filling variations on the cooked animal theme.

need to know

Currency Exchange Get some punts at **Northern Bank** *(78 Scotch St.; Tel 02837/522004; 9:30am-5pm Mon, 10:00am-3:30pm Tue-Fri).* There's a 24-hour ATM outside. You can also change money at the **tourist office** [see below].

Tourist Information The **tourist office** *(40 English St.; Tel 02837/521800; 9am-5pm Mon-Sat, 2-5pm Sun)* can give you the inside info *and* change your money for you. Talk about service.

Health and Emergency Emergency: *999;* Police: *(Newry Rd; Tel 02837/523311).* **Armagh Community Hospital** *(Tower Hill; Tel 02837/522341)* offers medical attention.

Pharmacies **Gray's Chemist** *(15-17 English St.; Tel 02837/522092; 9am-6pm Mon-Sat)* is centrally located and has friendly people working there, the kind of folks you'll be glad to buy drugs from if you're sick. On Sundays, at least one chemist in town is open for one hour in the morning. If you need a prescription filled on a Sunday, it's best to call a day ahead if possible to find out which chemist it will be.

Buses The **bus station** is on the Mall West *(Lonsdale Rd.; Tel 02837/522266).* Buses make the 90-minute trip to Belfast 20 times a day during the week, 15 times a day on Saturday, and 8 times a day on Sunday. For most other destinations, you must make a connection at Belfast.

Maybe you'd like to see the apple blossoms a little farther out in the country? In the summer, a bus service—you know, a tourist-oriented bus service to get from tourist destination to tourist destination—runs from the Mall and takes people to major tourist destinations around Armagh. Check with the tourist office for details.

Bike Rental Get pedaling at **Browne's Bikes** *(Scott St.; Tel 02837/522782; 9am-5:30pm Mon-Sat; £7 per day, £30 per week).*

Laundry Suds up your duds at **Squeeky Clean** *(11a Cathedral Rd.; 10am-5pm Mon-Sat).*

Postal The main **post office** *(31 Upper English St.; Tel 02837/510313; 9am-5:30pm Mon-Fri, 9am-12:30pm Sat)* is in the center of town, right across from all of the pubs on English Street.

Internet The computer retail store **Armagh Computer World** *(43 Scotch St., the second floor of Wisebuys; Tel 02837/510002; 9am-5:30pm Mon-Sat; armaghcw@aol.com; £4 per hour)* offers basic Internet services.

everywhere else

newcastle

The appeal of Newcastle is in its tourist trappings. If you don't take things too seriously, you can really enjoy the superficial revelry of this seaside town. Grotesque arcades heaped with greasy light bulbs nestle against fast-food stands built cheaply and decorated sparingly. It's all good enough for the onslaught of weekenders and summer day-trippers from Belfast looking to indulge in a bit of nonsensical fun. Only a block away from the Promenade, the long, main boulevard where most of the carny-type attractions lie, is the vast and haunting expanse of sandy beach looking out on the Irish Sea.

If you're into it, Newcastle is fun like a county fair is fun, minus the pig races. Beyond that, look to Mother Nature and she may reward you for the visit. Newcastle is the unofficial gateway to the Mourne Mountains, the 15 peaks that make up the best hiking terrain in the North [see **Mourne Mountains**].

The locals are geared up for the tourist trade, and face thousands of screaming kids and adults every year, so in general people are not dying to open up to you. It's still a friendly place, though, but with the detached attitude of any resort town. If you're just interested in hiking, the best time to come to this little hamlet of 7,500 people is in late spring or early fall. The temperatures are relatively warm, there is less rain, and you won't be bothered with crowds. If you want to be surrounded by kids of all ages goofing it up on the Promenade, come in July.

Newcastle has none of the rural quaintness of many other towns in Ireland, Northern or Republic of. Restaurants and shops along the Central Promenade are decorated minimally except for bright lights that draw you to the smells of sweet things and all thing fried, and the whiff of alcoholic libations. As it's under the jurisdiction of Britain, Newcastle reflects a very British taste in vacationland kitschiness.

wired

There are no cybercafes to be found, but the library at the **East Down Institute** *(Castlewellan Rd.; Tel 02843/722451; 8:30am-4:30pm Mon-Fri; £5 per hour),* a block from the bus station, has computers with web access.

neighborhoods

Newcastle is laid out like a starfish that's had two of its limbs ripped off. When you come into town, you'll probably be coming by bus (about a 45-minute trip from Belfast), which means that you'll be let off on **Railway Street,** on the north end of town and at one end of **Main Street.** All the sights are walkable from here.

From here, you can take Main Street, which turns into **Central Promenade** and boasts all the amusement attractions in town, some hotels, and the tourist office [see *need to know,* below]. Heading toward the water and bearing right will take you to **Downs Road,** where the beaches and youth hostel are.

bar, club and live music scene

Newcastle isn't really hip and doesn't have a great nightlife, but there are a few good pubs to unwind in after a day out in the hills. On summer weekends, the town buzzes at night with moms, dads, kids, and others wandering the streets, eating ice cream and browsing for souvenirs. It's good old-fashioned fun. Pubs are open daily and usually until 11:30pm. This is flexible, and you may find yourself getting kicked out around 1am on weekend nights. Pick up a *What's On in Down District* brochure from the tourist office for a monthly listing of live music and arts events.

One of the most lively pubs is **Quinn's Spirit Grocer** *(62 Main St.; Tel 02843/726400).* It's got a sort of 1950s America feel inside and has live rock, trad and jazz several nights a week. DJs spin seventies and eighties disco most Fridays. Dress for conquest, not subtlety.

Percy French *(Downs Rd.; Tel 02843/723175)* is a more upscale, Tudor-like watering hole with lots of polished wood, perfect pints, and friendly bartenders. Named after a mushy old 19th-century Irish songwriter, you'll find this pub in the Slieve Donard Hotel [see *crashing,* below]. It's a respite from the tackiness of Newcastle and while the crowd is generally older, moneyed folks, there is still good *craic,* or Irish for fun, to be had.

culture zoo

It's about kitsch, right? So just don't go looking for much high culture and you'll do fine.

Route 66 Museum *(94 Dundrum Rd.; Tel 02844/725-223; 10am-6pm daily Easter-Sep; 10am-6pm Mon-Fri, 2-6pm Sat-Sun, Oct-Easter).* This completely tacky collection of classic American cars and road memorabilia is a fun diversion. The classic 1959 white Cadillac, with the biggest fins known to man, is a sight to see.

eats

Dining out in Newcastle can be dirt-cheap if you grab fast food or pizza at one of the many local or international chain greasy spoons on Main Street or Central Promenade. The restaurants in town are nothing to write home about in terms of atmosphere, but if you're willing to pay a little more than fast-food prices, the food is pretty good. As is the case in most of Ireland, rich, filling variations on poultry and meat with sides of potatoes and boiled vegetables are the best options.

▸▸CHEAP

There are a few cafes that have good lunches on Central Promenade, one of the best being **Sea Salt** *(51 Central Promenade; Tel 02843/725027; 10am-6pm Mon-Sat; £4; No credit cards),* With a basic dining room in the back, this cozy little place caters to a slightly more health-conscious crowd and has good soups and sandwiches. Some stuff is organic, and they do dinner for around £15 on Friday nights.

▸▸DO-ABLE

The food at the charming little **Pavilion** *(36 Downs Rd.; Tel 02843/726239; Noon-10pm daily; bistro entrees £6-10, lunches £5-6, MC, V)* is hot and delicious. They feature a good variety of lighter fair and seafood is the highlight of the menu.

Toscana *(47 Central Promenade; 11am-11pm; £6; No credit cards)* is a good bet too, with pub food all day until 11pm—burgers, toasted cheese sandwiches, little personal pizzas and the like.

to market

If eating out has become a bit much, you can buy groceries at **Dunnes** *(Main St.)*. Especially handy if you're staying at the **Newcastle Youth Hostel** [see *crashing,* below], with it's enormous kitchen facilities.

newcastle

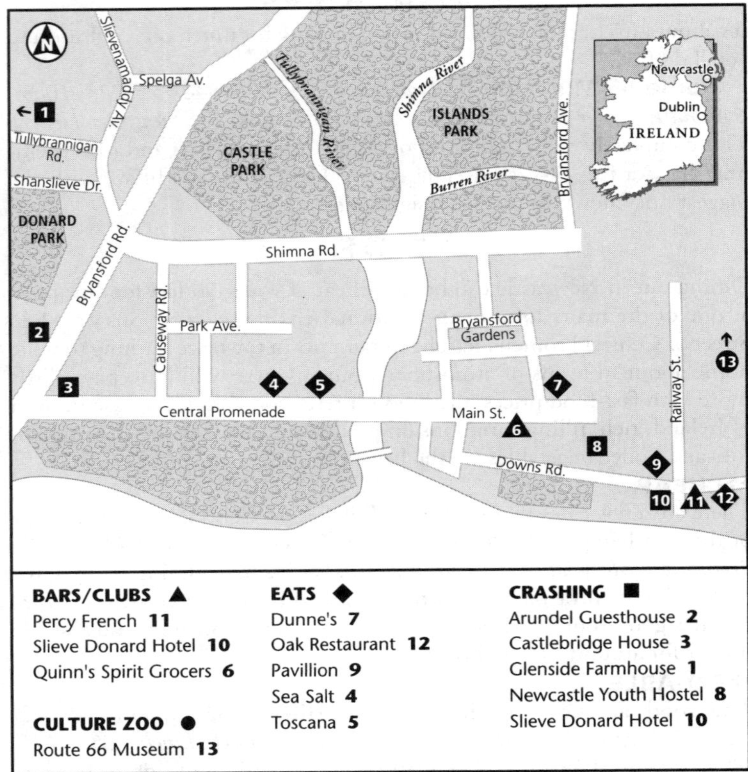

▸▸SPLURGE

The country-swank **Oak Restaurant** *(Downs Rd.; Tel 02843/724347; 3-10pm daily; MC, V)* in the Slieve Donard Hotel [see *crashing*, below] has delicious and pricey dinners for about £20. Decor is elegant-rustic and the food is delicately seasoned and rich as Texas tea.

crashing

Don't blow your wad on hotels in Newcastle—they're insanely expensive and there are plenty of B&B's (and one hostel) that are centrally located, cheap and cozy. The B&B's are all pretty similar, with clean rooms, enormous breakfasts, and friendly ladies taking care of you. You'll save a few pounds if you don't mind a bathroom down the hall.

▸▸CHEAP

The cheapest option for a bed is the **Newcastle Youth Hostel** *(32 Downs Rd.; Tel 02843/722133; £8.50 dorm, £1 towel rentals),* a stark hostel with a friendly staff and a kitchen that's big enough to feed busloads. The small TV room gets smoky when full, but is still fun to relax in. It's the only hostel in town, so call ahead in the summer. To get here, head down Railway Street toward the water and turn right onto Downs Road.

▶▶DO-ABLE

The popular **Castlebridge House** *(2 Central Promenade; Tel 02843/723209; £15-20 per person; No credit cards)* has an excellent view of the coast and is quite a comfortable B&B for its price.

The **Arundel Guesthouse** *(23 Bryansford Rd.; Tel 02843/722232; £16 single, £30 double; No credit cards)* is also a decent enough place smack in the middle of town. Bryansford Road is your last right on Central Promenade before it curves and turns into South Promenade.

Other do-able options include **Harbour House Inn** *(4 South Promenade; Tel. 040/623445)*, **Glenside Farmhouse** *(Tullybrannigan Rd.; Tel. 02843/722628)*, and **Drunrawn House** *(Central Promenade; Tel. 02843/726847)*.

▶▶SPLURGE

If you must blow your wad, the **Slieve Donard Hotel** *(Downs Rd.; Tel 02843/722681; £90 and up for single; MC, V)* is the place to do it. It's right on the beach, and has a restaurant and the Percy French pub in house [see *eats* and *bar, club, and live music scene,* above]. Toward Tollymore Forest Park, the **Glenside Farmhouse** *(Tullybrannigan Rd.; Tel 02843/722628; £15-20 single, £25 double; No credit cards)* has a B&B. To get here from the bus station, head down Central Promenade, take a right onto Bryansford Road, make a left onto Slivenamaddy Avenue, then the second left onto Tullybrannigan road and walk for about a kilometer. Not the most convenient option, perhaps, but this certainly is a good choice if you want to hike.

need to know

Currency Exchange Try **Northern Bank** *(60 Main St.; 9:30am-5pm Mon, 10am-3:30pm Tue-Fri)* or **First Trust Bank** *(28 Main St.; 9:30am-4:30pm Mon-Fri)*. Both banks have *bureaus de change* and 24-hour ATMs outside.

Tourist Information The **tourist office** *(10-14 Central Promenade; Tel 02843/722222; 10am-5pm Mon-Sat, 2-6pm Sun)* has info and brochures about accommodations and sights, and also sells handmade crafts from around the area—lots of hand-thrown pots and a scattering of decorative woodcraft and textiles. The **Mourne Heritage Trust** *(91 Central Promenade; Tel 02843/724059; 9am-5pm Mon-Fri; occasionally open on weekends for walks)*, further down on the opposite side of the street, has maps and info about walks in the Mournes. Definitely head here if you want to do some climbing.

Health and Emergency Police: *(South Promenade; Tel 02843/723583)*.

Pharmacies For your drugs and sundries, head to **Thornton's Chemist** *(49 Central Promenade; Tel 02843/723248; 9am-6pm Mon-Sat)*.

Bus Lines Out of the City There is no train access to Newcastle, so the bus or hitching are your options. **Ulsterbus** *(5-7 Railway St.; Tel 02843/72296)* will get you to Belfast directly about every hour (the trip takes one hour); to Dublin through Newry six-eight times a day (the trip takes two hours); or to Downpatrick or Strangford twelve times a day (20 minutes to Downpatrick, 40 minutes to Strangford).

Bike Rental Wikki Wikki Wheels *(10 Donard St.; Tel 02843/723973; £6.50 per day, £30 per week)* a stone's throw from the bus station, rents bikes.

Laundry Dirty Duds *(58A Valencia Place; Tel 02843/726190; £4.50)* offers self-service washers and dryers.

Postal Send your postcards from the **post office** *(33-35 Central Promenade; Tel 02843/722418; 9am-5:30pm Mon, Wed, Fri, 9am-12:30pm Tue, Thu).*

Internet See *wired,* above.

downpatrick

Downpatrick is a must-see if you want a sense of the tumultuous history of Christianity in Ireland. Home of the **Down Cathedral,** the purported burial place of St. Patrick, who died in the 5th century, this town is a feast of sacred sites—but not terribly lovely otherwise. The high ground in town, the Hill of Down, was in ancient times a fort for Norman kings and the Down County Museum has loads of displays on Saint Patrick, as well as the sordid lives of prisoners unlucky enough to land in the town's jail.

All of these are on or near **The Mall,** one admittedly pretty little street in the middle of town. Beyond the religious significance of Downpatrick, there isn't a lot to keep a visitor here for more than an afternoon. From the **Ulsterbus station** on **Market Street,** take a left and walk down to where **Irish, English,** and **Church Streets** converge to form the center of town. Little shops, pubs, and restaurants dot the streets. Standing here, you don't get the feeling that the town is supercharged and ready to launch into a new millennium—more like they're awaiting something to do. During the day, the pace is definitely bustling, but the energy is not feisty and defiant as in Belfast, nor leisurely and kitschy as in Newcastle, but more drab and dilapidated. At night, the pub scene seems almost inadequate for a town of around 10,000, although there are a few good spots to hang out if you end up liking the vibe of the town during the day. Folks in this sleepy little working town dominated by the cathedral are far from party animals, though, so perhaps it's just as well.

bar, club, and live music scene

Downpatrick doesn't really have a "scene," but if you want to go have a pint with the locals, **Denvir's Pub** *(14 English St.; Tel 02844/612-012)* is a

downpatric

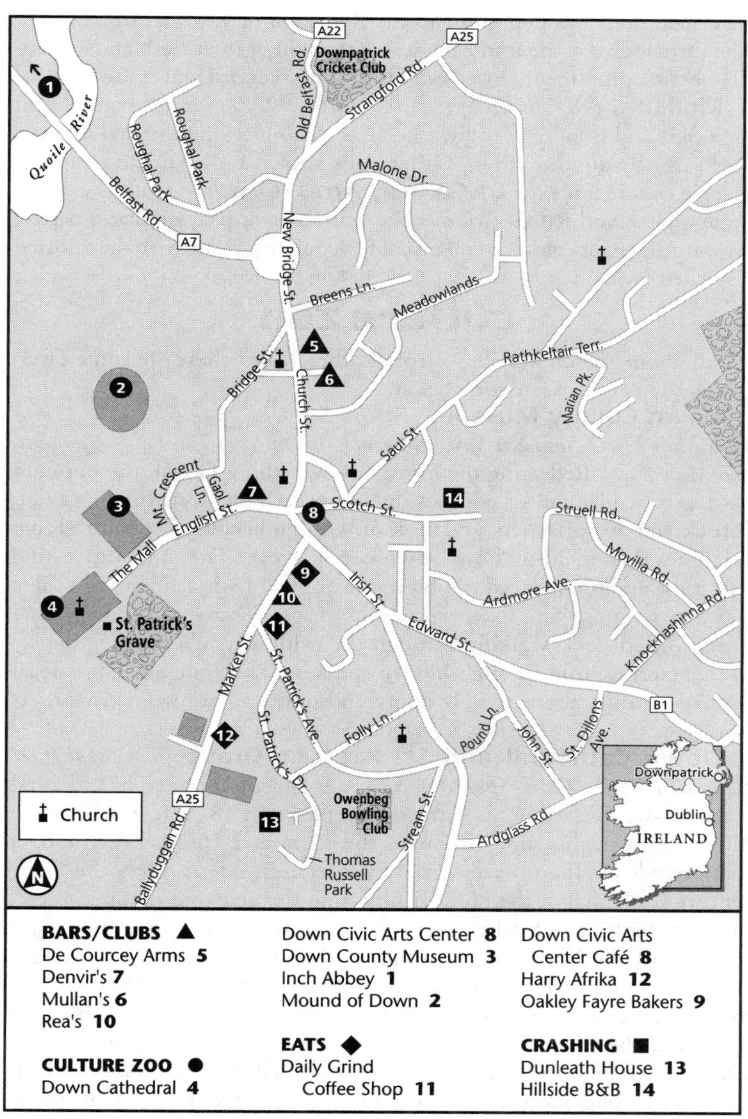
A22
A25
Downpatrick Cricket Club
Old Belfast Rd.
Strangford Rd.
Quoile River
Roughal Park
Roughal Park
Belfast Rd.
A7
Malone Dr.
New Bridge St.
Breens Ln.
Meadowlands
Bridge St.
Church St.
Rathkeltair Terr.
Marian Pk.
Saul St.
Mt. Crescent
Gaol Ln.
English St.
The Mall
Scotch St.
Struell Rd.
Movilla Rd.
Irish St.
Ardmore Ave.
Edward St.
Knocknashinna Rd.
St. Patrick's Grave
Market St.
St. Patrick's Ave.
St. Patrick's Dr.
Folly Ln.
Pound Ln.
John St.
St. Dillons Ave.
B1
A25
Church
Owenbeg Bowling Club
Stream St.
Ardglass Rd.
Ballyduggan Rd.
Thomas Russell Park
N
Downpatrick
Dublin
IRELAND
BARS/CLUBS
De Courcey Arms 5
Denvir's 7
Mullan's 6
Rea's 10
CULTURE ZOO
Down Cathedral 4
Down Civic Arts Center 8
Down County Museum 3
Inch Abbey 1
Mound of Down 2
EATS
Daily Grind Coffee Shop 11
Down Civic Arts Center Café 8
Harry Afrika 12
Oakley Fayre Bakers 9
CRASHING
Dunleath House 13
Hillside B&B 14

great, traditional pub dating back to the 17th century. It's got a colorful story too: the United Irishmen, great-great-great-great-grandparents of the IRA, held meetings here prior to the Rebellion of 1798 against Britain. The Denvir clan made it to America by the skin of their teeth and eventually became prominent citizens and the namesakes of Denver, Colorado.

Mullan's, *(48 Church St.; Tel 02844/612-227)* is another good spot for a pint and is quite friendly, too. Trad sessions happen several nights a week, usually around 10pm. Other pubs known for adequate to above-average *craic* include the **De Courcey Arms** *(Church St.)* with live music some nights, and **Rea's** *(Market St.),* with a great peat fireplace, perfect for warming your cold, wet self on cold, wet nights, along with the assorted dispirited locals.

culture zoo

It's all about the church (no surprises there), but there are some fascinating sights to be seen nonetheless.

Down County Museum *(English St.; Tel 02844/615-218; 11am-5pm Mon-Fri, 2-5pm Sat-Sun, June-Aug; 11am-5pm Tue-Fri, 2-5pm Sat, Sep-May; Free):* Reflecting the history of everything Down, the museum has a great collection of oddities, including exhibits featuring a wax St. Patrick, starving prisoners, and some old computer equipment and adding machines documenting how Down people work. The most interesting part is the audio-enhanced exhibit in the original 18th-century jail, where wax convicts pose with fixed expressions of agony, starvation, and general pissed-off-ed-ness. Walking through the exhibit, you'll listen endlessly to their stories, told through hidden speakers. There are also some local history exhibits about the economy and politics, and women workers in Down.

Down Cathedral and St. Patrick's Grave *(The Mall; Tel 02844/614-922; 10am-5pm Mon-Sat, 2pm-5pm Sun; Free):* The cathedral is a must-see for fans of St. Patrick. Completed in 1818, it stands on the Hill Of Down, the same ground as the 12th- and 16th-century abbeys that preceded it (both were sacked by foreign invaders). Only the 17th-century Cathedral of the Holy Trinity is now visible, but it contains elements of both of its forebears. It's not the most awe-inspiring holy place in the land, but the cathedral has a great, thundering organ and a "Judge's Box," where legal trials were once carried out, a reminder of the close historical links between the Irish church and state. People usually come here to look at the stone slab in the graveyard commemorating St. Patrick, who's said to be buried under the cathedral itself. The Mound of Down, a large lump of grassy earth in the shadow of the larger Hill of Down, was once a round hill fort of the Normans. Over the centuries, everything decayed, leaving just the mound behind. Stonehenge it's not, but it's got a pretty view of the town and makes for nice strolling grounds.

Inch Abbey *(About a mile northwest of town on the A7 Belfast; Tel 02890/235-000; 10am-7pm Tues-Sat, Apr-Oct; 10am-1:30pm Sat, Oct-Mar; special tours available on request):* Situated on the River Quoile,

Inch Abbey was founded in 1180 by John de Courcy, a Norman invader. This former Cistercian abbey illustrates how deeply rooted the Anglo-Irish conflict actually is. It was operational until the mid-16th century and for the entire time refused to admit the native Irish, instead importing monks from Lancashire in order to establish a strong English presence in the area.

Down Civic Arts Center A beacon of culture in town, the Arts Center seems a bit desperate for recognition, as in other towns where there are only a handful of things to do. Everything from opera to theater passes through here, so it's definitely worth checking out what's playing. The stuff that comes here originates in Belfast or Dublin, but can be cheaper to see, and you won't have to fight the crowds. There is also a gallery exhibiting contemporary Irish art and a cool café inside [see *eats,* below] that gives its profits to charity.

eats

Downpatrick is slim pickin's for eats, but there are a few places that serve good, basic traditional grub. A very handy place to grab lunch is **The Café** *(At the junction of English, Market and Irish St.; Tel 02844/615-283; 11am-4:30pm Mon-Sat)* inside the Down Arts Center [see *culture zoo,* above], where the cuisine is suitably zesty.

If you're looking for a hearty lunch at a lean price, go to **Harry Afrika** *(102 Market St.; No phone),* a little diner across from the bus station with cheap lunches and breakfasts, or the cool **Daily Grind Coffee Shop** *(21a St. Patrick's Ave.; Tel 02844/615-949; lunch about £4)* for the most savory sandwiches in town.

You can also find outstanding sandwiches, pies, and soda bread for under £4 at the **Oakley Fayre Bakers** *(52 Market St.; No phone).* Also, **Denvir's Pub** [see *bar, club, and live music scene,* above] has decent dinners featuring stews for about £8 until 9pm and bar snacks in the day for £2-3. The crowd is made up of Downpatrick's more upscale residents as well as tourists.

crashing

There are no hostels in Downpatrick, so it would behoove the budget traveler to head for Portaferry or Newcastle. If you want to stay, there are many B&B's around town, virtually identical, all perfectly pleasant, including the **Dunleath House** *(33 St. Patrick's Dr.; Tel 02844/613-321; £15-20 per person; No credit cards).* To get here from the Ulsterbus station, take the first right after the tourist office on Market Street onto St. Patrick's Avenue, then make a right onto St. Patrick's Drive. Also centrally located is the **Hillside B&B** *(62 Scotch St.; Tel 02844/613-134; £15-20 per person; No credit cards.* Other do-able options include **Hillcrest** *(157 Strangford Rd.; Tel 02844/612-583)* and **Havine Farm** *(51 Ballydonnell Rd.; Tel 02844/851-242).*

need to know

Currency Exchange Go to the **Bank of Ireland** *(80-82 Market St.; Tel 02844/612-911; 9:30am-4:30pm Mon-Fri, open at 10am Wed)* or

Ulster Bank *(2-8 Market St.; Tel 02844/613-064; 9:30am-4:30pm Mon-Fri; ATM available)* to improve your cash flow.

Tourist Information For information about all things Down, go to the **Down Center Tourist Information Center** *(74 Market St.; Tel 02844/612-233; 9am-5pm Mon-Fri; 10am-1pm/2pm-5pm Sat, Sep-Jun; 9am-6pm Mon-Sat, Jul-Aug).*

Public Transportation Bus service is not practical in Downpatrick. Catch a cab from **Downpatrick Taxis** *(Market St.; Tel 02844/614-515)* or **Call-a-cab** *(61 Irish St.; Tel 02844/613-329).*

Health and Emergency Police: *(Irish St; Tel 02844/615-011).* **Downpatrick Hospital** *(Irish St. and circular road; Tel 02844/613-311)* is centrally located.

Pharmacies **Deeny Pharmacist** *(30a St. Patrick's Ave; Tel 02844/613-794; 9am-1pm/2-5:30pm Mon-Fri)* is centrally located.

Trains and Bus Lines Out of Town To get in and out of Downpatrick, you'll find yourself at **Ulsterbus Depot** *(Market St.; Tel 02844/612-384),* whether riding by wheel or rail.

Postal Envelopes come and go via the main **post office** *(65 Lower Market St.; Tel 02844/612-061; 9am-5:30pm Mon-Fri, 9am-12:30pm Sat).*

mourne mountains

Roughly translated, "Mourne" means "Hikers' Paradise." Just kidding, but the Mourne Mountains do have a tremendous lot to offer even the most non-athletic Nancy boy who wants to get out and frolic in the great outdoors. From rolling hills to majestic vistas to desolate stretches of uninhabited territory dotted only with sheep, the Mournes have it all. Yes, there are oodles of sheep in them thar hills, and you can walk among them for inspiration while exerting yourself on foot; the breathtaking views make the exertion well worth it. Even the staunchest Marxist would approve of the amount of capital (in this case pleasure) produced per hiker in such a brief span of hours. It's hard to believe, standing in a valley between two majestic granite-accented peaks, that you're less than three miles from the sights and sounds of the Promenade in downtown Newcastle. The following are three separate ways to enter the mountains. **Donard Forest Park** is the immediate first choice as it's closest to Newcastle, but if you have extra time, check out the other two.

To get to the glorious peaks of the sunny north, head down Newcastle's Central Promenade till you see the signs for the Donard Forest. You'll take a right off the Central Promenade and head back to a large and generally uninteresting patch of park. Don't mind the vacationing shirtless men sprawled out on the grass handycaming their young nubile brides. Follow the path up the left-hand side of the park and you'll come to a little sign announcing Donard Forest. Situated at the foot of Slieve Donard, the highest peak in the Mourne range at 850 meters (over 2,600 feet), the Forest is a 280-hectare (280,000-acre) stretch of mostly coniferous woodland. It's the most convenient place to start hiking. Continue uphill past the sign and veer to the left into the forest. From there you can take four separate trails, three of which are for day-hikers; the fourth goes on for miles and could take days.

All the day hikes are lovely and very do-able for afternoon excursions. The **Pinewood Trail** is the best for scenery and walkability. For this trail, follow the red arrows and you'll hike up about a half-mile over some flat rocks until you reach a bridge and road bisecting your trail. Continue until you reach a barbed-wire fence and gate. In the distance, you'll see what looks like some kind of stone fort with a round roof nestled into the hillside. Don't worry, you haven't stumbled upon the jealously guarded compound of a paramilitary group. The "igloo" is for hikers who have been stranded in bad weather. Best times to hike are May-September, though careful hiking can be done anytime of the year. Always take rain gear; this is Ireland, after all, where there's almost as much water in the air as there is flowing out of the tap.

Hop the gate (or use the convenient latch which allows the gate to swing open), hike up to the igloo, turn around and you'll get a beautiful vista of the sea, the town, and the sheep, all laid out in spacious beauty. This path continues for miles up the Glen River through the beautiful saddle of the mountains. Rest on a big rock, have a picnic, commune with the sheep. Hiking from the bottom of the trail to the big rocks takes about two-three hours, so make sure you leave time to hike back in daylight.

As you start your ascent, You may notice a little vein of rock that runs through the hills. This is the **Mourne Wall,** a six-foot high wall than runs over hill and dale for 22 miles. The Great Wall of China it's not, but it's definitely a Good Wall. Accounts of its origin vary; some say it was built to keep in the sheep, others say it was a project for local men to work on during the economically depressed 1920s.

Another place to begin an ascent into the Mournes is **Tollymore Forest Park.** Its trails run along the 1,200 acres of lush parkland. If fishing is your thing, you can dip your pole into the salmon-stocked Shimna River. The **Tollymore Outdoor Center** *(Bryansford Rd.; Tel 02843/722158; Call for rates and schedules)* is on the grounds of the park and offers rock-climbing, canoeing, and other fun courses in the warmer months. The best months to come are June-August, when the weather is pretty sunny and warm. Call ahead for specifics as weather and crowds often determine what goes on. To get to Tollymore, on the northern side of the Mournes, head about two miles west of Newcastle on Tullybrannigan Road. You can take an Ulsterbus shuttle from Newcastle to Tollymore at 10am, noon, and 4:30pm. For a couple of punts, you'll be dropped off at the entrance to the park.

Castlewellan Forest Park, about five miles from Newcastle in Castlewellan, also has some good walking trails and contains the National

Arboretum, one of the best tree collections in Europe. Buses leave several times a day from Newcastle to Castlewellan. Off Main St. in Castlewellan, the park opens at 10am and closes at sundown, 5pm on Sunday. There are camping and barbecue sites, and a cafe. It has the usual sandwiches and candy bars that you can get anywhere else, but is the only place around here for a pre-made meal.

need to know

Hours/Days Open Tourist Information Head to the **Mourne Heritage Trust** *(91 Central Promenade; Tel 02843/724059; 9am-5pm Mon–Fri),* in Newcastle for great information about hikes and walks in the Mournes. They also have guided walks for free on Mondays and Saturdays. We highly recommend you pay a visit before heading into the hills.

Crashing Call the **Castlewellan Forest Park office** *(Off Main St. Castlewellan; Tel 02843/778664; 10am-sundown Mon-Sat, 10am-5pm Sun)* to book campsites in the park.

planning your trip

It may be well to begin with a caution, offered in this case by John Steinbeck in *Travels With Charley:* "A journey is like a marriage. The certain way to be wrong is to think you control it." Fair enough. A trip too tightly packed and planned, with no room for the spontaneous and unexpected, is often not worth the effort. And yet, when you are so poorly prepared that surprise runs riot, you might wish you'd stayed home. In travel, as in Buddhism, the middle ground is recommended. Lay down your plans like pavement, and then romp on the grass at will.

the lay of the land

Dublin sits on just about the same latitude as Edmonton, Alberta, and Bremen, Germany, but unlike those distinctly cold places, Ireland's capital is blessed with lush signs of life you'd normally expect to see only in the tropics: palm trees and bougainvillea. The milder Irish climate comes from the Gulf Stream, which originates in the Caribbean and sends its warm currents and tropical sea life northward to the Emerald Isle. On occasion it sends a hurricane as part of the bargain, but that's very rare even on the Irish Sea, which is notorious for its bad temper.

With a landmass of approximately 32,600 square miles, Ireland is roughly the same size as the state of Maine, though shaped somewhat differently. In rounded figures, it is at most 300 miles north to south, and 170 miles east to west. No point in Ireland is farther than 70 miles from one of its encircling waters: the Atlantic Ocean, the Irish Sea, and the St. George and North channels. It may seem strange, but in the past, the Irish rarely saw their offshore waters as a resource. Traditionally, the Irish disliked fish and avoided learning to swim. The sea was to be feared. It was perilous to cross, and, worse, its waves brought invaders, one after another.

The country's topography is unusual. Instead of its shores sloping to the sea and its interior rising to mountain peaks, the reverse is the case. Shaped like a saucer, Ireland's twisted, 2,000-mile coastline is, with a few notable exceptions, a breachless bulwark of mountains, cliffs, and highlands. Its interior is generally flat, a broad limestone plain made up of fertile farmland and raised bogs, graced with the occasional lake and wetland. Some would say that Ireland has only hills—its highest peak, Carantuohill in County Kerry, reaches to only about 3,400 feet. All would agree that Ireland has few crags. Most of its heights, whether mountains or hills, were rounded off and smoothed into graceful slopes tens of thousands of years ago by receding glaciers. Ireland's longest and greatest river is the Shannon, flowing 230 miles south and west across the midlands from its source in the Cuileagh Mountains of County Cavan to its estuary in County Limerick. The island's largest lake, Lough Neagh, occupies 153 square miles of counties Antrim and Armagh in the north.

One of Europe's least densely populated countries (third behind Finland and Sweden), Ireland is commonly described as unspoiled, even "untouched." Not so. Lovely as it is, the Irish landscape is no wilderness, and is certainly not untouched. For example, only about 1 percent of the hardwood forests have survived 6,000 years of deforestation. In fact, Ireland, once a rich source of timber for the British fleet, has imported virtually all of its wood for more than 200 years. The recent planting of pine forests around the island is only another, though more positive, instance of human intervention.

On the bright side, the predominance of small-scale mixed agriculture has long contributed to the preservation of an unusually wide range of flora and fauna in the Irish countryside, with the notable and famous exception of snakes and other reptiles. As it happens, Mother Nature, not St. Patrick, deserves credit for Ireland's "snakelessness"—all she gave to the island, herpetologically speaking, is one lonely type of common lizard, featured several years ago on a 32p postage stamp.

In recent years, Ireland has gone increasingly "green" in its policies. It has created a number of national parks for the sake of both enjoying and protecting the island's natural beauty. Four are open to the public: Connemara National Park in County Galway, Glenveagh National Park in County Donegal, Killarney National Park in County Kerry, and Wicklow Mountains National Park in County Wicklow. Others are planned, including Burren National Park in County Clare, which is currently under development.

The Regions in Brief

Ireland is a land divided many different ways, all of which are significant in finding your course through its history, along its roads, and amid its people.

The first and most recent division is between **"the South"** (the Republic of Ireland, Éire, or the "Free State") and **"the North"** (Northern Ireland, commonly and confusingly referred to as "Ulster"). The South is a sovereign, independent nation made up of 26 counties, while the North, with 6 counties, remains part of Great Britain. The line partitioning the land and people of Ireland into two political entities was drawn in the Anglo-Irish Treaty of 1921 and remains a matter of dispute. In simplest practical terms, for the tourist, the line between north and south represents a national border.

Still very much alive on the maps and in the minds of the Irish, however, is another, much older, Gaelic set of divisions corresponding to the four points of the compass. In this early scheme of things, Ulster is north, Leinster is east, Munster is south, Connaught is west, and the traditional center of Ireland is the hill of Uisneach in County Westmeath.

Next, there are the counties, which is how most Irish and visitors commonly orient themselves. These are the "states" of Ireland. Each has its own rep, and they all tangle in fierce athletic contests for national titles in Gaelic football and hurling. The island's 32 counties, grouped under the four traditional provinces of Ireland cited above, are as follows:

IN ULSTER (TO THE NORTH): Cavan, Donegal, and Monaghan in the Republic; Antrim, Armagh, Derry, Down, Fermanagh, and Tyrone in Northern Ireland.
IN MUNSTER (TO THE SOUTH): Clare, Cork, Kerry, Limerick, Tipperary, and Waterford.
IN LEINSTER (TO THE EAST): Dublin, Carlow, Kildare, Kilkenny, Laois, Longford, Louth, Meath, Offaly, Westmeath, Wexford, and Wicklow.
IN CONNAUGHT (TO THE WEST): Sligo, Mayo, Galway, Roscommon, and Leitrim.

Lastly, in more immediately practical terms for the tourist, Ireland may be divided into regions: the southeast, the southwest, the west, the northwest, the midlands (including much of the area that surrounds the Shannon River), and Northern Ireland. These, with several specific cities and their environs—Dublin, Cork, and Galway—make up the principal areas of interest for Ireland's visitors.

DUBLIN & ENVIRONS **Dublin** is ground zero for the profound, high-speed changes that are transforming Ireland into the Napster of Europe—young, innovative, and prosperous beyond all odds. What was old and venerable in the city remains so, but now it shares space with an all-out twentysomething Irish renaissance. It's that combination of ancient history and cutting edge that gives Dublin an amazing buzz—and keeps it distinctly Irish. The hippest music is still inspired by the most traditional, the coolest pubs have been around forever. There's every scene here you'd find in any big city anywhere—style, music, nightlife, culture—but if you head out of the city center you can be standing in the middle of prehistoric ruins in less than an hour. Or you can be walking around a tiny coastal village, hiking in the **Dublin**

Mountains, or lying on a beach in **County Wicklow**—all within an hour of the capital city.

THE SOUTHEAST With the warmest and driest weather in Ireland, the southeast coast generally provides an alternative to a pub for getting out of the rain. There are some really great sandy beaches that are definitely worth a visit, plus one of the coolest towns in the whole country: medieval **Kilkenny.** Going there feels almost as though you've been beamed down to an ancient town taken over by friendly party-aliens who left the place intact but added a bunch of bars and Mexican food joints. *We come in peace. Where are your super tacos and giant alcoholic beverages?* It's really amazing to hang around and socialize with your 21st century peers in a place where Vikings once chugged their cocktails from animal horns. It's also somewhat bizarre to squeeze your way through hordes of tourists whose idea of checking out an ancient town like **Waterford** is spending an inordinate amount of time and money at the gift shop in the crystal factory there. Pass 'em by, catch a few castles, and move on.

CORK & ENVIRONS Cork, Ireland's second largest city, is Dublin's rival in sport and stout but little else. Though many visitors have lost more than a weekend in rowdy Cork bars, the area's primary claim to fame is being a congenial gateway to the south and west of Ireland, which many consider Ireland's Oz, the ultimate destination. Within arm's reach of Cork are the truly impressive **Blarney Castle** (with its less impressive kiss-me stone), the culinary and scenic delights of **Kinsale,** the **Drombeg Stone Circle, Sherkin** and **Clear Islands,** and **Mizen Head.** Also in this region are the spectacular expanses of **West Cork.**

THE SOUTHWEST If you've ever been to Seattle, you know the secret to happiness in the rainiest corner of Ireland: There are more important things in life than staying dry. The once-remote splendors of **County Kerry** are no longer a secret, so be prepared to share the view. Next to the Book of Kells, the **Ring of Kerry** is the most visited attraction in Ireland, which is more of a warning than a recommendation. You're actually better off in the nearby **Killarney National Park,** where 25,000 acres of mountains, woodlands, waterfalls, and wildlife provides a welcome escape from tour buses and flash bulbs. Other highlights of this region are the **Dingle Peninsula** and the **Skellig and Blasket Islands.**

THE WEST The west of Ireland used to be considered one step above hell by British invaders who figured they'd take over the whole country forever by either killing off the Irish or banishing them to the rocky, desolate land of **Connaught.** Needless to say, the plan failed. Today tons of people—including British tourists—gladly fork over their hard-earned vacation money to enjoy the entire region, from the rocky and remote **Aran Islands** to the castles in **Dunguaire. County Clare's** natural beauty, the 700-foot **Cliffs of Moher,** and the limestone grasslands of the Burren are unforgettable.

GALWAY & ENVIRONS **Galway** is a thriving port and university city, pleasantly packed with international travelers and Irish youth. It's a great party town, slower-paced than Dublin and not as rowdy as Cork. Just beyond the city stretches **Connemara,** home to the greatest number of rocks you'll ever see in one place. The legendary **Aran Islands—Inishmore, Inishmaan,** and **Inisheer**—are just offshore, easily accessible by ferry.

THE NORTHWEST North of Galway is "Yeats country," the land that inspired William Butler Yeats to immortalize the "terrible beauty" of Ireland. The poet lived, wrote, and eventually was buried in **County Sligo,** which has the greatest concentration of megalithic sites in Ireland. You can be just driving or walking along almost any road and off to the side you'll see stone circles, passage tombs, dolmens, and cairns. Sligo town is better for mild nights than wild nights, but it's a fun place to meet people and socialize without major crowds. South of Sligo is **County Mayo,** access point to a string of islands, including **Inishbofin, Inishturk,** and **Clare. Achill Island**—Ireland's largest—is accessible by car. Head north of Sligo and you'll surely understand Yeats's bleak-is-beautiful mentality. This is especially true of **Donegal,** with its 200 miles of drenched, jagged coastline—and some of the finest surfing in the world. Nearby Leitrim is about as far from party central as you can get, but its unspoiled lakes are awesome if you like to fish.

THE MIDLANDS The thought of midlands, any midlands, is likely to bring yawns, and the lush center of Ireland, bisected by the mighty but lazy Shannon, is no exception. This is a land of pastures, rivers, lakes, woods, and gentle mountain slopes, an antidote to the barren beauty of Connemara and a retreat, in high season, from the throngs of tourists who crowd the coasts. The midlands have no cities, and their towns are not their attractions; the shores and waters of the Shannon and Lough Derg and of their many lesser cousins provide much of the lure. Outdoor pursuits—biking, boating, fishing, and hiking—are the reason to be here. You can also check out some historic sites, including **Birr Castle** and **Clonmacnois** (the ruins of a famous Irish monastic center).

NORTHERN IRELAND There are plenty of reasons to cross the invisible border into Northern Ireland, from the urban pleasures of **Belfast** and **Derry** to the stunning **Antrim coast** and the 37,000 black basalt columns of the **Giant's Causeway.** Don't let talk of "the Troubles" stop you from going to the cities in the North. Belfast is actually one of the safest cities in Europe in terms of street crime, and Derry is definitely one of the last semi-undiscovered cool cities anywhere. (Go soon, though; it's getting more popular every day.)

Visitor Information

To get your planning under way, contact the following offices of the Irish Tourist Board and the Northern Ireland Tourist Board. They're eager to answer your questions, and have bags of genuinely helpful information, mostly free of charge.

IN THE UNITED STATES

Irish Tourist Board, 345 Park Ave., New York, NY 10154; Tel 800/223-6470 from the U.S., or 212/418-0800; Fax 212/371-9052.

Northern Ireland Tourist Board, 551 Fifth Ave., Suite 701, New York, NY 10176; Tel 800/326-0036 from the U.S., or 212/922-0101; Fax 212/922-0099.

IN CANADA

Irish Tourist Board, 160 Bloor St. E., Suite 1150, Toronto, ON, M4W 1B9; Tel 416/929-2777; Fax 416/929-6783.

Northern Ireland Tourist Board, 2 Bloor St. W., Suite 1501, Toronto, ON, M4W 3E2; Tel 800/576-8174 or 416/925-6368; Fax 416/925-6033.

IN THE UNITED KINGDOM

Irish Tourist Board/Bord Fáilte, 150 New Bond St., London W1Y 0AQ; Tel 020/7493-3201; Fax 020/7493-9065.

Northern Ireland Tourist Board, 11 Berkeley St., London W1X 5AD; Tel 020/7766-9920; Fax 020/7766-9929.

IN AUSTRALIA

Irish Tourist Board, 36 Carrington St., 5th Level, Sydney, NSW 2000; Tel 02/9299-6177; Fax 02/9299-6323.

IN NEW ZEALAND

Irish Tourist Board, Dingwall Building, 2nd Floor, 87 Queen St., Auckland; Tel 0064/9-379-8720; Fax 0064/9-302-2420.

IN IRELAND

Irish Tourist Board/Bord Fáilte, Baggot Street Bridge, Dublin 2; Tel 01/602-4000; Fax 01/602-4100; www.ireland.travel.ie.

Northern Ireland Tourist Board, 16 Nassau St., Dublin 2; Tel 01/679-1977; Fax 01/679-1863.

IN NORTHERN IRELAND

Irish Tourist Board, 53 Castle St., Belfast BT1 1GH; Tel 028/9032-7888; Fax 028/9024-0201.

Northern Ireland Tourist Board, St. Anne's Court, 59 North St., Belfast BT1 1NB; Tel 028/9024-6609; Fax 028/9031-2424; www.ni-tourism.com.

Entry Requirements & Customs

ENTRY REQUIREMENTS

For citizens of the United States, Canada, Australia, and New Zealand entering the Republic of Ireland for a stay of up to 3 months, no visa is necessary, but a valid passport is required. Citizens of the United Kingdom, when traveling on flights originating in Britain, do not need to show documentation to enter Ireland. Nationals of the United Kingdom and

colonies who were not born in Great Britain or Northern Ireland must have a valid passport or national identity document.
For entry into Northern Ireland, the same conditions apply.

WHAT YOU CAN BRING TO IRELAND Since the European Union's (EU) introduction of a single market on January 1, 1993, goods brought into Ireland and Northern Ireland fall into two categories: (1) goods bought duty-paid and value-added-tax-paid (VAT-paid) in other EU countries; and (2) goods bought under duty-free and VAT-free allowances at duty-free shops.

Regarding the first category, if the goods are for personal use, no further duty or VAT needs to be paid. The limits for goods in this category are 800 cigarettes, 10 liters of spirits, 45 liters of wine, and 55 liters of beer. This category normally applies to Irish citizens, visitors from Britain, and travelers from other EU countries.

The second category pertains primarily to overseas visitors, such as U.S. and Canadian citizens. The following duty-free and VAT-free items may be brought into the country for personal use: 200 cigarettes, 1 liter of liquor, 2 liters of wine, and other goods (including beer) not exceeding the value of £34 ($52.70) per adult. There are no restrictions on bringing currency into Ireland.

The Irish and Northern Irish Customs systems operate on a Green, Red, and Blue Channel format. The first two are for passengers coming from the United States and non-EU countries. The Green Channel is for anyone not exceeding the duty-free allowances, and the Red Channel is for anyone with extra goods to declare. If you are like most visitors, bringing in only your own clothes and personal effects, choose the Green Channel. The Blue Channel is exclusively for use by passengers entering Ireland from another EU country.

In addition to your luggage, you may bring in sports equipment for your own recreational use or electronic equipment for your own business or professional use while in Ireland. Prohibited goods include firearms, ammunition, and explosives; narcotics; meat, poultry, plants, and their by-products; and domestic animals from outside the United Kingdom.

WHAT YOU CAN BRING HOME Returning U.S. citizens who have been away for 48 hours or more are allowed to bring back, once every 30 days, $400 worth of merchandise duty-free. You'll be charged a flat rate of 10% duty on the next $1,000 worth of purchases. Be sure to have your receipts handy. On gifts, the duty-free limit is $100. You cannot bring fresh foodstuffs into the United States; tinned foods are allowed. For more information, contact the **U.S. Customs Service** *(1301 Constitution Ave., P.O. Box 7407, Washington, DC 20044; Tel 202/927-6724)* and request the free pamphlet *Know Before You Go.* It's also available on the Web at www.customs.ustreas.gov/travel/kbygo.htm.

Citizens of the U.K. who are returning from a European Community (EC) country will go through a separate Customs Exit (the Blue Channel) for EC travelers. In essence, there is no limit on what you can bring back from an EC country, as long as the items are for personal use (this includes gifts), and you have already paid the necessary duty and tax. However, Customs law sets out guidance levels. If you bring in more than these levels, you may be asked to prove that the goods are for your own use. Guidance levels on goods bought in the EC for your own use are 800 cigarettes, 200 cigars, 1kg smoking tobacco, 10 liters of spirits, 90 liters of wine (of which not more than 60 liters can be sparkling wine), and 110 liters of beer. For more information, contact **HM Customs & Excise** *(Passenger Enquiry Point, 2nd Floor Wayfarer House, Great South West Road, Feltham, Middlesex, TW14 8NP; Tel 020/8910-3744, 44/181-910-3744 outside the U.K.; www.hmce.gov.uk).*

Canadians should check the booklet *I Declare,* which you can download or order from **Revenue Canada** *(Tel 613/993-0534; www.ccra-adrc.gc.ca).* Australians can contact the **Australian Customs Service** *(Tel 1-300/363-263 within Australia, 61-2/6275-6666 outside Australia; www.customs.gov.au/).* New Zealand citizens should contact **New Zealand Customs** *(Tel 09/359-6655; www.customs.govt.nz/).*

money honey

CASH/CURRENCY

The Republic of Ireland, unlike the United Kingdom, lies within the new "Eurozone." As of January 1999, Ireland has adopted the single European currency known as the "euro." Although the euro will not appear as hard currency until 2002, it is already the medium of exchange in the Republic. The punt, or Irish pound, no longer trades as an independent currency. Its value is permanently fixed at 1.27 euros. Consequently, the fluctuating value of the euro is of concern to you as a visitor, because the punt remains a fixed multiple of that value. In shops and elsewhere, prices already appear in both punts and euros; before we know it, punts will disappear from both signs and pockets. But that day is not yet upon us, so in this guide prices in the Republic are still given in punts. In converting prices in punts to U.S. dollars, we used the rate IR£1 = $1.40.

So far, the United Kingdom has resisted the euro and retained its traditional currency, the pound sterling, which continues to trade independently on the world currency market. Northern Ireland, as part of the UK, uses the British pound. The British pound is not legal tender in the Republic, and the Irish pound is not legal tender in the North. In converting prices for this guide, we used the rate £1 = $1.65.

In this volume, the £ sign symbolizes both the Irish and the British pound. The Irish pound is officially designated by the £ sign preceded by IR: IR£. Each unit of paper currency is called a "note." The pound notes, which are printed in denominations of £5, £10, £20, £50, and £100, come in different sizes and colors (the larger the size, the greater the value). There are still some £1 notes in circulation, although these are being phased out in favor of the £1 coin. (The old £1 note is a work of art, so try to find one before they disappear altogether.) Since 1971, the Irish monetary system has been on the decimal system. The pound is divided into 100 pence ("p"); coins come in denominations of £1, 50p, 20p, 10p, 5p, and 1p.

The British currency used in Northern Ireland, identified by engravings of British royalty, follows pretty much the same pattern as that of the Republic, with notes in denominations of £5, £10, £20, £50, and £100. Coins are issued in £1, 50p, 20p, 10p, 5p, 2p, and 1p denominations.

Note: The value of both the Irish and the British pound fluctuates daily, so it is best to begin checking exchange rates well in advance of your visit to gain a sense of their recent range. Deciding when and where to convert and how much is always a gamble. Shop around and avoid exchanging in airports and train stations. Banks are best, and on any given day one bank will offer a better rate than another. Any purchase on a U.S. credit card offers an exchange rate far more favorable than anything an individual is likely to negotiate, so I make a point of converting as little currency as possible and using my credit card to the max. Whatever you do, don't convert small amounts daily. The fees alone will impoverish you. Rates of exchange are available daily in most newspapers, and on the Net (try www.xe.net/currency/ or www.x-rates.com).

CREDIT CARDS

Leading international credit cards such as American Express, Carte Blanche, Diners Club, MasterCard (also known as Access or EuroCard), and Visa (also known as Visa/Barclay) are readily accepted throughout all 32 counties. Most establishments display on their windows or shop fronts the symbols or logos of the credit cards they accept. MasterCard and Visa are the most widely accepted, with American Express an often distant third. However, many banks (including Citibank) are beginning to add a service charge to every transaction made in a foreign currency; check with your card's issuer before you leave to avoid a nasty surprise when you get your bill.

ATMS

Any town large enough to have a bank branch (all but the smallest villages) will have an ATM, most likely linked to a network that includes your home bank. **Cirrus** *(Tel 800/424-7787; www.mastercard.com/atm)* and **Plus** *(Tel 800/843-7587; www.visa.com/atms)* are the two most popular networks. Use the toll-free numbers to locate ATMs in your destination.

Check with your bank to make sure the PINs on your bankcards and credit cards will work in Ireland.

TRAVELER'S CHECKS

Traveler's checks are something of an anachronism from the days before the ATM (automated teller machine) made cash accessible at any time, but some travelers still prefer the security they provide. You can get them at almost any bank, for a small service charge. American Express traveler's checks are also available over the phone by calling 800/221-7282 or 800/721-9768, or you can purchase checks online at www.americanexpress.com. AmEx gold or platinum cardholders can avoid paying the fee by ordering over the telephone; platinum cardholders can also purchase checks fee-free in person at AmEx Travel Service locations. American Automobile Association members can obtain checks with no fee at most AAA offices.

when to go

CLIMATE

You have to be psychic to predict Irish weather. The only thing consistent about it is how often it changes; the best of times and the worst of times may be only hours—or minutes—apart. The best you can do is hedge your bets: Odds are, east equals dry and west equals wet, except when that's wrong, which is slightly less than half the time. The driest and sunniest parts of Ireland are the northeast and the southeast—but don't count on it.

In Ireland, the thermometers, gratefully, are a lot less busy than the barometers. Temperatures are mild and fluctuate within what any New Englander would call "spring." The generally coldest months—January and February—bring frosts but seldom snow. The warmest months—July and August—rarely are hot. And remember, in Ireland any temperature over 70 degrees (Fahrenheit) is "hot," and 32 degrees is truly "freezing." Both are unusual. For a complete guide to Irish weather on the Net, including year-round averages and daily updates, consult www.ireland.com/weather.

When packing, think *layers* for any time of year.

In sum, the weather is neither the reason for coming to Ireland nor a reason for staying away, unless you're looking for the beaches of Mexico or Greece, which remain in Mexico and Greece.

HIGH & LOW SEASONS

It's not just the weather that's all over the map in Ireland, prices and crowds also go up and down in the course of the year. The precise difference between high and low season, however, varies greatly from one locale to another. At one extreme, there's Dublin, which really doesn't have a low season; it's always crowded, and prices there are always fairly high. At the other end of the scale, there's Cape Clear, where the tourism meter is perpetually low.

But there is one thing you can count on across the board:

Transatlantic airfares drop significantly in the winter months, which makes a trip to Ireland that much more affordable. And if you're not planning a major surfing safari, who cares if it's a bit chilly? That just makes the pubs more inviting and the tourist factor less annoying. Plus, outside of Dublin, the more off-season you are, the more negotiable will be your lodging. In many cases you can practically ignore any stated prices and simply ask for the innkeeper's best offer. The lowest prices that hotels are willing to tolerate in print are often appreciably higher than the lowest prices they're willing to accept on a given day when rooms might go empty. During April, May, and October you often can get simultaneously lucky with weather, crowds, and prices—especially in the Southeast, which tends to have a gorgeous early spring and a tourist season that doesn't really get going until summer.

HOLIDAYS

The Republic observes the following national holidays: New Year's Day (January 1); St. Patrick's Day (March 17); Easter Monday (lunar/variable); May Day (May 1); first Monday in June and August (Summer Bank Holidays); last Monday in October (Autumn Bank Holiday); Christmas (December 25); and St. Stephen's Day (December 26). Good Friday (the Friday before Easter) is mostly observed, but not statutory.

In the North, the schedule of holidays is the same as in the Republic, with some exceptions: the North's Bank Holidays fall on the last Monday of May and August; the Battle of the Boyne is celebrated on Orangeman's Day (July 12); and Boxing Day (December 26), not St. Stephen's Day, follows Christmas.

staying healthy

As a rule, no health documents are required to enter Ireland or Northern Ireland from the United States, Canada, the United Kingdom, Australia, New Zealand, or most other countries. If, in the previous 14 days, a traveler has visited areas where a contagious disease is prevalent, proof of immunization for such disease may be required.

If you have a condition that could require emergency care but might not be readily recognizable, consider joining Medic Alert (Tel 800/432-5378; www.medicalert.org). It provides ID tags, cards, and a 24-hour emergency information hotline. If you are diabetic, you can call the American **Diabetes Association** *(Tel 800/342-2383; www.diabetes.org/ada/c60e.asp)* for a Diabetes Travel Kit and other information for traveling with diabetes.

If you require the services of a physician, dentist, or other health professional during your stay in Ireland, your accommodations host may be in the best position to recommend someone local. Otherwise, you can call the **Irish Medical Council** *(Lynn House, Portabello Court, Lower Rathmines Road, Dublin 6; Tel 01/496-5588)* for a referral.

INSURANCE

It's a good idea to consider insurance coverage for health and accident, cancellation or disruption of services, and lost or stolen luggage. Travel insurance makes especially good sense if you're purchasing nonrefundable airline tickets or a package tour that requires you to pay up front.

Before buying any new coverage, check your own insurance policies (automobile, medical, and homeowner) to see if they cover the elements of travel abroad. Also check the membership contracts of automobile and travel clubs, and the benefits extended by credit card companies.

If you decide you need further coverage, consider one of the following companies, which specialize in short-term policies for travelers: **M.H. Ross Insurance Brokers** *(Tel 800/423-3632; e-mail: rosswiteby@aol.com);* **Travel Guard International** *(Tel 877/216-4885; www.travel-guard.com);* or **Travel Insurance International, Travelers Insurance Co.** *(Tel 800/243-3174).*

Travelers with Special Needs

STUDENTS

With almost half its population under age 25, Ireland is geared to students, whether you're planning to study or are just passing through. Two excellent source books can help you explore the opportunities for study in Ireland: *The Transitions Abroad Alternative Travel Directory,* an annual guide to living, learning, and working overseas, published by Transitions Abroad www.transitionsabroad.com; and *Work, Study, Travel Abroad: The Whole World Handbook,* compiled by the Council on International Educational Exchange (CIEE). Both are available in bookstores.

Ireland in general is extremely student-friendly. Most attractions have a reduced student-rate admission charge, with the presentation of a valid student ID card. A range of travel discounts are available to students, teachers (at any grade level, kindergarten through university), and youth (anyone under 25). For further information on international student, teacher, and youth identity cards and fares, call the national office of **Council Travel** *(Tel 800/226-8624; www.counciltravel.com).* The staff can make your reservations or refer you to the Council Travel office nearest you. Council Travel operates more than 40 offices in the United States and works through a network of world affiliates. (Even if you're not eligible for Council's student, teacher, and youth discounts, it offers full travel services, with the advantage of a growing network of local offices and overseas affiliates.)

In Canada, **Travel CUTS** *(200 Ronson St., Suite 320, Toronto, ON, M9W 5Z9; Tel 800/667-2887 or 416/614-2887; www.travelcuts.com),* offers similar services. **USIT/Campus Travel** *(52 Grosvenor Gardens, London SW1W 0AG; Tel 087/0240-1010 www.usitcampus.co.uk),* opposite Victoria Station, is Britain's leading specialist in student and youth travel.

In Ireland, Council Travel's affiliate is **USIT, the Irish Student Travel Service** *(19 Aston Quay, Dublin 2; Tel 01/679-8833; www.usitnow.ie).* In Northern Ireland, contact **USIT** *(Sountain Centre, College Street, Belfast BT1 6ET; Tel 028/9032-4073),* or at **Queens University Travel** *(Student Union Building, University Road, Belfast BT7 1PE; Tel 028/9024-1830).* In the United States, **USIT** is at *(891 Amsterdam Ave., New York, NY 10025; Tel 212/663-5435).* (For the hopelessly curious among you, USIT is the acronym for the organization's original name, "Union of Students of Ireland Travel," but as the man told me when I asked, "It doesn't stand for anything anymore. It's just USIT.")

U.S. firms offering educational programs to Ireland include **Academic Travel Abroad** *(Tel 800/556-7896 or 202/785-9000),* **Cultural Heritage Alliance** *(Tel 800/323-4466 or 215/923-7060),* and **Irish American Cultural Institute** *(Tel 800/232-3746 or 973/605-1991).*

TRAVELERS WITH DISABILITIES

A disability shouldn't stop anyone from traveling. There are more resources out there than ever before. The **Moss Rehab Hospital** *(Tel 215/456-5995; www.mossresorcenet.org)* has been providing friendly and helpful phone advice and referrals for years through its Travel Information Service. You'll find links to a number of travel agents who specialize in planning trips for disabled travelers here and through **Access-Able Travel Source** *(www.access-able.com),* another excellent online source.

You can join the **Society for the Advancement of Travel for the Handicapped** *(SATH; Tel 212/447-7284; Fax 212/725-8253; www.sath.org),* to gain access to their vast network of connections in the travel industry. Membership requires a tax-deductible contribution of $45 annually for adults, $30 for seniors and students.

Vision-impaired travelers should contact the **American Foundation for the Blind** *(Tel 800/232-5463)* for information on traveling with Seeing-Eye dogs.

For the past 30 years, the **National Rehabilitation Board of Ireland** *(24/25 Clyde Rd., Ballsbridge, Dublin 4; Tel 01/608-0400),* has encouraged facilities to accommodate people with disabilities. Consequently, more and more hotels and public buildings now have ramps or graded entrances and rooms specially fitted for wheelchair access. Unfortunately, many of the older hotels, guesthouses, and landmark buildings still have steep steps both outside and within. For a list of the properties that cater to the needs of patrons with disabilities, contact the National Rehabilitation Board in advance.

The **Irish Wheelchair Association** *(24 Blackheath Dr., Clontarf, Dublin 3; Tel 01/833-8241),* loans free wheelchairs for travelers in Ireland. A donation is appreciated. Branch offices are at Parnell Street, Kilkenny (Tel 056/62775); White Street, Cork (Tel 021/966354); Henry Street, Limerick (Tel 061/313691); and Dominick Street, Galway (Tel 091/771550), as well as in a range of other towns less frequently visited by tourists.

If you plan to travel by rail in Ireland, be sure to check out Iarnrod Eireann's Web site (www.irishrail.ie), which includes services for travelers with disabilities.

For advice on travel to Northern Ireland, contact *Disability Action (Portside Business Park, 189 Airport Rd. West, Belfast BT3 9ED; Tel 028/9079-1900).* The Northern Ireland Tourist Board also publishes a helpful annual *Information Guide to Accessible Accommodation,* available from any of its offices worldwide.

GAY & LESBIAN TRAVELERS

Gay Ireland has rapidly come out of the closet since homosexuality became legal in the North in 1982 and in the Republic in July 1993. Although the gay and lesbian community has received increasing support over the past several years, much of Ireland continues to discourage its gay population. In cities such as Dublin, Cork, and Galway, however, gay and lesbian visitors can find more formal support and an open, if small, gay community. Two essential publications for the gay or lesbian visitor to Ireland are the *Gay Community News* and *In Dublin* magazine. *Gay Community News* is a free newspaper of comprehensive Irish gay-related information published on the last Friday of each month and widely available in the city center. You can always find a copy at the National Lesbian and Gay Federation (see below), where it is published and where you can get advice on gay-related legal issues. The *Gay Community News* is also distributed by Books Upstairs, 36 College Green, across from Trinity College; Waterstone's on Dawson Street, also near Trinity; the Well Fed Cafe on Crow Street in Temple Bar; the George on South Great George's Street off Dame Street; and other progressive haunts.

The most comprehensive web site for Gay organizations, events, issues, and information throughout Ireland can be found on **Ireland's Pink Pages** *(http://indigo.ie/~outhouse).*

In Dublin, which comes out twice a month and is for sale at news agents and bookstores throughout the city, has a page that lists gay events, current club information, AIDS and health information resources, accommodations options, and helpful organizations.

The following organizations and help lines are staffed by knowledgeable and friendly people:

National Lesbian and Gay Federation (NLGF), (6 South William St., Dublin 2; Tel 01/670-6377; Fax 01/679-1603; http://homepage.tinet.ie/~nlgf), available Monday to Friday noon to 6pm

Gay Switchboard Dublin, (Carmichael House, North Brunswick Street, Dublin 7; Tel 01/872-1055; Fax 01/873-5737; gsd@iol.ie), Sunday to Friday 8 to 10pm and Saturday 3:30 to 6pm

Lesbian Line Dublin; (Tel 01/872-9911), Thursday 7 to 9pm

LOT (Lesbians Organizing Together), the umbrella group of the lesbian community, 5 Capel St., Dublin 1; Tel and Fax 01/872-7770), accommodates drop-ins Fridays 10am to 4pm. LOT also sponsors LEA/Lesbian Education Awareness; Tel and Fax 01/872-0460; e-mail: leanow@indigo.ie).

The Gay and Lesbian AA Group meets in Outhouse, 6 South William St., Dublin 2 on Friday evenings at 8pm

AIDS Helpline Dublin (Tel 01/872-4277), runs Monday to Friday 7 to 9pm and Saturday 3 to 5pm, offers assistance with HIV/AIDS prevention, testing, and treatment.

Gay and lesbian travelers seeking information and assistance on travel abroad might want to consult the **International Gay and Lesbian Travel Association (IGLTA** *(4331 North Federal Hwy., Suite 304, Fort Lauderdale, FL 33308; Tel 800/448-8550 or 954/776-2626; Fax 954-776-3303; www.iglta.org).* General gay and lesbian travel agencies include Family Abroad (Tel 800/999-5500 or 212/459-1800) for gays and lesbians; and Above and Beyond Tours (Tel 800/397-2681; www.abovebeyondtours.com) mainly for gays. Additional helpful resources include the Ferrari Guides, whose titles include: Gay Travel A-Z; Men's Travel in Your Pocket; Women's Travel in Your Pocket; and Inn Places. All four are published by Ferrari Publications, P.O. Box 37887, Phoenix, AZ 85069 (www.q-net.com). Women Going Places is available from Inland Book Company, P.O. Box 12061, East Haven, CT 06512. Also, Council Travel (Tel 888/COUNCIL for an office near you) can supply a free pamphlet called AIDS and International Travel that includes information on hotlines, HIV testing, blood transfusions, and traveling with AIDS overseas.

getting there by plane

About half of all visitors from North America arrive in Ireland on direct transatlantic flights to Dublin Airport, Shannon Airport, or Belfast International Airport. (Since March 27, 1994, transatlantic flights to the Republic are no longer required to stop in Shannon.) The other half fly first into Britain or Europe, then "backtrack" into Ireland by air or sea. In the Republic, there are seven smaller regional airports, all of which (except Knock) offer service to Dublin and several of which receive some EC international traffic. They are Cork, Donegal, Galway, Kerry, Knock, Sligo, and Waterford. In Northern Ireland, the secondary airports are Belfast City Airport and Derry City Airport. Services and schedules are always subject to change, so be sure to consult your preferred airline or travel agent as soon as you begin to sketch your itinerary. The routes and carriers listed below are provided to suggest the range of possibilities for air travel to Ireland.

FROM THE U.S.

The Irish national carrier, **Aer Lingus** *(Tel 800/474-7424; www.aerlingus.ie)* is the traditional leader in providing transatlantic flights to Ireland. Aer Lingus offers scheduled flights from Boston, Chicago, Los Angeles, Newark, and New York JFK to Dublin, Shannon, and Belfast International Airports, with connecting flights to Ireland's regional airports.

Note: Aer Lingus offers educational discounts to full-time students, which can be booked through CIEE/Council Travel (see above). It also sells an attractively priced Eurosaver Green Pass for those who want to combine an Aer Lingus round-trip transatlantic flight to Ireland with a side trip to Britain or the Continent, or a domestic flight within Ireland, including the North.

Icelandair *(Tel 800/223-5500; www.icelandair.com)* offers direct flights from North America to Europe via its hub in Reykjavík, Iceland. They offer service from Boston, New York, Baltimore/Washington, Minneapolis/St. Paul, Orlando, and Halifax (Canada) to Dublin and Galway (via London and a connecting flight on British Midlands, whom they have a partnership with). We think they're one of the coolest ways to get to Europe, not only because of their great service, but because of their Take-a-Break program: You can take up to a 3-day layover in Iceland on any of their flights (in either direction) for no extra charge.

Excellent transatlantic service is also provided by **Delta Airlines** *(Tel 800/241-4141; www.delta-air.com)*. It offers scheduled daily flights from Atlanta and New York JFK to both Dublin and Shannon, with feed-in connections from Delta's network of gateways throughout the United States.

Also offering daily transatlantic service to Ireland is **Continental Airlines** *(Tel 800/231-0856; www.continental.com)*, with two flights a day from their Newark hub, one to Shannon and one to Dublin. In addition, limited scheduled service from Chicago, Miami, Mexico City, and Washington, D.C. to Shannon is offered by **Aeroflot** *(Tel 888/340-6400).* **Royal Jordanian Airlines** *(Tel 800/223-0474)* flies twice a week, Mondays and Thursdays, to Shannon from Chicago.

BACKTRACKING FROM BRITAIN

Many travelers opt to fly to Britain and backtrack into Dublin (see "From Britain to Ireland," below). Carriers serving Britain from the United States include American Airlines (Tel 800/433-7300; www.aa.com), British Airways (Tel 800/247-9297; www.british-airways.com), Continental Airlines (Tel 800/231-0856; www.continental.com), Delta Airlines (Tel 800/241-4141; www.delta-air.com), Northwest Airlines (Tel 800/447-4747; www.nwa.com), TWA (Tel 800/892-4141; www.twa.com), United (Tel 800/241-6522; www.ual.com), and Virgin Atlantic Airways (Tel 800/862-8621; www.fly.virgin.com).

FROM LONDON TO DUBLIN

The following carriers operate air service from London to Dublin: **Aer Lingus** *(Tel 800/474-7424 from the U.S., or 020/8899-4747 in Britain);* **British Airways** *(Tel 0345/222111)* offered by **City Flyer Express** *(Tel 800/247-9297 from the U.S., or 0345/222111 in Britain);* **British Midland** *(Tel 800/788-0555 from the U.S., or 0870/607-0555 in Britain; www.iflybritishmidland.com);* **CityJet** *(Tel 0345/445588 in Britain; www.airfrance.fr);* and **Ryanair** *(Tel 0541/569569 in Britain; www.ryanair.com).* In addition to the London-Dublin routes, there are direct flights from London to Cork, Kerry, Knock, Shannon, and Waterford, as well as flights from over twenty other British cities to Ireland's airports.

Direct flights into **Belfast International Airport** *(www.bial.co.uk)* include flights by **British Airways** *(Tel 0345/222111; www.british-airways.com)* from Birmingham, Edinburgh, and London/Heathrow; and by **Virgin Express** *(Tel 800/891199; www.fly.virgin.com)* from London/Heathrow. In addition, there is service into **Belfast City Airport** *(Tel 01232/457745; www.belfastcityairport.com)* by a range of carriers, including British Airways flights from Edinburgh, Glasgow, Leeds, Liverpool, and Manchester and by **Jersey European** *(Tel 0990/676676)* from Birmingham, Bristol, Exeter, London Stansted, and London Gatwick: Service to Derry City Eglinton Airport is provided by British Airways from Glasgow and Manchester, and by **Ryanair** *(Tel 0541/569569 in Britain)* from London Stansted.

FROM THE CONTINENT

Major direct flights into Dublin from the continent include service from Amsterdam on **KLM** *(Tel 800/374-7747 in the U.S.);* Barcelona on **Iberia** *(Tel 800/772-4642 in the U.S.);* Brussels on **Sabena** *(Tel 800/952-2000 in the U.S.);* Copenhagen on Aer Lingus and **SAS** *(Tel 800/221-2350 in the U.S.);* Frankfurt on Aer Lingus and **Lufthansa** *(Tel 800/645-3880 in the U.S.);* Paris on Aer Lingus and **Air France** *(Tel 800/237-2747 in the U.S.);* Prague on **CSA Czech Airlines** *(Tel 212/765-6588 in the U.S.);* and Rome on Aer Lingus. Quite recently, **Cork Airport** *(www.cork-airport.com)* has passed Shannon and become the number two airport in Ireland, though it offers no non-stop trans-Atlantic service. Aer Lingus,

British Airways, KLM, and Ryanair are among the airlines flying into Cork and providing a rapidly growing network of connections with Great Britain and the Continent (see above for their contact info). Direct service to Shannon from the Continent includes Aer Lingus from Düsseldorf, Frankfurt, Paris, and Zurich, Aeroflot from Moscow, and Virgin Express from Brussels.

AIRFARE BARGAINS

Here are a few tips that might help you save some money upfront on airfare:

Take advantage of APEX fares. Advance-purchase booking is often the key to getting the lowest fare. You generally must be willing to make your plans and buy your tickets as far ahead as possible. Be sure you understand cancellation and refund policies before you buy.

Consolidators, also known as bucket shops, are a good place to find low fares, often below even the airlines' discounted rates. There's nothing shady about the reliable ones—basically, they're just big travel agents that get discounts for buying in bulk and pass some of the savings on to you. Some of the most reliable consolidators include **Cheap Tickets** *(Tel 800/377-1000; www.cheaptickets.com)*, **Council Travel** *(Tel 800/226-8624; www.counciltravel.com)*, **STA Travel** *(Tel 800/781-4040; www.sta.travel.com)*, **Lowestfare.com** *(Tel 888/278-8830; www.lowest fare.com)*, **Cheap Seats** *(Tel 800/451-7200; www.cheapseatstravel.com)*, and **1-800-FLY-CHEAP** *(www.flycheap.com)*.

Search the Internet for cheap fares—though it's still best to compare your findings with the research of a dedicated travel agent. Two of the better-respected virtual travel agents are Travelocity (www.travelocity.com) and Microsoft Expedia (www.expedia.com). See "Ireland Online," below, for further discussion on this topic and other recommendable sites.

Consider a charter flight. They're often a good value, though they offer fewer frills, and their tickets are ordinarily nonrefundable. From the United States, **Sceptre Charters** *(Tel 800/221-0924 or 718/738-9400)* operates the largest and most reliable charter program to Ireland. It flies to Shannon from Boston, Philadelphia, Chicago, and Los Angeles. Several companies in Canada operate charter flights from Toronto to Ireland, including **Signature Vacations** *(Tel 800/268-7063 in Canada or from the U.S. 800/268-1105)*, **Air Transat Holidays** *(Tel 800/587-2672 in Canada, or 514/987-1550)*, and **Regent Holidays** *(Tel 800/387-4860 in Canada, or 905/673-3343)*.

getting there by ferry

If you're traveling to Ireland from Britain or the Continent, especially if you're behind the wheel of a car, ferries can get you there. The Irish Sea has a reputation, however, so it's always a good idea to consider an over-the-counter pill or patch to guard against seasickness. (Be sure to take any pills before you set out; once you're underway, it's generally too late.)

The coast of Ireland is not so razor-straight as, say, the borders of Kansas. A number of passenger and car ferries cut across the wider gaps, shaving hours off point-to-point driving times. These routes operate between Tarbert, County Kerry, and Killimer, County Clare; Passage East, County Waterford, and Ballyhack, County Wexford; and Glenbrook, east of Cork City, and Carrigaloe, outside of Cobh.

Additionally, because Ireland includes a number of must-see islands, getting around includes getting on a boat now and then. Some boats, including all major ferries, have official licenses and offer regular scheduled service. Sometimes, however, making a crossing is a matter of staring out across a body of water to where you want to be and asking someone with a boat to take you there. Both methods work. To supplement the boat listings in this guide, you might want to request a copy of Information Sheet 50C—"Island Boat/Air Services"—from the Irish Tourist Board.

Prices fluctuate seasonally and depend on your route, time of travel, and whether you are on foot or in a car. It's best to check with your travel agent for up-to-date details, but just to give you an idea, the lowest one-way adult fare in high season on the cruise ferry from Holyhead to Dublin is £20 (that's British pounds, or $31). Add your car, and the grand total will be £149 (again, in pounds sterling, or $231.95). The web sites given below have regularly updated schedules and prices.

FROM BRITAIN

Irish Ferries *(www.irishferries.ie)* operates from Holyhead, Wales, to Dublin and from Pembroke, Wales, to Rosslare, County Wexford: For reservations, call **Scots-American Travel** *(Tel 561/563-2856 in the U.S., or 01/638-3333 in Ireland).* **Stena Line** *(Tel 888/274-8724 in the U.S., or 01233/647022 in Britain; www2.stenaline.com)* sails from Holyhead to Dun Laoghaire, 8 miles south of Dublin; from Fishguard, Wales, to Rosslare; and from Stranraer, Scotland, to Belfast, Northern Ireland. **Swansea/Cork Ferries** *(Tel 011792/456116 in Britain; www.swansea cork.ie)* links Swansea, Wales, to Cork. P&O European Ferries operates from Cairnryan, Scotland, to Larne, Northern Ireland (for reservations, call **Scots-American Travel** *(Tel 561/563-2856 in the U.S., or 01/638-3333 in Ireland; www.poef.com).* **Norse Irish Ferries** *(Tel 0151/9441010 in Britain; www.norse-irish-ferries.co.uk)* sails between Liverpool and Belfast. **Seacat Scotland Ltd.** *(Tel 800/551743 in Britain or 01/874-1231 in Ireland; www.team-packet.com)* operates ferries from Liverpool, England and Douglas, Isle of Man to Dublin; from Stranraer, Heysham, and Troon, Scotland to Belfast, and from Campbeltown, Scotland to Ballycastle, Co. Antrim.

FROM CONTINENTAL EUROPE

Irish Ferries sails from Roscoff and Cherbourg, France to Rosslare. For reservations, call **Scots-American Travel** *(Tel 561/563-2856 in the U.S., or 01/638-3333 in Ireland).* **Brittany Ferries** *(Tel 021/277801 in Cork; www.brittany-ferries.com)* connects Roscoff, France to Cork.

Note: Because the Irish Ferries company is a member of the Eurail system, you can travel free on the ferries between Rosslare and Roscoff or Cherbourg if you hold a valid Eurail Pass.

getting around ireland

Transport fares—air, ferry, train—are either "single" (one-way) or "return" (round-trip).

BY PLANE

Because Ireland is such a small country, it's unlikely you'll be flying from place to place. If you do require an air transfer, however, **Aer Lingus** *(Tel 01/705-3333; www.aerlingus.com)* operates daily scheduled flights linking Dublin with Cork, Galway, Kerry, Knock, Shannon, and Sligo.

BY TRAIN

Iarnrod Eireann/Irish Rail Travel Centre, 35 Lower Abbey St., Dublin 1 *(Tel 01/703-1839),* operates a network of train services throughout Ireland. With the exception of flying, train travel is the fastest way to get around the country. Most lines radiate from Dublin to other principal cities and towns. From Dublin, the journey time to Cork is 3 hours; to Belfast, 2 hours; to Galway, 3 hours; to Limerick, 2-1/4 hours; to Killarney, 4 hours; to Sligo, 3-1/4 hours; and to Waterford, 2-3/4 hours. For train departure times and fares, call (in Dublin) Tel 01/836-6222 Monday through Saturday 8:30am to 6pm, Sunday 9am to 6pm. Outside of regular business hours, call Tel 01/703-1842/1843. For rail inquiries anywhere in Ireland, call toll-free Tel 1850/366222. Iarnrod Eireann has an excellent interactive Web site (www.irishrail.ie) where you can map out and schedule all your comings and goings in Ireland. You'll find updated timetables for DART, Intercity, and Suburban lines, as well as useful links to other travel services.

Iarnrod Eireann/Irish Rail also offers an enticing array of weekend to week-long holiday packages or RailBreaks to practically every corner of Ireland, North as well as South. For details, contact the Irish Rail Travel Centre (see above).

In addition to the Irish Rail service between Dublin and Belfast, **Northern Ireland Railways** *(Tel 888/BRITRAIL or 028/9089-9411; www.raileurope.com)* operates three main routes from its hub in Belfast. They run north and west from Belfast to Derry via Ballymena; east to Bangor, tracing the shores of Belfast Lough; and south to Dublin via Newry.

BY BUS

Bus Eireann, with its hub at Busaras/Central Bus Station, Dublin 1 *(Tel 01/836-6111; www.buseireann.ie),* operates an extensive system of express bus service, as well as local service to nearly every town in Ireland. Express routes include Dublin to Donegal (4-1/4 hours), Killarney to Limerick (2-1/2 hours), Limerick to Galway (2 hours), and Limerick to Cork (2 hours). The Bus Eireann Web site at provides the latest timetables and fares for bus service throughout Ireland. Bus travel is usually affordable, reliable, and comfortable.

For bus travel within Northern Ireland, contact **Ulsterbus,** Europa Buscentre, 10 Glengall St., Belfast *(Tel 028/9033-3000; www.translink.co.uk).*

RAIL & BUS TRAVEL PASSES

For extensive travel by public transport, you can save money by purchasing a rail/bus pass or a rail-only pass. The options include the following:

Brit/Ireland Pass: For all standard-class rail travel throughout Great Britain and Ireland, including a round-trip ferry crossing on Stena Line. Valid for 1 month, it costs $528 1st class, $396 2nd class for 5 days of travel; $752 1st class, $566 economy for 10 days of travel. It must be purchased before departure for Ireland or Britain. Available from **BritRail** *(Tel 800/BRITRAIL, or 800/555-2748 in Canada; www.raileurope.com),* or from **CIE Tours International** *(Tel 800/243-8687 or 973/292-3438 from the U.S., 800/387-2667 in Canada; www.cietours.co).*

Emerald Card: This pass is good for rail and bus service throughout Ireland and Northern Ireland. It costs £200 ($280) for 15 days of travel within a 30-day period, £115($161) for 8 days of travel within a 15-day period. It's available from **Iarnrod Eireann/Irish Rail,** Travel Centre, 35 Lower Abbey St., Dublin 1 *(Tel 01/703-1839; www.irishrail.ie);* from **Busaras/Central Bus Station,** Dublin 1 *(Tel 01/836-6111),* at all major bus and train stations; or from **CIE Tours International** *(Tel 800/243-8687 or 973/292-3438 from the U.S., 800/387-2667 in Canada; www.citours.co).*

Eurail Pass: For unlimited rail travel in 17 European countries. It is not valid in Britain or Northern Ireland. In the Republic, the Eurail Pass is good for all rail travel, Expressway coaches, and the Irish Continental Lines ferries between France and Ireland. The pass must be purchased 21 days before departure for Ireland by a non-European Union resident. For further details or for purchase, call **Rail Pass Express** *(Tel 800/722-7151; www.eurail.com).* Also available from Council Travel and other travel agents.

Freedom of Northern Ireland: Seven days unlimited travel on bus and train in the North for £37 ($61.05), five days for £25 ($41.25) or one day for £10 ($16.50). It's available from **Northern Ireland Railways,** Central Station, East Bridge Street, Belfast *(Tel 028/9089-9411);* and **Ulsterbus,** Europa Buscentre, 10 Glengall St., Belfast *(Tel 028/9033-3000; www.translink.co.uk);* as well as all major bus and train stations in Northern Ireland.

Irish Explorer: For use in the Republic of Ireland, this pass is good for either 8 days of combined rail and bus services £100($140) or 5 days of rail only £83($116.20). It's available from **Iarnrod Eireann/Irish Rail** Travel Centre, 35 Lower Abbey St., Dublin 1 *(Tel 01/703-1839; www.irishrail.ie);* and **Busaras/Central Bus Station,** Dublin 1 *(Tel 01/836-6111);* as well as all major bus and train stations.

Irish Rover: For use in the Republic of Ireland and the North, this pass entitles you to 5 days of rail travel for £83($116.20). It's available from **Iarnrod Eireann/Irish Rail Travel Centre,** 35 Lower Abbey St., Dublin 1 *(Tel 01/703-1839; www.irishrail.ie),* and all major train stations.

Note: Three-day passes are good for any 3 days in an 8-day period;

5-day passes for any 5 days in a 15-day period; 8-day passes for any 8 days in a 15-day period; and 15-day passes for any 15 days in a 30-day period. The Emerald Card, the Irish Explorer, and the Irish Rover passes can be purchased in Ireland at most mainline rail stations and Bus Eireann ticket offices. In the United States, they're available from **CIE Tours International** *(Tel 800/243-8687).*

BY CAR

Although Ireland offers an extensive network of public transportation, the advantages of having your own car are obvious.

The disadvantages begin with the cost of rental and continue with each refueling. In high season, weekly rental rates on a compact vehicle begin at around $250 (if you've shopped around) and ascend steeply—but it's at the pump that you're likely to go into shock. Irish gas prices can easily be triple what you pay in the United States. The sole consolation is that Ireland is comparatively small, so distances are comparatively short.

Another fact of life on the road in Ireland is that space is limited. Most Irish roads and highways are surprisingly narrow, made to order for what many Americans would regard as miniature cars—just the kind you'll wish you had rented once you're under way. So think small when you pick out your rental car. The choice is yours: between room in the car and room on the road.

Unless your stay in Ireland extends beyond 6 months, your own valid U.S. or Canadian driver's license (provided you've had it for at least 6 months) is all you need to drive in Ireland. Rules and restrictions for car rental vary slightly and correspond roughly to those in the United States. (This was not always the case).

Highway safety—or the lack of it—has reached the level of a national crisis in Ireland during the last several years. The number of highway fatalities is shocking, and has caused Ireland to be ranked as the second most dangerous country in Europe in which to drive (only Greece is worse). So if you rent a car, be extra careful.

The excessive speed of many Irish drivers can be a fierce annoyance on the open road, the snail's pace of traffic in Dublin provides its own form of frustration. There is simply no point in renting a car for your time in Dublin. The pace of traffic in the capital's city center is now officially down to 8kph (about 5mph), as against an average of 15kph in most other European capitals. You're better off on foot.

A common concern for would-be motorists from abroad is the fact that the Irish, in both the North and South, drive on the left. The thought of this whitens some knuckles even before they touch the wheel, but don't worry, you'll catch on fast; there's nothing like the sight of an oncoming vehicle to remind you that you're in the wrong lane.

"Roundabouts" also take a little getting used to. Just remember: Always turn left into a roundabout and yield to vehicles on the right.

One signal that could be particularly misleading to U.S. drivers is a flashing yellow light at a pedestrian traffic light. This means yield to pedestrians, and proceed only if the crossing is clear.

There are relatively few major (extended, limited access, divided) highways to speak of in the Republic—only national (N), regional (R), and rural or unclassified roads. N50 and higher are primary roads; numbers lower than 50 indicate secondary roads. Regional roads usually have a name, not a number. In the North, there are two Major Motorways (M), equivalent to interstates, as well as a network of lesser A- and B-level roads. Speed limits are posted. In general, the limit for urban areas is 46kmph (30 mph), for open but non-divided highways 95kmph (60 mph), and for major motorways 110kmph (70 mph).

The enforcement of speed limits is becoming increasing stringent, and Irish roads have some built-in enforcers. Roads are often slick, with many bends and rises, any one of which can present a sheep or other four-legged pedestrian on very short notice. The low density of traffic on some of Ireland's roads can promote the deadly fantasy that you have the road to yourself. Don't wait to be contradicted.

Both the North and the South have appropriately severe laws on the books against drunk driving, and they will gladly throw them at you. Irish hospitality has its limits. Both also enforce the mandatory use of seat belts in the front seat, and the North extends that to rear-seat passengers.

Rentals: Major international car-rental firms are represented at airports and cities throughout Ireland and Northern Ireland. They include **Alamo-Treaty** *(Tel 800/522-9696 from the U.S.; www.goalamo.com),* **Auto-Europe** *(Tel 800/223-5555 from the U.S.; www.autoeurope.com),* **Avis** *(Tel 800/331-1084 from the U.S.; www.avis.com),* **Budget** *(Tel 800/472-3325 from the U.S.; www.budgetrentacar.com),* **Hertz** *(Tel 800/838-0826 from the U.S.; www.hertz.com),* **Murrays Europcar** *(Tel 800/800-6000 from the U.S.),* **National** *(Tel 800/227-7368 from the U.S.; www.nationalcar.com),* and **Payless/Bunratty** *(Tel 800/729-5377 from the U.S.; www.paylesscar.com).* It's best to shop around, because it is difficult to say who will be offering the best rate at any given moment, although Budget seems consistently quite competitive and tries hard to accommodate special circumstances and needs.

I strongly urge you to make car-rental arrangements well in advance of your departure. Leaving such arrangements until the last minute—or, worse, until your arrival in Ireland—can mean you wind up either walking or wishing you were. Ireland is a small country, and in high season, it can completely run out of rental cars—but before it does, it runs out of affordable rental cars. Discounts are common in the off-season, of course, but it's also possible to negotiate a decent deal for July and August, if you put in enough time and effort.

Auto Europe *(Tel 800/223-5555; Fax 207/828-1177; www.autoeurope.com)* offers superior rates and service on overseas rentals and long-term leases. Their agreements are clear, straightforward, and all-inclusive. Better yet, they can beat any bona fide offer from another company; ask for the "Beat Rate Desk." Another well-established firm offering long-term leases and rentals is **Europe by Car** *(Tel 800/223-1516).*

In addition, a variety of Irish-based companies have desks at the major airports and full-service offices in city or town locations. The leader among the Irish-based firms is **Dan Dooley/Kenning Rent-a-Car** *(Tel 800/331-9301 from the U.S.; www.dan-dooley.ie)*.

The car-rental rates quoted by many companies do not include the inevitable 12.5% government tax (VAT), nor do they include CDW (collision damage waiver) or insurance against theft of the rental vehicle. If you have your own auto insurance, you may be covered; check your existing policy before you pay for additional coverage you may not need. If you do not have your own auto insurance, and you rent with a credit card that provides free protection, be sure to call your card's customer service line to make certain there are no invisible or whispered restrictions on that coverage. Tell the company exactly where you are going, for how long, and let the staff assure you that all is well. (Note that while many cards offer collision protection, they do not cover you for liability.) One common hitch is that the complimentary CDW may be invalid beyond 30 consecutive days, which means you must return the car within 30 days and take out a second rental to extend the coverage beyond the 30-day limit. In 1999, Visa eliminated all coverage on rental cars in Ireland, and MasterCard limited its coverage. Be certain that your information is current. Always confirm the details of your coverage when you charge your car rental to your credit card. Make certain that the distinction between Ireland and Northern Ireland is clear both to you and to those with whom you are negotiating.

If you are renting a car in the Republic and taking it into the North (or vice versa), be sure to ask the car rental firm if the rental insurance the company provides covers cross-border transport. If not, you may be required to buy extra insurance. If you rent a car in the Republic, it is best to return it to the Republic, and if you rent it in the North, return it in the North (some firms charge extra for cross-border drop-offs).

Parking: Some small cities and most towns have free street parking, but larger cities confine parking to metered spaces or parking garages and lots. "Disc-parking" is also in effect in many places. Under this system, you buy a paper disc and display it for the time you are parked in a certain area. Discs in Dublin currently cost 40p to 80p (56¢ to $1.12) per hour of use; they're sold in most shops, hotels, and tourist offices. Some towns also follow the "pay and display" system, which is similar to the disc system: You buy a parking voucher (usually for 20p/28¢ to 40p/56¢ per hour) from a machine at the site and display the voucher for the time you are parked. Remember not to park on double yellow lines.

Dublin, in particular, has recently taken the gloves off in an effort to crack down on parking violations—so be extra vigilant there. The city is poised to hike the current fine of £15 ($21) to £65 ($91), which will likely be the slap you'll feel by the time this edition hits the stands.

In Belfast and other large cities in the North, certain security measures are in place. Control zone signs indicate that no unattended vehicle can be left there at any time. That means if you are a single traveler, you cannot leave your car; if you are a twosome, one person must remain in the car while it's parked. Also, unlocked cars anywhere in the North are subject to a fine, for security reasons.

Taxi & Hackney: Taxis and hackneys look very much alike. Both drive you where you ask them to, and the drivers collect a fee at the end and are quite likely to entertain you with stories. There are some significant differences, however. Hackneys are not allowed to wait at taxi "ranks" or display a sign atop their cars; they don't use meters; and they are not regulated by any municipal or state agency. In other words, they are private individuals doing business as drivers for hire. They agree with you on a fare, which could be more or less than the regulated fee a taxi would charge. Both taxis and hackneys advertise in the classifieds or "Golden Pages."

Driving Services: There is still another way of getting around Ireland by car. If cost is no concern, or if you can't shake the fear of the left lane, you might want to consider being chauffeured in style. The fleets of such services usually begin at ground level with a basic Mercedes sedan and stretch from there. If you're interested, contact **Carey Limousine International** *(Tel 800/336-4646; www.careyint.com),* whose 8-hour daily rate is currently around $450: In Ireland, with offices in Dublin and Shannon, we recommend Bord Failte-approved **Dave Sullivan Chauffeur Drive Limited** *(Tel 01/820-1076; Fax 01/820-6333; www.chauffeur.ie).* A typical 8-hour bottom line for two people in and around Dublin will run about $350. For larger parties, Chrysler Voyagers are available.

crashing

One of the best things about visiting Ireland is the variety of really great places to stay on the cheap. From hostels to farmhouses, you can easily find a bed—and usually breakfast—without ever having to even glance at a Holiday Inn. And if you're in the mood to splurge, you can stay in one of the many castles that accommodate guests. But don't avoid hotels altogether; many of Ireland's old hotels are more charming (and sometimes less expensive) than some B&Bs. Here's a sketch of what's out there.

HOSTELS

Hostels provide remarkably appealing accommodations at a fraction of the cost of even a modest bed-and-breakfast (see Hostels directory). There are two national hostel organizations; **An Oàige,** the Irish Youth Hostel Association (61 Mountjoy St., Dublin 7; Tel 01/830-4555, Fax 01/830-5808; www.irelandyha.org) in the Republic and **YHANI,** Youth Hostel Association of Northern Ireland (22-32 Donegal Road, Belfast, BT12 5JN; Tel 028/9032-4733, Fax 028/90439699; www.hini.org) in the North. If you come across a reference to HINI (Hostelling International Northern Ireland), don't be confused; it's another name for the same organization. The Websites for these organizations can give you all the info you'll need on becoming a member and using the hostel system.

BED & BREAKFASTS

Throughout Ireland, in the cities and in the sticks, private homes are often open to lodgers, by the night or longer. A warm bed and a solid, hot breakfast can be expected, and other meals are negotiable. While most B&Bs are regulated and inspected by Tourism Quality Services (look for the shamrock seal of approval), approximately 12,000 premises are under no external supervision. Regulated or not, they are all different, as are your hosts. Establishments without governmental supervision or approval are not necessarily inferior to those stamped with the green shamrock. Approval involves an annual fee, as well as specific restrictions that some proprietors prefer not to embrace.

For a modest fee, the Irish Tourist Board will send a detailed listing of roughly 2,000 approved B&Bs, complete with a color photo of each. Needless to say, you receive the personal touch when you stay in someone's home, and more often than not, this is a real bonus. For those on the move (spending only a night or two in each location) and on a budget, this choice is often hard to beat.

HOTELS & GUESTHOUSES

Be Our Guest, a full guide to the hotels and inns of Ireland, is distributed by the Irish Hotel Federation and is available from the Irish Tourist Board. It's also online at ireland.iol.ie/be-our-guest/. Hotels and guesthouses, depending on their size and scope, offer a good deal more than a bed and a meal—everything from nightclubs to golf courses. Some were castles in a former life, others have been elegant hotels from birth, and many are nondescript.

The governments of the Republic and of the North inspect and rate all approved hotels and guesthouses. In the Republic, hotels can aspire to five stars, but guesthouses can reach no higher than four. In the North, hotels receive one to four stars, and guesthouses are either grade A or grade B. The least expensive options might cost no more than a home-style bed-and-breakfast, and the most expensive can be over 10 times that.

FARMHOUSE ACCOMMODATIONS

The vast majority of Irish farms—more than 150,000 in all—are relatively small and remain family-owned and -operated. In recent years, many of these farms have opened their doors to visitors. They offer an attractive alternative to hotels, guesthouses, and more standard B&B homes, particularly for families. The Irish Farm Holidays Association produces an annual book that lists farmhouse accommodations throughout the country. It is available from the Irish Tourist Board.

Farm holidays can take various forms, from one-night-at-a-time bed-and-breakfasts to extended self-catering rentals. Many of the farmhouse accommodations, in addition to breakfast, offer high tea, a full dinner, or both. Some are exactly what you'd imagine—full working family farms in untouched, often spectacular surroundings—while others stretch the meaning of farm to include country houses with a garden and a dog nearby, or guesthouses that are more "lodging with greenery" than "farm with lodging."

SELF-CATERING

If you want to stay a while and establish a base, you might want to consider renting an apartment, townhouse, cottage—or even a castle if you just received a major inheritance. Self-catering is a huge trend in Ireland, and the range of available accommodations is startling. The minimum rental period is usually 1 week, although shorter periods are sometimes negotiable off-season. For families or small groups, this is definitely a bargain way to go.

In high season, in both the Republic and the North, a cottage sleeping seven could cost anywhere from $250 to more than $1,000 per week. Both the Irish Tourist Board and the Northern Ireland Tourist Board prepare helpful annual guides to self-catering.

If you are the nesting type, this could be a good option. Contact **Trident Holiday Homes** *(15 Irishtown Rd., Irishtown, Dublin 4; Tel 01/668-3534; Fax 01/660-6465; www.thh.ie)* for rentals throughout Ireland; **Elegant Ireland** *(15 Harcourt St., Dublin 2; Tel 01/475-1632; Fax 01/475-1012; www.elegant.ie)* for a major splurge in anything from a castle to a fine Georgian manor house; **Cashelfean Holiday Houses** *(Durrus, County Cork; Tel 027/62000; Fax 027/62012; www.cashelfean.com)* for seaside properties in County Kerry; **Rent an Irish Cottage** *(85 O'Connell St., Limerick, County Limerick; Tel 061/411109; Fax 061/314821 www.rentacottage.ie)* for fully equipped traditional cottages in the west of Ireland; or **Rural Cottage Holidays Ltd.** *(St. Anne's Ct., 59 North St., Belfast BT1 1NB; Tel 028/9024-1100; Fax 028/9024-1100)* for beautifully restored traditional cottages hosted by nearby local families in Northern Ireland.

PRACTICAL MATTERS

Rates: Room charges quoted in this guide include 12.5% government tax (VAT) in the Republic of Ireland and 17.5% VAT in Northern Ireland. They do not (unless otherwise noted) include service charges, which are usually between 10% and 15% (most places add 12.5%). Most hotels and guesthouses automatically add the service charge onto your final bill, although in recent years many family-run or limited-service places have begun the practice of not charging for service, leaving it as an option for the guest. Home-style B&Bs do not ordinarily charge for service.

If you have a talent for it, room prices in hotels—especially privately owned hotels in the off-season—are negotiable. A polite way to find out is simply to ask, "Is that your best rate?" or "Can you do a little bit better?" Don't try the cowboy-style method of slamming a fistful of bills down on the reception desk and saying, "Fifty bucks, take it or leave it." That approach not only won't lower your rate, it may also get you kicked out of the place for good.

Terminology: The Irish use the phrase "en suite" to indicate a room with private bathroom. A "double" has a double bed, and a "twin" has two single beds. An "orthopedic" bed has an extra-firm mattress. Queen- and king-size beds are not common except in large, deluxe hotels.

Reservations: Many hotels can be booked through toll-free numbers in the United States, for rates as much as 40 percent lower than what you get if you just walk up to the front desk. For those properties that do not have a U.S. reservation number, the fastest way to reserve is by telephone, Fax, or e-mail. Fax and e-mail are advisable, because they give you a written confirmation. You can then follow up by sending a deposit check (usually the equivalent of one night's room rate) or by giving your credit card number.

If you arrive in Ireland without a reservation, the staff members at the tourist offices throughout the Republic and Northern Ireland will gladly find you a room using a computerized reservation service known as **Gulliver.** You can also call the Gulliver line directly *(Tel 00800/668-668-66).* This is a nationwide and cross-border "freephone" facility for credit-card bookings, operated daily 8am to 11pm. Gulliver is also accessible from the United States *(Tel 011800/668-668-66).*

Quality & value: Despite the various systems of approval, regulation, and rating, accommodations in Ireland are quite uneven in quality and cost. A budget hostel might be cleaner and more accommodating than a guesthouse or hotel and cost only a third as much. It's always wise to consult a fellow traveler or a reliable guidebook in booking your lodgings (which, of course, is what you're doing). If possible, always ask to see your room before committing yourself to a stay. In any given lodging, the size and quality of the rooms can vary considerably, often without any corresponding variation in cost. This is particularly true of single rooms, which can approach boarding-house standards even in a semi-luxurious hotel. Don't be discouraged by this, but be alert so you're not disappointed.

Many lodgings close for a few days or more on and around Christmas, even when they announce that they are open year-round. If you plan to visit Ireland during the Christmas holidays, double-check that the hotels, restaurants, and attractions you're counting on will be open.

eats

Ireland has a wide range of restaurants in all price categories. The settings range from old-world hotel dining rooms, country mansions, and castles to skylit terraces, shop-front bistros, riverside cottages, thatched-roof pubs, and converted chapels. And you can get every kind of food, from cheap Mexican to fancy French; what's available now is a far cry from the old stereotype of corned beef and bland boiled potatoes.

RESERVATIONS

Except for self-service eateries, informal cafes, and some popular seafood spots, most restaurants encourage reservations. The more expensive restaurants absolutely require reservations because there is little turnover—once a table is booked, it is yours for the whole lunch period or for the evening until closing. Seatings for Friday and Saturday nights (and Sunday lunch) are often booked a week or more in advance at some places, so have a few options in mind if you're booking at the last minute.

TABLE D'HÔTE OR À LA CARTE

Most restaurants offer two menus: *table d'hôte,* a fixed-price three- or four-course lunch or dinner with a variety of choices; and *à la carte,* a menu offering a wide choice of individually priced appetizers (starters), soups, main courses, salads or vegetables, and desserts (sweets). The table d'hôte menu is a good option if you're at a really good restaurant and you want to eat each and every course on the fixed-price menu. Otherwise, go for à la carte; you can choose exactly what you want to eat without paying for all those extra courses.

If you want to try a top-rated restaurant but can't afford dinner, have your main meal there in the middle of the day by trying the table d'hôte set lunch menu. You'll experience the same great cuisine at half the price of a nighttime meal.

TIPPING

Meal prices at restaurants include 12.5% VAT in the Republic of Ireland and a 17.5% VAT in Northern Ireland, but that doesn't include the tip. Some restaurants add a 10-15% service charge and others leave the tip up to you. This can be confusing for a visitor, but each restaurant normally prints its policy on the menu. If it is not clear, ask.

When no service charge is added, tip as you normally would in the United States, 15-20% depending on the quality of the service. If a service charge has already been added to your bill, leave an appropriate amount that will total 15-20% if service has been satisfactory.

SPECIAL DEALS

Some restaurants offer a fixed-price three-course tourist menu during certain hours and days. These menus offer limited choices, but are usually lower in price than the restaurant's regular table d'hôte menu. Look for a tourist menu with a green Irish chef symbol in the window, listing the choices and the hours when the prices are in effect.

pubs

Pubs are the mainstay of Irish social life. There are more than 10,000 throughout the country, in every city, town, and hamlet, on every street, and at every turn. A pub is not just a cocktail lounge with a cute name, it truly is a public house where people gather for conversation and a pint or maybe some inexpensive "pub grub." Pub grub is often a lot better than its name suggests; in recent years, many pubs have converted or expanded into restaurants, serving excellent unpretentious meals at prices that leave you plenty of change for another pint.

PUB HOURS

In the Republic of Ireland, pubs are open 10:30am-11:30pm hours Monday through Saturday, May through September; they close a half-hour earlier the rest of the year. On Sunday year-round, bars are open 12:30-2pm and 4-11pm; nightclubs and discos close at 2am. In the North, pubs are open 11:30am-11pm Monday through Saturday, 12:30-2pm and 7-10pm on Sunday, year-round.

sightseeing & shopping

SIGHTSEEING DISCOUNTS

You can stretch your vacation fund a bit by purchasing a Heritage Card, which entitles you to unlimited admission to more than 100 attractions all over Ireland operated by Dúchas, the Heritage Service. These include castles, stately homes, historic monuments, national parks, and more. The card, which costs £15 ($21) for adults or just £6 ($8.40) for students, is available from participating attractions or by credit card at Tel 01/647-2461 (check out www.heritageireland.ie). Just get it the first time you visit a Heritage site; it only costs a few bucks and you'll be really mad at yourself if you don't and then realize a week later how much you would have saved.

Detailed information about National Trust attractions in Northern Ireland is available from the Northern Ireland Tourist Board.

VAT REFUNDS

When shopping in the Republic of Ireland and Northern Ireland, bear in mind that the price of most goods, excluding books and children's clothing and footwear, already includes valued-added tax (VAT), a government tax of 17.36%. VAT is a hidden tax—it is already included on the price tags and in prices quoted to you.

As a visitor, you can avoid paying this tax, if you follow a few simple procedures. (EU residents are not entitled to a VAT refund on goods purchased or to duty-free shopping in airports and other transit terminals).

The easiest way to make a VAT-free purchase is to arrange for a store to ship the goods directly to your home, but then you have to pay for shipping, so you might not save that much in the end.

You'll probably end up carting most of your stuff home with you, which means you'll have to pay the full amount (including VAT)when you buy it, then get a refund later. There are a few different ways to get the refund.

STORE REFUND

For a store refund, get a full receipt at the time of purchase that shows the name, address, and VAT paid. (Customs does not accept cash register tally slips.) Save your receipts and get them stamped at the Customs Office at the airport or ferry port when you leave the country. A passport and other forms of identification (driver's license) may be required. Then you have to send the stamped receipts to the store where you made the purchase, and they'll send you a VAT refund check. Most stores deduct a small handling fee for this service.

CASH REFUND

Global Refund (Tel 800/566-9828) is one of several private companies offering a cash refund on purchases made at thousands of shops that display a variety of stickers, such as "Tax Back," "Cash Refund," and "Tax Saver." Refunds can be collected in the currency of your choice as you depart from Dublin or Shannon Airport. The nominal fee for this service is calculated on the amount of money you spend in each store. These booths are open year-round (except December 25 and 26) in the arrivals halls of Dublin Airport and Shannon Airport.

To get a refund, do the following:

1. Make purchases from stores displaying an appropriate sticker, and be sure to get VAT-refund vouchers from these participating shops each time you make a purchase.
2. Fill out each form with your name, address, passport number, and other required details.
3. When departing Ireland, have any vouchers with a value of over £200 ($280) stamped and validated by a Customs official.
4. Go to the VAT-refund booth corresponding to your vouchers at Dublin Airport (Departures Hall) or Shannon Airport (Arrivals

Hall), turn in your stamped forms, and receive cash payments in U.S. or Canadian dollars, British pounds sterling, or Irish punts.

MAIL-IN REFUND

If you are departing from Ireland through a ferry port, or if you don't have time to get to the ETS booth before you leave, you can send your stamped vouchers to the appropriate VAT refund company and receive a refund by mail, or have your refund applied to your credit-card account.

phones

In the Republic, the telephone system is known as Telecom Éireann; in Northern Ireland, it's British Telecom. Phone numbers in Ireland are currently in flux, as digits are added to accommodate expanded service. Every effort has been made to ensure that the numbers and information in this guide are accurate at the time of writing. If you have difficulty reaching a party, the Irish toll-free number for directory assistance is Tel 1190. From the United States, the (toll) number to call is Tel 00353-91-770220.

Local calls from a phone booth cost 20p (28¢) within the Republic of Ireland, and 20p (33¢) in the North for the first minute. The most efficient way to make calls from public phones is to use a Callcard (in the Republic) or Phonecard (in the North). Both are prepaid computerized cards that you insert into the phone instead of coins. They can be purchased in a range of denominations at phone company offices, post offices, and many retail outlets (such as newsstands). There's a local and international phone center at the General Post Office on O'Connell Street.

Overseas calls from Ireland can be quite costly, whether you use a local phonecard or your own calling card. If you think you will want to call home regularly while in Ireland, you may want to check out some of the low-rate international phone cards available over the Internet or open an account with Swiftcall (toll free in Ireland Tel 0800-794-381; www.swiftcall.com). Its rates represent a considerable savings, not only from Ireland to the United States but vice versa (handy for planning your trip as well as keeping in touch afterward). **Premiere WORLDLINK** *(Tel 800/432-6169)* offers an array of additional services for overseas travelers—such as toll-free voice-mail boxes, Fax mail, and news services—which can be crucial for keeping in touch when you don't know where or when you can be reached.

To place a call from your home country to Ireland, dial the **international access code** *(011 in the U.S., 0011 in Australia, 0170 in New Zealand, 00 in the U.K.),* plus the **country code** *(353 for the Republic, 44 for the North),* and finally the number, remembering to omit the initial 0, which is for use only within Ireland (for example, to call the County Kerry number 066/00000 from the United States, you'd dial 011-353-66/00000). To reach directory assistance, dial Tel 1190 within Ireland. From the United States, the (toll) number to call is Tel 00353-91-770220.

To place a direct international call from Ireland, dial the **international access code** *(00)* plus the **country code** *(U.S. and Canada 1, the U.K. 44, Australia 61, New Zealand 64),* the area or city code, and the number (for example, to call the U.S. number 212/000-0000 you'd dial 00-1-212/000-0000). Several widely used toll-free international access codes are: **AT&T** *1-800-550-000,* **Sprint** *1-800-552-001,* and **MCI** *1-800-55-1001.* Note: to dial direct to Northern Ireland from the Republic, simply replace the 028 prefix with 048. To place a collect call to the United States from Ireland, dial 1-800/550-000 for USA Direct service.

fast facts

AMERICAN EXPRESS

The only American Express offices in Ireland are in Dublin, Galway, and Killarney. There are no longer offices in the North. In an emergency, traveler's checks can be reported lost or stolen by dialing collect 1-44-1-273-571-600.

BUSINESS HOURS

Banks are open Monday through Wednesday and on Friday from 10am to 12:30pm and from 1:30 to 3pm, on Thursday from 10am to 12:30pm and from 1:30 to 5pm. Some banks are beginning to stay open through the lunch hour. Most business offices are open from 9am to 5pm, Monday through Friday. Stores and shops are open from 9am to 5:30pm Monday through Wednesday and Friday to Saturday, and from 9am to 8pm on Thursday. Some bookshops and tourist-oriented stores also open on Sunday from 11am or noon until 4 or 5pm. During the peak season (May through Sept), many gift and souvenir shops post Sunday hours. Some country towns have an early closing day when shops close at 1pm. For more exact regional shopping hours, see individual chapters.

CLOSING TIMES

It is often the case with "Attractions" that new visitors will not be admitted 30 minutes prior to the stated closing time; so, for example, don't expect to slip into a museum or castle at 4:35, even though it offically closes at 5pm.

CURRENCY EXCHANGE

Currency-exchange services, signposted as **BUREAU DE CHANGE,** are in all banks and at many branches of the Irish post office system, known as **An Post.** A bureau de change operates daily during flight arrival and departure times at Dublin airport; a foreign currency note-exchanger machine is also available on a 24-hour basis in the main arrivals hall. Many hotels and travel agencies offer bureau de change services, although the best rate of exchange is usually given at banks or, better yet, when you use your credit card for purchases or expenses.

DENTISTS

For listings, look under "Dental Surgeons" in the Golden Pages (yellow pages) of the Irish telephone book or in the Yellow Pages of the Northern Ireland telephone book—or better yet, ask your innkeeper for advice. Expect to pay up front.

DOCTORS

If you need to see a physician, most hotels and guesthouses will contact a house doctor for you. We have given referral services for the greater

Dublin area in chapter 4. Otherwise, consult the Golden Pages of the Irish telephone book or the Yellow Pages of the Northern Ireland telephone book. As with dentists, expect to pay for treatment up front and be reimbursed after the fact by your insurance company.

DRUGS & FIREARMS

The laws against the importation of illegal drugs and firearms are quite severe and will be enforced. Consult the nearest Irish or Northern Ireland consulate before presuming to bring any firearm into Ireland.

DRUGSTORES

Drugstores are usually called "chemist shops" or "pharmacies." Look under "Chemists—Pharmaceutical" in the Golden Pages of the Irish telephone book or "Chemists—Dispensing" in the Yellow Pages of the Northern Ireland telephone book.

ELECTRICITY

The standard electrical current is 220 volts AC in the Republic of Ireland, 240 volts in Northern Ireland. Most hotels have 110-volt shaver points for use in bathrooms, but other 110-volt equipment (such as hair dryers) will not work without a transformer and a plug adapter. Computers and sensitive electronic equipment may require more than the standard over-the-counter voltage converter. Some laptops have built-in converters. Consult the manufacturer of your computer for specifics. In any event, you will always need a plug adapter.

EMBASSIES/CONSULATES

The **American Embassy** is at 42 Elgin Rd., Ballsbridge, Dublin 4 *(Tel 01/668-8777);* the **Canadian Embassy** at 65/68 St. Stephen's Green, Dublin 2 *(Tel 01/678-1988);* the **British Embassy** at 33 Merrion Rd., Dublin 4 *(Tel 01/205-3700);* and the **Australian Embassy** at Fitzwilton House, Wilton Terrace, Dublin 2 *(Tel 01/676-1517)*. In addition, there is an **American Consulate** at 14 Queen St., Belfast BT1 6EQ *(Tel 028/9032-8239)*.

EMERGENCIES

For the Garda (police), fire, or other emergencies, dial Tel 999.

INTERNET ACCESS

Public access terminals are no longer hard to find in Ireland; they're now in shopping malls, hotels, and even hostels, especially in the larger towns and more tourist-centered areas. Additionally, there are an increasing number of internet cafés sprouting up across the island.

LIQUOR LAWS

Individuals must be age 18 or over to be served alcoholic beverages in Ireland. Restaurants with liquor licenses are permitted to serve alcohol during the hours when meals are served. Hotels and guesthouses with licenses can serve during normal hours to the public; overnight guests, referred to as "residents," can be served after closing hours. Alcoholic beverages by the bottle can be purchased at liquor stores, at pubs displaying "off-license" signs, and at most supermarkets.

Ireland has very severe laws and penalties regarding driving while intoxicated, so don't even think about it.

MAIL

In Ireland, mailboxes are painted green with the word *POST* on top. In Northern Ireland, they are painted red with a royal coat of arms symbol. From the Republic, an airmail letter or postcard to the United States or Canada costs 45p (63¢) and takes 5 to 7 days to arrive. Pre-stamped aerogrammes or air letters are also 45p. From Northern Ireland to the United States or Canada, airmail letters cost 39p (64¢) and postcards 34p (56¢). Delivery takes about 5 days to a week.

NEWSPAPERS/MAGAZINES

The national daily newspapers in the Republic of Ireland are the *Irish Times, Irish Independent,* the *Irish Examiner,* the *Herald,* the *Star,* and the *Evening Echo.* The national Sunday editions are the *Sunday Independent, Sunday Press, Sunday Tribune, Sunday World,* and the Irish-language *Anola.* Prime dailies in the North are the *Belfast Newsletter,* the *Irish News,* and the *Belfast Telegraph.* For up-to-date listings of events throughout Ireland, the biweekly *Event Guide* is free and widely available.

POLICE

In the Republic of Ireland, a law enforcement officer is called a Garda, a member of the Garda Siochana (guardian of the peace); in the plural, it's Gardai (pronounced gar-dee) or simply "the Guards." Dial Tel 999 to reach the Gardai in an emergency. Except for special detachments, Irish police are unarmed and wear dark blue uniforms. In Northern Ireland, you can reach the police by dialing Tel 999.

RADIO/TV

In the Republic of Ireland, RTÉ (Radio Telefis Éireann) is the national broadcasting authority. There are two nationwide TV channels: RTÉ 1 and Network 2; a new Irish-language channel, and TnaG (Teilifís na Gaelige); and six nationwide VHF radio stations: Radio 1, 2FM, Radió na Gaeltachta (in Irish and English), FM3 (offering classical music), Today F.M., and RTÉ Cork. Smaller local stations serve specific regions. In North America, RTÉ radio is available through the Galaxy 5 satellite and at www.rte.ie. RTÉ, jointly with Telecom Éireann, owns and operates Cablelink Ltd., which provides a range of cable and satellite channels from Britain and farther abroad.

The latest addition to the Irish airwaves is TV3, Ireland's first independent and wholly commercial station.

In the North, there are Ulster Television, BBC-TV (British Broadcasting Corporation), and ITN-TV (Independent), plus BBC Radio 1, 2, and 3. Satellite programs via CNN, SKY News, and other international operators are also received.

REST ROOMS

Public rest rooms are usually simply called "toilets," or are marked with international symbols. In the Republic of Ireland, some of the older ones still carry the Gaelic words *Fir* (Men) and *Mna* (Women). The newest and best-kept rest rooms are found at shopping complexes and at multistory car parks. Some cost 10p (14¢) to enter. Free rest rooms are available to customers of sightseeing attractions, museums, hotels, restaurants, pubs, shops, theaters, and department stores. Gas stations normally do not have public toilets.

SAFETY

The Republic of Ireland has enjoyed a traditionally low crime rate, particularly when it comes to violent crime. Those days are not entirely over, but they do regrettably seem to be passing, especially in the cities. By U.S. standards, Ireland is still very safe, but not safe enough to warrant carelessness. Take normal precautions to protect yourself and your belongings.

The gardai advises you not to carry large amounts of money or important documents like your passport or airline tickets when strolling around. Leave them in a safe deposit box at your hotel. As usual, don't leave cars unlocked or cameras, binoculars, or other expensive equipment unattended. And ask your hotel or other travelers which areas are safe and which are not.

Most people are a bit more uptight about traveling in Northern Ireland because of the political unrest that has prevailed there for the past 30 years. It's not likely to be an issue, but to ease your mind, you can contact the Northern Ireland Tourist Board to obtain the latest safety recommendations before you go. Also, the U.S. Department of State 24-hour hotline *(Tel 202/647-5225)* provides travel warnings and security recommendations, as well as emergency assistance.

TAXES

As in many European countries, sales tax is called VAT (value-added tax) and is often already included in the price quoted to you or or shown on price tags. In the Republic, VAT rates vary—for hotels, restaurants, and car rentals, it is 12.5%; for souvenirs and gifts, it is 17.36%. In Northern Ireland, the VAT is 17.5% across the board. VAT charged on services such as hotel stays, meals, car rentals, and entertainment cannot be refunded to visitors, but the VAT on products such as souvenirs is refundable. (For full details on VAT refunds for purchases, see *VAT Refunds* above.)

TIME

Ireland follows Greenwich Mean Time (1 hour earlier than Central European Time) from November through March, and British Standard Time (the same as Central European Time) from April through October. Ireland is five time zones earlier than the eastern United States (when it's noon in New York, it's 5pm in Ireland).

Ireland's latitude makes for longer days and shorter nights in the summer, and the reverse in the winter. In June, there is bright sun until 11pm, but in December, it is truly dark at 4pm.

WATER

Tap water throughout the island of Ireland is generally safe to drink, though contamination of ground water and private wells is an increasing problem. If you prefer bottled water, it is readily available at all hotels, guesthouses, restaurants, and pubs.

YELLOW PAGES

The classified section of telephone books in the Republic of Ireland is called the Golden Pages (on line at *www.goldenpages.ir*). In the North, it's the Yellow Pages.

IRELAND ONLINE

TRAVEL-PLANNING WEB SITES

By Lynne Bairstow

WHY BOOK ONLINE?

Online agencies have come a long way over the past few years, now providing tips for finding the best fare, and giving you suggested dates or times to travel that yield the lowest price if your plans are at all flexible. Other sites even allow you to establish the price you're willing to pay, and they check the airlines' willingness to accept it. However, in some cases, these sites may not always yield the best price. Unlike a travel agent, for example, they may not have access to charter flights offered by wholesalers. Online booking sites aren't the only places to reserve airline tickets—all major airlines have their own Web sites and often offer incentives (bonus frequent flyer miles or net-only discounts, for example) when you buy online or buy an e-ticket.

The best of the travel planning sites are now highly personalized; they store your seating preferences, meal preferences, tentative itineraries, and credit-card information, allowing you to quickly plan trips or check agendas.

In many cases, booking your trip online can be better than working with a travel agent. It gives you the widest variety of choices, control, and the 24-hour convenience of planning your trip when you choose. All you need is some time—and often a little patience—and you're likely to find the fun of online travel research will greatly enhance your trip.

WHO SHOULD BOOK ONLINE?

Online booking is best for travelers who want to know as much as possible about their travel options, for those who have flexibility in their travel dates, and for bargain hunters.

One of the biggest successes in online travel for both passengers and airlines is the offer of last-minute specials, such as American Airlines' weekend deals or other Internet-only fares that must be purchased online. Another advantage is that you can cash in on incentives for booking online, such as rebates or bonus frequent-flyer miles.

Business and other frequent travelers also have found numerous benefits in online booking, as the advances in mobile technology provide them with the ability to check flight status, change plans, or get specific directions from handheld computing devices, mobile phones, and pagers. Some sites will even e-mail or page a passenger if their flight is delayed.

Online booking is increasingly able to accommodate complex itineraries, even for international travel. The pace of evolution on the Net is rapid, so you'll probably find additional features and advancements by the time you visit these sites. The future holds ever-increasing personalization and customization for online travelers.

STAYING SECURE

More people still look online than book online, partly due to fear of putting their credit-card numbers out on the Net. Secure encryption, and increasing experienced buying online, has removed this fear for most travelers. In some cases, however, it's simply easier to buy from a local travel agent who can deliver your tickets to your door (especially if your travel is last-minute or if you have special requests). You can find a flight online and then book it by calling a toll-free number or contacting your travel agent, though this is somewhat less efficient. To be sure you're in secure mode when you book online, look for a little icon of a key (in Netscape) or a padlock (in Internet Explorer) at the bottom of your Web browser.

Booking and Discounts on Line

We highly recommend **Arthur Frommer's Budget Travel Online** *(www.frommers.com)* as an excellent travel-planning resource. Of course, we're a little biased, but you'll find indispensable travel tips, reviews, monthly vacation giveaways, and online booking. Among the most popular features of this site are the regular "Ask the Expert" bulletin boards, which feature Frommer's authors answering your questions via online postings.

Subscribe to **Arthur Frommer's Daily Newsletter** *(www.frommers.com/newsletters)* to receive the latest travel bargains and inside travel secrets in your e-mailbox every day. You'll read daily headlines and articles from the dean of travel himself, highlighting last-minute deals on airfares, accommodations, cruises, and package vacations.

Search Frommer's **Destinations** archive *(www.frommers.com/destinations)* of more than 200 domestic and international destinations for great places to stay and dine, and tips on sightseeing. Once you've researched your trip, the **online reservation system** *(www.frommers.com/booktravelnow)* takes you to Frommer's favorite sites for booking your vacation at affordable prices.

TRAVELOCITY

www.travelocity.com; www.previewtravel.com; www.frommers.travelocity.com

Travelocity is Frommer's online travel-planning and booking partner. Travelocity uses the SABRE system to offer reservations and tickets for more than 400 airlines, plus reservations and purchase capabilities for more than 45,000 hotels and 50 car-rental companies. An exclusive feature of the SABRE system is its Low Fare Search Engine, which automatically searches for the three lowest-priced itineraries based on a traveler's criteria. Last-minute deals and consolidator fares are included in the search. If you book with Travelocity, you can select specific seats for your flights with online seat maps, and also view diagrams of the most popular commercial aircraft. Its hotel finder provides street-level location maps and photos of selected hotels. With the Fare Watcher e-mail feature, you can select up to five routes and receive e-mail notices when the fare changes by $25 or more.

Travelocity's Destination Guide includes updated information on some 260 destinations worldwide—supplied by Frommer's.

Note to AOL Users: You can book flights, hotels, rental cars, and cruises on AOL at keyword: Travel. The booking software is provided by Travelocity/Preview Travel and is similar to the Internet site. Use the AOL "Travelers Advantage" program to earn a 5% rebate on flights, hotel rooms, and car rentals.

ONLINE TRAVELER'S TOOLBOX

Exchange Rates *www.x-rates.com*

See what your dollar is worth in pounds.

Mapquest *www.mapquest.com*

The best of the mapping sites that lets you choose a specific address or destination; in seconds, it will return back a map and detailed directions. It really is easier than calling, asking, and writing down directions. The site also links to special travel deals and helpful sites.

U.S. Customs Service Traveler Information
www.customs.ustreas.gov/travel/index.htm

HM Customs & Excise Passenger Enquiries *www.open.gov.uk*

Canada Customs and Revenue Agency *www.ccra-adrc.gc.ca*

Australian Customs *www.dfat.gov.au*

New Zealand Customs Service *www.customs.govt.nz*

Planning a shopping spree and wondering what you're allowed to bring home? Check the latest regulations at these thorough sites.

Visa ATM Locator *www.visa.com/pd/atm*

MasterCard ATM Locator *www.mastercard.com/atm*
Find ATMs in hundreds of cities around the world. Both include maps for some locations and both list airport ATM locations, some with maps.

The Weather Channel *www.weather.com*
Weather forecasts for cities around the world.

CHECK YOUR E-MAIL

You don't have to be out of touch just because you don't carry a laptop while you travel. Web browser–based free e-mail programs make it much easier to stay in e-touch.

With public internet access available in all of the principal cities and an increasing number of small towns, it shouldn't be difficult for you to log on regularly during your travels in Ireland. In a few simple steps you can set yourself up to receive messages while overseas from each of your email accounts.

The first step to uninterrupted e-mail access is to set up an account with a freemail provider, if you don't have one already: **hotmail.com** is one among scores of companies offering this service. The advantage of freemail is that all you need to check your mail from anywhere in the world is a terminal with internet access; since most internet café computers aren't set up to retrieve POP mail, this is the best option. Most freemail providers will allow you to configure your account to retrieve mail from multiple POP mail accounts, or you can arrange with your home ISP to have your mail forwarded to the freemail account.

Once in Ireland, you can use this book to find internet cafes in Ireland's cities and principal towns; we've listed them in the **Wired** sidebars throughout the text. In areas where internet cafes haven't yet appeared, we've often been able to find internet access in the local public library, and you'll find several internet-savvy libraries listed in the guide. Many hostels now provide internet access for residents, as do an increasing number of hotels. If you do travel with a laptop, you'll be glad to find that not only hotels but quite a few guesthouses provide a telephone jack in all rooms for dial-up access; many internet cafes also provide an Ethernet hook-up for travelers who want to surf the internet from their laptop.

There are also some helpful online resources for finding internet cafes in Ireland. The best general guide for finding the nearest internet cafe is http://netcafeguide.com/ireland.htm. For a limited listing of internet cafes in Irish cities, visit home.netcom.com/~pohallor/ireland/isp1.htm; for cities in Northern Ireland, try www.thenisite.com/internet.htm.

best ireland web sites

By Mark Meagher

Also check the Web sites listed in the **Wired** sidebars, as well as in the individual hotel and attractions listings, throughout this book.

COUNTRY GUIDES

D-Tour: A Visitor's Guide to Ireland for People with Disabilities *http://ireland.iol.ie/infograf/dtour*
This site offers various resources for disabled travelers in Ireland, including extensive listings of wheelchair-accessible accommodations.

Go Ireland *www.goireland.com*
Similar in scope to the Irish Tourist Board site listed below, GoIreland.com is a well-organized guide to lodging, dining, pubs, getting around, entertainment, sightseeing, and car rentals. Click on "Itineraries" to get ideas for sample tours through various regions. You can even trace your Irish roots on this site.

Heritage of Ireland *www.heritageireland.ie*
Though this site is hindered somewhat by awkward use of frames, it's quite a lovely tour of Ireland's historic attractions. From the home page, click on "Historic Sites" to see images and descriptions of attractions by region and town. Other sections cover maps, tours, and an "A-Z" guide to the country.

Interactive Ireland *www.iol.ie/~discover/*
An excellent compilation of Irish links. The site includes a gazetteer of Irish towns with brief descriptions of attractions, accommodations, and restaurants; abundant links provide further information. Be sure to scroll through the long, eclectic list of links on the home page: It's a fascinating assortment of information on all things Irish.

Ireland.com *www.ireland.com*
Presented by the Irish Times, this site includes late-breaking news and perspectives from Dublin's major newspaper. A section called Dublin Live includes advice on lodging, entertainment, attractions, food and drink, sport, and weather. You can see live views of Dublin's O'Connell Bridge, and find tips on getting around, such as the following warning about trying to get anywhere quickly during the commute hour: "The greatest ever work of fiction produced in Dublin is the bus timetable."

Ireland for Visitors *http://goireland.about.com*
This compendium of Web sites from About.com includes dozens of categories, from Dining to Package Tours to Travelogues. While this site is comprised primarily of links to other Web sites, you'll also find some short feature stories about Ireland.

Irelandseye.com *www.irelandseye.com*
This whimsical site isn't focused solely on travel—you can seek out the supernatural on the "ghost watch" webcam or generate random Irish proverbs, ("If you lie down with dogs, you'll rise with fleas."). Beyond proverbs, you'll find excepts from numerous guides to Ireland for sale at the site, including lodging listings, magazine-style features, history, and suggested tours.

Irish Tourist Board (Bord Failte) *www.ireland.travel.ie*
The most comprehensive online guide to travel in the Republic of Ireland, the official site of the Irish Tourist Board (Bord Failte) provides information for most tourism facilities. You'll find an exhaustive events calendar, the latest tourism news, and access to Gulliver, an online accommodations booking service. There are also links to several web sites devoted to specific regions within Ireland: click on "Associated Sites," then "Regions of Ireland."

Island Ireland *http://islandireland.com/*
This is the best place to begin your search on any topic related to Irish culture, the arts, geneology, or the outdoors. There aren't many broken links, and each site is screened for the quality of its content. Especially fascinating is the list of "good sites from around the country," an eclectic collection of online information from each of Ireland's counties.

Northern Ireland Tourist Board *www.ni-tourism.com*
Other than the flamboyant introductory page, this site offers a no-nonsense interface and abundant pages packed with all the information you'll need to get started planning your travels in Northern Ireland. For exploration in depth, however, you'll have to look elsewhere—text descriptions are brief and images often absent, an inconvenience when you're trying to assess a particular B&B, restaurant, or pub.

LODGING SITES FOR IRELAND

Many of the sites in the section above include accommodation listings. The sites below are devoted exclusively to lodgings in Ireland. In addition to the sites below, you can go to worldwide hotel directories (such as All Hotels, www.all-hotels.com) and search the Ireland listings.

Accommodations in Ireland *www.lodgings-ireland.com/*
A helpful compendium of the best marketing groups for specialty accommodations in Ireland. Included you'll find "Hidden Ireland," a collection of privately owned castles and country manor houses (plus a few elegant townhouses); "Ireland's Blue Book," a selection of upscale hotels, manor houses, and B&Bs across the country; "The Great Fishing Houses of Ireland"; and "Irish Farmhouse Holidays," a list of tourist board-approved B&Bs on working farms.

An Oige: Irish Youth Hostel Association *www.irelandyha.org*
An Oige operates 34 youth hostels around Ireland, most of them in beautiful rural locations and many in buildings of historical interest. The site provides photos, locator maps, bus and rail info, contact numbers, and internet booking.

Be Our Guest *www.beourguest.ie*
The official site of the Irish Hotels Federation, this is a comprehensive list of hotels that you can search by location or desired amenities. Most listings include pictures of the properties, rates, number of rooms, facilities, and contact information.

Elegant Ireland *www.elegant.ie*
If you're eager to rent a 14-bedroom medieval castle with professional staff, then look no further. There are some humbler houses for rent as well, though the selection of properties is decidedly upscale. For each house you'll find photos, description, prices, and amenities.

Hotels and Travel: Ireland *www.hotelstravel.com/ireland.html*
A nice selection of lodging choices, well organized by county and city. Some of the listings (which include prices, amenities, and descriptions) link to hotel's own Web pages, where you can explore images of the hotels and rooms, and, in some cases, availability.

Irish Accommodations *www.transatlan.com/ireland/*
Whether you're looking for a B&B, hotel, or guesthouse, this site has extensive listings, including prices, brief descriptions, pictures, e-mail (if available), and, for some properties, reviews.

Town and Country Homes *www.townandcountry.ie*
The most comprehensive list of B&Bs in Ireland, this site includes every B&B approved by the Irish Tourist Board (Bord Failte). You'll find images of the properties, prices, number of rooms, and nearest town.

FOOD & DRINK

Guinness *www.guinness.ie*
A very slick site, showcasing the remarkable flair for advertising that has been a trademark of Guinness since its beginnings. Check out the animated screensavers, read a history of Guinness, or get tips on brewing your own.
Pub Reviews from the Virtual Irish Pub. www.visunet.ie/vip/pubguide/

A collection of reviews for pubs throughout Ireland submitted by visitors to the site.

Sheridans Cheesemongers *www.irishcheese.com*
Numerous local cheesemakers throughout Ireland have perfected their products in recent decades, resulting in nothing short of an Irish cheese

renaissance. Sheridans, with shops in Dublin and Galway, is one of best resources for exploring Ireland's cheese heritage. The best feature of this no-frills site is a (partial) gazetteer of Irish cheeses with photographs and descriptions. You can also order the cheeses and have them delivered to your door (within the European Union).

A Taste of Ireland www.thecia.ie/tasteofireland
A guide to member restaurants of Euro-Toques, an association of chefs and restaurant owners devoted to promoting local produce and traditional recipes throughout Europe. Most descriptions are minimal, but a few include links to restaurant web sites with menus and photos. There's a lot more to Irish cuisine these days than boiled potatoes, and this site helps you find the delicacies.

DUBLIN

The Event Guide *www.eventguide.ie*
The online presence of Dublin's eponymous free weekly, this site chronicles the city's cultural life. You'll find current listings for Dublin's clubs, theaters, cinemas, and concert halls interspersed with interviews, profiles of performers, and some information on events outside Dublin.

Ostlan Dublin Restaurant Guide *www.ostlan.com*
A searchable database of Dublin restaurant reviews. The site's official reviewers don't offer much in the way of criticism; better are the more candid opinions offered by visitors to the site. There's a concise pub guide, and an interesting forum for online discussion.

Sonaco City Guide to Dublin *www.sonaco.com/cityguide/Dublin/*
The best thing about this site is the extensive list of Dublin attractions. The descriptions are cursory, but links are provided for attractions with their own web site. Descriptions include hours of admission and a contact telephone number.

Temple Bar Properties *www.temple-bar.ie*
Here you'll find abundant information on Temple Bar, Dublin's new cultural hub. The heart of the site is a calendar of events, many of them free of charge. Sophisticated graphics and a simple interface make navigating this site a pleasure.

AROUND IRELAND

Belfast: Life@Belfast *www.belfastcity.cjb.net*
The best parts of this site are its virtual tours. Enjoy images of Belfast's legendary pubs or take a historical tour. You'll also find information on entertainment, shopping, and getting around.

Cape Clear Island *www.oilean-chleire.ie/*
A collection of information and links for Cape Clear, Ireland's southernmost inhabited island. Be sure to visit the Cape Clear Island Bird Observatory site.

Clare Ireland *www.clareireland.com/*
On this site featuring all things related to County Clare, you'll find visitor information, links to local news and weather, a helpful message board, and a genealogical service.

Cork-Guide *www.cork-guide.ie/corkcity.htm*
You'll find dozens of lodging options and restaurants to choose from on this exhaustive city guide. Also listed are attractions, shops, entertainment options, nightclubs, and pubs.

Derry Visitor and Convention Bureau *www.derryvisitor.com*
An online guide to one of Northern Ireland's principal cities, with abundant information and links.

Galway.net homepage *www.galway.net*
The links to accommodations, restaurants, pubs, and shops are far from comprehensive. Most listings include a photo and brief descriptive text; many have links to a very schematic interactive map of the city. One of the best features of this site is a county Galway events calendar, with links provided for the major venues.

Web Guide to Sligo *www.sligo.ie*
Includes an excellent guide to archaeological sites in county Sligo, an interesting virtual tour of Sligo Abbey, information on W.B. Yeats, and a calendar of current events. The listings of accommodations and restaurants are very basic.

OTHER WORTHWHILE SITES

AllExperts.com *www.allexperts.com*
This is a site where fellow travelers volunteer to answer your questions about Ireland. Search for "Ireland," pick an expert, and zap that person your question via e-mail. Some experts specialize in a city (Dublin) while others have more general interests (golf, pubs, etc.).

Ireland's Pink Pages *http://indigo.ie/~outhouse*
A list of resources compiled by the Outhouse, Dublin's lesbian, gay, bisexual, transgendered and transvestite community center. You can search by region for B&Bs, bars, helplines, and other information. Another useful address is *www.gcn.ie,* the home of Gay Community News, Ireland's largest gay monthly.

Irish Architecture Online *www.archeire.com*
This fascinating site illuminates Ireland's medieval castles, Georgian monuments, and modern buildings. There are links to numerous architectural sites of interest, including Architectural Dublin, the Irish Architectural Archive, the Irish Georgian Society, and several sites featuring the works of individual Irish architects.

Mad Maps *www.mad-map.ie/*
Navigate your way through eight of Ireland's most popular cities using these colorful hand-drawn maps. Street names are indicated, and you can zoom in on the places that interest you. There's also a search by street name, but very few streets are currently listed.

The Megalith Map *www.megalith.ukf.net/*
An interactive map providing information and links for each of Ireland and Great Britain's stone circles and stone rows.

Stones of Ireland *www.stonepages.com/ireland/ireland.html*
A site documenting Ireland's archaeological heritage, including tombs, stone forts, dolmens, standing stones, and stone circles.

Unison Irish Regional Newspapers Online *www.unison.ie/allpapers.php3*
A news service providing access to articles from Irish regional newspapers. Other features include world and national news, weather, and a travel advisor.

GETTING AROUND

Aer Rianta *www.aer-rianta.ie*
Information for the three principal airports in the Republic of Ireland: Dublin, Shannon, and Cork. Includes arrival and departure info, daily advisories for each airport, and basic maps of the terminals.

Belfast International Airport *www.bial.co.uk*
Information for Belfast's largest airport, with flights from the U.K. and a handful of cities in continental Europe.

Bus Eirean *www.buseireann.ie*
Bus schedules and fares for the Republic of Ireland's national bus service.

Irish Ferries *www.irishferries.ie*
Get information on ferry travel between Ireland, Britain and France from one of Ireland's largest ferry companies.

Iarnrod Eirean *www.irishrail.ie*
Timetables, fares, and general information for rail travel throughout the Republic of Ireland, including Dublin's DART and Suburban rail lines.

Northern Ireland Railways *www.nirailways.co.uk/*
A guide to rail travel in Northern Ireland, with timetables and route maps.

hostels appendix

The source for all hostel listings and hostel-resource information below was the website for An Óige, the Irish Youth Hostel Association, a member of the International Youth Hostel Federation: **www.irelandyha.org.** An Óige is the Irish link in a chain of 6,000 youth hostels located in 66 countries; there are approximately 34 hostels in Ireland. Membership in An Óige enables travelers to stay and take part in hostel activities in Ireland and abroad, often at a discounted price.

Website information is subject to error of course, and is constantly being updated. Rates range from 5—13£ per person, and vary by season. Please check the site, **www.irelandyha.org,** before planning your trip.

COUNTY CORK

Allihies (Na hAilichi)
Cahermeelabo, Allihies,
Beara Peninsula, Co. Cork
Tel: 027/730-14
Fax: n/a
E-mail: n/a
Open: June 1-Sept 30
Desk hours: 5pm-10am
# of beds: 34

Cape Clear Island (Oilean Cleire)
South Harbour, Cape Clear Island
Skibbereen, Co. Cork
Tel: 028/391-98
Fax: 028/391-98
E-mail: n/a
Open: March 1-Nov 30
Desk hours: 5pm-10am
# of beds: 48

Cork International Youth Hostel (Corcaigh)
No. 1&2 Redclyffe,
Western Road, Cork
Tel: 021/543-289
Fax: 021/343-270
E-mail: n/a

Open: n/a
Desk hours: 24 hours
# of beds: 102

COUNTY DONEGAL

Crohy Head (Au Cruach)
Crohy Head, Dungloe,
Co. Donegal
Tel: 075/219-50 or 075/211-54 (members)
Fax: n/a
E-mail: n/a
Open: Apr 21-Sept 30
Desk hours: 5pm-10am
# of beds: 36

Errigal (An Earagall)
Errigal, Dunlewy,
Gweedore, Co. Donegal
Tel: 075/311-80
Fax: n/a
E-mail: errigalhosteleircom.net
Open: n/a
Desk hours: 5pm-10am
# of beds: 46

COUNTY GALWAY

Ben Lettery (Binn Leitri)
Ben Lettery,
Ballinfad, Clifden,
Co. Galway
Tel: 095/511-36
Fax: 095/511-36
E-mail: n/a
Open: Apr 21-Sept 30
Desk hours: 5pm-10am
# of beds: 50

Doorus (Duros)
Doorus House,
Kinvara, Co. Galway
Tel: 091/631-73 or 091/637-512 (Members)
Fax: 091/631-73
E-mail: n/a
Open: n/a
Desk hours: 5pm-10am
# of beds: 56

Galway Youth Hostel (Gaillimh)
St. Mary's College.
St. Mary's Road,
Co. Galway
Tel: 091/528-710
Fax: 091/527-411
E-mail: n/a
Open: July 1-Aug 25
Desk hours: 24 hours
# of beds: 150

Killary Harbour (An Caolaire Rua)
Rosroe, Renvyle,
Co. Galway
Tel: 095/434-17
Fax: n/a
E-mail: n/a
Open: Mar 1-Sept 30, weekends all year
Desk hours: 5pm-10am
# of beds: 44

COUNTY KERRY

Ballinskelligs (Baile en Sceilg)
Prior House,
Ballinskelligs, Co. Kerry
Tel: 066/792-29
Fax: n/a
E-mail: n/a
Open: Apr 21-Sept 30
Desk hours: 5pm-10am
# of beds: 22

Black Valley (An Coimin Dubh)
Black Valley, Beaufort,
Killarney, Co. Kerry
Tel: 064/347-12
Fax: n/a
E-mail: n/a
Open: Mar 1-Nov 30
Desk hours: 5pm-10am
# of beds: 50

Dunquin (Dun Chaoin)
Dunquin, Ballyferriter
Tralee, Co. Kerry
Tel: 066/915-6121 or 066/915-6145
Fax: 066/915-6355
E-mail: n/a
Open: n/a
Desk hours: 5pm-10am
# of beds: 52

Glanmore Lake (Gleann Mor)
Glanmore Lake, Lauragh
Killarney, Co. Kerry
Tel: 064/831-81
Fax: n/a
E-mail: n/a
Open: Apr 1-Sept 30
Desk hours: 5pm-10am
# of beds: 36

Killarney International Hostel (Cill Airne)
Aghadoe House,
Killarney, Co. Kerry
Tel: 064/312-40
Fax: 064/343-00
E-mail: anoigekillarney.ie
Open: n/a
Desk hours: 24 hours
# of beds: 190

Valentia Island (Oilean Dairbhre)
Knighstown, Valentia Island
Co. Kerry
Tel: 066/761-41
Fax: n/a
E-mail: n/a
Open: June 1-Sept 30
Desk hours: 5pm-10am
# of beds: 40

COUNTY KILKENNY

Foulksrath Castle (Caislean Ratha)
Foulksrath Castle,
Jenkinstown, Co. Kilkenny
Tel: 056/671-44 or 056/676-74
Fax: 056/671-44
E-mail: n/a
Open: n/a
Desk hours: 5pm-10am
# of beds: 50

COUNTY LIMERICK

Limerick (Luimneach)
1 Pery Square,
Limerick
Tel: 061/314-672
Public Tel: 061/410-718
Fax: 061/314-672
E-mail: n/a
Open: n/a
Desk hours: 24 hours
# of beds: 66

COUNTY MAYO

Cong (Cunga Fheichin)
Lisloughrey, Quay Road,
Cong, Co. Mayo
Tel: 092/460-89
Fax: 092/464-48
E-mail: n/a
Open: n/a
Desk hours: 24 hours
# of beds: 102

Traenlaur Lodge (An Trian Lair)
Traenlaur Lodge, Lough Feeagh,
Newport, Co. Mayo
Tel: 098/413-58
Fax: n/a
E-mail: n/a
Open: Apr 21-Sept 30
Desk hours: 5pm-10am
# of beds: 32

Westport (Cathair na Mairt)
Club Atlantic, Altamount Street,
Westport
Tel: 098/266-44 or 098/267-17
Fax: 098/262-41
E-mail: n/a
Open: Mar 10-Oct 31
Under 18 rates not available in July/Aug.
Desk hours: 24 hours
# of beds: 140

COUNTY TIPPERARY

Ballydavid Wood (Eatharlach)
Ballydavid Wood House, Glen of Atherlow,
Bansha, Co. Tipperary
Tel: 062/541-48
Fax: n/a
E-mail: n/a
Open: Mar 1-Nov 30
Desk hours: 5pm-10am
# of beds: 40

Mountain Lodge (Cuilleanach)
Mountain Lodge, Burncourt,
Cahir, Co. Tipperary
Tel: 052/672-77

Fax: n/a
E-mail: n/a
Open: Mar 1-Sept 30
Desk hours: 5pm-10am
# of beds: 30

COUNTY WEXFORD

Arthurstown (Colman)
Coastguard Station,
Arthurstown, New Ross,
Co. Wexford
Tel: 051/389-411
Fax: n/a
E-mail: n/a
Open: June 1-Sept 30
Desk hours: 5pm-10am
# of beds: 32

Rosslare Harbour (Ros Lair)
Goulding Street,
Rosslare Harbour, Co. Wexford
Tel: n/a
Fax: n/a
E-mail: n/a
Open: n/a
Desk hours: Caters for hostellers using night ferry sailings
# of beds: 68

COUNTY WICKLOW

Ballinclea (Baile an tSleibhe)
Ballinclea, Donard,
Co. Wicklow
Tel: 045/404-657
Fax: 045/404-657
E-mail: n/a
Open: Mar 1-Nov 30, weekends all year
Desk hours: 5pm-10am
# of beds: 40

Baltyboys (Loch Bhaile Coimin)
Baltyboys, Blessington,
Co. Wicklow
Tel: 045/867-266
Fax: 045/867-032
E-mail: n/a
Open: Mar 1-Nov 30, weekends all year
Desk hours: 5pm-10am
# of beds: 36

Glencree (Gleann Critigh)
Stone House, Glencree,
Co. Wicklow
Tel: 01/286-4037 or 01/276-6142
Fax: 01/276-6142
E-mail: n/a
Open: n/a
Desk hours: 5pm-10am
# of beds: 40

Glendaloch International Youth Hostel (Gleann Da Loch)
The Lodge,
Glendalough, Co. Wicklow
Tel: 040/445-342
Fax: 040/445-690
E-mail: n/a
Open: n/a
Desk hours: 24 hours
# of beds: 120

Glenmalure (Gleann Maolura)
Glenmalure,
Greenane, Co. Wicklow
Tel: none
Fax: none
E-mail: n/a
Open: July 1-Aug 31, Sat nights all year
Desk hours: 5pm-10am
# of beds: 16

Knockree (Cnoc Riabhach)
Lacken House,
Renvyle, Co. Wicklow
Tel: 012/864-036
Fax: 012/762-722
E-mail: n/a
Open: n/a
Desk hours: 5pm-10am
# of beds: 58

Tiglin (Gleann Mor) (Devil's Glen)
Tiglin,
Ashford, Co. Wicklow
Tel: 040/449-049
Fax: 040/449-049
E-mail: n/a
Open: n/a
Desk hours: 5pm-10am
# of beds: 50

COUNTY DUBLIN

Dublin International Youth Hostel (Atha Cliath)
61 Mountjoy Street,
Dublin 7
Tel: 018/301-766
Fax: 018/301-600
E-mail: dublininternationalanoige.ie
Open: n/a
Desk hours: 24 hours
# of beds: 350

sports appendix

To many first-time visitors, the concept of "sports" in Ireland conjures mostly images of sitting around in a pub, putting back a few pints of stout while watching football—or football hooligans—on TV. And tales of how it rains all the time hardly make the Emerald Isle sound like a place anyone would go for hiking, biking, or other outdoor pursuits. But the truth is, it doesn't truly *rain* rain all the time, and the Irish sure don't let a little mist stop them from doing whatever they want, whenever they want, from golfing or hiking to windsurfing or biking. And the same is becoming true of their visitors. The days are long gone when the most aerobic thing tourists did in Ireland was tracing their roots. Practically every corner of Ireland is packed with opportunities for outdoor pursuits.

biking

Biking is the best way to see the Irish landscape in its many forms, from barren bogland to crashing surf to inland lakes. The distances are quite manageable: in a week or two you can bike through several of the regions described in this guide or explore one in greater detail. And you don't have to camp-out just because you're on a bike; there are loads of hostels, B&Bs, and hotels that are happy to accommodate touring cyclists who don't want to deal with the extra weight of a tent and sleeping bag.

And you don't have to do your whole trip on a bike; day trips on two wheels can be a great way to stretch your legs after spending too much time in a bus or a train. Rentals are available in most towns that cater in any way to tourists.

Roads in Ireland are categorized as M (Motorway), N (National), or R (Regional); some still bear the older T (Trunk) and L (Link) designations. For reasons of scenery as well as safety, you'll probably want to avoid the busier roads. The R and L roads are always suitable for cycling, as are the N roads in outlying areas where there isn't too much traffic. The disadvantage of the smallest roads in remote areas is that they are rarely signposted, so you should have a good map and compass to be sure of your way. In some areas of the west and northwest, *only* the N roads are consistently signposted.

WHERE TO RIDE

Anyone cycling in Ireland should be prepared for two inevitable obstacles to progress: wind and hills. Outside the midlands, there are hills just about everywhere, and those on the back roads can have outrageously steep grades. Road engineering is rather primitive—instead of having switchbacks on a steep slope, roads often climb by the most direct route. The prevailing winds on Ireland's west coast blow from south to north, so by traveling in the same direction you can save a lot of effort over the course of a long tour.

Cyclists have long favored the coastal roads of the southwest, west, and northwest. Note: The quiet roads and rugged scenery of the **Dingle Peninsula** are perfect for a bike ride; you'll have to become an expert at dodging tour buses if you ride the **Ring of Kerry**; **Donegal** is one of Ireland's hilliest regions, so you'll have to pump-and-grind to get to the country's most spectacular coastal and mountain scenery.

Also ideal for cycling are Ireland's many islands; you can bring your bike on all passenger ferries, often for no extra charge, and the roads have little or no traffic. Some of the best islands (with accommodations) are **Cape Clear** in County Cork; **Great Blasket Island** in County Kerry; and the **Aran Islands** in County Galway.

RENTAL AND BYOB TIPS

If you plan to do a serious bike tour, you should bring your own bike unless you're traveling with an outfitter who'll supply a good one for you—rental models are often impossibly heavy and clunky, not to mention unreliable. Ask your airline about the cost of bringing your bike; some carriers charge around $75, while others will take bikes for free if they're properly packed and take the place of one of your allowable checked bags.

If you must rent a bike for your tour, at least bring your own helmet (many places don't rent them and the ones they do rent tend to be of the one-size-fits-all variety), panniers (rental saddlebags are unbelievably flimsy), and cycling shoes. Some people bring their own pedals and attach them to the rental bike. Your best bet for decent rentals for long trips (100 miles or so) is to reserve in advance from national companies, such as Raleigh Rent-A-Bike and Rent-A-Bike Ireland, where you can usually get a bike that fits you and arrange a one-way rental throughout the country.

OUTFITTERS & RESOURCES

If you want to design your own itinerary and bike independently, several rental agencies with nationwide offices permit one-way rental. Try Ireland's largest bike rental outfit, **Raleigh Ireland** *(Raleigh House, Kylemore Road, Dublin; Tel 01/626-1333; Fax 01/626-1770)* or **Rent-A-Bike International** *(58 Lower Gardiner St., Dublin; Tel 01/872-5399; Fax 01/874-4247).* Mountain and cross-country bike rental rates average £10 ($14) per day, £40 ($56) per week. The negotiable one-way drop-off fee, where available, averages £15 ($21).

If you want to ride with a pack while somebody else serves as your ground crew, check out **Irish Cycling Safaris** *(Belfield House, UCD, Dublin; Tel 01/260-0749; Fax 01/706-1168; www.kerna.ie/ics/).* It's run by Eamon Ryan and family, who offer trips to practically every part of Ireland. Or hang out with **Backroads** *(Tel 800-GO-ACTIVE or 510/527-1555; www.backroads.com)* or **VBT** (formerly Vermont Bike Tours *(Tel 800/BIKE-TOUR; www.vbt.com),* two U.S. companies that take care of everything from your bike to your butt (they have great support vans, commonly known as "sag wagons"), and include your meals and accommodations in local inns and cool little hotels, all in one price. It ain't cheap, but it can really be fun if you get a good group of people (make sure to ask about the age range of your particular group before you book your trip).

If you'd just as soon skip the group thing but want a little help organizing your independent adventure, consult **Celtic Cycling** *Lorum Old Rectory, Bagenalstown, County Carlow; Tel 0503/75282; Fax 0503/75455; www.celticcycling.com).*

hiking

Hiking has become really popular in Ireland, especially since the creation of a network of 25 marked long-distance trails. The first to open was the 82-mile **Wicklow Way,** which begins just outside Dublin and proceeds through rugged hills and serene pastures. Others include the **South Leinster Way,** the **Beara Peninsula,** the **Kerry Way,** the **Dingle Way,** and the **Ulster Way.** Most trails are routed so that meals and accommodations—whether in B&Bs, hostels, or hotels—are never more than a day's walk apart.

The long-distance routes are the best-marked trails in Ireland, although the standards for signposting will seem surprisingly inadequate to those familiar with similar trails in America. It is generally assumed in Ireland that walkers possess a map and compass and know how to use them. Markers are frequently miles apart, and often seem to be lacking at crucial crossroads. Because trees on Irish hillsides rarely impede visibility, a post or cairn on each summit usually indicates the way between two peaks. You're expected to be able to find your own way in between. A compass becomes crucial when a fog blows in and all landmarks quickly disappear. Be warned: This can happen quite unexpectedly, and the safest strategy when you can't see your way is to stay exactly where you are until the fog clears.

MAPS

Guides with maps for most of the long-distance trails in Ireland are available from bookstores, shops, and tourist offices in the local area. Many of the relevant guides can be obtained from **An Óige, the Irish Youth Hostel Association** *(61 Mountjoy St., Dublin 1; Tel 01/830-4555),* or in the

North from **YHANI, Northern Ireland's Youth Hostel Association** *(22 Donegal Rd., Belfast, BT12 5JN; Tel 028/9032-4733).* Ordnance survey maps are available in several scales; the most helpful to hikers is the 1:50,000—1 1/4 inches to 1 mile—scale. This series is currently available for all of Northern Ireland and a limited number of locations in the Republic. The 1/2-inch-to-1-mile series covers the whole country in 25 maps, and local maps are available in most shops. They indicate roads, major trails, and historic monuments in some detail. Although they are on too small a scale for walkers, they are all that is available in many areas. For ordnance survey maps, contact **Ordnance Survey Service** *(Phoenix Park, Dublin 8; Tel 01/802-5300),* or **Ordnance Survey of Northern Ireland** *(Colby House, Stranmillis Court, Belfast BT9 5BJ; Tel 028/9066-1244; www.osni.gov.uk).* The Irish Tourist Board's booklet *Walking Ireland* and the Northern Ireland Tourist Board's *An Information Guide to Walking* are both very helpful. Other excellent resources include *Best Irish Walks,* edited by Joss Lynam (Passport Books, 1995); and *Irish Long Distance Walks: A Guide to the Waymarked Trails,* by Michael Fewer (Gill and Macmillan, 1993).

TOURS

Sometimes it's fun to see things through locals' eyes, which is what you'll do if you sign up for a walking/hiking tour at **Ballyknocken House B&B** *(Ashford, County Wicklow; Tel 0404/44614; Fax 0404/44627; £285-295 ($400-415) week; £178-188 ($250-$265) 4 nights and 3 days).* Their 2- to 7-day walking tours of the Wicklow Mountains—for individuals or groups—include lodging, meals, and transport to and from the trailheads. The owner of Ballyknocken House, Mary Byrne, really knows the trails, so she can help you set up a route that suits your interests and level of fitness. If you like the whole tour thing, you'll be in luck in the West of Ireland; for a wide selection of guided walks in the Burren, from a day to a week or more, contact **Burren Walking Holidays** *(Carrigann Hotel, Lisdoonvarna; Tel 065/7074036; Fax 065/7074567).* In the southwest, contact **SouthWest Walks Ireland** *(40 Ashe St., Tralee, County Kerry; Tel 066/712-8733; Fax 066/712-8762; e-mail: swwi@iol.ie).* For a full walking holiday package to County Kerry, consult BCT Scenic Walking *(703 Palomar Airport Rd., Suite 200, Carlsbad, CA 92009; Tel 800/473-1210; www.bctwalk.com).*

The Northern Ireland Tourist Board *(www.ni-tourism.com)* has a walking and hiking page that lists self-guided tours, 14 short hikes along the Ulster Way, and names and addresses of organizations offering guided walks throughout the North. For walking holidays in Northern Ireland, contact **Walk Ulster** *(Bleach Green Centre, Lurgan Rd., Banbridge BT32 4LU Tel 028/4066-2126).*

golf

With nearly 300 championship courses and many others of lesser repute, Ireland has devoted a greater percentage of its soil to the game of golf than has any other country in the world. The Irish landscape and climate, like those of Scotland, are custom-designed for some of the fairest fairways, greenest greens, and most dramatic traps you'll ever encounter. And there is never a shortage of 19th holes.

And the best part of all is that the game is not confined to people with incomes that would rival A-Rod or Madonna. Membership fees at private clubs are reasonable, and greens fees for walk-ins are often quite modest, especially on weekdays and at off-peak hours.

RESOURCES

Apart from the tourist boards, which are glad to supply brochures on golfing holidays, these are the principal organizations to contact for detailed information: the **Golfing Union of Ireland** *(Glencar House, 81 Englington Rd., Dublin 4; Tel 01/269-4111; www.gui.ie)* and **Golfing Ireland** *(18 Parnell Sq., Dublin 1; Tel 01/872-6711; Fax 01/872-6632; e-mail: golf@iol.ie; books tee times and arranges itinerary for 28 clubs in Ireland).*

horseback riding

Ireland is a horse-loving country, and in most areas you can find a stable offering trail rides and instruction. The Association of Irish Riding Establishments (AIRE) is the regulatory body that accredits stables, ensuring adequate safety standards and instructor competence. Riding prices range from £10 ($14) to £25 ($35) per hour; expect to pay £15 ($21) on average. A list of accredited stables throughout the country is available from the Irish Tourist Board.

A great variety of riding options can be found to suit different interests and levels of experience. Pony trekking caters primarily to beginners, and you don't need experience. Trail riding over longer distances requires the ability to trot for extended periods, and can be quite exhausting for the novice. Riding establishments also commonly offer such advanced options as jumping and dressage, and some have enclosed arenas—an attractive option on rainy days. Several establishments have accommodations and offer packages that include meals, lodging, and riding. Post-to-post trail riding allows a rider to stay at different lodgings each night, riding on trails all day.

The **Irish National Stud** and the **Curragh** in County Kildare are ground zero for horse racing, which means there are lots of really good stables nearby where you definitely can avoid getting saddled up on a nag. The **Wicklow Hills** in County Wicklow have a number of fine riding establishments, as do counties **Wexford, Tipperary,** and **Galway,** and most of the **Northwest.**

HORSEY HOLIDAY TOURS

Stables and equestrian centers that provide riding holiday packages include **Horetown House** *(Foulksmills, County Wexford; Tel 051/565771),* **Dingle Horse Riding** *(Ballinaboula House, Dingle; Tel 066/915-2199: www.dinglehorseriding.com),* **Glen Valley Stables** *(Glencroff, Leenane, County Galway: Tel 095/42269),* and **Beech Cottage** *(Dromahair, County Leitrim; Tel/Fax 071/64110).* You can get a free copy of *Equestrian Holidays*

Ireland from the **Irish Tourist Board** or **Equestrian Holidays Ireland** *(P.O. Box 590, Limerick; www.ehi.ie).*

fishing

With a coastline of more than 3,472 miles, a plethora of lakes and ponds, and countless creeks, rills, streams, and rivers, Ireland offers an abundance of prime fish habitats. The sport of catching those fish—referred to by the Irish as angling—is a cherished tradition. If you're around anytime between March and September, check out some of the festivals and competitions; contact the **Irish Tourist Board** well in advance if you want to participate in the competitions. Among the festivals are Killybegs International Fishing Festival and the Baltimore Angling Festival in July, and the Cobh Sea Angling Festival in September.

FINDING THE FISH

For "sea angling," try **Killybegs,** the **Killarney** area, the **Blackwater River** near Cork, and **Kinsale.** Freshwater fishing spots inn the West include **Lough Corrib, Lough Conn,** and **Lough Mask.** You also might want to consider the **Shannon River** and its lakes, especially **Lough Derg.**

RESOURCES

Fishing seasons are as follows: salmon, January 1 to September 30; brown trout, February 15 to October 12; sea trout, June 1 to September 30; course fishing and sea angling, all year. A license is required for salmon and sea trout angling; the cost is £3 ($4.20) for 1 day, £10 ($14) for 8 days, £25 ($35) annually. For all private salmon and sea trout fisheries, a permit is required in addition to the license. Prices vary greatly, from £5 to £150 ($7 to $210) per rod per day, although most permits run £20 to £25 ($28 to $35).

A helpful brochure, *Angling in Ireland,* details what fish can be caught where. It is available from the **Central Fisheries Board** *(Balnagowan House, Mobhi Boreen, Glasnevin, Dublin 9; Tel 01/837-9206; Fax 01/836-0060).* Another helpful resource, *The Angler's Guide,* is published by the Irish Tourist Board. Permits, licenses, and specific information can be obtained from local outfitters or the Central Fisheries Board.

In Northern Ireland, you must get a rod license from the **Fisheries Conservancy Board** *(1 Mahon Rd., Portadown, Craigavon, County Armagh; Tel 028/3833-4666),* or in the Derry area from the **Foyle Fisheries Commission** *(8 Victoria Rd., Derry BT47 2AB; Tel 028/7134-2100).* A permit may also be required; information can be obtained from local outfitters or the **Department of Culture, Arts and Leisure** *(Interpoint Centre, York St., Belfast BT4 3PW; Tel 028/9052-3434; Fax 028/9052-3121).* A rod license costs £10 ($14) for 8 days; permits run £9 ($12.60) a day or £45 ($63) for 8 days. You can find a wealth of information and contacts in *An Information Guide to Game Fishing,* available from any office of the Northern Ireland Tourist Board.

SCOOP: TROUT & SALMON

Yeats imagined his ideal fisherman *"climbing up to a place/ where stone is dark under froth," and vividly pictured "the down-turn of his wrist/ when the flies drop in the stream."* Anglers visiting Ireland are free to do so, because they don't need a license to take brown trout, and many a small stream or mountain tarn offers free fishing. Be sure to check with the local tourist office or tackle dealer before dropping your line. The trout might not be very large, but they will make a sweet dish for supper. Free advice: Bring rods, reels, and waders with you, because gear rental is rarely available. Suitable flies can always be bought locally.

If your quest is for larger brown trout, head for the bigger lakes where the underlying rock is limestone rather than granite. Go to **Oughterard** in County Galway, or **Ballinrobe** and **Pontoon** in County Mayo to get to Lough Carrib, Lough Mask, and Lough Conn, respectively. No permit is required, but you need to hire a boat and an experienced boatman. May and June are the best months, as they are for the great midland lakes that can easily be reached from **Mullingar** in County Westmeath. The lakes around **Ennis** in County Clare fish well in March or April. Excellent brown trout fishing can also be had in the rivers of **County Cork** and *County Tipperary,* where you usually have to apply to the local angling club for a visitor's ticket.

Many rivers and lakes hold good stocks of salmon and sea trout. Sea trout run from late June through August. There are two main salmon runs: the spring run of older, bigger fish and the "grilse" run in June and July. Opening and closing dates vary from river to river, but most waters are open from March through September. A license (obtained locally) is required, and advance booking is a necessity for the more famous locations, such as the Salmon Weir pool in Galway City and the Ridge pool in Ballina. Serious anglers reserve accommodations by the week in centers like Waterville in County Kerry and Newport in County Mayo. If you are touring by car, it is always worth inquiring locally. Day tickets are often available from hotels or angling clubs.

Two excellent books by Peter O'Reilly, *Trout and Salmon Rivers of Ireland* (3rd edition, 1995) and *Trout and Salmon Loughs of Ireland* (1987) give full coverage of the waters available.

(The source of the scoop on trout and salmon is J. V. Luce, author of an Irish favorite, *Fishing and Thinking.*)

Kayaking

Known as "canoeing" in Ireland, this sport enjoys considerable popularity. Winter is whitewater season; frequent rains fill the rivers enough for good paddling. By early summer, most whitewater streams are reduced to a trickle. One exception is the **Liffey,** which is dam-controlled and has some minor rapids upstream from Dublin that are sometimes passable during the summer months.

Sea kayaking is much better suited to the Irish landscape and climate. It can be done year-round and permits access to one of the island's greatest treasures: its remote seacoast.

In a sea kayak, the wonders of the Irish coast can be investigated at close hand. You'll find caves and tiny inlets, out-of-the-way cliffs and reefs inhabited by abundant seabirds, colorful crustaceans, seals, and the occasional dolphin. Many islands are within easy reach of the mainland, and with experience and good conditions, a sea kayaker can reach any of Ireland's island outposts.

A number of adventure centers offer kayaking lessons, and a few schools are devoted solely to kayaking. Some of them will rent equipment as long as you can demonstrate adequate proficiency—call ahead to make arrangements if that is what you plan to do. For those new to the sport or unfamiliar with the Irish coast, a guided excursion is the best option.

The deeply indented coast of **West Cork** and **Kerry** is a sea kayaker's paradise, with clear water, cliffs rising to dizzying heights, and rocky shorelines so full of caves in some places that they seem hollow. The west of Ireland offers many tiny islands and remote spots to explore.

RESOURCES

For the latest information on kayaking throughout Ireland, surf the web to the **Irish Canoe Union** *(www.irishcanoeunion.ie).* Or get some hands-on instruction from **Jim Kennedy** *(Maria's Schoolhouse, Union Hall, County Cork; Tel 028/33002),* a former world champion in kayak marathon racing, who teaches and guides excursions along the spectacularly beautiful West Cork coast. If you're so hard-core you want your whole vacation to be about kayaking, contact **Delphi Adventure Center** *(Leenane, County Galway; Tel 095/42307; Fax 095/42303)* or the **National Adventure Centre** *(Ashford, County Wicklow; Tel 0404/40169; Fax 0404/40701).*

diving

With visibility averaging 49 feet and occasionally reaching 98 feet—and many wrecks to explore—the west coast of Ireland is a great place for divers. In fact, it offers some of the best scuba diving in Europe.

The Irish dive season generally starts in March and ends in October, although specific dates depend on your comfort zone. Outside these months, weather and ocean conditions could make jumping into the sea unappealing for some. The PADI open-water diver certification is the minimum requirement for all dives; most schools also offer introductory dives for novices.

The rocky coast of **West Cork** and **Kerry** is great for diving, with centers in Baltimore and Dingle. On the west coast there are many great locations, one of which is the deep, sheltered **Killary Harbour.** Northern Ireland offers many interesting dives, with more than 400 named wrecks off the coast, and many in the **Irish Sea** and in **Belfast Lough.**

RESOURCES

The **Irish Underwater Council** *(Comhairle Fo-Thuinn, 78A Patrick St., Dun Laoghaire, County Dublin; Tel 01/284-4601; Fax 01/284-4602; www.scubaireland.com),* an association of more than 70 Irish diving clubs in the world diving federation, has information on diving, dive centers, and dive hotels (no pun intended) throughout the Republic, and publishes the *CFT Guide to Dive Sites* and other information on exploring the

Emerald Isle's emerald waters. **UK Diving** *(www.ukdiving.co.uk* features information on diving in the North, including a wreck database you can access either through a conventional listing or by pinpointing on a map. Wrecks are marked as red dots, which can be clicked on to find more information.

Irish dive centers and schools include **Oceantech Adventures** *(Dun Laoghaire, County Dublin; Tel 01/280-1083 or 800/272822 toll-free in Ireland; www.oceantechadventure.com),* **Baltimore Diving & Watersports Centre** *(Baltimore, County Cork; Tel 028/20300; Fax 028/20300),* **Dingle Marina Centre** *(Dingle marina, Dingle; Tel 066/915-2422; Fax 066/915-2425; e-mail: divedingle@tinet.ie),* and **Scubadive West** *(Renvyle, County Galway; Tel 095/43922; Fax 095/43923; www.scubadivewest.com).*

windsurfing

Windsurfing has become so popular in Ireland that the really primo spots are host to virtual flotillas of colorful sails and wetsuits when conditions are good. But some of the best places are in remote areas of the west coast, so they're rarely crowded. There are windsurfing schools that rent boards all over Ireland, especially on the southeast and southwest coasts.

Ireland's water quality is some of the best in Europe; nearly 90 percent of its beaches surpass EU voluntary guideline levels. When you're at a beach, look for a blue flag bearing a circular logo and the current year to be assured of the highest standard in water quality. To find a complete listing or to check out a particular beach in advance, go to *www.blueflag.org.*

COOL SPOTS

In Dublin, the most popular spot is **Dollymount Beach; Salthill,** behind Dun Laoghaire Harbour, is another good choice. In the southeast, try **Brittas Bay** (County Wicklow), **Cahore** (County Wexford), and **Rosslare** (County Wexford). **Dunmore East** (County Waterford), **Dungarvan** (County Waterford), and **Cobh** (County Cork) are good in the south. The most challenging waves and winds are in the west, at **Brandon Bay** on the Dingle Peninsula, **Roundstone** in Galway, **Achill Island** in Mayo, and **Magheroarty** and **Rossnowlagh** in Donegal.

RESOURCES

Equipment rental and lessons are widely available on Ireland's coasts and lakes. Try the **Surf Dock Centre** *(Grand Canal Dock Yard, Ringsend, Dublin; Tel 01/668-3945; Fax 01/668-1215),* the **Dunmore East Adventure Centre** *Dunmore East, County Waterford; Tel 051/383783; Fax 051/383786),* **Oysterhaven Windsurfing Centre** *(Oysterhaven, Kinsale, County Cork; Tel 021/770738; Fax 021/770776),* **Jamie Knox Adventure Watersports** *(Maharees, Castlegregory, County Kerry; Tel 066/713-9411; www.jamieknox.com),* and in the North, the **Ardclinis Activity Center** *(High Street, Cushendall, County Antrim; Tel/Fax 028/2177-1340).*

about the authors

Camille DeAngelis is an art history student at New York University with a minor in Irish Studies. She is the Opinion Editor of the Washington Square News, NYU's daily student newspaper, and enjoys making a mockery of convention and inflaming the tempers of overpaid bureaucrats whenever possible.

Tom Haslow was born and reared in the Adirondack mountains of upstate New York and studied film at NYU. He is now a squirrel trying to get a nut in the New York City movie business. In Ireland, Tom learned that the most important part of any trip is the people you meet. He would like to thank those in every pub, club and bog he visited for teaching him something about life.

d

f

g

S